COLLECTION DEVELOPMENT
FOR LIBRARIES

TOPICS IN LIBRARY AND INFORMATION STUDIES

General Editors: **G.E. Gorman,** School of Information Studies,
Riverina-Murray Institute of Higher Education,
Wagga Wagga, New South Wales.
Ronald R. Powell, School of Library and Informational Science,
University of Missouri-Columbia,
Columbia, Missouri.

COLLECTION DEVELOPMENT FOR LIBRARIES

G.E. Gorman and B.R. Howes

Topics in Library and Information Studies

BOWKER-SAUR

London Edinburgh Munich New York
Singapore Sydney Toronto Wellington

In association with
Centre for Information Studies
Riverina-Murray Institute of Higher Education
Wagga Wagga New South Wales

(First published 1989)
Reprinted 1990

British Library Cataloguing in Publication Data

Gorman, G.E. (Gary Eugene), *1944–*
  Collection development for libraries. –
  (Topics in library and information studies)
  1. Libraries. Stock. Management
  I. Title II. Howes, B.R. III. Series
  025.2

  ISBN 0-40830–100–7

Library of Congress Cataloging-in-Publication Data

Gorman, G.E.
  Collection development for libraries / G.E. Gorman and B.R. Howes.
  448 p. 21.5 cm. – (Topics in library and information studies)
  Bibliography: p.
  Includes index.
  ISBN 0–40830–100–7.
  1. Collection development (Libraries)
  I. Howes, Brian R. (Brian, Richard), *1930–*. II. Title. III. Series.
  Z687.G65 1989
  025.2 – dc 19   89-579
                                                    CIP

Bowker-Saur is part of the Professional Publishing Division of Reed International Books, Borough Green, Sevenoaks, Kent TN15 8PH

Cover design by Calverts Press
Printed on acid-free paper
Printed and bound in Great Britain by
Biddles Ltd, Guildford and King's Lynn

ABOUT THE AUTHORS

G.E. Gorman (BA cum laude, MDiv, STB Hons., DipLib, MA, ALAA, FLA) is Graduate Course Coordinator in the School of Information Studies at the Riverina-Murray Institute of Higher Education. He has had many years' experience in academic and research library collection development and regularly serves as a consultant in this area. He has previously been Lecturer in Librarianship at the Ballarat College of Advanced Education, International Organizations Librarian at the Institute of Development Studies (University of Sussex), Information Retrieval Officer at Christian Aid, a tutor and chaplain at Oxford University. He is the author of more than fifty articles in various fields and of several books, including *The South African Novel in English* (G.K. Hall), *Theological and Religious Reference Materials* (3 vols., Greenwood Press), *Guide to Current National Bibliographies in the Third World* (2nd rev. ed., K.G. Saur). He is also Advisory Editor of the Greenwood Press series, Bibliographies and Indexes in Religious Studies; Joint Book Review Editor of the *African Book Publishing Record*; Joint Editor-in-Chief of *Riverina Library Review;* Assistant Editor of *Library Acquisitions: Practice and Theory;* General Editor of Topics in Australasian Library and Information Studies (Centre for Information Studies) and of the new Butterworth series, Topics in Library and Information Studies.

B.R. Howes (BA, MA, ALA) is Senior Lecturer in the School of Information Studies at the Riverina-Murray Institute of Higher Education. He has previously taught at Loughborough Technical College, Loughborough University of Technology, College of Librarianship Wales and the University of Ibadan. He is the author of articles on book reviewing, library legislation and education for librarianship, and has published *A Checklist of Some Recent Australasian Antiquarian Book-Dealers' Catalogues, Guide to Fine and Rare Australasian Books* and *Second-hand and Antiquarian Book-Dealers in Australia: A Directory.* He has worked in academic and public libraries in Australia and Germany, collects in some areas of children's books and is the co-proprietor of a small publishing firm, Magpie Books.

CONTENTS

LIST OF FIGURES

ACKNOWLEDGMENTS

The authors are grateful to the many students who, unwittingly or otherwise, have assisted in developing the views and ideas discussed in this work, and also to those professional colleagues who over the years have argued strongly for a more informed and professional approach to all aspects of collection development. We wish to thank Cathy Sheahan for her wordprocessing assistance, and we express our special gratitude to Dr Lyn Gorman for her editorial and indexing services, but retain for ourselves responsibility for all errors or omissions which might appear in the work.

Given the significant emphasis on readings in this volume, we also wish to thank all individuals, publishers, organizations and journals for permission to reprint materials. We hereby acknowledge the various permissions as follows:

American Library Association, Office of Rights and Permissions, for Judy Horn, "Government Publications" and Marcia Tuttle, "Serials", both in *Selection of Library Materials in the Humanities, Social Sciences and Sciences*;

Anthony Arthur and the editor and publisher of *Australian Academic and Research Libraries* for Anthony J. Arthur, "Collection Management - an Australian Project";

the editor and publisher of *Collection Management* for Robert W. Evans, "Collection Development Policy Statements: The Documentation Process"; Blaine H. Hall, "Writing the Collection Assessment Manual"; Robert D. Stueart, "Weeding of Library Materials - Politics and Policies"; Jutta Reed-Scott, "Implementation and Evaluation of a Weeding Program";

the editor and publisher of *College and Research Libraries* for John Rutledge and Luke Swindler, "The Selection Decision: Defining Criteria and Establishing Priorities";

the Graduate School of Librarianship at Monash University and Professor Jean Whyte for John Adams, "More than Librarie Keepers." In *Books, Librarians and Readers in Colonial Australia: Papers from the Forum on Australian Colonial Library History Held at Monash University, 1-2 June 1984*;

the editor and publisher of the *Journal of Academic Librarianship* for Robert L. Burr *et al.*, "Six Responses to 'A Rationalist's Critique of Book Selection for Academic Libraries'"; Dennis W. Dickinson, "A Rationalist's Critique of Book Selection for Academic Libraries"; Dorothy A. Koenig, "Rushmore at Berkeley: The Dynamics of Developing a Written Collection Development Policy Statement"; Beth Macleod, "*Library Journal* and *Choice*: A Review of Reviews";

the publisher of *Library Acquisitions: Practice and Theory* for Jennifer Cargill, "Collection Development Policies: An Alternative Viewpoint"; Eric J. Carpenter, "Collection Development Policies: The Case for";

the publisher of *Library Resources and Technical Services* for Y.T. Feng, "The Necessity for a Collection Development Policy Statement";

the publisher of *Library Research* for Abraham Bookstein, "Sources of Error in Library Questionnaires";

the editor and publisher of *New Library World* for George McMurdo, "User Satisfaction";

the St. Joseph Public Library and its Director, Dorothy Sanborn Elliott, for St. Joseph Public Library, *Materials Selection and Collection Review Policy*;

the editor and publisher of the *Serials Librarian* for Laura Neame, "Periodicals Cancellation: Making a Virtue out of Necessity";

the State Library of Victoria and the State Librarian, Jane La Scala, for State Library of Victoria, *State Library of Victoria Selection Policy*;

William Paterson State College and Director of the Sarah Byrd Askew Library for William Paterson State College of New Jersey, Sarah Byrd Library, *Collection Development Policy*;

Eric Wainwright, Deputy Director General of the National Library of Australia, for Eric W. Wainwright, "Collection Adequacy: Meaningless Concept or Measurable Goal?" In *Collection Management in Academic Libraries: Papers Delivered at a National Seminar, Surfers Paradise, Queensland, 16th-17th February 1984.*

INTRODUCTION

Edward Evans tells the story of a library science lecturer who gives her students the following advice: "On the first day you go to work in collection development ask to see the written policy so you can study it. When they tell you they don't have one, faint. By the way, you need to practice fainting and falling so you don't hurt yourselves - not many libraries have written collection development policies."[1] If we were to give students in Britain, Canada, Australia and other countries similar advice, the profession would quickly become noted for its bruised and probably comatose bodies. There is on the whole relatively little in the way of planned collection development, let alone formal policies, so most librarians would be unconscious most of the time. However, there are signs that the situation is improving. Most library schools in the anglophone world now devote at least some time to collection development in their curricula, although few provide anything like the detailed treatment recommended in the 1985 "Guidelines for Collection Development Courses".[2] Many libraries have written documentation in support of collection development (as distinct from formal policy documents), but this seems to be mainly the larger organizations - national, state and academic libraries. Very few public, school or special libraries have made any attempt to plan or devise a systematic approach to collection development. Several eminent librarians are agitating effectively and vociferously for planned collection development, and a handful is even writing on this subject. Overall, though, many more librarians and students need to be convinced of and trained in the techniques of effective collection development. The general purpose of this volume is to contribute to this twofold aim - to convince and to train. In particular it seeks to assist those who are or will be directly involved in collection development planning, in conducting use and user studies, in selecting and weeding library materials.

With this objective in mind, we have divided the work into three sections, covering collection development policies, collection evaluation and use studies, and selection and weeding of materials. These sections, totalling nine chapters, are supplemented by a select bibliography. Each section consists of a small number of chapters devoted to specific topics, and each of these chapters includes an explanation of the theoretical basis of the topic, a discussion of the main points and of the coverage of those points in the literature, and a guide to the practical application of the methodology and techniques adopted by those working in the field. Each chapter is then complemented by a number of readings chosen especially for the manner in which they either explain in greater detail some of the issues touched upon in the chapter, or illustrate how the techniques discussed have been applied in particular situations.

In Chapter 1 we address the question of why a library should even bother to have a collection policy, and it is interesting to note that this is one area in which many librarians have expressed strong opinions. We have explored the basis of these opinions and make a firm recommendation that flexible and well constructed policy statements are not a luxury, or even simply "useful", but are in fact essential parts of the administrative and professional armoury.

Chapter 2 then leads on to the very practical area of policy development and the construction of policy statements, an area in which considerable confusion over the difference between selection, acquisitions and collection development (and even collection evaluation) seems to arise. We address the areas that ought to be covered by collection development policies and provide details of sample policy statements to demonstrate not only where they excel but also where they are inadequate.

Chapter 3 presents the detail of policy formulation and offers descriptions of the methods used by those who have already produced policy statements and also advice to those about to attempt the exercise, recommending a very structured approach which requires that the policy itself be revised regularly and often, with continual fine-tuning.

The second part of this book focuses on collection evaluation. In Chapter 4 we ask why it is necessary to have procedures for collection evaluation; this is one area in which we can report both quantity and quality in the available literature. In contrast a well documented lack of interest in libraries as information sources combined with an as yet underdeveloped set of survey techniques suggest that librarians still have a long way to go in their efforts to find out who does and does not use libraries. In Chapter 5 we explore the tools and techniques available to librarians, making frequent reference to the various attempts that have been made to construct and use effective measuring instruments.

Part 3 covers the even more practical areas of selection and weeding. We have taken the viewpoint that weeding is an integral part of the selection process, and not simply a dirty job to be avoided if at all possible. Chapter 6 opens with a discussion of the "wants or needs" dilemma, the resolution of which is basic to any attempt to develop effective selection procedures. The differing environments in which selection takes place in different kinds of libraries are addressed, and the most important of the selection strategies are discussed in detail.

Chapter 7 covers the main approaches to the selection of sources of information for collection development, using a simple scheme of classification designed specifically for this book, analyzing the characteristics of each of the classes represented and offering one example of each class or sub-class. Throughout this chapter, and Chapter 8, we stress the necessity for the stock selector to examine each tool in use in terms of its ability to evaluate as well as to provide bibliographical details, and we lay strong emphasis on the need for complete understanding of the rules for inclusion and exclusion used in each tool.

Chapter 8 comprises a listing of the works discussed in Chapter 7, with more detailed description added where necessary. We have attempted in these two chapters to outline a method by which students can come to grips with an otherwise confusing variety of selection tools, and practising librarians can complete their own collections of relevant tools.

Chapter 9 covers both the rationale behind the weeding of collections and the methods that are in use or are recommended. It will be noted that we do not use ugly euphemisms but prefer to regard an unused or unwanted book in the same light as any other weed, simply a plant growing in the wrong place. By way of illustration we include a simple, stylized example of how one would go about weeding one section of a public library collection, to demonstrate how the various theories and practical applications come together in a working programme.

References

1   G. Edward Evans, *Developing Library and Information Center Collections* (2nd ed. Library Science Text Series. Littleton, Colo.: Libraries Unlimited, 1987), p. 65.

2   G.E. Gorman, "Guidelines for Collection Development Courses in Australian Library Schools." *Education for Librarianship: Australia* 3, 1 (1986): 38-45. See also "Discussion of 'Guidelines for Collection Development Courses in Australian Library Schools'," *Education for Librarianship: Australia* 3, 3 (1986): 36-41.

PART 1

COLLECTION DEVELOPMENT POLICIES

CHAPTER 1

THE RATIONALE FOR COLLECTION DEVELOPMENT POLICIES

Reasons for Policy Statements

A written collection development policy statement is intended " ...to clarify objectives and to facilitate coordination and cooperation, both within a library or library system and among cooperating libraries.... If it is well done, it should serve as a day-to-day working tool that provides the necessary guidelines for carrying out the majority of tasks within the area of collection building."[1] As Gardner intimates, such a policy serves a broad range of functions, and in fact he continues by setting forth a dozen reasons why a collection development policy statement should be formulated. In his view such a document performs the following tasks:

1. forces staff to think through library goals and commit themselves to these goals, helps them to identify long- and short-range needs of users and to establish priorities for allocating funds;
2. helps assure that the library will commit itself to serving all parts of the community, both present and future;
3. helps set standards for the selection and weeding of materials;
4. informs users, administrators and other libraries of collection scope, facilitates coordination of collection development among institutions;
5. helps minimize personal bias by selectors and to highlight imbalances in selection criteria;
6. serves as an in-service training tool for new staff;
7. helps assure continuity, especially in collections of any size, provides pattern and framework to ease transition from one librarian to the next;
8. provides a means of staff self-evaluation, or for evaluation by outsiders;
9. helps demonstrate that the library is running a business-like operation;
10. provides information to assist in budget allocations;
11. contributes to operational efficiency in terms of routine decisions, which helps junior staff;
12. serves as a tool of complaint-handling with regard to inclusions or exclusions.[2]

How wonderful this sounds - a written collection development policy does everything that one could ever hope for, and then some. But is this really so, and is it even necessary? Historically one could argue that it is in fact a needless luxury. After all, Sir Thomas

Bodley did not begin his collection by formulating a policy statement, and the Bodleian Library today still does not enjoy the benefit of such a document. Few - if any - of the great librarians of the past ever bothered with anything so mundane; they simply relied on their genuine passion for literature and inbred instinct for what was "right" when collecting. Purely on the basis of these traits they were able to build unsurpassed collections, and no one would deny that the British Library, the Library of Congress, the Bibliotheque Nationale, the university libraries of Cambridge and Oxford, Harvard and Yale are among the world's great repositories of recorded knowledge. They may be eccentric, idiosyncratic and eclectic, but great nevertheless - and all without benefit of a written collection development policy.

None of these libraries has formulated until comparatively recently a written collection development policy. The reasons for this are not difficult to trace; according to Adams in his survey of the nineteenth century Australian scene, "to some extent this is understandable when we examine the management structure of the libraries of the period, where the role of librarian was usually shown to be little more than caretaker or curator of the collections."[3] In museums, colleges, universities, seminaries and public libraries the librarian had few professional responsibilities and certainly little involvement in selection, which was the prerogative of the library committee in most cases. On the whole libraries of the late nineteenth and early twentieth centuries exhibited an eclectic, serendipitous and highly personal approach to collection building, as John Adams clearly indicates in his interesting historical overview (pp. 10-16).

Today, of course, several of these libraries do have written, publicly available policy statements. Why might they now regard collection development policies as important? Probably the most basic reason is that they provide guidance through the forest of documentation. This is important in all fields, whether agricultural economics or nineteenth century literature. The nature of modern documentation may be characterized as unspeakably complex, diverse and amoeba-like. In terms of geographical, chronological and linguistic breadth the material in which any library has an interest spans a broad spectrum of countries, periods and languages. This recorded knowledge encompasses all aspects of human experience; it is truly multi- , inter- and cross-disciplinary. Furthermore, disciplines are constantly changing their nature and focus as new trends rise and fall. Thirty years ago area studies of any sort were almost unknown, and even ten years ago no self-respecting scholar dared mention Australian studies. Today African studies is officially enshrined in centres at many British and American universities, as is development studies in its various forms. New literatures in English, bio-ethics and other fields become established with frightening regularity. As these fields wax and wane, they exert significant impact on the nature, quality and quantity of recorded knowledge; and all of this becomes reflected in what libraries collect.

In addition to the complexity, flux and blurring of boundaries apparent in modern recorded knowledge one faces the problem of volume. Look, for example, at religion as a relatively typical area of knowledge. In this one discipline there are some 150,000 American titles in print according to *Religious Books in Print,* and *Ulrich's International Periodicals Directory* shows more than 2500 theological serials in existence. If one considers all fields of knowledge, the scale of current output is far more daunting. In the United Kingdom there were issued in 1985 alone 41,254 new titles and 11,740 new editions and reprints, for a total of 52,994 titles. The 1987 edition of *Ulrich's* lists 68,770 current serials, while the *Serials Directory* records a staggering 113,000 extant titles.[4] In addition to the USA and the United Kingdom the USSR, France, Germany and Japan are all major producers of printed literature.

Given these characteristics of published literature, how does the librarian proceed to build an adequate or representative collection in any field? Two ways followed in the past have been the way of the expert or the way of the clerk. Today the volume and complexity of recorded knowledge prevent one from being an expert in more than a tiny fragment of any field; gone forever are the days of the Baroque man in terms of broad understanding and genuinely informed, catholic tastes. At the same time the alternative of the clerical function, of ordering what one is told to purchase by others, is neither satisfying nor acceptable professionally. It is the information professional who is trained to find out about literature and who, de facto if not de jure, ought to be charged with selecting appropriate materials. But this means that collection development should be regarded as a "scientific" enterprise operating in accordance with established criteria, techniques and methods; it is these elements that become formalized into a policy statement which has at least some of the functions noted above by Gardner.

Frankly, a number of these reasons or justifications seem dangerously near the edge of acceptability, and one could argue that Gardner makes excessive claims for collection development policies. Indeed John Horacek dissects Gardner's arguments point-by-point, suggesting that these claims are not only unrealistic but also irrelevant in the academic library context.[5] However, this list does embody some of the more important arguments to be advanced in favour of a written collection policy. Essentially Gardner is arguing, at least by implication, that a policy is a planning document. Devising a policy is a means of engaging in self-examination and reflection, which today is essential for rational, coherent growth of a collection. All work in a library becomes routine, and routine often becomes a substitute for vision, especially in smaller libraries where one may lack the support of professional colleagues. Users change, needs change and resource availability changes; a policy can help one to be aware of these changes by acting as a collection of baseline data for current operations and, ideally, a starting point for future development. Essentially, then, a policy is useful because it forces or encourages one to think through the library's goals and place them in some sort of perspective, a context anchored in the present and directed towards the future. This means that a policy is primarily a planning device; this is equivalent to points one, two, seven and ten advanced by Gardner.

The Planning Function

As part of its planning function, the collection policy seeks to identify and develop an appropriate response to perceived user needs, both present and future. This ensures that the library establish priorities for the allocation of funds and that it commit itself to serving all sections of the user community. It is with respect to this aspect that opponents of collection policies become most vociferous in their criticism. Horacek, among others, says that serving all parts of the community (however defined) is impossible. Because libraries today are cutting services to existing clients by cancelling serial subscriptions and decreasing monograph orders, how can they afford to think even in passing about the needs of future users? Inadequate funding, in other words, makes rational, directed development an unattainable ideal. As funding is unpredictable, so too is the collecting of library materials.[6] Well, one might suggest that this is precisely why libraries need to have clearly articulated collection development policies. Such policies are contracts between users and their libraries; and like all good contracts they indicate the parameters within which services can be delivered. Thus a collection policy states on one hand the priorities that must be supported at all costs, and on the other it specifies areas that should receive attention when funding increases to more generous levels. Without a policy that is both flexible and far-sighted the library is engaged merely in spending money on materials for the collection, not in systematic development which makes rational use of limited financial resources. In other words it is professionally irresponsible not to have a document which will help librarians to husband their resources more carefully as a means of providing more and better materials for future generations of users.

The External Communication Function

In addition to its planning function a policy possesses a communication function. It informs users, administrators and other libraries of the nature of a given collection; in other words it communicates internally and externally and in this equates substantially with Gardner's fourth point. Looking first at the external mode, Horacek and others take exception to this function as well, stating that it is irrelevant in countries where there is no national collection development plan. That is if a national library or other information agency in a country has not mounted a formal national drive to coordinate collection development, why should smaller, more parochial institutions expend energy in this area? There are two answers to be advanced here. First, if a national library cannot be relied upon to lead the way in other areas, why should one wait for it in this case? There is no national collection development plan, but why should that stop an individual library from developing its own plan? Second, must one start with a giant leap, or is it more feasible to start with a tiny step? Begin today with one individual library, hoping tomorrow to influence a consortium, next week a state or province, eventually the nation in a "bottom-up" approach to national collection development. In other words one library or group of libraries can take the lead by showing that policies can be developed, that they can serve a useful communication function in coordinating development within clearly defined network or consortia boundaries.

Communication among libraries, of course, also relates to the financial aspect of planning. As the ALA *Guidelines* state, "widespread budgetary constraints and the growth of interlibrary cooperation for shared resources and service networks have given impetus to analyze collection activity in universally comprehensible terms."[7] Libraries need to save money, or at least spend it more carefully, and one way to do this is by communicating with one another about rationalization of resources; this is precisely what a collection development policy is designed to do.

The Internal Communication Function

Communicating with other libraries is only part of the overall dialogue. Within institutions the library also needs to communicate with its community - users, staff and administrators. There needs to be dialogue in particular with both the library's clients (users of all types) and its masters (whether local authority, parent company or academic institution); these are the people with whom libraries have contractual obligations and to whom they are responsible in one way or other. Preparing a policy statement requires consultation with the user at all levels, and this can be the beginning of an ongoing dialogue and continuing involvement of library clients. Surely this can be an important way to generate not only goodwill but also commitment, both of which aid the library and protect it from attack. While not necessarily part of the user community in the normal sense, administrators must be encompassed within the internal communication process for very practical reasons. Normally they come to the librarian and ask, "What in the world are you doing with all this money?" With a policy one can be on the offensive for a change; using the policy statement, the librarian can indicate to the exchequer that particular types of materials in specified subject areas are being purchased as a matter of policy. The collection development policy, then, is an outgrowth of effective professional responsibility and a means of expressing operational efficiency - Gardner's ninth point.

The Inflexibility of Policy Statements

The foregoing should indicate that it is possible to disarm critics who attack collection development policies as planning or communication devices. Less quickly defeated, though, are those who criticize on the grounds of inflexibility, because they often point to practical experience with policies that have become enshrined as gospel. Cargill is but one example of critics in this category.

> ... If librarians are coping with developing their collection without *written* policies, why then engage in an exercise known to be time-consuming and difficult to prepare? The existence of a written policy does not guarantee that a balanced collection will result. The policy, if written, represents an ideal rather than a realistic situation. How can such policies be accurately interpreted? Academic libraries need the flexibility and freedom to make selection choices without being tied to a written policy.[8]

Policies, then, are often seen as inflexible documents. What happens as new disciplines emerge, as a community profile alters, as multiculturalism becomes increasingly prevalent, as funding decreases? To the degree that policy statements are static, they do inhibit the librarian's response to such changes; and unfortunately many policies exist which, because of the time and effort involved in their preparation, have become inflexible codes. However understandable this may be due to costs, staff shortages and plain inertia, it really does miss the whole point and purpose of a collection development policy. After all, a key purpose of a written policy statement is to define both the stability and *flexibility* in the collection building process. Just as collections grow and develop, so should policies. What the librarian attempts to do in devising a policy is to use the past to nurture the present, to ensure stability rather than rigidity. A policy is no substitute for awareness of changing needs or informed criticism of collection building; rather it is a framework for ongoing review. Once formalized a policy must never be regarded as fixed for eternity. If collections are to grow and change in response to a host of factors, then their policies must be flexible enough to guide them. Therefore, while the policy forms a basic framework for projected growth, it must also be reviewed at regular intervals to ensure that it continues to provide an acceptable and viable pattern for effective collection building. Certainly this is a primary assumption in Chapters 2 and 3.

References

1   Richard K. Gardner, *Library Collections: Their Origin, Selection and Development* (New York: McGraw-Hill Book Company, 1981), p. 22. A less ambitious view is taken by William A. Katz in *Collection Development: The Selection of Materials for Libraries* (New York: Holt, Rinehart and Winston, 1980), pp. 19-20.

2   *Ibid.*, pp. 222-224.

3   John Adams, "More than 'Librarie Keepers'." In *Books, Libraries and Readers in Colonial Australia: Papers from the Forum on Australian Colonial Library History Held at Monash University, 1-2 June 1984,* ed. Elizabeth Morrison and Michael Talbot (Clayton, Vic.: Graduate School of Librarianship, Monash University, 1984), p. 93. It was probably only at the end of the nineteenth century that selection (one component in the collection development process) began publicly to exercise the professional imagination of these managers. See, for example, Spofford's 1890 essay "The Choice of Books" reprinted as "A Guide to Book Selection." In *Ainsworth Rand Spofford: Bookman and Librarian,* ed. John Y. Cole (The Heritage of Librarianship Series, no. 2. Littleton, Colo.: Libraries Unlimited, 1975), pp. 110-127.

4   *Serials Directory: An International Reference Book* (3 vols. Birmingham, Ala.: EBSCO, 1986).

5   John Horacek, "Collection Development Policies." In *Collection Management in Academic Libraries: Papers Delivered at a National Seminar, Surfers Paradise, Queensland, 16th-17th February 1984,* ed. Cathryn Crowe, Philip Kent and Barbara Paton (Sydney: Library Association of Australia, University and College Libraries Section, 1984), pp. 11-18.

6   *Ibid.*

7   American Library Association, Collection Development Committee, *Guidelines for Collection Development,* ed. David L. Perkins (Chicago, Ill.: American Library Association, 1979), pp. 9-10.

8   Jennifer Cargill, "Collection Development Policies: An Alternative Viewpoint." *Library Acquisitions: Practice and Theory* 8 (1984): 47.

READINGS ON THE RATIONALE FOR COLLECTION DEVELOPMENT POLICIES

There are, as indicated at the opening of this chapter, many arguments to be advanced in favour of collection development policies. Only the major arguments in two areas, planning and communicating, have been discussed here; these can be regarded as among the most important functions of policies in any context and appear time and again in policy documents as their raison d'etre. The many other reasons offered in support of policy documents have been described elsewhere in some detail, as the bibliography indicates. From many possibilities we have selected two succinct summaries of the arguments for written collection development policies. Y.T. Feng (pp. 17-21) believes strongly that such policies are important for several reasons: they enhance self-examination and reflection, encourage consistent and balanced growth, offer protection against outside pressures and facilitate resource sharing. In a similar vein Eric Carpenter (pp. 21-23), following the lead of Baughman and Mosher, suggests that written policy statements introduce rationality into collection development in a way that no other process can and that they force libraries to address their several audiences clearly and logically.

We regard these views put forth by Feng and Carpenter as representative of the more legitimate arguments that will prove correct in the long term. There are, however, serious arguments against the need for and viability of collection policy statements, and these cannot be ignored. Unfortunately, many of the published arguments are related to specific situations and so lack general application. One exception is the paper by Jennifer Cargill (pp. 24-25), which suggests that institutional realities operate against either the need for or possibility of written collection policy statements - time and money, flexibility and freedom, realism and responsiveness are all offered as reasons why policies are neither possible nor necessary. Such arguments are likely to be presented far less politely in the real world, so one must be prepared to counter them firmly and logically.

One problem with much of the discussion about collection development policies is the way in which the requirements of a particular context and a singular historical moment seem to muddy the water. Whether arguing for or against policies, one must be prepared to take the broader view, to consider consequences in some future time. To facilitate such an historical perspective we open these readings with John Adams' encapsulation of the largely non-professional but well-intentioned ethos of nineteenth century libraries (pp. 10-16). As this article quite clearly suggests, libraries have made amazing progress in a century. It also indicates, albeit obliquely, that great collections can be created out of personal tastes, cultured bibliophilia and felicitous bequests. All of this must be kept in mind as one considers the nature and function of structured collection development policies.

John Adams, "More than 'Librarie Keepers'." In *Books, Libraries and Readers in Colonial Australia: Papers from the Forum on Australian Colonial Library History Held at Monash University, 1-2 June 1984*, edited by Elizabeth Morrison and Michael Talbot, 93-101. Clayton, Vic.: Graduate School of Librarianship, Monash University, 1984.

It is perhaps rather ironic that the history of libraries and librarianship in nineteenth century Australia is most reticent about the real achievements of the librarians who were, after all, responsible for the maintenance of the libraries. To some extent this is understandable when we examine the management structure of the libraries of the period, where the role of librarian was usually shown to be little more than caretaker or curator of the collections.

The British library scene provided enough precedent in all types of libraries from the subscription libraries to the mechanics' institutes and the later municipal public libraries. Frank Beckwith in a paper on the eighteenth century proprietary libraries in England provides a useful summary of the situation in such libraries:

> The librarian was clearly no more than the custodian of the books and the stern administrator of rules laid down for him. His post was no sinecure and he (or she, for women were not refused office, being probably better able to survive on the modest competences attached to the office) was not overpaid.... Rule upon rule hemmed him in; no initiative was possible or expected; he was the very humble servant of the proprietors.[1]

This would have been the essence of the position of librarians in Australian libraries from the pioneering Australian Subscription Library to the hundreds of mechanics' institutes and schools of art scattered across the face of the continent by the end of the century. Indeed it is often quite difficult to learn much about the librarians who served these libraries, even in many cases their very names.

The Australian Subscription Library employed a number of librarians over the forty-four years of its existence, few of them at all memorable. They were circumscribed in their role, being little more than clerks. They were responsible to the Secretary and to the Committee of the Library for the maintenance of the library and the collections, the management of the reading room and the operation of the circulation system. The by-laws of the Library called for the Librarian to keep a series of registers, a stock book, a deposit book (of books lent to the Library for the use of members), a catalogue, an issues book and a book of fines and forfeits. The Librarian was expected to keep a record of overdues to report to the monthly Committee meetings and to send out the appropriate overdue notices. He was expected to be in attendance on subscribers from 10 a.m. to 5 p.m. and again from 7 p.m. to 11 p.m.[2]

As Case has pointed out in his study, *Librarians in New South Wales*, the real control of the selection of the bookstock and the development of library policy was firmly in the hands of the Library Committee. The Librarian, he suggests, "was expected to be a cipher contributing nothing but deference to the members and dusting to the collection". Even the cataloguing and general organisation of the bookstock was not his responsibility. The status of the first librarians can be seen in their salary - Peter Cook, "Librarian and dispenser", earned £40 a year. Few could be induced to stay long in the post, and of some librarians, there seemed to be a particular inclination to drunkenness. At least one librarian, John Fairfax, soon moved on to become pioneer editor of the *The Sydney Morning Herald.* Only with P.J. Elliott as librarian was there an improvement in his role for he acquired an assistant, had more say in the book vote and earned £255 a year.[3]

The first mechanics' institutes often combined the posts of Secretary and Librarian. The Van Diemen's Land Mechanics' Institution Secretary was to act as Librarian and was to "have the care and management of, and be personally accountable for, all printed Books, Charts, Maps, Paintings, Engravings and Furniture, and such other property of the Institution of every description as is not by the next rule, or may not hereafter be, confided to the Curator (of the Museum), and make out and keep a detailed catalogue or list thereof, distinguishing Donations by the names of the Donors, and transmitting a Copy, dated and certified as a true copy, to the Trustees forthwith, and afterwards quarterly and correcting such catalogue or list or copy as circumstances may require". There were also the numerous standard duties of a Secretary.[4]

At the Sydney Mechanics' School of Arts the Library laws set out the nature of the records to be maintained by the Librarian, who was in this case not the Secretary, such as the "proposing book" in which members wrote in their suggestions for purchase, the stock book, the manuscript catalogue and the circulation register. As with other libraries he was responsible for the maintenance of the collection and the operation of the circulation, while the Committee held on to real management of the Library. An interim measure of the initial set of laws is of interest when it decreed:

> Till the next Annual General Meeting the Library shall be under the Superintendence of a Chief Librarian, assisted by twelve sub-librarians, chosen from the general body of the Members, who will engage to attend one week each, in rotation, to execute the several duties of Librarian.

At the least the bookstock was then quite small and the hours were just 7 to 9 p.m., Monday to Saturday.[5]

Secretary-Librarians were general throughout mechanics' institutes right into this century. In the dual role they have more cause to be remembered, even honoured, like Robert Band, the Secretary of the Sydney Mechanics' School of Arts who died while returning to England after some years in the post, and James Harrison, the Secretary-Librarian of the first Geelong Mechanics' Institute which he had founded, linking this job with his role as newspaper editor and bookseller.

The rules of mechanics' institutes and schools of art generally differed little in their statement of the role of librarians. As late as 1899 the Newrybar School of Arts near Ballina in New South Wales included in its regulations a statement that the custodian or librarian:

> ...shall be appointed by the Committee and shall, as the Committee may determine from time to time, have the immediate charge of all books, etc., connected with the Library and reading room. He shall keep an issue book, and enter therein the number of every volume issued, and to whom and the date when issued and when returned, and shall furnish a report of the state of the Library, etc. to each quarterly committee meeting, and a general report to the Secretary at least 14 days previous to each annual meeting.[6]

The Maclean Mechanics' Institute also in New South Wales in its rules issued in 1906 saw the librarian's role as having charge of the buildings, being responsible for their cleanliness, lighting, etc., for the maintenance of order in the Reading Room and Premises generally, and for the exclusion therefrom of persons who were not members, accepting such visitors as should be introduced by the Committee members. In this latter case the hours of the Reading Room were 9 a.m. to 10 p.m. Monday to Saturday, 10 a.m. to 6 p.m. Sunday.[7]

Even with the Council-controlled libraries the role of librarians was no different. The Committees or the Councils were, as before, responsible for the selection of bookstock and the formulation of policies, and quite often, the preparation of catalogues of the collections where a bookseller may be employed or an enthusiast on the Committee. Nevertheless it was inevitable that the Librarian had a close interest in the bookstock and came to know the subscribers and their wants so that he could provide high standards of reader assistance, even if no more than a patient ear for their regular narratives of their life, activities and problems. Several librarians, generally remembered as being elderly, were fondly recalled by a number of people in their biographies and reminiscences. The limited nature of the catalogue and the rather broad classification of the collections meant that readers were more dependent on the Librarian and his knowledge of the bookstock for guidance. A Librarian dedicated to his or her task with a real sense of service could be said to be in their limited way offering notable standards of professionalism.

Outside mechanics' institutes, libraries existed attached to schools, churches and Sunday schools, to societies and institutions of all kinds. In many cases there were librarians, generally employed in a voluntary capacity from among willing teachers or committee members. Even here, the roles of librarians could be determined by regulations such as with the Australasian Wesleyan Methodist Church in 1885 which listed rules for librarians of Sunday Schools:

> The Librarian shall take charge of the library, make a complete catalogue of the books, keep them in good order and enter in a proper book the issue and return of every volume lent, with their period during which they are kept; he shall also furnish to the Committee a quarterly report of the state of the library and the number of books issued therefrom.[8]

Again the control of the selection of bookstock was in the hands of the relevant committee, but it would be reasonable to expect that in these cases the librarians would be active members of the committees. Societies and clubs would also generally arrange to appoint one of their members to be librarian responsible to the committees or special library committees, a practice which is still current today.

The more scholarly libraries such as those of theological colleges and the libraries of cathedrals and of the scholarly societies and professional institutes were not always to be managed by appointed librarians, and often left to wait for the occasional bibliophile enthusiast who would voluntarily organise and catalogue the collections. Many such collections came as large single donations and were stored without any real attention for years until such an enthusiast would arouse some concern for the collection and its proper maintenance. With this initial encouragement a more formal library committee might be appointed with a secretary again acting as librarian. Such a library would at least have the attention of a knowledgeable book lover who could apply his unique skills to its organisation.

Libraries established for Government institutions could provide the basis for a more professional approach to their maintenance, even though the position of librarian might be a relatively low public service position. The roles of such librarians may have differed little from those of subscription libraries and institutes and could be expected to be carried out by junior clerks, perhaps as a side activity to their ordinary clerical duties. Even so, a scholarly collection could require a librarian with some reasonable education to ensure the proper organisation of the specialised materials. An example of one such library, that of the Australian Museum in Sydney, can illustrate. The Secretary of the Museum acted as Librarian and, under the Act of Incorporation 1899, was to keep a register of all books in the library, entering them in a library catalogue, maintaining a borrowers' register, to check on overdues and to follow them up to ensure their return, to provide reports on the collection, to write letters of thanks to the donors of items for the collection, and to organise appropriate inter-library loans to approved institutions.[9] No mention is made here of selection but there were indeed few purchases. Almost all material was donated. The Trustees were responsible for approving purchases as for any other costs to be incurred.

The role of librarians in universities and colleges may have differed little from the above, but there was more likely to be some degree of academic standing in the qualifications of such librarians. Initially the libraries were the responsibility of the Registrars or their staff, but assistants could be appointed to look after the libraries once they were large enough and needed to be properly organised and supervised. Dr Bride, a Doctor of Laws at Melbourne University, spent many years as assistant librarian until his appointment as Chief Librarian of the Public Library of Victoria. In smaller institutions the librarians might well be enthusiasts from among the teaching staff, who could be expected to have a stronger personal interest in the development of the collection and the cataloguing of it relatively free of interference from any committee or authority. Again, purchases would be few, the collections springing from generous donations.

Parliamentary libraries, when established, were often managed in the early stages by a member of the clerical staff such as was the case of the Legislative Council Library in New South Wales where in the 1840s Richard O'Connor, the Assistant Clerk, served as Librarian.[10] Later in the century the post of Librarian was recognised and each colony could boast of such librarians holding their respective posts for many years, although few could be as well remembered as Denis O'Donovan of the Parliamentary Library in Queensland.

O'Donovan's story is well told in a useful biographical article by Robert Longhurst in the *Australian Library Journal* in June 1975.[11] He brought to his position a valuable and extensive scholarly background for he had been professor of Modern Languages and Literature at the College des Hautes Etudes in Paris as well as lecturer at the University of Paris; editor of *L'Ami de la Religion*, a leading Catholic layman and author of the highly regarded *Memories of Rome*. He arrived in Melbourne in 1866 and lectured at the Public Library and worked for the formation of Schools of Design. He became Parliamentary Librarian in Brisbane in 1874 where he was to be greatly respected for his scholarship and significant role in the cultural and religious life of that city. As librarian he was responsible for the complete restoration of the library, developing a catalogue organised by an alphabetico-analytical system unique for its time and which was to win him recognition around the world. He was honoured by the Queensland Government which recommended him for the award of CMG. The catalogue was not his only concern for he was particularly concerned to develop collections which would have the greatest value for members of parliament in carrying out their roles, with serials and legislative reference materials being acquired and promoted. O'Donovan has every right to be named one of the first really professional librarians in Australia.

The major public libraries were the only other real training ground for professional librarianship such as we might know it. Again, because of the size and scope and significance of these collections, their scholarly nature and the greater degree of effective management required, the librarians appointed to these libraries needed to demonstrate a scholarly background and good management skills. Many of those who served as chief librarians had just such background, while their initiative in organising and cataloguing the collections, their dedication to implementing more efficient reader services and their role in encouraging the employment of well-educated staff and training them indicates just how closely they reached what we would regard as true professional status.

Among the earlier librarians was Robert Cooper Walker, first Librarian of the Free Public Library of Sydney at the age of thirty-six in 1869. He was the son of a clergyman headmaster and had served several years as Government clerk, rising to senior rank before he became for a short time Inspector of Public Charities and then Chief Librarian. While he was not so much a scholar, his administrative skills and personal initiative enabled him against all odds to develop a significant collection, to start a lending service and promote the idea of a truly National Library in Sydney.[12]

With regard to the Public Library of Victoria one may be tempted to say that its greatest librarian was Sir Redmond Barry, scholar and bibliophile supreme who, as Chairman of the Trustees, spent a great deal of his time attending closely to the personal affairs of the Library and playing a dominant role in the development of its collections. The first Librarian, Augustus Henry Tulk, was a man after his own heart, a highly regarded scholar, profoundly knowledgeable in both the classics and modern literature, and a veritable bibliophile who, like his mentor, had personal knowledge of the book trade in Europe. He organised and catalogued the collection but the users depended a great deal on his own knowledge of what was in the collection and where, even to the very pages, the information required could be obtained. Edmund La Touche Armstrong, a successor to the post of Chief Librarian, was to write of him:

He was to some extent a Librarian of the old school, and to say that is to pay the memory of the man no mean compliment.... He had not the combination of scholarship and practical librarianship of Panizzi, but he had the wide reading and the real love of books that so often marked the old-time librarian or keeper. He was not the man to devise means to supply promptly whatever information might be required. There was no need for haste, and what was worth getting was worth waiting for, if it could not be supplied from his own capacious memory. So he had none of the aids to readers that are so necessary in modern libraries.... It was as a collector and a book lover, rather than a Librarian, that the services of Augustus Tulk were valuable.[13]

Dr Thomas Francis Bride as Chief Librarian from 1881 brought good management skills as well as local scholarship and experience as a librarian to the position. With the help of another scholar-bibliophile with bibliographic experience, Dr Gagliardi, he was able to produce a much more efficient catalogue of the collection as well as better organisation of the resources. He actively promoted better reference services, and was concerned to employ bright young graduates as clerks to train them to a career in librarianship. He started a Lending Library and was the leading architect in the building up of what was to be regarded by visitors as one of the finest libraries in the world in its day.

We cannot leave our account of colonial librarians without paying homage to Henry Charles Lennox Anderson who became Principal Librarian of the Free Public Library of Sydney in 1893 after a long career in the New South Wales Public Service, principally as teacher and agricultural chemist, and first Director of Agriculture in that colony, founder of the Hawkesbury Agricultural College. He came to librarianship rather reluctantly when his department was closed down and he received the Free Library appointment. He never really regarded that he was a career librarian but was a good public servant and he returned to the position of Director of Agriculture in 1906.

Nevertheless as Chief Librarian he became dedicated to his role, and was to achieve world recognition for his cataloguing rules. He kept abreast of contemporary overseas library developments by instituting such reforms as reclassifying the collection by the Dewey Decimal Classification system. He became an ally of David Scott Mitchell, working with him personally cataloguing his collections and eventually having the satisfaction of seeing this valuable collection of Australiana presented to the State. He must also be remembered for his training classes for staff and for the employment of women as clerks. One at least, Margaret Windeyer, was a graduate of the Library School of New York and was appointed cataloguer. It is interesting to note that before her time Christopher Brennan, the noted academic and poet, was Chief Cataloguer of the Library.

In 1897 Anderson attended the Second International Library Conference in London at which he gave a paper on library work in New South Wales. He referred to his staff at the time, stating that it "consists entirely of the inferior sex at present, but", he went on, "I believe that our Public Service Commissioners consider our work peculiarly suited for women". The women were only able to be appointed as clerks and had little career structure, while the bright young men, well educated and selected after a competitive examination, were encouraged to think of themselves progressing through the Public Service generally and not just remaining in the Library. He went on:

> I hold classes for the junior officers, which I have found invaluable for training these assistants to thoroughly understand our own system of cataloguing and indexing, and to deal intelligently with the public whom we have to serve. We have to deal with all classes of the community, and I have found that the young men who come first into contact with visitors must be far more than messengers: my aim has therefore been to enable them to be of use to the inquirer for information, and thus leave the assistant librarians and myself free for our own special duties. I can speak highly of the good feeling engendered in the younger members of the staff by these classes, and have always the satisfaction of feeling that I have ready to my hand a succession of men well fitted to accept higher duties in our own or any other similar library, and to efficiently fill any vacancy that may arise on our own staff.[14]

Anderson brought in, then, a new approach to the career of librarianship which was genuinely taking the career into real professional status. With the new century librarians were to emerge as truly professional, a far cry from the older curator positions which, nevertheless, were to linger on into our day in many smaller libraries. Here in Anderson's time were the germs of the development of the profession of librarianship in Australia.

In 1896 the establishment of the Library Association of Australasia at the Intercolonial Conference of Librarians in Melbourne helped to generate a professional approach to librarianship among the new stream of library assistants in the public libraries and in some other major institutions. Professional literature from Britain and the United States was being read, systems studied and adopted, and ideas being shared by this group who included J.R.G. Adams and W.H. Ifould of South Australia, E. La T. Armstrong and E. Morris Miller of Victoria and James S. Battye of Western Australia among others. With their story comes the next chapter in the development of librarianship in Australia.

References

1   Frank Beckwith, "The Eighteenth-Century Proprietary Library in England." *Journal of Documentation* 3 (1947): 9.

2   *Catalogue with Rules, Regulations and Bye-Laws for the Conduct of the Australian Subscription Library and Reading Room* (Sydney, 1830), pp. 9-10.

3   F.M.B. Cass, *Librarians in New South Wales: A Study* (Adelaide: Library Board of South Australia, 1972), pp. 5-6.

4   *Rules of the Van Diemen's Land Mechanics' Institution* (Hobart Town, 1843), p. 10.

5   *The Laws of the Sydney Mechanics' School of Arts* (Sydney, 1833), pp. 14-17.

6   Newrybar School of Arts, *Constitution, Rules and Regulations and By-laws* (Ballina, 1899).

7   Maclean Mechanics' Institution, *Rules and By-laws of the Institution* (Maclean, 1906).

8   Australasian Wesleyan Methodist Church, *Laws and Regulations* (Melbourne, 1885), Rule ix-6, p.109.

9   Australian Museum, Sydney, *Act of Incorporation ...* (Sydney: Government Printer, 1899), pp. 18-19.

10 R.L. Cope, "The Genesis of the NSW Parliamentary Library." *Australian Library Journal* 17, 1 (February 1968): 30-31.

11 Robert Longhurst, "Personalities from the Past: Denis O'Donovan." *Australian Library Journal* 24, 5 (June 1975): 214-216.

12 G.D. Richardson, "A Man of Zeal and Application." *Australian Library Journal* 25, 9 (August 1976): 242-243.

13 Edmund La Touche Armstrong, *The Book of the Public Library ... 1856-1906* (Melbourne: Melbourne Public Library, 1906), p. 112.

14 H.C.L. Anderson, "Library Work in New South Wales." In *Second International Library Conference, London 1897: Papers* (London, 1897), p. 94.

Y.T. Feng, "The Necessity for a Collection Development Policy Statement." *Library Resources and Technical Services* 23, 1 (1979): 39-44.

"The Library is the heart of education," we are told. When the Widener Memorial Library was first built in the midst of Harvard Yard, there were some professorial grumblings about its "ungainly size" which prompted the famous and beloved (at least by librarians) retort from George Kittredge: "You could destroy all the other Harvard buildings and, with Widener left standing, still have a university." But I am sure even the architect of that building would not mistake Professor Kittredge's remark for an aesthetic appreciation of his edifice. True, buildings are important, just as clothes are important. "The basic elements of any library are books, people, and buildings," and, to quote Lawrence S. Thompson, "in precisely that order of importance." In other words, the heart of the library lies in its collections.

The foundations of the Boston Public Library were not made of bricks and mortar but rather the private collections of books and documents from Edward Everett, George Ticknor, Theodore Parker, and a munificent gift from a Boston boy made good, Joshua Bates, a systematic, intensive, global acquisition program to stock the new library with "a collection of books in as many departments of human knowledge as possible." The three-year Bates plan itself netted the fledgling institution some 27,000 volumes, "purchased in the great book marts of Europe." And these are the cornerstones that made the BPL [Boston Public Library] a research library.

So, collections are important. And collections have to be built continuously. Learning, so goes a Chinese saying, is like sailing against the tide: if you don't advance, you retreat. So does a library collection. A first-rate collection, if not properly nurtured, will invariably deteriorate - and not merely in its physical aspect. But growth is a complex and many splendored thing. We grow taller and indeed sometimes shorter as we grow older; we grow fatter or thinner, stronger or weaker, prettier or, alas, homelier; we grow older but many feel younger; we become happier or sadder, and if we are blessed, wiser and kinder. A collection also grows in a myriad of ways. It may grow in size, it may grow in market value, and it may grow in its relevance and use. It may grow in the scope of its coverage, and it may grow in the depth of its specialization; or, it may just grow, amoebalike, by means of pseudopodia - in this case, a mixture of available funds and articulate personal preferences, whether from the librarian or the user.

And somehow, in each case, it implies a collection development policy; for even the conspicuous lack of it describes a practice that reflects a certain philosophical rationale. And many libraries, while not in possession of a written collection development policy statement, nevertheless do operate with certain goals, objectives, and guidelines when selecting the materials to be acquired. And while some libraries follow detailed collection development policies with minute subject breakdowns and specific imprint requirements, others may opt to pursue their task with broad outlines and general objectives. And, either way, good library collections have been developed. But we are here this morning to consider the need for a written collection development policy statement, or rather, a standardized statement to allow comparison and facilitate cooperation.

Do we need it? And if so, why? In these days of universal fiscal constraints, it is only natural to bemoan the information explosion and to contemplate library ecology. Budgetary limitations necessitate the setting of priorities, which in turn requires a reexamination of goals and objectives and the definition of the precise role and function of the institution. In this sense, the present shortage of money is perhaps a blessing in disguise in that it forces us to think. Here, at the very outset, I should like to say that I don't believe we should formulate collection development policy to save money. In fact, I don't believe the prime purpose of the library is to save money. Consortia, networks, resource sharing all are important, but the purpose of librarianship is to provide better library service, not to reduce library expenditure. If library A chooses not to subscribe to certain journals or purchase other books because it can rely on the holdings in library B, it can claim to have improved its service only when it thereby can use the money "saved" to subscribe to other journals or purchase other books which otherwise would not be available to its users. Resource sharing must be progressive, not regressive. Library consortia as well as technological innovation may very well cost money instead of saving money, but the governing criterion lies in the services increased and improved, not in the dollar figure decreased. If saving money be the primary goal, there is no surer way than simply to close down the library.

Returning to the rationale for a collection development policy, one may ask why it should be desirable to have a written statement. First of all, the very process of writing one affords the opportunity for self-examination and reflection, two essential ingredients for growth and renewal. All work, however creative or interesting at the beginning, can easily settle down to a routine that sometimes breeds boredom and blurs, if not kills, vision. Times change, people change, our needs change, and our resources change. What's best for the past may not always be best for the present, not to mention the future. Collection development policy, once defined, must serve at once as a base for current operation and as a springboard for future growth.

The second reason, which is the raison d'etre for any collection development policy, is that such a statement assures a consistent and balanced growth of library resources. Book selectors, be they faculty members or librarians, specialists or generalists, are, like the rest of us, susceptible to personal preoccupations and not immune from the temptations of the popular and the trendy. Sound development of a collection must pay due attention to long-term needs as well as immediate demands, from the smallest popular library to the largest research institution. The difference lies mainly in the kinds of materials collected and in the degree of intensity in collecting. In referring to "the temptations of the popular and the trendy," I am concerned not merely with best-sellers and gadgetry. The "temptations" can be scholarly and serious but nonetheless inappropriate in terms of the goals and objectives of the specific institution. And consistency also means a continuous commitment to a set of policies regardless of the personal interests and specialties of those who select the books. Professors and librarians come and go, but the books in the libraries stay. A library collection is not merely an assembly of books, not even an assembly of good books; they have to relate to each other. There has to be a rationale for the presence of these, but not others. And that rationale is provided in the collection development policy statement.

And that statement also seeks to insure the desired balance between the subject matters covered. This, of course, does not mean equal depth of coverage, nor equal allocation of book funds; it does mean a considered definition of emphasis from the perspective of the whole. Furthermore, a clearly stated policy serves to remind and alert the book selectors of the legitimate needs of the inarticulate as well as the articulate members of the community, and this is equally important in an academic library and public library.

Two supplementary, and perhaps practical, reasons for the formal establishment of collection development policy are:

1. To provide a guarantee against undue special interest pressure. This is perhaps particularly, but by no means exclusively, true in public libraries. A well-defined policy statement should serve to resist undue pressure to include irrelevant materials as well as to exclude unpopular or controversial materials. How many of us can recall with relief the occasions on which we could graciously refuse a gift or request for material of limited value on the grounds that the subject matter, or the format, or the language fell outside...the library's established collection development policy? And how often we have pointed with pride and conviction to our credo that the library "must provide free access to all points of view on public questions."

2. To serve as a vehicle to facilitate interlibrary cooperation and resource sharing. Union lists provide the means by which libraries share what they already own. Coordinated collection development policies provide the means by which the libraries can share their future resources. And in order that such cooperation can be operable, terminologies need to be standardized, and criteria need to be comparable. Hence the RTSD [Resources and Technical Services Division] "Guidelines".

However, the standardization of guidelines does not mean uniformity of goals and objectives. Each library serves a unique community, be it a township, metropolitan city, high school, multiuniversity, or the United Nations. The library must therefore first of all know its community and assess the needs of all segments of the community, not merely the conspicuous and the vocal. For the objectives and goals of the library must be to serve the whole community. Merely meeting the demands of the known and the articulate cannot assure the development of a collection that will serve the immediate present and the long-term future. Perhaps I should add here a word of caution. In setting goals and objectives, it behooves us to be realistic - realistic in seeking the attainable, realistic in accepting what's needed, not what's attractive, and realistic in defining one's own role, not somebody else's.

No man is an island, and no library is totally self-sufficient. But there are degrees of self-sufficiency, and libraries are fundamentally different from one another. As a result, each library needs to assess its own resources. Collection development requires not only maintaining a balanced growth but also building on strength. A strong collection needs to grow to retain its eminence. This is no vainglorious indulgence. Scholarship is better served by one great collection than two or three incomplete ones. And in our days of library cooperation, it is only logical that we taken into consideration the resources of other accessible libraries. I said "accessible," because cooperative collection development is only feasible when resources can be readily shared. Pie-in-the-sky pronouncements of cooperative enterprises lead only to disappointment and worse, distrust, and thus do a great disservice to our profession.

A collection development policy statement must therefore define the library's goals and objectives, identify the short-term and long-term needs of the community it serves, assess the degree of strength and weakness of its existing resources, and determine the depth and scope of its acquisition policy. The "meat" of such a statement usually consists of a listing of subjects, with accompanying annotations indicating the degree of coverage recommended. Delimitations by language, date, format, and cost offer further refinements. As in the case of almost all library tools, the usefulness of such an instrument, especially if it is a detailed one, will be greatly enhanced if an index is provided.

And now, some thoughts on what a collection development statement is *not* or should *not* be. First, a collection development statement is not a substitute for book selection. At best, it defines a framework and provides parameters, but it never selects a specific book. Each title has to be individually chosen, whether by means of blanket order, approval plan, or a corps of specialist book selectors. And no matter how specific and detailed the collection development policy statement may be, individual judgment still needs to be applied in the last analysis. Collection development charts the forest, but it does not plant the trees.

Further, a written statement, whether broadly outlined or specifically itemized, should not be fossilized for eternity. Just as institutions grow, collections grow; so should the collection development policies grow. The strength of tradition lies in the proper use of the past to nurture the present, and the purpose of such a policy statement is to assure stability, not rigidity. Therefore, the presence of a written policy statement cannot be a substitute for intelligent discernment, nor for an ever-alert awareness of the changing needs of the community it serves. For this reason, too, therefore, it is highly desirable, indeed imperative, that such a statement undergo regular, periodic review.

Even the dictum of "building on strength" mentioned earlier is not an immutable law. There may be times when it is wiser to "call it quits." The continuous maintenance of a collection, regardless of its intrinsic worth and accompanying prestige, must always be justified by its relevance - immediate or potential - to the community it serves. And ultimately, perhaps by its contribution to scholarship and knowledge in general. One does not collect just for the sake of collecting.

And sometimes it may be more appropriate to give up or transfer some responsibilities to other institutions which are better equipped to assume them. One must not be afraid to admit past errors or to change directions when good judgment so indicates; not should one be trapped in one's own past virtues. We need constantly to use our judgment and exercise our right - indeed, duty - to think, and sometimes having a piece of paper in front of us may make us forget that duty.

To confuse what's good for one library with what's good for another is to be intellectually lazy or socially irresponsible. Many factors come into play. What's adequate for one first-rate library may not be adequate for another. For years I watched with considerable concern some undergraduate libraries dutifully acquiring titles listed in the Lamont Library Catalog, thinking perhaps that if they had everything Lamont had, they too would serve their students well. But Lamont has Widener next door, not to mention Houghton and the dozens of other library facilities in the Harvard University system. Often what's unwanted by one library may well be treasured by another. A collection of third-rate novels adds little to the quality of a suburban public library, but the same collection may fit in well in a special collection which makes a large research library great.

And speaking of large libraries, perhaps we should remind ourselves once more that size is not synonymous with excellence, maybe not even eminence. Quantity does not assure quality, although neither does it preclude it. The nineteenth-century pipe dream of acquiring every worthwhile book has long evaporated in the puff of twentieth century information explosion. True, very large collections of books are necessary to scholars, whether the books are used frequently or not, and indeed many will not be used frequently. And libraries, at least some libraries, are repositories as well as circulating entities and as such need to be both diverse and deep. But just as no newspaper can really print "all the news that's fit to print," neither can any library collect all the books that seem desirable to collect. Indeed, to seek and even to acquire everything is not to have the best. Harvard University Library prizes the preeminence of its collections by their excellence, not their size. Its book collection is always selective. And a well-coordinated smaller collection is indeed much more useful than a topsy-turvy mass of unguided growth. Acquisition requires skill, and book selection requires judgement. Collection development policy statement is a guidepost, not a crutch.

A good collection development policy statement does not guarantee a good library collection, but it helps. To decide what to select and what not to select requires the courage to choose - to choose what to have, and what not to have, however tempting. And a sound collection development policy provides both a rationale and a reminder, lest vanity or timidity should lead us astray.

Eric J. Carpenter, "Collection Development Policies: The Case for." *Library Acquisitions: Practice and Theory* **8, 1 (1984): 43-45.**

"Why should I spend my precious time drafting another policy statement?" mutters the hard-pressed Ohio academic librarian in 1983. "Especially one that is apt to stir up faculty members? Writing a collection development policy is a waste of time! I have too many other pressing commitments. Both our library staff and the acquisitions budget have been cut. Besides, it'll get the faculty 'involved' in library matters, 'stirred up,' and asking questions such as 'Why is the book budget for my department so small?'"

Such questions are no doubt on the minds of at least some academic librarians in Ohio in 1983 - perhaps even a few at this conference. My reply to such questions begins with a simple assertion - You can't afford not to! You can't afford not to have written collection development policy statements in the 1980s.

Collection development policies serve three major functions that are necessary for any library attempting to build collections in a rational manner. Collection development policies serve as: planning documents, tools for communication, and a basis for resource sharing with other libraries.

An academic library cannot have a program of collection development without eventually completing a written policy statement. James Baughman asserts that collection development consists of three essential elements: planning, implementation, and evaluation.[1] Without these a library is engaged only in acquiring - spending money and adding books - not in rationally and systematically developing its collection. Writing a collection development policy compels the librarian to develop a rationale, a plan for acquiring materials - to ask, What is the library acquiring, and why? What is the mission of our college/university and library, and what materials will the library acquire to support that mission? These questions should be answered in a written policy stating the institution's mission and describing each academic program supported by the library.

Library materials to be acquired in support of these programs should be described by subject, format, and language in accordance with ALA's *Guidelines for Collection Development*.[2]

A written collection development policy also provide a basis for rational planning and allocation of the acquisitions budget. It helps establish priorities for the allocation of resources to support specific stated needs. In lean fiscal years, the policy states collecting priorities that must be supported at all cost. In rare years of plenty, the policy specifies the collection areas that should receive priority if any unexpected gifts or grants happen to become available for materials purchases.

Collection development policies also serve as communications tools. Paul Mosher states that collection development is a process that "should constitute a rational, documented program guided by written policies and protocols and should reflect, in a sense, a contract between library users and library staff as to what will be acquired, for whom, and at what level."[3] Our patrons should know what we are buying and why.

A collection development policy permits a library to address several audiences. In the academic library, faculty and students are the most important audience - the users with whom we make the contract to collect materials. Preparing a policy for collecting in an academic library requires consultation with faculty members (and perhaps students) to develop policies and set priorities. Such librarian/faculty communication should be an ongoing process. If it is not, the preparation of a collection development policy can be the occasion for beginning such a dialogue. Faculty and library staff engaged in book selection are another important audience. For them, particularly for new bibliographers, the selection policy serves as a training document that guides their daily activity in selection, collection evaluation, and weeding.

Library administrators are another audience. "What are those acquisitions librarians/bibliographers doing with all the acquisitions dollars?" ask library directors. The policy supplies a ready answer to them, as it does to university or college administrators, deans, or provosts who ask the same question of the library annually when the budget is prepared. Speaking at the Pilot Collection Management and Development Institute at Stanford in 1981, Raymond Bacchetti, Vice-Provost of Stanford University, warned librarians to "approach budgeting with responsible alternate forms and levels of programs and service so that the definition of collection development remains in professional hands". In other words, Bacchetti warned the audience, "You define what can be delivered at certain levels of expenditure and identify the consequences of those alternatives. This provides substance to the budget process and forces attention to the issues as you define them, not as someone defines them for you."[4] Having a written collection development policy permits the academic librarian to work effectively with provosts as astute as Bacchetti.

The final audience for a collection development policy consists of a library's consortia partners, other libraries with which one attempts to share resources. Guideline 1.3 in *Guidelines for Collection Development* states the matter clearly: "Widespread budgetary constraints and the growth of interlibrary cooperation for shared resources and service networks have given impetus to the pressure to analyze collection activity in universally comprehensible terms".[5]

The *Guidelines* provide a tool for documenting and comparing collection strengths and buying patterns and overlaps among consortia members. Oberlin is a member of the Northeast Ohio Major Academic Libraries (NEOMAL) consortium. In 1981 NEOMAL conducted a buying overlap study using the *LC Classification: National Shelflist Count* breakdown in the *Guidelines*. Our objective was to discover if we could develop a resource sharing agreement to eliminate unnecessary duplication. We learned a good deal about each other's collections even though we eventually came to the conclusion that because of pressing local needs there was little we could do to prevent duplication of essential titles by member libraries.

What NEOMAL tried to do was develop a conspectus similar to that originally developed by the RLG libraries and described by Nancy Gwinn and Paul Mosher in an excellent article recently published. They define *conspectus* as a "breakdown of subject fields in such a way as to allow distributed collection responsibilities for as many fields as possible".[6] RLG has developed a conspectus based on the combined collection development policies of member libraries. It is an overview, or summary, arranged by subject, of existing collection strengths and future collecting intensities of RLG members. This summary has been developed into a database that is part of the RLIN system. The Association of Research Libraries is currently exploring the possibility of using the RLG format to develop a nationwide collection development policy or conspectus. The development of this valuable tool was made possible only because each member library devoted the necessary energy to writing a policy based on local needs.

While the individual patron in an academic library may know nothing about the RLG *Conspectus*, he or she is vitally concerned about one question, "Will my library have the book I want on the shelf when I need it?" If that person's library has a collection development policy statement, the patron is more likely to be able to answer the question, "Yes, there's the book I want, and I found it just in time to read for that paper I have to finish tonight and hand in tomorrow."

References

1   James C. Baughman, "Toward a Structural Approach to Collection Development." *College and Research Libraries* 38 (1977): 242.

2   American Library Association, Collection Development Committee, *Guidelines for Collection Development,* ed. David L. Perkins (Chicago: American Library Association, 1979).

3   Paul H. Mosher, "Fighting Back: From Growth to Management in Academic Library Collection Development." A paper delivered at the Pilot Collection Management and Development Institute at Stanford University, July 6-10, 1981, p. 4.

4   Raymond F. Bacchetti, "Reason, Politics, and Collection Development." A paper delivered at the Pilot Collection Management and Development Institute at Stanford University, July 6-10, 1981, p. 4.

5   *Guidelines for Collection Development,* p. 1.

6   Nancy E. Gwinn and Paul H. Mosher, "Coordinating Collection Development: The RLG Conspectus." *College and Research Libraries* 44 (1983): 131.

Jennifer Cargill, "Collection Development Policies: An Alternative Viewpoint." *Library Acquisitions: Practice and Theory* 8, 1 (1984): 47-49.

The case FOR written collection development policies has been articulated in the literature for many years. The topic is regularly addressed in publications as well as serving as the focus of numerous conferences and workshops around the country. The question remains: Is a written collection development policy really necessary? One might also ask: Is a written collection development policy prudent? And who should have the power or authority to make such policy decisions: faculty, librarians, the director?

The question also arises: If these written policies are such an important factor, then why don't all academic libraries have them? Wouldn't more libraries have drafted collection development polices and have them available for examination if they are such a vital ingredient? The philosophy or theory of collection development and evaluation is still developing. It is a difficult concept to grasp and implement. Collection development might also be considered more of an artform than a structured concept. Creating a workable document that can be applied to the selection process is exceedingly difficult. Relatively few policies have existed long enough for their impact on their respective collections to be examined and analyzed. AND, if libraries are coping with developing their collection without WRITTEN policies, why then engage in an exercise known to be time-consuming and difficult to prepare? The existence of a written policy does not guarantee that a balanced collection will result. The policy, if written, represents an ideal rather than a realistic situation. How can such policies be accurately interpreted? Academic libraries need the flexibility and freedom to make selection choices without being tied to a written policy.

On a regional basis, universities and colleges may attempt to engage in cooperative purchasing with their neighboring institutions. But how effective are such agreements? Academic libraries must support their own curriculum first. Cooperative purchasing is particularly difficult to conduct in comprehensive universities which must purchase in all areas.

Within the institution itself, the primary interests and mission of the university or college must be well known before it is possible to have a written policy within the library. The aims, objectives and institutional mission must exist in great detail before a library can even begin to adapt objectives to its collection development policy or to formulate cooperative relationships with other institutions. In the changeable climate of the 1980s, an institution's future curriculum may be vague or even unknown. Research goals may be unclear. If a written policy is attempted, it will most likely become dated before it reaches its final form simply because of the institution's lack of decision about programs of study and research. Lack of continuity in an institution's central administration can even make it unwise to attempt to create and rely on a written policy. This may be particularly true of a university or college that is changing from a humanistic approach to education to a technological approach. Indeed, within an institution, a collection development policy can easily become a political issue as faculty, sensitive about the needs of their own disciplines, see colleagues in other disciplines receiving preferential treatment. This political climate can lead to situations in which segments of the academic community become alienated from the library.

Faculty members are hired without consulting librarians. However, new faculty and their subject specialties must ultimately be supported. A collection development policy that does not reflect a specific research area will make it difficult for the library to respond to a faculty researcher's needs. Similarly, as new disciplines emerge, an inflexible existing policy makes it difficult to make critical purchasing decisions quickly in response to new demands. As faculty leave, an existing policy slows the process to cease collecting in areas that are no longer relevant. Of particular importance today is the fact that enrolment fluctuations do produce a marked effect on purchasing and that libraries should be able to move quickly rather than being tied to a restrictive policy. There is a real danger in inhibiting librarians with static statements. And if faculty happen to control the funds and the selection process, collecting will reflect their particular interests rather than the goals of following a set policy.

Within the library itself, the hiring of selectors in specific fields indicates what subject areas are considered worthy of special emphasis or support. These selectors are hired for their competence in assessing the needs of the collection. Why hinder them with a stated policy that could prevent them from reacting quickly to changes and shifts in the curriculum, faculty, and student body? As enrolment changes, and some disciplines grow or decline, the selector should be free to respond quickly.

Academia in the 1980s

A formal, written and approved collection development policy leads inevitably to inflexibility. Particularly in the 1980s, flexibility is desirable. We must be able to respond instantly to changes in the academic community. Purchasing must always reflect current needs. Indeed, few institutions can realistically afford to acquire anything but currently available materials. That's all that is affordable, considering today's rapidly escalating costs for library materials and the present trend toward austerity in higher education. We cannot acquire materials simply because a policy mandates their purchase: we must purchase according to actual, demonstrated need. Budgets are all too frequently unstable and future funding is unsure. As if this were not enough, there's another funding concern. The source of funding for a particular library is critical. If a given library becomes increasingly dependent on grants and gifts for a portion of its funding, any plan for systematic collection development is impossible. In such instances, funding dictates how the collection grows. Conversely, if you have a large funding windfall, spending must take place rapidly and there's often little or not time to consider a policy.

With our rapidly changing technology, we must find ways to remain open to purchasing a variety of new types of materials, not just the traditional books, periodicals, and microforms. We will be approaching the collecting of new types of materials and must have the flexibility to respond to demands without becoming bogged down in elaborate policies which take meetings, negotiations, and dialogue to change.

In summary, we must be realistic. We must be responsive to change. Writing collection development policies is time-consuming. They are difficult to compile and review. They can impose unneeded limitations on the acquisition of materials. They do not reflect the day-to-day reality of rapidly changing campus needs. They are administrative or management tools which can be identified - but in the final analysis are they worth all the time, effort, and politics that go into their creation? I think not. As an alternative, I propose that libraries adopt a general statement of purpose, one that becomes the focal point of an ongoing dialogue between faculty and librarians, thus serving to institutionalize both stability and flexibility in the delicate process of collection building.

CHAPTER 2

FORM AND CONTENT OF COLLECTION DEVELOPMENT POLICIES

Collection Development, Selection or Acquisitions?

Before one can decide what to put into a collection development policy statement there must be absolute clarity about what this policy is and how it impinges upon other collection-related statements. Theoretically this should pose no problems, yet existing policies and discussions in the professional literature suggest that confusion is the norm rather than the exception. In the simple matter of terminology, for instance, three terms seem to be used interchangeably: "collection development policy", "selection policy" and "acquisitions policy". Thus Elizabeth Futas has compiled a volume entitled *Library Acquisition Policies and Procedures*; the National Library of Australia has its *National Library of Australia Selection Policy* and William Paterson State College its *Collection Development Policy*. The list could and does go on, indicating that many libraries have policy statements issued under a confusing array of names, yet they all contain essentially the same type of data.[1]

This apparent confusion is also reflected in, or perhaps even derives from, the professional literature on collection development; for example, Bartle and Brown list eighteen "common features of selection policies" in terms of content:[2]

1. objectives of the library
2. community and its needs identified
3. purpose of the selection process
4. functions of the library
5. context of selection
6. authority for selection policy
7. responsibility for implementation
8. priorities (types of use and categories of material)
9. controversial issues
10. censorship
11. categories of exclusions
12. Statement on Freedom to Read
13. selection criteria
14. collection standards: quantity
15. collection development targets

16. selection methods: organization
17. acquisitions categories and coverage
18. ordering methods.

This is both an ambitious and somewhat confusing list of typical policy features, and the authors suggest that they can be grouped into three categories: selection policies, acquisition policies, development policies. "From the foregoing 'resources selection policy' can be seen as a blanket term covering a range of topics, from library aims at the starting point, through selection policy in the narrow sense, to acquisition procedures and stock circulation as a practical outcome."[3]

There are, then, serious misunderstandings that appear to have arisen as a result of the inconsistent use of descriptors for collection development policy statements. A collection development policy is not a selection policy, nor is it an acquisitions policy; and no effective policy statement will try to encompass all of these areas in a single document for one very simple reason: they are fundamentally different in intention and content. Both selection and acquisitions policies are basically procedural statements indicating in some detail how policies are to be implemented and by whom. Underpinning and preceding these statements are the actual collection development policies, which provide a rationale for the existence of collections and indicate what they will contain for the foreseeable future. These policies, then, deal with "why" and "what" issues, while selection and acquisitions statements address the practicalities of "how" and "who". Perhaps the clearest way to highlight the distinctions is to think in terms of a hierarchy. The highest level in this hierarchy is the planning function, policy formulation; from this flows selection, which involves decisions about what to include or exclude. Selection, in other words, is a direct function of collection development in that it applies the principles stated in the collection development policy document. As Feng suggests, "it is the decision-making process concerned with implementing the goals stated earlier."[4] While the criteria and methodology for selection are separate from collection development planning, they are certainly not independent of planning as embodied in a policy document. Acquisitions, the third level in the hierarchy and the one that actually gets material into the library, is the process that implements selection decisions which have arisen from the collection development plan. The hierarchical relationship among these three components of collection building, and the nature of the written documents which guide them, are summarized in Figure 1.

In the hierarchy of policy-selection-acquisitions three questions are asked and answered in sequence: why? what? how? The policy document addressing the first of these and the procedural statements answering the remaining questions clearly have different intentions and, to some extent, different audiences. Therefore, to consider them as one and the same is both inaccurate and confusing. The collection development policy should be regarded particularly, but not exclusively, as a document for public consumption - the external communication function discussed in Chapter 1 - because it explains the goals, purposes and functions of the library collection and the principles according to which it is built. Selection and acquisitions policies, best termed "manuals" or "statements", are primarily internal documents because they explain for the benefit of library staff and selectors the procedures to be followed in choosing and acquiring materials. The selection procedures statement indicates who is responsible for deciding what is to be acquired, and it presents the criteria used to evaluate materials. The acquisitions procedures statement indicates the process to be followed in obtaining materials, listing the various methods (direct order, distributor, etc.) and when they are to be applied. This distinction is an important one that should be reflected in a more careful and consistent use of accurate terminology, not to mention greater standardization in terms of content. The most descriptive term for the document under discussion is "collection development policy".

POLICY

Collection Development Policy

* statement of general principles
* why the collection exists
* what it shall contain
* internal and external audiences

PROCEDURE 1

Selection Procedures Statement

* statement of specific practices
* how to implement the collection development policy
* who does selecting
* criteria for selecting materials
* primary internal audience of selectors

PROCEDURE 2

Acquisitions Procedures Statement

* statement of specific practices
* how to implement selection decisions
* who does acquisitions work
* statement of specific acquisitions procedures
* internal audience of acquisitions personnel

Figure 1. Summary of Policy and Procedures Statements

Components of the Policy

At its simplest the collection development policy statement, in addressing the "why" of the library and its collection, presents a general indication of needs and priorities in the light of institutional goals, formulates specific parameters within which materials will be collected and identifies the breadth and depth of coverage to be achieved for each subject area. There are, then, two basic components to the written document: (1) a general policy statement and (2) a statement of collection levels. In treating these two elements (outlined in Figure 2) one must distinguish between judgements which can be summarized in an introductory statement and those which must be made in some detail for each subject or form division. In the ALA *Guidelines for Collection Development* the "Guidelines for the Formulation of Collection Development Policies" outlines these sections under four rubrics which, although not followed in more than general terms in this text, give a good indication of the logical arrangement of policy statements.[5] First, there should be an analysis of general institutional objectives; second, detailed analysis of the policy for subject fields; third, detailed analysis of the policy for form collections where required; fourth, indexes. If this sounds relatively straightforward and simple, there are two points

I. General Policy Statement

A. Introduction - establishes policy framework and scope

B. Statement of Philosophy - purpose of institution and library, overview of needs and priorities

C. Objectives of the Library - user groups, programmes and requirements, general subject boundaries, inclusions and exclusions generally, cooperative arrangements

II. Statement of Collection Levels

A. Classified Subject Analysis - standard classification scheme, code of density, intensity and policy levels

B. Index - subjects and other access points

Figure 2. Content of a Collection Development Policy

to keep in mind. The first of these is a plea for flexibility and adaptability. Any presentation of guidelines should not constitute a set of rubrics to be followed slavishly but in fact must be adapted to individual library situations; the diversity of collecting programmes, the varied and changing needs of users and the special requirements of specific subjects all mean that the components may vary significantly from policy to policy. To see this one need only compare a range of written policy statements, for example, those included as readings at the conclusion of this chapter. The other point is perhaps more crucial: the components of the policy are far more complex and detailed than any listing of categories would suggest. The following discussion, therefore, is intended to indicate this complexity, but it must be remembered that not all policies will treat matters in the same way.

The General Policy Statement

The general introduction or general policy statement is crucial, for it presents the individual library's philosophy of collection development, which in turn serves as a framework for the more precise definitions to follow. This broad statement tries to make several points. It states the mission of the library (in relation to objectives of the parent institution where appropriate); it identifies the major groups and programmes which the library serves; it defines the general priorities regarding selection (inclusions and exclusions, languages, duplication, etc.); and it may say something about reliance on cooperative agreements and networks. In practice this general policy statement is often separated into three distinct parts: introduction, statement of philosophy, parameters of the collections.

Introduction. The most general section of the policy document is the introduction, as it seeks to establish a framework within which the document is to be viewed. To do this it addresses several questions. Why was the policy developed? What is its scope, and what is the intended audience? How was the policy formulated, and who was involved in this process? These points may be treated in a few lines or a few paragraphs - at the most two to three pages. The *State Library of Victoria Selection Policy* (pp. 48-58) provides a reasonable example of this introductory material. Such information, while not essential, is useful because it establishes parameters; it tells the user what he might expect and what not to expect. It sets the general tone for what follows.

Statement of Philosophy of the Institution/Collection. Having established the raison d'etre and overall scope of the policy in the opening pages, one now moves into more specific areas. In particular why does the institution exist, and how does the library assist in fulfilling this purpose? Very often this section draws on legislation or similar documentation that gives the library its legal entity; the *National Library of Australia Selection Policy*, for instance, refers to the National Library Act (1960) and its requirements. This theoretical section also often includes or at least refers to various professional body statements on intellectual freedom, access to information, promotion of reading, etc. All of this is aimed at providing an overview of the needs, priorities and aims of the institution and its library. Again, the *State Library of Victoria Selection Policy* adequately covers this in its Introduction (pp. 48-58).

Parameters of the Collections. This differs from the preceding section in that it begins to provide specific information on the user community, the subject coverage of the collections, programmes supported by the collections, limitations of the collections, cooperative arrangements. One of the more succinct summaries of the content of this section of a policy statement is provided by Phyllis Van Orden, who calls it "knowing the community", and the following comments are derived from her five-fold schema.[6]

First, the policy delineates specific components of the user community; that is, one identifies the several groups within the population (whether institutional or general public) to be served. It is by understanding the clientele that one is able to determine needs and programmes to be supported by the collections. Second, then, the policy describes the kinds of programmes and user requirements that the library services. This is "a statement specifying types of subject coverage to be included in the collection, for example, instructional, informational, and recreational materials or those that support particular teaching methods, student organizations, or special user groups."[7] Third, the policy derives from both the user community and user requirements a statement of the general subject boundaries within which the collection is to develop. This is an essential prerequisite for the detailed subject analysis that forms the bulk of the policy, as it delimits the disciplinary framework within which the library operates - and by implication or statement those areas *outside* the operation. Fourth, the policy statement is now in a position to indicate inclusions and exclusions in specific categories: forms of materials, languages, geographical areas, multiple copies. That is, form restrictions are listed or, more positively, all formats to be included in the collection are listed; the same applies to a series of statements specifying the languages, geographical foci and any other variables to be included or excluded. In addition this fourth point states the collecting policy with regard to multiple or duplicate copies of materials. Fifth and finally, the parameters of the collection need to be clarified in terms of relations with, and reliance on, other libraries, cooperative arrangements and networks. Thus there must be a clear statement not only of programmes in which the library is participating but also of the library's responsibility in such programmes.

Statement of Collection Levels

The general policy statement, then, has identified the library's mission, its main user groups and programmes, the subject boundaries and overall inclusions and exclusions. Following this important task of parameter definition, the second major section of the policy addresses the central issue: a detailed listing of subjects together with annotations indicating the strengths and weaknesses of existing resources and the degree of recommended coverage. This in a sense is the point of the discussion in Chapters 4 and 5, because without collection evaluation and user analysis one cannot make decisions about levels at which subjects will be collected in future. One must first understand the present adequacy or inadequacy of the collection and the way in which it is being built and used; on the basis of this information informed decisions can be made about projected collection building.

Ideally all of these data ought to be summarized in the subject analysis section. Therefore, one formalizes in the policy document the following: present state of the collection, present level of collecting, future level of collecting. In other words the policy should indicate in some very clear manner collection *density* (extent of existing collections), collection *intensity* (current collecting activity, which may well differ from activity which produced the present density) and collection *policy* (the desired level for future collecting, which may differ from both density and intensity). To be fully comprehensible a policy must include these distinctions in order to avoid confusing what has been, what is and what is hoped for.

The key to indicating these levels for each subject category and to communicating them clearly is a standardized coding language. Humpty Dumpty could declare with certainty, "when *I* use a word, it means just what I choose it to mean - neither more, nor less ..."; but he met a rather sticky end. To avoid having a policy statement meet a similar fate it is necessary to define collecting levels in terms that are concrete and specific enough to carry the same meaning to all interested parties, both individuals and institutions. Today there is really only one standard code that is being accepted by all types of libraries - that devised by the American Library Association (reproduced in the Appendix, pp. 35-36) and translated into a numeric code by the Research Libraries Group (Figure 3). This code, or indeed any other, must be evaluated with extreme care before adoption. As Sheila Dowd suggests, adequate collection codes should address two problems. "The first difficulty is the definition of collecting levels in terms sufficiently concrete to be applied in a comparable way by all institutions using them."[8] The second is the problem of getting people to address precisely the same focus when applying a code. "Distinctions between what always has been, what is today, and what ought to be often merge...into a twilight of blurred judgments...."[9] In deciding whether to use the ALA/RLG code or whether to devise a unique code tailored specifically to the requirements of a specific collection, one must ask two questions. First, is the code suitable for all sections of the collection, all collections in the library, all libraries in the system? Second, can the code be applied equally effectively in addressing collection density, intensity and policy?

ALA *Guidelines*	RLG *Conspectus*
A comprehensive	5 comprehensive
B research	4 research
C study	3 study
D basic	2 basic
E minimal	1 minimal
	0 not collected

Figure 3. Comparison of Collection Strength Codes

Most policies devised today use the established ALA codes, although many libraries outside North America have been loath to adopt the American system. However, the widespread international acceptance of the RLG *Conspectus* (see Chapter 3), which converts the ALA codes into a numerical sequence, means that fewer libraries are finding it feasible or advisable to "go it alone" in terms of collecting level codes.[10] Despite this trend towards adoption of the ALA/RLG system, each library will have to decide this issue in terms of its specific needs, and no definitive guidance can be offered out of context.

Once chosen, this uniform set of collecting level codes is applied to the subject analysis. Although subject organization is the structure normally adopted in policy statements, this takes one of two forms in most cases. One, for example that employed by the St. Joseph Public Library (pp. 58-67), follows fairly broad subject rubrics ("Religion", "Social Sciences", etc.); this form can occur in either a classified order or in a simple alphabetical sequence. Some maintain that this results in a more readable document appealing to all types of users who may wish to consult the policy. Equally, however, this approach, whether classified or alphabetical, has the disadvantage of being too imprecise for many professional users or incompatible with the detailed classification of the actual collections. A second, more structured approach permits greater detail by following more closely the classification scheme of the library for which the policy is devised. Thus the St. Joseph Public Library, which is classified according to Dewey, uses the Dewey Decimal Classification for its subject analysis. Such schemes have the advantage of being far more specific than general subject categories, and they also form a lingua franca spoken by most libraries. The level of specificity in this approach will vary in accordance with the nature and depth of the actual collections and the classification scheme in use. The University of California (pp. 102-115), for example, uses the Library of Congress classification and in its policy employs such headings as "GC Oceanography", "GC1015 to 1572 Marine Resources and Pollution", etc. In this instance it is interesting to note the rigorous and detailed adherence to Library of Congress in the classed analysis, compared with the somewhat general following of Dewey in the class analysis of many public library policies. Once again, each library must decide for itself the best method for presenting its subject analysis; the policy extracts accompanying this chapter should assist in the decision-making process.

In the ALA *Guidelines for Collection Development* analysis by physical format is suggested as an additional section following the subject analysis. This may be necessary in rare instances, but on the whole forms should be treated in the same way as other non-subject categories. That is, if it is possible to generalize about languages, chronological periods, geographical areas or forms (and it very often is), then such generalizations about these variables should appear earlier in the policy to simplify matters. Only changing variables should be included in the detailed subject analysis. In the State Library of Victoria policy, for example, format is treated quite adequately in a single paragraph within the introductory section.

The coded subject analysis is the core of the collection development policy. As such, it should be fully accessible for all possible requirements, and this means adequate indexing. As the ALA *Guidelines* suggest, "...an index should be appended which correlates subject terms to class numbers. Individual libraries may also wish to index by academic programs, library units, or other key words or concepts."[11] Although this implies a classified subject analysis, detailed subject indexing should accompany any policy statement regardless of its analytical arrangement; few policies provide this much access assistance.

In summary a written collection development policy is a complex document which benefits from clear and logical organization. The most commonly accepted shape of a policy statement is one which proceeds from generalities to specific details, as the preceding discussion has indicated.

Appendix. ALA Collection Level Codes[12]

The codes defined below are designed for use in identifying both the extent of existing collections in given subject fields (collection density) and the extent of current collecting activity in the field (collecting intensity).

A . Comprehensive level. A collection in which a library endeavors, so far as is reasonably possible, to include all significant works of recorded knowledge (publications, manuscripts, other forms) for a necessarily defined field. This level of collecting intensity is that which maintains a "special collection"; the aim, if not the achievement, is exhaustiveness.

B . Research level. A collection which includes the major published source materials required for dissertations and independent research, including materials containing research reporting, new findings, scientific experimental results, and other information useful to researchers. It also includes all important reference works and a wide selection of specialized monographs, as well as an extensive collection of journals and major indexing and abstracting services in the field.

C . Study level. A collection which supports undergraduate or graduate course work, or sustained independent study; that is, which is adequate to maintain knowledge of a subject required for limited or generalized purposes, of less than research intensity. It includes a wide range of basic monographs, complete collections of the works of important writers, selections from the works of secondary writers, a selection of representative journals, and the reference tools and fundamental bibliographical apparatus pertaining to the subject.
NOTE: Some college librarians have expressed a need for further refinement of the "Study level" code for use by libraries without comprehensive or research level collections, to enable them to define their collecting policies explicitly enough to meet the needs of network resources planning. We include the following optional subcodes for such institutions.
(1) Advanced study level. A collection which is adequate to support the course work of advanced undergraduate and master's degree programs, or sustained independent study; that is, which is adequate to maintain knowledge of a subject required for limited or generalized purposes, of less than research intensity. It includes a wide range of basic monographs both current and retrospective, complete collections of the works of more important writers, selections from the works of secondary writers, a selection of representative journals, and the reference tools and fundamental bibliographical apparatus pertaining to the subject.
(2) Initial study level. A collection which is adequate to support undergraduate courses. It includes a judicious selection from currently published basic monographs (as are represented by *Choice* selections) supported by seminal retrospective monographs (as are represented by *Books for College Libraries*); a broad selection of works of more important writers; a selection of the most significant works of secondary writers; a selection of the major review journals; and current editions of the most significant reference tools and bibliographies pertaining to the subject.

D. Basic level. A highly selective collection which serves to introduce and define the subject and to indicate the varieties of information available elsewhere. It includes major dictionaries and encyclopedias, selected editions of important works, historical surveys, important bibliographies, and a few major periodicals in the field.

E. Minimal level. A subject area in which few selections are made beyond very basic works.

References

1   F.R. Bartle and W.L. Brown, in "Book Selection Policies for Public Libraries." *Australian Library Journal* 32, 3 (1983): 5-13, mention thirteen Australian public library policies which reflect this confusing use of terminology, and there are bound to be others. "Selection" policy seems to be the most common Australian usage for "collection development" policy. It should be noted, however, that the National Library of Australia is adopting the latter name for its policy currently under revision. Undoubtedly this decision will trickle down to the similar naming of policies by other libraries.

2   *Ibid.*, pp. 10-11.

3   *Ibid.*, p. 11.

4   Y.T. Feng, "The Necessity for a Collection Development Policy Statement." *Library Resources and Technical Services* 23, 1 (1979): 39.

5   American Library Association. Collection Development Committee, *Guidelines for Collection Development*, ed. David L. Perkins (Chicago, Ill.: American Library Association, 1979), pp. 6-8

6   Phyllis J. Van Orden, *The Collection Program in High Schools: Concepts, Practices and Information Sources* (Littleton, Colo.: Libraries Unlimited, 1985), pp. 79-80.

7   *Ibid.*, p. 79.

8   Sheila T. Dowd, "The Formulation of a Collection Development Policy Statement." In *Collection Development in Libraries: A Treatise, Part A,* ed. Robert D. Stueart and George B. Miller, Jr. (Foundations in Library and Information Science, Vol. 10. Greenwich, Conn.: JAI Press, 1980), p. 75.

9   *Ibid.*, p. 78.

10 In Australia, for example, the National Library of Australia, the universities and several state libraries have all decided to adopt the ALA/RLG collecting level codes in place of those devised some years ago by the National Library. Also, libraries in Canada, Scotland and England are using *Conspectus* - and thus the ALA codes - in assessing and describing their collections.

11 American Library Association, *op. cit.*, p. 8.

12 *Ibid.*, pp. 3-5.

READINGS ON THE FORM AND CONTENT OF COLLECTION DEVELOPMENT POLICIES

This chapter has sought to show that the content of a collection development policy can be framed within certain clearly defined parameters, and it has suggested that there is an identifiable logic to this framework. To some extent the article by Bartle and Brown (pp. 38-48) supports both contentions. In it the authors maintain that the library's intentions with regard to the provision of resources can be represented to the wider community in a policy statement. But they also admit that the production of an adequate policy statement is a task attempted by many and achieved by few. To improve the chances of success they offer suggestions for the content of a typical "selection" policy; while we do not agree in full with these suggestions, they do show how order, consistency and logic can be achieved.

The degree to which policy documents embody these characteristics is indicated in the remaining readings, all of which are collection development policies. The choice of policies is purposely eclectic, reflecting not only libraries of various types - state, public, academic - but also documents of varying quality and sophistication. The introductory information discussed above appears at its most adequately detailed in the *State Library of Victoria Selection Policy;* accordingly, the relevant extracts are reproduced here (pp. 48-58). However, smaller libraries may well find this level of description daunting - and indeed it is perhaps more appropriate for major state or university libraries. By way of contrast one might study the St. Joseph Public Library *Materials Selection and Collection Review Policy* (pp. 58-67). Although a far more modest effort, this document indicates one way in which basic, general comments can offer reasonably clear guidance in developing collections. The same applies to the *Collection Development Policy* of William Paterson State College (pp. 67-84). One might expect an academic library policy to differ in many respects from that of a public library; quantitatively, for instance, academic library collection development policies have tended to provide almost excessive detail with regard to the nature of the collections, level of description and subject breakdown. The William Paterson State College policy offers a simplified alternative that may appeal to many academic librarians who until now have contemplated a policy document with more than a degree of scepticism.

No policy reproduced here, however, achieves what we regard as the optimum level of information and treatment. This indicates in part the difficulty in achieving the ideal policy, but it is also a function of space in these pages. The most adequate comparisons can be made by studying detailed policies firsthand; there are many such documents available, and some are reproduced in Elizabeth Futas' *Library Acquisition Policies and Procedures* (2nd ed. Phoenix, Ariz.: Oryx Press, 1984).

F.R. Bartle and W.L. Brown, "Book Selection Policies for Public Libraries." *Australian Library Journal* 32, 3 (1983): 5-13.

It is easy to criticise as I shall demonstrate in the rest of this paper but before I proceed to do so I should thank all those who have provided me with their book selection policy statements. The fact is that it is extremely difficult to produce an adequate book selection policy statement and the State Library of Tasmania (in common with many others) has failed to do so. We have pondered the problem at length but have so far failed to produce a document which we consider worthy of publication.

Perhaps more than ever before, public libraries in recent times have produced a variety of documents which are claimed to be resources selection policy statements. The motivation to produce such statements springs from a number of sources, including accountability in hard times, and bewilderment at the range of expectations and demands placed upon public libraries.

At best, selection policies are seen as signposts to the future development of services; at worst, a bulwark behind which to hide when the political, moral and sectarian flak starts to fly. A resources selection policy statement is of value only when it is a public document, the purpose of which is to tell the community what the library thinks it is doing in providing the kinds of resources it provides, why and for whom it is providing these resources and how it is intended to make them available. Furthermore, a resources selection policy statement has value for the librarian in that it is the principal supporting document for the organisation's objectives and suggests which courses of action should be taken to achieve those objectives.

So many selection policies are something other than what they claim to be that I want to begin by mentioning the kinds of policies I am not talking about. Those of the type included in Boyer and Eaton[1] are predominantly statements of rules and procedures for the categories of materials to be obtained and for their location and use within the library system; they are acquisitions policies and to my mind a quite separate and lesser order of policy statement. What, then, are the defining characteristics of a resources selection policy?

In the first instance a selection policy is one of a number of mutually supportive statements concerning major aspects of public library service, each of which stems from a principal and all-embracing exposition of library purpose. Companion documents to a selection policy may address such areas as reference and information services, services to minority groups, standards for library buildings, the library's position in relation to children, students and education generally, and the role of the library beyond the provision of resources and related services. Each of these policy statements takes the principal document as its starting point and seeks to elaborate the themes relevant to its own area of concern.

Unless there already exists a general statement of the objectives of the library service it would seem to be impossible to produce any other document detailing library policies in specific areas. A selection policy document cannot be a substitute for an objective statement, it is totally dependent on it. The public library's objectives statement must indicate whom it considers it exists to serve and the general requirements of the community which it claims as the reason for its existence.

The problem about producing general objectives statements for public libraries is that we tend to finish up with generalities such as those in the UNESCO *Public Library Manifesto*[2] which invoke high principles but which are far removed from the everyday realities of providing public library service in general or in allocating useful materials in particular. The UNESCO *Manifesto*, however, may well be the basis on which your public library and mine build their own harder-headed statements of objectives.

For my money, in recent years the most lucid expression of what libraries are all about was given by Daniel Boorstin, Librarian of Congress, when addressing the 1979 White House Conference on Library and Information Services.[3] Boorstin's theme was the distinction between information and knowledge, and the need for librarians to keep in mind the primacy of knowledge, which in this context is the happy combination of "amusement" and "instruction". As Boorstin said: "the autonomous reader, amusing and knowledging himself, is the be-all and end-all of our libraries".

The State Library of Tasmania, after some hard thinking, put together a document, *Public Library Objectives*[4] which was subsequently endorsed by the Tasmanian Library Board in April 1981. It takes the form of a general rationale for the public library service, and emphasises its role as an entry point into the whole range of recorded knowledge. The statement identifies four major areas of responsibility - objectives if you like - which seek to satisfy the identifiable needs of:

a) the individual to develop his knowledge of the social, political, economic, cultural and natural environment as a means of understanding and interacting with that society of which he is a part, thereby developing his full potential as an individual.

b) the organisation or common interest group to successfully pursue that goal for which it has been created.

c) the individual in pursuit of the creative and practical use of leisure.

d) the individual seeking entertainment.

In broad terms the objectives indicate the types of use for which public library services are intended and organised. However, the document also attempts to indicate some circumscription by discussing limitations on the service which can or should be provided. In other words, the document does not claim that the public library is for every man in all his roles. It recognises that there are going to be many instances where the public library is not able, nor is it its proper role, to meet all library needs. The State Library of Tasmania document also attempts to explain the Library's role relative to formal education. Having done all these things the objectives then imply categories of users and levels of resources provision which the selection policy can develop. Having suggested where the general policy fits into the scheme of things, I now want to do the same but in more detail for the resources selection policy.

As with all the public library's policies the selection policy forms part of the pattern of information, explanation and accountability that government owes to the public at large. As a statement of purpose and intention the policy enables the politician, the library user and other interested persons to question the library's objectives and the implied means of attaining them. It also permits some comparison between aims and performance. In its opening paragraph Wade Shire Library's selection policy pinpoints what should be a primary function of all such statements: Book selection policy is intended to implement the general objectives of the library. By this I take to be meant that the selection policy, and its companion statements, are the first link in the chain leading from the library's aims to their realisation.

The notion of justification may seem rather defensive, but in fact it is entirely appropriate that the public library should be seen to be conscious of its responsibility in using public funds and providing public services. A statement concerning the provision of resources is one form of accountability which the library can proffer as a means of reassuring the public that its efforts conform with their needs.

There is a problem in that the public at large has limited perceptions of the library's role, and its view of what it wants may be substantially different from our view of what we think it needs. Much of the purpose of a selection policy comes back to this question of giving the public the means of assessing how well the library is doing its job. The public is entitled to know what are the library's service priorities; the selection policy is a principal source for finding out.

Resources selection priorities should be seen to follow logically from the broader library objectives and be a more specific expression of them. To say, as does the State Library of Tasmania's *Public Library Objectives*, that a principal aim is satisfying the needs of the individual to develop his knowledge of the social, political, economic and cultural environment in which he lives by the provision of material across as wide a range of subject areas as possible at a level which is able to satisfy general needs, may be a worthwhile general objective for a public library, but it gives only the broadest terms of reference for a selection policy. Without a more specific statement of objectives and priorities, such as that provided by a selection policy, the public has no basis for determining the value of what the library is trying to achieve. We are all familiar with the complaining reader who asks "How can you justify having so many books on x subject when you have so few books on y subject".

From the staff point of view a well articulated selection policy permits the setting down of acquisition objectives which in turn can be related to whatever standards of service the public library is pursuing. Camberwell-Waverley's selection policy establishes the broad principle of

> ...a representative collection of classic and current fiction, including works of notable contemporary writers. Fiction acquisition is not restricted to works of high literary merit, but includes fiction of interest to the clientele of the library.

Within this broad framework, presumably, staff are able to determine more specific priorities between categories of fiction. Such priorities between categories of fiction, when linked to standards of bookstock of the type published in the LAA's *Interim Minimum Standards for Public Libraries*[5] and the NZLA *Standards for Public Library Service in New Zealand*[6] can be translated into clear courses of acquisition activity. At the same time they become the means by which the library's performance can be evaluated.

The question is: does the library user know what these acquisition priorities are other than by inference from what is available on the bookshelves? It seems unlikely. How, then, is the library user to obtain the answer to three questions:

1.   What are the library's resources provision and selection priorities?
2.   What standards of resources service is the library aiming at?
3.   How well is it performing at present?

The selection policy should provide the means for answering each question. Similarly, the selection policy should also be a vehicle for staff education and motivation by establishing who is responsible for implementing the policy. From it there should be developed an annual acquisitions priorities document based on the financial allocations the library is seeking in its budget and, when the actual budget allocation is known, the working document for the year's programme of acquisitions.

I have already suggested that a selection policy exists within the broader context of a public library policy, but this notion of a predetermining framework doesn't end there. The ideas and attitudes underlying a selection policy are formed through a wide range of influences which act as determinants and constraints. Principal among these must be the community, its expressed needs and anticipated demands. Other influences which spring readily to mind include the geographical characteristics of the area served, the nature of financial restraints upon collection development, legal implications of resources provision, the role of other organisations within the community, and the professional philosophy of those formulating the selection policy.

The truism that the community is the major determinant of selection policy still leaves open the question of how librarians see the community and which of its perceived needs they choose to acknowledge. Most selection policies seem alive to the many claims on library services, usually going so far as to identify some of the many groups within society - particularly the disadvantaged ones. The problem is, having recognised the claims of the community as a whole, how to formulate in a selection policy the particular responses that book selection can make and the order of priority of these responses?

The different emphases in service one might find in Blacktown as opposed to Manly or Sunshine in comparison with Malvern may belie policies which, if published, would appear substantially the same. This being so, does the diversity of selection priorities stemming from different service priorities suggest a selection policy which is too generalised to be useful, and is therefore ignored? or one which is flexible enough to allow professional interpretation of changing circumstances? For example, I doubt if the assertion in St. Kilda's selection policy that "...the library is obliged to maintain a seriousness of purpose...and should not compete in the field of lowest common denominator entertainment..." means that St. Kilda does not purchase popular recreational reading.

The alternative to clearly defined priorities, however, is a confusion of purpose which results in a gradual undifferentiated paring away of all services, essential and peripheral, until the service as a whole is undermined. Unless we have developed clearly stated orders of priority there is a real danger that in times of financial stringency we will keep on doing more and more less and less satisfactorily.

There are many libraries with incomplete runs of major periodicals and journals, gaps in reference coverage and inadequate holdings of standard fiction, non-fiction and children's titles which would now be in better shape if they had systematically pursued a selection policy with clear priority guidelines. We will not be able to take the politically hard decision of eliminating some elements of service provision in order to preserve those which we regard as central and which are the main justification for our existence unless we are supported by a public document which has been endorsed by our political masters. By juxtaposing, as I did earlier, two pairs of library services, I implied differences of degree in demographic and socio-economic complexion which prompt the formulation of selection policy guidelines - often with practical and specific outcomes. Sutherland Shire, for example, refers in its policy to the high proportion of young people in the area; Wade Shire points to the diversity of ethnic groups, both of which factors find expression in particular selection emphases.

Each library's organisational response to a given population spread must also have a bearing upon the emphases of its selection policy. Local authorities serving densely populated areas through a few strategically placed service points will view stock development and maintenance in a different way from country shires working with fragmented collections spread over many rural communities. The latter is well expressed in Central Gippsland's comment:

> The organisation of a library service has a direct bearing on the selection of materials. The Central Gippsland Regional Library Service is...designed to make its resources available over a large area through a branch library network.

> Each branch has a reference collection and a circulating collection. The quantity and range of materials in stock at a particular branch at a particular time is determined by space restrictions and by budgetary restrictions.

Despite the organisational problems inherent in this type of library service the policy statement emphasises the need for a wide-ranging materials selection policy leading to a well-rounded and balanced collection. The emphasis upon a single integrated collection despite the widely dispersed nature of the resources seems to me a particularly significant approach to materials selection - one which should be stressed in the selection policy.

(One area which I don't propose giving time to, although it is a fundamental part of any selection policy, relates to the criteria we use when selecting resources, that is, criteria concerning the intrinsic qualities of the materials under consideration. I think there is sufficient agreement about what are the criteria, if not about their precise application, to warrant my gliding over the subject.)

At the same time there is an aspect of selection criteria which is worth mentioning. Circumstances sometimes arise in which the library will wish to depart from its normal selection standards. Reasons underlying this are frequently to do with types of user or scarcity of materials, or both. However, it seems that some libraries do not quite have the nerve to carry through the logic of their intention. One policy, while stressing the need to attract new users by the provision of paperbacks, cassettes, magazines, easy books, toys, audio-visual material and art prints, also adds the rider that the resources allocation should not devote too high a proportion to purely recreational type material.

It would be interesting to know what is "too high a proportion of expenditure" on purely recreational type material. It would also be interesting to define this material. We are all familiar with the pressure that arises when we find we are unable to supply sufficient copies of the new popular titles, and yet very few of us have any policy statement about our obligation to meet the demands that are created by the wide publicity given to (say) *The Thorn Birds* or the *Brideshead Revisited* kind of super-promotion. I do not know of any library that says it will not attempt to meet excessive demands on particular titles or fill the bottomless pit of very light fiction demand; in fact libraries usually have an unwritten policy that they will not meet this demand. The librarians then are in a weak position when the unsatisfied demands are converted into political pressure.

It is difficult to see how a selection policy can have any real point unless it takes as its central issue the question of library users and their needs. Only from an attempted identification of user needs can inferences be drawn about the types of service and resources appropriate. I say attempted identification because I realise that the question of defining user needs raises issues which cannot be answered here. Unfortunately, it is precisely on this question that most policy statements fall down. Libraries seem content to stipulate the types of service they regard as necessary, and the materials underpinning the service. There is little attempt to analyse the user needs which are seen as prompting those services and resources. I do not regard statements of the kind "... As the interests of the community are wide ranging so should be the selection of materials..." as particularly rigorous. Nor, for that matter "...the library purchases books about sex for such users as parents, adolescents, young people contemplating marriage, newly married couples, teachers, social workers, clergymen and physicians." Few selection policies come to grips with the library user in explicit terms. Others seem overly ambitious in their objectives:

> The establishment of priority collection development of those types of library materials which will attract new users and new groups of users, whilst continuing to develop a high standard for present users.

Cornucopia approaches of this kind give no basis for a realistic selection policy; they usually result in acquisitions objectives which have absolutely no prospect of attainment. As I have indicated elsewhere it is better to do fewer things well than all things poorly.

Selection policies differ markedly in their approach to the question of resources interdependence among library systems. Most seem oblivious to the possibilities of cooperative selection. An exception is the joint statement of the Toowoomba Municipal Library and the Darling Downs Institute of Advanced Education which defines some principles for a working relationship and describes specific acquisitions and collection development arrangements. Others confine themselves to matters relating to subject specialisation schemes.

As I explained earlier the State Library of Tasmania's objectives document does attempt to address the question of what it will not do and whom it will serve. In doing so it indicates the library's obligation to act as the link between its own resources and those of other collections. What we have not done is to attempt a joint selection policy statement. A question we in Tasmania have before us at the moment and one on which we hope a research study will shortly be undertaken is "What are the respective roles of public children's libraries and school libraries?" I am not aware that anyone has seriously addressed this vital question.

The recent publication of the *National Library of Australia Selection Policy*[7] focuses attention upon the inter-relationship between the national, state and local levels of collection development. Although it should act as a precipitant for many other policy statements from all types of libraries, I'm not sure that this will be the case. The policy is a detailed enumeration of the subject areas and levels of collecting activity with which the

National Library is concerned. The principal authority for this policy, the National Library Act 1960, is other than in a few predictable areas - Australiana, Pacificana, Parliament and Government - either vague or silent on the question of what the National Library should collect. As Burmester's account of the National Library's collections shows, the more [sic] is owed to historical accident than premeditated action. It cannot be said, then, that the National Library of Australia's acquisitions policy stems from a fully coherent and integrated concept of national collection building. The policy says little about the collection development role of the National Library of Australia vis a vis other institutions. It is more a case of "this is what we are collecting, now what about you?"

For their part, I doubt if public libraries, even at the State level, can use the National Library of Australia policy as a point of reference for articulating their own statements. Putting aside local responsibilities, which clearly complement the National Library of Australia's role, large public libraries probably find themselves in much the same situation, having a broad range of resources needs to satisfy the various collection strengths already firmly committed. The likelihood of a nationally integrated acquisitions policy has, if anything, been made less likely by the National Library declaring its hand.

Characteristics of Selection Policies

Examination of a number of Australian public library selection policies reveals many common features (and some not so common) and a diversity of ways of expressing them. The following table indicates the most frequently occurring characteristics:

Table 1. Common Features of Selection Policies

1.	Objectives of the library
2.	The community and its needs identified
3.	The purpose of the selection process
4.	The functions of the library
5.	The context of selection: needs, quality, funding, cooperation
6.	Authority for selection policy
7.	Responsibility for implementation
8.	Priorities: types of use and categories of material
9.	Controversial issues
10.	Censorship
11.	Categories of exclusions
12.	Statement on Freedom to Read
13.	Selection criteria
14.	Collection standards: quantity
15.	Collection development targets
16.	Selection methods: organisation
17.	Acquisitions categories and coverage
18.	Ordering methods

Closer examination of the features listed below suggests three broad groupings as shown in Table 2.

Table 2

Selection Policies	1.	Objectives of the library	Why and
	2.	Community and needs identified	for/by whom
	3.	Purpose of the selection process	
	4.	Context of selection	
	5.	Authority	
	6.	Responsibility	
	7.	Priorities of use and category	
	8.	Controversial issues	
	9.	Censorship	
	10.	Statement on Freedom to Read	
Acquisition Policies	11.	Functions of the library	What done
	12.	Selection criteria - application	
	13.	Acquisition categories, coverage	
	14.	Selection methods	How done
	15.	Acquisition methods	
Development Policies	16.	Collection standards	Which level
	17.	Collection development targets	

From the foregoing "resources selection policy" can be seen as a blanket term covering a range of topics, from library aims as the starting point, through selection policy in the narrow sense, to acquisition procedures and stock circulation as a practical outcome.

The most substantial public library selection policy to appear in Australia is one approved recently by the Library Board of Western Australia.[8] It is a second edition of that first prepared by Ali Sharr in the 1960s and now substantially rewritten and expanded. Running to over thirty pages of text, the scope and detail of the document make is a major statement of the direction to be taken by public libraries in Western Australia from now into the next century. The publication should be read in conjunction with the Library Board's *Operational Standards for Public Libraries in Western Australia* published last year. The policy deserves some attention.

At the outset it clearly identifies itself as being concerned with book provision in general as well as selection, with practice as well as policy. The first section firmly establishes the context of the policy by setting out the purpose and objectives of the Board. In proper organisation management style the aim or purpose of the Board is succinctly stated as to satisfy "to the fullest extent possible the needs and wants of the Western Australian public for the information and enjoyment that are to be had from all forms of recorded materials". One could get into an interesting discussion - part semantic and part philosophical - about the implications for library services of this particular form of words, but it isn't strictly relevant to this paper. Nor need I comment on the six means by which the Board achieves its purpose, nor, for that matter on the ten objectives which give directional clarity to the means, other than to make the point that the general statement seems more preoccupied with the organisational arrangements for providing services than with indicating what are the societal needs upon which the services are premised.

The publication as a whole is an approachable document well suited to public dissemination and in typically West Australian style. Where else would you find the question of popular lending services expressed thus:

> It would on the other hand, be difficult to justify the provision of a wholly recreational service, the government does not, after all, provide purely recreational activities, such as the trots, free!

Or this extract from the introduction:

> I remain steadfast in my belief that book selection and collection building lie at the centre of the art and craft of the librarian. When all the computerised systems that nowadays take our fancy have been forgotten, when it no longer matters what classification schemes or codes of cataloguing were used in an age gone by, users of libraries will judge the success or failure of earlier library managers by virtue of the collections they established and the assistance they were able to give to the scholars of the day. We all hear a great deal about Dr J.S. Battye, the foundation Principal Librarian of the Public Library of Western Australia. He was for fifty years a leading figure in Western Australian educational, literary and library circles. Yet little emphasis is placed in the folklore of WA librarianship on the systems in which he believed - and his preference for one cataloguing code over another - on his understanding of statistical methods or his reliance on classification schedules. We are told stories - both those that tend to his good reputation, and those that detract from it - of his ability as a book selector and collection builder. Indeed, the rise and decline of the old Public Library of Western Australia seem in large part to be coincident with periods of great achievement and periods of stagnation in Dr Battye's book selection.

Reading further one finds the policy statement to be primarily concerned with the implementation of policy, and "how done" - resources provision, stock ratios, location of materials, collecting emphasis, etc. More than a third of the publication is given over, in the manner of the National Library of Australia policy, to summarising the principal subject areas for collection building in the State Reference and Battye Libraries - in effect an acquisitions statement. It seems to me significant that the section head "Book Selection Policy" comprises only two pages, and that matters concerning selection procedures for the State Reference Library and Circulation Division occupy most of the space.

What emerges from the Western Australian publication and from all the other policy statements I have read is a suspicion that there may be no such thing as a resources selection policy. It may be that a statement of this kind can find expression or be inferred only from among the whole range of complementary policies already mentioned. Perhaps a selection policy has no separate entity? If this is the case, then it follows that librarians, when formulating general library policies, must keep in mind that resources selection impinges upon, and in turn is affected by, policies in all the service areas of public library activity.

The problem that the National Library, state libraries and public libraries have in developing selection policy statements which are coherent and will stand up to critical examination is that they are organisationally independent. Other libraries are part of another institution which they serve and which itself has objectives. The selection policies of school libraries, university libraries and special libraries stem directly from the objectives of their parent bodies. Their clientele is circumscribed and their charter is clear. Our problem in the public library is that there is no limitation on our client group, and if we are to have a charter, or institutional objectives, from which to develop our selection policy statements, we must produce them ourselves.

When the world is your oyster you need a very sharp sword to open it. If we are to produce the documents needed to justify our existence and explain what we do and why we do it, we will need to spend more time at the grindstone.

References

1   Calvin J. Boyer and Nancy L. Eaton, *Book Selection Policies in American Libraries: An Anthology of Policies from College, Public and School Libraries* (Austin, Tex.: Armadillo Press, 1971).

2   *Unesco Bulletin for Libraries* 26, 3 (1972): 129-131.

3   Daniel J. Boorstin, "Remarks...at the White House Conference on Library and Information Services." *Special Libraries* (1980): 113-116.

4   State Library of Tasmania, *Public Library Objectives* (Hobart: State Library of Tasmania, 1981).

5   Library Association of Australia, *Interim Minimum Standards for Public Libraries* (Sydney: Library Association of Australia, 1972).

6   New Zealand Library Association, *Standards for Public Library Service in New Zealand* (Rev. ed. Wellington: New Zealand Library Association, 1980).

7   National Library of Australia, *Selection Policy for Library Materials: Draft* (Canberra: National Library of Australia, 1980).

8   Library Board of Western Australia, *Book Provision and Book Selection Policy and Practice* (Perth: Library Board of Western Australia, 1982).

Policy statements consulted and not cited elsewhere in the text are:

Camberwell-Waverley Regional Library Materials Selection Policy (June 1973)
Materials Selection Policy of the Central Gippsland Regional Library Service (June 1981)
Gold Coast City Council (extract from Council papers, 1969/70)
Hurstville Municipal Library: Book Selection Policy (1978)
The Objects of the Kempsey Shire Library (August 1978)
Lane Cove Public Library: Collection Development Policy (extract from Council papers, October 1981)
Marrickville Municipal Library: Acquisition Policy (1978)
St. Kilda Public Library: Policy Statement on Selection of Books and Related Materials (1974?)
Shellharbour: Resource Acquisition and Allocations Policy (1978)
Sutherland Shire Council: Libraries Department Policy: General Acquisitions (n.d.)

Toowoomba Municipal Library and DDIAE Resource Materials Centre (1978)
Wade Shire Library: Library Selection Policy (n.d.)
Western Sydney Reference and Information Service Study: Objectives for Selection and
Services (n.d.)

**State Library of Victoria, *State Library of Victoria Selection Policy*.
Melbourne: Library Council of Victoria, 1986. pp. iii-vii, 1-12.**

(a) pp. iii-vii

Preface

Late in 1982 the Public Service Board of Victoria conducted a management review into
the operations of the Library Council of Victoria. Central to the recommendations
following the review was the gathering together of related functions into a number of
operating Divisions. Within the Technical Services Division was to be a selection unit to
develop policy and to coordinate the selection of material for the collections of the State
Library of Victoria.

With the appointment during 1983 of the members of the Corporate Management Group,
each of whom was to direct and manage one of the newly-formed divisions, there came
the first opportunities to set in train many of the recommendations made by the
Management Review Committee. By August 1983 it seemed to the Director, Technical
Services, that the most effective means of managing the selection of materials was to
recognise and utilise the considerable expertise also in the Information Services Division
in particular. Whilst the control and coordination of selection could quite properly be
vested in Technical Services, it was postulated that individual interest and/or subject
specialisation already present in a majority of professional staff could be turned to positive
advantage by involving them in the future development of the collections.

There had been a widespread perception that the practice of selection was insufficiently
dispersed amongst staff. Nor did staff necessarily understand the context within which
particular decisions to acquire were made since there was no written selection policy, and
no specific budget allocations were made for types of material or collections. An
introductory document was drawn up in 1982 at the request of the State Librarian, and
this provided a basis for this selection policy.

These factors, then, led the Director, Technical Services to establish in August 1983 a
Selection Committee which had as its members the Director, Technical Services
(chairperson), the Director, Information Services, the La Trobe Librarian, the Reader
Services Librarian and the Resources Development Librarian. The last position was
subsequently replaced by the newly-established position of Acquisitions Librarian, who
acts as secretary to the Committee. The first and most important brief of the Selection
Committee was to establish a selection policy for the development of the collections of the
State Library of Victoria. The ongoing brief of the Selection Committee is to provide a
formal forum for the selection of particular materials. The selection policy was to take into
account other library collections, especially in Victoria, as well as the major client groups

to whom present and likely future services would be offered. It subsequently became clear that in order to make useful comparisons or to provide links with other collections, it would first be necessary to find out in some detail and in a systematic way, more about the State Library of Victoria's collections as they had developed since 1856.

In order to begin the complex task of measurement and evaluation of the collection as a necessary precursor to any attempt at drafting policy statements, the Selection Committee, in September 1983, established a number of working groups. It was expected that their findings and preliminary selection policy statements would be completed, assessed and re-drafted in fuller form for publication in mid-1984. This turned out to be a far more demanding exercise than envisaged and the Selection Committee was overwhelmed with documentation.

Regular monthly meetings soon became weekly ones and this selection policy has emanated from weekly meetings of two hours each held nearly every week since January 1984. As the selection policy developed, it became apparent that some areas needed further work, and these were referred back to working groups for further detail and discussion, prior to re-drafting by the Selection Committee. Collegiate collaboration has been one of the highlights of the entire process, and the Selection Committee wishes to acknowledge the substantial contributions made by so many staff. The Committee had the difficult role of trying to see each subject in the context of the whole and to ensure consistency.

In particular, I wish to acknowledge the contributions of the individual members of the Selection Committee - Anne Beaumont, Moira MacKinnon, Dianne Reilly, Derek Whitehead. Their efforts were unflagging and thoroughly competent. Derek Whitehead as Secretary performed the Herculean task of bringing together all of the documentation stemming from the initial collection measurement and analysis, the recommendations of the staff members responsible for each subject and the discussions of the Selection Committee itself. The Selection Policy document as it stands is the result. I commend it to you for your consideration.

Readers of this document will, we hope, be quick to point out its deficiencies and to make constructive suggestions for its improvements.

Frances H. Awcock
Director, Technical Services

(b) pp. 1-12

Introduction

This introduction deals with the following:

1   The Role of the State Library of Victoria
2   The Determinants of the Selection Policy
3   The Purposes of the Selection Policy
4   The Principal User Groups
5   Materials Acquired
6   Collection Levels
7   Other Issues

1. The Role of the State Library of Victoria

The Library Council of Victoria 1965 sets out as one of the functions of the Library Council of Victoria

" to maintain and develop the State collection of library material" (s.11(b)).

The State Library of Victoria maintains a collection of library materials which is the principal public collection for the people of Victoria. It exists both to serve their current needs for library materials and information, and to develop a collection which is part of the heritage of the State. The State Library of Victoria, in common with the public libraries of Victoria, is accessible without charge to all.

As such, the role of the library and the development of its collections are not circumscribed by the policies and activities of a parent body, as is the case with an academic or special library, for example. The library exists to serve the information needs of the Victorian community. However, although the information and materials needs of Victorians are potentially universal, the resources of the State are not. A selection policy is therefore necessary because the library must choose which of the available materials it will acquire. Approximately 675,000 monograph titles are published each year throughout the world, a quarter of them in the English language, and there are over 200,000 current serial and newspaper titles published.

Moreover, it would be both wasteful and impractical for the State collection to attempt to duplicate the collections of other institutions within the State, or to serve potential user groups for which other accessible collections exist. The State Library of Victoria must select the emphases in collecting most appropriate to an institution of its nature, and most needed by the Victorian community. Priorities in both current service and in the preservation of materials for future generations must be set.

2. The Determinants of the Selection Policy

The selection policies of the State Library of Victoria are determined by four principal factors.

In the first place, the statutory responsibilities of the Library Council of Victoria are central to its policies for acquiring materials.

Secondly, the needs of its potential and current users are an essential determinant of selection policies. Such needs include the expressed needs of current users of the collections, but also the perceived needs of groups which do not at present use the library extensively. In determining the needs which it is most appropriate for the collections of the State Library of Victoria to meet, account is taken of the composition of the Victorian population, known patterns of demand for library resources, particular subjects of current or likely future interest, and the needs of government, institutions, groups and associations.

Thirdly, in determining its priorities the State Library of Victoria takes into account the collections of other institutions. The library gives priority in developing its collections to those people or institutions whose needs are not specifically provided for by other collections (such as those of schools, tertiary educational institutions or research institutions) and which no other libraries have an obligation to provide. Where the availability of material in other collections to the general public is limited, the State Library of Victoria may attempt to facilitate access through means, such as inter-library loans, other than purchase of additional copies of titles.

Finally, the State Library of Victoria takes into account its own particular advantages and strengths in developing its collections. For example, legal deposit provisions make the State Library of Victoria particularly appropriate as the repository for the major collection of Victorian imprints; long-standing arrangements with governments for the deposit of their publications make the library an appropriate centre for the development of government publications collections. The State Library of Victoria also considers the existing strengths of its collections if further developing those collections. In addition, to its responsibilities to the State of Victoria, the State Library of Victoria's collections are a major national resource, and the library's historical role imposes a consequent responsibility in the future development of its collections.

The State Library of Victoria avoids unnecessary duplication of the resources of other libraries within the state, and is unable to make good the collection weaknesses of other libraries in their primary areas of collecting responsibility. It attempts through consultation and cooperation with other libraries to avoid unnecessary duplication of expensive works. However, duplication of the resources of other institutions may be unavoidable because of limitations on general public access to other collections, or the discarding policies of other libraries, or substantial public interest in and demand for particular kinds of materials.

The State Library of Victoria exercises leadership in promoting the development of library collections and services which will collectively meet information needs of people throughout the State.

3. The Purposes of the Selection Policy

There are three aspects of the development of collections of the State Library of Victoria: evaluation of the collections as they have been developed over the last century and as they are now; current and future goals in maintaining and developing these collections in accordance with the policies and goals of the Library Council of Victoria; and priorities for the current budget period.

This policy deals primarily with the second of these aspects and sets out a broad framework of priorities for the development of the collections in the near future. The policy is capable of application to greater funds than are now available for expenditure on books and materials. Therefore priorities will need to be set or reconsidered regularly in accordance with funds allocated and the policy can only be fully implemented should adequate funds be available. Other factors relevant to setting priorities include current and changing patterns of user needs, long-term collection development considerations and the directions given by the library's corporate plan, which was being developed when this selection policy was written. Such priorities will be set within the bounds of this selection policy.

The policy is based upon a relatively brief survey of the collections and takes the existing collections as its starting point. A great deal of further work is necessary for an adequate description of the present collections.

The policy does not encompass all aspects of collection development. It does not deal with the mechanics of selection or of acquisition, and is essentially concerned with the choice of materials for the collection and with the selection of materials by subject, format, language, or other characteristics.

The policy has four main purposes.

Firstly, it is a planning tool, and exists within the context of the overall goals and objectives of the Library Council of Victoria.

Secondly, the policy is a management tool, and exists to provide a greater degree of consistency and continuity in the selection policies and practices of the library. A wide range of library staff is involved in the selection of materials for the collection. It is necessary in order to ensure consistency of practice between different staff and continuity over time that clear and coherent guidelines be set out for all to follow. It is essential that staff involved in selection work towards the same collection development goals and that these be followed regardless of changes in personnel.

Thirdly, the policy is a communication tool, and provides information to a number of groups other than staff involved in selection. These include users of the library and the public in general, and the policy indicates what may be expected to be found within the collection, what may not, and provides reasons. The policy is a means of accountability to both the public and the Government.

Finally, the policy is intended to facilitate cooperation. It is intended, like the selection policy of the National Library of Australia, to be a vehicle for national and state cooperation in the development of library resources. To this end the terminology used in the policy and the collection levels used generally follow those of the National Library of Australia.

4. The Users of the State Library of Victoria

All residents of Victoria are freely entitled to use the collections of the State Library, but in planning the development of its collections the library must necessarily give priority to some user groups. In the same way that it cannot acquire all possible materials, so it cannot equally serve all possible user groups.

The user or client groups set out below reflect the major priorities of the library's collection development policies; however, the Library Council of Victoria's corporate plan, to be completed during 1986, will address issues of service priorities in greater detail.

A. *The Informed Reader*

A major target group of users may be characterised as the informed reader (the term includes users of non-written material). In most subject areas this is the group to which the development of the collections is directed.

The group may be characterised as people with a relatively advanced level of knowledge and interest but who are not professionals or specialists in the areas of their interests. They may lack access as of right to the major academic and special library collections, either because they are not students or academic staff, or are not employed in the area of their interest. Alternatively, there may not be advanced collection at all in their areas of interest. For these groups of users, the library complements the collections of public libraries. They consist of a very wide variety of subject interest groups, such as people involved with particular social issues, family or local historians, political lobbying groups, collectors and restorers, people wishing to enhance their appreciation of art, music or natural history, and those handling their own legal affairs.

B. Libraries

As a central focus for the Victorian state network of libraries, the resources of the State Library of Victoria are available to all libraries within the state, either through inter-library loan or through referral of their users to the State Library. In building its own collections the State Library pays attention to the roles of public and other libraries and attempts to complement their resources.

For many purposes the State Library of Victoria is the centre for a network of public libraries, and its resources are an important supplementary resource for public libraries and their users. It plays a major coordinating role in locating and obtaining material in other libraries for its own users and those who use public libraries.

C. Occupational Groups

The State Library of Victoria acquires materials to support occupational groups which do not always have access to appropriate resources through professional or other institutional libraries; for example, an extensive reference service is maintained for business.

D. Professional Researchers

The State Library of Victoria is a research library in that over wide areas its collections are of a level appropriate to support formal and informal research. In many areas these collections include material not held elsewhere in the state or in Australia; in particular, the library holds an unparalleled collection of material relating to all aspects of life in Victoria. However, although the library continues to develop some subjects at a research level, its major collections appropriate to support advanced research are now primarily in areas relating to Victoria and Australia.

E. Students

Secondary and tertiary students are substantial users of the State Library of Victoria's resources, but are not a primary target group in the development of those resources. The State Library regards these groups as principally served by school, college, university and other institutional libraries. Should students wish to use its resources, however, every effort is made to provide assistance to them.

A higher priority is given to adult learners, and in particular to those who are not studying towards formal qualifications and may lack access to substantial library resources.

F. *Reference Services*

The State Library of Victoria maintains an extensive range of resources to support a wide-ranging and comprehensive reference and information service to the general public, to public and other libraries, and to all Victorians regardless of whether or not they fall into major target user groups. The maintenance of an up to date collection of reference sources is a high priority in the acquisition of materials; such materials include, for example, a wide range of national bibliographies, international telephone directories, bibliographical works, and encyclopedias from as many countries as possible.

5. Materials Acquired for the Collection

Library materials can be categorised in a number of ways, and such ways include: subject matter, place or country of origin, language of the work, physical format, means of acquisition, and intended purpose. A cross-tabulation of all of these means of categorising library materials would produce many thousands of possible categories for consideration.

This policy is primarily arranged by subject, and the subject arrangement is based upon and follows as closely as practicable the Dewey decimal classification system by which the library's collections are arranged. However, some attention to other means of describing the collections, such as format, is also necessary, and where appropriate throughout the policy reference is made to such other means. The arrangement of this policy by subject is the clearest means of arrangement, and enables comparison with the policies of other institutions. Other relevant means of description of the collection include the following:

A. *Format*

While the collections of the State Library of Victoria have throughout its history been dominated by printed material, other formats, in particular pictures and manuscripts, have always been included. Appropriate formats in which material may be acquired now include the whole range of printed books, pamphlets, newspapers and serials, microforms, pictures in various formats, manuscripts and recorded oral history, printed music, maps, ephemeral publications, audio and video recordings, photocopies, and information available on-line.

In developing the collections, material is acquired where possible in the most appropriate formats, as indicated by reasons of economy, user needs and preferences, durability, ease of use, frequency of use, and relevance to the subject.

B. *Imprints and Language*

This policy includes a statement on area studies, which considers the geographical and language orientations of the collections of the State Library of Victoria. Throughout the policy material produced in Victoria, or by Victorians, or about Victoria and Victorians, is acquired at the most comprehensive level, while collection of material relating to other parts of Australia is also emphasised strongly. In determining collection levels for other places of publication and for languages other than English, attention is paid to existing strengths, actual demand, the ethnolinguistic composition of the State's population, cultural and other connections, and the proximity of other places to Australia. These points are discussed in greater detail in the policy on area studies.

C. *Method of Acquisition*

Although the collections of the State Library of Victoria are substantially built up and maintained by purchase of materials, other methods of acquisition have always played a very important part in collection development, and continue to do so. These methods include legal and government deposit, donation, exchange, and creation of material (such as the creation of oral history recordings).

As a general rule the same principles are applied to all materials considered for acquisition. Shortage of funds may result in collection development goals not being met through purchase. Where shortage of funds limits purchasing, donated material is still acquired at the higher level set out in this policy. It is recognised that the acquisition of material by any means involves a cost, in particular a staff cost.

The library is entitled to receive, under the legal deposit provisions of the Library Council of Victoria Act 1965, one copy of every printed item published in Victoria. Material published by the Victorian Government and its instrumentalities is deposited with the library under the terms of the Premier's Department Circular 85/5 and its predecessors. These form the basis of the Victorian research collections of the library.

A number of other deposit arrangements also exist with other governments, such as those of the United States, the United Kingdom, and Canada, as well as arrangements with the Australian Government Publishing Service and with many international organisations. In view of its central position within the State's library system, it is an appropriate role of the State Library of Victoria to act as a deposit library for governments and other bodies. These deposit collections involve the addition of material according to source rather than subject matter, and therefore the subject range of such collections is wider than that of the general collections.

The State Library receives a very large number of donations from individuals and organisations within Victoria and elsewhere. Because of its public accessibility and central role, it is widely seen as an appropriate repository for collections and items which donors wish to make generally available. Donation of material under the terms of the Taxation Incentive Scheme is also encouraged. The State Library of Victoria also encourages public and other libraries in Victoria to transfer to it materials which are no longer useful to those libraries, but which have an enduring value, are appropriate in terms of the State Library's selection policy, and make a contribution to the resources of the State.

Where material is unlikely to be obtained in other ways the library may obtain it from time to time on exchange. Because it is the principal library maintained by the Victorian Government, the State Library of Victoria maintains agreements with state and national libraries in Australia and overseas, as well as with other institutions such as galleries.

The State Library of Victoria also creates materials for the collection, obtaining microform or photocopied copies of important materials, commissioning photography or oral history recordings and in other ways.

D. *Purpose*

In acquiring materials the State Library is primarily concerned with those materials which are appropriate to activities such as research, serious reading, the pursuit of a variety of interests, and informal or self-education. It is not concerned to acquire curriculum materials for educational courses.

6. The Collection Levels Used in This Policy

This selection policy uses the four collection levels adopted by the National Library of Australia in its selection policy (*National Library of Australia Selection Policy*, Development of Resource Sharing Networks: Networks Study, 17. Canberra: NLA, 1981).

Representative: "limited to current materials for information and reference processes", "a small number of items to represent the class of material."

Selective: "overall coverage permitting limited research."

In depth: "thorough, strong coverage."

Comprehensive: "the ultimate aim is to achieve complete coverage."

However, in order to apply these levels it was found necessary to define them in greater detail than that provided by the National Library. In the definitions below each level is defined approximately in terms of monographs, serials, indexes and abstracts, reference material, and language coverage. Most of these terms are readily understood, but it is necessary to define what is meant by reference material.

Reference material is commonly defined as material published for consultation rather than for continuous reading. It includes: bibliographies, dictionaries, encyclopedias, yearbooks, manuals, bibliographic sources, indexes and abstracts, handbooks, directories, atlases and gazetteers, government reference sources, and "standard" or "general" works. The last are understood as single monographs which treat the whole of a fairly broad subject area (such as the Cambridge History of...) from an authoritative standpoint.

The four levels are further defined as:

Representative level. This includes a very broad coverage of reference works and selected standard works; a highly selective coverage of monographs oriented towards non-specialists; serial coverage limited to titles which cover the field broadly for a non-specialist readership; English-language coverage only; and access to appropriate online databases.

Selective level. This includes a thorough coverage of reference works of all kinds, including standard works; seminal retrospective monographs and a good selection (up to a third of English-language output) of current monographic publishing for the informed non-professional interested in the area; a selection of the major authoritative journals and a good selection of serials with a broad appeal; basically English-language coverage, but with some material, depending on the subject-matter, in other original languages; and access to major relevant online databases. Coverage at this level provides a good introduction to the subject and a guide to materials available elsewhere. Reference materials are regularly kept up to date.

In depth level. This includes a thorough coverage of reference works of all kinds, including all standard works; major retrospective works and the collected writings of major authors in the field, with selections from minor authors; in general a wide range of current monographs in English and other languages; an extensive selection of scholarly journals and a good coverage of other serial literature in English and other languages; access to all relevant online databases. Coverage at this level should be able to support research and should enable the library user to keep abreast of current developments in advanced research in the subject. Purchase of microform collections and of large formed collections should be considered at this level. The collections should be kept thoroughly up to date.

Comprehensive level. It is not expected that this level would be applied to subjects other than Victorian-related areas. Coverage includes all published monographic and serial material; active retrospective purchasing; access to all relevant online databases; acquisition of published non-book materials in the subject (such as audio and video material), maintenance of collections of ephemeral material; purchase of all published material regardless of language; purchase of all published microformat material unless it duplicates existing print holdings unnecessarily; purchase of original materials, such as manuscripts and pictures.

It should be noted that in applying these collection levels, this policy expresses levels for each subject appropriate to its goals and objectives. The achievement of the levels assigned within this policy is always dependent on appropriate levels of financial support.

7. Other Issues

Duplication of Materials. In general it is the library's policy to avoid duplication of materials. Additional copies are acquired of items required for more than one public service point, and of materials for which the library's responsibility is both to preserve for future use and to provide for current use; in particular, a high proportion of material acquired on legal deposit and from the Victorian Government and its instrumentalities is duplicated.

Retention of Materials. The State Library of Victoria follows a policy of indefinite retention for most materials acquired. Where materials are considered for discard, the obligation of the library to retain and preserve materials as part of the heritage of the State is the over-riding consideration and material is only discarded when it falls into clearly defined categories and when other relevant conditions are met. Factors relevant include operational factors (such as the time and cost of selecting materials for discard, amending records and disposing of discarded material); conservation and preservation factors (such as the physical condition of the material); and selection factors (such as the degree to which information and content is unnecessarily duplicated within the collection; the obsolescence of information on specific subjects which are not primary subjects of emphasis in the collection; and the existence of copies in other collections).

Where material is discarded, it will be offered to other institutions should this be appropriate.

Responsibility for Selection. The selection of materials is coordinated and directed by the Acquisitions Librarian (within the Technical Services Division), in cooperation with the Selection Committee where matters of policy or significant individual items or subscriptions are concerned. A wide range of staff of the Library Council of Victoria is involved in day to day selection of materials, and outside advice may be sought where special expertise is needed. The State Library of Victoria welcomes recommendations from its users for the acquisition of materials within its collecting areas.

Although a formal programme for materials selection has yet to be set in place, the Selection Committee considers all items with a monetary value of $150 (a figure to be reviewed annually, having regard to the delegations set by the Victorian Government for expenditure). The Committee also considers all serial titles recommended for subscription, as well as items being duplicated across the collections where the decision to duplicate is likely to result in heavy or controversial expenditure. More expensive items are recommended for purchase to the State Librarian, often for subsequent deliberation by the Library Council of Victoria. The Library Council is responsible for the management of its Trust and Endowment Funds, the interest from which is often used to purchase items of particular historic importance which cannot be acquired from the books and materials vote, allocated as part of the normal government budgetary cycle.

St. Joseph Public Library, *Materials Selection and Collection Review Policy.* **St. Joseph, Mo.: St. Joseph Public Library, n.d.**

I. Authority and Purpose of the Policy

Authority for making and adopting regulations regarding the operations of the library is granted to the Board of Directors by the Charter of the City of St. Joseph and the Statutes of the State of Missouri. In this regard, the library director coordinates and supervises the selection of materials and delegates to department heads the responsibility for making recommendations for purchase. The director has the right to reject or recommend any item contrary to the recommendations of the staff and should be able to answer to the Board and the public for any selections made.

The purpose of this policy is to: (a) enable staff members of the St. Joseph Public Library who make recommendations for the selection of materials to work with greater consistency toward the stated goals and objectives of the library, thereby developing stronger collections and allocating financial resources more wisely and methodically; (b) inform library staff, patrons, administrators, Board members, and the public as to the scope and character of existing collections, and the plans for their continuing development; (c) provide guidelines which will assist in the allocation of funds to various departments to purchase current materials, to round out the collection, and to fill in gaps.

II. Principles Governing the Formulation and Application of the Policy

The development and implementation of any policy governing the operations of the library must be in harmony with the library's mission, set forth as follows:

The St. Joseph Public Library attempts within its financial means to collect, to organize, to make accessible, and to disseminate print and nonprint resources and to guide both users and potential users in the use of these resources to meet the following goals:

Meeting informational needs of individuals and groups;
Facilitating informal self-education;
Encouraging wholesome recreation and constructive use of leisure time;
Supporting the educational, civic, and cultural activities of groups and organizations;
Providing supplementary resources on subjects for which individuals are undertaking formal education.

Approved by the Board of Directors
St. Joseph Public Library
January 9, 1980

In addition, the basis of the materials selection and collection review policy may be found in two codes to which the Board of Director subscribes, the Library Bill and Rights and the Freedom to Read Statement.

III. Clientele to Be Served

Because the library cannot meet all the demands placed upon it, the Board has adopted the following policy regarding priorities of service to different groups and the expenditure of funds:

Service Groups

The St. Joseph Public Library has served and, as long as funds permit, will continue to serve a wide spectrum of age groups with a variety of interests. The library will place emphasis on service to the following segments of the community:

Adults

Recognizing that out-of-school adults comprise the largest single group of users, the library will make its first priority providing for their informational, self-educational, and recreational needs.

Among other services, the library will also give special attention to older citizens when they come to the library, extensive telephone and in-house service to the business community and upgraded service to those who are either economically or educationally disadvantaged. Outreach services will continue through the Books by Mail Program and Bookmobile stops and will be provided, when time and staff permit, to the institutionalized, the homebound, and to the handicapped.

Preschoolers

The St. Joseph Public Library has traditionally assumed a high level of responsibility for programming for preschoolers, since no other agency provides this kind of service. The library will continue to target this age group in the interest of encouraging in the formative years the development of an appreciation of the library's resources.

Students in Elementary through Secondary Schools

Special programs both in the schools and in the library are provided for young people, especially those in elementary school. However, in view of the development of school libraries at all levels, the St. Joseph Public Library will cooperate with school libraries in an attempt not to duplicate materials or services, especially those which relate to a specific curriculum. However, the Public Library will attempt to respond to general informational, recreational, and cultural needs regardless of their relationship to school assignments, and will encourage a continuous use of the public library.

College and University Students

The St. Joseph Public Library will not attempt to meet curricular needs of college and university students, recognizing that academic libraries exist for this purpose alone. Rather, the Public Library will cooperate with academic libraries, especially the Hearnes Learning Resources Center at Missouri Western State College, in an attempt to meet noncurricular needs of this age group.

Approved by the Library Board of Directors at their May 14, 1980 meeting.

IV. Criteria for Materials Selection and Collection Review

The established criteria for selection, withdrawal, and replacement of materials in all nonfiction areas for all age groups are:

Contemporary or permanent value;
Authority, skill, competence, reputation and significance of the author;
Reputation and standards of the publisher;
Clarity, accuracy, logic, objectivity, and readability;
Social significance;
Comprehensiveness and depth of treatment;
Appropriateness and effectiveness of the medium to the content;
Quality and suitability of the physical format to the library;
Attention of critics and reviewers;
Public demand;
Importance of the subject matter;
Accessibility to the title through indexes and bibliographies;
Price;
Availability of materials elsewhere in the region or through interlibrary loan;
Potential use;
Budgetary limitations;
Need for duplicate materials in the existing collection;
Space limitations.

Moreover, criteria for selection, withdrawal, and replacement of works of imagination - fiction, drama, and poetry - also include:

Representation of a significant genre or national culture;
Originality;
Literary quality;

Strength of characterization and plot;
Sustained interest;
Authentic reflection of human experience.

Since libraries are seldom able to examine a work under consideration, the following selection aids are ordinarily used to evaluate a particular title:

The Booklist
Choice
The Horn Book
Library Journal
New York Times Book Review
Publishers Weekly
School Library Journal
Wilson Library Bulletin.

Other sources are also used. Bibliographies and lists prepared by other libraries and subject authorities are checked. Occasionally publishers' brochures are consulted.

Public Library Catalog, Fiction Catalog, and other standard catalogs are checked in considering replacements.

V. Policies by Subject (by Dewey Decimal Classification)

000 Generalities

Bibliographies of certain subjects are purchased where there is a demonstrated need for further resources beyond the library's holdings. They are also used by the staff as buying guides.

Materials relating to library science are selected primarily for the professional development of the staff.

Encyclopedias for general reference use and for circulation are selected using the regular criteria. An attempt is made to replace major titles at least every two or three years. Encyclopedias on specialized subjects are purchased for the Reference Department of the main library only.

To meet reference needs many titles in continuations will be replaced every year. Certain others can be used for two or three years without having a negative effect on the quality of service given.

When needed, many series are purchased in their entirety; however, individual titles of series may also be selected.

100 Philosophy

The library selects representative material from all the areas included in this classification: metaphysics; knowledge; special philosophical viewpoints; psychology; ethics; ancient, medieval, and oriental philosophy; and modern Western philosophy.

In the area of popular philosophy, parapsychology, and occultism, public demand is a major consideration in the library's selection.

200 Religion

In accordance with the selection criteria, the library continues a tradition of collecting widely on the subjects of the Bible; Christian doctrinal theology; religious orders; the history and denominations of the Christian church; other religions of the world; and comparative studies of religions. The tenets of the Library Bill of Rights are carefully adhered to in the interest of providing understanding amongst the members of different religions. Sectarian materials of an inflammatory nature which tend to foster intolerant attitudes are collected only if they have historical or research value.

The personal religious convictions of individuals or groups of staff members should not influence the selection of materials in this area.

300 Social Sciences

The library attempts to provide materials of interest to the general reader on statistics, political science, economics, public administration, social pathology, education, commerce, and customs.

As many viewpoints as possible are represented on both controversial and noncontroversial subjects. No attempt is made to purchase materials of interest only to specialists.

Popular and standard reference materials are purchased on the subject of law. No attempt is made to purchase encyclopedic or case law. Other titles of interest and value only to attorneys are also not purchased.

A continuing emphasis is being placed on the purchase of materials of interest to local businesses.

400 Language

The 400's include general works on language and linguistics in English and other languages. A heavy emphasis continues to be placed on the history, study, and use of the English language, and a wide variety of dictionaries are purchased for reference use.

"English to foreign language" and "foreign language to English" dictionaries in the major European languages are purchased for the Reference Department of the Central Library.

No recent attempt has been made to purchase either fiction or nonfiction materials in foreign languages.

500 Pure Sciences

The library purchases for the general, nonspecialist reader materials written at various levels of difficulty on mathematics, astronomy, physics, chemistry, paleontology, life sciences, botanical sciences, and zoological sciences.

No attempt has ever been made to collect in great depth on any of these subjects for practicing professionals, undergraduate students, graduate students, or researchers.

600 Technology (Applied Sciences)

In the applied sciences the library purchases extremely heavily in some areas and less so in others.

Because of the bequest by Wayne M. Tookhaker, the library purchases many materials for the lay citizen on such subjects as drugs, diseases, diet, and preventive medicine.

A few basic texts and handbooks are collected in the field of engineering. Books on electronics and automotive repair are purchased in large quantities for both circulation and reference to meet strong popular demand.

The library purchases many titles on farming and gardening, homemaking, pet care, and managerial services.

Works dealing with chemical technologies and manufacturing are limited to those recommended specifically for public libraries.

In the field of building skills, including carpentry and heating and ventilation, the library purchases heavily.

700 The Arts

An attempt is made to provide representative coverage of both major and minor artists, periods, and media.

"How to" books in public demand are also included.

For the reference collection the library has always purchased heavily in the field of antiques.

A heavy emphasis continues to be placed on handicrafts, sports, and other recreation.

800 Literature (Belles-lettres)

Essays, poetry, drama, short stories, and selected works of criticism on these forms are included, but exhaustive literary criticism on any author is not maintained. Titles on techniques of communication such as professional writing and public speaking are also purchased.

Heavy preference is given to British and American literatures, but representative work of the literature of other countries is collected to some extent in translation. Special emphasis is also given to the work of the recipients of recognized awards such as the Pulitzer Prize and the National Book Award.

A major criterion for selecting from the large quantities of drama and poetry published is inclusion in popular indexes.

900 General Geography and History

The library collects works on all periods of history with heavy emphasis on American. Standard, up-to-date travel guides for parts of the globe of interest to the community are purchased.

Books about local places, events, and people are usually acquired.

Political, geographical, and historical maps and atlases are collected for reference and circulation.

Biographies are routinely collected for well-known persons. A strong emphasis has always been placed on genealogy and local history.

VI. Policies by Format of Material

Books

Hardbacks
Most books selected for the library, especially those considered to be of lasting value, are purchased in hardback.

Paperbacks
Books of ephemeral interest, mainly for recreational reading, are obtained in paperback. Occasionally a title of lasting worth to the collection will be available only in paperback. The subject matter or age level of a book will also make a paperback copy more appropriate.

Textbooks
Textbooks are acquired only if they are the best source of background information or specialized treatment of a subject.

Slides

The library makes no attempt to purchase slides of any size.

Films and Filmstrips

Because of the accessibility of films through the library's membership in the Missouri Libraries Film Cooperative, 16mm films are not purchased, with rare exceptions made for films of seasonal interest not usually available through the Cooperative.

Filmstrips are purchased infrequently, usually to enrich inhouse library programs.

Newspapers

The main library subscribes to the *St. Joseph Gazette* and *News-Press* and to about fifteen other newspapers from major US cities. One local regional newspaper is taken, and donations of other small newspapers are occasionally made. The main library will continue its commitment to subscriptions for newspapers from Kansas City, Washington D.C., Chicago, New York, and St. Louis.

Microfilm files are also kept on St. Joseph newspapers. In addition, subject vertical files are maintained on the *Gazette* and *News-Press* at the main library.

The branch libraries subscribe to St. Joseph newspapers.

Records and Cassettes

Record albums representing many different styles and periods of music are collected at the main library, and to a much lesser degree at the branches. Records for teaching languages and skills such as typing are also purchased. Cassettes of music, literature, and subjects of popular interest are purchased for adults particularly to meet the needs of the visually handicapped. Cassettes obtained for children usually supplement print materials.

Printed Music

The library no longer buys sheet music, although a small collection from previous years remains. Collections of music in book form are purchased, however; in addition to meeting a need for circulating materials, these books are useful for reference questions on the lyrics of popular music.

Pictures

The library occasionally collects pictures for use in vertical files or for promotion activities.

Maps

Separate maps are collected mainly for major cities and local municipalities. Most maps for reference use are contained in atlases.

Pamphlets

Inexpensive, ephemeral, and timely pamphlets are collected to supplement the regular book collections. They are periodically reevaluated and weeded.

Periodicals

For the most part, selection criteria for periodicals are the same as those for books and other materials. Periodicals are purchased which are important to reference work and general research work in the various subject areas as well as for general and popular reading. An attempt is made to ensure that periodicals taken are indexed in the major periodical indexes held by the library.

Government Documents

As a Federal Depository, the St. Joseph Public Library collects approximately 25% of the documents available through that program. The regular selection criteria apply to government publications, with heavy emphasis placed on popular demand and anticipated needs of the community.

Manuscripts and Rare Books

The only manuscripts and rare books which are collected are those dealing with local history and specialized reference needs.

Microforms

The library is making an increasing effort to collect in microform certain government publications available in that format as well as back issues of periodicals taken. In both cases the regular selection criteria apply.

Framed Prints and Sculpture

The library maintains a collection of framed prints and small pieces of sculpture which are available for circulation. This collection is financed wholly by donations from the Runcie Club. An attempt is made to include representative reproductions from major periods in the library of Western art.

VII. Handling of Complaints Regarding Library Material

A patron who questions any material in the library may register his or her opinion in writing on the form "Patron Comment on Library Materials", and the matter will be referred to the direction under the guidance of the Materials Selection Committee of the Board of Directors.

A disputed book will not be removed from the shelves because of a complaint until such recommendation by the Materials Selection Committee is reviewed and approved by the Board as a whole.

VIII. Gifts

Funds available from government sources have not kept pace with the needs of the community. Therefore, the policy of the St. Joseph Public Library is to encourage donations of materials, or gifts of money for the purchase of materials, which meet the stated selection criteria.

Furthermore, the library accepts gift books with the understanding that those which would enrich the library collection will be retained, and others disposed of in an appropriate manner - by giving them to other libraries or institutions or by selling them. In accordance with selection criteria, out-of-date material, duplicates of items for which additional copies are not needed, and material in poor physical condition will not be added to the collection.

The library accept gifts with "strings" regarding subject matter only if they meet a recognized need in the collection.

The library cannot make a commitment to keep any collection or group of books on a special shelf apart from other books in the library. The library by necessity reserves the right to intershelve gifts with other materials on the same subject.

Individual volumes will be marked with bookplates identifying the donor. Donors are encouraged to consult the library director in advance concerning donations of materials.

IX. Review of This Policy

This materials selection and collection review policy should be reviewed regularly to ensure that changes in goals and objectives, needs of users and potential users, priorities and budgetary conditions are confronted and reflected in it.

Moreover, the policy should also be coordinated with appropriate other libraries in the vicinity so that librarians are assisted in selecting and withdrawing materials in conformity with the needs and resources of the northwest Missouri area.

William Paterson State College of New Jersey. Sarah Byrd Askew Library, *Collection Development Policy.* **Wayne, N.J.: William Paterson State College of New Jersey, 1982.**

TABLE OF CONTENTS

*These documents are not reproduced from the policy but are readily available in the ALA's *Intellectual Freedom Manual.*

I. Introduction

Collection development policies are designed for use as planning tools and as means of communicating the collection goals and policies of libraries. Such policies reflect the reality that all libraries, no matter how large or of what type, are constrained from accumulating all informational materials in all subject areas by limitations in funds, space and staffing. In the face of these constraints, libraries can maximize their effectiveness by establishing collection goals and priorities and the concomitant policies and procedures to implement them.

In its function as a planning tool this collection development policy provides College and Library decision-makers with information necessary for allocating funds for library materials. As a communications tool it provides the guidelines for establishing priorities for the selection of library materials and the criteria for the withdrawal of materials from the Library collection. Whereas the policies are specific, they will be interpreted broadly as the situation may demand.

While the Library staff is ultimately responsible for the quality of the collection, to a great extent the selection of new library materials and the withdrawal of materials from library collections are shared functions. Materials can be requested by librarians, teaching faculty, and College administrators, and librarians work closely with coordinators from academic departments to ensure that the materials needed by the College are added to the collection. Input from the teaching faculty is particularly important with respect to withdrawal of materials from the General Collection and the cancellation of serial subscriptions. The selection and withdrawal processes are described in more detail in Section III of this document.

The Library supports a series of policy statements by the American Library Association and the Educational Film Library Association concerning the responsibilities of librarians and libraries in making materials available to the public. Copies of these documents are included in Appendix A, "Freedom to Read Statement", Appendix B, "Library Bill of Rights", Appendix C, "Intellectual Freedom Statement", and Appendix D, "Freedom to View". [These documents are not reproduced from the policy but are readily available in the ALA's *Intellectual Freedom Manual.*]

This document presents the first phase of a two-step process. It enumerates the collection goals of the Library and synthesizes its policies and procedures on the selection and acquisition of different types of materials. During the second phase, the collection will be analyzed in terms of the subjects presently represented, and the extent of future collecting activities in each subject area will be detailed.

The policies which apply to the selection and acquisition of all materials are presented first, followed by policies pertaining to specific types of materials or to materials in specific Library collections.

II. Collection Development Goals Statement

The *primary goal* of the Library with regard to the maintenance and development of the collection is: to acquire and make available those information resources which are needed to support the instructional programs of the College.

The Library will also pursue three *secondary goals*. While these are subordinate to the primary goal, all three demand equal emphasis:

to acquire and make available those materials needed for research by faculty and administrators which will be frequently used and of long-term value to the College community;

to acquire and make available library materials for general information in subject areas not included in the curriculum of the College;

to collect and preserve all important materials related to the history and development of William Paterson College.

All materials acquired by the William Paterson College Library will conform to the goals of the collection development efforts of the Library.

III. Materials Selection and Withdrawal

A. Selection of Library Materials

All librarians, teaching faculty, and College administrators are encouraged to submit requests for both print and non-print materials which fall within their areas of expertise and which conform to the collection policies presented in this document. The cost of these materials will be charged against the appropriate Library account. Materials Request Forms and copies of the monthly Library Budget Report are available from the Collection Development Office.

In an effort to develop a collection which supports the instructional program of the College each librarian is assigned to select materials in specific subject areas and to be the library coordinator (i.e., contact person) for the corresponding academic departments. Acting in this liaison capacity, the focus of the library coordinator's departmental contacts is the faculty member whom the chairperson appoints to serve as the departmental coordinator. The role of the departmental coordinator is to encourage faculty to submit requests for materials which fall within their areas of expertise, to bring any problems or questions concerning Library policies and procedures to the attention of their library coordinator and to apprise the library coordinator of any changes in the curriculum which would impact on Library use. The library coordinators are responsible for notifying departmental coordinators of changes in policies and procedures which may affect their departments, apprising them of new library materials which may be useful to members of their departments, and serving as troubleshooters for the departments they contact. The Collection Development Librarian supervises the efforts of the library coordinators and also determines whether requested materials conform to the goals, qualitative guidelines, and the selection and acquisition policies presented in this document.

B. General Guidelines for Selection of Materials

The following guidelines are presented to assist librarians, faculty, and administrators in selecting quality materials for inclusion in the Library collection. *It is recognized that some of the criteria included in these guidelines are more important than others and that the quality of content should be more heavily weighed than other guidelines.* Therefore, exceptions for materials which do not meet all of the criteria listed below will be made whenever possible.

Print Materials

Content Quality

In the case of fiction, titles should have received favorable published reviews by reputable critics, or should be considered quality literature by other literary authorities including members of the College community. In the case of non-fiction, the materials acquired should present data accurately and priority will be given to titles authored by authorities in their fields or by those representing a consensus of expert opinion. The literary style should be readable and the author's meaning clear. Non-fiction titles should have accurate and complete bibliographic references and indexes.

Physical Quality

The materials to be acquired should have evenly spaced print and a type face which is large enough to be easily legible. Bindings should be sturdy, attractive, and easy to open. Margins should be wide enough to allow rebinding and to allow reading and photocopying without breaking the binding. Illustrations should be appropriate to the content of the book, and conveniently positioned within the printed text. Art reproductions, maps, and photographs which complement printed text should be in focus and have consistent and accurate color tones.

Publishers

The print materials to be purchased should be the products of publishers with high standards of quality in general and reliable reputations specifically with respect to the subject matter and type of print material to be acquired.

Non-print Materials

Content Quality

The non-print materials to be acquired should be those materials which, in the opinion of reputable reviewers or experts within the College community, present ideas and information in an accurate and well-organized manner, and which employ a style of presentation appropriate for the medium, the subject matter, and the intended audience. Materials which will not become outdated due to their timeless subject matter or their manner of presentations will be favored. Items such as games which require them should have instructions for use which are clear and easy to understand.

Technical Quality

The technical quality of purchased materials should meet professional standards, i.e., sound formats should be clear and visual formats should be in focus and have consistent and accurate color tones. The ratio of visuals to sound should be appropriate.

Physical Quality

Only those non-print titles produced on the highest quality materials will be purchased. Film stock should be of non-deteriorating quality in which no silver nitrate is left on the stock. Audio tape and cassette materials should be on medium to high grade mil stock to avoid stretching and breakage. Preview prints will be returned to the distributor/producer and only fresh prints will be accepted for purchase. Printed guides to audio-visual materials should be produced on durable paper in legible, easy to read type.

Distributors/Producers

Audio-visual materials will be purchased only from reputable distributors/producers. Films will be purchased only from distributors which sell replacement footage. Other types of media will be purchased from established companies in order to assure easy replacement.

C. Withdrawal of Materials

Materials are withdrawn from the Library in order to maintain a current, active, and useful collection which reflects the goals of the Library. In addition, the shortage of space has necessitated the withdrawal of materials from the General Collection and the decline in the Library's purchasing power has forced the cancellation of serial subscriptions. In these withdrawal programs consultation with the teaching faculty is especially important as a safeguard against the withdrawal or cancellation of materials with special qualities or significance.

A unique set of withdrawal criteria is used for each type of library material. These criteria are established by the Collection Development Librarian, in consultation with other librarians and teaching faculty, as appropriate. For library materials which do not fall into serial or series categories these sets of criteria are based on combinations of some of the following characteristics:

Obsolescence,
Language in which the material is written,
Appropriateness of subject matter to the collection,
Quantity and recency of past use,
Number of copies in the collection.

Characteristics to be used to develop criteria for the cancellation of serial or series subscriptions or standing orders are:

Existence and availability of indexes,
Language in which the material is written,
Appropriateness of subject matter to the collection,
Past use,
Cost of continuing subscription/standing order.

Materials withdrawn from one collection may be transferred to another with the approval of the appropriate librarians. Withdrawn materials are sent to the New Jersey Deposit and Exchange Collection.

D. Criteria for Withdrawal of Library Materials

The criteria used to identify titles for withdrawal from the collection are reviewed on a regular basis by the Collection Development Libraries and the appropriate Library department heads. The criteria currently in use are listed below.

1. General Collection

All superseded editions of General Collection titles become candidates for withdrawal. Decisions to withdraw are made by the Collection Development Librarian on a title-by-title basis.

All damaged, lost and long-overdue General Collection titles become candidates for withdrawal. Decisions to withdraw or replace are made on a title-by-title basis by appropriate Library coordinators in consultation with the Collection Development Librarian.

All General Collection titles acquired prior to 1975, which have not circulated since then and whose authors are not listed in the second edition of *Books for College Libraries* become candidates for withdrawal. Lists of candidates, arranged by subject, are compiled and sent to all Deans, department chairpersons, departmental and library coordinators, and individual faculty members in the appropriate departments. Faculty members can expect to receive a list of candidates pertaining to their departments approximately once every two or three years. However, all faculty members are notified whenever a withdrawal list has been distributed. Faculty members are invited to select titles to be returned to the collection and are asked to respond to each list by a specified date. These faculty selections are then reviewed by the Collection Development Librarian.

2. Reference Materials

The Reference Department has established specific withdrawal policies for many of the reference titles for which revised or superseded editions are regularly received. Superseded editions of titles for which polices have not been formulated become candidates for withdrawal. Decisions to withdraw these titles and to revise established withdrawal policies are made by the Head of Reference in consultation with the Collection Development Librarian.

3. Documents

Superseded editions of materials housed in the Government Documents Collection become candidates for withdrawal. Decisions to withdraw are made by the Documents Librarian on a title-by-title basis.

All New Jersey State documents which have been in the collection for five years become candidates for withdrawal. Decisions to withdraw are made on a title-by-title basis.

4. Serials

Each year librarians and teaching faculty review serial holdings and evaluate titles which receive infrequent use. Recommendations for cancellation and retention are made in light of curriculum needs and budgetary considerations.

5. Audio-visual Materials

All damaged audio-visual materials become candidates for withdrawal. Decisions to withdraw or replace are made on a title-by-title basis by the Head of the Audio-visual Department. Amount of use and obsolescence are important factors in these decisions.

6. Vertical File

Obsolete materials are withdrawn from the Vertical File Collection at the discretion of the reference librarian in charge of the vertical file.

IV. General Policies

A. Materials Exceeding $100.00

All requests for single titles which exceed $100.00 require the approval of the Collection Development Librarian who will consult with the requestor's Dean. Excepted from this rule are serials, series, 16mm film and video recordings which require the approval of the Periodicals/Serials or Film/Video Committee (Sections V.j, V.k, and V.b).

B. Out-of-print and Facsimile Materials

All requests for out-of-print and facsimile editions must be approved by the Collection Development Librarian before they can be processed.

C. Foreign Language Materials

In general, the Library does not acquire materials in foreign languages other than those needed to support the foreign language programs offered by the College. Requests for foreign language materials which are not intended to support these programs must be approved by the Collection Development Librarian.

D. Gifts

Gifts of library materials are accepted at the discretion of the Collection Development Librarian with the understanding that there are no conditions attached to their disposition. Only those materials which prove to be in good physical condition and which conform to the collection goals, guidelines, and policies are actually added to the collection. All others are discarded or sent to the State Library Deposit and Exchange Collection.

All gifts are acknowledged by the Collection Development Librarian. However, the appraisal of gifts for tax purposes is the responsibility of the donor. In general, the Library conforms to the "Statement on Appraisal of Gifts" developed by the Association of College and Research Libraries.

Monetary donations to the Library for the purpose of purchasing library materials are accepted subject to the approval of the Library Director.

V. Specific Format and Collection Policies

In addition to the general guidelines already presented, there are Library policies and procedures which apply only to library materials in specific formats and/or to those housed in specific collections within the Library. These policy statements are presented below.

A. Archives

In the absence of an official College archives, the Library endeavors to collect and organize as many of the documentary records of the College and its predecessors as space and personnel constraints permit. Examples of official archival documents are: minutes of the Board of Trustees meetings; reports of the President, Deans and Departmental Chairpersons; and official files of the College administrators where available. Other official documents include minutes of the activities of faculty departments and student organizations, as well as reports and publications issued about the College by the New Jersey Department of Higher Education, accrediting bodies, and pertinent bargaining agents.

The Archives Collection also contains some non-official materials relating to the facilities, students, and history of the College and to College sponsored events. Most of these materials take the form of clippings from newspapers and magazines, although appropriate materials in all types of media are accepted for inclusion in the Archives Collection.

The Archives Librarian is responsible for selecting materials for the collection. In most cases single copies of materials are added. Duplicate copies of materials for which the Archives Libraries anticipates heavy use may be acquired.

B. Audio-visual Materials

The purpose of the Audio-visual Collection is to provide all members of the William Paterson College community with access to art and information in audio-visual forms. The Audio-visual Collection is meant to serve a College-wide audience. It is not intended to replace or supplement specialized collections, such as those in the Art and Music Departments, which are being developed elsewhere on campus. Whereas the Audio-visual Collection is largely comprised of adult-level titles, the collection also includes a representative sampling of juvenile materials.

All requests for the purpose of adult level, audio-visual materials are forwarded to the Audio-visual Department for review. The Head of the Audio-visual Department may modify any media requests to conform to the Audio-visual Department software preference and is responsible for the disposition of any general audio-visual materials funds.

The following types of software are presently included in the Audio-visual Collection, although some may not be acquired in the future. Requests for types of media not included below are considered on a title-by-title basis. In general, however, only software which is compatible with Library owned hardware is purchased and preference is given to materials which can be repaired within the Library.

Cassettes, Records and Reel-to-Reel Tapes

Standard cassettes are the preferred audio medium because of their easy storage, portability, and long-term durability. Only those recordings unavailable on cassettes are purchased in other audio media. Open reel-to-reel tapes and 33.3 rpm stereophonic records are the only acceptable alternative media.

It is recognized that the Library cannot meet all the audio needs and tastes of the variety of groups comprising the William Paterson College community. However, a representative audio collection has been developed consisting of recordings in the following categories:

    a.   Music - primarily classical music, opera, jazz and children's songs.
    b.   Theatre - primarily show music, plays and dramatic readings.
    c.   Spoken Word Recordings - primarily lectures, seminars, stories, debates and proceedings.

Recordings in other categories, such as comedy and popular music, are considered for purchase and inclusion in the collection on a title-by-title basis by the Collection Development Librarian in consultation with the Head of the Audio-visual Department.

Slides and Filmstrips

All slides must be 2" x 2" in size. Whenever a choice of medium is offered, slide sets are preferred over filmstrips.

Multi-media Kits

Multi-media kits include any combination of slides or filmstrips, with cassettes, reel-to-reel tapes or records. When kits are purchased and a choice of media is offered, cassettes are preferred to tapes and records, and slides are preferred to filmstrips. The Library does not purchase individual parts of multi-media kits.

Transparencies

Transparencies and transparency masters are purchased. Whenever possible, transparencies are acquired framed.

Loop Films and 8mm Films

In general, Library materials are not acquired in these formats. However, exceptions may be made by the Head of the Audio-visual Department.

Motion Picture Films, Video Tapes, and Video Cassettes

In general, 16mm film and video recordings are rented rather than purchased. The cost of rental is borne by the appropriate academic School. The Audio-visual Department does, however, assist faculty in locating titles on specific subjects and ordering information (distribution, price, etc.), and forwards film/video rental requests.

Titles for which a librarian or teaching faculty member anticipates a minimum of five uses per year for five years are considered for purchase from the Library materials budget of the School of the requestor. Requests are made on a Film/Video Request Form and must be approved by the appropriate Dean and the Film/Video Committee.

The Film/Video Committee meets several times each year, depending upon the volume of requests it receives, to preview requested titles. It is composed of the librarians in the following positions:

Head of the Audio-visual Department
Associate Director for Collection Management
Audio-visual Services Librarian
Collection Development Librarian, Chair

The library coordinator for the subject area of the title being considered, the requestor, and the appropriate Dean, are also invited to attend the screening. Requestors receive written notification of the decision of the Committee.

The Film/Video Committee follows the general guidelines for non-print materials (Section III.B) to assure the acquisition of quality films and video materials. In addition, the Committee also considers the following characteristics in relation to each title requested:

Appropriateness of the subject to the collection,
Anticipated use of the title 5 times per year for 5 years,
Favourable reviews,
Unavailability of title from easily accessible loan or rental sources,
Cost.

The Committee may make an affirmative decision even when a requested title does not have all these characteristics. However, it is unusual for the Committee to approve requests for titles which do not possess the first two characteristics.

As a rule, when a choice of media is available, 16mm film is preferred for both purchase and rental over video tape and video cassette. When video recordings are acquired 3/4" U-matic cassettes are the preferred format.

Miscellaneous Media

The following types of materials are usually housed in the Audio-visual Department. Teaching faculty and librarians may submit requests to purchase materials from their library departmental allocation on Materials Request Forms. With the exception of materials purchased for the Curriculum Materials Department, all acquisitions of these types of materials must have the approval of the Collection Development Librarian.

Games - limited to education and simulation games.
Realia - including actual objects, samples and specimens used to relate classroom teaching to real life, especially of peoples studied.
Pictures - including all art originals, photographs, post cards, posters and sturdy prints.

C. Curriculum Materials

The primary purpose of curriculum materials is to support the professional curriculum of the School of Education and Community Service. These resources are intended to be used by students in their efforts to develop the skills needed to identify, select, and evaluate the materials they will use in teaching. All juvenile print materials, all elementary and secondary level textbooks, and the most heavily used of other types of print curriculum materials are housed in the Curriculum Materials Department.

The juvenile print materials range in reading and interest level from pre-kindergarten through twelfth grade, although an emphasis is placed on materials for pre-kindergarten through eighth grade. Included in the collection are fiction and non-fiction monographs, picture books, basic reference materials, such as encyclopedias and dictionaries, and a small number of children's periodicals.

The Library collects those elementary and secondary level textbooks which cover subject areas in which the School of Education and Community Service offers teacher certification. Whenever possible, teachers' editions of textbooks and the workbooks and activity books accompanying textbooks are acquired.

Other types of curriculum materials include courses of study or curriculum guides (on microfiche and in hard copy), bibliographies, mediographies, activity books, and selection aids for juvenile print and non-print materials.

As in the case of print materials, audio-visual curriculum materials focus on pre-school through grade 12 audiences with emphasis on elementary level materials. Types of materials included in this collection are cassettes, records, filmstrips, and 8mm film loops. In general, multi-media kits are purchased in their entirety, although individual kits in a series may be acquired. All acquisitions of realia must have the approval of the Curriculum Materials Librarian. Only audio-visual materials that accompany books in the Collection are housed in the Curriculum Materials Department. All other juvenile audio-visual materials are housed in the Audio-visual Department of the Library to allow them to circulate.

The Curriculum Materials Librarian is responsible for the selection of materials appropriate for the Curriculum Material Collection. Any exceptions to the general rules set out in the "Curriculum Materials" section of this document must be approved by the Curriculum Materials Librarian. The librarian selects materials for the Collection on the basis of favourable reviews, inclusion on standard lists and bibliographies, and faculty recommendations.

In general, hard copy editions are preferred to paperbacks. With the exceptions of the Newbery and Caldecott Award winning titles, duplicate copies of titles are not purchased for the Curriculum Materials Department. Duplicate copies of some of the materials housed there may, however, be found in other collections within the Library.

D. Dissertations

The library does not routinely acquire academic dissertations. Doctoral dissertations are ordered upon faculty request, and requests from students are accepted when accompanied by written recommendation from a member of the teaching faculty. The Library does not, however, acquire unpublished master's theses. Whenever possible, dissertations are acquired on microfiche.

E. Documents

The term "documents" applies to publications issued by both the United States government and the State of New Jersey. Included in this category are publications generated from all government branches - legislative, judicial, executive - and their respective agencies and departments. The Documents Librarian is responsible for the selection of these documents as well as for the selection of privately published materials, such as indexes and abstracts, which facilitate their use. County and municipal documents of local interest or which pertain to important issues or events may be considered for purchase by the Documents Librarian on a title-by-title basis.

The Library acquires all congressional hearings and joint committee reports. These and the majority of the other federal documents purchased by the Library are acquired on microfiche through a commercial vendor. Titles not available from the commercial vendor are acquired from the Government Printing Office.

As a Secondary Depository for New Jersey State documents the Library receives the majority of the New Jersey documents as they are issued. Additional New Jersey State publications are acquired on the recommendation of the Documents Librarian. New Jersey documents are housed in the Documents Collection and are maintained in accordance with the New Jersey State Depository rules and regulations.

Whereas all non-reference New Jersey documents are housed in the Documents Collection, the federal documents which are currently being acquired are integrated in the Reference, Microform and General Collections. Decisions to add documents to the General Collection are made by the Documents Librarian. However, the addition of documents to the Reference Collection requires the approval of the Head of Reference.

Because of space considerations, the acquisition of documents in microformat is preferred to hard copy. Hard copies of documents already owned in microformat will not be purchased. Exceptions to this rule will be made on a title-by-title basis by the Documents

Librarians in consultation with the Collection Development Librarian and other librarians, as appropriate.

F. General Collection

The General Collection consists of adult-level, hard copy, cataloged print materials shelved in open stacks on the second floor of the Library and available for loan to patrons. The majority of these materials are monographs and individual series titles. However, certain series and non-periodical serials (Sections V.J and V.K) may be designated as circulating materials by the Periodicals/Serials Committee. As a rule textbooks are not acquired for the circulating collection.

In general, the Library does not purchase more than three copies of any one title. Duplicate copies of titles includes in the Reference, Curriculum Materials, New Jersey, or Miscellany Collections may be acquired for the General Collection with the approval of the Collection Development Librarian. The Collection Development Librarian must also approve the addition of superseded editions of reference titles and the intra-library transfer of any materials into the General Collection.

Whenever possible, materials are acquired for the General Collection in paperback editions. Exceptions to this rule may be made by the Collection Development Librarian for oversized items and for titles for which heavy use is anticipated.

C. McNaughton Book Service

A small collection of books, unrelated to the curriculum and faculty research interests, are leased from the McNaughton Book Service for recreational reading and general information purposes. Each month the Collection Development Librarian selects additional titles for this collection from an availability list supplied by the McNaughton company.

H. Microforms

The purpose for acquiring microform titles is to provide patrons with access to materials which are unavailable in hard copy, or which, in hard copy, would be too costly or occupy prohibitively large amounts of space. All requests for materials on microform are reviewed by the head of Periodicals and Microforms in consultation with the Collection Development Librarian. Requests for serials and series on microforms are also reviewed by the Serials Committee as outlined in Section V.K of this policy. The Head of Periodicals and Microforms in consultation with the Collection Development Librarian is responsible for deciding which format will be acquired when requested titles are available in both hard copy and microform editions.

The acquisition of microform titles is considered on a case-by-case basis, with anticipated amount and type of use being important factors in decision-making. The potential amount of space the microform edition would save and the difference between the cost of the microform and hard copy editions are other important considerations. In general, indexing and/or abstracting services, and monographs which are not part of a series are not acquired in microform or converted to microform. However, all periodical titles which are to be held for more than one year are acquired in microform whenever possible.

The Library acquires only those microforms which are compatible with Library owned hardware and storage facilities.

The preferred microformat is 4" x 6" negative polarity microfiche, although, when microfiche is unavailable 16mm negative polarity microfilm will be acquired. Reduction ratios between 12 x and 24 x for both microfilm and microfiche are also preferred. Microforms of those materials which the Library is acquiring for archival purposes are purchased on silver halide film/fiche. When available, all other microforms are acquired on Diazo or Vesicular film and fiche. When preferred formats are not available the Library may purchase 35mm microfiche, microfilm with reduction ratios of 24 x to 48 x, and positive polarity film and fiche. The Head of Periodicals and Microforms considers such factors as convenience in reading, copying, and storing microform materials in making purchasing decisions. As a general rule the Library does not acquire materials on micro opaques, or microfiche with reduction ratios greater than 48 x. Purchase of other types of microforms is considered on a case-by-case basis by the Head of Periodicals and Microforms in consultation with the Collection Development Librarian.

The purchase of microform titles is made only after detailed information is obtained from the publisher. When necessary purchase may be delayed until the Head of Periodicals and Microforms can examine the quality of the microforms and the bibliographic access to them. Only those titles which evidence adequate bibliographic access are approved for purchase.

I. New Jersey Collection

The purpose of the New Jersey Collection is to acquire and preserve materials related to the history, geography, geology, and culture of New Jersey. Toward this end efforts are made not only to acquire such materials as they are published, but also to acquire appropriate out-of-print monographs on the State as they become available. The Library does not, however, collect genealogies.

In addition to monographs, the New Jersey Collection, which is housed in the Special Collections Room, also includes a selection of important serials and series related to New Jersey history, geography, geology, and culture. A vertical file containing newspaper clippings and other ephemeral materials related to New Jersey history, and a selection of state and federal documents on the geology of New Jersey are also part of this collection. Many of the historical, topographical, and geological maps of New Jersey are technically part of the New Jersey Collection but for preservation and storage purposes they are housed in map cabinets located in the Reference Department.

All acquired materials which relate to New Jersey are considered candidates for inclusion in the New Jersey Collection. However, only those materials which are approved for inclusion by the Special Collections Librarian will be housed there. When duplicate copies are considered useful and if the cost permits, additional copies of materials to be located in the New Jersey Collection are purchased and housed in other appropriate Library Collections.

Some New Jersey library materials are not included in the New Jersey Collection because of their format, subject area, and/or the limited amount of space available in the Special Collections Room. These materials are housed in other Library collections as appropriate. Audio-visual materials on New Jersey, for instance, are housed in the Audio-visual

Department and microforms on New Jersey are filed in the Microform Collection. The Reference and Curriculum Materials Collections also contain materials on New Jersey, and the Government Documents Collection includes New Jersey graphs, series, and serials in the General Collection which are duplicates of New Jersey related materials which the Special Collections Librarian has decided are inappropriate for the New Jersey Collection. All of the New Jersey related materials which are not housed in Special Collections must be acquired in accordance with the criteria pertaining to the collections in which they are housed.

J. Reference Collection

To a greater degree than any other collection in the Library, the Reference Collection addresses the goal of providing research materials which go beyond curriculum-related needs. A strong Reference Collection, not limited to curriculum-related subjects, but reflecting greater depth in those areas is therefore maintained at William Paterson College. To the extent resources permit, the Library also identifies and provides access through the location of bibliographic citations (at times using automated techniques), to materials in specialized areas and subjects which go beyond the sophistication of the materials in other Library collections. Although source materials may not be available in-house, user access to them may be provided via referral to other appropriate libraries and/or inter-library loan service.

The Reference Collection includes several categories of print formats:

Compendia which are either:

  a. Primarily statistical or biographical and arranged for quick access to information;
  or
  b. General in scope and designed to be consulted for specific facts;
  or
  c. Guides to the literature of subjects;
  and

Bibliographic aids which are either:

  a. General in scope (i.e., covering more than one author or facet of a subject) issued as monographs;
  or
  b. Indexes and abstracts issued as serials.

In addition, the Reference Collection may include other titles which are generally considered to be standard reference tools (i.e., represented in standard bibliographies or reference works), as well as those which are locally regarded as reference tools because of use patterns peculiar to the William Paterson College community or because of necessity for universal availability. Examples of materials which fall into the latter category are the law and business services.

Any title which meets these criteria may be housed in the Reference Collection at the discretion of the Head of Reference regardless of who ordered it or the collection for which it was originally intended. In general, only one copy of a title is housed in the Reference Collection, but when appropriate, duplicates of titles housed there are purchased and added to other collections in the Library. Older reference titles or superseded editions which are still usable may be transferred from Reference to other Library collections by the Head of Reference in consultation with the Collection Development Librarian and other librarians, as appropriate. The Head of Reference is also responsible for the disposition of the reference materials budget and for decisions concerning format.

K. Serials

Because of the importance of continuing in runs the acquisition of each serial title usually results in budgetary commitment which is carried over from year to year. For this reason requests for any publication issued in successive parts at regular intervals which is intended to continue indefinitely will be reviewed with special care. For the purpose of this policy, newspapers, in addition to periodicals, annuals (reports, yearbooks, etc.), and memoirs, proceedings and transactions of societies are considered serials.

Requests for serial title subscriptions, standing orders, and back files may be made by librarians and teaching faculty on Periodical/Serial Request Forms. All such requests are considered by the Library Serials Committee which meets three time each year (March, July and October).

The Serials Committee is composed of the librarians in the following positions:

Head of Reference
Head of Periodicals and Microforms
Associate Director for Collection Management
Director of Library Services
Collection Development Librarian, Chair

Librarians who have recommended serial subscriptions or who select materials for various disciplines are invited to attend Serials Committee meetings when relevant requests are being considered. The Library begins receiving subscriptions and standing orders with the first issue of the calendar year whenever possible. Members of the teaching faculty and librarians who request subscriptions or standing orders receive written notification of the Committee's decision within two weeks of the Committee meeting.

In reviewing each serial request the Committee considers the characteristics presented below. Those listed in Group A are of greater importance than those listed in Group B, and so forth. However, all characteristics in a given group are weighted equally.

Group A

- Appropriateness of the subject matter to the collection.
- Ability to access the title through an index which is available at the William Paterson College Library.

Group B

- Anticipated use as reflected by the title's relevance to courses frequently offered on campus.

- Favourable reviews.
- Reliable publisher.
- Predominance of articles written in English.

Group C

- High quality and appropriateness of physical format.
- High usage of similar titles already owned by the Library.
- Cost which is justifiable based on the Committee's perception of the title's value.

The Committee may make an affirmative decision even when a requested title does not have all these characteristics. However, it is unlikely that the Committee will approve requests for titles which do not possess both Group A characteristics. When reviewing a request for back files the Committee considers the amount of use received by those volumes of the titles the Library already owns.

After approving a request the Serials Committee determines whether the Library should keep all or only the latest year's issues. It also determines where non-periodical serial titles will be housed. The Collection Development Librarian, in consultation with other librarians as appropriate, may modify this decision at a later time. In general, all periodical titles which are to be held for more than one year are acquired in microform whenever available.

I. Series

As in the case of serials, agreement to subscribe to or place a standing order for a series requires that the Library commit funds over a long period of time. For this reason requests for series are reviewed in the same manner as serial requests, although in determining whether to subscribe to a series title the Serials Committee may place less emphasis on the ability to access the title through an index. Series requests will be subject to all other policies and procedures outlined in the "Serials" section of this policy (Section V.K).

Individual titles in a series may be acquired as separate monographs without making a commitment to place a standing order for the entire series.

M. Special Collections

In addition to the New Jersey Collection, the Special Collections Room houses the three types of titles described below. These three collections, like the New Jersey Collection, are the responsibility of the Special Collections Librarian.

Autographed Copies - The majority of titles in this category are complimentary copies of works authored by members of the College faculty. The Library accepts all monographs authored and signed by the College faculty members for inclusion in this collection.
First and Limited Editions - Titles in this category are first editions and limited editions of major works by prominent American and British authors of the 19th and 20th centuries. This collection is being maintained at its present level.
Miscellaneous Titles - These materials have been housed in the Special Collections Room for preservation purposes. Most are out-of-print, or have unusual or rare formats or

bindings, although some of the volumes included in this collection are expensive and/or unusual facsimile editions.

After requests for out-of-print and facsimile materials are approved by the Collection Development Librarian (Section IV.B), the Special Collections Librarian decides which are to be housed in the Miscellany Collection. Any other materials which the Special Collections Librarian identifies as requiring preservation due to specialized format are also housed with the Miscellaneous Titles.

N. Vertical File

The purpose of the vertical file is to augment other Library collections by providing quick and easy access to pamphlets, clippings, fliers, and other ephemeral material. The emphasis in this collection is on materials covering topics of current interest. However, other materials for which there may be occasional or sporadic demand are also housed there.

Most pamphlets of 49 pages or less, regardless of the collection for which they were originally intended, are considered for inclusion in the vertical file. The Head of Reference will have complete discretion as to which materials will be housed there.

CHAPTER 3

FORMULATION OF THE COLLECTION DEVELOPMENT POLICY

Given the content of collection development policy statements and the uses to which these documents are put, one basic characteristic of the policy formulation process should be immediately apparent: the exact procedure to be followed cannot be stated definitively outside the unique context of a specific library. It is essential to keep this point clearly in mind throughout the ensuing discussion, which assumes a larger, probably academic, library as a typical policy-generating environment. While the general principles and procedures remain constant, they will need to be scaled up or down, altered and revised in accordance with a given library's collection size, staffing arrangements, user groups and budget.

As Figure 4 on the following page shows, there are typically six stages in policy formulation; each of these stages is crucial in the success of a written policy and should be understood in detail before beginning the process.

Policy Committee Staffing

Like nearly all library activities one begins by forming a committee, but in this case the appointed committee actually achieves its goal - formulation of a written policy. The general responsibility of this group is to oversee and direct the entire process, from staffing to promulgation of the final document. Within this broad charge the committee performs three initial tasks: (1) engages in substantial discussion about assumptions, purposes and goals to be achieved; (2) determines general parameters and deadlines; (3) sets staffing for the project. Each of these tasks is an essential prerequisite for the efficient functioning of the project. The first point helps not only to clear the air of misconceptions and false assumptions but also to clarify exactly why the project is being undertaken, and this sets the tone and overall goal of the process.

All of the discussion, argument and disagreement implied in this part of the task is necessary to ensure coherence and unity of purpose in an activity which has long-range implications for the library and its collections. The second point, determining parameters and deadlines, is a means of keeping the project on target. More than most types of applied research, collection development policy formulation involves so many variables and incorporates so many possible ramifications that a detailed map is necessary to keep the policy staff from wandering down interesting byways or simply becoming lost. Similarly, it is essential to keep staff working to strict deadlines if the project is ever to be completed.

Figure 4. Policy Formulation Procedure

In practical terms the staffing determined by this committee is probably the most crucial factor in the likely success or failure of the project; it must be fully representative of both the users and the community and embody the expertise needed to complete the policy document. In effect this means that all sectors of the community must be represented on the committee, including administrators, department heads, students, general public, staff from other local institutions and libraries, etc. In addition anyone within the library with responsibility for collection development, selection and acquisitions should be on the committee. It is from this second, in-house group that the staff for drafting the policy, collecting and analyzing data are drawn. A committee constituted in this manner has several advantages. First, it is representative of all groups who have at least a notional interest in the collection, whether as users, administrators or professionals. This in turn means that the policy theoretically has more chance of incorporating requirements of the widest possible public, and it also means that the policy cannot be criticized as an example of elitism. Many collection development policies in the past have been written by librarians for other librarians; if users and administrators are involved, they will help ensure that his does not happen. Rather, the policy statement will be directed towards all interested parties, both internal and external. Second, the involvement of staff with collection development responsibilities means that all professional needs in the collection development sphere have a reasonable chance of being considered and that the committee includes the professional expertise needed for collection evaluation, user analysis and policy formulation duties.

It is the in-house professionals on the committee who in effect form the working party, while the full committee acts as a control body and advises on the content of the draft policy. Once one has decided exactly who on the library staff will collect and evaluate data, determine collection levels and produce the draft document, it is necessary to put one of these people in control of the overall process; as any experienced committee observer knows, without rather firm direction a working group tends to dissipate its energies rather ineffectively. In a small library the person responsible for both the full committee and the working party probably will be the librarian; in larger libraries the chief or deputy librarian will likely chair the full committee, while the collection development or acquisitions librarian will assume responsibility for directing the working group.

Preliminary Matters Determined

This person and the team constituting the working group have as their first priority establishment of the exact steps to be followed in formulating the draft policy and of a realistic timetable for completion of each step. In addition tasks must be allocated to each staff member, with clear instructions on what is to be done by when. But before staff proceed with their tasks a common sense of purpose must be achieved, and this involves decisions about several features of the draft policy. In particular descriptions and definitions of collection levels as described in Chapter 2 should be considered. Will the ALA *Guidelines* be used? Or will the library, for some special reason, want to utilize some other code? The ALA collection level descriptors, and their coding in the RLG *Conspectus*, are adequately detailed and readily understood throughout the profession; their gradual adoption in the anglophone world suggests that the use of any other code in future by larger libraries will be counterproductive in terms of professional credibility and possible cooperative activities. A useful rule in this respect is the fewer changes, the better; if the American model is suitable despite its bias towards large academic or research collections, then the working group would be advised to adopt this as its analytical framework.

Allied with the adoption of an appropriate terminology for describing collection levels is the need to decide upon subject descriptors. What classification scheme will be used? Will broad or narrow descriptors be employed? Normally the answer to the first question is determined by the scheme already used in the library; it would be foolish to utilize some other set of descriptors given the lack of a definitive table of equivalency for classification terminology. On the other hand there are times when consideration of the wider audience may warrant adoption of descriptors other than those currently used - for example, if the policy is to be employed heavily to assist in resource sharing in a consortium of libraries using a classification scheme other than that employed in the collection being analyzed.

More problematic, though, is whether to use broad or narrow terminology within a given classification scheme. As discussed in Chapter 2, some libraries prefer rather broad rubrics, maintaining that this results in a more readable document. However, such broad categorizations as "English literature" or "church history" are not precise enough for most analytical purposes. This lack of precision raises the possibility that collecting activity in certain areas may be overlooked or that cross classification may result. For example, if one uses "Bible", "church history" and "doctrine" in religious studies, how do these cope with biblical history, early church history and doctrinal history? In other words, the use of broad subject areas in the policy tends to produce a document lacking in clarity, as well as producing overlap and perhaps omission of some categories. It is preferable, then, to utilize a more detailed breakdown of subjects; but one always follows the shape and content of the library collection with regard to detail. As Koenig points out in the University of California experience, "ND (Painting) as given had to be refined both geographically and chronologically by the subject specialist; the result - 41 new categories."[1] While the ALA *Guidelines* are most satisfactory for collection levels, they are less than helpful in determining level of detail for descriptors. It is, as Evans indicates, uneven and inconsistent, "...providing for instance eleven subdivisions for Spanish literature but only two for botany. It is a compromise that is likely to please no one: too detailed for small public or school libraries, hopelessly inadequate for subject specialized libraries...."[2] In short one needs to use a level of subject description best suited to the individual library.

Having reached agreement on these essentials, members of the working group are then in a position to proceed with collection analysis in accordance with the techniques outlined in Chapters 4 and 5. To do this effectively one requires a data analysis or subject profile form; this should be a practical data collecting and data analysis form, one that both reflects the actual collection and suits the needs of the projected policy statement. Consequently, it must be suitable for the collection analysts and possibly appropriate for reproduction in the policy document. One such form is appended to Dorothy Koenig's article (pp. 102-115); this is probably most suitable for large academic or research libraries. A simpler variation now being used in some much smaller teaching libraries appears in Figure 5 below. Note that this includes columns for the subject classification and descriptors, collecting level codes and other variables which the working group feels are significant. During the collection analysis process each of the variables is coded for density and intensity; on the basis of these data and specified institutional goals the third level (future policy) is determined by the working group. There is also a column for notes, which may cover special aspects of the subject, specific exclusions or inclusions, exceptions to the collecting levels, etc. The use of the form and how data are to be collected must be clear to all members of the team; this implies the need for training sessions prior to data collection and analysis. Another important preliminary activity is the collecting of other policies and of statements of procedures such as that reproduced in "Rushmore at Berkeley" (pp. 102-115). If one can find such policies and statements relevant to one's own situation, they may well serve as blueprints or at least aids in determining pitfalls to be avoided; the compilation of extracts from North American policies by Elizabeth Futas is invaluable in this respect.[3] To some extent existing policies will help determine both framework and detail, and other documentation - some of it noted in the Part 4 bibliography - has similar value (pp. 374-378). Robert Evans adequately outlines the various kinds of sources from which documentation might be collected, but note that some of his assumptions reflect the typical confusion between collection development policies and selection procedures. Nevertheless, the essential points are these: one should take time to collect adequate documentation both on the particular library and on policy statements generally; and, particularly with regard to the latter, one should be quite openly willing to use this to guide and inform one's own policy formulation activities. Librarians often commit themselves to re-inventing the wheel, and this is one instance where to do so would be pointless. One may need to build a wheel suited to a specific need, but existing patterns often can be used effectively for this purpose.

Subject unit: _____   Name of evaluator(s): _____

Dewey Class	Descriptor	Collecting Level Codes			Language Codes			Notes
		1	2	3	1	2	3	

Columns 1, 2 and 3 under Collecting Level, Language and any other desired variables indicate the following: 1 = strength of existing collection (density), 2 = current level of collecting activity (intensity), 3 = level of collecting appropriate to institutional goals (collection development policy). In each column one enters the appropriate collection level code according to ALA *Guidelines*, RLG *Conspectus*, etc.

Figure 5. Sample Data Form for Collection Development Policy

Draft Policy Formulated

The committee has been formed, the working group and its coordinator determined; procedures have been outlined and scheduled, and the general shape and content of the policy have been determined. Collecting level codes and subject descriptors have been agreed upon, and data collecting procedures have been explained. Finally, supporting documentation of all types has been collected. At long last the working group is ready to fulfil its role, and it does this in two ways.

First, an attempt is made to draft the general policy statement outlined in Chapter 2. As this includes a statement of institutional philosophy and objectives, the background documentation already collected will be useful here. Similarly, any existing documentation about the library should help when stating the general subject coverage of the collections, purpose of the library and range of programmes. This is not as straightforward as it sounds, because here librarians are forced to think through their professional priorities, match them with institutional realities and arrive at a compromise. Furthermore, staff may well disagree markedly about institutional priorities, service needs and professional standards. To paraphrase a Yiddish saying, put two librarians together and there will be three opinions. This situation is not aided by the fact that many parent institutions lack clearly defined goals and purposes, and it therefore becomes the library's task to articulate such principles for the very first time in its policy statement. Conflict, uneasiness and perhaps even ill feeling may result, but the final statement of aims and goals will be worth the trauma to the extent that it gives staff a sense of common purpose.

To some extent potential difficulties in this process can be avoided if the working group has detailed knowledge of the user community; this information provides hard data needed to define the user categories and describe their needs, both of which are done in the general policy statement. These data are derived from the results of user surveys and use studies, which is why these must be conducted. If they have not been performed already, surveys must be completed and analyzed at the draft policy stage. Given the complexity of user and use studies as described in Chapters 4 and 5 and the substantial work involved in producing a draft policy, it is inadvisable to leave surveys to this stage. Assume, therefore, that use and user studies have been completed at some earlier time and that analyzed data are available for use in the draft policy. The working group uses these data to make concrete statements about user categories served by the library, their perceived and real needs, the types of services and collections maintained to meet these needs.

The second activity of the drafting committee is to prepare the detailed statement of collection levels, and this must be derived from a collection analysis or evaluation as described in the following two chapters. Very few libraries ever undertake such an analysis except for the purpose of devising a collection development policy, which means that substantial data on the collections are not readily available at this stage. Therefore, this is normally the juncture at which a collection evaluation is done. Using whatever method has been deemed appropriate at the earlier planning stage, the working group collects data needed to determine collection density and collection intensity; this is the most labour-intensive segment of the entire process and will take the greatest amount of time. However, the time and effort are well spent, as the resulting data provide the key facts around which the core of the policy is developed.

Once density and intensity have been determined, the group returns to a less mechanical task - determining the desired level for future collecting. While data on the extent of the existing collection's current collecting activity are crucial in this task, one also relies on data collected during user and use studies, on understanding of community and institutional needs, on likely constraints in terms of staff and finance, on projections of future needs and demands, on possible trends in networking and resource sharing. All of this is thrown into the broth, and again members of the working group argue, discuss, analyze and compromise until acceptable codes are reached for each area. Because it is frustrating and painful, there is a tendency to avoid this third component in collection analysis; yet the major role of a written policy is not to indicate what *has been* and what *is* but rather what *will be*.

Throughout the process of collecting data for the policy statement the working group chairman has maintained active involvement, controlling, directing and resolving differences. At the final drafting stage this person should assume editorial responsibility for putting the policy together. The chairman cum editor, having collected the individual subject statements, should compile them by class (if indeed a classified arrangement is to be followed). At this point discussions about future collecting levels can be held among all concerned selectors to reconcile conflicting judgments and refine the data into a statement of proposed library policy. These meetings to establish consensus can contribute greatly to the education of the library staff and to the reinforcement of their sense of common purpose. Also, even before the policy statement is finished selectors broaden their understanding and clarify their views of collecting goals and responsibility by examining library-wide practice in a subject field.[4] Thus many may and should contribute at this point, but only one individual should have editorial duties in order to ensure consistency in the final product. Like any careful editor the working group chairman will ensure that the policy follows the outline, that it is factually accurate, that it does not misrepresent the institution or its goals, that it is written in clear and unambiguous English and that it is produced to a high standard. In many cases a library will be judged by its policy statement; this should be a guiding concern at the compilation stage. When the document has been prepared, checked and corrected, it is presented to the full policy committee for evaluation.

Draft Policy Reviewed and Revised

The problem with dividing the policy formulation process into a series of steps is that it fosters the notion of discrete activities completed independently of preceding or succeeding events, when in reality each of the stages is interdependent. To ensure that the committee is aware of this complex interrelationship, the working group, if it is functioning effectively and is politically astute, will solicit advice from, and the continuing cooperation of, the policy committee and its chairman throughout the drafting stage. Consequently, the committee members will not be presented with a document which seems totally foreign, and this will help the committee to evaluate the draft more thoroughly and sympathetically. The committee has been constituted to represent the institution and its administration, professional staff, user groups and outside expertise. All of these interests must analyze the policy section by section from their particular viewpoints and offer critical guidance about necessary changes. This review may well include input from other concerned parties, as it did at the University of California (pp. 102-115), or it may involve submission to a governing body or local council, as in the case of school and public libraries. Every library will have its unique institutional requirements with regard to review and approval of the draft policy; no matter what this might involve it is essential that the policy committee and its working group in particular act in accordance with the review recommendations, providing they are in keeping with the spirit and intention of the policy statement. Often this is psychologically difficult, for long hours have gone into formulating the policy and defending its conclusions; but if the policy is to succeed and receive final approval it must be in a form acceptable to the library's masters. Therefore, the working group revises the policy accordingly, ensuring that such revision remains true to the data collected during user and use studies and the collection evaluation process.

Policy Implemented and Disseminated

When completed, the revised collection development policy is ready for implementation. In the past this has meant distribution primarily for use in-house only by those staff concerned with selection and acquisitions; it is rather unusual in Australian libraries for policies to be generally available to the public or even to reference, circulation or technical services staff. Because of this very limited distribution, policies on the whole have been produced in the cheapest possible manner from typescript. Fortunately, this is beginning to change with the realization that policies are important planning and communication documents and therefore deserve to have a more professional physical appearance. This approach is to be encouraged by any library that takes the time to prepare a policy. Once the policy exists, it should not merely be implemented but should also be available for wide distribution; if this means a more costly document, then the library can make it available for purchase. Because the policy is a major achievement, it should be heralded as such, perhaps even to the extent of a public, or at least institution-wide, launching. In other words, if the policy statement profiles the library, why not give it a *high* profile? This will assist significantly in the communication function discussed in Chapter 1.

Implementation is the less glamorous but certainly more important activity, and every effort must be made to familiarize all staff with the use and role of the collection development policy. All staff members involved in the selection and acquisition of library materials must be fully cognizant of the document's content and use; as they will have been party to the formulation process, this should not pose problems. But all other staff who handle, process and use library materials should also be familiar with the policy. The best way to achieve this familiarity is through meetings or even an in-service programme in which staff learn how to use the policy, how to explain its purpose and how to handle questions which the policy might answer.

Ongoing Evaluation Process

With the formal, written policy in place and being used to help shape the library's development the tendency is to sit back and let the system operate unhampered. However, every librarian experienced in the drafting of a policy statement will say that this attitude merely engenders a dangerous sense of immutability. Librarians must remember that the collections being guided by the policy are constantly growing and changing in response to new needs and developments. Consequently, the policy directing the collections should also be susceptible to change and development. If it is not, the result will be a policy which becomes superseded and thus unusable; this will mean total revision of the existing policy document through replication of all the stages described in this chapter, and librarians want to avoid this situation at all costs.

It is highly recommended, then, that some procedure be established at the outset for ongoing review of the policy, for evaluation on a regular basis and for revision as required. On a regular schedule each subject section of the policy should be scrutinized by appropriate personnel, and the entire policy should be reviewed on an annual or biennial basis. While this may seem overly ambitious, it is the only way to avoid complete rewriting of the policy or its discard. Such ongoing revision should be built into the job descriptions of professional staff, probably the selection or acquisitions librarian for the most part. This will enable fine tuning rather than far more costly engine replacement.

References

1   Dorothy A. Koenig, "Rushmore at Berkeley: The Dynamics of Developing a Written Collection Development Policy Statement." *Journal of Academic Librarianship* 7, 6 (January 1982): 346.

2   Robert W. Evans, "Collection Development Policy Statements: The Documentation Process." *Collection Management* 7 (1985): 66.

3   Elizabeth W. Futas, *Library Acquisition Policies and Procedures* (2nd ed. Phoenix, Ariz.: Oryx Press, 1984).

4   Sheila T. Dowd, "The Formulation of a Collection Development Policy Statement." In *Collection Development in Libraries: A Treatise, Part A,* ed. Robert D. Stueart and George B. Miller, Jr. (Foundations in Library and Information Science, Vol. 10. Greenwich, Conn.: JAI Press, 1980), p. 86.

5   *The State Library of Victoria Selection Policy* (ISBN 0-909962-51-0) is available for A$10.00 from The Accountant, Library Council of Victoria, 328 Swanston Street, Melbourne 3000, Australia.

READINGS ON FORMULATION OF THE COLLECTION
DEVELOPMENT POLICY

In this chapter the focus has been on practical activities to be undertaken when attempting to formulate a policy that contains the elements outlined in Chapter 2. These activities have been stated in a way that should be applicable to any library environment with appropriate modifications. The readings are intended to supplement this discussion in two ways: by giving additional details in support of our general remarks, and by giving a concrete example of how a specific policy has been formulated.

Accordingly, the article by Robert Evans (pp. 95-102) discusses the actual process of putting together a policy statement. He considers composition of the policy committee, use of the ALA *Guidelines* and sources of documentation that require analysis for the policy. With particular reference to the experience in New York State and at one college of the State University of New York, Evans also discusses the problems of determining collection levels, reconciling ideals with practices and the treatment of interdisciplinary areas.

Following this general analysis, we turn to a concrete, "how-we-did-it-here" case study. In "Rushmore at Berkeley" (pp. 102-115) Dorothy Koenig presents a detailed account of how one very large university library system engaged in - and successfully completed - a three-year collection development design process. More than that, she shows how a library can cope quite adequately despite severe logistical problems. Her article should give confidence to anyone contemplating the preparation of a written collection development policy.

Robert W. Evans, "Collection Development Policy Statements: The Documentation Process." *Collection Management* 7, 1 (1985): 63-73.

Few would doubt that a library's policy statement on collection development and management is a Good Thing (capital G, capital T, *a la 1066 and All That*). This is so because the creation of the document requires two kinds of commitment: the commitment to intellectual effort toward a certain end; and the commitment of the library's most valuable resource, the time of its staff, to that same end. The commitment should ideally be made by all of the members of a staff, since the product is going to affect the resources that all of them have available for the performance of their jobs. The commitment must certainly be made by those with administrative responsibility for the assignment of resources such as staff time and acquisitions dollars.

A look at the literature on the creation of collection development policy statements and a look at the statements themselves reveal quickly that a great many of these documents have been written in defense of intellectual freedom and as barricades against the censors, particularly of course in school and public libraries. As Michael Benedict pointed out in a paper in 1978, those who feel that something should be in the library will be less vocal than those who think that something should not be in it.

In the middle 1970s articles about the value of the policy document as a management tool began to appear in the literature, culminating in the publication of the ALA *Guidelines* in 1978. The impetus for this movement came from the large scholarly libraries, members of ARL, but the scene was set for the extension of the technique to libraries of all types and sizes, and a standard of language and mechanics has been laid down. In New York State the plan required for the distribution of regional coordinated collection development aid is apparently to be based upon this standard, thus providing many with a powerful incentive to apply the techniques of the *Guidelines* in their own shops.

How does a library organize to produce a collection development policy document? Common to all descriptions of this process are the words: "A committee was appointed." This common characteristic underlines the fact that no matter what the composition of the committee may be, how it is put together, or how it organizes its work, there is going to be a lot of discussion in this process, and some of it may be heated. But that discussion should be of enormous value to the participants, as they take apart what they are doing, examine assumptions, hear each other's points of view, and put it all back together again.

Who is to work on the document depends, of course, on the:

> size of the staff and the amount of staff time that can be devoted to this activity;
> organization of the library in terms of departments, branches, etc.;
> distribution of responsibility for collection development and for the allocation of funds.

All writers suggest user involvement - patrons, students, faculty, executives whose departments depend upon the special library, and so on - in these discussions. The presence of users at the creation of the document should not only help to anchor the discussions in the real world but also act as insurance against a phenomenon, pointed out by Michael Benedict, in which the document is thought of as something safe that is placed between the librarian and the reader, stifling communication with the public.

The first step, then, is to determine who will work on the production of the policy statement, and ideally this will be as many as possible of those who have collection development responsibilities, along with a leavening of laymen. The second step is to put someone in charge who can take a fairly long-range view of the operation and who can also charm, threaten, cajole, do whatever is necessary to keep the activity going.

The committee's first activity should be to analyse and schedule the steps needed to produce a collection development policy statement. These may include the following:

First, consideration of the definitions of collection levels published in the *Guidelines*, or the need to adapt them or write new ones to suit the library's specific mission and clientele, (more will be said later on this step);

Second, consideration of what statements will be necessary for specific formats if films or gifts or computer software, for instance, are to be given special treatment, as well as what auxiliary statements should be included, such as those standard ALA documents, The Library Bill of Rights, the Freedom to Read statement, and so on. A preliminary table of contents is a very good idea even if the final product takes some unexpected directions and looks rather different from one's initial expectations;

Third, collection of precedents, whether achieved through examination of existing documents (and some libraries are lucky enough to have them), picking the brains of those who are doing the work without the guidance of a formal statement, or through collection analysis;

Fourth, determination of the breadth or narrowness of the subject descriptors to be used, and finally the application to them of the levels of collection development.

Finally your chairman, who must have a surgically precise editorial hand in addition to all of his or her other virtues, puts it together, and sends a draft round again to all concerned for comment and emendation.

In order to keep the process moving and to avoid spending a great deal too much time and effort on some minor aspect of the document, it is a good idea to set up a timetable to match the outline of procedure, indicating which portions of the process can be done simultaneously and how many weeks will be devoted to each step.

The great step forward provided by the *Guidelines* is one in the direction of standardization. If comparisons among institutions are to be made, the form and terminology of policy documents must have certain elements in common. It seems clear therefore that the less each library fiddles with the definitions of collection levels in the *Guidelines*, the better off everyone is, even though a library may have a mission with features unusual enough to require some adjustment or extension of the ALA definitions. The recently published definitions of the New York State Library are a case in point. The library's primary clientele is the legislature, and its collecting levels are stated in terms of legislative needs. They are, however, fairly easy to equate with ALA's levels A to E and O.

When it comes to subject descriptors, there is a good deal less unanimity, and probably not so much need for common language. The level of detail of the descriptors used for the abbreviated version of the Library of Congress classification scheme in the *Guidelines* leaves something to be desired. It is internally uneven, providing for instance eleven subdivisions for Spanish literature but only two for botany. It is a compromise that is likely to please no one: too detailed for small public or school libraries, hopelessly inadequate for subject specialized libraries such as those of medical schools or art museums. Some of LC's terminology also needs updating. Many of us have materials on solar energy in LC's class TJ, the rubic for which is Mechanical Engineering and Machinery. In support of our programs in environmental science and ethology my own library has materials on wildlife in SK, for which the descriptor is "Hunting Sports".

In short, it appears that we ought to stick as close as possible to the definitions of collection levels that appear on pages 3-5 of the *Guidelines* but feel a great deal more freedom to adopt whatever set of descriptors suits our own collections. The regional coordinated collection development aid program in New York State seems to have recognized this, among other things, permitting the use of terms such as women's studies and city planning, describing interdisciplinary fields that do not appear in the Library of Congress classification.

Much of the work to be done on a collection development policy statement is the unearthing and codification or formalization of documents and practices already in existence. This is not to say that it is easy, since the basis for a library's mission statement, for instance, may be well buried. Some selection officers find it difficult to formulate a statement of what they are doing. And there may well be general and fairly determined disagreement with what is going on, when the statement is finally placed upon the table. What follows is a short list of sources, possibly already in existence, which for the sake of convenience is divided into sources of the framework and sources of detail.

Many of us will want to begin the framework with statements on intellectual freedom such as those referred to above. On the basis of examination of policy statements, it is clear that the national association carries some weight in these matters, a factor we should perhaps keep in mind as discussions of the role of ALA vis a vis its divisions continue. Secondly there may be documentation of the political considerations that have a bearing on collection policies. The requirements of the governing or sponsoring authority or body should be searched out, and it is to be hoped that these statements will not have been made completely obsolete by the passage of time. There are also such fairly obvious sources of statements of purpose as college catalogs, charters, and the tacit objectives of businesses and public institutions.

The sources of the detail that will add form to the outline may include the following. For academic libraries, curricular planning is all important. New programs in the offering, new courses within existing majors, and the phasing out of old programs will obviously change what happens in collection development and management, and it is essential that academic collection development officers know what is contemplated on a consistent and coherent basis as well at this point in the creation of the policy statement. It is useful to note that an idea once floated in academe has a kind of half-life, even if it seems to have been thoroughly shot down. Thus, a proposed new program may not actually come into being, but some of its elements may linger on and recur in slightly different guise in established programs.

Knowledge of the community to be served is clearly useful, whether it is a community of scholars or of businessmen or the more heterogeneous community served by the public library. The sources include user surveys, census data, course enrolments, business and other economic trends, analysis of circulation trends and the expression of user interests. One of my great regrets is that in my own library we allow a great deal of useful information on users' needs to escape us at the circulation desk. We have a study in progress that is meant as a partial remedy to this situation; but it moves slowly and its result will not be a complete solution to the problem.

Collection analysis receives careful attention in the ALA *Guidelines*. It should lead, in the process of developing the policy statement to the analysis of precedent among book selectors, all of whom have certain rules of thumb, area collections that they know are developing or should be developing, authors and classes of authors who are collected or excluded. The essential activity is to elicit these precedents in discussion and then reduce them to written form for the information and possibly criticism of all. It is a process of picking the brains of people who have been doing the job, and it should result in a document which will guide them and their successors. Again, all commentators on this subject agree that the worst situation for librarians assuming new collection development responsibilities is to have no guidance in writing from their predecessors.

Another important element is the coordination of the library's policies with other available resources. Do the public and the school or local college libraries have any agreements or understandings about backing each other up and to what extent? Are there agreements among local institutions, public and private, about the allocation of collection development responsibilities. Are these agreements formal or implicit? If there is an agreement or assignment of roles, are the resources involved actually freely available to users? The technology of resource availability is one of the fastest moving areas of librarianship. It is changing rapidly, and has changed since the publication of the *Guidelines* as increasing numbers of titles can be identified easily because of retrospective conversions and union listing in the databases of the bibliographical utilities.

No amount of bibliographic information can solve our problems, however, if the collections are not in fact open to the users of other libraries. In New York State the regional plans required for coordinated collection development aid should provide a usefully broad picture of relative strengths and weaknesses. We have indeed progressed since 38 member libraries of METRO produced a joint profile of their collections in 1976, a document that because of the subjectivity of its application and the delay in its dissemination has not been very widely used.

Most libraries will also have certain subject area commitments resulting from the development of strong collections in the past or as the result of gifts, for instance, that have created deposits of strength. It is to be hoped that these historic strengths remain useful to the library's patrons. The process of developing the policy statement is a good occasion for cool and critical examination of them, in any case.

The customary format of the document, then, includes in whatever order: (1) some general statements regarding intellectual freedom and the governance and mission of the library; (2) definitions of collection levels; (3) the application of these levels to a set of subject descriptors, however broadly or narrowly stated; (4) if necessary, statements on specific formats such as non-text materials or sources such as gifts or depository documents requiring separate attention; and (5) in a complex library some attention to the differences between the main library and branches or departments.

There are several problems with the application of the collecting levels to the subject areas in which the library collects. The first of these is subjectivity in the selectors. Two librarians on the same staff who are familiar with the collecting patterns in a field such as economics may very well disagree on the level to be assigned to LC's classes HB through HG. In particular, it is difficult in practice to distinguish the Advanced Study Level from Initial Study Level, levels C.1 and C.2 in the *Guidelines*. Patient and scrupulous discussion may be combined with shelf list measurements, expenditure levels, etc., and perhaps a little honest horse trading to produce a general agreement and satisfactory result within the library. The problem of different standards in the application of the definitions from one library to another is one for which no ready answer is available. In New York we are about to see how well the definitions in the *Guidelines* work in comparing unlike libraries as the coordinated regional plans emerge.

A second problem area is the reconciliation of ambition with actual practice, and included here is the difficulty created by budgetary fluctuations. A library may know that in order to support its institution's business management programs, it should be collecting at the advanced study level, while it is in fact going on from year to year with the same few journal subscriptions and buying only an occasional monograph. Because of its large numbers of students and faculty in the management field and because of its intention to support their work, should it show itself as collecting at the C.1 level or at the D level? The answer must be that the library should show its actual and present practice as honestly as possible. It may be that the document will show in a gloss that this is an area that gets first priority for upgrading when funds are available to employ a selector and to buy the materials. One treatment that did not work comes to mind. In my own library in a period of budgetary contraction we tried two columns for each subject descriptor. One was the actual level at which we thought we were collecting, while the other column represented what we felt was the level at which we ought to be collecting, the feasible and the ideal. This so overloaded the policy document that it contributed in large measure to the fact that we simply stopped paying very much attention to it.

The *Guidelines* of course recommend distinguishing various collecting levels for the same subject on the basis of past, present, and expected future practice. Experience suggests that this leads to difficulties. The information asked for in this instance is the sort of thing that could very well be considered an individual selector's annotation on the institutional document rather than a necessary and complicating part of the central effort. In most small and medium-sized libraries, and in libraries working at this exercise for the first time in particular, the maxim should be KEEP IT SIMPLE. For the purpose of the policy statement, a balance must somehow be struck between present and readily foreseeable future activity, and the selection of the appropriate collection level designator made on that basis. Since updating is part of the process, one can leave the upgrading of collection levels to the day when one feels that is actually taking place at that level.

A second problem suggested by the planners of this conference is the balance of long and short-term objectives. To this might be added the treatment of intellectual and social fads. Here the whole weight of the document and the exercise of producing it comes down on the side of long-term goals and the reduction of fads to their proper scale. The same thing may be said in academic libraries of the extracurricular interests of faculty members. The utility of the policy statement is to place these individual quirks in the perspective of the institution's objectives.

A third problem, alluded to earlier, is the multidisciplinary area where the interests of two or more selectors may overlap, an area that may very well not have an adequate descriptor in the classification scheme (if one chooses to go that route), or where owing to classification practices the material is scattered rather than being brought handily together in one place. Such subjects as black studies, women's studies, city planning, and so on, have been suggested. There is no reason why the library should not add a descriptor to the list or change the terminology or add to existing headings to reflect its collecting interests. The library may also wish to indicate in the policy statement that while several selectors may have an interest in a field, one of them has the ultimate responsibility for it. City planning may be of interest from the point of view of architecture, demography and other social sciences, design, urban history, and so on. It is possible that the library's perception of what it is doing will be heightened by the determination that the selector for one of these fields has primacy. One great advantage to a systematic journey through the classification scheme and the assignment of each class and descriptor to a selection officer on the library staff, is that it reveals subject fields that have in effect fallen through the cracks, fields that may be of interest to the institution but are receiving the attention of no one.

Finally a decision must be made on the balance between what may be termed the barebones approach and the provision of detail in the policy document itself. It is possible that there are fields in which the descriptors can be delimited in such a way as to provide some detail without creating a document with the size and weight of a volume of Mansell. In many fields where, for instance, most small and medium-sized libraries collect only as the subject pertains to the United States, this can be indicated with ease and without adding much verbiage. At Purchase we found two or three ways to show that we collect plays in literatures where we collect nothing else. Generally, however, it is suggested that the document should be kept as compact as possible and that individual selection officers should be expected to annotate their own portions of the document for their own guidance and that of their colleagues and successors.

No institution's objectives remain forever the same, and no library's mission is without the possibility of change. The world of scholarship itself changes as new interfaces emerge and in some cases become new disciplines. The library should therefore include provision in its plans and in the format chosen for the collection development policy document for updating the document on a regular basis. Some such device as an annual update session at the first staff meeting in October suggests itself. The discussion might take the form of review of statistical measurements against the document or a presentation on new developments in the institutional mission or outside factors, such as funding or new areas developing in the world of publishing. It might also take the form of a review of individual selectors' notes on their sections of the classification scheme or a discussion of overlapping interests. Whatever transpires, whether the document needs to be changed or not, the discussion is bound to be a useful one for the implementation of the policy on a day to day basis. If the initial effort was thoughtfully and carefully done, need for change should be minor and will probably be the result of exterior influences, such as the introduction of new programs in a college's curriculum.

The SUNY [State University of New York] College at Purchase experience with a selection policy statement has been mentioned a couple of times, and will be gone back to now on the possibility that as a kind of case study it may be of value.

First it should be explained that the SUNY College at Purchase is both a new institution with a VERY largely librarian-formed collection and a very participatory library staff. The librarians meet weekly, and have a set of rules and standing committees under which we function as a division of the college faculty. All libraries have subject responsibilities for both the development and the interpretation of the collection. In 1974 or 1975, when Columbia University was first attempting an automated application of a set of collecting level definitions to subject descriptors as a means of rationalizing the policies of their departmental libraries, copies of their definitions were obtained and turned over to our Collection Development Committee. The committee, headed by a bright and energetic young librarian, took the bit in its teeth, restated the definitions in what we thought were our own terms, and began the process of applying them to the Library of Congress classification scheme. They also produced a list of format statements they felt were desirable, and assigned them to the appropriate members of the staff. This list became the table of contents of our document, although not all of the statements were actually written, and some of them still have not been.

We produced a draft document, and it then became the responsibility of each of the selectors to take it to the faculty in the disciplines for which he or she was responsible. We got some valuable input that way, but not much of it resulted in change in the draft document. We used the draft as part of our self-study for accreditation in 1977, and later when dollars became scarce, added to it the ideal/feasible breakdown described earlier.

That was the point at which the whole thing became something of a bore. The librarian who had chaired the committee work on the document left us, and new staff members came and went, some of them probably without knowing of the existence of the policy document.

Publication of the ALA *Guidelines* served as a reminder that further work was needed. And as discussion of the regional coordinated collection development aid in New York State began, the document was dusted off to see what was retrievable. The librarians discussed the matter as a committee of the whole, and decided two things: (1) to take the collection development levels from the *Guidelines* verbatim and abandon our attempt to set up our own definitions; and (2) that some of our format statements were no longer acceptable. The selectors concerned wrote new format statements that were criticized and redrafted in general meetings. A new statement of basic premises was written; and we went through the LC classification and assigned to each librarian the classes for which we were responsible as selectors. In January we were at last ready to go over the thing, class by class, each one presenting his or her own view of what we were doing for each field. Levels were assigned, and discussed. And the library director took a day off to put it all together. It should be added that the date, the 14th of March 1983, when this paper was to be presented, gave the director and therefore the rest of the staff a powerful push forward.

The result is still a draft. We are now in the process of taking it back to the faculty to secure their agreement or disagreement, as the case may be. We still have a number of format statements to write, but the most important ones are present. We have learned some fairly powerful lessons in the process about our own practice, and there are a couple of fairly important points on which we have so far only agreed to disagree. It should be possible for us, however, to keep this up to date in the future without a great deal of effort, and certainly each of us knows a good deal more about what we are doing both individually and collectively

Bibliography

Buzzard, Marion L. "Writing a Collection Development Policy for an Academic Library." *Collection Management* 2 (Winter, 1978): 317-328.

Futas, Elizabeth, ed. *Library Acquisition Policies and Procedures*. Phoenix, Ariz: Oryx Press, 1977.

Koenig, Dorothy A. "Rushmore at Berkeley: The Dynamics of Developing a Written Collection Development Policy Statement." *Journal of Academic Librarianship* 7, 6 (January 1982): 344-350.

Osburn, Charles B. "Planning for a University Library Policy on Collection Development." *International Library Review* 9 (1977): 209-224.

Pettit, Katherine D., ed. *Collection Development: Papers Presented April 6, 1978 by the Acquisitions Round Table at the Texas Library Association's 65th Annual Conference.* ED183142.

Dorothy A. Koenig, "Rushmore at Berkeley: The Dynamics of Developing a Written Collection Development Policy Statement." *Journal of Academic Librarianship* **7, 6 (1982): 344-350.**

The interest to the profession of the development of a coordinated, written Collection Development Policy Statement for Berkeley lies in the collection's size, decentralization, and complexity.

The stated objective of the library regarding collections is to identify, acquire, organize, and disseminate all forms of recorded information which are pertinent to existing research and instructional programs. The magnitude of the library's task has grown exponentially as has the scope of the university's curriculum. In 1869 the University of California opened with an inaugural enrolment of fewer than 200 students. The university had been chartered in 1868 by the state with the expressed mandate:

> The University shall have for its design to provide instruction and thorough and complete education in all the departments of science, literature, art, industrial and professional pursuits, and general education, and also special courses of instruction in preparation for the professions of Agriculture, the Mechanic Arts, Mining, Military Science, Civil Engineering, Law, Medicine, and Commerce, and shall consist of various Colleges....[1]

The academic environment of 1978 at the University of California at Berkeley described in the interim report of the Collection Analysis Project is still recognizable in 1981 as the enrolment approaches 30,000. The report describes the library's support of 236 separate [undergraduate] fields of study, some as individually tailored as "Holism and Environmental Problems," the "Mammalian Genetic Process" and "Theater Politics." Equal scope for innovation among traditional disciplines is found at the graduate level where 34 Interdisciplinary Groups have been structured to coordinate study toward the doctor's degree: 68% (23) of these Interdisciplinary Groups are in the Sciences; 32% (11)

are in the Humanities and Social Sciences. The Graduate Division has also encouraged the informal establishment of ad hoc individual programs leading to the PhD degree. There are 109 departments offering a total of 83 masters and 98 doctors degrees, both academic and professional. Not included in the masters count are the departments that award the master's degree only to students pursuing work toward the PhD. If one considers the 34 Interdisciplinary Groups as well, Berkeley offers 132 established programs leading to the PhD degree. Six inter-campus joint doctoral programs and 13 concurrent degree programs on the Berkeley campus are also offered to meet the needs of graduate students.[2] Such is the current scope of the continuing challenge to library resources.

Academic complexity is compounded by the institutional complexity of the library. The General Library of the University of California at Berkeley is a system comprising the Main Library, 21 branch libraries, the Moffitt Undergraduate Library, and the Bancroft Library which houses the library's special collections including Western Americana, Californiania, and rare books. In addition, a number of institutes and departments on the Berkeley campus maintain libraries which are independent of the General Library system. These are commonly called the nongeneral libraries, e.g., Institute of Governmental Studies (IGS) library, Institute of Transportation Studies (ITS) library, and the Water Resources library.

The size of the collection is also a factor to be taken into account. As of June 30, 1981 the University Library at Berkeley had 5,927,773 volumes, an annual growth of 2.9 percent over the previous year. It subscribed to 104,607 current serial titles, an increase of 2.4 percent.

RUSHMORE is a catch phrase which was coined when selectors - book fund managers - faced the task of defining on paper the policy that informed their book selection practice in support of these complex research and instructional needs of the academic enterprise at Berkeley. The purpose of this account is to provide a description of this process and to record the strategies used to engineer not only an effective methodology of collection development design but also the facilitation of the successful cooperative effort of 65 book selectors who realized its initial goal - a coordinated policy statement.

Contract

In February 1977 a contract was drawn up between the Board of Trustees of the Leland Stanford Junior University and the Regents of the University of California. This contract bound the two universities to establish a program to further the sharing of library resources through (1) developing a coordinated acquisition policy, (2) granting of direct borrowing privileges to faculty, graduate students, and academic personnel, (3) introducing reciprocal lending privileges to eligible users by all campus libraries, except the undergraduate libraries, and (4) providing for the rapid movement of books and patrons between the two campuses.[3] This ambitious cooperative program was made possible by two grants, one each from the Alfred P. Sloan and the Andrew W. Mellon Foundations (Contract No. 76-10-3).

The first priority set forth in the grant proposal's summary of the three-year program objectives states,

There needs to be established a clear statement of book selection policies which allows curators [book selectors] to choose from scholarly production those materials needed currently by teaching and research programs. In this program the two universities will plan a joint and coordinated acquisition policy document which will be the blueprint for more efficient selection of materials...and which will serve as a model for other cooperative efforts.[4]

Design

In February 1977 the author was appointed Berkeley's Collection Development Policy Statement Coordinator on a half-time basis. This position involved close work with Sheila Dowd, Assistant University Librarian for Collection Development and Reference Services, and the members of the General Library's Selection Committee to create a standardized format for the responses to be elicited from individual selectors. We made an early basic decision to organize the policy statement by the Library of Congress Classification Scheme. The LC classification is a lingua franca among librarians, and we wanted to facilitate the possibility of future interlibrary dialogue structured on comparability of categories. We next recognized the utility of selecting those classification breakdowns chosen as organizational elements for the *National Shelflist Count*, whose function is the biannual comparison of the growth and decline of holdings among participant academic libraries.[5]

Besides looking ahead to cooperative decisions in acquisitions policy between Berkeley and Stanford, we wanted to ensure that selectors, in assessing their choices of what titles to purchase in support of Berkeley's needs, would be forced to consider the whole range of human knowledge. Because of the vagaries of classification, for example, the Biology Library needed to record in the VM class (Naval Architecture) its minimal-level collection on diving research. This is relevant to the effect of underwater pressure on the physiology of divers. One would not necessarily expect an aspect of human physiology to be classed in Naval Architecture. In this way we hoped that all collected subjects would be noted and that none would be neglected through oversight. We also expected areas of benign neglect as well as pockets of unwarranted duplication to be spotlighted.

This project was the first attempt to formulate a written, coordinated statement documenting library-wide direction of collection shaping. The information explosion and financial constraints no longer permitted an amorphous growth of collections.

Information Meeting

In late April 1977 we convened a meeting to explain to all General Library selectors in what ways their active participation in the project was essential. Each of the 65 selectors had special subject, area, or language expertise. Many were associated with individual academic programs or congeries of departments. Most had highly developed territorial instincts: *my* faculty, *my* discipline, *my* interdisciplinary nexus. Since there had never been a general meeting of selectors qua selectors before, the necessity for coordination became more apparent as the extent of provincialized decentralization was recognized.

In order to reinforce the idea of the library as a whole, at this initial meeting an exercise based on LC proof slips was introduced. Samples of 28 diverse proof slips were distributed and the following directions were given: Look at each title and note your judgments. Do you think this book should be in an academic library like Berkeley? Should it be in your unit? If not, should any other unit consider it for purchase? What unit, if any, has primary responsibility for books on this subject?

Some titles were so obviously inappropriate for Berkeley's collection that they provoked no discussion at all, e.g. *Strange Stories, Amazing Facts: Stories That Are Bizarre, Unusual Odd, Astonishing, and Often Incredible.* But several proved to be so equivocal they occasioned lively and lengthy exchanges of differing points of view. A case in point is *A Climber's Guide to Glacier National Park.* During the discussion of our separate judgments, some selectors agreed that Berkeley should not be expected to provide guidebooks for climbers, but to our concerted surprise three selectors individually informed the group that the title already sat appropriately on their respective shelves - one copy in the Forestry Library that buys books by policy on all national parks, including their recreational uses; another copy in the Bancroft Library because the original edition of the book was published by the San Francisco-based Sierra Club, and the Bancroft Library purchases a copy of every title published by the Sierra Club, and a third copy in Moffitt Undergraduate Library, which supports the current interests of undergraduates. Each purchase had been made in accord with a policy well known to and easily articulated by the collecting unit. As more judgments on different titles were openly discussed, the LC proof slips served their purpose as a means to heighten the interest of the group in the central question, "Now what are we really going to do to get our policy well defined?"

At this point we directed attention to the breakdown of the LC classification that would be used in defining policy (see Appendix 1: Sample Profile Sheet). For each of the 700 subject categories listed, the selector was asked to line out those that had no application whatsoever to his or her collecting practice. The written explanatory notes acknowledged that the breakdown provided might not be adequate to express all shades of actual policy. In instances where the given breakdown was not sufficiently refined to permit an accurate statement of collection development policy, the selector was encouraged to append an analysis of his or her policy by a more specific breakdown. As it turned out later, when the individual responses were correlated, selectors added about 600 individual categories, nearly doubling the number of descriptors. Thus, it was here we relied heavily on the participation and experience of each selector to break down general categories into more specific and meaningful indexes. For example, ND (Painting) as given had to be refined both geographically and chronologically by the subject specialist; the result - 41 new categories.

Workshops: Methodology

All selectors were required to attend one session of a three-hour workshop repeated seven times during the first week of May 1977. The explicit assignment before they came to a scheduled workshop was to have filled out one line on any of the profile sheets, which were oversize, 11 x 17 inches. During the workshops we began to refer to them as subject profile sheets, and they were massive profiles. Someone made the mental link of massive profiles with Mt. Rushmore, and the manageable term RUSHMORE easily displaced its tongue-twisting alternative - the Collection Development Policy Statement Project.

Significant decisions in designing the format of the profile sheets were (1) to follow the American Library Association's guidelines for collection development and (2) to force three judgments to be made of the library's collecting level on every subject under consideration. Summaries of the definitions proposed by the guidelines are Code 1 = Comprehensive level (collecting exhaustively in the subject field); Code 2 = Research level (collecting source materials required for dissertations and independent research); Code 3 = Study level (collecting materials to support undergraduate and graduate course work); Code 4 = Basic level (collecting materials to introduce and define a subject) and Code 5 = Minimal level (collecting marginally).[6] The three judgments asked for from selectors were labelled columns, x, y and z. The x column represented an evaluation of the collection already sitting on the shelves; the y column described the level of current collecting activity at the time of the response; the z column expressed the selector's opinion of the policy level desirable to support current and continuing academic program needs. The three judgments taken together indicated trends in changing levels of support either planned or de facto. For example, in the draft Policy Statement under GC (Oceanography) (see Appendix 2: Sample page from the draft Policy Statement), the Engineering Library records its policy decision to collect the aspect of ocean engineering at a research level at which it has not collected at all in the past. A jump from collecting level 0 to 2 could have been interpreted as the introduction of a new PhD program, an individual professor's new research interest, or as the selector stated in this case, "They discovered oil in the North Sea." Here are some typical numerical sequences with the noted trend translated into possible interpretations:

x	y	z	Interpretations
-	5	5	Did not collect in the past
4	-	5	Did not collect at present
4	5	-	Think it appropriate not to collect in future
2	2	2	Maintaining appropriate research strength
2	3	2	Current funding inadequate to do proper job
2	3	4	Phasing down
-	4	3	New program support
4	4	4	Continued basic support
4	3	2	New PhD program

In the final printout of the draft Policy Statement the y column was suppressed because it was three years out of date, but the program field exists in the database for periodic reappraisals in the future. An important distinction that emerged in the selector's grappling with the nuances of the definitions of collecting levels was the firm understanding that the z column represented a policy decision. It was by no means to be thought of as shelflist count. The number of books on the shelves does not in itself make a research collection; quantity is no automatic measure of adequacy.

In considering arbitrary language codes A through O, selectors were asked to be sure to take into account in their evaluation serials and all materials received through exchange agreements. Selectors had a natural tendency to be more aware of titles they personally chose for purchase from publishers' announcements, reviews in scholarly journals, LC proof slips, etc. They tended to be less aware of much of the material in foreign languages arriving on serial standing orders, approval plans, and exchange. However, the collecting level and language coverage expressed in the draft Policy Statement are representative of the whole collection without regard to the route by which the titles found their way to Berkeley. For ease of recognition in the final policy, the letter language codes are expressed as mnemonic abbreviations: e.g. "All applicable languages (i.e., no exclusions)" is represented by ALL, not the letter A; "English primarily, other languages selectively" is abbreviated ENG+, not B, and so forth.

Other qualifying factors needed definition for each subject breakdown on the distributed profile sheets: chronological exclusions and strengths, geographical exclusions and strengths, form of material collected (newspapers, manuscripts, maps, etc.), aspect, and primary responsibility. If the limits to a unit's collection of materials could not be expressed fully in codified form, the aspect column allowed the selector to indulge in free language to get his or her distinctions across. For example, the Anthropology Library could specify under QL737.9 (Primates) that its emphasis is on the social behaviour of primates, not physical characteristics. Under the same class number the Biology Library could note its emphasis on anatomy and physiology, not social behaviour. In the final display Berkeley's holdings can in sum be a true research collection, but different aspects of any subject may be concentrated in two or more locations. Individually collections can be lacking; when appraised as a whole they may be superior. Throughout the Policy Statement complementary shared responsibility points up the need for continuing consultation between and among selectors to prevent unwarranted and unconscious overlap.

Respondents were asked to indicate whether they believed they had primary collecting responsibility for materials in any given classification. They were encouraged to indicate what unit they thought responsible if they disclaimed the responsibility themselves. These responses were very useful as later springboards to discussion among selectors in any one large subject area, e.g. the social sciences. When the individual responses were tabulated, problems leapt to view: areas where no one claimed abiding interest, subjects where three units each dubbed themselves the responsible locations, fields where Unit A said that Unit B had the responsibility and B gave it to C who knew that it belonged to A all along. An example of such irresolution was Human Nutrition (QP141), neither fully claimed nor rejected by Public Health, Agriculture, and Biology libraries. This ambivalence resulted in an unevenly developed total collection.

Individual Responses

In contrast to the later subject-centered discussion groups, for the purpose of the workshops held during the first week of May there was no effort made to get librarians together who had similar areas of expertise. In fact, dissimilar backgrounds were seen as an advantage to stimulate debate in order to reach a common understanding of the conceptual framework and terminology distinctions used on the profile sheets. It was important to ensure that the judgments expressed by each selector would be mutually intelligible. Though the goal was to arrive at a normative use of the project's concepts, the exact idea of what constitutes a research collection turned out to be difficult to pin down.

Selectors worked dialectically to explore this elusive concept through debating the important distinctions between quantity and quality, primary works and derived works, original sources and translations, etc. Selectors found that their sense of a growing common understanding of the definitions of collecting levels was facilitated by trading examples of specific titles. If the methodology of the whole project was to succeed, this shared understanding of the meanings of the definitions of collecting levels had to be its firm foundation. A "2" collection had to be judged qualitatively the same from location to location or comparability would be flawed and credibility diminished.

The following timetable was suggested for the completion of individual responses: three weeks for individual assessment, two weeks for consultation with appropriate faculty members, a week each for exchange of views among colleagues within a unit and among interdepartmental selectors, two weeks for reevaluation, one week for consolidation of the statement for each collecting unit. Although the deadline for submitting the statement to the coordinator was July 15, 1977, a few were not received, due to unforeseen pressures, until December.

Library-wide Coordination

Each response was equivalent to a best-guess policy statement for each collecting unit. During the first months of 1978 the author set about correlating the individual selector's responses by subject breakdown, adding to the scheme those additional refinements necessary to express policy as practiced, e.g., "Fish Culture and Fisheries" was not sufficient. We needed to add sealing, sea otters; crustacea, shellfish; whale fishery, seaweed, turtles; angling. Finer discriminations are as necessary to express what a library does not collect as to emphasize what it does. If one has a study-level collection in sealing (3) and a minimal-level collection in angling (5), one is forced to make such distinctions.

The selectors expressed continuing interest which heightened when subject-centered discussion meetings of appropriate selectors were convened. The mix of people attending these topical discussions was not the usual, since meetings within the library system are most often organized along administrative lines. For instance, for the first time the selector of science materials for the Moffitt Undergraduate Library as well as the history of science librarian working out of the Bancroft Library joined the deliberations of the departmentally constituted physical science librarians when the Q-QE classes were under discussion. General agreement among selectors could be punctuated by surprising revelations at any point. No one would expect that QB500-903, Descriptive Astronomy, would elicit a discussion of moon rocks which led to a consideration of extraterrestrial geology, which alerted those present to the fact that the Engineering Library has a definitive collection of this type of material in so far as it is a NASA depository. The Policy Statement's potential for reference referral became increasingly clear.

During the weeks and months that these fruitful exchanges of information took place, a sense of an organically whole library was being built up informationally bit by bit in the minds of the participants, and some ingrained attitudes began to change. Shared expertise can have more than incremental benefits. Discussions which began in a policy meeting might continue later by telephone as afterthoughts emerged and points of view were modified. Territorial edges eroded. Seemingly small decisions were indicative of major changes to come. For instance, traditionally the Biology Library collected "fish" from a natural history point of view, and the Agriculture Library was responsible for "fisheries" in all their commercial aspects. Users as well as reference personnel in other parts of the library system would be confused by an unarticulated policy no matter which branch, Agriculture or Biology, was consulted first. Choosing a potentially ambiguous example, the author checked Berkeley's holdings to see in what locations one would find Eleanor Clark's *Oysters of Locmariaquer* - in the Main Loan Stacks as literature, in the Biology Library for its discussion of the physical characteristics and life cycle of the oyster, or in the Agriculture Library as a longitudinal study of the impact of the oyster industry on the fluctuating economy of Brittany. In fact the title is owned by the Main Loan Stacks, the major authors collection in the Humanities Graduate Service, Moffitt Undergraduate Library, and the Agriculture Library. The Library of Congress classified it in SH371 (Shellfish), a category for which the Biology Library now has primary responsibility. As a result of one of the natural history discussion groups, the Agriculture Library volunteered to cede its responsibility in "Fisheries" (LC classification SH) to the Biology Library and to maintain only a local basic collection. Two of the implications of this fiat are that some journal titles will have to be transferred from Agriculture to Biology, and regular users of the two locations will have to be reeducated to the change in policy. The ready availability of the Policy Statement at all public service points will enable reference librarians to be currently correct in their referrals.

The subject-centered discussion groups benefitted greatly by the institutional memories of long-tenured selectors at Berkeley. Activated by the topic under discussion and review, their memories produced pockets of special collections that needed to be recorded as strengths: manuscripts of Horace, emblem books housed in the Rare Book collection, eighteenth century Irish pamphlets as well as other gifts and bequests that lend special enrichment to Berkeley's collection. At the other end of the spectrum, new selectors, by participating in these discussions, were given an overview of the Berkeley collection in the context of its several and related locations. Moffitt Undergraduate Library librarians, who regularly rotate their selection assignments, were particularly vocal in expressing how useful and to the point they found this shared experience to be. Throughout the calendar year 1978 Berkeley selectors explored the range of human knowledge as recorded in the total collection.

Internal Review Process

The spring of 1979 was used for internal library review of the emerging descriptions of the collections and of the resulting decisions arrived at by subject-oriented selectors. The Selection Committee functioned well as a sounding board during the design stage of the RUSHMORE format. At first it seemed natural that they should again serve as a reflective body to review the results. But by the nature of its structure the Selection Committee of 1979 was not the same group of people as its 1977 predecessor. Continuity is served by having the ex officio member and three continuing members carry over from year to year. In 1979 six new members coming from different backgrounds had to be informed of the project's prior progress. Sharing with the committee the results of the selectors' discussions quickly settled into an interesting process of education; the background and the results to date had to be explained. Going over all this ground again was time-consuming and, from the point of view of the coordinator, unproductive. After experimentation, we found the most effective review and decision-making group to be made up of three people: the Assistant University Librarian (AUL) for Collection Development and Reference Services (she had the authority to make necessary decisions in case of deadlock); the library expert on any large LC subject classification under discussion (he or she had the understanding necessary to explain current or projected policy); and the policy statement coordinator (she was the single person who had directed and participated in the whole process from its beginning).

Data Programming

In the spring of 1979 the AUL and the Coordinator met with the Head of the Library Systems Office to discuss the desired computer-produced format and the necessary components of a final product. The information in the database has the potential to deliver a variety of products tailored to identified needs. It could generate a total statement reflecting the policies of any single library location. It could provide a policy profile for any academic department or program indicating the collecting levels of those subjects relevant to its instructional and research needs. It could list the areas of knowledge in which the library collects in East Asian languages, and so forth.

At this stage of programming, a final column was added to the display format, a column labelled "Cooperative Reliance." This was a spinoff in response to information supplied by some selectors when they wished to indicate intercampus resources for materials not collected at Berkeley, e.g. the medical collections at UC San Francisco and UC Davis for books about surgery. The names of 19 potential cooperating partners were codified by abbreviations and included in the introduction to the draft Policy Statement. For this first draft, only those reliances are stipulated where formal agreements already exist between Berkeley and other libraries, e.g. Berkeley's firm and well-articulated agreements in complementary collecting responsibilities with the neighboring Graduate Theological Union. It is likely that this column as well as the aspect column (designated "Notes" in the final product) will be used to express the detailed agreements arrived at by Berkeley and Stanford in their joint collecting policy.

During the time that the programming was being worked out, the AUL for Collection Development and Reference Services and the Collection Development Policy Coordinator collaborated in writing an introduction and planned the structure of the appendices and indexes to supplement the Classed Analysis, A - Z. The table of contents of the draft Policy Statement reflects the balance of philosophical generalities with the specifics thought necessary to present the well-rounded picture of collection development at Berkeley. An augmented subject index was prepared as well as a simple index matching academic departments and the LC classes most likely to be of interest to them. A roster of Berkeley selectors, their collecting responsibilities, library locations, and telephone numbers was appended to establish ready lines of communication for the feedback this document is expected to generate among faculty and others interested in directing and commenting upon the selection process within the Library.

Faculty Review

In May 1980 the first draft policy was distributed to all selectors, library and campus academic departments, the nine University of California campuses and Stanford, the members of the Research Libraries Group, etc. All selectors were reconvened as a group for a second informational meeting also in May 1980 almost three years to the day from that introductory session in 1977. The purpose of the meeting was to tie up loose ends, share the sense of a large task cooperatively completed, and shift mental gears to the next major stage of the process, offering to the faculty the library's best current statement of its support of the academic departments it serves. Selectors had the opportunity to discuss those approaches that might prove most effective in eliciting productive faculty response to the policy statement in all of its components, for instance a sense of the adequacy or inadequacy of the subject index. What are the terms that a professor looks for automatically in his or her discipline but cannot find? How can selectors elicit faculty members' differing perceptions of collecting levels appropriate to support their own research and instructional needs? It is hoped that differing expectations will be clearly articulated and satisfactorily resolved. In reviewing the draft policy statement, the faculty has the opportunity to heighten its own awareness of the selector's angst about needing to know what directions academic research is taking so the library can make appropriate and timely response. If this continuing dialogue between library and faculty is successful, the fine tuning of the Berkeley and Stanford joint acquisitions policy can be as productive and financially beneficial as the contract between the two research libraries was optimistic.[7]

Appendix 1: Sample Profile Sheet

UNIT _____ SELECTOR _____

L.C. CLASS	DESCRIPTOR	LANGUAGE CODES			COLLECTING LEVEL CODES			QUALIFYING FACTORS						
								OTHER CHRONOLOGICAL		GEOGRAPHICAL		FORM	ASPECT	PRIMARY RESPONSIBILITY
		X	Y	Z	X	Y	Z	EXCLUSIONS	STRENGTHS	EXCLUSIONS	STRENGTHS			
F1000-1170	History: British America, Canada													
F1201-1392	History: Mexico													
F1401-1419	History: Latin America (General)													
F1321-1577	History: Central America													
F1601-2151	History: West Indies													
F2155-2183	History: Caribbean Area													
F2201-3799	History: South America													
G1-890	Geography (General)													
G1001-3102	Atlases													
G3160-9980	Maps													
GA1-87	Mathematical Geography													
GA100-1999	Cartography													
GB	Physical Geography													
GC	Oceanography													
GF	Anthropo-geography													
GN1-295	Physical Anthropology													
GN307-686	Ethnology and Ethnography													
GN700-875	Prehistoric Archaeology													
GR	Folklore													
GT	Manners and Customs (General)													
GV1-198	Recreation													
GV201-553	Physical Training													
GV557-1197	Sports													
GV1200-1570	Games and Amusements													

Appendix 2: Sample Page from Draft Policy Statement

UNIVERSITY OF CALIFORNIA, BERKELEY	THE GENERAL LIBRARY			COLLECTION DEVELOPMENT POLICY	CLASSED ANALYSIS
LOCATION	LEVEL OF EXISTING COLLECTIONS	COLLECTING POLICY LEVEL	LANGUAGES	NOTES	COOPERATIVE RELIANCE
GAI TO 87 ----- MATHEMATICAL GEOGRAPHY -----					
*MAIN	3	3	ALL		
REFE	3	3	ALL		
UNDE	4	4	ENGL		
GA100 TO 1999 ----- CARTOGRAPHY -----					
BANC	2	2	ALL	Within Bancroft area and time scope.	
EART	4	3	ALL	Curriculum support	
*MAIN	3	3	ALL	Historical emphasis	
MAPS	4	4	ENGL+		
UNDE	4	4	ENGL		
GB ----- PHYSICAL GEOGRAPHY -----					
BANC	4	4	ALL	Within Bancroft area and time scope.	
*EART	2	2	ENGL+	Emphasis on Geomorphology	
EAST	5	4	E ASI		
ENGI	3	2	ALL	Coastal Geomorphology, Hydrology	
ENVI	3	3	ENGL+	Landscape Architecture Applications	
*MAIN	2	2	ALL	Exception: Current English language materials collected by EART.	
REFE	3	3	ALL		
UNDE	5	5	ENGL		

GC ----------------------- OCEANOGRAPHY -----------------------

*BIOL	4	4	ENGL+	Biological and Biochemical
*EART	4	4	ENGL+	Physical and Chemical
EAST	4	5	KOR	
ENGI		2	ALL	Ocean Engineering
MAIN	4	3	EUR-E	Strength: Soviet exchange material
UNDE	4	4	ENGL	

GC1015 to 1572   MARINE RESOURCES AND POLLUTION

DOCS	3	3	EUR-W

GF ----------------------- ANTHROPO-GEOGRAPHY, HUMAN ECOLOGY -----------------------

EAST	3	3	E ASI
*ENVI	3	2	ENGL+
MAIN	4	4	ALL
UNDE	3	3	ENGL

* INDICATES PRIMARY RESPONSIBILITY.

References

1   *An Act to Create and Organize the University of California,* Assembly Bill 583, Introduced in the California Legislature by Mr. [John W.] Dwinelle, March 5, 1968, p.1.

2   Sol Behar *et al., Collection Analysis Project Interim Report* (Berkeley, Calif.: University of California, The General Library, 1978), pp. 41-42.

3   Stanford University Contract for Sharing of Library Resources/The Regents of the University of California. Contact No. PR 2329 (Stanford, Calif.: Stanford University, 1977), pp.1-2.

4   UCB - Stanford Research Library Cooperative Programs, "A Proposal" (1976), p.7.

5   *Titles Classified by the Library of Congress Classification: National Shelflist Count* (Berkeley, Calif.: University of California, The General Library, 1977).

6   *Guidelines for the Formulation of Collection Development Policies, Preliminary Edition* (Chicago, Ill.: American Library Association, Resources and Technical Services Division, Resources Section, Collection Development Committee, 1976), pp. 3-4.

7   Libraries or individuals wishing to purchase a copy of Berkeley's *Collection Development Policy Statement*, preliminary edition, January 1980, should make their cheques out to the Regents of the University of California and mail their requests to: Librarian's Office, General Library, University of California, Berkeley, CA 94720, USA. The price per copy is $10.00.

PART 2

COLLECTION EVALUATION, USE AND USER STUDIES

CHAPTER 4

PROCEDURES FOR COLLECTION EVALUATION

The Reasons Why

It is almost axiomatic that one should ask why any particular job is being planned, or carried out before one starts on the work itself; there seems little sense in doing anything at all unless one has first worked out good reasons for doing it. Put at its simplest, evaluation is no more, and no less, than the measurement of how good an item is for its particular purpose; however, as any such measurement must be made in terms of "good for what?", it is obvious that any evaluation can proceed profitably only if the purpose of the object being evaluated is first defined, effectively setting not only the terms of the evaluation but also the criteria against which the object will be measured. Thus answers to the question of why one need bother with the tedious and costly processes of collection evaluation begin to suggest themselves: the librarian must first find out how good the collection is and then find ways to improve it, and, as every library should be established for a definite purpose, collection development can help determine objectively how and by whom the collection is being used and to what extent its expressed purpose is being fulfilled. Evaluation of a collection through use and user studies should lead to a more objective understanding of the scope and depth of the collection, including its weaknesses and strengths, and may be used as a guide for collection planning, budgeting and decision-making.

There are three main reasons for subjecting a collection to evaluation:

professional - is the collection doing its job?
economic - can the expense of doing that job be justified?
administrative - how can the various aspects of performance be assessed?

In this chapter and the next an examination is made first of the theoretical basis of the evaluation of library collections and second of the steps that must be taken in order that the theory should be put into practice, and the chapters lean heavily on the paper by Anthony Arthur (pp. 131-140), which describes the methodology and procedures used to plan the establishment of collection development policy and to provide policy recommendations in the area of collection evaluation, budget allocation and selection in a library serving a multi-level tertiary institution.

Although one expert in the field is said to have had as his primary aim the evaluation of collections for "optimizing storage of the collection",[1] a more important concern must be to find out whether the library is achieving its objectives and satisfying its users, as collection evaluation is a function of collection development and is related to the planning, selection and pruning of collections. This basic concern of collection evaluation embodies a number of aims:

1. to search for more accurate understanding of the scope, depth and utility of collections;
2. to prepare a guide to and a basis for collection development;
3. to aid in the preparation of a collection development policy;
4. to measure the effectiveness of a collection development policy;
5. to determine collection adequacy or quality;
6. to help rectify inadequacies in library holdings and to suggest ways to improve them;
7. to focus human and financial resources on areas most needing attention;
8. to aid justification for book budget increases;
9. to demonstrate to administrators that something is being done about the demands for "more money";
10. to establish the existence of special strengths, as well as weaknesses, in the collection;
11. to check the need for weeding and collection control, and to establish areas of priority of need.

These aims are listed in a descending order of importance, which is most emphatically not to say that those at the bottom of the list are unimportant, but rather to stress that those at the top should be regarded as of greater significance, specifically because the primary concern of any collection development exercise is to aid the library in achieving the particular objective of satisfying its users. Thus the first five aims listed here would need to command the most attention. The need to understand the present state of the collection underpins all the other aims, as on that understanding are built the subsequent tasks of preparing guides and policies for collection development, and of measuring the effectiveness of those policies. It is from this stage that one then develops measurements of the adequacy of the collection, so that attention can be further focused on the areas in which the collection is less than adequate, and on the practical measures that must be developed to rectify these shortcomings. These are generally encompassed in the aims specified in the list as 6 and 7. The political nature of all operations involving evaluation of performance, and the possible re-allocation of resources such as this is highlighted in 8 and 9, in which one takes steps to ensure not only that the library is moving towards a better service for its clientele, but also that those who control the purse strings are made aware of this in the hope that a certain loosening of these purse strings may follow as a result of this heightened awareness. The last two aims listed are the necessary operations that follow from the previous steps. Once the library has identified its aims, has developed measures of adequacy and inadequacy, and has convinced the administrators that funds ought to be made available, then it must set about establishing the specific weaknesses and strengths of its collections and taking steps to rectify those weaknesses and build on those strengths. Some less obviously important reasons have also been suggested: to provide better means for bibliographers to learn about specific parts of collections and to provide data for coordination with other libraries in their collection development programmes.

It is obvious, then, that it is important to have the goals and mission of the institution in mind at all times, as well as to remember the impact on coordinated collection arrangements with other libraries, so that librarians must first have a clear idea of the purpose of the collection, and then understand the objectives of the evaluation. Perusal of user studies can lead quite easily to a sense of frustration for administrators if the librarian is uncertain about the objectives of the institution, or the purposes of the particular evaluation, and thus does not make it clear to the administrators what steps are being recommended as a result of the findings, and what might be the likely results of action or lack of action.

In general it is accepted that the gathering of data on costs, effectiveness and efficiency, or of the results of any performance measurement operations, ought to aid any administration in its endeavour to make better, more rational decisions, or to produce better, more useful plans, and in the long term to increase the overall efficiency of the institution. However, it is not at all clear to what extent the provision of useful and accurate information necessarily affects the ultimate actions of decision-makers. "Decision-making" has been defined "...as the process whereby information is converted into action...[so that] decision making is largely concerned with the processes of acquiring, controlling, and utilizing information to accomplish some objective."[2] While this has value as a rational view of decision-making, it does not take into account other factors that affect the process, such as organizational variables, the political realities of power play in the organization, the personal ambitions, strengths and weaknesses of individual members of the staff, the innate conservatism of organizations, and the managerial competence of the decision-maker. It is naive in the extreme to believe that decision-makers, even in libraries, are always rational, thoughtful beings who can be relied upon to weigh carefully and judiciously all the factors and then make the best choice in the circumstances. It is of course not only the administrative decision-makers who can be suspected of not always making decisions designed to provide benefits for the organization; there is little doubt that many librarians taking part in surveys and studies often see little reward for themselves personally, and some even suspect that the knowledge of actual costs and performance could well lead to the questioning of the viability of some operations, with consequent changes in the status quo.

In many ways, because of the intensely political nature of macro-decision-making in any organization, it is probably more important for the librarian to establish good interpersonal relationships with the administrators than it is to produce well documented reports; while such reports will never hurt the librarian's case, the information on its own is not likely to produce results unless the political spadework has first been done. Nevertheless, despite all these necessary cautions, one must assume that evaluative methods are needed to determine the scope, quality, accessibility and usefulness of existing collections so that development can proceed in line with current needs and future goals, and remember that the major objective is to analyze the collection as a functioning unit.

A Paradigm of Collection Evaluation

It is accepted that the mark of a professional in any field is that he applies himself to supplying what his professional expertise tells him the client needs, rather than what the client wants, or says he wants. There is a difference between these three concepts of need, actual demand, and expressed demand, which is covered in greater detail in Chapter 6; and, while published work on this area in librarianship seems not to concern itself with "subconscious needs", there is little doubt that librarians must be concerned particularly with "yet un-expressed demand". The information supply agency must be managed in such a way that its clients' needs can be anticipated as much as possible and material is made available at the earliest expression of any demand.

It is possible to outline the sequence of the formulation of this information need in this fashion: an actual but unexpressed need is developed, and is followed by the conceptualization of the need in the mind; a formal statement of the need in a natural language is made and is followed by a formal statement of the need in an interface language (that is, one used by the information providing agency). However, one major problem is that a need for information may be less obvious or less spontaneous than at first appears. Steven Chweh designed a survey instrument with a list of fifty criteria library patrons might use to judge standards of quality in a library, and although most of these criteria had to do with information or information sources, the two most highly desired services were related to availability of material rather than with the provision of information.[3] It may well be that the measure of library quality has rather more to do with users' perceptions of how well it provides what they ask for and rather less to do with any perceived ideas of quality or any schedules of users' needs that information managers may have put together. Because it seems well established that there is no real quantitative relationship between user attitudes towards a library and the quality of that library, it may follow that, as far as planning and decision-making are concerned, it is not necessarily of any value to the librarian who is concerned with a quality collection to know which parts of his service most satisfy the users.

Although this kind of approach does not suffer from the major problem inherent in user studies, in that it does not need to demonstrate how to measure need, it indicates that it is dangerous to ignore the political problems. While it might be the professional duty of the librarian to supply what he thinks people need, it may also be a political and economic necessity to meet their expressed demands, as there is a great deal of evidence to suggest that the budget decision-making process is very much influenced by user satisfaction. The facts indicate that whether a library service is really any good is less important than whether the users, and in particular the decision-makers, think it is so, the placebo effect operating here as much as in medicine. This area of collection development practice is the subject of the thought-provoking paper by McMurdo (pp. 140-146) in which the question of the perceived value of a collection is given some searching attention.

It has also been argued that user studies ought to be about people rather than about the technical details of information management systems and that they also ought to be about the use that people make of information of all sorts, not just about how some people use some information, so that studies should concentrate both on the users and on the factors that are visible to them; the point must be stressed that it is dangerous to assume that a change must be socially or politically acceptable to users simply because it is technically possible.

There are also suggestions that studies based on the operations of "intermediaries" (that is, information professionals or librarians) are much less useful than are those based on information users, and that user studies in general consider factors that are really beyond the control of the managers of information systems. The range of variations in individual use patterns is so great, and so far out of the control of these information systems managers, that it may be better to concentrate on the organizational variables, which are both less variable and also more controllable. Describing an individual in terms of personal attributes helps very little, because the need to use a library is "situational", that is, a user will find himself in a situation in which "...an information practitioner would be useful,"; the reason why he is using the library has little to do with any personal factors.[4] Other studies show that the only real difference between the library user and the non-library user in general is that one group uses libraries and the other group does not. There seem to be real differences between the normal and legitimate kinds of uses made of library and information services, surveys, research, study, idle curiosity, pleasure reading, information gathering for day-to-day tasks, recreation, simple time wasting, but sometimes these differences are hard to define or difficult to see.

It is important also to remember that the information-gathering methods used by workers in different professional fields vary considerably, and that ease of access seems to be the most important single criterion, with relevance, pertinence, accuracy and currency of information being relatively less important. A research worker prefers to ask an accessible colleague rather than to go to a library, and overall there is little doubt that to many people a library means little as a source of information. Comparison of a survey made in 1950 with another made in the early 1970s shows that in this respect the situation appears not to have changed during those two decades; the 1972 thesis concludes that the information systems relied on by community groups trying to effect social change were entirely informal and interpersonal, the library playing no role in supplying information for any of the activities studied.[5]

This lack of interest in libraries as information sources is well documented, and if one looks, for example, at the techniques of biologists engaged in research, one finds that they read very few journals, publish in even fewer themselves, strongly resist the temptation to expand the number read, and identify a small number of key journals and read only those.[6] In fact these library users cope with what was once called the information explosion by largely ignoring it; they simply do not read a major part of their professional literature. A study of the amount of research (defined as "the discovering of new knowledge") that was duplicated simply because the traditional library method, a subject literature search, either was not done or was not successful, calculated that 750 research teams could have been employed with the money spent on unnecessary duplication of research in Great Britain each year.[7]

There is also the question of the "value" of the material to the user. Greene's study of browsing is limited in many ways, but nevertheless has some interesting conclusions: browsing in the stacks came out as the method most frequently used by faculty to locate books they subsequently borrowed, but when those books were ranked in terms of perceived usefulness, books found by browsing turned out to be least useful. Browsing (that is, searching along the shelves and picking out items that look interesting) resulted in more borrowing than did other methods, but also in the discovery of what subsequently were classified as the least useful books.[8]

One must be careful not to assume that use patterns or information needs are similar in different classes of library users, but it is evident that only limited use is made of library services by undergraduate students; and other studies have disclosed that the average faculty member is only barely aware of the services available in academic libraries.[9] Much the same attitude shows up in studies of public library use; there is little doubt that a minority of the population belongs to and actually uses public libraries, and only a small part of that minority is responsible for most of that use, so that if more use of public libraries in particular is wanted, it may be more profitable to concentrate on those people who are actually using them, rather than to try to attract non-users. The position seems to be that, although librarians can identify some factors such as education, family life pattern and environment that allow the prediction of library use, there are other demographic factors that appear to have no effect, and those factors that do have an effect seem to account for a small part of library use.[10]

The various findings that lead one to these conclusions may be closely related to another very serious problem in use studies, one that has been glossed over or ignored, possibly because it is too hard to solve. An assumption is made that if a researcher or librarian wants to know something about people, the simplest way to find out is to mount a survey to ask them, but recent studies have shown that a considerable amount of the variation reported in library "use" may be no more than variation in interpretation of the meaning of the word "use". Even the most common words mean different things to different people, and thus will have a serious effect on survey results. The question of different interpretations of meaning is attacked by Bookstein, who finds that much work has yet to be done before such studies have any practical significance.[11] It is difficult to demonstrate with any degree of certainty that the use of libraries has any definite influence on anything else, because the question of the identification of the factors that provoke library use is still wide open for study. Use studies provide very little help when it comes to collection development, because, despite the fact that librarians and other researchers have been studying library users for many years, we still do not have a satisfactory understanding of why people do, or do not, use libraries.

Essential Steps in Survey Design

The essential steps in the design, planning and operation of use and user studies, whether user-centred (in that concentration is on the individual person as the unit of analysis, with "user" being defined as the person using the book, periodical or segment of the collection) or collection-centred (in that the techniques rely on an examination of the collection and focus on the size, scope, depth and significance of the collection), are set out below. It should be obvious that they differ in no important respect from the requirements for any respectable piece of research.

Set Purpose and Objectives. Define the purposes of the study and the specific objectives to be met; ask if the information being sought is really needed, and precisely how it will be used when it is gathered. For instance, there is little point in taking exact measurements of several different aspects of the manner in which specific titles in a collection are used by the readers if the objective is purely to discover what there is about certain specific bibliographical sources that might influence the decisions of those readers to use or not to use those titles. A measurement of specific title use could be influenced by any of a number of quite unrelated factors, such as the popularity of that title at the time because it appeared on television, its inclusion in a reading list for an essay, the lack of any suitable alternatives for the user at the time of need, the diffidence of users in making use of an inter-library loan service or the lack of such a service in the first place, the difficulty users experienced in the bibliographical identification of the title, or the difficulty they had in finding it on the shelf. Even though all this other information may be useful as measures of other aspects of library service, it is not relevant in the measurement of the use of a particular reference source for identification.

Equally, there is no point in trying to find out how those users came to specify those particular titles, which bibliographies they used, how they managed or did not manage with the catalogue, or whether they had any problems of communicating with library staff, if the purpose of the investigation is to establish the relationship between the physical relocation of a certain section of a collection and its subsequent usage. All that is necessary in this case is to chart the relationships between physical location and use, not those between bibliographical identification and use. In practice this would mean that in this example a question extracting information on how library users obtained their information would not be relevant, no matter how carefully the question is phrased, how accurately the answers are recorded, and how precisely the results are tabulated and analyzed.

Assuming that the objective is to establish the relationships between physical location and subsequent usage patterns in specific subject areas and that an accurate and relevant answer could be produced, the next step is to ask what would be done with the information once it is gathered. Again the precise charting of the variability of use throughout the survey period will be of little practical value unless it is to be used in the planning of the relocation of part of a collection in an attempt to induce greater use of that part. Even then it may still be of little value if the reasons the section of the collection is not used are not related to the physical location of that section but are instead a factor of bibliographical redundancy, or of the unsuitable nature of the material. It is imperative that a causal relationship can be shown to exist between two factors before they are measured, as it is possibly the most elementary error in survey design at this level to assume that an observable action which precedes a second observable action is necessarily the cause of that second action; that is, the dictum *post hoc ergo propter hoc* must be demonstrated, not merely assumed.

Review Previous Research. Survey previous studies in similar fields, remembering that in the example used above, a similar field could be a study of the usage patterns of the same class of readers but in a different collection in the same library, a study of a similar kind of usage in any number of similar collections not in the same library, or a study of the use or non-use of a library of a similar kind, whether or not it includes the question of physical relocation. There is much to be learned from an evaluation of the objectives and the methods used in other surveys; at the least some insights could arise, and at best a plan or an instrument that could be adapted might be revealed. A basic tenet of any form of research ought to be that it builds on previous studies in the same field, so that it is a necessary part of a project to describe and understand what has already been done in the field, and not the least important reason is to avoid the danger of simply repeating a previous study without the rigorous controls necessary for the repetition to be regarded as a comparable replication.

Select Data to Be Collected and Methodology. Determining the precise data to be gathered and the methodology to be followed are necessary in order for the librarian to be certain of what answers are needed well before the questions are developed to elicit those answers. To vary the example, it may be judged valuable to know what are the peak times of use of a particular part of a library in order to arrange maximum staffing at those times, and minimum staffing at other times, so that any measures of use, of seat occupancy, or of internal traffic flow that do not pinpoint maximum usage rates and also precise times will be of little value. Any number of averages, or measures of central tendency, can be produced which will paint an accurate and meaningful picture of the usual or normal usage rates, and measures can easily be included which will show the deviation from those norms, but it would be necessary to know what is the maximum usage rate (however it is calculated), and also when that maximum usage occurs. Given that maximum usage rates and time must be discovered, the questions on internal traffic flow must be phrased to allow for the measurement of multiple use by each individual, duration of use, purpose of the passage, length of time of the passage, reasons that particular route was taken, and possible alternative routes. It is not necessary, in this example, to know when the journey began or ended, but it would be necessary to know why a user who was simply passing through found it desirable to use that route. Thus a question framed to elicit the information that "X people began their passage through this section at Point Y and ended it at Point Z" will not provide useful information, whereas a question that discovered that "X people entered at Point Y because Item A, needed for initial reference, is close to hand, and left by Point Z because the results of the use of Item A needed to be used again outside the section" could indicate that a simple relocation of Item A might overcome at least one traffic problem (it may of course cause others, but that is why all survey results need evaluation). Had the question been framed simply to elicit the information that users entered at Point Y to use Item A, then the decision to move Item A to another location might have produced no change in the traffic pattern, as it could still have been necessary for the users to pass through that area in order to get to Item B.

Select Population Sample. Having determined what data are to be gathered and which methodology is to be employed, the librarian then selects the sample of the population to be studied, which will certainly mean the careful study of a reputable textbook on survey design and the understanding of the simplest facets of sampling technique.[12] If it were possible to count or measure all the items in a given group at any one time, it would then be possible to describe those items in terms of the characteristics of the group, and to indicate which of the items did not fit neatly into the description and to what extent they were atypical. However, as even the fastest counting takes time, during which the items counted may change, and the most exact measurement is always an approximation between one grade on the scale and the next, then any count or measurement becomes an approximation. For all practical purposes, counting all the volumes in a particular part of a collection would produce a figure accurate enough for use, but as that method is the most costly way of doing the job, the surveyor relies on selecting some members of the group, measuring or otherwise describing the characteristics of that sample, and assuming that such a measure accurately describes the group. That is, if the sample is accurately taken, the characteristics of the sample approximate those of the group from which it was taken, or, as it is known, the "population". There are numerous factors to be taken into account in sampling.

1. The sample must be such that every member of the stratum being sampled (not necessarily the total population) has an equal chance of being selected, otherwise bias will be introduced.

2. Generally a large sample, if properly selected, will produce more accurate results, but as the cost of sampling increases at a rate greater than does that accuracy, then a trade-off must be made between sample size, sample accuracy, and total cost.

3. The sample must be of that part of the population being studied, and must be taken under conditions such that no hidden bias is introduced.

4. Because any sample will produce figures that merely "approximate" the total population, a decision must be made at the time the survey is being planned on the

level of precision (that is, how accurate is the approximate answer?) and the level of confidence (that is, how confident can the surveyor be that a true answer would have fallen within the range indicated by the sample?)

Each of these factors will be affected by sample design and by cost, and to put it simply, a trade-off is always necessary between cost, accuracy and reliability; although a bad sample, no matter how much it costs, will still be a bad sample, a good sample can be a remarkably accurate and useful method of estimating the characteristics of a total population.

Analyze Data. Determining the methods of analysis of the data, or of the observations, is much less of a chore in these days of computer-based data management, but the basic problems remain. It is necessary first of all to edit the data that have been returned from the survey instruments and make certain that the coding decisions made when the instrument was designed are not ignored. Many of the problems of coding can stem from the different meanings attached to the same words by different people, so it is essential that the classification or coding scheme used is one devised for the purpose and implemented by the surveyors. It is pointless, for instance, to ask the respondents to show whether the book used was (a) reference, (b) quick reference, (c) lending stock, (d) fiction, (e) non-fiction, or (f) serial, as any one title could conceivably be placed in any one of these categories by different respondents. It is essential that the questions be framed so that the information provided requires the coder, not the respondent, to make the decision how to code the answer. A further essential step, closely related to the problem of sampling and response rate, is a decision on how to handle incomplete responses, or what to do about non-response, as it is a basic but oft-repeated mistake to assume that a tendency disclosed in those answers that are returned would be reflected in the number that are not returned. Indeed, it may even be wise in many cases to assume that the tendency would have been exactly the opposite; that is, if the 70 per cent of those surveyed who did respond all indicated they used a section of the library because it had the material they needed, it may be wise to assume that the 30 per cent who did not respond might well have not been able to find the material they required, and that was the reason they did not respond. The second part of the analysis is the decision on the form of the graphic presentation of the results, which must be such that it describes the overall pattern accurately and simply, because that is the basic aim of statistical method. Simple tabulation, showing numbers, totals, percentages and various averages may be suitable in some applications, while bar charts, pie charts or scatter diagrams may be more suitable in others. The test is always that the presentation method should be clear, simple and accurate, and should reflect the characteristics of the population studied.

Facilitate Replication. Last of all, be prepared from the outset to chart the passage taken through the particular exercise (a) for the benefit of others who may want to try the same kind of exercise, as it is a necessary part of the professional life of the librarian to disseminate useful information, (b) for the design discipline that such charting imposes on the exercise itself, and (c) to make it possible for the whole exercise to be repeated under similar conditions simply so that the results can be verified. While it is becoming more and more necessary in these days of large centralized databanks to assure respondents that their replies and information will be kept only as long as needed for inclusion in totals, will not be identifiable, and will be destroyed as soon as processed, it is also necessary for the survey instruments and the methods of analysis and interpretation to be preserved so they can be examined and re-used.

Steps in Constructing the Survey Instrument

It is important that the subjectivity of the various measures of the quality of collections be reduced as much as possible by the use of quantitative techniques which not only count items of stock and the numbers of times they are used in some way or another, but also measure the interactions between users and the library's services as well as its stock. This is not to argue that quantitative measures, which count items and actions, are necessarily always more useful or more accurate, as the wrong kinds of analytical measures may be used, irrelevant factors may be counted, the most accurate statements may be misinterpreted, and simple mistakes may be made in the statements themselves. As the evaluation of any collection must be done with some specific purpose in mind, it is imperative that techniques of analysis be chosen that are appropriate not only for the task but also for the institution, which means the question of the aims and objectives of the institution, and thus of its library, is paramount. With this in mind, the surveyor should begin the evaluation with the identification of the specific questions to be asked, starting always by asking what kind of information is needed, which will suggest what answers are required and thus what questions should be asked, and also by questioning whether that information may be available alternatively from other sources. It is also of paramount importance that the chosen processes measure and evaluate those aspects that do have an effect, as it would seem that despite the fact that librarians and other researchers have been studying library users for many years, there is still no satisfactory understanding of why people do, or do not, use libraries, mainly because traditional approaches have relied on descriptive factors rather than on causal factors, and librarians are unable thus to predict future library patron behaviour or patterns of future library use. A discussion in detail of the technique of collection evaluation forms the basis of Chapter 5.

References

1   F.W. Lancaster, *The Measurement and Evaluation of Library Services* (Washington, D.C.: Information Resources Press, 1977), as quoted by Paul H. Mosher in "Collection Evaluation in Research Libraries: The Search for Quality, Consistency, and System in Collection Development." *Library Resources and Technical Services* 23, 1 (Winter 1979): 20.

2   Charles R. McClure, "A View from the Trenches: Costing and Performance Measures for Academic Library Public Services." *College and Research Libraries* 47 (1986): 324.

3   Steven S. Chweh, "User Criteria for Evaluation of Library Service." *Journal of Library Administration* 2, 1 (1981): 35-46.

4   Douglas L. Zweizig and Brenda Dervin, "Public Library Use, Users, Uses: Advances in Knowledge of the Characteristics and Needs of the Adult Clientele of American Public Libraries." *Advances in Librarianship*, Vol. 7, ed. Melvin Voigt (New York: Academic Press, 1977), p. 250.

5   *Ibid.*, pp. 237-238; Pauline C. Wilson, *A Community Elite and the Public Library: The Uses of Information in Leadership* (Westport, Conn.: Greenwood Press, 1977).

6   K.L. Blaxter and M.L. Blaxter, "The Individual and the Information Problem." *Nature* 246 (1973): 335-339.

7   John Martyn, "Unintentional Duplication of Research." *New Scientist* 377, 6 (1964): 338.

8   Robert J. Greene, "The Effectiveness of Browsing." *College and Research Libraries* 38 (1977): 313-316.

9   A study reported by Peter Mann in 1976 indicated that students in technology at the University of Sheffield tended to make very little use of the library and concluded that "...there is no apparent connection between failure in examinations and a lack of borrowing or purchase of books." Peter H. Mann, "Undergraduates and Books: The University Lecturer." In *Books and Undergraduates: Proceedings of a Conference Held at Royal Holloway College, University of London, 4th-6th July 1975*, ed. Peter H. Mann (London: National Book League, 1976), p. 9.

10   Carol L. Kronus, "Patterns of Adult Library Use: A Regression Path Analysis." *Adult Education* 23 (Winter 1973): 115-131.

11   Abraham Bookstein, "Sources of Error in Library Questionnaires." *Library Journal* 4 (1982): 85-94.

12   There are many useful texts available in this area. One of the standard works is C.A. Moser and G. Kalton, *Survey Methods in Social Investigation* (2nd ed. London: Heinemann, 1971). A more recent and equally useful general research text is Paul D. Leedy, *Practical Research: Planning and Design* (3rd ed. New York: Macmillan, 1985). Specifically for research in library science there is the widely available, comprehensive volume by Charles H. Busha and Stephen P. Harter, *Research Methods in Librarianship: Techniques and Interpretation* (Library and Information Science Series. New York: Academic Press, 1980). Also worthwhile is Ronald R. Powell, *Basic Research Methods for Librarians* (Library and Information Science Series. Norwood, N.J.: Ablex Publishing Company, 1985).

READINGS ON PROCEDURES FOR COLLECTION EVALUATION

This chapter has attempted first of all to explain the reasons why any system of collection evaluation is necessary, and then to establish the methodology by which such evaluation might profitably be pursued, inherent in which is an outline of the problems that are likely to be met while the operation is in train. The basics of such operations are covered in detail by Anthony Arthur (pp. 131-140), who undertook a consultancy at Swinburne Library, an establishment serving a multi-level tertiary institution (both a college of technical and further education and a college of advanced education). The aim of the consultancy was to establish a collection development policy and to provide recommendations on collection evaluation, including procedures for the evaluation of the collection, the funding of various areas, the establishment of responsibility for selection and weeding. The methodology was based very substantially on the American Library Association's *Guidelines for Collection Development* and made use of collection-centred evaluation, while emphasizing use-centred techniques. This paper is especially useful for its statement of the difference between the various kinds of techniques and Arthur's definitions of these techniques, contrasting his own method with others such as the use of expert evaluation. The various kinds of surveys can be grouped into six classes; although some doubts could well be raised about the applicability of some of these methods, they are set out in such a fashion that the paper is a necessary starting point for practical work in this field.

Some of the questions raised in this chapter are also covered by McMurdo (pp. 140-146), who sets out very strongly the case both against the need for more user studies and also against the usual simple acceptance of the argument that it must be of value to know what people think of a library because such opinions are a measure of the value of that library. McMurdo effectively demolishes such a naive approach and argues convincingly that it is not necessarily of much use to know what users think of a library (or any other operation, for that matter), if those users do not have a sufficiently broad grasp of what might be possible, rather than merely (as seems most usual) a rather sketchy knowledge of what is currently offered to them.

Anthony J. Arthur, "Collection Management - an Australian Project." *Australian Academic and Research Libraries* **17**, 1 (1986): 29-38.

Swinburne Library is a central library which serves a multi-level institution with both a College of Technical and Further Education and a College of Advanced Education. At the end of 1984 it served over 11,000 students and held in its collection 242,000 items, including 165,000 monographs. Little used titles are stored in a closed access stack.

The collection management project undertaken during 1983 and 1984 had its origins in Swinburne Library's need to find a solution to the problem of a rapidly expanding collection for which there was no storage space within Swinburne.

In 1982 and 1983 the Library had taken measures to alleviate this problem, removing excess duplicates and low use unique titles, which were identified by a specially written computer program analysing data from Swinburne's in-house automated circulation system. Teaching staff were invited to vet the items to be relocated or discarded.

While these exercises succeeded in removing sufficient items from the Library's shelves to make space available for several years' new acquisitions, they drew strong criticism from some academic staff who opposed the removal of material from the Library and/or disagreed with the criteria being used.

They also highlighted the need for a total review of the Library's collecting practices.

Objectives of the Consultancy

In response to this situation the author was appointed as consultant, on secondment from Melbourne College of Advanced Education, Institute of Early Childhood Development, with the brief to establish a collection policy and develop policies and procedures for: evaluation of the adequacy of the collection, appropriate funding of the various areas of the collection, the appropriate division of responsibility for selection of library materials between library and teaching staff and the discard and relocation of library materials. Thus the problem of space was placed firmly in the context of the management of the collection as a whole.

Methodology

The methodology of the project was based on the American Library Association's *Guidelines for Collection Development*[1] and the addendum on use and user studies[2] which provided, for each of the areas of the brief, a theoretical discussion of the topic, practical guidelines to follow and reference to the original works on which they were based. Further direction was provided by the published Australian works on the writing of collection policy statements, [3, 4] on aspects of collection use[5] and on selection practices.[6]

In this project the major task of writing the collection policy and the related task of evaluation of the adequacy of the collection, integrated collection-centred and use-centred techniques of evaluation, with an emphasis on the latter. Collection-centred evaluation is described in the ALA *Guidelines* as focussing on "the size, scope, depth and significance of the collection (using such) techniques as checking lists, catalogs, bibliographies, (and) looking over materials on the shelf and compiling statistics",[7] while use-centred evaluation is based on various surveys of the library's capacity to meet its users' needs.

Collection-centred methods were used in the writing of the collection policy in that teaching staff evaluated the collections they used and described what they perceived to be a desirable collection. Use-centred techniques, i.e. use and user studies, were employed to obtain objective data about the collection and how it was used, to balance these statements of perceived need by the academic staff.

The collection policy was to be formulated from the data from the user studies and the collection goals identified by teaching staff tempered by the capacities of the Library to achieve them given the constraints of space, finance and staffing.

This approach contrasts with other work undertaken in Australia which had focussed on writing collection policies using evaluation by expert librarians or teachers alone (collection-centred evaluation) or where use and user studies were carried out outside the perspectives of collection management.

Surveys

The key surveys, apart from the major work of the collection policy survey were:

1. an Availability Study (alternatively known as a user and stock failure study)
2. a study of interlibrary loan requests
3. two surveys of periodicals use
4. a survey of Swinburne staff on selecting items for the Library
5. an in-house use study (study of use of monographs within the Library).

The information from the latter two, while primarily intended to provide data for the development of policy in the areas of selection responsibility, and discard and relocation respectively, also provided useful information about collection use. A variety of approaches was used to complete all these surveys over a relatively short time, basically 11 months. For example, the Availability Study has been carried out with the participation of the RMIT [Royal Melbourne Institute of Technology] Department of Librarianship which had developed a useful model. The data were analysed by two RMIT students. The SPSSX program used to process the data was written by one of the lecturers in the Swinburne Maths Department.

The survey of staff selection practices was conducted by students of the Swinburne Graduate Diploma of Urban Sociology, who used a questionnaire based on a rough draft of a survey originally carried out at the University of Queensland,[6] modified extensively by the consultant and the Swinburne Library staff.

This approach was not without its drawbacks in terms of control and meeting deadlines, but it did provide resources for carrying out important surveys that could not otherwise have been performed.

It should also be pointed out that the requirement for extra staff in carrying out a large number of surveys in a short period of time is quite high, including interviewers, checkers, typists, reference staff drafting collection policies, attendants marking all items to be reshelved, and Circulation staff following up overdue items which are part of samples. Just about all of the Library staff were involved in some aspect of the project.

The Collection Policy

The collection policy was intended from its inception to be not only a policy but a political document in that it would be a blueprint for the development of the collection (and development includes relocation and discard). This is one of the major reasons why the departments were requested to supply the bulk of the information for the policy, and especially the evaluations of each Dewey area of the Library collection they used, and the needs of those areas for development, which would comprise a major part of the collection policy. Another reason was that, in common with most other CAE [college of advanced education] libraries, teaching staff at Swinburne undertook most of the selection of Library materials and thus are de facto "subject experts". Politically also, close involvement in the survey work on the part of the departments was felt likely to encourage their later support for the completed policy as well as increasing their understanding of the purpose of the project. To emphasize the importance of the project the Swinburne librarian and the consultant formally met with all the deans, and heads of TAFE [technical and further education] Divisions, and then with the heads of every department. It was intended to convey in very strong terms that the Library was engaged in a project to improve management of its collections and services and that it wanted to involve the teaching staff in the management process.

The Collection Policy Survey Form

The form of the policy was to comprise separate statements by all departments defining their general objectives and a detailed analysis of the subject areas of the collection they used. To bring together all this separate departmental information about each collection, a subject index in Dewey order has been compiled. This shows which departments use which collections and clearly indicates areas where more than one department has an interest in the collection.

This can be consulted when any area has been identified for development or discard and relocation and all departments with an interest can be involved.

Departments were surveyed by questionnaires, on which librarians filled in as much of the detail as possible from their own knowledge. This was to reduce the workload on the departments and to provide extra guidance for them. The form comprised two parts - a departmental profile and a collection assessment section. The profile was to provide details of the courses and subjects taught, levels of study (undergraduate, graduate diploma, etc.), the number of enrolments, statements of departmental attitudes to the provision of multiple copies, textbooks etc., details of departmental research, planned new courses, and finally a statement of their assessment of the adequacy of their budget allocation for library materials.

The second section was a detailed description of the areas of study, the Dewey ranges for materials supporting these areas and an assessment of these collections (a department might have to complete between three and twenty forms depending upon the range of areas of the collection drawn on in teaching).

The assessment was in terms of the adequacy of the number of books in each section, the number of multiple copies, the currency of the material and whether there were enough periodicals to support current course needs and whether back runs of periodicals were adequate. An assessment of the non-book and reference collections for each area was also requested. Respondents were then requested to identify any areas in which they believed extra or different material was required and to put these areas into priority order for development. Finally, they were asked to assign a qualitative level to the collection as it existed and the level they would like to see the collection reach.

While the definition of level of the collection followed the recommendations from the Acquisitions Special Interest Group's "Study Session on Selection Policies" held at the 1982 LAA [Library Association of Australia] Biennial Conference[8] (i.e. a division into Representative, Selective, In Depth, and Comprehensive), the Selective category was divided further into two sub-sections to reflect the greater amount of undergraduate material in the Swinburne collection. These were based on definitions for college libraries taken from the ALA *Guidelines* and were "Initial Study Level - a collection which is adequate to support undergraduate courses" and "Advanced Study Level - a collection which is adequate to support graduate diplomas but is less than research intensity".

As described previously, in the methodology section, the departmental statements about the need for development of an area or its development to a higher level are to be modified by the Library and priorities for development set. They will then be discussed with each department with the view to obtaining agreement on the modifications and on the priorities. When negotiations have taken place with each department priorities for the development of the collection as a whole would be set.

To facilitate these discussions and to provide a framework for continuing collection management, including liaison with departments and ongoing collection evaluation, a structure was established. This includes as its main elements a Collection Management Librarian and Collection Development Groups for each department. The document which will set out the agreed priorities for collection development will be an appendix to the Collection Policy known as the Collection Management Plan.

Collection Management Librarian

Because of the wide range and complexity of tasks involved in ongoing collection evaluation and development, especially the time consuming task of coordinating liaison between the Library and the departments, a full-time position was established. This librarian will also be responsible for policy development in a range of areas such as discard and relocation, collection maintenance and regional cooperative collection development.

Administratively, this position is part of the Acquisitions and Collection Management Section.

Collection Development Groups

In order to provide a formal structure for the discussions with departments about their collection development needs and priorities, these groups are being established for each teaching department or division to participate with the Library in continuing collection development, evaluation and review. Their membership includes a representative from each major subject grouping in each department, the Collection Management Librarian, the liaison Librarian for the department and the Periodicals Librarian and Audio-visual Librarian when required.

Among the other tasks of these groups is to provide a channel for communication between the Library and the department on specific collection development matters, to take part in ongoing evaluation of the collection and to offer advice in establishing short and long term goals for collection development. It also seems likely that they will participate in the process of selection of items for relocation or discard.

Collection Management Plan

This document includes the agreed statements about further development of the Library collection made by each department and also the priorities for development mutually agreed. It will also include quantifications and costing of the individual departmental needs for development.

Finally, it would draw these departmental plans together, set them in overall priority order and detail what financial resources should be allocated to them. In this way a clear statement is available of the overall needs of the collection for development, the current priorities, the costs, and a timetable for their completion.

Collection Evaluation through Use and User Studies

Most of the different types of use and user studies described by the ALA were utilized, including: circulation studies, survey of user opinion, availability studies and in-house use studies.

Circulation data were examined to identify user populations and patterns of use, the purpose being to establish whether any areas were high or low use.

Staff opinions were canvassed through both the Collections Policy Survey and also the Survey of Swinburne Staff on Selecting Items for the Library where the "experts" were the individual teaching staff who were surveyed. In the context of establishing who selected, how much they selected, why they selected and the sources they used, the respondents (in this case the whole teaching staff) were asked to provide an evaluation of the collection. Assessment was in terms of the adequacy of the collections of monographs, periodicals and audio-visual materials to meet teaching needs. Further, they were asked to evaluate their adequacy for such major purposes as research, consultancies, and preparation of a manuscript for publication.

These individual responses were analysed down by faculty of the respondent and compared to the department evaluation contained in the Collection Policy Survey.

The Availability Study used the model developed by McIntyre at RMIT and fully described by Broadbent.[9] During a one week survey a sample of 2500 people were interviewed as they left the Library and asked whether they had been looking for specific items and whether they found them. Unlike the previous surveys mentioned, in this one the majority of the respondents were students. The main measure of collection adequacy was the "reader satisfaction rate", which is a percentage figure based on a comparison of the number of known items the users reported seeking and the number they found. In Swinburne's case the rate compared favourably with those in similar studies conducted elsewhere and indicated a high degree of satisfaction, i.e. the Library had a high percentage of the items users wanted. This overall rate was examined by user categories to ascertain any area which differed significantly from the average, indicating possible weakness in that collection in terms of meeting its users' needs.

The survey also covered areas such as availability of items, techniques of searching for material and the reasons why people were present in the Library.

A survey of all interlibrary loan requests for 1983 was conducted to identify any weaknesses in the collection indicated by any department requesting more than average amounts of material on one subject or by identifying frequently requested periodical titles which should perhaps be held. Several titles were identified and recommended for purchase.

The Audio-visual Librarian carried out a separate survey of the adequacy of that collection, looking at loans records, to provide information to be incorporated in this project.

This wide range of surveys provided direct evaluation of the existing collection by departments and teaching staff, and indirect evaluation by other user groups through the various use and user studies. They provided both objective data and a comprehensive profile of the adequacy of the existing collection and its capacity to meet users' needs.

Discard and Relocation of Library Materials

As it was the problem of lack of space that prompted the project, there was some emphasis on work in this area.

It became apparent that the problem was being exacerbated by the changing goals of the academic programme following upon the growth of higher degrees and the growing expectation that teaching staff should pursue research and the Library should support both, by building research level collections.

Although all possible ways of expanding the capacity of on-campus storage were investigated and the most practical of these recommended for adoption, it was nevertheless clear that within a few years all available space would be filled and, each year, almost as many items would have to be relocated or discarded as were acquired. Investigation then focussed on the most effective and economical ways of selecting materials for discard and relocation, at the same time looking at methods of securing the cooperation of the teaching departments in this process.

In-house Use Survey

Among the aspects of collection use surveyed for this purpose were in-house use and browsing use of the collection.

As noted earlier, the Library was already relocating or discarding materials which had little or no use as measured by circulation. These were identified by a computer program which analysed circulation records, but it was not known to what extent these items were used in the Library and hence were of value to users.

In this survey, conducted over a ten week period, the definition of in-house use was narrowly restricted to items left on tables and sorting shelves. All items reshelved were marked every time they were reshelved. A random sample of titles from the whole collection was taken from the shelf list. Samples were also taken from twelve specific Dewey areas to see what, if any, variation occurred in different areas of the collection.

The books identified were checked for marking and for date stamps, indicating use in-house or loan use respectively. The results showed that for the collection as a whole around 6% were used in the Library but did not circulate. There was considerable variation in such use, ranging from a high of 9% for the 790s to a low of 2% for the 370s. It would seem that, except in those areas recording low in-house use percentages in this survey, it was unwise to base decisions about the discard of items on circulation data alone.

Browsing Use

Data from the Availability Study were analysed to establish what percentage of the total items sought were looked for by users browsing and if there were any areas of the collection accessed substantially in this way. Overall the study indicated that about 15% of those seeking items in the Library did so by browsing. Respondents from one faculty reported using this approach in 40% of searches. These figures suggest that in any relocation programme a significant proportion of material in some subject areas may have to remain in the Library, as it is accessed primarily by browsing.

Periodicals

For periodicals a different approach was taken. The aim was to test the hypothesis (suggested by earlier analysis of interlibrary loan requests) that the main use of periodicals was centred on issues published in the last fifteen years, with a view to storing or discarding those published earlier, were the hypothesis proven.

The two surveys conducted to test this consisted of an analysis of overnight loans over a semester, and an examination of in-house use, as measured by items reshelved over a ten week period.

The method employed was the same employed in the survey of in-house use of monographs. Over 75% of the uses, recorded in both periodicals use surveys, were of issues published since 1980 and a further 15% to 20% within the period 1970-1979, thus confirming the hypothesis.

Recommendations about Discard and Relocation

Although these surveys indicated that selection for discard and relocation on the basis of low circulation use alone was not a foolproof approach to the problem, the high cost of title by title selection led to the recommendation that selection continue to be on the basis of loan history but with input from the Collection Development Groups. It was hoped that the negative attitudes of teaching staff to the process might be reduced if they were involved through these groups. Participation in the group would allow members to gain experience of the process of collection development as a whole. It was suggested that the groups might select "core-titles" in their subject areas and that these could be tagged on the circulation database so that they would be exempted from the automatic selection process.

Other recommended approaches were that rates of selection should be varied according to whether it was a high or low use subject area, whether a high percentage of those using it browsed or not, differing obsolescence rates of the material and the proportion of in-house to circulation use.

As a means of reducing the number of unique titles that would have to be treated it was recommended that the current and relatively automatic process of discarding low use duplicates and duplicate copies of earlier editions of textbooks should continue.

Appropriate Funding

The relative success or failure of the present system of budget allocation, where each department is allocated an amount from Library funds based on student numbers, was measured by examination of data from a number of surveys.

In response to a direct question in the Collection Policy Survey about the adequacy of their budget allocation, the majority of departments reported that they were satisfied with the total amount, but many were dissatisfied with the proportion allocated by the Library to the different areas of monographs, periodicals and audio-visual material. Most departments wanted a larger proportion in the last two categories.

The Availability Study gave an indirect measure of the success of the allocation procedure in terms of the measure known as the "Reader Satisfaction Rate" (noted above) with students from at least one faculty having a rate well below average. This was interpreted as an indication that their faculty allocation may have been too low.

On balance, the evidence suggested that allocation using student numbers as a basis has been generally satisfactory. It was recommended that the process be modified by the agreed priorities from the Collection Policy, and that it take into account such factors as differential prices for books in different subject areas. It was further decided that there be a separate allocation for areas needing development.

Appropriate Division of Responsibility for Selection

At Swinburne the teaching staff take the main responsibility for selection with assistance from the Library which distributes book reviews, publishers' blurbs, and "on-approval slips" from Blackwell and Bumpus-Haldane.

As one of the aims of a collection policy is to enable selectors to work with greater consistency toward defined goals, a survey was undertaken to establish the extent to which staff were selecting according to any guidelines or overall plan, or whether they selected simply to support their own interests. Staff were also asked about the main reasons for selection, e.g. selecting to support teaching or research, and their main sources of information. The results indicated that the collection was being developed in a very haphazard manner - less than 30% reported any awareness of departmental guidelines to assist selection, and close to 60% believed that their department had a more ad hoc approach to library ordering, leaving it to individual staff members rather than having an overall plan.

Further, the assistance provided by the Library was not rated particularly highly, with the exception of the provision of publishers' blurbs.

Departments should have become more conscious of the need for planning the development of collections in their areas through the actual exercise of completing the Collection Policy Survey. The existence of the Collection Development Plan and the Collection Development Groups should provide more guidance in this area and provide a basis for a collection being built on more logical grounds.

Conclusion

What has been described in this paper is only the broad outline of the surveys and analysis that went into the full report to the Swinburne Librarian.[10]

At the end of 1985 edited drafts of the Collection Policy had been discussed with and accepted by a number of departments and Collection Development Groups were being set up. In these areas there is much goodwill toward the project and management of the collection is becoming reality.

Swinburne has collection management policies that can be used both as planning tools and communication devices. The emphasis on use and user studies has given a more objective understanding of the collections and how they are used, enabling decisions about resource allocation to take a place in a more rational way.

In an environment where libraries have increasingly to justify their budgeting and space needs, and hence formalize and modify their collection management practices, this project has demonstrated that, given appropriate resources, a library can usefully follow ALA *Guidelines* in an Australian setting.

References

1   American Library Association. Collection Development Committee, *Guidelines for Collection Development*, ed. David L. Perkins (Chicago, Ill.: American Library Association, 1979).

2   Dorothy E. Christiansen, C.E. Davis, and Jutta Reed Scott, "Guide to Collection Evaluation through Use and User Studies." *Library Resources and Technical Services* 27(1983): 434-440.

3   Juliet Flesch, "Collection Development at Melbourne University Library." *Australian Academic and Research Libraries* 14, 11 (March 1983): 21-27.

4   Jo McLachlan and Isabella Trahn, "A Method of Collection Evaluation for Australian Research Libraries." *University of New South Wales Library Annual Report* (1982): 51-61.

5   L.B. McIntyre, *Stock Failure in RMIT Central Library 1978-1981* (Melbourne: Royal Melbourne Institute of Technology, Department of Librarianship, 1981).

6   Joy Guyatt, *Towards a Collection Development Policy: A First Essay* (St. Lucia: University of Queensland, Tertiary Education Institute, 1981).

7   Christiansen, *op.cit.*, p. 434.

8   "Editorial Note." *Australian Academic and Research Libraries* 14 (1983): 36.

9   Marianne Broadbent, "Who Wins? Who Loses? User Success and Failure in the State Library of Victoria." *Australian Academic and Research Libraries* 15(1984): 65-80.

10   Copies of the full report are available for purchase from the Swinburne Library, John St., Hawthorn, Vic. 3122 (A$30 + A$5 handling prepaid).

George McMurdo, "User Satisfaction." *New Library World* 81, 958 (1980): 83-85.

User studies proliferate in the literature of librarianship and information science. As early as 1967 one bibliography of library user studies contained 547 references.[1] The popularity of the user study is probably a function of the service-orientation of contemporary library philosophy. Librarians have become increasingly sensitive to user requirements and the user study offers a means of defining a library's clientele, establishing levels of demand for various services, and tailoring those services to meet the interests of that clientele. While some user studies have restricted themselves to gathering data about patterns of library use, many aim at evaluating users' attitudes to the library, and assessing the degree of satisfaction being achieved.

The majority of user studies have based their data collection on interviews, questionnaires, participant observation, diaries and intuition. Such techniques are inherently subjective and the data they yield lack the authority of more objective studies. It has been observed of the general run of user study that:

Generalisations based upon data yielded by heterogeneous investigations of varying merit are of arguable validity and are certainly not universally applicable: each will be false in some circumstances.[2]

The methods used by librarians to gather information about their clients have generally lacked scientific rigour. This failure is evidenced by, on the one hand, little sign of this literature progressing according to a logical structure. The volume of publishing activity should by now have produced a sophisticated body of knowledge. In reality, lack of both scientific technique and methodological uniformity has generated a rambling, redundant literature little of which is competent to be used as a foundation of further work.

The solution to this problem obviously lies in the development of more stringent investigative techniques, though it is possible that librarians may find discouraging the process of accumulating empirical knowledge through scientific research.[3] At any rate, the point being made here is that while there is a consensus that user studies are a worthy topic, current methodology frequently undermines the confidence with which the result of such studies can be accepted.

With particular regard to studies of user satisfaction, however, even if the data were to be obtained by acceptable methods, there is still a considerable area of doubt as to how far librarians should be influenced by the preferences of their users. A number of writers [4, 5, 6] have cautioned that the attitudes of users may bear little relation to the provision of a good library service. Menzel, for example, argues that "valuable information" may well not be the information that users are aware of wanting.[4] Stecher is more emphatic, stating that:[5] There is no valid quantitative relationship between user attitudes and the quality of the library. This viewpoint approximates to the doctor-patient analogy raised during discussion of librarianship's status as a profession. Patients do not write their own prescriptions. The doctor who allowed his patients to decide their own treatments would be in breach of his ethical code. Analogously, the library user is not fit to decide how a library should function in order to serve his own best interests. Certainly, the user is the final arbiter in judging the relevance in relation to his own needs of any document supplied to him by the library, but he is not qualified to comment on how the system which supplied that document should operate. To take any other viewpoint negates the training deemed necessary to becoming a professional librarian.

Consequently - as far as planning and decision making is concerned - it is not necessarily of value to the librarian to know which aspects of his service engender user satisfaction. While it is possible that under certain conditions user satisfaction will in fact coincide with what would be professionally regarded as good library service, it is not axiomatic that there will be a consistent correlation. For all practical purposes user satisfaction must be disregarded as anything other than a supportive measure.

Although user satisfaction is therefore of limited direct value to practical library decision making, it would be unpragmatic to disavow totally the concept of user satisfaction. Wills offers a perceptive comment on this subject:[7]

Making decisions about a library's operation based on user's preference is considered unwise because users do not know what they want in terms of information services. However, there is a counter argument. To ignore the political basis of library decision making is unrealistic. There is a great deal of evidence that the budget decision making process is very much influenced by users' satisfaction with a library system.

Wills is acknowledging a fact of life. Librarians have always been plagued by inability to quantify the value of their services and thus objectively justify budget requests. Even in the academic sector where libraries have traditionally been assumed to have value "per se", librarians are facing new pressures to justify their budgets. Conventional library objectives and evaluation techniques tend to be inwardly directed. Performance measures such as exposure time, item-use-days, effective user hours, retrieval time, precision, recall, and statistics of internal library operations, though highly meaningful within the profession, will generally be unintelligible to the user.

In recent years modern management techniques have been applied to library resource allocation. The Planning Programming Budgeting System,[8] cost benefit,[9] and cost-effectiveness[10] have been introduced with some success to demonstrate library effectiveness, but have generally foundered over quantification of the ultimate benefit of information in terms of value to the user. A recent study of criteria actually being used for the evaluation of library performance surveyed sixty-two libraries' annual reports which included 774 criteria of various types, but failed to locate a single instance of cost-effectiveness or cost-benefit being used as criteria.[11] So, while librarians may ultimately need to perfect objective techniques of financial analysis, in the short term Wills'[7] comment about user satisfaction influencing budget decision making may be the pragmatist's alternative, and it is clear that many user studies - though ostensibly aimed at gauging demand or identifying areas for development - are also, consciously or unconsciously, "taking the temperature" of user attitudes.

Sensitivity to user attitudes is entirely healthy and the librarian who paid no attention to the view of his users would be regarded as having severe communication problems. The difficulty about user attitudes arises when one recalls Stecher's premise that there is no valid relationship between user attitudes and quality of library service.[5] The realistic librarian thus has to pursue both the goal of quality library service and the goal of user satisfaction in the disconcerting knowledge that the two may be independent. The implication is that through inattention to user attitudes - or even through pursuing a policy, in their best interests, but unpopular with users - a professionally competent librarian might be negatively perceived. The corollary to this implication is arguably more insidious in that an incompetent librarian might survive by concentrating on maximizing user satisfaction as an end in itself.

This article has introduced the notion of user satisfaction as an end in itself, to be pursued perhaps as a surrogate for actual quality of library service, of which it may be independent. To explore further this notion hypotheses will be set up which hold that under certain conditions user satisfaction may not only be independent of, but actually contradictory to professional interpretations of good library service. These hypotheses will relate to situations in which some form of delay is imposed on the library user.

Delay in Delivery of a Document

By inspection it would seem indisputable that delay in access to a document will generate user dissatisfaction. Nevertheless, a number of studies of the effect of delay in the supply of inter-library loan material do not support this expectation,[12, 13] and Houghton[14] found that: "It would appear that delay is not a critical factor as viewed by librarians: only ten per cent of the respondents reported any inconvenience." This finding is startling by itself. However, it is even possible that user satisfaction can actually be increased by delay. Consider the user waiting for his reservation or inter-library loan to be supplied. Over and above the objective value that document has, the user invests the waited-for-item with subjective value which relates to the act of waiting. Simmell[15] has suggested that even where objects possess no intrinsic value, a substitute for this is furnished by the mere difficulty of acquiring them.

It is important to note that we are talking only about the subjective value of the document, for otherwise a logical extension of this argument leads to the absurd position of a user - faced with the option of immediate access or delay - preferring delay. This argument finds support in the literature of social psychology from a number of closely related concepts including dissonance,[16] inequity[17] cognitive balancing and congruity,[18] which are collectively known as balance theories. The basic postulate of the balance theories is that there is a need for socialised humans to maintain an equilibrium between psychological investment and perceived rewards.

In the case of the library user waiting for a document, the imbalance created by the investment of waiting time is reduced by the subjective worth of the document when it is finally delivered. Conversely a document delivered immediately will be attributed a lower subjective value.

Restricted Access to the Librarian

A comparable balance effect may apply when a user has to wait to speak with a librarian. For example, Schwarz observes that in seeking professional help a client will not always be encouraged by the granting of an immediate appointment, or discovering an empty waiting-room when he arrived for the appointment.[19] Schwarz notes that: "...services to which we have immediate access - which we can acquire without waiting - are of relatively little value to us." There is a parallel between this observation and the perennial debate over professionals or non-professional manning of library service-points. The view advocating the use of non-professionals is exemplified by Jestes:[20] "Professional librarians, although still immediately available to any patron, would be freed from many interruptions and better able to concentrate on collection development."

Wheeler states the case for the opposition:[21] "The idea that inquiries should be presented to inexperienced persons and fed upward to those qualified to help is disservice and inconvenience to readers, partly because the inexperienced do not know where the question should lead." An unconsidered side-issue in this debate is the possibility that by restricting access to the professional librarian, users' eventual satisfaction with whatever information or service the professional eventually provides may be increased. For if the professional librarian is to be directly available, then: "Such ease of access may speak unfavourably of the server's scarcity as a social or economic resource: it may disconfirm the worth of his service. In contrast, those who confront obstacles to service tend to have more confidence in its value, once it is acquired."[19] Thus, by distancing himself from the user by means of non-professional intermediaries, the librarian is not only "better able to concentrate on collection development, etc.", but when he actually does provide a direct personal service to the user, that service will be more highly valued and accepted with greater confidence.

Considering the implications for the profession of these hypotheses, first, one prerequisite to the attainment of professional status (in the sociological definition) is the formulation of, and adherence to, a code of ethics. The independence between user attitudes and quality of library service is potentially an ethical question. Goode, for example, discussing censorship, cites a survey in which nearly two-thirds of the sampled librarians involved in book selection decisions reported instances of not buying books which were thought to be controversial.[22] Goode's observation with regard to this dilemma - and presumably it would be valid to extrapolate this observation to all instances where user attitude diverges from quality of service that there is a: "...simple ethical duty to follow professional principles...and to ignore lay opinion as irrelevant and incompetent." The ethical problem of this divergence is synthesised by a recent paper which studied the relationship between public relations activities and budget allocation in public libraries.[23] The use of promotional techniques may be useful for bringing the library to the attention of the potential user. Ethical questions arise, however, when PR work provides a short-cut to a larger slice of the budgetary cake. We have to differentiate between, on the one hand, a user lobby for enhanced funding which has been genuinely generated through contact with, and appreciation of, the existing library service, and on the other hand, an apparent user lobby which has actually been whipped up by skilful PR activities and may bear little relation to the existing, and possible undeserving, library service.

Secondly, with regard to the more specific hypotheses about waiting behaviour, where user satisfaction was not only independent of, but actually contrary to, professional interpretations of quality library service, librarians are faced with the opportunity to exploit the user. It would hypothetically by possible for a Machiavellian librarian to use behaviour and procedures which would enhance the user's satisfaction beyond the level actually merited by the library service. The point here is that it becomes the ethical duty of the librarian, and the profession as a whole, to recognise the existence and potential of these phenomena and - if they are judged to be against users' interests - to thereafter shun their use.

To summarize, this speculative article has at best provided a novel viewpoint on an existing body of literature. Its observations have sought to be thought provoking, but they are always essentially hypothetical and thus of little practical value until validated (or rejected) experimentally. Those hypotheses relating to the paradoxical effects of waiting may be considered esoteric, or even contrived. Nevertheless, if librarianship is to attain the status of a profession in the sociological sense - and there are strong reasons for pessimism - the inadequacy of the existing librarian-user relationship must be resolved.

Intellectually, the librarian must work within the client's limitations, instead of imposing his professional categories, conceptions, and authority on the client. In other professions, too, the practitioner must understand the client's notions, but enough to elicit adequate information and cooperation from him. The practitioner can solve the problem even if the client never understands what the professional is doing.[23]

We in librarianship need to subject the librarian-user interface to rigorous scientific study to enable the development of methodologies which will allow us to "diagnose" a user's information requirements as accurately as a doctor might diagnose his physical ailments. Until this level of understanding is attained, and the librarian is free to work to his own intellectual limitations, rather than those of this clients, the librarian is doomed to be: ...a gatekeeper who can exclude almost no one; a guardian who can protect primarily against vandals and thieves; a stock room custodian who must hand over any of his stock even if he is sure the person really wants or needs something else.[22]

References

1   L.C. Deweese, "A Bibliography of Library User Studies." In *Report on a Statistical Study of Book Use*, ed. A.K. Jain (CFSTI, 1967).

2   C.W. Hanson, *Introduction to Science-information Work* (London: Aslib, 1971), p. 51.

3   G. McMurdo, "Psychology and Librarianship: An Appraisal of the Potential of Experimental Psychology in the Study of Librarian-Client Behaviour." *Aslib Proceedings* (June 1980).

4   H. Menzel, "Can Science Information Needs Be Ascertained Empirically?" In *Communication, Concepts, and Perspectives*, ed. L. Thayer (Spartan Books, 1967).

5   G. Stecher, "Library Evaluation: A Brief Survey of Studies in Quantification." *Australian Academic and Research Libraries* 6 (March 1975): 1-19.

6   Richard H. Orr, "Measuring the Goodness of Library Services: A General Framework for Considering Quantitative Measures." *Journal of Documentation* 29, 3 (September 1973): 315-332.

7   G. Wills, and C. Oldman, *The Beneficial Library* (BLRD Report 5389. London: British Library, 1977).

8   D. Mason, "PPBS: Application to an Industrial Information and Library Service." *Journal of Librarianship* 4, 2 (April 1972): 91-105.

9   M.S. Magson, "Techniques for the Measurement of Cost-benefit in Information Centres." *Aslib Proceedings* 25, 5 (May 1973): 164-185.

10   A.D.J. Flowerdew and C.M.E. Whitehead, *Cost-effectiveness and Cost/Benefit Analysis in Information Science* (OSTI Report 5206. London: Office of Scientific and Technical Information, 1974).

11   John J. Knightly, "Overcoming the Criterion Problem in the Evaluation of Library Performance." *Special Libraries* 70, 4 (April 1979): 173-178.

12   D. Barr and J. Farmer, "Waiting for Inter-library Loans." *BLL Review* 5, 1 (1977): 8-12.

13   M. Stuart, "Some Effects on Library Users of the Delays in Supplying Publications." *Aslib Proceedings* 29, 1 (January 1977): 35-45.

14   B. Houghton and C. Prosser, "A Survey of the Opinions of British Library Lending Division Users in Special Libraries on the Effects of Nonimmediate Access to Journals." *Aslib Proceedings* 26, 9 (September 1974): 354-366.

15   G. Simmel, "Philosophie des Geldes." In *George Simmel: On Individuality and Social Forms*, ed. Donald N. Levine (Chicago, Ill.: University of Chicago Press, 1971), pp. 43-69.

16   L. Festinger, *A Theory of Cognitive Dissonance* (Stanford: Stanford University Press, 1957).

17   J.S. Adams, "Towards an Understanding of Inequity." *Journal of Abnormal and Social Psychology* 67, 5 (1963): 422-436.

18 R.B. Zajonc, "The Concepts of Balance, Congruity, and Dissonance." *Public Opinion Quarterly* 24 (1960): 280-296.

19 B. Schwarz, "Waiting Exchange and Power: The Distribution of Time in Social Systems." *American Journal of Sociology* 79, 4 (1974): 841-870.

20 E. Jestes and W.D. Laird, "A Time Study of General Reference Work in a University Library." *Research in Librarianship* 2, 7 (1968): 9-16.

21 J. Wheeler and H. Goldhor, *Practical Administration of Public Libraries* (New York: Harper and Row, 1962), p. 324.

22 W.J. Goode, "The Librarian: From Occupation to Profession." *Library Quarterly* 31, 4 (1961): 306-318.

23 P. Berger, "An Investigation of the Relationship between Public Relations Activities and Budget Allocation in Public Libraries." *Information Processing and Management* 15, 4 (1979): 179-193.

CHAPTER 5

METHODS OF COLLECTION EVALUATION

Kinds of Evaluation Studies

In this chapter the question of how collections can be evaluated is discussed, as it has yet to be demonstrated conclusively that the size of a library collection alone can be taken as a measure of its worth. Because of this, it is necessary to establish some measures that indicate the worth of a library,[1] and it becomes necessary to make some basic assumptions, such as: use of a book is a measure of its value, past use of books is a valid indicator of likely future use, circulation figures are an indication of the actual use of an item, or measurements of use in the library are indicators of use outside the library.

The most important argument against this approach is that measures of past use show what was done, whereas what ought to have been done is perhaps more important. Underlying methods of analysis of use or user statistics there is a basic assumption that value is directly proportionate to use. However, it might be suggested that availability of material, rather than ideas of perceived value, is the most significant factor affecting material use, so that measurement of use is a doubtful method of measuring value, even though it may well be a good measure of availability; and that to calculate future use in terms of present use is almost certain to guarantee the status quo - "more of the same". There is also an implied assumption underlying these studies that knowing what people need can be translated into a service that people will use to satisfy their needs.

While a distinction between *use studies* and *user studies* may be valuable, it is preferable to concentrate on the difference between *user-oriented* and *library-oriented* studies. Many studies, both user-oriented and library-oriented, assume that use of the literature of a subject is equivalent to a search for information; but there can be many reasons for using literature, and information seeking may be only one of those. The processes of evaluating a collection presume that the evaluation is taking place for a particular purpose, and thus a method appropriate for that purpose must be chosen. Considerations as basic as "what are the institution's missions and goals?" need definition, and the precise purposes of the study must be spelled out. For instance, if the purpose is evaluation for comparison with other collections for planning purposes, methods differ from those used if the evaluation is for certification of a new degree programme supported by a library collection. It is essential that the study be designed with an overall view of its usefulness and applicability. As a starting point, any approach to use or user studies needs to ask these questions:[2]

1. What is the goal of the study?
2. What are the parameters of the study? (Which segments of the collection are to be studied? What kinds of samples are to be taken of the population? Which specific aspects of collection development are to be analyzed?)
3. Which aspects of collection use are to be analyzed?
4. Can the necessary information or significant data be gathered?
5. Is the method appropriate for the purpose?
6. What is the possible range of findings that might result from the surveys?
7. What are the practical benefits that might result from any findings?
8. What are the implications of the process itself in terms of likely impact on services, operations and the political environment in which the library operates?

The essential steps in the design, planning and operation of use and user studies were mentioned in the previous chapter. To recap, they are:

1. Define the purposes of the study and the hypotheses to be studied. Ask if the information is really needed, and exactly how will it be used.
2. Survey any previous relevant studies.
3. Determine the specific data to be gathered and the methodology to be used.
4. Select the sample to be studied.
5. Determine the methods of data analysis or observation.
6. Determine the methods of presentation and utilization of results, including dissemination.
7. Document the development of the study to help in replication and to provide supporting data.

In general, evaluation methodologies may be grouped into three classes: (1) user-oriented measures; (2) collection-oriented measures; (3) non-quantifiable measures.[3]

User-oriented Measures

Use and User Studies. These must measure actual use by users, and they assume that heavy use of a collection necessarily means it is a "good collection". An implicit assumption in this approach is that a measure of the use of a book is a measure of its value to the library and thus to society. This assumption is the basis of the work on collection weeding by Slote, in which he argues that in weeding one is aiming to reduce the stock to a core collection that will satisfy 95-99 per cent of present use as measured by loan statistics.[4] While it is not difficult to collate figures that indicate classes of books that have not been used in the past, and thus are likely not to be used in the future, it may not be possible to do the same for individual items in the collection. Nevertheless, there is little doubt that the best method of establishing likely future use of any individual work is its "shelf-time period", that is, the time the work has remained on the shelf since it was last issued, or (in the case of very recent acquisitions) since its accession. Most writers have now accepted that past use is the most reliable indicator of likely future use in large research libraries, although they stress that there are great variations in different subject areas and that the method needs to be applied with extreme caution.

There are many problems inherent in the use and user studies approach. First, it is necessary that some statistics have already been gathered, for at least a reasonable period; and should these statistics not be available, then some sampling must be employed, which could be sampling of the total collection, or a form of sampling of current use such as current loans. In addition to this there is the problem that statistics gathered on the use of certain parts of any collection do not necessarily reflect the use of other parts, or of different uses of the same parts; for instance, measures of undergraduate use of an academic library do not reflect the research value and use of that collection. There are also problems in measuring "in-house" use, as most of the methods either rely on user cooperation or on staff who are involved in other work at the time, or are used in uncontrolled areas of the library; the details are discussed later in this chapter.

Further problems are caused because the method measures demands rather than needs and thereby raises the important question of whether measures of what has actually been required in the past should be taken as reliable indicators of what ought to be needed in the future. It is necessary at all times to consider the question of whether academic libraries, for instance, should be considering expanding the outlooks of their students rather than necessarily limiting library collections to catering for the current outlook. Not of least importance is the fact that any surveys of actual users must of necessity ignore potential users, unless it is to be assumed that the potential users will have the same needs and make the same demands as do existing users. Extrapolation and the forecasting of future use can be effective only if the likely requirements of potential users can be estimated; the more closely the forecast is based on current use, the more likely it is to reinforce the current patterns of use.

It is also vital to ask what is the real meaning of "use" as it is understood by library patrons being surveyed, as a landmark study by Abraham Bookstein established that there was considerable variation in what library patrons understood by the words "use" and "read", and that the term "use" seemed generally to be linked in the minds of respondents with some measure of "usefulness", rather than with the simple act of "making some use of".[5] In addition, there were different reactions to the concept of "using a library", in that some respondents did not necessarily see "using a library" in the same light as "using a book from that library". Each survey instrument must be designed with the utmost care, so that the basic concepts of validity and reliability are made an integral part of the instrument.

Finally, familiarity with the bookstock will influence the advice and recommendations given by staff to patrons. It is almost inevitable that where professional advice is offered by a librarian there will be a tendency to recommend material that is familiar to that librarian or has recently come to his notice, thus influencing the results of any "use study", no matter how internally valid that study may be; survey instruments must be designed to take this phenomenon into account and to minimize it.

Document Delivery Tests. These are used to assess the capability of the library to provide its users with the items at the time they need them. They must measure the extent to which the collection is adequate to provide the material needed in specific subject areas, the speed with which the material is provided, the effort the user is required to expend in order to get results, and the level of precision of the system expressed by its ability to provide what is needed and to filter out what is not needed. While it is certainly important to design the study so that it does not interfere with normal work routines, this introduces the problem that a time and a method that best suit staff requirements and best fit into work patterns may not be the best in terms of objective measurement. One might almost assume the reverse to be true: for instance, a time that suits work patterns could well be a "slack period" and would measure a "non-typical" delivery pattern. An effective approach would be to design an instrument that lists a number of documents (or references to them) thought to be those most likely to be needed by the users, and then to determine how many of the items are owned by the library, how many are available at the time, and how long it takes to make them available. Although the technique is said to simulate the processes employed by a user who walks into the library and searches for a document, it may be difficult not to introduce unconscious variations. The best way, of course, would be to make use of "real-time" situations, but this would almost certainly result in some unnecessary complications; it could not only lower the quality of the service being offered at the time but also introduce an unmeasurable bias.

Among the advantages of document delivery tests are these: they provide objective information on the ability of the system to satisfy specified user needs; the data can be comparable and therefore compared among different libraries; they are not difficult to design, to understand, or to instal. However, these advantages are counterbalanced by several disadvantages: it is difficult to compile a list of representative citations for use in checking the actual delivery procedures; they require repeated comparable tests; since the staff who perform the tests will be familiar with the library's routines, the results can underestimate the problems faced by users, who are not so well versed in the techniques of using libraries.

Shelf Availability Tests. These form in most senses a subset of the document delivery tests, and are used to determine whether or not items presumed to be in the collection are actually available to users. Danton reported on work done on the collections of some German research libraries that had been badly damaged in the war of 1939-1945 and showed that in some libraries up to 40 per cent of the collection was considered not worth replacing.[6] This would indicate that a considerable part of the collections of those libraries was "redundant", and if that were so of these carefully selected research collections, it is reasonable to assume that it might be even more so in some of the rather haphazardly collected public and academic libraries elsewhere, so that simple measures of what is, or is not, available when asked for may have little to do with any measures of value. These figures correspond quite well with those of Trueswell, when he surveyed two libraries in an American university and calculated that 99 per cent of the circulation requirements could have been met by 25 and 40 per cent respectively of the two collections.[7]

These tests have several advantages: they do report failures of real users, and are thus more likely to reflect what is actually happening, rather than what is thought to be happening; they can be used to identify reasons for user failure outside the scope of collection development policies, and thus can be useful for other purposes; they can easily and readily be replicated. Among their disadvantages are the fact that they depend on the cooperation of users; the design and operation of each study is difficult and time-consuming; they do not identify the needs of non-users.

Circulation Studies. These studies are used to identify the less used parts of a collection for weeding, to identify a core collection, perhaps for duplication or special treatment, or to identify use patterns of selected subject areas for adjustment of funding and collection development practices, and also to identify user populations. The methods used certainly reflect current circulation patterns, but the basic problem remains that although circulation may be a measure of what was done in the past, it is not necessarily a measure of what ought to have been done, or of what is likely to be done in the future. The statistics kept must show loans by different classes of borrowers and of different classes of materials and must also measure different loan periods. Some method of comparison of the loans figures in specific subject areas with those of acquisitions in the same areas should also be included.

Advantages of circulation studies include the following: the data are easily arranged for analysis; they allow flexibility in the duration of the study; sample size can easily be adjusted to suit changing circumstances; the units are easily counted; the information is objective. Among the disadvantages one may cite these: they exclude in-house consultation and thus are almost certain to under-represent actual use; they reflect only successes, and do not record user failures; they may be biased through the inaccessibility of heavily used material; they could fail to identify low use caused by the predominance in the collection of obsolescent or low quality material.

In-house Use Studies. This final approach can be used to record the use of material consulted in the library. In-house user studies give a more complete picture of in-house use than do other methods, and they can be used in conjunction with circulation studies for more accurate information on specific parts of the collection. On the other hand, they rely on user cooperation, so they are difficult to use in "uncontrolled" areas; certain aspects of timing and of the non-recording of materials in circulation may bias results; and they also reflect only successes and do not report failures. In construction they tend to mirror the procedures used in the other types of studies mentioned above, and do not need to be covered in detail at this stage, except for a mention of some points of their construction and operation that would be peculiar to them. It is necessary to define precisely what is meant by "in-house" and for that purpose some kind of marking of material is used so that it can be seen if it has been disturbed, and use is more narrowly defined by taking into account only material taken from the shelves and left on tables for re-shelving. Because there is also a considerable amount of variation in use of different parts of a collection, it would be unwise to make any decision on the basis of "in-house" studies that could not be verified and supported by other kinds of measures.

Collection-oriented Measures

The second group of evaluation methodologies comprises collection-oriented measures. The principal methodological approaches include the selection and application of relevant standards, the use of checklists and verification studies, and the use of citation analysis. In general collection-oriented measures are based on an assumption that the collection should be moulded to a "stimulus-response" pattern designed to satisfy the needs of those who use libraries most frequently.

They are best thought of as a group of statistical descriptions of collections, concentrating on size, subject areas, usage, expenditures and other factors. The principal methodological techniques are those dealing with size and patterns of growth, and comprise the investigation of the question of minimum collection size in relation to level and size of specific demand areas, such as teaching programmes, taking into account the budget in relation to the same kinds of areas. Statistics on size are easily available, easily understood and are easy to compare, but, as has been stressed earlier, may be of questionable use when one is measuring the value of a collection.

Verification Studies. One of the most important methodologies is the application of verification studies which are measurements of the resource adequacy of the collection to supply materials in demand, requiring the checking of standard lists and bibliographies.

They are easy to summarize and to compare and can be used to measure "quality" of the collection; but they need to be matched with the library's specific objectives and require appraisals by library users and experts.

The lists used to check the collections may be standard "checklists", for example, those published by the H.W. Wilson Company.[8] These comprise listings put together for quite specific purposes such as to allow a teaching institution to supply all the material necessary for the preparation of essays and project papers, and for independent background reading, or composite lists such as the various guides to reference books which are often used as checklists for establishing core collections. The weaknesses of this kind of checking are: the various lists must of necessity be out-of-date as soon as they are published; they tend to reflect what is already in the collections of similar libraries, or even in the very libraries using them to check, so that they lead to conformity in collections. In extreme cases they may well have been the same lists that were used by the library in the past to build up its collection, and thus would be of no use at all in an evaluation. It is essential that any such lists be assessed for their suitability for the particular library, and indeed in cases such as these specially designed lists may be the only answer. The checking may also cover only a small part of the library's holdings in any specific subject area, and could well overlook many important works held by the library but not listed in the checklist. One variation is to evaluate the library against listings of sources used by scholars in the preparation of well-known works, and in effect to ask whether such books could have been written using only the resources available in that library. This method has the attraction that not only will it check the collection at a practical as well as a theoretical level, but also it will check the holdings in many peripheral subject areas that might have been covered by the works in question. Another variation is to make up the initial list from several reviewing and selection tools, assuming that the appearance of any specific title on a multiplicity of lists is an indication of its acceptance as a worthwhile acquisition.

It has been mentioned previously that a basic assumption underlies methods of analysis of use or user statistics, which is that value is in some way proportionate to use, and that to measure use of items is *ipso facto* to measure their value.

Citation Analysis. One seemingly more accurate quantitative measurement of use is the technique of citation analysis, another form of checklist approach, relying on published research to establish standards of quality. It can be useful in fields in which no standard lists exist; however, it does under-represent material which is important but which is otherwise undercited, such as review articles, and annual summaries in particular discipline areas. There is also the danger of a "closed circle" of reference leading to citations which result in a further reference, and the method relies on the assumption that more heavily cited material is more likely to be used than is less heavily cited material. Enough has been said in this and previous chapters about the dangers of equating "use" with "value" for the usual caveat to be understood here. Studies have shown that a small core of works contains a substantial part of the relevant literature in any subject area; indeed the study of this effect, which in reality is no more than a "local" application of statistically normal distribution, has become almost a minor "growth industry" in librarianship in recent years, with the generous application of Bradford's law to some areas of very doubtful relevance.[9]

The advantages of citation analysis are that: data are easily arranged; the method is simple and thus studies can be replicated with comparative ease; the method can help to identify trends in published literature; the lists can be compiled easily using online databases. On the other hand, disadvantages include the following: surveyors may find it difficult to select source items to reflect specific needs; certain sub-areas in any one discipline may have use and citation patterns which are different from those of the general literature; research patterns in some subjects do not lend themselves to citation study; the time that elapses between the writing of a paper, its publication and subsequent citation, and the measurement of the citation pattern may not reflect changes in the discipline or in publishing patterns, and when used in isolation, for all its apparent "arithmetical respectability", the technique can be a questionable measurement for use in collection development decisions.

In fact, there are many good reasons why it is dangerous to accept that citation analysis and citation use studies provide much useful information at all. The practising librarian, searching for ways to apply accurate measures of use to a collection, needs to exercise extreme care when using this method. One problem is that there is a variety of reasons for citing references: the author may not cite all the papers he used; works that were cited may not have been used very much at all; some ideas may be incorporated without reference to their source; papers that oppose an argument may not be cited, or may be cited simply to be refuted; and references may be included simply in order to "dress up" a paper. In addition, citation of a friend or a superior, or simply the seminal and prestigious works in the field, is not unknown. There are several papers that cover this weakness of the citation analysis method, and it is recommended that they be given some attention. Two quotes from a paper by Herner and Herner, for instance, give an idea of the flavour of this kind of problem: "How people get information and what they cite are frequently quite different....The second fallacy is the extreme subjectivity involved in trying to divine why an author cited a publication...."[10]

The other major problem associated with measuring use by citation is the question of whether external use measured by loan figures can be used in any way as a measure of "in-library" use. Although some research shows a high correlation between measurements of use of volumes in the library and a count of volumes taken out on loan, other work suggests there is some danger in basing any kinds of management decisions on this type of correlation.[11] It is also quite likely that a different situation exists altogether with periodicals, and it is likely that analysis of citations is of little use for comparing journals which have been made accessible by their reference in the indexing and abstracting journals with those not in the various indexing journals.

Nevertheless, and despite the evidence that can be amassed against the efficacy of citation analysis for measuring use, it is still seen as one useful tool. Koenig says, "What is important tends to be what is cited";[12] and Baughmann, in a study of works on sociology, lists those monographs that received five or more citations and refers to them as "...thereby representing some of the best in sociology."[13]

Non-quantifiable Measures

The third group of measures, the non-quantifiable measures which rely on the collation and assessment of opinions rather than on the counting of observable or measureable incidents generally comprises surveys of user opinions, which have as their primary stated goal the determination of how well the library's collections meet users' information needs. Because "use" can only be measured when it is a recordable transaction, even the most sophisticated use study cannot disclose whether the material that was used was in fact what was needed, or indeed whether any result other than the mere transaction itself was achieved. Thus it becomes necessary not only to survey the users to ask questions about the degree of satisfaction felt, but also to use the services of experts in order to get critical assessments of the quality of the material, and it is perhaps in this kind of study that the weakness of using those who are responsible for the selection of the stock in the first place to evaluate its effectiveness shows up so clearly, as the "self-fulfilling prophecy" so well described (even if unconsciously) by Evans demonstrates.[14] His paper describes a study of the patterns of use of books selected by several different methods and shows the following: those books that were selected by librarians in reader services are used most, those selected by technical services librarians are used slightly less often, those selected by faculty account for even less use, and those received in the library as a result of some kind of blanket order acquisitions process are used least. Evans shows no sign of recognizing the effect that familiarity with those works selected personally would have on the kinds of works recommended by library staff to their users - precisely the same effect that would influence non-quantifiable studies. This position is supported by other studies which illustrate that it is important to understand why a book is not being used, not merely to record the fact that it is not. Although one can conclude that lack of use in most categories of library materials seems to result from the processes of change in the needs and desires of patrons, rather than from initial poor selection by library staff, it could well be that a major reason for non-use of particular items might be the failure of staff, both librarians and faculty, to understand properly the need to introduce the reader to the work that is best suited to his particular need at that time, rather than to a work that is most familiar to the staff member, or is the most readily available.

Non-quantitative user studies have the following advantages: they can be used for the qualitative evaluation of the effectiveness of the collections and services in meeting users' needs; they provide information to help librarians solve specific problems, to modify particular programmes and to assess needs for new services; they define the make-up of the community of library users, identify groups that need to be better served, provide feedback on successes as well as on deficiencies, and improve public relations; they assist in the education of user communities and in identifying changing trends and interests; they are not limited to the simple measurement of existing data; they permit direct feedback from users; they can be as simple or as complex as is desired (or can be afforded). Their disadvantages are almost as numerous: they measure demands rather than needs; it is difficult to design a sophisticated survey; data analysis is difficult; the passivity of some users as well as the eagerness of others to provide answers that please the surveyors can make surveying difficult.

It is important that the assumption not be made that any collection is in fact satisfying its users because those users seem not to have many specific grievances; many users simply may not be aware of services that are offered, so they cannot judge what may have been more satisfactory for their purposes. As well as these disadvantages, some users simply may not cooperate, thus skewing results; the method may focus on user interests more than on collection development policies; and as the surveys consider only actual and not potential users they cannot take into account input from non-users. Problems arise also from the propensity of users to provide information that might well reflect their intentions or their memories rather than provide an accurate portrayal of the past or of future needs.

It is important also to bear in mind the effect on public relations that studies of this type could have, for as well as being instruments designed to provide detailed information which could be used for collection development, they can also be used to gain support for the library's overall policy as well as for the particular project by the encouragement of cooperation with the users.

The normal pattern for studies of this kind includes either a set of specific structured questions plied through interviews or questionnaires, or a set of rather more general open-ended queries, using the same kinds of methods. In libraries where there is the chance for the surveyors to have access to a more closely structured clientele it is possible to cooperate with representatives of the various groups in the design and application of survey instruments that will test the ability of the collection to meet demands and standards in specific areas Reference should be made to the paper by Wainwright (pp. 166-173), in which he canvasses at greater length several of the issues covered in this chapter, and also to the paper by Chweh,[15] which inter alia lists and discusses ten of the forty-seven categories of measures which might be applied by users to evaluate library services. It is important also to remember that "non-users" may also be offering their own evaluation of the service simply by their failure to find any reasons for using it. The librarian must always bear in mind that the very characteristics of the problems on which information is being sought may themselves have a greater bearing on information-seeking behaviour than do such items as the personal or work-related characteristics of the seekers. These factors stress the point made earlier that under normal circumstances searchers will regard convenience as more important than accuracy, and will tend to be satisfied with what is available rather than to extend the search.

References

1   The seminal study in this area, and to date the most used, is that of Clapp and Jordan, who produce convincing arguments for the measurement of collection adequacy by the use of a formula that began with the statement of a base number of volumes to which are then added more volumes, the additional number being calculated according to separate quite specific factors. They use lists of required titles, produced by academics in each discipline area, to establish the base of 42,000 volumes, which they argue is the minimum number needed regardless of factors such as subjects taught or student numbers. They then suggest that additional volumes be added, the numbers calculated by adding sixty volumes per full-time member of teaching staff, ten volumes per full-time student, 2400 volumes for each subject area in which work is done at master's level, and 16,000 for areas in which doctoral work takes place. There is nothing immutable about the numbers, or the factors, and the approach can be used in any library, with the factors and the numbers of volumes being adjusted to suit local conditions. The topic is also covered by G. Edward Evans, *Developing Library and Information Center Collections* (2nd ed. Littleton, Colo.: Libraries Unlimited, 1987), pp. 316-330.

2   As these questions have been discussed in detail in Chapter 4, it is necessary only to mention them again at this point.

3   For examples of practical applications of the methods to be discussed in the balance of this chapter see Anthony J. Arthur, *Collection Development: A Report to the Swinburne Librarian* (2 vols. Hawthorn: Swinburne Ltd, 1985); Bruce C. Bennion, "The Use of Standard Selection Sources in Undergraduate Library Collection Development." *Collection Management* 2, 2 (1978): 141-152; Gary D. Byrd, D.A. Thomas and Katherine E. Hughes, "Collection Development Using Inter-Library Loan Borrowing and Acquisitions Statistics." *Bulletin of the Medical Library Association* 70, 1 (1982): 1-9; Pauline A. Scales, "Citation Analyses as Indicators of the Use of Serials: A

Comparison of Ranked Title Lists Produced by Citation, Counting and from Use Data." *Journal of Documentation* 32, 1 (1976): 17-25; Eric J. Wainwright and John E. Dean, *Measures of Adequacy for Library Collections in Australian Colleges of Advanced Education* (2 vols. Perth: Western Australian Institute of Technology, 1976).

4   Stanley J. Slote, *Weeding Library Collections - II* (2nd rev. ed. Littleton, Colo.: Libraries Unlimited, 1982).

5   Abraham Bookstein, "Sources of Error in Library Questionnaires." *Library Journal* 4 (1982): 85-94.

6   J. Periam Danton, "The Subject Specialist in National and University Libraries with Special Reference to Book Selection." *Libri* 17, 1 (1967): 42-58.

7   Richard A. Trueswell, "A Quantitative Measure of User Circulation Requirements and Its Possible Effect on Stack Thinning and Multiple-copy Determination." *American Documentation* 16 (January 1965): 20-25.

8   These tools are covered in detail in Chapters 7 and 8, but another good example of the type is *Books for College Libraries: A Core Collection of 40,000 Titles* (2nd ed. Chicago, Ill.: American Library Association, 1975).

9   Bradford's law states that if scientific journals are arranged in order of decreasing productivity of articles on a given subject, they can be divided into a nucleus, which contains the journals specifically devoted to the subject, surrounded by a number of zones or groups, each with a significantly smaller number of relevant articles. See S.C. Bradford, *Documentation* (London: Crosby Lockwood, 1948), p. 116.

10   Saul Herner and Mary Herner, "Information Needs and Uses in Science and Technology." *Annual Review of Information Science and Technology* 2 (1967): 2.

11   William E. McGrath, "Correlating the Subjects of Books Taken out of and Books Used within an Open-stack Library." *College and Research Libraries* 32, 4 (1971): 280-285; Geoffrey Ford, "Stock Relegation in Some British University Libraries." *Journal of Librarianship* 12, 1 (1980): 42-55.

12   Michael E.D. Koenig, "Citation Analysis for the Arts and Humanities as a Collection Management Tool." *Collection Management* 2, 3 (1978): 249.

13   James E. Baughman, "Some of the Best in Sociology: A Bibliographic Checklist Created by the Unusual Technique of Citation Counting." *Library Journal* 98, 18 (15 October 1973): 2977.

14   G. Edward Evans, "Book Selection and Book Collection Usage in Academic Libraries." *Library Quarterly* 40, 3 (July 1970): 297-308.

15   Steven S. Chweh, "User Criteria for Evaluation of Library Service." *Journal of Library Administration* 2, 1 (Spring 1981): 35-46.

16   This topic is covered in greater detail in Wainwright and Dean, *op. cit.*

READINGS ON METHODS OF COLLECTION EVALUATION

This chapter has attempted to explore the practical problems of the design and application of studies of the use of libraries, or of their users, and the differences between "use studies" and "user studies", with a further discussion of the possibility that a division into "user-oriented" or "library-oriented" studies may be more practical. It is argued that current levels of sophistication in both the design and the application of studies of libraries and library use are such as to cause grave concern, and that a much more rigorous approach to these problems is needed before any reliable methodology can be developed. The not uncommon assumption that more use of a library necessarily is ipso facto a good thing, and that the measurement of use is also a measurement of value, is further questioned, and the basic types of study are discussed in some detail. Some of the further problems inherent in the basic idea of "asking people what they want" are explored in the study by Bookstein (pp. 158-165) which sought to determine what library users understand by words such as "use" and "read", and led to some very strong suggestions about the need for a great deal more care in the construction of survey instruments than has been evident in the past in library surveys. By way of contrast a statement of the traditional approach is presented in the paper by Eric Wainwright (pp. 166-173), in which he discusses the operation of the standard forms of collection evaluation in an attempt to determine the adequacy of library collections in Australian colleges of advanced education. Neither the methodology nor the conclusions break new ground, but they do provide a detailed exposition of the method.

Blaine Hall (pp. 173-182) stresses the importance of a collection evaluation manual, which, he says, should provide not only an outline of the techniques that are needed if the librarian is to conduct a proper exercise in collection evaluation, which includes gathering the data, analyzing it, and reporting the results, but also a statement of the rationale for the complete exercise, which ought to begin with a statement of the specific objectives before leading on to details of the measurement techniques and the reporting formats.

Abraham Bookstein, "Sources of Error in Library Questionnaires."
Library Research 4 (1982): 85-94.

Introduction

Crucial to any analysis of a library's effectiveness is the proper collection of data on how that library's resources are being used. The tradition of user studies has stemmed out of a recognition of this need. Probably the most common methodology appearing in these studies is the questionnaire survey. The impetus behind this approach is simple; if one wishes to know something about people, the simplest and most natural way to proceed is by asking them. We proceed in this manner when dealing with the problems that come up in everyday life; it is not surprising that we extend this approach to problems demanding more precise information. Perhaps because of the apparent simplicity of this approach, studies based on questionnaires are often naively designed, with little consideration as to the validity of the data produced. Indeed, although hundreds perhaps thousands of studies have been published in the library literature using questionnaires, we know of none that examine the impact of the questionnaire itself on how individuals respond to questions about their library activity.

Although our concern here is with the use of questionnaires in library research, the problem that we are considering is more general. Whenever we carry out a research project, we are trying to reach conclusions from data generated by inherently faulty techniques. Sensitivity towards the distortions introduced by research techniques has a long history (see e.g. Selltiz, Wrightsman, and Cook, 1976 for an overview of the problem of response bias). This development perhaps culminates in the classic paper of Campbell and Fiske (1958), which systematically discusses how the instrument we use must be considered as an important factor determining our results. This means, before we reach a conclusion based on research data, we must keep in mind the possibility that *how* we collected the data may be as much a cause of the data taking the form they do as is the reality being probed.

Although the naturalness of questionnaires obscures the extent to which they may colour the responses, it is necessary for us to learn the extent to which questionnaires influence responses if we are to make intelligent use of survey data. Questions such as these have been studied; some of the results are presented in research reports and textbooks on questionnaire design (e.g., Payne, 1951; Kahn and Cannell, 1957; Bradburn and Sudman, 1944). The results are not encouraging. Researchers have become aware that in many situations the questionnaire is not a neutral instrument but a device that may itself distort the response, sometimes seriously.

Our concern in this paper is with one facet of this problem: the extent to which people differ in how they understand commonly used words describing library activity. In particular, the purpose of this study is to examine explicitly how people differ in their understanding of the questions that appear in library-user surveys. For example, patrons are often asked quantitative questions regarding their "use" of the library or one of its services, or, in other contexts, of books and journals. If people do indeed differ in their application of the term "use" to various acts, then, for example, two people whose experiences in a library are identical may, when asked about the extent of their library use, give very different answers, although both may sincerely be trying to cooperate with the investigator. Thus, a considerable portion of the variability reported in library use may in fact be variability in how one interprets what constitutes a use of the library.

One of the reasons library research is carried out is to discover the character of individual differences with regard to library involvement: We want to know how a "typical" member of a population behaves, and also the degree of variability within the population. People differ, and we expect to find differences in their behavior and attitudes towards libraries. But, if people interpret the terms we use differently, this will contribute a component to the variation in the responses beyond that reflecting the true differences in which we are interested. If the effect is large, it may in fact dominate our findings. Although we expect an error component in any research result, we wish to emphasize that the degree of error may be quite large, and be caused by differences of interpretation of even the simplest words appearing in the questionnaire, whose meanings we tend to take for granted.

Nor is there any reason to believe that this error component is random. Not only may the differences in interpretation influence the variability of the responses, but they may also systematically distort the findings and lead to biased results. Thus, by studying how people interpret words such as "use", we learn about a source of error in questionnaire design, and also gain an important insight into people's perceptions of the library and its services.

A similar source of ambiguity lies in the differences in how people interpret quantitative adverbs, such as "sometimes", "rarely", and "often." In this study, we probed a small number of people to see whether differences in interpretation of these terms are a source of ambiguity for the results of a library survey.

Methodology

The methodology of this study is very simple. We first wish to observe that our objective was not to estimate in some way a true "population value" for the divergence in interpretation of terms appearing in library surveys. Indeed, given the variety of conditions under which library surveys are in fact carried out, it would be difficult, if not impossible, to identify the population that should be represented. Instead, we sought to learn whether there is reason to believe that in a group of people such as might be approached in a library survey, a significant variety of interpretation is likely. As a first attempt to assess this, we chose a group of people easily available to us: students taking a methodology course at the University of Chicago and their acquaintances. The advantage of using this group, besides convenience, is its relative homogeneity. The variability in age, educational level, and area of specialization was likely to be less than would be the case among a more typical set of survey respondents. In addition, many of the respondents were interested in library problems, and were likely to be sensitive to issues related to how a library was used. In other words, this was a group of people that one would expect, *a priori*, to show a minimum of variation in how questions regarding library activity are interpreted. If any degree of variation exists among a group such as this, we would have reason to be very seriously concerned about the degree of variation in interpretation that would be exhibited by a more heterogeneous group of people less interested in library matters. Thus, our results represent a conservative estimate of how much people answering survey questions differ in their understanding of what they are being asked.

The logic behind our methodology can be clarified by comparing it to a more standard approach: Usually, survey research depends heavily on randomized sampling. Randomization is a powerful tool in that it assures the representativeness of the sample, and disassociates the findings from the selection method. Thus in a random sample, the conclusions drawn from the data are strengthened in that the claim that the results are an artifact of how the sample was selected cannot be sustained. Given the inappropriateness, for the reasons noted above, of randomized selection here, a different approach had to be taken to give validity to our data and make implausible the possibility that the effect is due to how we selected our subjects. To support the existence of an effect, we selected a sample in which the selection mechanism was most likely to diminish the likelihood of that effect occurring. If even here an effect is found, then we can reasonably expect such an effect in a more diverse group of people.

The study was carried out, of course, by means of a questionnaire. Since a small number of people (43) were involved at this stage, each could be given a careful explanation as to the purpose of the study, and any questions could be answered. The questionnaire consisted of two parts. The first attempted to get at how people interpret words such as "use". It consisted of descriptions of a number of situations that often occur in a library, or of types of contract with reading material. For each, it asked the respondents whether they would, if asked in a questionnaire about their use of the library or of reading material, answer that they had used it if they experienced the situation described.

The second group of questions probed how people use adverbs such as "seldom" or "often", and whether usage varies with context. Again, situations were described, and respondents were asked to indicate the appropriate adverb to describe that situation.

To get additional information about the impact of a questionnaire form on responses, two forms of the questionnaire were administered, one of which had slightly different wording for several questions. Our concern was whether the difference in the choice of words might influence how people responded to the question.

Results

Interpretations of the Term "Use"

In preparing this project, we expected that individuals would differ in their response to commonly appearing questions. However, considering the homogeneity of our respondents, we were surprised at the extent to which respondents did differ. The results are given in Table 1.

For some questions, our respondents showed a large degree of agreement. For example, 39 respondents (91%) would say they "used" a library if they read an issue of one of its journals from cover to cover, although, even here, 9% of our respondents have a definition of "use" that they would not apply to this activity. Similarly, 91% of our respondents would not describe as a book use the activity of looking at the publisher and copyright data of a book they found on the shelves, but were not previously aware of, if this information was enough to indicate to them that they should not further explore the book. Other examples of activities in which a consensus existed were: going to the library to use the rest room (18% considered this a use) and arranging to meet a friend at

Table 1. Responses to Questionnaire Probing Interpretation of the Term "Use" in Library Context. Data Give Percent of Respondents Describing Activities as Library Uses.

Activity	Percent Yes	Percent No
Use library if:		
Check out book - find out useful	100	0
Read a library-owned magazine or journal cover to cover	91	9
Read article referred to, but find not useful	88	12
Duplicate known journal article belonging to library	81	19
Check spelling of author's name in catalog	70	30
Use library as reading room	62	38
Unsuccessful attempt to check out a book	53	47
Return book to library	32	68
Meet friend	21	79
Use rest room	18	82
Use or read book or journal if:		
Occasionally scan journal of peripheral interest	67	33
Examine indexes of book for further use	53	47
Examine book only to see how diagrams are presented	49	51
Skimming book - not finding useful	47	53
Skim introduction before returning as not useful	20	80
Examine only publisher and copyright data	9	91

the library (only 21% considered this to be a use of the library). Interestingly everyone described checking out a book as a use of the library, even though that book was found not to be "useful".

But for a wide range of very common types of library activity, marked differences of interpretation emerge. Examples with substantial disagreement regarding the use of library material include:

1. Taking a book from the shelves only to see how various conventional diagrams and graphs are now being presented in textbooks (49% yes, 51% no).
2. Looking through an index of a book to get an idea of the content for future use (53% yes, 47% no).
3. Skimming a book, reading a small section, and not finding the book useful (5=47% yes, 53% no).

A number of respondents indicated they would have described the above actions as a library use, through they did not consider them as book uses, again suggesting a degree of discrimination on the part of respondents to distinctions that could be overlooked by a questionnaire designer. However, when asked directly about library use, about one third would not describe a use of the catalog to check the spelling of an author's name as a library use; and 38% would not describe using the library's reading room as an example of library use. We thus find substantial disagreement in answers to direct questions regarding rather fundamental types of library activity.

Apparently, the term "use", when applied to contact with a book, has a variety of connotations. To many people, it seems that a book is "used" provided it turns out to be "useful", and that use involves extended immediate reading of it. This has serious implications in interpreting survey data, since many would argue that a library is providing a real service in making books available to patrons in such a way that patrons can decide whether or not a book has any value for them. Similarly, although books are printed to be read, a patron interested in learning about publications trends in an area of interest is being well served by a library that permits him to scan a number of books to obtain an impression of such trends, even if he reads none of them. Yet half of our respondents would not consider such an interaction as a use of the book. This is particularly interesting since one would expect the group of subjects being questioned to be particularly likely to represent libraries as providing useful services. If the designation of "use" as applied to interactions with libraries parallels that of interactions with books, then the public may be very seriously underestimating in questionnaires the extent to which it uses its libraries, and it certainly does so for uses of library materials. Here, differences in interpretation may result in biased results.

But many of the activities occurring in libraries, and of value to their patrons, do not involve stored documents directly. For example, many people use the library for its unique store of bibliographic information. Nonetheless, we saw that a third of our respondents did not consider using a library's catalog to corroborate the spelling of an author's name as a use of the library. Similarly, 20% of the respondents did not consider using library equipment to duplicate an article in a library-held journal as a use, if they were already aware of the existence of the article. Other activities, such as returning a book, was not considered a library use by about 70% or our respondents, yet processing such activities do incur substantial costs for the library. (Here, some respondents considered the return of the book as an activity following a use, but not a use in itself.) Again, it seems that there is a tendency, not shared by all, of restricting use directly to reading. For this reason it was interesting to see how respondents would react to frustrated use, so defined. Here the extent of involvement of library personnel seemed to be influential. Thus about half of our respondents would feel they used the library if they tried to check out a book, but found it wasn't available, causing them to plan a return next week. On the other hand, if a recall request was made, this figure rises to about 90%. Five people, however, still felt that a use was not made of the library in such circumstances. If the book was successfully checked out, all of our respondents would designate that interaction as a use, even though the book was not useful. Thus, though an unsuccessful interaction with the book was not designated a use if the book was not checked out, the process of checking out the book somehow sanctified the interaction and raised it to the level of a use.

Interpretations of Adverbs of Frequency

Questions relating to the frequency with which an activity occurs are clearly of interest to library management. It is commonly believed that it is easier for respondents to answer such questions with verbal designators of frequency, such as "often" or "sometimes", than to give an exact numerical value. The value of such a device depends, however, on there being a common understanding as to what these terms mean - the very vagueness that makes the use of such phrases appealing may compromise the validity of the responses. In our questionnaire, we included a number of items essentially of the form: If you used the library once a week, would you describe the activity as occurring: rarely, seldom, etc.? On the questionnaire used here, four versions were used, each having only a single frequency designation. As expected, the question relating frequency of activity to verbal designation again showed variability. For example, "using" the library once a week was described by one person as "very frequently" and by two persons as "rarely", the other respondents being divided between "seldom", "sometimes", and "often" with the median category being "sometimes". On the other hand, asking questions this often at the reference desk was perceived as "often" by over half of those responding to this question (this was the median category), and no one applied the designation "rarely". Similarly, almost everyone believed using a library or its catalog less than once a year was a rare event, but less than half would characterize that degree of use of a scholarly index as an event that occurred rarely. Looking at the variety of interpretations possible for an adverb of quantity, we find that when applied to the use of the card catalog, "rarely" meant anything from once a week to less than once a year, with a similar spread for "rarely" as applied to use of the library. In virtually every case, the interpretation spread across three or more categories, with four or five categories being quite common.

A closer examination of the individual responses suggested at least three possible sources of variability. The most obvious was that people do indeed mean different things when they use verbal descriptions of quantity. But it also seems that another source of variability was that some people were using an absolute scale of quantity, in which, say, once a year is "rare" regardless of what it describes, whereas other respondents were influenced by context. (These two categories may not be that different. People having absolute scales may in fact be using a class of commonly occurring activities to which they were referring. My experience, however, was that some people have great difficulty saying how often something that occurs "frequently" occurs, independent of a referent, while other people readily provide an answer.) Among the latter group, some seemed to have an absolute sense of how often a catalog, for example, must be used for it to be used "very frequently," whereas others related the frequency to their own use patterns. The end result of this analysis is a sense of unease about how a study depending on these designations can be interpreted. Again, the differences of interpretations of these adverbs of quantity may affect the variability of the responses, and perhaps also introduce a bias.

Discussion

Responses to questionnaires have a compelling certainty about them. Once collected, each question has associated with it a definite YES or NO, or else a precise number. It is possible to summarize these as simple fractions or as averages, to create tables or, if additional authority is desired, to carry out more complex analyses via the computer and some acronymed body of software. It is very easy to lose sight of the fact that when a person responds to a question, he is expressing not only some truth about himself but also how he is interpreting the q estion and his understanding of the terms he uses to express his answer. Our study suggests that the degree of variation in how people interpret even the simplest terms is considerable, even among a group of people almost designed to minimize this variability. Thus, should we find that 25% of a group of people say they do something "often" it is possible that 25% engage in that activity often, but also that all do so, with only 25% choosing to characterize themselves in this manner. Also very serious is the possibility that how terms are interpreted is related to other variables in the study, for example, education level. Such an interaction would tend to introduce or exaggerate the relationship between these variables and measures of library activity.

Research in other contexts has come to similar conclusions. Payne (1951) gives many examples of how changing a few words in a question in a seemingly innocuous way produces a striking change in the response pattern. Simpson (1944) in a pioneering study, has shown how varied the meanings of such words as "never", "always", or "sometimes" are. These findings were corroborated by Hakel (1968),[7] and for adjectives such as "few", "some," "several," etc., by Hoyt (1972). Pepper and Prytulak (1974) studied the impact of context on how people interpret these words. The second part of this study was intended to get an overall impression of the degree to which people differ in interpreting adverbs of quantity in a library context. Its results lead us to the following conclusions:

1.   It is crucial that we slow down the use of questionnaires as a tool for research on substantive questions and subject the questionnaire itself to the scrutiny of research. More, and extended, studies of this kind should be carried out on larger and more diverse populations. Ideally such questionnaires should contain fewer items than ours and be directed at a more restricted problem area - we are concerned, for example, about the extent to which questions were interacting in our own questionnaire. There is some indication that respondents were formulating answers to questions using their answers to other questions as a frame of reference.

2.   The questionnaire designer must be very sensitive to the choice of words used. For example, in an earlier study, we used the phrase "only to use the rest room" to mean, "for the sole purpose of using the rest room". The results led us to question whether the term "only" may have influenced the response. For this reason, in the current project we used two forms, one using the term "only", the other omitting it. The results were mixed. In two such questions, no effect was observed. In a third question, 60% of the respondents described themselves as using a book when the "only" was absent, and only 39% did so when "only" was present in the description of the activity. The results did not achieve statistical significance, probably because of the size of the sample, but they strongly suggest that at least for some activities, slight changes in terminology could radically change the results. Another example, in the context of our study, is the appearance of terms like "useful" in questions relating to library "use".

3.   We believe that the appearance of broad terms such as "use" in questionnaires stems from the impulse to get at a wider range of information with a single question. It would be advisable for researchers to attempt to get accurate information about more narrowly focussed problem areas, if probing broader questions results in no real information at all. We wonder whether this is why, after thousands of user studies, the consensus is emerging that we really know

very little about how patrons behave in, and respond to, libraries. We also suspect that the use of general, vague terms sometimes masks the failure of the researcher himself to think out what the critical areas are in which information is desired, and how to obtain it. Clearly, an important first step in any research project should be a precise statement of what the problem being researched is.

4. Given the inevitability of error in any research design, new approaches should be explored to limit and control this error. For example, concern about bias is prevalent in discussions about questionnaire design. Since it cannot be eliminated, we wonder whether intelligent use cannot be made of bias in questionnaires. An example would be to distribute two forms of the question, each mildly biased in opposite directions. This should produce results surrounding the true answer, but also give information on the susceptibility to bias of the question and the strengths with which people hold opinions on that problem area - an important parameter often overlooked.

We conclude that, although asking questions often gives satisfactory results in the informal interactions one experiences in the course of life, this procedure can result in serious distortions if used naively in a quantitative investigation. It is suggested that before a further study is made in which the questionnaire is a component, an effort should be devoted to understanding how people are responding to questions about their activities in a library.

References

N.M. Bradburn and S. Sudman, *Improving Interview Method and Questionnaire Design* (San Francisco, Calif.: Jossey-Bass, 1979).

D.T. Campbell and D.W. Fiske, "Convergent and Discriminant Validation by the Multitrait-multimethod Matrix." *Psychological Bulletin* 56 (1959): 81-105.

M.D. Hakel, "How Often Is Often?" *American Psychologist* 23, 7 (1959): 533-534.

J.S. Hoyt, Jr., *Do Quantifying Adjectives Mean the Same Thing to All People?* (Minneapolis, Minn.: University of Minnesota, Agricultural Extension Service, 1972).

R.L. Kahn and C.F. Cannell, *The Dynamics of Interviewing* (New York: John Wiley and Sons, 1957).

S.L. Payne, *The Art of Asking Questions* (Princeton, N.J.: Princeton University Press, 1951).

S. Pepper and L.S. Prytulak, "Sometimes Frequently Means Seldom. Context Effects in Interpretation of Quantitative Expressions." *Journal of Research in Personality* 8,1 (1974) 91-101.

C. Selltiz, L.S. Wrightsman and S.W. Cook, *Research Methods in Social Relations* (3rd ed. New York: Holt, Rinehart and Winston, 1976).

R.H. Simpson, "The Specific Meanings of Certain Terms Indicating Differing Degrees of Frequency." *Quarterly Journal of Speech* 30, 3 (1944): 328-330.

Eric J. Wainwright, "Collection Adequacy: Meaningless Concept or Measurable Goal?" In *Collection Management in Academic Libraries: Papers Delivered at a National Seminar, Surfers Paradise, Queensland, 16th-17th February 1984*, edited by Cathryn Crowe, Philip Kent and Barbara Paton, 1-10. Sydney: Library Association of Australia, University and College Libraries Section, 1984.

In developing the title for this paper, I was conscious of being asked to provide a paper on the topic of "measuring collection adequacy". Implicit in that title was the suggestion that the adequacy of a collection can be measured. Such a proposal seems beguilingly simple. However, I know from my own research some years ago that there could be some difficulties:

> No single techniques may be regarded as adequate for complete evaluation purposes, nor does the whole range of techniques available provide any certainty of arriving at measures of collection adequacy which may be asserted irrefutable.[1]

In writing more recently about the evaluation of academic library collections, Broadus has written that this "...may well be doomed to frustration. To measure the ultimate value of the collection to the university and to society is simply beyond us and may always be so".[2] In perhaps the best and certainly the most honest examination of the concept of adequacy in recent years, Michael Moran went further in writing:

> Is it possible to point to a library collection and say with justification that it is either adequate or inadequate? The correct answer to the question should form a fundamental axiom of librarianship. Much of the literature assumes the answer to be Yes; however, a logical and linguistic analysis will show that the answer should actually be no....[3]

Why should this be so? Primarily because both the words "measuring" and "adequate" imply quantification. To "measure" means to "ascertain the amount of", while the meaning of "adequacy" is "sufficiency". Immediately it must be asked, adequacy for what? Clearly for a variety of purposes. If measurement is to be applied to a collection, then this implies that the purposes of the collection can be delineated in a way that allows them to be linked to certain measurable events involving the collection.

In order to answer whether this is possible, we need to ask some basic questions about academic libraries and their operations today. It is important to obtain answers because to quote the American Library Association's *Guidelines for Collection Development*, "Every library collection should be established for a definite purpose".[4] This presents the first problem. The purposes of academic libraries seem at first sight to be quite simple and mirror those of the institution the library serves. Most library standards contain statements such as "The library's collections shall comprise...recorded information...for educational, inspirational and recreational purposes".[5] This of course belies [sic] the question. We can define an academic library collection's purposes as to meet the needs of:

1. undergraduate and postgraduate students in the completion of their course requirements;
2. academic staff in their teaching assignments;
3. postgraduate students and academic staff in pursuit of their individual research;

4. all members of the university in exposure to the major ideas of civilisation and the promotion of their intellectual, social and cultural development;

and possibly,

5. the institution's administration;
6. the community around the institution (although there are very few academic libraries that have accepted that their collections should be developed specifically for such a purpose).

Immediately this raises a further problem. For there to be any meaningful attempt to provide measures which relate collection adequacy to such broad needs, the needs require analysis in much more detail. The process of needs analysis is fundamental to the development of collection policies, and I contend that it is impossible to measure the adequacy of a collection, or even evaluate it at all without some clear delineation of the detailed purposes of the collection.

Once again this leads to a further problem. What is "adequacy" in relation to these purposes? There is "physical adequacy" in the sense of the direct availability of relevant material in the collection when it is needed by users, and also, as Chapin has pointed out "bibliographic adequacy",[6] in the sense of materials which enable users directly or indirectly to find and obtain materials and information from sources within the library, or from other resources. Bibliographic adequacy is gradually becoming more important with the development of more resource sharing. Online databases are replacing some of the reference materials providing the main basis for bibliographic adequacy in the past, and we are in an era when it can often be faster, and occasionally may even be cheaper, to obtain the publication from outside one's own library than from within it, if extended searching and recall from loan has to occur.

Again, further problems are raised. What do we mean by "direct availability"? Can we separate collection adequacy from library adequacy? If a library's collection is to meet the demands of users, let alone their needs, then the extent to which it is successful is dependent not only on the extent of the collection, but on the availability of the collection. An available collection requires a whole range of library services, from effective catalogues to reference assistance, signposting to reshelving procedures. In practice it is not sensible to separate the theoretical adequacy of a collection from its practical availability.

Further, can we today regard any academic library collection in isolation? Or is the adequacy of its collection affected by the availability of alternative resources, either locally or nationally. I would argue yes - if the availability of alternative resources improves either in scope or speed of access, then one's own library collection may be "adequate" at a lower level, as part of the total extended set of collections available to users within an acceptable time.

A further difficulty is that "needs" of users are not the same as their "demands". It is very unlikely that we can measure adequacy properly in relation to needs. Many measures of adequacy assume that a need is met if a user finds an item sought on the shelf or borrows it. It is very difficult to measure whether in fact the item meets the user's underlying need for information, as the user often cannot make such a judgement until the item is read carefully. Personal experience suggests that needs are only partly met in most cases.

Once we find ourselves dealing only with "demands" in applying measures, the problem of circularity arises. Library users are realists and tailor their actions to their expectations. A collection could meet a high proportion of expressed demands, yet be inadequate to meet the educational purposes of an institution, because the users do not have sufficient expectations of their institution's library to place many demands upon it.

A further difficulty is that most academic library collections do not simply serve the immediate needs or demands of their users. For an academic library collection to be truly adequate, relevant material must be available when required, and this implies provision for the future. The extent to which this is needed varies, but in any substantial research institution a large part of the collection is not used at any particular time, but may well be used in the longer term. This fact affects very substantially what kinds of measure can be applied to research collections, and indeed it may be questioned whether adequacy to meet future needs is measurable at all.

There are then some substantial difficulties in the attempt to measure collection adequacy. They have led me to conclude that it is not possible to "measure the adequacy" of an academic library collection in a way that truly reflects its capacity to meet both current and future needs of its potential users. This does not necessarily mean that quantitative measures of adequacy have no purpose. For example, there is some good evidence to suggest that various standards and formulae developed in relation to collections have had a useful political and planning use in being held up to academic administrations and funding bodies as targets to be aimed at. My own research for the colleges of advanced education rested primarily on this premise. However, we should not delude ourselves into thinking that such quantitative measures have any real meaning in the extent to which they reflect the ability of our collections to meet the needs of our users.

But this does not mean that library collections cannot be systematically improved in relation to satisfying those needs and, after all, this is the only aim of "measuring collection adequacy". The answer to the dilemma is I believe to move from the aim of measuring adequacy to the wider concept of collection evaluation or overall collection assessment. This is not just a matter of semantics. "Evaluation" means "to determine the value" of something and this is a subjective concept which introduces ideas of quality, rather than necessarily involving measurement.

In preparing this paper I have been surprised to find that almost no new ideas on collection evaluation have been brought forward over the past ten years. Several of the older surveys of collection evaluation methods such as those by Bonn[7] and Lancaster[8] remain useful, although the most convenient summary is probably now the American Library Association's *Guidelines for the Evaluation of the Effectiveness of Library Collections*.[9]

Collection evaluation methods may be grouped fairly conveniently as suggested by Gardner and Webster in their excellent Collection Analysis Project manual[10] into collection-centred and client-centred evaluation methods. Another way of looking at this division is to consider the two groups as firstly, measures based on either perceptions of adequacy or recommended materials from outside the library's own clientele, and secondly as evaluations based on a library's own current users' expressed needs. Both have their uses, but provide different kinds of measure, and therefore vary in their appropriateness to different kinds of academic libraries.

1. Collection-centred evaluation methods

(a) Statistical comparisons. These include comparisons of collection size, rates of growth, acquisitions expenditures, etc., either over a period of time or in comparison with other libraries. These comparisons have been extended in some cases to complex multiple regression techniques aimed at eliciting predictive factors for collection adequacy.

(b) Comparison of holdings against "standard" formulae or recommendations. The most well known example would be the Clapp-Jordan formula,[11] although there are now a fairly large number relating to colleges and universities in various countries.

Both these quantitative types of measure in my view have mainly political uses in being used by librarians as arguments for upgrading their own resources in comparison with other institutions or the "standards". It is unlikely that such measures have any real relation to the adequacy of the collection in serving the needs of a particular institution unless more automatically equates to more adequate. Nevertheless, their is no doubt that, other things being equal (which is rarely the case), a larger collection is likely to serve a particular user group more effectively than a small collection, but I doubt whether anything more specific can be said.

(c) Direct evaluation of the collection by a person familiar with the literature of a subject. Such an examination may reveal size, scope, depth, significance and recency of a collection if carried out by a subject expert. Care needs to be taken that examination of the shelves is conducted in conjunction with the shelflist because of material missing from the shelves, but the work carried out by Spencer Routh[12] at the University of Queensland indicates what can be done through this method by a knowledgeable person.

(d) Checking library holdings against lists of publications, including citations. There is a vast array of lists which have been used for this purpose. Amongst the most common are specialised subject bibliographies, lists of periodicals, citations in relevant publications, course reading lists, printed catalogues of major or specialised libraries. While most citation studies are straightforward, Lopez[13] has developed an interesting evaluation technique of weighted citations tracing through successive citations from an original highly relevant bibliography.

(e) Document delivery tests. This is a technique developed by Orr[14] allowing an extended checklisting approach, which also tests the time it takes for a sought item to become available in a library.

In my view, these three methods depend for effectiveness on the existence of a detailed collection development policy which outlines the collection level required. The concept of collection levels will no doubt be dealt with in the next paper, but typical approaches are those of the National Library of Australia[15] and the Research Libraries Group.[16] Unless there is a clear concept of the depth and scope of collection required in a particular subject area, it is unlikely that a list chosen for checking or testing will be valid as the basis for considering holdings in that area. All checklisting approaches rest on the assumption that the list or sample used is appropriate to the needs of the users of the particular collection being evaluated and that is unlikely to be the case for many published lists, particularly the more general ones. Most of these methods are inadequate in isolation, but nevertheless they are capable of providing a good current picture of parts and even the whole of an academic library collection when taken together. The University of New South Wales, for example, has used several methods[17] to create its own picture of parts of the collection. I suspect, however, that these collection-centred techniques are really useful, other than for political purposes, only if repeated over a period of time in a particular library, rather than being used for interlibrary comparisons. They are, however, the only measures that can hope to provide a basis for evaluating the likely effectiveness of the collection to meet future user needs, albeit often in an unspecific way.

The use of citation studies for evaluation of collections has come into vogue in recent years, but I am in agreement with Maurice Line's view that "...no measure of journal use other than one derived from a local use study is of any significant practical value to libraries"[18] for the evaluation of an individual collection. Line does agree that there are certain exceptions to this general view. For example, highly ranked journals in general citation studies that are not acquired by a library, which appear to be within the subject scale of its users, are worth examining for the collection. Similarly, citation lists based on source journals well used in a particular library can indicate journals outside a core subject that might be valuable for local users.

2. Client-centred evaluation methods

These include:

(a) User opinions. While these relate directly to the needs of users and can reflect changing interests and trends quickly, users are often subjective or inconsistent and their interests may be focused more narrowly than the collection policy as a whole.

(b) Availability and failure studies. This is an area which has received some considerable development in recent years, although the basic techniques go back to the work of Line[19] and of Urquhart and Schofield[20] in the early 1970's. More recently the techniques have been refined and developed by Kantor and his associates[21, 22] as availability analyses. Basically, the studies are analyses of the results of real attempts by library users to find particular items sought in the library and the reasons why they are unsuccessful. The importance of availability studies is in pinpointing not only which items sought by users have not been acquired by the library, but areas of weakness in systems and services, e.g. catalogue use success, unavailability because of loan, items missing or misshelved, etc. Kantor[23] and Schwarz[24] have recently developed techniques for using simulated searches weighted to allow for the effects of circulation, which reduces the cost of availability studies.

(c) Analysis of user requests, e.g. interlibrary loan, catalogue searches. Analyses of user requests may pinpoint areas of the collection which are not adequately serving users, but the statistics may be difficult to interpret unless the extent of requests in particular areas are related to the total demands of different user groups on the library collections.

(d) Expectation surveys. This is a relatively new technique, which has been used by the Office of Management Studies[25] and a few other investigations[26] examining the expectations of library users in being able to find items they seek in the collection. Changes in expectations over a period of time or very different expectations on behalf of different user groups can indicate inadequacies in the collection, particularly if studied in conjunction with availability studies.

Few of these client-centred methods are very useful in isolation, but together they help to provide data on gaps in holdings and the availability problems of the collection. Most suffer from problems of cost, and survey techniques can be expensive if samples large enough to be valid are used, but the refinement of the techniques in recent years allows libraries to draw on methods which have been fully tested elsewhere. The major drawback with all client-centred evaluation methods is that they can only provide an evaluation of the collection's adequacy in relation to the current demands of library users. They provide no information on how effective the collection is likely to be in meeting the needs of future users.

Advances in technology are having some effects on the ease with which some evaluations can be made. The major impact has been on the ability of libraries to conduct statistical analyses. For example, machine-readable catalogues and circulation systems now allow circulation data to be correlated with holdings in particular classifications. More recently, online catalogues have started to allow analyses of the searches conducted at the catalogue. Quantitative data is now available in many libraries on holdings in the collection, for example, by date of distribution, by language, etc. thus allowing much more quantitative support data to be available when evaluating different subject areas. The development of online searches has enabled outputs to be analysed in relation to a library's holdings. Similarly, with the development of machine-assisted interlibrary loan networks, we can expect more cost-effective analyses of interlibrary loan requests which can be linked back to the collection strengths or weaknesses.

This improved statistical basis for collection analysis can be extended to the national and regional level. For example, we could envisage the comparison of holdings in various libraries in different subject areas, based on comparisons of the numbers of items held in different classifications. While there is some crudity in such analyses, it would provide us with a far better idea of the major collections in Australia covering a particular subject, or say, relating to a particular author. The networks potentially allow overlap studies to be conducted on the holdings of libraries in a region, which will indicate the quantitative adequacy of libraries in the area. A further useful development is foreshadowed by the Research Libraries Group in the United States, who have developed an online system for recording collection development policies in detail using the system of collection levels for each subject.[27]

None of these developments in themselves are solutions to the intrinsic problems of measuring collection adequacy. However, each adds to the armoury of techniques that are available for overall collection assessment. While measuring collection adequacy in the true quantitative sense is not possible, nor, in many cases, are attempts to quantify useful, there are now a variety of evaluation methods which, used in combination, allow a library to build up a clear picture of the content of its collections. If, in parallel, a library has built up a detailed set of collection development policies, a proper evaluation of the collection can be made, even if we are still short of an overall measure of adequacy. The benefits of collection evaluation are in understanding a collection, and allowing its rational planning; they do not rest on pseudo-scientific quantification.[28] To quote Hazen, "Some essential variables are not now subject to quantification. Others may never be. Nevertheless, neither the facile associations of the formulas, nor the statistical sophistication of narrow-gauged quantitative studies, should prevent us from attempts to grasp the whole".[29]

References

1   E.J. Wainwright and J.E. Dean, *Measures of Adequacy for Library Collections in Australian Colleges of Advanced Education: Report of a Research Project Conducted on Behalf of the Commission on Advanced Education* (Perth: Western Australia Institute of Technology, 1976), vol. 2, p. 82

2   R.N. Broadus, "Evaluation of Academic Library Collections: A Survey of Recent Literature." *Library Acquisitions: Practice and Theory* 1 (1977): 154.

3   M. Moran, "The Concept of Adequacy in University Libraries." *College and Research Libraries* 39, 2 (1978): 85.

4   American Library Association, Collection Development Committee, *Guidelines for Collection Development*, ed. David L. Perkins (Chicago, Ill.: American Library Association, 1979), pp. 9-19.

5   Association of College and Research Libraries, "Standards for College Libraries." *College and Research Library News* 9 (1975): 278.

6   R.E. Chapin, "Limits of Local Self-sufficiency." In *Proceedings of the Conference on Interlibrary Communication and Information Networks Warrenton, Virginia, September-October 1970*, ed. R.E. Chapin (Chicago, Ill.: American Library Association, 1971), p. 54.

7   G.S. Bonn, "Evaluation of the Collection." *Library Trends* 22, 3 (1974): 265-304.

8   F.W. Lancaster, *The Measurement and Evaluation of Library Services* (Washington D.C.: Information Resources Press, 1977). Ch. 5, Evaluation of the collection; Ch. 7, Evaluation of document delivery capabilities.

9   American Library Association, *op.cit.*

10 J.J. Gardner and D.E. Webster, *The Collection Analysis Project: An Assisted Self-Study Manual* (Washington, D.C.: Association of Research Libraries, 1980).

11 V.W. Clapp and J.T. Jordan, "Quantitative Criteria for Adequacy of Academic Library Collections." *College and Research Libraries* 26, 5 (September 1965): 371-380.

12 S. Routh, *Subject Strengths of the University of Queensland Library* (Mimeographed. St Lucia: University of Queensland, 1978).

13 M.D. Lopez, "The Lopez or Citation Technique of In-depth Collection Evaluation Explicated." *College and Research Libraries* 44, 3 (1983): 251-255.

14 R.H. Orr *et al.*, "Development of Methodologic Tools for Planning and Managing Library Services. II: Measuring a Library's Capability for Providing Documents." *Bulletin of the Medical Library Association* 56, 3 (1968): 241-267.

15 *National Library of Australia Selection Policy* (Development of Resource Sharing Networks: Networks Study No. 17. Canberra: National Library of Australia, 1981).

16 N.E. Gwinn and P.H. Mosher, "Coordinating Collection Development: The RLG Conspectus." *College and Research Libraries* 44, 2 (1983): 128-140.

17 J. McLachlan and I. Trahn, "A Method of Collection Evaluation for Australian Research Libraries." *University of New South Wales Library Annual Report* (1982): 51-61.

18 M.B. Line, "Rank Lists Based on Citations and Library Uses as Indicators of Journal Usage in Individual Libraries." *Collection Management* 2, 4 (1978): 313-316.

19 M.B. Line, "The Ability of a University Library to Provide Books Wanted by Researchers." *Journal of Librarianship* 5, 1 (1973): 37-51.

20 J.A. Urquhart and J.L. Schofield, "Measuring Readers' Failure at the Shelf." *Journal of Documentation* 27, 4 (1971): 273-286.

21 P.B. Kantor, "Availability Analysis." *Journal of the American Society for Information Science* 27, 5 (1976): 316-318.

22 T. Saracevic, W.M. Shaw and P.B. Kantor, "Causes and Dynamics of User Frustration in an Academic Library." *College and Research Libraries* 38, 1 (1977): 7-18.

23 P.B. Kantor, "Demand-adjusted Shelf Availability Parameters." *Journal of Academic Librarianship* 7, 2(1981): 78-82.

24 P.J. Schwarz, "Demand-adjusted Shelf Availability Parameters: A Second Look." *College and Research Libraries* 44, 4 (1983): 210-219.

25 Gardner and Webster, *op.cit* , pp. 9-18.

26 K.A. Frohmberg, P. Kantor and W.A. Moffett, "Increases in Book Availability in a Large College Library." *Proceedings of the 43rd Meeting of the ASIS* (1980): 292-294.

27 Gwinn and Mosher, *op. cit.*

28 P.H. Mosher, "Collection Evaluation in Research Libraries: The Search for Quality, Consistency, and System in Collection Development." *Library Resources and Technical Services* 23, 1 (1979): 16-32.

29 D.C. Hazen, "Modelling Collection Development Behavior: A Preliminary Statement." *Collection Management* 4, 1/2 (1982): 1-14.

Blaine H. Hall, "Writing the Collection Assessment Manual." *Collection Management* **6, 3/4 (1984): 49-61.**

As libraries grow larger in collections and staff and become more complex, the problems of managing and controlling that growth increase dramatically. This problem is particularly evident in collection development where larger budgets and the decentralization of acquisitions decisions make consistency and standardization difficult. Daniel L. Perkins [9] wisely recommended a collection development manual to guide the collection development program and to assure the smooth functioning of the acquisition and processing operations. But of similar value to a library can be a collection assessment manual to assure that collections are regularly and systematically monitored and evaluated, essential considerations of any well-managed collection development program.

As an outgrowth of the ARL [Association of Research Libraries] Collection Analysis Project (CAP) conducted at Brigham Young University in 1978-79, the library developed its *Collection Assessment Manual*.[3] The suggestions and recommendations here are based on the experience and results of this manual development process.

Importance of a Manual

There is, of course, no lack of published material on library collection evaluation. The excellent surveys of the collection evaluation literature by Bonn [1] and Lancaster [5] together list 268 articles and books in their bibliographies. Lancaster notes that "more work has been performed on the evaluation of collections...than any other facet of the library....[5:165]

A manual, however, can be a valuable collection evaluation tool for a number of reasons. First, it can aid uniformity and consistency among the various assessors and, over time, assure comparability of results. Second, it can save considerable time by eliminating the necessity for each evaluator to study the voluminous literature on collection assessments to determine which measurement or assessment techniques to use and how to use them. Many libraries, in fact, may not have this literature readily available. Third, it can establish a common purpose, rationale, and standardized procedures for conducting collection evaluations. Fourth, it can provide training, direction, and guidance to evaluators for developing their professional competence in conducting collection assessments and interpreting and reporting the data obtained.

Perkins[9] distinguishes two types of collection development manuals - the training manual and the reference manual. Similar distinctions can and need to be made for the collection assessment manual. Both should include specific measurement techniques and implementation methodology, reporting requirements, etc., required by the library. But the reference manual might simply be a procedures manual containing only the measurement techniques adopted by the library, a step-by-step methodology for implementation, forms, etc. This manual would be particularly appropriate for smaller libraries with few evaluators and rather homogeneous collections or any library that has established a set procedure for conducting assessments. For most larger libraries, however, with many collections developed at various collecting levels with varied assessment objectives, a rigid step-by-step procedural or reference manual might be too simplistic to work well.

A training manual, on the other hand, can provide additional information to enable the assessor to understand: (1) the purposes and objectives of the library's assessment program; (2) the planning process required by the library in determining the objectives for a given assessment, including the resources in personnel, supplies, and equipment necessary for successfully completing the project; (3) the measurement techniques and methodologies from which to select their advantages and disadvantages, the purpose and value of the data they produce, and how to employ them; (4) suggested methods for analyzing the data obtained from employing the various techniques; and (5) reporting requirements.

A training manual, in brief, can prepare professional librarians to make professional decisions and to develop tailor-made evaluation programs to meet a variety of assessment objectives. This is important in many libraries, since all collections do not require full-scale assessments in every instance, particularly when subsequent assessments of a collection may only require updating information in a limited number of areas rather than a full-scale evaluation.

Deciding on the type of manual to develop, then, is basic and should be decided at the outset according to local assessment requirements.

Planning the Assessment

Only through careful planning can a collection assessment be systematic and thorough enough to produce accurate and reliable data. The manual should, therefore, outline the assessment planning process. The BYU *Manual* establishes five basic premises the assessors should keep in mind as they plan an assessment project:

1. Assessments are to be performed to obtain data for more effective collection development decisions.

2. Assessments should consider how well collections are meeting the needs of both present and potential users.

3. Assessments should be based on a current collection development policy statement for the collection being assessed.

4. Explicit objectives or outcomes to be achieved from the assessment should be written and approved by the Collection Development Librarian.

5. Subjectivity as to collection quality should be reduced by using a combination of both collection-centred and client-centred measurement techniques and objective data.[3:11]

By considering these basic premises, the assessor will be able to develop an assessment plan that is sound and will guarantee worthwhile results. Each library, of course, should establish its own basic premises and can also develop a planning form, and, if needed, use this form in a formal review/approval process for each projected assessment.

The manual should also specify the procedure for doing the planning. The following considerations should be included:

(1) Selecting the collection or part of the collection to be assessed. A number of factors might govern this - the size of the collection and the time and resources available to assess it, changing needs or demands of library clientele or institutional requirements, consortium or network commitments, accreditation requirements, a weeding program, etc. It would also be helpful for the library to

develop a long-range assessment plan, especially in larger libraries, to assure that all parts of the collection receive appropriate evaluation.

(2) Reviewing the collection policy statement. This review ensures that the collection policy reflect current thinking as to collection level, types of materials and formats required, language focus, and the relationship of the collection being assessed to other collections within the library or to network or consortium commitments. This policy review is necessary because the data obtained from collection measurement can only be interpreted in terms of the collection purpose and objectives. Obviously a collection assessment can provide new or additional data to help update collection policy statements, but this does not eliminate the need to begin an assessment with as up-to-date a policy as possible.

(3) Determining the objectives to be achieved by the assessment. This step is crucial for worthwhile results. Some assessments may require full-scale measurement of size, growth rate, comparison to established subject bibliographies or lists, patron opinions as to collection quality availability and accessibility measures, etc. Other assessments may require only one or two of these measurements.

An objective may be stated in rather general terms; e.g., "to determine the strength and weaknesses of the juvenile literature collection." But this may not help the selector determine exactly what needs to be measured and which techniques to use. Thus, the plan should include the specific questions that need to be answered about the collection to determine its strengths and weaknesses, such as:

Are there sufficient copies of heavily requested titles?
Is the budget adequate to obtain sufficient new titles?
Are there duplicate or non-used titles that should be weeded?
Are library or institution programs anticipated that will affect the adequacy of the collection?
Are there sufficient journal subscriptions?
Can patrons readily find the materials they need?

This kind of question, when made a part of the assessment planning process and when required by an assessment manual, helps assessors plan more thoroughly and also suggests the kinds of measurements required to complete the project.

(4) Selecting the measurement techniques to be used in the assessment. Since each measurement technique has been development to obtain certain kinds of information about a collection, the techniques must be selected carefully in terms of the objectives previously established. A shelf list measurement, for instance, can show the gross size of a collection, but it cannot show how accessible the materials are to patrons or how current and up-to-date the collection is. Nor can it show how good the collection is, even though we often assume that bigger is better. If the objective is to assess quality, other techniques must be used, although examining gross size may be a good place to start. The training manual should include a variety of measurement techniques from which assessors may choose and a discussion of the important considerations in their selection and use.

(5) Estimating the resources required to conduct the assessment. Full-scale assessments can be time consuming and represent a significant commitment of

library resources. The manual should establish some preliminary estimates of the time and type of library personnel (professional or clerical) required to perform some common assessment tasks. Card catalog checking, for instance, requires a minimum of one minute of clerical time per citation when an alphabetized list is used, and a document delivery test takes from four to ten hours. The profession could perform a useful function by establishing some uniform time estimates for various assessment activities. Over time, of course, an individual library can come up with standards of its own that will enable assessors to prepare fairly accurate resource estimates, and these should become a useful part of the assessment manual.

Measurement Techniques

The heart of the assessment manual should be a discussion of measurement techniques. Assessment literature distinguishes between quantitative and qualitative, objective and subjective, and collection-centred and client-centred methods of evaluation. Ideally, the measurement methodology should help reduce subjectivity of judgment as much as possible. But as the ALA *Guidelines for Collection Development* cautions:

> Available methods for determining the value of a collection are not completely objective or free of interpretation by the evaluators, nor are they foolproof in their application and outcome. However, procedures are available which can reduce individual interpretation.... If applied and administered carefully, or if used in combination with one another, the procedures can demonstrate with reasonable assurance how well a collection satisfies the purpose of the library as perceived at any one time.[8:10]

The assessment manual should provide a convenient arrangement for assessors to select from the various measurement techniques those that will provide a reasonably objective and quantitative approach to both collection-centred and client-centred methodologies.

The collection-centred approaches generally treat the collection as a resource and attempt to show its size, rate of growth, and its quality in relation to some external standard, e.g., a list or bibliography of recognized quality or a standard established by a professional organization for a type of library or for a professional or educational program.

However, librarians are well aware that good collections do not necessarily create satisfied clients. Materials, even if acquired, are not always immediately available on the shelf, and even when they are, users do not always find them on the shelf without difficulty and delay. Client-centred methods, therefore, attempt to measure the utility of the resource. Only by measuring the quality of actual and perceived use can the library really determine the usefulness of its collection development program to its patrons. Patron surveys can be used to determine user perception of their needs and the library's success in meeting those needs. And a number of availability, accessibility, and document delivery capability measures can indicate the success of the library in meeting patron demand on collections.

A convenient arrangement for the assessment manual is to have separate chapters on the collection-centred and client-centred approaches. The various measurement techniques can then be introduced and explained and the implementation procedures spelled out step-by-step with appropriate forms and analysis procedures provided. The assessor, then, has everything necessary to select and apply the measurement techniques to achieve the specific objectives for a given assessment project.

The advantage of this arrangement is its flexibility. No assessor will be expected to use every technique for every assessment, but the manual can be developed to provide as little or as much as is necessary for an ongoing assessment program for any library.

Collection-centred Techniques

The manual developer has a number of collection-centred measurement techniques from which to choose. The BYU *Manual* includes compiling statistics, list checking, direct observation, and applying standards.

Compiling Statistics

Counting and compiling statistics are frequently used to describe collections. These include such measures as gross size, volumes or titles added per year, percent of growth, circulation, unfilled requests, expenditures and formulas. The BYU *Manual* excludes formulas, unfilled patron and ILL requests and expenditures either for lack of adequate records or for their inappropriateness to evaluating individual subject collections. But each library should make its own determination.

The advantages of using numerical and statistical data are that they (1) are often readily available (possibly from various online systems), (2) lend themselves to comparison with similar data from other libraries or internally over time, and (3) help eliminate subjectivity. Their disadvantages are that (1) the significance of the figures may be difficult to interpret in terms of judging collection quality and (2) they may be inaccurate because of improper recording or inadequate definition of the categories or units to be counted (the title vs. volume problem is a good example).

Checking Lists

Checking lists against holdings has long been used to measure the quality of library collections. In many research libraries, it is often the major, if not the sole, measure used. If the lists are carefully selected with consideration of the peculiar or unique purposes of the collection and the patrons and programs it serves in mind, it can provide excellent results. It also results in buying lists for collection improvement. Obviously, lists previously used as buying guides for the collection being assessed or lists that are out-of-date or not representative of the library's interests, collection levels, or purposes will not provide satisfactory results. The training manual should provide information to help assessors select appropriate lists.

Applying Standards

Applying standards to evaluate library collections can sometimes produce worthwhile results. Regional accrediting associations and many professional societies and associations have established standards for academic libraries, as have some state and national library associations. In recent years, however, the emphasis in some of these standards has been on quality rather than quantity and on judging the adequacy of a collection in terms of institutional goals and objectives. The most recent thrust is on outputs rather than on inputs. Outputs, as noted earlier, lend themselves of course to client-centred measurements in determining the utility of a collection.

Most standards are expressed in broad general terms that require interpretation by the assessor, but standards should be considered in library collection assessments since they often carry considerable weight with funding authorities. However, standards must be related to the goals and objectives of a specific library or institution, and should be considered as establishing minimums, not maximums.

The assessment manual can provide at least a sample of some of the standards statements available for various subjects or types of libraries or can specify the standard adopted by the individual library.

Client-centred Techniques

Only by measuring the quality of the actual and perceived use of its collections can a library really determine the usefulness of its collection development program to its patrons. Assessors have at their disposal two ways of obtaining information about the utility of a collection: (1) asking patrons for their perceptions of the collection or (2) measuring appropriate aspects of use or delivery potential.

Opinionnaires

Opinionnaires are a useful tool in the assessor's arsenal of techniques, but they must be used with caution. Designing a brief, unambiguous survey instrument is not easy, nor is the validating, the administration, the tabulating or analyzing of the results always a simple matter. Used too often, such forms become not only a nuisance but may also create antagonism rather than eliciting useful information. Moreover, users are often passive, inconsistent, and uncooperative, and the opinions of ill-informed respondents often receive as much weight as those of well-informed and experienced users.

However, carefully planned and executed surveys can help the library (1) identify levels and kinds of user needs, (2) reflect change in patron interests and trends, (3) refine collection and service goals and objectives, (4) and reach those patrons whose attitudes and opinions may not otherwise be communicated to the library.

Users may be surveyed on (1) their needs for various types of materials and services; (2) their perception of the adequacy of collections to meet their needs; (3) their ideas for improving collections, services, and policies; and (4) their use of various types of material and services.

The assessment manual should include examples of survey instruments used previously in the library or by other libraries. Assessors may then use those appropriate for their purposes or modify or adapt as needed. For either use, the examples can save each assessor from reinventing the wheel. The BYU *Manual* includes questionnaires used previously to survey faculty in English, chemistry, and Latin American studies; several instruments developed during the CAP study, i.e., "Faculty Research Survey," "Graduate Student Library Research Survey," "Needs Survey of Major Academic Units," "Faculty Periodicals Survey," "Faculty Interview Checksheet," plus an "Importance/Success

Survey" instrument from the ARL *CAP Manual* and the user survey instrument developed by MIT for their CAP study.

But perceptions of the utility of a collection are not always accurate or quantifiable, and a user-centred assessment as well as the assessment manual should include quantifiable measures of the usefulness of a collection.

Availability and Accessibility Measures

The literature contains references to a number of useful availability and accessibility measures that show the likelihood of patron requests being satisfied and in what length of time. Some also help pinpoint what library practices or policies might be changed to improve the quality of service. Orr's[7] "Document Delivery Capability" combines both availability (the probability that a patron will find desired items on the shelf when needed) and accessibility (the time required to obtain the item) into one numerical index number by measuring both the adequacy of the collection and the speed with which the library can meet patron demands.

Kantor[4] developed an availability test using data provided by catalog users as they conducted author or title searches. His test measures the level of immediate patron satisfaction and pinpoints one or more of five causes for patron failure or dissatisfaction, i.e., (1) failure of the library to acquire the item, (2) patron failure to use the catalog correctly, (3) failure to find the book because it is circulating, (4) failure of library procedures, and (5) user failure to find correctly shelved items.

Kantor also developed for the *CAP Manual*[2] measurements of accessibility that measure the time required to perform various library functions that might be slowing down the process of getting materials to patrons, e.g., acquisition, repairing, searching, reshelving, ILL, weeding, reclassifying. These tests can help libraries detect bottlenecks or unnecessarily long procedures that frustrate user access to materials and services.

Circulation Statistics

Another important measure of utility is provided by circulation statistics. With the wide use of computerized circulation systems, numerous possibilities are becoming available to measure and study collection use. The number of circulations per individual item (useful in determining the need for multiple copies or changes in loan policies), the number of circulations by classification of materials and patrons, and the percentage of holdings circulating by classification are several possibilities. The assessment manual should indicate whatever the individual library is capable of providing from its circulation system and the procedures for obtaining and using this information in the assessment process.

Periodical Use Measures

We included in the BYU *Manual* a periodical use measurement developed by Shaw[10] at Case Western, which required a simple procedure of placing colored dots on each bound volume of a journal as it is reshelved after its initial use during the study period. However, this technique determines only use or non-use of a volume, not the number of uses per volume. To measure uses per volume, we modified the Shaw technique by putting a 1" square label on the spine at the first reshelving and making a hash mark for subsequent shelvings.

Other Considerations

Since the assessment manual should be as useful as possible, each library should include whatever features will make it work best for local needs. The BYU *Manual* includes a policy and methodology for conducting assessments for special purposes, e.g., for storing, discarding, or obtaining alternate formats (microforms, etc.) and for assessing and updating approval program profiles using reports from approval plan vendors.

Another essential element should be a chapter on reporting assessment results. Mosher[6:29] lists nine items a good report should include:

1. the reason why the evaluation was conducted;
2. the nature and goal of the evaluation;
3. the method or methods used;
4. problems encountered (particularly those that may have affected the results);
5. general comments about the collection;
6. a summary of specific strengths and weakness;
7. suggestions for additional measurements or analyses and recommended methods;
8. peripheral discoveries or observations of use to this library;
9. a plan or campaign of action to improve collection in areas of *undesirable* weakness, with lists of specific items or types of materials needed and cost estimates, where appropriate.

The report should probably also include a description of the clientele the collection serves and the purposes for which the collection is being developed. Including in the manual examples of good reports and illustrations of the effective use of charts, graphs, tables, etc., and any other specific requirements required by the individual library will help to ensure effective assessment reports.

At BYU we also found appendices valuable additions to the manual. These include:

1. agencies accrediting academic programs at BYU, giving address and phone number and current accreditation status of the BYU program;
2. most recent ALA standards for university libraries;
3. statistical aids, including sampling principles and techniques, tables of sample sizes, and random number tables;
4. a list of readings on collection assessments that contributed to the principles and methodologies included in the manual (the master copy of the *Manual* also includes copies of many of these sources, as a help to assessors who wish to read more about a principle or measurement methodology).

Finally, the authors should decide on a workable format for the manual. At BYU we chose a looseleaf format and a chapter paging system (1.1, 2.1.) to facilitate revisions and additions as use of the manual suggests the need for such changes.

Conclusion

Although developing an assessment manual requires a lot of effort, that effort is well invested. A good collection development manual can help to insure more carefully planned and purposeful evaluations, less time wasted by assessors in determining their evaluation strategies, more meaningful reports, and ultimately better collection development decisions.

References

1. George S. Bonn, "Evaluation of the Collection." *Library Trends* 22 (January 1974): 265-304.

2. Jeffrey J. Gardner and Duane E. Webster, *The Collection Analysis Project: Operating Manual for the Review and Analysis of the Collection Development Function in Academic and Research Libraries. CAP Manual* (Washington, D.C.: Association of Research Libraries, University Library Management Studies Office, 1978).

3. Blaine H. Hall, *Collection Assessment Manual* (Provo, Utah: Brigham Young University Library, 1981). ERIC Document ED217852.

4. Paul B. Kantor, "Availability Analysis." *Journal of the American Society for Information Science* (September-October, 1976): 311-319.

5. F.W. Lancaster, *The Measurement and Evaluation of Library Services* (Washington, D.C.: Information Resources Press, 1977).

6. Paul H. Mosher, "Collection Evaluation in Research Libraries: The Search for Quality, Consistency, and System in Collection Development." *Library Resources and Technical Services* 23 (Winter 1979): 16-32.

7. Richard H. Orr *et al.*, "Development of Methodologic Tools for Planning and Managing Library Services: II. Measuring a Library's Capability for Providing Documents." *Medical Library Association Bulletin* 56 (1968): 241-267.

8. American Library Association. Collection Development Committee, *Guidelines for Collection Development*, ed. David L. Perkins (Chicago, Ill.: American Library Association, 1979).

9. David L. Perkins, "Writing the Collection Development Manual." *Collection Management* 4 (Fall 1982): 37-47.

10. W.M. Shaw, Jr., "A Practical Journal Usage Technique." *College and Research Libraries* 39 (November 1978): 479-484.

PART 3

SELECTION AND WEEDING OF RESOURCES

CHAPTER 6

SELECTION PRINCIPLES AND PRACTICES

Basic Principles in Selection

In *Developing Library and Information Center Collections* Edward Evans presents a masterful summary of what he terms the "theory" of selection based on eleven major textbooks published between 1925 and 1985.[1] Despite this extended analysis the principles can be summarized in three words: need versus want, or "quality versus demand" in Evans' words. From this one issue stem all principles upon which genuinely responsible and responsive selection is built.

To begin with it indicates that the user above all else is the central focus of selection, the raison d'etre upon which collection development, technical services and information services are built. Therefore, a librarian may argue quite legitimately that the selection of library materials should aim at providing the users with exactly what they want. Another librarian, though, may argue with equal fervour that the library, as a socially responsible institution, should qualify this approach by selecting the *best* material available that meets the users' demands. A third librarian may go further, stating that the library should select simply the best there is without worrying about demand.

The most succinct summary of the need versus want debate is presented by Robert Broadus, who sets forth the case for each side clearly and objectively.[2] In his analysis of the case in favour of user wants Broadus implies that proponents put forth five basic arguments:

1. a librarian does not have the right to impose his views about what is best for his users;
2. people should be provided with what they will use, not with materials that will sit on shelves unread;
3. collecting what people want does not automatically mean that only one level of quality will be the result, because users are different enough that their wants will result in a broad range of qualities;
4. if users financially support the library, they have a right to determine exactly what goes into the collection;
5. giving people exactly what they want ensures that they will read, and this helps to build an important habit.

Claims made in support of emphasizing user needs include, according to Broadus, the following:

1. the library has an obligation to meet user needs by supplying high quality materials;
2. the library has a positive obligation to educate its users, and it does this by exerting constructive influence on thought and attitudes;
3. the library is not in competition with newsagents and bookshops, both of which supply what readers want very effectively;
4. the library ought to be improving the reading tastes of its users, and it can do this by providing information which otherwise might not be available or not be chosen;
5. without motivation public reading tastes on the whole are remarkably mundane and disinclined toward "the best" in any field.

As one might imagine, both sides of the issue have been argued with equal vigour and conviction, and no one has yet proposed an argument from either perspective that is totally convincing. Each librarian must reach his own decision and take a clear position in the need versus want debate; this position will determine to a great extent what one selects for the collection. The most flexible position which draws on the strengths of both arguments, and therefore one with much to commend it, lies somewhere in the middle. This position draws on the following points:

1. the library exists to serve its users and therefore must take account of what they want;
2. but if the librarian selects only what his users want, these people are not being given a chance to improve their knowledge and tastes;
3. if presented with qualitatively superior materials along with exactly what they want, users may begin to appreciate and use the former;
4. the library, to facilitate its recreational, informational and educational objectives, has an obligation to cater to all tastes, both high and low;
5. the librarian as a professional selector should be trusted both to select high quality materials in accordance with user needs and to supply their wants.

Basic Requirements for Effective Selection

In many ways these principles draw substantially on ideas first articulated by the noted Indian librarian, S.R. Ranganathan. In *Library Book Selection* he discusses the five "laws" of librarianship, and these impinge directly on our modern understanding of selection.[3] These laws are: (1) books are for use; (2) every reader his book; (3) every book its reader; (4) save the reader's time; (5) a library is a growing organism. Clearly these guidelines go beyond selection principles and set the framework for practical understanding as well. The librarian, or anyone else involved in selection for that matter, must have a strong commitment to these laws as they relate to selection. In the end that commitment is more important than any number of procedures, allocation of responsibilities, policy statements, complaint-handling systems or collection of selection tools. In our view the serious selector must remember - and practise - a handful of basic principles. These are stated here not with biblical certainty but as starting points for developing one's own foundations for effective selection.

1. The selection process is related to other professional activities and is dependent on them both for policy decisions and practical procedures. Selection is part of the overall collection development process and must be viewed in this perspective.

2. One should update professional competence by regular reading in the literature concerning the principles and practices of collection building, selection, publishing, reviewing and acquisitions.[4]

3. One must have an intimate knowledge of the library's purpose, its collections and its user groups. These are the key factors in effective, responsible selection of library materials.

4. A good selector will develop over time a sound understanding of how the publishing industry and the book trade operate; this includes how library materials of all types are generated, distributed and sold.

5. One should become fully familiar with the publishing policies, advertising media, publicity outlets, names of senior editors and general reliability of those publishers whose lists are most directly relevant to the library's collection-building requirements.

6. One should become fully familiar with the key reviewing media and should read reviews regularly in order to keep abreast of critical opinion on books and other library materials.

7. One should become fully familiar with trade and national bibliographies and should understand their strengths and weaknesses with regard to the library's collection-building requirements.

8. One should always make independent but well-informed judgments about what materials are to be selected for a library, as the competent professional is in the best position to determine the right materials for the specific collection and its users.

The Selection Environment

Selection in all types of libraries occurs within a set of common factors. First, it is done on the basis of existing collection requirements and user needs and wants with regard to subjects, formats and level of content. Second, it proceeds within a carefully determined budget, with funds allocated to specific subject areas or other categories suitable to the library. Third, it involves a structured approach to the identification and evaluation of potentially suitable library materials. Within this threefold set of factors there are many permutations, depending largely on the specific variables which apply to the different types of libraries.

Public Libraries. Ranging from the very large and impressive state library collections to a few hundred volumes in small branch libraries, the collections of public libraries all share a common characteristic - diversity. Because user groups in the public library setting range across the entire social and cultural spectrum, the selection of materials must reflect and cater to this diversity. The genuinely responsive public library will work to meet the educational, informational and recreational requirements of the full range of age groups, educational levels, multicultural factors and interests represented in its service area. In practice this means that educational and informational needs are at least matched by recreational requirements, with this last category receiving far more attention than in other types of libraries. Consequently, current titles produced by trade publishers receive the greatest emphasis in public library selection, as these materials are most suited to the general interests of the community.

Most selection is done by the librarian, and it is not unusual for the senior librarians of a regional library service to do virtually all of the selecting. It is more the norm, though, for the chief librarian to rely on input from other librarians, including those serving branches and mobile services. Occasionally this democratization of selection extends to the formation of a selection committee, but for a variety of reasons this approach seems to have lost much of its popularity among librarians. It is an unwieldy system; consensus is difficult to achieve; regular meetings prove almost impossible to arrange; representation of all user interests creates too large a committee; responsibility for selection is removed from the librarian, who after all is trained in this procedure. Still, there are some public libraries that prefer this method, defending it on the ground that it involves both local authority and community members with positive ramifications in two areas. First, justification of expenditure is easier if the local authority has been involved from the outset; second, library materials are more easily defended against challenges if members of the community have been involved in their selection.

Indeed complaints about library materials tend to occur more in public libraries than in almost any other environment, with the possible exception of schools. Critical rumblings are as likely to come from local government officials as from the general public. Therefore, selection in public libraries takes greater account of public sensitivity to issues and subjects than in most other types of libraries. In practice this means heavy reliance not only on positive reviews in "trustworthy" sources but also on careful examination of titles received on approval or by purchase. Although this may apply especially to children's materials, it should also be an important consideration in juvenile and adult materials involving race, sex, politics and religion - everything that is really interesting in life.

Because speed of supply is essential in order to meet user demand generated by advertising and reviews in the popular press and other media, public libraries tend to make heavy use of approval plans, visits by publishers' representatives, trade literature promotions and timely reviews in the mass circulation magazines and newspapers. All of these permit rapid, often first-hand, evaluation, and this helps to ensure that materials are acquired before or while they are being sought by users. Other selection procedures are not ignored, including standing orders, browsing in bookshops and use of the standard library selection tools (*Wilson Library Bulletin*, etc.); but these generally aid in selecting educational and informational materials, while other methods are preferred for recreational materials.

School Libraries. If public libraries have a particular concern for the community's recreational requirements (but not to the exclusion of other needs), then school libraries have a special commitment to educational needs of students and curriculum support for teachers. If public libraries are characterized by heterogeneous user populations, then school libraries may be said to serve homogeneous user groups. These groups also form a captive audience, since students must read what is deemed appropriate for the curriculum by teachers and librarians. Selecting educational materials for an identifiable range of students engaged in a specific set of curriculum modules may appear rather simpler than it is, but there are once again a number of variables to be considered.

First of all, children have a range of educational needs and abilities, whether at primary or secondary level; all of these needs and abilities must receive attention if the library is to serve its developmental function in the educational process. In addition to the students, of course, teachers and administrators have some right to expect curriculum support and other professional materials in the school library, and this expectation adds yet another level to be considered. It must be noted, however, that few school libraries have budgets that permit selection of more than a handful of teacher-oriented materials and that for the most part state education department libraries are regarded as the primary source for such literature. Second, a wide range of subjects and disciplines must be covered in a school library, from such areas as literature and history to science and technical or practical subjects. Third, school libraries tend to have a greater variety of materials in their libraries because of the heavy reliance on audio, visual and other non-print media in teaching. Therefore, the subject range, educational needs and levels and formats are all sufficiently broad to make selection a difficult and time-consuming activity in school libraries.

To this extent school and public libraries may be rather similar, but in selection procedures they differ significantly. Most school libraries do not in theory or practice rely as heavily on the librarian to do most of the selecting as is the case in public libraries. Instead the teaching staff provide substantial input in terms of both selecting and evaluating materials; the Sample Evaluation Form (Attachment B in Appendix B) is based on one devised for teachers. In addition school administrators and students to some extent are encouraged to become involved in the selection of materials. Occasionally this range of selectors is formalized into a committee, but normally the teacher-librarian relies on a more informal arrangement and retains the final decision on selection for himself. The additional variable here, of course, is the school principal, who often exercises significant control over what is selected.

Obviously the problem of challenged materials can be particularly difficult in school libraries because of the young readers and the involvement of parents in their reading. This suggests that collection development policies and statements of selection procedures should have a major place in school libraries, as indeed they should in public libraries. As Evans states, "because the media specialist normally is responsible for what is purchased and because more parents and others are actively concerned about both formats and contents of materials children will be exposed to, having clearly stated collection goals and selection criteria allows everyone to operate as efficiently (and safely) as possible."[5] Many more teacher-librarians, therefore, should pay attention to developing formal policy statements and perhaps to establishing selection advisory committees to help defuse censorship before it becomes an issue.

Selectors in school libraries rely heavily on published reviews, and there is a number of reviewing journals catering specifically to materials for children and young adults. Some of these are treated in Chapter 8. According to Belland, teacher-librarians rank favourable reviews as the most important factor because they have "...neither the time nor the commitment to analyze materials in terms of a particular curricular need. They defer judgment to those persons who are professionally involved in reviewing a wide variety of materials."[6]   On the whole this assessment is also true of the Australian situation, although school librarians here do still rely on recommendations and evaluations by teachers, on approval plans and other means of previewing materials. Previewing, in fact, plays a greater role in selection in this environment because of the amount of non-print material acquired for school libraries.

Academic Libraries. Higher education embraces a multitude of institutional types, from "junior colleges" to teacher training colleges to large universities. When speaking of academic libraries, therefore, one encompasses an extremely broad range of collections. They may be devoted to relatively few subjects in an institution with a narrow teaching focus (an agricultural college, for example), to a broader but still not full disciplinary range (a technical college or polytechnic), to all disciplines at all levels (a college or university offering undergraduate and postgraduate degrees). In addition to subject focus there is a notable disparity in levels of readership; users at a technical college, for example, will be rather different in their abilities and needs from students and staff at a major university. Nevertheless, the tertiary sector embraces all of these variations, and this must be kept in mind when thinking in general about selection in academic libraries.

While the user community in an academic library may appear to be heterogeneous in terms of the range of subjects studied - even a smaller college of advanced education offers hundreds of subjects in several degree programmes - it is in fact relatively homogeneous within itself and has definable boundaries of reading interests. That is, disciplines are being studied at specific levels, from basic undergraduate to advanced research, and both disciplines and levels can be determined accurately from the institution's clearly defined teaching activities. There is generally substantial documentation upon which selectors can draw for information about user interests and needs: institution handbooks, course syllabi, research reports, etc.

Selection in academic libraries exhibits a number of characteristics that set it apart from other types of libraries. First, these libraries deal more intensively as a matter of course with the international booktrade. While Western Europe and North America may be their primary foci, many also select widely from Asian, African, Latin American and Pacific sources. This means that the selection sources must be representative not only of all subject areas but also of various regions. Second, languages tend not to be a limiting factor in academic libraries. Public libraries with multicultural user groups and special libraries in science and technology will have some foreign language materials, but it is the academic libraries which collect most heavily in foreign languages either in support of specific language-linked programmes or because a reasonable percentage of users can read materials in other languages. Third, academic libraries on the whole use a broader and more detailed range of selection tools. Trade publications, national bibliographies, reviewing journals, scholarly journals, indexing services - these and more are used in the normal course of events by selectors in academic libraries. Fourth, selection is less the preserve of professional librarians in academic libraries than in any other type. As Dickinson (pp. 214-224) suggests, the academic staff are expected to have significant input in the selection process. The assumption is that academic staff, as experts in their disciplines, are also experts in the most suitable literature in these disciplines for their library's collections. While one may question this assumption, and may cite the example of subject or area studies librarians who act as selectors, the norm is for selection to be out of professional hands at least to a significant degree. The librarians in academic libraries tend to select for non-circulating collections (reference works) and to monitor the selection by academic units. This monitoring procedure can be formalized quite usefully by the appointment of discipline librarians with responsibility for liaison with individual schools or departments in the selection of library materials.

These librarians have responsibility to select material not specifically recommended by the teaching staff and to ensure a balance is maintained within their particular subject areas. They bring to the notice of the academic staff material considered of value and interest.[7]

While this helps to give the library a modicum of control over selection, it is really through allocation of the book vote to departments and schools that most effective control is exercised. While the book vote is specifically for acquisitions, it has obvious repercussions on selection if librarians, when monitoring the expenditure of funds, can suggest that items are excessively costly or that a high percentage of the vote is being spent on specific topics in a discipline.

Special Libraries. Special libraries form at one time the largest, most disparate and least easily identified group of libraries. They range from small collections in a single room of a commercial firm or professional body to the multi-branch scientific and technical libraries of a country's major government research agencies. Also included in this group are a number of academic libraries which, because of the highly specialized nature of their collections, have the narrow subject focus more typical of special than academic libraries. At the University of London, for instance, there are specialized research libraries in art, classical studies, psychiatry, legal studies, United States studies and many other quite specific disciplines.[8]

Obviously, then, a narrow subject focus is most typical of the special library collection, and this is matched in most cases by currency of collections (except in special academic or research institute libraries). On the whole working collections in special libraries tend to be no older than twenty-five to thirty years, although retrospective collections may well be relegated to closed access storage. Also, a high proportion of the collection is devoted to serial titles - as much as 80 per cent in libraries with a scientific or technical orientation. As in academic libraries these collections are characterized by a significant proportion of foreign and foreign-language materials.

These characteristics of special library collections suggest a number of features common to selection for such libraries. It is, first of all, most likely for there to be a single professional in charge of the library operation, or at least for collection development not to be the responsibility of a professional appointed for this specific purpose. The librarian tends to be a subject specialist, as it is assumed that a professional with intimate knowledge of the field will be the best person to understand both user needs and their information requests. These specialists, as in academic libraries, rely heavily on users to suggest items for selection; but unlike colleagues elsewhere they cannot place much reliance on standard selection tools because they are either not specialized or not current enough. Information from publishers and suppliers and reliance on indexing and abstracting sources play a higher than expected role in selecting materials for such in-depth collections.

A final but most significant characteristic of selection in special libraries is the reliance on intimate, often relatively formal, knowledge of user information requirements. Because user profiles are so specialized, the librarian necessarily constructs a unique and detailed picture of each user's information needs much more readily than in other information settings. In libraries offering special dissemination services, including regular online searches and SDI (Selective Dissemination of Information), these profiles may be developed as part of a formal procedure; in other instances they may accrue simply as part of the librarian's daily contact with the users. However arrived at, such profiles are of special significance in the selection process. Given the frequent availability of these formal or informal user studies in the special library sector, special librarians are in a unique position with regard to the preparation of written collection development policy statements, which as yet have not become popular with this type of information centre.

Selection Strategies

By and large selection in libraries of all types is on an item-by-item basis, with selectors in the library or elsewhere in the institution selecting specific titles from a variety of secondary bibliographic, previewing and reviewing sources. At the same time, though, a certain amount of selection can be "automated" and delegated to various functionaries in the booktrade by a variety of means, most usually approval plans, blanket orders and standing orders. While these are normally discussed under the rubric of acquisitions, they do in fact have a selection function in that suppliers do the selecting in accordance with a specific profile and thus give librarians additional time for the time-consuming business of item-by-item selection.

Approval Plans. In this method of selecting and acquiring materials the library supplies a vendor with a detailed profile of the library's requirements in specific areas plus budgetary limits and depends on the supplier to select and regularly supply materials within the parameters indicated. The library then evaluates the materials supplied and returns those that it feels are unsuitable. Given the expense involved in administering approval plans, it is to the advantage of both library and supplier to have a profile that is extremely accurate and detailed, and for this reason a written collection development policy may well serve as a suitable profile. When a plan is functioning effectively, there will be few or no returns, although the advantage is that the library does have the right to evaluate and return any item supplied. From the library's standpoint, then, it is a means of selecting on the basis of first-hand evaluation, which is often not possible in any other purchase method. From the vendor's viewpoint, it is a way to boost sales by providing libraries with a package of materials which otherwise might be overlooked.

In addition to the obvious advantage of allowing evaluation of an item before acquisition approval plans save library time and money that would be absorbed by the selection of a single item and the subsequent generation of an individual order. They also theoretically are able to provide materials more quickly, thereby resulting in a higher rate of currency in selection than might otherwise be possible. However, this implies that the vendor is doing his job well, which may not be the case. Therefore, and this raises the issue of disadvantages, the library must be prepared to monitor the approval plan, and this means having in operation an effective monitoring programme rather than an ad hoc evaluation system. Katz offers 12 per cent as a rough guide to efficiency; that is, if returns exceed this figure, the plan should be revised or cancelled. He goes on to say, though, that "there is disagreement on the percentages of returns. Some vendors and librarians say the percentage of returns should be no more than 4 per cent."[9] Whatever percentage is deemed significant for a given library, it implies the need to monitor approval plans. Monitoring in turn costs time and money, and there is available very little information on the actual costs of this as compared with item-by-item selection. When monitoring, one must be on the lookout for what the plan is excluding as well as what it is including, remembering that the sense of security engendered by a market-oriented supplier may result in potentially wanted materials that are not supplied being out of print by the time they come to the library's attention. This raises the other major problem with approval plans: they may supply more than the library expects, or they may supply less. In either case the plan is being less than desired as a selection device, but on the whole the popularity of this method suggests that it functions reasonably well.[10]

Blanket Orders. Both blanket orders and standing orders (the latter described in the next section) are less thoroughly defined than approval plans. The former tend to operate with the larger trade publishers, while the latter are usually limited to smaller specialist publishers; but there are several other subtle differences that distinguish these two types of selection procedures. In a blanket order agreement the library does not offer the supplier or publisher a profile. Rather the librarian instructs the vendor to supply every title in a specific subject area, within a specific price range, in a specific form or genre (all trade books, all fiction, etc.), in a certain language, from a specific geographical region or other variable of the library's choosing. The library sets these fairly broad parameters and relies on the supplier to provide titles accordingly. Traditionally blanket orders have not carried the right of return, and this tends to remain the case with publisher operated plans. Other suppliers (agents, for example) are permitting a limited return privilege with some blanket order agreements.

The major advantages of blanket orders are two. First, they carry a very high discount for titles (typically no less than 30-35 per cent), and this combined with the savings made in the cost of an item-by-item order makes such a selection method most attractive. Second, blanket orders on the whole operate very efficiently in terms of getting titles to libraries soon after their publication. On the other hand a blanket order agreement, like an approval plan, does require monitoring, with the attendant costs and time involved. Also, the general lack of return privileges and trade publication focus of this method mean that it is not suitable for all types of libraries. In particular blanket orders are less used by academic and special libraries, both of which rely more on standing orders.

Standing Orders. Similar in intention to blanket orders, a standing order is used most often in two specific situations: where a continuation or a series in a specific field is likely to be of ongoing interest to the library or where a publisher, generally technical or professional, has such a specific list that the library would probably select every item anyway. While such an arrangement may carry a limited right of return, on the whole this is not the case. Instead a unit price discount (often in the 30 per cent range) may be offered if the library places a standing order with the publisher or supplier. The assumption in the case of continuations or series titles is that all items will be up to the standard of the title which generated the standing order, yet any librarian can show that this is not always the case. Indeed, some will say that publishers use standing orders to generate sales which otherwise might not occur and in fact often develop series for this very reason. Today many libraries, particularly academic and special libraries which traditionally have been important standing order buyers, no longer use this selection method but prefer to order on an item-by-item basis. Recognizing this, some publishers and suppliers now operate standing orders with on approval privileges. Here the library places an order for a series or continuation, and the supplier offers right of return. The disadvantage, of course, is that this arrangement may not carry the same discount as a straight standing order. It must be remembered, too, that standing orders must be monitored in the same way as serial subscriptions, and this adds to the cost. On the whole standing orders with specialist publishers for all of their titles engender fewer problems, as their subject focus is unlikely to change.

Approval plans, blanket orders and standing orders are effective selection devices as long as they provide materials within the library's collection profile in a timely and accurate manner. When monitoring indicates that any automatic selection procedure is functioning inefficiently, it is important that the library act to renegotiate or cancel the agreement. One must remember that these procedures are not meant to be soft options but that they are meant to save time, and thus money, which can be spent in more involved areas of selection. When they begin costing more time or money for any reason than item-by-item selection, they no longer have a role as selection aids.

Criteria for Selection

One of the standard texts on book selection makes this daunting statement: "in considering an individual item the selector should ideally judge it against the rest of the subject literature and against the library's holdings of that literature. In other words selection of one item cannot be made in a bibliographical vacuum."[11] In the same breath Spiller adds that this is an unachievable ideal in all but a few libraries. No sooner has one recovered from the shock of Spiller's initial statement, however, than one is faced with eight detailed pages on how to examine individual items for selection. According to Spiller, the selector must consider eight categories: date, author, structure and research method, level, physical presentation (format, binding, illustrations, typography), readability, index and bibliography.[12]

Finding even this rather detailed set of categories too niggardly, some professionals have gone even further in devising criteria for evaluating materials. Perhaps the pinnacle of detail has been achieved by Kenneth Whittaker, who devotes an entire textbook to the methods and sources for assessing books.[13] All of this detail he condenses into an appendix of seven broad criteria, but these are broken down into fifty sub-categories. Whittaker's seven categories, rather different from Spiller's, are: people, plan, contents, organization, design, production and placing; these criteria and their sub-categories are displayed fully in Appendix A.

In truth even experienced selectors blanch at this massive list of categories. While the beginner may well wish to begin with such a detailed listing in order to develop a thorough set of selection practices, the contention in this section is that such an approach obfuscates the goal of selection with an unnecessarily confusing plethora of criteria. Instead it may be productive to consider a much smaller set under two broad criteria: (1) content and its presentation, (2) form. Certainly the basic consideration in selection must be the quality of the product in terms of its content; as this can be enhanced or weakened by physical presentation, format can be regarded as a secondary criterion. Within these two broad categories it is useful to consider six sub-categories. Alternatively, Rutledge and Swindler (pp. 236-246) present a model consisting of six selection criteria; their presentation should be read in conjunction with the following suggestions. However, the intention must be to develop a proficiency in evaluation such that selection proceeds automatically, thereby obviating the need for slavish obeisance at each of these points.

Authority of Creators. Here one is concerned with the qualifications and reputation of those who have created the material. Creators include authors, publishers and, in the case of audio-visual materials, producers. To understand their suitability as producers of a given title one asks a range of questions. What are the author's qualifications, and has he written other works in the same area? What is the author's reputation as indicated in the reception of his other publications? How reputable is the publisher, and is it known as a producer of works in this particular field?

Scope. Here one is concerned with the breadth and depth of coverage afforded by the work, including both intended and actual coverage. What does the work set out to do, and does it achieve this? Is it meant to be a detailed analysis of the subject addressed, or is it meant to present a broad overview? Is it meant to be exhaustive or selective in its coverage? To determine this one examines the introduction and contents, comparing the work with titles of similar scope; or at least one relies on a surrogate, normally a review which provides this information. If the material achieves its stated purpose and fills a gap in the collection, then it is worth selecting.

Treatment and Level. Equally, though, one expects the scope to be treated in a way that is appropriate to the work's intended audience. Who, according to the author, is most likely to read the work? To see whether the audience intention is achieved, one looks for content that is pitched at the right level and that talks neither down to nor above the reader. This is more difficult to achieve than one might imagine, and it is best assessed by looking at the language, illustrations, reader aids and overall "user friendliness" of the work in terms of table of contents, bibliography, notes and index.

Arrangement. Treatment and level lead naturally to arrangement and in the evaluation process are often treated together. Here one looks at the organization of content, paying special attention to both content and format. In particular how clearly set out is the development of ideas, and how logically does the author present his case? The material should be arranged in a way that facilitates the development and logic of the text. Access to information should be facilitated by such features as the table of contents, bibliographic references and index as appropriate. In other words is the arrangement (topical, chronological, biographical, etc.) suitable to the subject, and is access promoted by appropriate retrieval features?

Format. This component in the overall impression made by the material figures in several of the preceding categories but is important enough to warrant consideration on its own, particularly when considering non-book material. In particular one is concerned with technical and aesthetic considerations. Has the material been produced to a high standard physically, and is it likely to stand up to substantial use? Paper, print and binding in the case of book materials should be evaluated; one expects an item to be physically durable and at the same time presented in an aesthetically acceptable manner. Are the illustrations appropriate and produced to a high standard? Is the typeface clear and appropriate to the text? In the case of audio-visual materials, is the quality of sound and visual imagery clear and appropriately expressive? All aspects of format can affect the usefulness of a work, but these features should not override the primary concern with intellectual content of material.

Special Considerations or Special Features. Finally, one evaluates two closely related criteria. Does the work have special features that set it apart from (and ideally above) all similar works? If so, do these features mean that the item should be selected or rejected? Here there are so many possibilities related to the various forms and uses of documentation that generalization is difficult. Essentially, though, one looks for something special that will give an item some positive benefit to the users in the context of a particular collection. If one is examining a new indexing service, for example, does it cover a comparatively higher percentage of serials in the library than its closest competitor? Does a particular children's encyclopedia contain more attractive colour illustrations than some other encyclopedia for the same audience? Does a new textbook cover a field so much more thoroughly than the competition that it can replace several titles already in the collection? These and similar issues, most of them of a comparative nature, should be considered in the final analysis. One would include price as a comparative factor.

While this set of criteria may be simpler than those proposed by either Spiller or Whittaker, one should not be lulled into thinking that selection is necessarily a simple task. For the librarian who is absolutely up-to-date with the latest authors, intellectual trends and user demands in a field, selection may indeed count as a minor activity in terms of mental energy; but such librarians are almost non-existent. For most professionals selection will be a demanding task requiring the skilful balancing of funds, collection strengths and weaknesses, user needs and demands and other available materials. To wend one's way through this maze of competing and sometimes conflicting demands evaluation according to ASTAFS (Authority, Scope, Treatment, Arrangement, Format and Special considerations) can be one usefully concise formula.

Selection Procedures Statement

In Chapter 2 a clear distinction was made between collection development policies and selection procedures statements. The former focuses on why the collection exists and what it shall contain, whereas the latter should be a statement of specific practices with regard to how materials are selected and by whom. A statement of selection procedures, then, is an administrative device designed to facilitate implementation of decisions about materials based on collection development policy guidelines. If most libraries lack written collection development policies, so they also lack written selection procedures statements. As in most administrative matters requiring consistency over time, it is helpful if procedures can be formalized in a written statement. There are at least six reasons for advocating the adoption of a formal selection procedures statement, and many of these echo the rationale for having a written collection development policy:

1. sets standards for procedures to be followed;
2. reduces the likelihood of bias and personal influence;
3. provides continuity despite staff changes;
4. serves as an orientation device for new staff;
5. provides guidelines for complaint handling;
6. assists in weeding.

All of these reasons can be summarized as providing practical guidance in who should select and how selection is done. This practical guidance is most effectively contained in a detailed statement consisting of an outline of general procedures and a set of related attachments as indicated in Figure 6.

Selection Responsibilities. Essentially a written procedures statement must address two questions: who shall do the selecting and how shall the procedure be organized? With reference to the first question the choice is a combination of library staff and users, ideally a balance between the two within the institutional constraints outlined above. Within the library selection may be done by the chief librarian (or only librarian); it may be done by division or department heads engaged specifically for this task (collection development

I. Main Procedures

A. Selection Responsibilities

B. How Selection Is Organized

C. General Guidelines for Selection

D. Handling of Gifts and Donations

E. Criteria for Weeding

F. Handling of Complaints

II. Attachments

A. Sample Request Form

B. Sample Evaluation Form

C. Statement on Freedom to Read

D. Request for Review of Library Materials

Figure 6. Content of a Selection Procedures Statement

librarian, acquisitions librarian); it may be done by subject or area specialists; or it may be done by other professional staff as part of their general duties (reference librarians, technical services librarians). Whichever applies, it should be stated clearly in the written document. Outside the library selection should involve input from users of all types, and these should be specified clearly: administrators, institution staff, students, teachers, general public, etc.

To facilitate and encourage participation of these groups it may help to have a simple, easily understood request form. The form should have space for all essential information needed to identify an item: author, title, number of volumes, place of publication, publisher, date of publication. It is also helpful to have the selector indicate series and volume number, source of information, price and pagination; but all of this will be determined at the verification stage in the acquisitions process. Finally, one wants to know who has selected the item and, in an attempt to determine priorities, why it has been selected. In an academic library this might be for teaching, research or background reading, as Attachment A shows. Finally, since the selection form may double as an acquisitions processing form, it may well include relevant verification and processing information on the verso. This form should be reproduced in the procedures statement, with copies readily accessible to selectors both within and outside the library. One should be careful to distinguish between this and an evaluation form (Attachment B), which is intended to solicit opinions about the value and content of an item. This and any other form will appear as an attachment to the selection procedures statement.

How Selection Is Organized. Having indicated who does the selecting, the statement addresses the second question: how is selecting done? The selection request form is the link between the two questions, because in a sense the question of "how" determines the simplicity and level of detail in the form. If selection is limited primarily to library staff, the form can be a detailed acquisitions form; if selection is handled mainly by non-professionals, the form should be simple enough to encourage their participation in the selection process.

Normally selection is built around the variables outlined in the collection development policy and in part reiterated in the third section of this procedures statement ("General Guidelines for Selection").The basic principle is that selection responsibilities are determined by the type of library and by the environmental or institutional context. Therefore, this part of the statement of selection procedures should indicate clearly and precisely who has responsibility for what and who is responsible to whom. If a selection committee is used, who chairs the committee and who appoints the members? How often does the committee meet? What are its terms of reference? If selection is the responsibility of individuals outside the library, how is this responsibility allocated and monitored? What recourse does the librarian have if his external selectors fail to perform adequately? If selection is done jointly by internal and external selectors, what are the lines of demarcation? Who selects reference materials, serials, decides on multiple copies, etc.? All such questions should be addressed in the statement so that there is no doubt about responsibility and so that the newest member of staff has a clear grasp of procedures.

General Guidelines for Selection. Once the statement has addressed the questions of who and how, it turns to the matter of what to select; here it presents only general guidelines derived from and based on the collection development policy. For example, general selection sources (*Choice, Wilson Library Bulletin*) might be listed, together with categories of more specific types of sources (publishers' catalogues, scholarly journals, indexing services, etc.). Such listings have two functions. First, they help ensure that the named sources are used by selectors; second, they remind selectors of the other types of sources that they ought to be using. In some libraries this second function is extended by actually naming specific sources within each type, but obviously this cannot be done in libraries selecting across a broad range of subjects. In addition to indicating standard selection tools and types of sources this section of the statement might list the languages in which materials are selected, or perhaps other limitations which apply across the range of materials. It might also offer other guidelines, such as "select no popular fiction" or "select only materials which have received at least three positive notices". And of course one will want this list of guidelines specifically to exclude racist and sexist materials, to indicate that all points of view are to be represented, or any other position that applies to the individual library. In other words all selection criteria derived from, or at least compatible with, the collection development policy should be stated here. This will enable all selectors to operate within the same set of guidelines.

Handling of Gifts and Donations. The next area addressed by the selection procedures statement is how to handle gifts and donations. Many a librarian has come to grief over what donors regard as cavalier treatment of their gifts, so it is useful to spell out precisely how gifts are to be evaluated. Basically a donated item is to be taken into the collection according to the same criteria applied to purchased items. Therefore, the statement should say this and should also indicate that gifts are received on the understanding that they may be disposed of in a manner deemed appropriate by the librarian. On a more positive note valuable donations are sometimes offered to libraries with conditions attached; no library wants to close the door on such gifts, so it is useful to indicate acceptable conditions (e.g., an endowment required to support a collection offered on the understanding that it is housed or catalogued separately). The library needs maximum room to manoeuvre in its treatment of gifts, and this section should be worded to assure that freedom.

Criteria for Weeding. Closely related to the treatment - and discard - of gifts is the procedures whereby a collection is weeded, and it is sensible for a selection statement to say something about weeding, often termed "deselection" in the US and "relegation" in the UK. The library may well have included a section on weeding in its collection development policy; if so, this needs to be taken into account at this stage. Essentially weeding involves a number of basic decisions that should be outlined in the selection procedures statement. These decisions involve criteria for weeding, scope of weeding procedures, frequency and certainly purpose. Criteria, scope and frequency should be noted in the statement, together with a general allocation of staff responsibilities. All of this is discussed more fully in Chapter 9, but once again such issues must be covered in the procedures statement so that there is no confusion about who is responsible for what and when. Although these points have been addressed by comparatively few libraries in any consistent or thorough manner, the growing emphasis on "responsive" collections, particularly in special and school libraries, suggests that weeding and discard procedures will become important topics in the near future.

Handling of Complaints. Complaints about and censorship of library materials have been controversial issues for many years, if not for centuries. Accordingly, every library should be prepared to deal with complaints about what the collection contains, and this means having specific guidelines to follow. Extensive discussion of procedures and guidelines is provided by Frances Jones in *Defusing Censorship*,[14] but the simplest and most practical method is to have a written statement of complaint-handling procedures and a standard form to be completed by potential censors. The written statement should be made available, along with a copy of the collection development policy, at the first hint that an item in the collection is being challenged. The complaint-handling form should be completed only if a formal complaint is to be lodged. The exact procedure, who is to be involved and the documentation to be utilized must all be stated clearly in this final part of the statement of selection procedures. The entire statement should be readily accessible not only to selectors but also to all users, as this often alleviates the need for complaints to go beyond an informal discussion. Appendix B presents a sample statement of selection procedures, including complaint handling.

Appendix A.   Checklists for Information Books and for Fiction[15]

Checklist for information books

1   *People*
(a)   Author
(b)   Editor etc.
(c)   Artists and photographers
(d)   Designer
(e)   Printer etc.
(f)   Publisher

2   *Plan*
(a)   Subject or theme
(b)   Origins
(c)   Aim
(d)   Audience
(e)   Variant issues
(f)   Special services
(g)   Related works

3   *Contents*
(a)   Standing
(b)   Research: methods and sources
(c)   Soundness
(d)   Length
(e)   Scope
(f)   Detail
(g)   Viewpoint
(h)   Bias
(i)   Balance
(j)   Level
(k)   Style
(l)   Accuracy
(m)   Up-to-dateness
(n)   Revision
(o)   Permanence
(p)   Bibliographical
(q)   Visual information
(r)   Special features
(s)   Supporting material
(t)   Effect

4   *Organization*
(a)   Arrangement
(b)   Contents list
(c)   Indexes
(d)   Cross-references
(e)   Headings

5   *Design*
(a)   Format
(b)   Layout
(c)   Legibility
(d)   Aesthetic aspects

6   *Production*
(a)   Methods
(b)   Craftsmanship
(c)   Materials

7   *Placing*
(a)   Price
(b)   Comparisons
(c)   Uniqueness
(d)   Quality
(e)   Usefulness

Checklist for fiction

1   *People*
(a)   Author
(b)   Editor etc.
(c)   Artists and photographers
(d)   Designer
(e)   Printer etc.
(f)   Publisher

2   *Plan*
(a)   Subject or theme
(b)   Origins
(c)   Aim
(d)   Audience
(e)   Variant issues
(f)   Special services
(g)   Related works

3   *Contents*
(a)   Standing
(b)   Research: methods and sources
(c)   Observation
(d)   Inventiveness
(e)   Length
(f)   Plot
(g)   Setting
(h)   Characters
(i)   Level
(j)   Approach
(k)   Style
(l)   Spirit
(m)   Permanence
(n)   Visual information
(o)   Supporting material
(p)   Effect
(q)   Power

4   *Organization*
(a)   Arrangement
(b)   Contents list
(c)   Indexes
(d)   Cross-references
(e)   Headings

5   *Design*
(a)   Format
(b)   Layout
(c)   Legibility
(d)   Aesthetic aspects

6   *Production*
(a)   Methods
(b)   Craftsmanship
(c)   Materials

7   *Placing*
(a)   Price
(b)   Comparisons
(c)   Uniqueness
(d)   Quality
(e)   Usefulness

Appendix B. Sample Statement of Selection Procedures[16]

A. Selection Responsibilities

1. The Chief Librarian has overall responsibility for selection and for the management of selection duties, but the regular operation of selection activities is organized and monitored by the Collection Development Librarian in consultation with the Chief Librarian.

2. Selection responsibilities should be regarded as a privilege, with opportunity for all sections of the user community to share in this activity.

3. Accordingly, Request Forms (Attachment A) should be readily available at all service points and to all staff and users.

4. Academic staff are expected to assume responsibility for selection of materials in their respective disciplines and teaching areas.

5. Librarians, in consultation with subject specialists as required, shall assume responsibility for selecting general library materials, including non-circulating stock (reference materials, serials, etc.).

6. Any library material acquired on approval or standing order, by gift or any other means should be subject to detailed evaluation by any person deemed appropriate. An Evaluation Form (Attachment B) should be used for this purpose.

B. How Selection Is Organized

1. While all users and all library staff are encouraged to select materials, most selection responsibilities devolve on specific individuals and should be organized in a systematic manner.

2. Selection by academic staff should be organized on a departmental basis, with a member of staff in each department acting as the library liaison officer. It is the responsibility of this officer to monitor selection by his colleagues and both to pass requests to the library and to receive requests for assistance and evaluation from the library.

3. Each department in the institution should have assigned a liaison librarian to serve as a link and contact point for staff in each department and to maintain communication with the departmental liaison officer described in 2. The liaison librarian will ensure that the relevant catalogues, notices, evaluation requests, etc. are distributed to the liaison officer and will monitor the level of selection activity by departments. *[Departments and their liaison librarians may be listed as an attachment.]*

4. Liaison librarians and departmental liaison officers shall meet at least quarterly with the Collection Development Librarian to discuss such issues as are deemed important.

5.   Selection by library staff should be under the direct supervision of the Collection Development Librarian with regard to general library materials, with reference to liaison librarians for materials of specific subject interest

C.   General Guidelines for Selection

1.   Library materials should support and be consistent with the general goals and objectives of the library as outlined in the Collection Development Policy.

2.   Library materials should meet high standards of quality in both content and presentation.

3.   Library materials should be appropriate for their subject area and for the needs, abilities and interests of those for whom the materials are selected.

4.   Library materials should have overall aesthetic, literary, entertainment or social value.

5.   Library materials should have been prepared by competent and qualified authors and producers.

6.   Library materials should be selected to foster respect for and understanding of all ethnic, cultural, social, religious and gender groups in Australia's multicultural, pluralistic society.

7.   Library materials should be selected for their strengths rather than rejected for their weaknesses.

8.   Biased or slanted library materials may be selected to meet specific objectives and to ensure that all viewpoints are represented in the collection.

9.   Physical format and appearance of library materials should be suitable for their intended use and users.

D.   Handling of Gifts

1.   Gifts and donations are to be received positively and are to be treated as important supplements to regular collecting activities.

2.   However, they are subject to the same selection guidelines as all library materials and are to be evaluated according to the criteria outlined in C.

3.   Gifts which fall outside parameters of the Collection Development Policy or the selection guidelines may be disposed of without prejudice to the donor or the library.

4.   Any donation or gift requiring special treatment or handling may require financial support from the donor.

5.   Upon receipt of a gift or donation the librarian should make it clear that such material is accepted in accordance with these conditions.

E.   Criteria for Weeding

1.   Weeding is an important component of collection management and should receive the same attention as selection.

2.   Weeding should be regarded as an ongoing process and should be conducted by library staff as part of their selection activities.

3.   Library materials are to be weeded in accordance with collection requirements as stated in the Collection Development Policy and in keeping with selection guidelines outlined in C.

4.   Any library material outside the parameters of the Collection Development Policy should be considered for weeding.

5.   Obsolete library materials should be deselected and replaced by current materials within collection development and selection guidelines.

6.   Superseded editions of titles should be weeding and replaced by current editions.

7 .   Materials that are incomplete, irreparably damaged or in otherwise poor condition should be weeded and replaced with appropriate titles.

F.   Handling of Complaints

1.   Any member of the public served by the library may lodge a complaint about material in the collection, and the library staff are to respond professionally to such a complaint in accordance with the following guidelines.

2.   Initially the complaint shall be dealt with informally but immediately, with the senior librarian on duty explaining the selection criteria and collection development policy guidelines. A copy of the Collection Development Policy and the ALA's Statement on Freedom to Read (Attachment C) or other appropriate document should be made available to the user at this point.

3.   The librarian should explain how the challenged item falls within the library's guidelines and that it is a responsible policy to represent all opinions and attitudes in a collection.

4.   If the complaint is not resolved in this way, a Request for Review of Library Materials (Attachment D) should be completed by the user and passed to the Chief Librarian immediately. Note, however, that the form should be accepted only when completed in full.

5.   The Chief Librarian should call a meeting of the Library Committee or special Complaint-handling Committee as soon as feasible, presenting the Committee with all evidence necessary to decide on the validity of the complaint. The Committee should include not only library staff but also representatives of all user groups. The user lodging the complaint should be invited to attend the meeting.

6.   The Committee should issue a written decision of its findings signed by all Committee members; a minority report, signed by dissenting members, should also be issued if required. This report should then be filed with the appropriate authority, and a copy should be sent to the user lodging the complaint.

7.   The written decision should be regarded as adequate defence should the same item be cause for complaint in future.

Attachment A. Sample Request Form
(front)

Author

Title, No. of Vols., Series

Publisher   ISBN

Place of Publication

Date of Publication

No. of Students No. of Copies   Semester 1 2 19   Reading List_____
                                                     Prescribed Text_____
                                                     Background R_____

Proposer   School

(back)

LIBRARY USE ONLY

Held by Library at: WML   MU   CRC   MC   CLANN U.C.No..................

    same ed.   call no.
    ....copies   Contact Librarian
    earlier   Date
    .... ed.   Inits.
    o/o
    not held

Sources Checked   AMRS no. ....

    ABIP   BIP   Acquisitions Dept.
    ANB   NUC   Date
    BBIP   Trade Cat.   Inits.
    BNB   Other

Attachment B. Sample Evaluation Form

Author: _____ Title: _____

Edition: _____ Series Title: _____

Publisher: _____ Place: _____ Date: _____

Format [tick one]: Book Film Filmstrip Phonodisk Tape
                              Other
Appropriate Users:_____

Curriculum Uses Include: _____

Information Uses Include: _____

Personal Uses Include: _____

Criteria [tick one]: Poor Fair Good Superior Comments

Authoritativeness: _____

Accuracy or credibility: _____

Organization: _____

Appropriateness of content: _____

Aesthetic quality: _____

Technical quality: _____

Overall rating: _____

Recommendation [tick one]: Add 1 copy   Add   copies
                           Do not recommend   Uncertain   Why?
Evaluator:_____
Date:_____

Attachment C. *Statement on Freedom to Read**

The freedom to read is essential to our democracy. It is continuously under attack. Private groups and public authorities in various parts of the country are working to remove books from sale, to censor textbooks, to label "controversial" books, to distribute lists of "objectionable" books or authors, and to purge libraries. These actions apparently rise from a view that our national tradition of free expression is no longer valid; that censorship and suppression are needed to avoid the subversion of politics and the corruption of morals. We, as citizens devoted to the use of books and as librarians and publishers responsible for disseminating them, wish to assert the public interest in the preservation of the freedom to read.

We are deeply concerned about these attempts at suppression. Most such attempts rest on a denial of the fundamental premise of democracy: that the ordinary citizen, by exercising his critical judgment, will accept the good and reject the bad. The censors, public and private, assume that they should determine what is good and what is bad for their fellow-citizens.

We trust Americans to recognize propaganda, and to reject it. We do not believe they need the help of censors to assist them in this task. We do not believe they are prepared to sacrifice their heritage of a free press in order to be "protected" against what others think may be bad for them. We believe they still favor free enterprise in ideas and expression.

We are aware, of course, that books are not alone in being subjected to efforts at suppression. We are aware that these efforts are related to a larger pattern of pressures being brought against education, the press, films, radio, and television. The problem is not only one of actual censorship. The shadow of fear cast by these pressures leads, we suspect, to an even larger voluntary curtailment of expression by those who seek to avoid controversy.

Such pressure toward conformity is perhaps natural to a time of uneasy change and pervading fear. Especially when so many of our apprehensions are directed against an ideology, the expression of a dissident idea becomes a thing feared in itself, and we tend to move against it as against a hostile deed, with suppression.

And yet suppression is never more dangerous than in such a time of social tension. Freedom has given the United States the elasticity to endure strain. Freedom keeps open the path of novel and creative solutions, and enables change to come by choice. Every silencing of a heresy, every enforcement of an orthodoxy, diminishes the toughness and resilience of our society and leaves it the less able to deal with stress.

Now as always in our history, books are among our greatest instruments of freedom. They are almost the only means for making generally available ideas or manners of expression that can initially command only a small audience. They are the natural medium for the new idea and the untried voice from which come the original contributions to social growth. They are essential to the extended discussion which serious thought requires, and to the accumulation of knowledge and ideas into organized collections.

We believe that free communication is essential to the preservation of a free society and a creative culture. We believe that these pressures towards conformity present the danger of limiting the range and variety of inquiry and expression on which our democracy and our culture depend. We believe that every American community must jealously guard the freedom to publish and to circulate, in order to preserve its own freedom to read. We believe that publishers and librarians have a profound responsibility to give validity to that freedom to read by making it possible for the readers to choose freely from a variety of offerings.

The freedom to read is guaranteed by the Constitution. Those with faith in free men will stand firm on these constitutional guarantees of essential rights and will exercise the responsibilities that accompany these rights.

We therefore affirm these propositions:

1.   It is in the public interest for publishers and librarians to make available the widest diversity of views and expressions, including those which are unorthodox or unpopular with the majority.

Creative thought is by definition new, and what is new is different. The bearer of every new thought is a rebel until his idea is refined and tested. Totalitarian systems attempt to maintain themselves in power by the ruthless suppression of any concept which challenges the established orthodoxy. The power of a democratic system to adapt to change is vastly strengthened by the freedom of its citizens to choose widely from among conflicting opinions offered freely to them. To stifle every nonconformist idea at birth would mark the end of the democratic process. Furthermore, only through the constant activity of weighing and selecting can the democratic mind attain the strength demanded by times like these. We need to know not only what we believe but why we believe it.

2.   Publishers, librarians, and booksellers do not need to endorse every idea or presentation contained in the books they make available. It would conflict with the public interest for them to establish their own political, moral, or aesthetic views as a standard for determining what books should be published or circulated.

Publishers and librarians serve the educational process by helping to make available knowledge and ideas required for the growth of the mind and the increase of learning. They do not foster education by imposing as mentors the patterns of their own thought. The people should have the freedom to read and consider a broader range of ideas than those that may be held by any single librarian or publisher or government or church. It is wrong that what one man can read should be confined to what another thinks proper.

3.   It is contrary to the public interest for publishers or librarians to determine the acceptability of a book on the basis of the personal history or political affiliations of the author.

A book should be judged as a book. No art or literature can flourish if it is to be measured by the political views or private lives of its creators. No society of free men can flourish which draws up lists of writers to whom it will not listen, whatever they may have to say.

4. There is no place in our society for efforts to coerce the taste of others, to confine adults to the reading matter deemed suitable for adolescents, or to inhibit the efforts of writers to achieve artistic expression.

   To some, much of modern literature is shocking. But is not much of life itself shocking? We cut off literature at the source if we prevent writers from dealing with the stuff of life. Parents and teachers have a responsibility to prepare the young to meet the diversity of experiences in life to which they will be exposed, as they have a responsibility to help them learn to think critically for themselves. These are affirmative responsibilities, not to be discharged simply by preventing them from reading works for which they are not yet prepared. In these matters taste differs, and taste cannot be legislated; nor can machinery be devised which will suit the demands of one group without limiting the freedom of others.

5. It is not in the public interest to force a reader to accept with any book the prejudgment of a label characterizing the book or author as subversive or dangerous.

   The idea of labeling presupposes the existence of individuals or groups with wisdom to determine by authority what is good or bad for the citizen. It presupposes that each individual must be directed in making up his mind about the ideas he examines. But Americans do not need others to do their thinking for them.

6. It is the responsibility of publishers and librarians, as guardians of the people's freedom to read, to contest encroachments upon that freedom by individuals or groups seeking to impose their own standards or tastes upon the community at large.

   It is inevitable in the give and take of the democratic process that the political, the moral, or the aesthetic concepts of an individual or group will occasionally collide with those of another individual or group. In a free society each individual is free to determine for himself what he wishes to read, and each group is free to determine what it will recommend to its freely associated members. But no group has the right to take the law into its own hands, and to impose its own concept of politics or morality upon other members of a democratic society. Freedom is no freedom if it is accorded only to the accepted and the inoffensive.

7. It is the responsibility of publishers and librarians to give full meaning to the freedom to read by providing books that enrich the quality and diversity of thought and expression. By the exercise of this affirmative responsibility, bookmen can demonstrate that the answer to a bad book is a good one, the answer to a bad idea is a good one.

   The freedom to read is of little consequence when expended on the trivial; it is frustrated when the reader cannot obtain matter fit for his purpose. What is needed is not only the absence of restraint, but the positive provision of opportunity for the people to read the best that has been thought and said. Books are the major channel by which the intellectual inheritance is handed down, and the principal means of its testing and growth. The defense of their freedom and integrity, and the enlargement of their service to society, requires of all bookmen the utmost of their faculties, and deserves of all citizens the fullest of their support.

We state these propositions neither lightly nor as easy generalizations. We here stake out a lofty claim for the value of books. We do so because we believe that they are good, possessed of enormous variety and usefulness, worthy of cherishing and keeping free. We realize that the application of these propositions may mean the dissemination of ideas and manners of expression that are repugnant to many persons. We do not state these propositions in the comfortable belief that what people read is unimportant. We believe rather that what people read is deeply important; that ideas can be dangerous; but that the suppression of ideas is fatal to a democratic society. Freedom itself is a dangerous way of life, but it is ours.

*   Adopted 25 June 1953 and revised 28 January 1972 by the Council of the American Library Association. Reprinted by permission from the ALA Office for Intellectual Freedom, *Intellectual Freedom Manual* (2nd ed. Chicago, Ill.: American Library Association, 1983), pp. 87-91.

Attachment D. Request for Review of Library Materials

Author:_____

Title:_____

Publisher:_____ Date of publication: _____

Request initiated by _____

Telephone: _____ Address: _____

Complainant represents [tick one]: him/herself organization

If organization, give name: _____

1. Specify what you object to in the book (indicate pages)._____

2. What do you think might be the results of reading or viewing this material?_____

3. What do you think is good about this material?_____

4. For what age group would you recommend the material?_____

5. Did you read or view the entire work or just parts of it?_____

6. Are you aware of the judgment of this material by reviewers or evaluators? _____

7. What do you believe is the theme of the material? _____

8. What would you like the library to do about the material?
_____

9. What material would you recommend in its place? _____

_____

Signature of Complainant:_____ Date: _____

References

1   G. Edward Evans, *Developing Library and Information Center Collections* (2nd ed. Library Science Text Series. Littleton, Colo.: Libraries Unlimited, 1987), pp. 82-107.

2   Robert N. Broadus, *Selecting Materials for Libraries* (2nd ed. New York: H.W. Wilson Company, 1981), pp. 30-51.

3   S.R. Ranganathan, *Library Book Selection* (New Delhi: Indian Library Association, 1952).

4   Key journals are *Collection Management, Library Acquisitions: Practice and Theory, The Serials Librarian, Library Resources and Technical Services, College and Research Libraries* and the *Journal of Academic Librarianship.*

5   Evans, *op. cit.*, pp. 116-117.

6   J. Belland, "Factors Influencing Selection of Materials." *School Media Quarterly* 6 (1978): 117.

7   Riverina College of Advanced Education, Information Resources Centre, *Policy Statements and Guidelines* (Wagga Wagga: Riverina College of Advanced Education, 1982), p. 10.

8   These are regularly listed in that excellent directory, *Libraries in the United Kingdom and the Republic of Ireland* (15th ed. London: Library Association, 1989).

9   William A. Katz, *Collection Development: The Selection of Materials for Libraries* (New York: Holt, Rinehart and Winston, 1980), p. 164 n.24.

10 The 1981 Association of Research Libraries survey indicated that 85 per cent of ARL libraries used approval plans. See T. Leonardt (ed.), *Approval Plans in ARL Libraries* (Washington, D.C.: Association of Research Libraries, Office of Management Studies, 1982), pp. 11-15.

11 David Spiller, *Book Selection: An Introduction to Principles and Practice* (3rd ed. London: Clive Bingley, 1980), p. 82.

12 *Ibid.*, pp. 83-90.

13 Kenneth Whittaker, *Systematic Evaluation: Methods and Sources for Assessing Books* (Outlines of Modern Librarianship. London: Clive Bingley, 1982).

14 Frances Jones, *Defusing Censorship: The Librarian's Guide to Handling Censorship Conflicts* (Phoenix, Ariz.: Oryx Press, 1983).

15 Whittaker, *op. cit.*, pp. 145-147. Needless to say, the efficient evaluator in many library settings will rely on published reviews for assistance in working through these, or any other set of, criteria. A great deal is being written on the nature, value and effectiveness of reviews and reviewing. See, for example, A.J. Walford (ed.), *Reviews and Reviewing: A Guide* (London: Mansell Publishing, 1986), and Bill Katz and Robin Kinder (eds.), *The Publishing and Review of Reference Sources* (New York: Haworth Press, 1987).

16 This sample statement is based in part on the model selection policy of the Iowa Department of Public Instruction as presented and discussed by Phyllis J. Van Orden in *The Collection Program in Schools: Concepts, Practices and Information Sources* (Library Science Text Series. Littleton, Colo.: Libraries Unlimited, 1988), pp. 95-105. A similar but less detailed model is presented by Jones, *op. cit.*, pp. 143-147.

READINGS ON SELECTION PRINCIPLES AND PRACTICES

In this chapter all aspects of selection have been covered, from basic principles to practical procedures and from staff involvement in choosing titles to user complaints about materials that have been selected. In the final analysis selection is a complex process by which librarians and others choose materials for their collections. If Chapter 6 has highlighted this complexity and the many variables involved in the selection process, it is unlikely that the librarian will find much in the professional literature to provide simple solutions to a complex set of problems. Most aspects of selection have generated considerable interest in print, with perhaps the key issues discussed being *who* does selection and *how* it is done.

Accordingly, the readings for this chapter open with two papers on selection by a particular group, academics in colleges and universities. Dennis Dickinson (pp. 214-224) argues that book selection is more properly and more adequately done by academics than librarians, because the latter simply do not possess superior ability in collection building. Such a view may trouble many librarians, who believe that part of their professional responsibility lies in the area of selection. Indeed, as one might expect, much literature on this topic disagrees with the views put forth by Dickinson. Typical are the immediate responses to Dickinson by Robert Burr and five other librarians and academics (pp. 225-236). They argue that librarians *do* have the necessary expertise, that they are committed to objective selection, that they are above academic politics, that they know the market and the needs of users and that they are professionally qualified to select materials. This argument over user versus librarian selection can be extended to libraries of all types and is an issue of perennial significance in collection development.

Less contentious than who does selection, but equally important, is how the selection decisions are made. This chapter has presented several sets of selection criteria and has argued in favour of one particular scheme. This should be compared with the carefully developed proposal by Rutledge and Swindler (pp. 236-246). Here the criteria are also grouped into six major categories, and within each category they are arranged in order of relative importance. Their proposed scheme provides librarians with a holistic and quite explicit model for making selection decisions, as well as a mechanism for assigning a specific priority to each selection. A model such as theirs can be useful in relating collection development to fiscal responsibilities and can also assist in promoting cooperative collection development.

Dennis W. Dickinson, "A Rationalist's Critique of Book Selection for Academic Libraries." *Journal of Academic Librarianship* **7, 3 (1981): 138-143.**

ra-tio-nal-ism: A view that an appeal to reason and experience rather than to the non-rational (emotion, intuition, faith, revelation, or authority) is to be employed as the fundamental criterion in the solution of problems.[1]

More than ten years ago Daniel Gore put forward "A Modest Proposal for Improving the Management of College Libraries" which was that only one whose training, experience, and values are substantially the same as the library's clientele can effectively administer an academic library. Therefore, he argues, academic libraries should be run by persons who are both teachers and scholars, i.e., members of the faculty rather than professional librarians.[2]

In the decade since Gore's article appeared, however, there has not been any noticeable tendency among academic libraries to follow his advice, except in the nugatory sense that more librarians have achieved at least nominal "faculty status." The reason for this seeming indifference may be that Gore cast his net too broadly. That is, the management of academic libraries is something which most faculty members are probably neither interested in nor particularly well suited for by either temperament or training. Nonetheless, one area in which both faculty members' and librarians' interests converge is in development of a library's collection; and thus there is at least one aspect of library operation, i.e., book selection or collection development, to which Gore's arguments are particularly germane.[3]

The notion of faculty selection of materials for academic libraries is by no means a new one. It was almost exclusively the pattern in the German institutions of higher learning which served as models for American universities established during the nineteenth century, and was, along with much else, adopted almost without change by the latter. From that time until the 1960s there existed in this country considerable support for the view that faculty members are best qualified to select materials for the library which serves their institution. In recent years, however, allegedly because critical evaluation of existing library collections raised questions about the effectiveness of faculty selection, there has been a growing sympathy with and tendency toward shifting selection responsibility to librarians and away from faculty members.[4] As a result, responsibility for book selection and collection development is now divided between faculty and librarians in various ways as described by the following tripartite taxonomy of libraries according to their roles in the selection of materials:

1. Self-effacing libraries...disclaim almost all responsibility for the development of the collection.

2. Libraries in which materials are selected by the faculty with the aid and advice of the library...book selection...left almost entirely in the hands of the faculty...library staff supplement and round out faculty buying in the various fields and select those works which are not specifically needed for the work of the particular departments.

3. Libraries in which materials are selected by the library with aid of the faculty.[5]

Among American academic libraries, numerous examples may be found to illustrate each of the three types described above and none of them appears to be dominant.[6] There is little agreement on which approach to collection development is to be preferred. There is even less sound empirical evidence on which to base a decision. In the light of this last, what follows is a rationalist's argument for the hypothesis that "better" (more useful) collections will result if teaching and research faculty select materials for the library than if that responsibility is relegated to librarians.[7]

Librarian Selectors - the Real and the Ideal

American academic libraries have, in fact, not gone to a completely unadulterated system of librarian selection. The American professorate has not abandoned its interest in building library collections, and academic librarians, while anxious to preserve their prerogatives, are, nonetheless, receptive to faculty participation in collection development activities.[8] Even the most outspoken proponents of the view that book selection for academic libraries should be in the hands of librarians hedge by urging that the latter seek the aid and advice of the faculty in discharging their responsibilities.[9]

Few would likely disagree with the statement that "the primary function of any college or university library collection is to support in some way the traditional disciplines offered in the curriculum."[10] That being the case, it is not surprising to find a corollary which holds that "of all the ways in which to evaluate the library's collection, finding out what its users think of it comes closest to an evaluation in terms of the library's objective or mission."[11] In arguing for this point, Bonn avers that

> serious users (e.g., faculty, research workers, professional people) are likely to be expert or at least be knowledgeable in the literature of their fields and their evaluation of the collection will indicate its actual strengths and weaknesses as well as providing information regarding the kinds of demands which will most likely be made on it.[12]

There is, however, a curious and vitiating logical circumlocution here. As pointed out above, one of the major reasons for the shift away from faculty selection in American academic libraries is purported to be that critical evaluation of existing collections called its efficacy into question. Now, however, librarian selectors are urged to call on these very faculty for advice and counsel in the prosecution of their own collection development activities. The reason for this conundrum would seem, at least in part, to lie in the fact that so called subject specialists in libraries are often laboring under more or less severe handicaps and, in fact, have no choice but to rely on the expertise of faculty members when evaluating a collection or selecting books.[13]

The term "subject specialization" has, at best, a very loose definition. It is more appropriate to speak of librarians' subject responsibility than to refer to them as subject specialists, since in most cases the breadth of subject responsibility assigned to any given librarian of itself makes ludicrous the notion of specialization. Given the preponderance of librarians with liberal arts backgrounds, many individuals are necessarily assigned responsibility for subject areas in which they have only the most rudimentary qualification, if any.[14]

Librarians generally agree that knowledge of the library's clientele is essential for effective selection and believe that bibliographers or subject specialists are necessary in order to gather information about an academic library's consistency. There is, however, a glaring inconsistency in the argument that a special apparatus must be set up to facilitate faculty influence over collection development but that the faculty should not, themselves, engage directly in the activity.

Apparently to avoid facing this contradiction, one finds in the literature explanations such as the following of the need for bibliographers and subject specialists in libraries:

> These new positions [subject specialists] first appeared on university staffs as the growth of budgets and collections made some assistance to faculty selectors necessary and as area study programs came into curricula. They had the added benefit of assisting balanced development of collections thereby compensating for the zeal of certain specialists and changes in faculty.

> ...book selection responsibilities are being assigned to library staff specialists [because]...the remarkable increment in the pace, intensity, and activities of modern academic life...leaves faculty members with little time or inclination for book selection...[15]

It appears, however, that the ability of libraries to meet demands placed on them has actually been declining during his same period due, among other things, to: (1) increasing rates of publication in all formats; (2) growing specialization on the part of scholars and researchers with a consequent increase in number of volumes required to provide a constant amount of useful information per user; and (3) the merger of aspects of formerly separate disciplines making it difficult to predict the user of a work once assignable to a definite set of individual or discipline; all of which are aggravated by the shrinking purchasing power of libraries.[16] This simultaneous increase in librarian selectors and decrease in library performance suggests that a system of subject specialists or bibliographers within the library may not be the best mechanism for improving library service under present circumstances and, in fact, may be counter-productive.

The Case for Faculty Selectors

The obvious alternative for academic libraries, and one which would go directly to the problems outlined above, is to place responsibility for selection outside the library and with the teaching faculty.[17] In the first instance, it is clear that in spite of cumbersome, complicated, and expensive systems of librarian selectors and bibliographers, many reasonable demands placed upon the academic library today simple are not being met.[18]

Secondly, it seems likely that, on the one hand, a better job of selection might be done by someone not disadvantaged and encumbered in the way that librarian selectors are; and, on the other, that the library as a system might derive certain advantages from placing those jobs which require very different conditions of employment from the vast majority of other library jobs outside the library and in an environment where the requisite conditions already exist. In sum, it would seem that selection responsibilities are organic to an academic department, but, at best, can be forced mechanically into the structure of a library. There is a kind of family resemblance between the duties and responsibilities of a selector and the teaching and research faculty which does not obtain between the collection development role and others necessary to the operation of a library - arguments in favour of faculty status for librarians notwithstanding. In an academic institution the place to locate responsibility for book selection would, then, seem to be with the teaching and research faculty.

The specific arguments which may be marshalled for a system of faculty selection are several and most stem from widely accepted beliefs regarding book selection. There is, for example, the "...seldom stated but always present assumption that the book selector must have a knowledge of the library users in order to function effectively."[19] It is also true that "library staff are making distinct efforts to relate collecting priorities more closely to the academic program and research activities on the local campus."[20] Furthermore, it is alleged that the addition of subject specialists to library staffs has, perhaps more than anything else in recent years, served to strengthen library/faculty liaisons, and therefore increases knowledge of the community served by the library.[21] Finally, a study by Evans has shown that there it little, if any, significant difference between the philosophical points of view of faculty members and librarians engaged in selection activities.[22]

If Evans is right, then consider the following: "Unfortunately, very little serious study has been done on the decision-making process in book selection. A substantial part of the [library] profession is unprepared to mold collection goals, available materials and available funds into a workable selection model...."[23] If librarians have no particular expertise in the mechanics of collection development which would compensate for their comparative lack of substantive knowledge in the field for which they select, then one is led inevitably to the conclusion that faculty are better qualified as selectors than their library counterparts.

The foregoing implies that all else being equal, the closer the relationship of the teaching faculty to the collection development process, the more successful the latter will be. It follows from this that placing collection development responsibility with the teaching faculty directly, whereupon the relationship between the teaching faculty and collection development functionaries becomes one of identity, should provide the best possible results. It is clear from the literature, however, that this is not a very popular view with librarians in spite of its inherent logic.

There has been at least one attempt actually to verify the supposition that selection by library staff members is to be preferred over selection by faculty members. Evans, in the same study mentioned earlier, has shown that, based on use as a criterion of value, selection by librarians is superior to that by faculty members, and that both of these methods result in a higher ration of books used than the third most common means of acquiring books for academic libraries, i.e., blanket-order or approval plans.[24] However, what Evans classes under the general rubric or "faculty selection" is a very mixed bag and certainly does not even approach an ideal system for faculty selection. In discussing faculty participation in book selection, Evans points out that

> frequently only one person is assigned selection work for a department. However, this person is usually not given released time to do the work nor given the responsibility for collection development; he is expected to receive suggestions from colleagues; in short he acts more as a liaison person than as a departmental bibliographer.... The librarian book selector, however, is usually charged with the

responsibility and authority for collection development and does not expect nor is expected to depend upon other librarians' suggestions to carry out his work.[25]

But, as seen above, the librarian book selector does expect and is expected to depend on the library's clientele - especially faculty - for suggestions to carry out his work. Thus, it appears that Evans, in this respect, is drawing a distinction without a difference.

Probably no one knows very much about how scholars in general use library resources; and necessarily so, for at the level of abstraction required to make statements encompassing all scholars there can be no utterances which are both significant and true. Some librarians, nonetheless, represent themselves as having such knowledge. In fact, however, it usually turns out to consist principally of high-level abstractions, trivialities, folk wisdom, and platitudes which may or may not have a basis in fact, e.g., "mathematicians don't use libraries"; "scientists are only interested in journals - and current issues at that"; "humanists need large amounts of retrospective materials", etc.

On the other hand, a faculty member who is actively engaged in teaching and research in a particular discipline knows - at least implicitly - whether and how he or she uses the library, and is probably only slightly less sure how many of the other members of his or her department use it as well. Simply put, faculty members have been, and continue to be, socialized into their disciplines and can, therefore, make collection development decisions based upon information not available to most librarians.

Finally, dismantling the costly collection development apparatus in the library should result in a smaller and, therefore, less expensive library staff. The savings achieved could be put directly into the book funds with an obvious beneficial effect.[26] The remaining library staff would, of course, retain responsibility for all other aspects of library operations except selection and could concentrate their efforts on things most librarians are best equipped to do, that is, on reference service, technical processing, curatorial work, and general library management. Such a plan would make more accessible a larger, better selected, and more adequate collection and generally improve the library's value to its patrons.

On the other side of the equation, a structured and workable arrangement that makes designated faculty members primarily responsible for book selection would seem to be a step in the direction of "self-imposed management: for faculty, recommended by Peter Drucker, and would provide one opportunity, however modest, for implementing a systematic program of professional development for individual faculty - especially those who, according to Drucker, need to be "repotted".[27]

The Problem of Faculty Accountability

Faculty selection for libraries has, in the past, been less than totally successful, not due to any lack of qualification on the part of faculty selectors, but rather because of a lack of commitment to the enterprise. What is truly at issue in the question of selection by teaching and research faculty versus librarians is clearly not ability, but rather, accountability. The argument quickly comes down to a contention that collection development is best accomplished by library staff members not because they have more knowledge - either extensive or intensive - of the fields for which they select, but because they can be held responsible for actually selecting books in a way that faculty members usually cannot or, at least, have not been.

It seems apparent that one who is active in a particular discipline and has day-to-day contact with others in the same discipline can - if he but will - do a better job of selection in that field than can a full-time library staff member who is charged with collection development duties in more than one discipline and burdened with an indefinite number of almost complete extraneous chores.[28] Few reasonable individuals would likely argue with the foregoing, and the notion of faculty selection should, therefore, be more palatable to those who approach the question objectively if only a way could be found to deal with the problem of faculty accountability.

A Model for Faculty Selection

Arguments for Faculty as Selectors

One way of achieving the best of both worlds would be to create a position in each academic department which would formally incorporate the duties and responsibilities of any other faculty members with those of a selector for a specific discipline. The incumbent of such a position would be obligated, on an appropriate scale, to teach and do research in his discipline just as any other faculty member, but would also be contractually responsible for book selection in that discipline and be given adequate time to discharge this responsibility. The ratio between normal faculty and bibliographic responsibilities specified in the contract would vary from department to department, of course, but the latter should always be subsidiary to other activities. In order to preserve this balance, some large and library-dependent department, e.g., history, might elect to have more than one bibliographer to cover various spatial and temporal divisions of the field as deemed necessary. In many - probably most - cases it should be possible simple to substitute book selection for a portion of the faculty member's committee work and other required "community service" activities and thereby avoid increased costs.

In addition to the advantages of faculty selection outlined above, such a system would make the person doing the selection for a particular discipline directly accountable to the academic department most immediately concerned, and his retention, promotion, tenure, etc., would depend as much on evaluation of his performance as a selector as it would on traditional criteria used to evaluate faculty. This, along with peer pressure, would provide an effective incentive for faculty selectors, first of all, to be attentive to their selection responsibilities, and secondly, to consider the collective interests of departmental faculty in making selection decisions.

The fear that selection, if left to faculty, would be dominated by the few who pursue only their own parochial interests at the expense of their more numerous but less concerned and aggressive colleagues could thereby be allayed. Also, by lodging responsibility for selection in the department itself, major questions of collection development could be considered in faculty meetings just as any other question which affects the enterprise in which the faculty is collectively engaged.

Under such an arrangement, all members of a given faculty would have an opportunity to influence the collection development process directly, immediately, and equally. Selection policies would be adjusted to changes in curricula and research at the earliest possible moment, since the same people who determine the former would also be party to decisions affecting the latter. This highly desirable real-time synchronization of academic program with library collection development activities is possible only in an indirect and largely ineffectual form in institutions which rely on library staff members as selectors.[29] There would seem to be no other way to achieve such broad-based participation in collection development as a system of faculty selection would provide.

The often heard complaint that faculty selection is unduly influenced by immediate needs and, therefore, adversely affects the long-term research value of collections is spurious on its face. The ability to divine what may be needed 10, 20, or 50 years in the future to support then current research needs is clearly at least as available to a faculty member who is actively engaged in teaching and research as it is to a library staff member who is not. It is probably true, as has been suggested, that it is only the active scholar who can limit the future direction of research in his field.[30]

Arguments for Librarians as Selectors

The argument for librarians as selectors based on the latter's presumed greater clairvoyance is not particularly forceful. It stems from a confusion of two essentially different responsibilities of libraries: archival responsibilities and library/information system responsibilities. That is, any book, no matter its monetary worth, has only intrinsic artistic or historical, i.e., archival, value unless and until it meets a user. It then acquires another set of values, called user values, which from the standpoint of a library viewed as an information system is the most valid measure of any item's worth. This latter is evident from the fact that academic libraries make acquisitions based almost exclusively upon the anticipated probability that a given item will, in fact, be used and evaluate collections in terms of the actual use rate.[31] So long as no one uses a particular book it has only archival value; its informational value remains unactualized. If the academic library's job is to build collections that will be used and further the goals of the educational institution which it serves, i.e., to concentrate on the information system responsibility rather than the archival, then preference should be given to near-term utility even if it comes at the expense of long-term research value - which it probably will not.[32]

Long-Term Research Needs versus Immediate User Needs

Although commonly believed, it has, to the author's knowledge, yet to be shown that a collection developed to meet current user needs is, by virtue of that fact alone, any the worse as a research collection. In any case, it will be necessary, as acquisition budgets continue to shrink when measured by real buying power, to rethink the relationship between relatively unpredictable, long-term research needs and highly predictable, immediate needs created by the academic program itself. It will likewise become increasingly necessary to base collection development decisions more and more heavily on the latter. In such an environment the argument used against faculty selection, based on the alleged short-term perspective which they adopt with respect to collection development, is converted instead to a powerful argument for such a system.

In spite of pervasive notions to the contrary, American academics are overwhelmingly teachers rather than scholars. The small scholarly subgroup which does exist is located almost exclusively at a limited number of institutions whose primary focus is on research.[33] Moreover, library statistics consistently show that faculty use of the library constitutes only about 10 percent of total use and that much of it is related to teaching rather than research. Clearly, for most academic libraries, emphasis on serving research needs can easily be exaggerated.[34]

Consideration of the relationship between relatively immediate user needs and what are believed by some to be antithetical, long-term research needs is, however, made difficult by at least two factors. The first of these is the lack of any meaningful, descriptive standards for assessing research collections, and thus assaying or even comparing the quality of such collections is largely an exercise in subjectivity.[35] In point of fact, a formidable argument has been made that it is logically impossible to make interinstitution comparisons and that only the faculty of a given institution can determine the adequacy of its library holdings.[36]

"Balanced" Research Collections

The second factor is a widely held assumption that research collections must be "balanced". Quite apart from the lack of any meaningful definition of the term "balance," it is not intuitively clear that a balanced collection is necessarily desirable. With ever-shrinking library budgets, one effect of an attempt to develop a balanced collection will be to distribute increasingly scarce resources over a constant or growing number of subject areas competing for support. The result of this situation, if continued for a sufficient amount of time, will be to produce an "oatmeal" collection, i.e., one which, while perhaps extensive in subject coverage, is uniformly bland, shallow, and undistinguished. It should be clear from what has been said above that the vast majority of research collections in American academic libraries until very recently, i.e, the late 1950s or early 1960s, were developed almost exclusively by faculty selectors assisted by a few enlightened scholar librarians, and the ones that can truly be called centres of excellence in all probability do not now and did not at any period in their history, have "balanced" collections. Rather they would seem to consist of collections with great strength in some areas and something considerably less in others.

Faculty selection presumably would lead to the development of collections which, while perhaps "unbalanced" are nonetheless distinguished in at least some areas. Since faculty have a better and more constantly up-to-date knowledge of the field for which they buy, the collection development efforts could be sharply focused. Consequently, the possibility of retaining the centres of excellence built during the era in which faculty dominated the selection process would be greatly enhanced.

Cooperative Collection Development

This view has been reflected in programmatic statements in the area of cooperative collection development. A recent report defined the latter as "a program among a fixed group of libraries to acquire all materials with a defined scope and to eliminate unnecessary duplication through agreement to share those materials."[37] The authors of the report determined that "the only valid method of meeting library needs of citizens is the adoption of 'user orientation' as the basis for acquisitions at the local level - a local library being defined as any library...in its function of serving its primary clientele." The report notes that "this change in basic philosophy will result in high use collections geared to primary clientele, thus easing the establishment of a cooperative collection development program to meet the needs of those seeking less frequently used materials."[38] The report further recommends that resource development at the local level be designed to meet user needs. This does not mean that a library will meet all user needs, but it does mean that every request and need should be considered, and that "standards of quality or literary merit should not be imposed."[39]

The recommendations of the report are well taken and can be disregarded only at risk of producing, over time, uniformly anemic, homogeneous, mediocre, and duplicative collections that do not have the resources to satisfy a majority of demands made on them by their primary clientele. Such disregard will have the addition deleterious effect of rendering interlibrary cooperation less and less effective in making up the deficiencies in any given collection. With shrinking resources, pursuing balance as the ultimate value will eventually lead libraries to the point where virtually all collections are essentially the same except for their size. That is, it will become increasingly true, as De Gennaro points out, that "all too frequently, cooperation is merely a pooling of poverty."[40]

Summary and Conclusion

The foregoing has attempted to show that book selection for academic libraries is best left to the teaching and research faculty of the institution and that arguments for librarian selection are less than persuasive if not simply wrong-headed. The argument for librarian selectors based on their alleged superior ability to build collections in academic libraries simply cannot withstand close scrutiny. Virtually all of the evidence gainsays the contention and leads one to the conclusion, that if the problem of accountability can be dealt with, faculty are, on balance, better equipped to select materials for an academic library than are librarians. Arguments to the contrary appear to be based on no more than an unsupported and insupportable belief that librarians, for reasons unspecified, possess a magic power of transmutation which renders books over which they murmur cryptic incantations somehow more valuable than those not receiving their ministrations. It is interesting to note however, that this latter turns out to be, also, a passing fair definition of alchemy.

References

1 *Webster's Third International Dictionary of the English Language,* 1971.

2 Daniel Gore, "A Modest Proposal for Improving the Management of College Libraries." *Educational Record* 48, 1(1967): 89-96.

3 James F. Govan, "Community Analysis in an Academic Environment." *Library Trends* 24, 3 (1976): 541-556.

4 George S. Bonn, "Evaluation of the Collection." *Library Trends* 22, 3 (1974): 265-304 and David O. Lane, "The Selection of Academic Library Materials: A Literature Survey." *College and Research Libraries* 29 (September 1968): 364-372.

5 Harry Bach, "Acquisition Policy in the American Library." *College and Research Libraries* 18 (November 1957): 446-447, quoted in Lane, *op. cit.,* p. 62.

6 Kathleen McCullough, Edwin D. Posey, and Doyle C. Pickett, *Approval Plans and Academic Libraries: An Interpretive Survey* (Phoenix: Oryx, 1977), p. 62.

7   For an elaboration of the arguments against selection by librarians alluded to herein, see: Dennis W. Dickinson, "Subject Specialists in Academic Libraries: The Once and Future Dinosaurs." In *New Horizons for Academic Libraries* (New York: K.G. Saur, 1979), pp. 438-444.

8   Bonn, *op. cit.,* p. 295.

9   J. Periam Danton, "Subject Specialists in National and University Libraries, with Special Reference to Book Selection." *Libri* 17 (1967): 42-58.

10   Govan, *op. cit.,* p. 545; see also Richard De Gennaro, "Copyright, Resource Sharing and Hard Times: A View from the Field." *American Libraries* 8, 8 (1977): 430-435; Michael Moran, "The Concept of Adequacy in University Libraries." *College and Research Libraries* 39 (March 1978): 85-93; Helen Welch Tuttle, "An Acquisitionist Looks at Mr. Haro's Bibliographer." *Library Resources and Technical Services* 13, 2 (1969): 170-174.

11   Bonn, *op. cit.,* pp. 279-280.

12   *Ibid.*

13   *N.B.* Much may be made of alleged differences between collection evaluation and book selection. Some will contend that these are both distinguishable and distinct enterprises. However, while they are clearly distinguishable, they are not distinct in fact, being no more than different facets of the same enterprise, i.e., collection development. They are distinguishable only in point of time, one occurring before the fact and one after. They are otherwise isomorphic in spite of the obfuscating mythology of librarianship. In the sometimes tortured language of the philosophy of science, book selection involves prediction of use while evaluation involves "retrodiction". The sole difference between these two activities, aside from their relative temporal location with respect to a given event, is the amount of information available to the agent. This virtual isomorphism is tacitly acknowledged in the fact that "weeding" a collection - which may be viewed as evaluation in action - is now frequently referred to as "deacquisition".

It may also be argued that there is such a thing as evaluation per se, i.e., simply identifying the strengths and weaknesses of a collection. However, assuming a dynamic collection, unless such an effort is used as the basis for decisions respecting further acquisitions or deacquisitions, it is for all practical purposes a null concept and an exercise in futility. As such, it can have nothing to do with collection development.

14   J.E. Scrivner, "Subject Specialization in Academic Libraries: Some British Practices." *Australian Academic and Research Libraries* 5 (1974): 113-122.

15   Govan, *op. cit.,* p. 548 and Danton, *op. cit.,* p.49.

16   Charles B. Weinberg, "The University Library: Analysis and Proposals." *Management Science* 21, 2 (1974): 130-140.

17   Tuttle, op. cit., p. 173.

18   C.K. Byrd, "Subject Specialists in a University Library." *College and Research Libraries* 27 (May 1966): 191-193; Robert P. Haro, "The Bibliographer in the Academic Library." *Library Resources and Technical Services* 13, 2 (1969): 163-169; Govan, op. cit., p. 546.

19 G. Edward Evans, "Book Selection and Book Collection Usage in Academic Libraries." *Library Quarterly* 40, 3 (1979): 297-308.

20 Govan, *op. cit.*, p. 543.

21 *Ibid.*, p. 548.

22 Evans, *op. cit.*, pp. 303-04.

23 Hendrick Edelman, "Redefining the Academic Library." *Library Journal* 101, 1 (1976): 53-56.

24 Evans, *op. cit.*; Gayle Edward Evans, "The Influence of Book Selection Agents upon Book Collection Usage in Academic Libraries" (PhD dissertation, University of Illinois, 1969).

25 Evans, *ibid.*, p.40.

26 Byrd, *op. cit.*, p. 193; Haro, *op. cit.*, p. 169.

27 Peter F. Drucker, "The Professor as Featherbedder." *Chronicle of Higher Education* 13, 20 (1977): 24.

28 There is some evidence, albeit inconclusive, that one's particular job in a library may have some minor effect on the ability to select useful materials; but it appears to be essentially indicative of the fact that some library jobs, i.e., most technical service positions, provide nothing in the way of useful information for selection, while others with public service responsibilities provide slightly more than that. Evans, "Book Selection and Book Collection Usage", *op. cit.*, p. 304.

29 Govan, *op. cit.*, p. 346.

30 Tuttle, *op. cit.*, p. 173.

31 Robert W. Burns, Jr., "Library Use as a Performance Measure: Its Background and Rationale." *Journal of Academic Librarianship* 4, 1 (1978): 4-11.

32 Moran, *op. cit.*, pp. 86, 90.

33 De Gennaro, *op. cit.*, p. 434; Edelman, *op. cit.*, pp. 54-55.

34 De Gennaro, *op. cit.*, pp. 433-434.

35 Bonn, *op. cit.*

36 Moran, *op. cit.*, pp. 85, 90.

37 Illinois State Library. Cooperative Collection Development Subcommittee of the Research and Reference Center Directors, "Toward Cooperative Collection Development in the Illinois Library and Information Network" (Springfield, Ill.: Illinois State Library, 1977), p. 25.

38 *Ibid.*, p. 26.

39 *Ibid.*, p. 27.

40 De Gennaro, *op. cit.*, p. 434.

Robert L. Burr, *et al.*, "Six Responses to 'A Rationalist's Critique....'"
Journal of Academic Librarianship 7, 3 (1981): 144-151.

Robert L. Burr, "A Pragmatist's View of Book Selection for Academic *Libraries.*"

Few librarians would challenge Dickinson's statement that "one area in which both faculty members' and librarians' interests converge is in development of a library's collection." Both groups have a mutual concern that selection decisions be the best possible decisions, for collection development may be operationally defined as "the cumulative and holistic effect of decisions made about the addition, retention, and deletion of library materials."

The debated issue is whether librarians or teaching/research faculty will tend to make better decisions. Dickinson's case for the superiority of faculty decisions appears to rest upon four types of arguments: an argument to effectiveness, an argument to efficiency, an argument to economy, and an argument to superior knowledge. None of these arguments is convincing, at least in my judgment.

Dickinson challenged the effectiveness of librarian selection by noting that "many reasonable demands placed upon the academic library today are simply not being met." The statement is probably true. It was equally true when, as Dickinson also notes, it prompted serious questions about the effectiveness of faculty selection. I suggest that the questions raised about effectiveness have less to do with the identity of the selector than the natural superiority of hindsight to foresight.

It is then argued that librarians are "disadvantaged and encumbered" by other duties and responsibilities, that "selection responsibilities are organic to an academic department, but, at best, can be forced mechanically into the structure of a library." The demands of preparing lectures, meeting classes, grading papers, holding office hours, advising students, attending committee meetings, drafting grant proposals, and other duties which routinely burden faculty members do not strike this observer as being any less distracting than reference work or cataloging or administration. Dickinson's proposal to restructure the academic department, with appropriate modification of the usual criteria for promotion and tenure, sounds suspiciously like mechanical force to me.

The argument to economy suggests imply that the salaries paid to librarian selectors would be spent for more materials, to the benefit of all. Not so! When the burden of selection is transferred to the faculty, one may safely predict a demand for lessened faculty responsibilities in other areas - a demand best met by hiring additional faculty. There is another option: extra stipends for faculty who find themselves facing the prospect of working the same number of hours per week as the average librarian. And since the approach of this paper is avowedly practical, one should also consider the claims of the athletic scholarship fund to the unforeseen bonanza.

The argument to the superior knowledge of the faculty is not one which can be dismissed lightly. Dickinson identifies three specific areas in which the knowledge of the faculty is claimed to be superior to that of librarians. Each of these claims merits careful consideration.

Dickinson as well as previous authors has suggested that knowledge of library users is an important element in successful materials selection. Despite some rather serious reservations, I am prepared to concede that members of the teaching/research faculty may have superior knowledge of the library needs and habits of their immediate colleagues. However, I would argue that librarians enjoy a significant advantage with respect to knowledge of how students and other important clientele use the library. This is an important point since Dickinson notes that "library statistics consistently show that faculty user of the library constitutes only about 10 percent of total use." Acceptance of the faculty claim would seem to imply that knowledge of the few is more important than knowledge of the many. I disagree.

Knowledge of the institution and its curriculum and research programs, is another desideratum. Contrary to Dickinson's claim, I consistently find librarians better informed about their institutions - including the touchy issues of institutional priorities - than any equivalent group of teaching/research faculty. The reason for this will soon by obvious to anyone who spends some time in the faculty lounge. Librarians, to their great credit, are one of the few groups in academe who regularly communicate with faculty (and students) in all disciplines.

More than anything else, the claim of the faculty to select library materials rests upon the supposition of superior subject knowledge. Lurking behind the debate over subject expertise is the specter of a librarian, sans PhD, threatening to substitute his or her judgment about what should be acquired for that of the faculty member with a PhD in the discipline. This is a myth which ought to be firmly cast aside.

The truth of the matter is that the selector, whatever his or her status, typically makes a decision based upon a survey of the literature or book review authored by Professor X, of Institution Y, appearing in Journal Z. Both librarians and faculty selectors use basically the same tools to guide decision making. Insofar as both tend to rely heavily upon the subject expertise of a third party, the intramural haggling over academic credentials seems to have little point.

If the selection process is essentially one of validation of opinion as claimed here, two things appear to be critical to the success of the effort. The selector must first have easy access to a broad spectrum of relevant opinion, accompanied by adequate time in which to consider it. The earlier discussion of Dickinson's argument to efficiency concluded that neither librarians nor teaching/research faculty could claim significant advantage with regard to the latter. I would argue that libraries do enjoy a significant advantage, if only by virtue of their location, in the matter of access. It is the library which receives the relevant journals, prepublication announcements, indexes, abstracts, and so forth, which selectors must use. Wholesale dispersal of such material to faculty offices makes no sense from a service point of view, and its wholesale reproduction is poor economics.

Although the largest part of the previous discussion has attempted to show merely that the claims advanced in favour of a faculty selection model are by no means proven, the conclusion advanced regarding the superior access to selection tools enjoyed by librarians is but one of several points which might be made in favour of a librarian selection model.

It is unfortunate but true that selection decisions are often influenced as much by economics as by intellectual merit. More and more, the question "Should we buy it?" includes an unstated "Can we afford it?" The faculty selection model presumes a distributed materials budget; otherwise librarians would have to select from faculty selections the items actually purchased. A librarian selection model offers at least the hope of a more flexible approach wherein the too frequently observed internecine battle over departmental expenditures might be avoided. A librarian selection model also offers some hope for the future of interinstitutional resource sharing and joint collection development. Knowledge of subject materials available elsewhere and the conditions under which they can be accessed seems to be a unique and important contribution of librarians to decision making about selection.

Despite Dickinson's claim to the contrary, I would argue that librarians do have a "particular expertise in the mechanics of collection development" which is an important asset. A major element of this expertise is nothing more than a synthesis of the knowledge possessed about users and their needs, institutional priorities, appropriate selection tools, budgetary constraints, the availability of extramural resources, and so forth. A second ingredient is a knowledge of the structure of a subject literature including such issues as how the literature is produced, the preferred formats in which it appears, the bibliographic conventions which guide access to the literature, and so forth.

I would like to conclude by suggesting that librarians are best able to bring to the selection process the sine qua non of success: a commitment to the enterprise. Selection responsibilities are organic not to the academic department but to the library. From ancient times librarians have embraced the responsibility to select, organize, preserve, and make available for use the recorded knowledge of mankind. I believe the available evidence will confirm that we have done the job rather well. Despite the momentary crisis of self-confidence within the profession, I believe we should continue to do the job.

Murdo J. MacLead, "Some Social and Political Factors in Collection Development in Academic Libraries."

Dickinson's provocative and stimulating essay, an appeal to rationalism, relies more on the ingredient of reasoning, and less on the ingredient of real-life experience, in its formulations. I will illustrate this tendency in the following points, then add a brief reflection of my own.

1. Librarians live the most precarious professional lives in all of academe. Among all of those with professional degrees in the university or college environment, they work the longest public hours, enjoy the least job security (few have academic or faculty tenure), and are among the lowest paid. Because of these working conditions academic librarians have to struggle against low morale, against the condescension of other professional colleagues, and against the lack of available time for personal research and professional development. As a group, academic librarians also have been handicapped by the fact that most of them are women, victims of an underprivileged condition which surely needs no further elaboration here, and that many are the "second earners" in family groups, and thus subject to location in geographic situations where a rational judgement would tell them that the market for librarians is saturated. The opposite is also true. Professional librarians find themselves compelled to leave advantageous situations because the "main earner" of the family has received a promotion.

Academic administrators, responding unwillingly or enthusiastically to market conditions or supply and demand, use these conditions to further depress salaries and other working conditions. The difficulties created by oversupply of professional librarians may be especially active in universities with large and vigorous schools or faculties of library science. Such degree-producing faculties sometimes depress the local market and thus adversely affect the working conditions of academic librarians in the same university and in other academic institutions within its region, given the relative lack of logical mobility enjoyed by specialized "second earners".

This harried professional existence is now further threatened by the exigencies of difficult budgetary times. Academic administrators ritually proclaim the central importance of the library to education and intellectual life, but just as expedientially cut library budgets, partly because the library and its users often do not compose a strong pressure group. (Often administrators are supplied with ammunition of dubious scientific validity by library schools which point to low library "use" of materials or financial waste. Some library schools are emerging as leading obstacles to professional librarians, library users, and thus to the growth of intellectual life in general.)

Belatedly, academic librarians are beginning to react to these threats. The movement for equal rights for women has helped considerably. So too has the movement toward unionization of academic faculties. University administrators, badgered by federal, state and local governments to appoint more women and minorities, often find that relabelling existing professional staff as faculty is faster, easier, and less expensive than searching for new candidates. Librarians, hesitantly flexing these new muscles, are looking for new areas of power and responsibility as they search for more autonomous and fulfilling professional lives. Much of this expansion of status and function by academic librarians is not finely tuned - it is too new and unsophisticated to have elaborated a coherent program - and it may well be, as Dickinson argues, that in some cases these librarians are pushing into areas where, from the pure point of view of organization logic, they do not belong. But any arguments, such as this one, which does not include recent political and social experience in its equations, must be described as more theoretical than rational.

2.   Dickinson presents the responsibility for collection development as a battleground between faculty and encroaching librarians. This smacks of the strawman. As he admits, most academic libraries select materials by some cooperative system, formal or informal, whereby librarians and faculty consult and interact. I know of no academic library where this is not the case. So what Dickinson is discussing, presumably, is a shift in emphasis away from the faculty end of the continuum toward the librarian end, a trend he wishes to reverse. Experience would indicate that such shifts in emphasis depend less on the formulation of general policies, however rational they may be, and more on local and idiosyncratic factors such as the degree of dedication and bibliographilia of individual faculty and collection librarians, relationships of harmony between the two groups, the divisions of political power within the institution, the perceived nature of the library (i.e., teaching, research, or both), and above all, on the locus of acquisition budget subdivision and assignment.

3.   Dickinson proposes to increase faculty enthusiasm and participation in collection development by offering greater rewards. Again, this seems rational but flies in the face of reality, that is, experience. The departmental representative is often selected in one of two ways. (a) He or she is the local bibliomaniac and volunteers. (b) The department assigns a number of extracurricular and nonresearch tasks and faculty members taken turns over the years at both the pleasant and unpleasant ones. (In undemocratic departments, the lore goes, the more unpleasant the task, the more junior the faculty

member who gets saddled with it.) These practices lead to three problems with Dickinson's proposals for incentives and accountability. First, the tendency in this era of budget difficulties is to increase faculty workloads, especially classroom teaching, and to cut rewards for other activities. Secondly, and more specifically, if the departmental library representative were to be more scrupulously scrutinized and rewarded or punished for performance, so too, in very little time, would be the departmental undergraduate adviser, graduate adviser, admissions officer, departmental curriculum and schedule supervisor, assistant chairperson, and in some cases, the graduate student placement officer. Obviously such a massive system of scrutinies, allied to the other work of tenure, review, and promotion committees, would be endless and unwieldy. It would be vetoed by deans in any case, who wish for more classroom and research productivity and are unwilling to give credit for these departmental chores. Finally, how would department members judge their library representative? The representative quickly becomes the most knowledgeable, often the only knowledgeable member of the department on library matters, and all know that his or her main constraint is the size of the departmental library budget. Selections, as peers recognize, are limited above all by that factor. Some members may disagree with the selections or emphasis, but faculty generally sympathize with the library representative. They realize that he or she has developed some expertise and must be left to do the best possible with a totally inadequate budget. To judge a person involved in such activity would be considered by most faculty to be presumptuous, pointless (it would lower the unpaid, amateur enthusiasm of the departmental bibliomaniac).

It must be clear by now that I am in favor of a cooperative arrangement for collection development. In one area, however, I emphatically favor librarian dominance. The head of collection development should be in charge of the dividing up among departments and schools of the acquisitions budget. The collection development specialist is especially well placed to obtain independent information from the academic administration as to strong and weak departments and as to future emphasis and deemphasis of programs. The specialist is also well placed to survey departmental library activities through bibliographers and through personal observations. Which departments are enthusiastic users and purchasers, which lackadaisical? The head of collection development is uniquely placed, in fact, to divide up the pie sensibly. Faculty turn such financial apportionment into battlegrounds of politics and prestige.

If librarians and faculty fail to cooperate over collection development, a common interest for some different and some similar reasons, then let both beware. The wolves are at the door and the acquisition budget is a poorly protected piece of raw meat.

Angela Poulos, "The Best of Both Worlds."

Much of the literature of collection development and book selection comes from the 1960s when money available for higher education created rising expectations for all involved in the academic enterprise. Unfortunately, too few planners looked beyond the demographic reality of that decade and established institutional priorities which cannot be maintained in the economic realities of the 1980s. In an effort to allocate resources more realistically, Dickinson proposes reductions in the amount of library budget devoted to staff salaries resulting in more funds for books.

I agree with many aspects of Dickinson's proposal for faculty selection of materials, since faculty participation in this capacity has been most valuable at my institution, but I take issue with some specific suggestions. His definition of collection development is limited to selection. His model for extracting responsibility from faculty selectors is commendable but is no more achievable in the present academic environment than are other "voluntary" alternatives. To alter present practices will take time. Selection for a library collection used heavily as an instructional laboratory is different from a collection used for research. The former emphasizes quantity and breadth, while the latter requires depth and selectivity. An academic library serving both functions will find the user of approval plans and librarian selectors appropriate for many aspects of its collection.

The first consideration in using faculty selectors exclusively is establishing who will be held responsible for the quality and performance of the library's collection. If the collection is deemed inadequate by accreditation agencies, the library director rather than faculty members will be asked to take the appropriate steps necessary to improve it. The university informs the library director of its priorities through budget support given to various departments, and he or she must formulate plans for correcting the deficiencies based on those priorities.

Dickinson's model for establishing faculty selection responsibility has some useful components and some deficiencies. Faculty members are effective in selection, but they report that promotion, tenure, and merit decisions are based primarily on scholarship and successful teaching. Additional service opportunities have little appeal. In departments where the faculty depends heavily on library resources, peer pressure on the faculty liaison is a powerful incentive to his or her prompt performance of selecting responsibilities. Librarians must monitor the faculty selection, however, to be certain that all departments are obtaining books.

Problems of continuity in selection arise when faculty members leave campus for one to three months several times during the year. Many departments annually appoint the newest member to be faculty liaison, but his or her knowledge of faculty research and teaching interests or collection strengths and weaknesses will need time to develop. Librarians often work closely with faculty in subject areas over a long period and provide this essential continuity.

Librarians, even those with additional subject degrees, will agree that they need faculty assistance in selection. Faculty members selecting books outside their specific teaching and research areas, however, encounter the same selection dilemmas as subject area librarians. If Dickinson's model is to be successful, pressure on faculty and departmental chairs to continue participation will have to be employed by library staff. The task is not impossible, but librarians must be prepared in meet resentment, frustration, and refusal from faculty members who are being asked to teach more hours of larger undergraduate classes and to produce more research as conditions for their continued employment.

Deacquisition is essential for a quality collection, and faculty participation in this process is important. Although research libraries seldom discard the last copy of any item they acquire, collections of many teaching institutions are badly in need of evaluation to remove multiple copies of outdated textbooks, superseded curriculum materials, and secondary sources. Faculty members often refuse to take responsibility for the removal of books from the collection; thus, librarians must assume it.

In large research libraries the collection development operation is expensive, and substantial portions of university resources are allocated to develop and maintain nationally recognized research collections. Although smaller universities and colleges may have some areas of research excellence, they emphasize teaching activity. Subject area librarians in small and medium-sized libraries serve as reference librarians, as liaisons for multiple subject areas, as committee members for university, library, and professional organizations, and as researchers. The added cost of collection development provided by librarians in the majority of libraries is not very large, and reductions in the number of librarians needed are unlikely without concomitant reductions in service. Adoption of the Dickinson model would result in collections more closely reflecting the curriculum needs and faculty research interests of a particular institution, but librarians must still coordinate the interests of various departments.

Approval plans can be used efficiently with faculty participation. Faculty members assist in profile development and review, and they select with the book in hand rather than from publishers' information. Librarians select for departments lacking interest in this activity. This arrangements reduces the possibility that large numbers of little-used titles will be purchased. Since approval selections of libraries supporting similar curricula will be heavily used, duplication of materials is appropriate. The unique character of research collections will continue to be a product of faculty selection.

Faculty support of cooperative collection development will be essential if it is to be successful. The viability of this concept has not been thoroughly tested to date, and cost-benefits to libraries are not known. Librarians must examine the concept critically for their particular institutions before committing resources to expensive and ineffective procedures. Cooperative collection development will be successful when institutions can agree to share promptly materials collected in areas of tangential interest. Faculty members will be receptive to cooperative collection development only if they are convinced of its value and are involved in planning for it at their institutions.

This response to the Dickinson model is an attempt to be eclectic and rational. Using reason and experience, we will select from among the various methods those which best enable us to provide the instructional and research materials needed by our faculty and students.

David H. Stam, "A Modest Case against Faculty Selection."

Despite Ralph Waldo Emerson's statement that "it is not observed that librarians are wiser than others," a strong and rational case can be made, at least in larger academic and research libraries, for placing the responsibility for collection building with librarians rather than with the Hobby-Horsemen of the faculty. I have little quarrel with Dickinson's arguments as applied to small and medium-sized college libraries where the collection must respond to immediate curricular needs best determined by teaching faculty responsible for answering those needs. However, when those faculty enter the areas of their own research, even in small colleges, they become particularly dangerous to the collection development process, bringing biases and self-serving motives to collection growth which do not necessarily serve the institutional mission. While there is no disputing against their Hobby-Horses, there is a question as to whether the institution should saddle and groom them, or carefully rein them in.

The Germanic model of the seminar or institute library which Dickinson cites is a good case in point. These were collections build around one person or one school. In this country, as far as I know, only Johns Hopkins University truly emulated this model, and it could do so in the 1870s because of the accessibility of a good general collection nearby, the Peabody Library. Eventually, of course, a more general or comprehensive approach had to be taken, but the evil effects lingered on. When Professor Hugh Kenner joined the English faculty at Johns Hopkins in the early 1970s, he made some pertinent observations on the growth of that collection, which had been shaped by faculty. He discovered in his own fields of study an erratic collection lacking many standard works (among them several of his own) but including many esoteric items. His speculation, which I found confirmed in other fields, was that faculty had used the selection process to add to the library not works that they required for their own personal/professional libraries, but that might have some tangential use for their research or that of their own students.

Faculty understandably tend to ignore cooperative collection development and borrowing arrangements if there is any possibility of their owning the material. In the best of all possible worlds, librarians would also candidly ignore such relationships in hopes of developing great collections, but library administrators required to make compromises among a vast range of demands have to take a different view.

We should also remember that collections are relatively permanent while faculty members have been notoriously transient. Should a medium-sized college or even a medium-sized university put substantial resources into developing specialized collections in Tudor geneology, Icelandic literature, or microbiology for faculty who aspire to move on to Harvard, Cornell, or Yale, possible leaving behind an investment on which there is little return? The danger is real and I doubt that a hypothetical model of faculty accountability will solve the problem. Dickinson's solution of placing the onus of accountability on the academic department seems to me to be an invidious way of putting academic departments in competition with one another at the expense of the library and the institution, especially in interdisciplinary areas where collection building overlaps many fields.

I am not arguing against faculty involvement in the selection process - it is crucial to teaching programs, and especially in the reserve department (where they so frequently let us down). But librarians should have the major responsibility - and with it they must have intimate knowledge of the curriculum and research programs of their institutions and must develop close working relations with faculty in all fields. Although there has been a marked increase in the subject competencies of academic libraries, they cannot know everything or even keep up in their own specialties. They need and gratefully accept any help they can get. But in the interests of balance, comprehensiveness, and responsibility to a wide variety of users, the basic responsibility for collection growth should remain in their hands.

J. Periam Danton, in his classic study on *Book Selection and Collections*, describes the problem of faculty selection as unregulated, uncoordinated, isolated decisions made in no coherent way. Citing the 1936 Waples-Laswell study, he says:

> Of nearly five hundred English, French, and German works in the fields of the social sciences judged by specialists in those fields to be of primary scholarly importance, Harvard held 63 percent, and the universities of Chicago, California, and Michigan, 49, 40 and 31 percent respectively. The New York Public Library,

on the other hand, where book selection is, of course, entirely the responsibility of a corps of subject specialist librarians, held 92 percent ... The differences were not the result of disparity of financial means... The difference lies largely in the chancy nature of almost exclusive reliance upon faculty initiative and industry.[1]

My own institution may not be doing quite so well today, but we are at least free of the distortions of faculty selection. Our librarians know the market and the realities of availability as faculty seldom would. They know intimately what a wide variety of users want, need, and ask for as faculty never could (except for their own specialized needs). They are fully dedicated to serve those needs, as faculty are not. They are in the best position to build collections for present use and for posterity.

Reference

1   J. Periam Danton, *Book Selection and Collections: A Comparison of German and American University Libraries* (New York: Columbia University Press, 1963), pp. 74-75.

Charles B. Osburn, "Collection Development Needs Professional Management."

Thank goodness for Dennis Dickinson's argument in favor of faculty, rather than librarian, selection of library materials! After all it make abundantly good sense that, since we get our best information straight from the horse's mouth, we ought to have the horse do the work. This would eliminate the middle man, i.e., the library selector; and, heaven knows, we have tolerated just about enough in the past 15 years from these prima donnas. Dickinson's model for faculty selection is clear in its logic, the extension of which I find particularly attractive. For example, I can see it all, now: The vast, but well organized, team of faculty selectors receives allocations from a faculty committee, which is chaired, depending upon local style, either by the debate coach or the wrestling coach. The icing on the cake is the logical conclusion, which proves the value of the whole process because, at long last, the director of libraries is finally and totally free of the heavy burden of collection development responsibilities.

Dickinson has selected some truths, organized them in a logical sequence, and followed their direction to extreme. Like any other reader of this kind of argument, I could easily take each major point and draw an opposite conclusion - without any more proof than Dickinson offers, however. Rather than take that approach, I prefer to offer some generalizations that I think cast doubt on the usefulness of the extreme model presented in the Dickinson article and suggest my own views.

I have taken special pains in the recent past to elaborate my belief that academic libraries (at least the large ones) have evolved to a high degree of independence within the university and that this is not good. The present position of collection development is extreme, just as Dickinson's model is extreme, only in the opposite direction. Surely, the best selection is that which is informed by an understanding of faculty activity and by perceived trends, but managed by the library. It is a far more complex job than it was thought to be by librarians 15 to 20 years ago - and more so than Dickinson makes it out to be, now. I do not believe that the average faculty member is more likely to be a good selector than the average librarian.

On the basis of my own professional employment over the past 20 years in six universities, my overall impression of Dickinson's extreme model is that it is most naive. Like Dickinson, I am no expert in the sociology of the professoriat. However, my experience tells me that, with the exception of some projects in the science and engineering fields, faculty members are strong individuals, unaccustomed to understanding and working for an ill-defined common good. Consequently, they appear as a group to be highly irrational, not subject to the laws of logic and reason as we know them. However, these characteristics contribute very significantly to the strength of academia and, therefore, should be protected. Selectors need to be managers of policy, budget, and people, and in control of a knowledge of broad subjects and their literatures. Selectors should not be subject specialists, which faculty members are, and in that regard Dickinson is quite right in recommending that we acknowledge a distinction between subject specialization and subject responsibility in the library.This has been a growing trend, however, for at least the last five years, as far as I can tell.

In this connection, I have one other general observation. Dickinson suggests that the information we need for the purpose of selection comes almost entirely from local faculty. That is only a part of the story, for specialized faculty interests have to be interpreted and perhaps expanded in the context of trends in the broader discipline. Otherwise, we will not be able to anticipate needs as they arise in the course of the next year or two (*n.b.*: I'm not referring to the 50-year projections that Dickinson ridicules), and we will not be able to develop the core of resources that is both needed by thesis writers and essential to cooperative collection development. All of this is to repeat that we need informed, communicating managers, not subject specialists, as our selectors.

It is true that we have not yet used our library organization in the most effective way to manage collections, but that is not, alone, sufficient reason to scrap the organization and adopt an extreme position that tends to get us off the hook. I disagree very strongly with Dickinson's proposed model, but his stimulating and well-written article allows us to examine some old problems from a different perspective, and that is a valuable opportunity at this juncture in our history.

Alfred Garvin Engstrom, "Methods of Fruitful Collaboration."

I agree wholeheartedly with Dennis Dickinson that college and university faculties should have a powerful shaping influence in developing the contours of growing academic library collections. But I sharply disagree with the extreme "alternative" by which he carries his major arguments and with his cavalier conception of the functions and abilities of specialist bibliographers on library staffs.

Part of my disagreement may arise from Dickinson's arguments being more applicable to small undergraduate libraries than to those of rapidly developing teaching- and research-oriented libraries like my own. But my essential criticism is that there are methods of collaboration available between faculty and library specialists that should resolve much of the problem that Dickinson sees largely in terms of extremes.

Until the 1950s a great part of my university's collections, at least in the areas of my special interest (the humanities, especially French literature, language, and civilization), were shaped largely by the faculty in terms of various curricula and the interests of outstanding professors. Annual budgetary allotments to the departments were small, and departmental book and periodical selection was a crucial but not heavy task. Since then (with, for example, nearly 130,000 volumes added to the overall library collection during the past year) the matter of book selection has become a very large and time consuming responsibility. No single representative of any large scholarly department could afford the time and effort required to keep up with all the new orders, unless he or she were relieved of a large part of teaching and committee work and gave up much scholarly research so as practically to become a rather ill-prepared semiprofessional bibliographer.

A few years ago our Chief Bibliographer, after consultation with the Library, the Administrative Board of the Library, and the book chairpersons in various departments, drew up an outline of three plans for library acquisitions with varying degrees of faculty participation. The decision of the broad, after careful deliberation in which departmental book chairpersons took part, was for a "Moderate Centralization" plan. This provided that Bibliographical Services with its specialists (who, in my field of interest, tend to have PhD degrees in the general area concerned or in an adjacent subject area, as well as the MLS degree) would take care of most orders for current publications with advice from departmental book chairpersons, but with generous annual allotments left in departmental budgets for the use of the various book chairpersons to fill gaps in retrospective materials.

Very fine relationships of enthusiastic cooperation between departmental book chairpersons and the professional specialist bibliographers are being established within this framework. I have found invaluable the notices of collections for sale, the special catalogs, and the great variety of miscellaneous professional information provided by this relationship. Over the years Bibliographical Services has furnished me with thousands of "goldenrod" and other slips for newly purchased and cataloged volumes that were clearly identified in my discipline, with very helpful bibliographical data on library call numbers. Thus I have had continuous, detailed information on our collection's development in my field and have been able to pass on details of individual books purchased to colleagues most immediately concerned.

Apart from the general blanket orders from university presses and the numerous standing orders from publishers' special collections in the various fields, for French purchases we have drawn up for the specialist bibliographers lists of our own existing special collections that we want to expand, lists of the special interests of individual professors, and lists of French authors (rated 1, 2, or 3 by our scholars in the order of importance for our work and collections); and new developments in our curriculum have been indicated for collection purposes. As a result, far more has been accomplished than would have been if the departmental book chairperson in the area had been the sole organizer of the whole, and an ordered plan has been provided for the future, much of which can be carried out by informed and concerned specialists in Bibliographical Services. Thus, by a combination of professional bibliographical information, skills, and experience with particular departmental knowledge in the field, we have, in my judgement, resolved to our very great academic benefit the supposed dilemma that Dickinson considered in his essay.

The greatest university research libraries have, of course, long since established procedures in book and periodical selection that satisfy most faculty needs, and highly specialized bibliographers are necessarily an integral part of their organization. For college and university libraries that are currently developing into significant research centres, the presence of specialist bibliographers is essential, and a closely organized interrelationship between them and departmental book chairpersons is an invaluable means of ensuring the faculty influence that Dickinson rightly desires in developing collections. But it is not a choice between one or the other - rather a very present call for both in a carefully planned and clearly organized cooperation.

Much depends upon the qualifications of the individuals involved and upon the nature of the relationship between the professional bibliographers and the various book chairpersons; but with a careful selection of personnel, good faith is likely to result when plans and organizations are clear and are the outgrowth of careful discussion and good will. My one experience, after many years as one of my department's book chairpersons for library purchases, has been a very happy one in the present relationship with Bibliographic Services and its professional specialist bibliographers. I am more grateful to them than I can say for their knowledge and enthusiasm and skillful and imaginative cooperation. I feel that we are working together as colleagues in a magnificent enterprise at the very heart of my university's essential program.

John Rutledge and Luke Swindler, "The Selection Decision: Defining Criteria and Establishing Priorities." *College and Research Libraries* **48, 2 (1987): 123-131.**

This article discusses the specific selection criteria used in making collection development decisions. The criteria are grouped into six major categories, and within each category they are arranged in order of relative importance. The proposed schematization provides librarians who have collection development responsibilities with a holistic and explicit model for arriving at a selection decision as well as a mechanism for assigning a specific priority to each selection. Use of such a model can help to rationalize selection decisions; it relates acquisitions effectively and convincingly to a library's fiscal environment; and it promotes cooperative collection development.

A German proverb states, "Whoever has the choice, also has the misery." Making choices is no easy business, yet selecting materials is one of the principal functions of collection development officers. Even in libraries that rely heavily on approval plans, selectors must review titles individually to ensure an effective collection development program. Despite the centrality of selection decision making to the collection development process, there are few tools that offer practical assistance for the performance of this intellectual task, particularly in academic settings. Moreover, the guides found in the published literature are not truly comprehensive, and none provides a practical means of relating selection to a library's acquisitions budget. While a collection development officer may be called upon to select or reject hundreds of titles during the course of the working day and is generally proficient at making these choices, he or she could still benefit from a convenient tool that rationally organizes the factors contributing to an acquisitions decision. This would be particularly helpful if funds are insufficient for acquiring all appropriate titles or if the library is seriously attempting to implement cooperative collection development programs.

Selection officers typically receive little assistance from their own library when making decisions. Even the best and most widely known collection policies merely state what a library ideally would select in a world without financial constraints, while a few policies also indicate the existing level of collecting.[1] A unique tool, the *Bibliographer's Manual*, proposed by the collection development staff of the University of Texas at Austin Library, serves as a guide to the collection development system and selection procedures rather than to the decision-making process itself.[2] A more general guide used in many libraries is ALA's *Guidelines for Collection Development*.[3] This otherwise useful handbook covers the formulation of a collection development policy and the evaluation of the results of selection, but does not deal with the specific selection decision-making that is central to the collection development process.

Earlier Approaches to Selection

The task of setting forth the criteria use to select materials for libraries offers an intriguing challenge and has appeals to many other writers. During the past few years, as the field of collection development has matured, a number of texts have appeared. As one would expect, certain themes are common to all attempts - quality of the materials, relationship to the patrons, cost - to name only the most frequent. Usually, however, treatments of selection decision-making are very general, discursive, and incomplete. Moreover, the selection criteria are often tied to the scope and organization of specific tools.

An examination of major works by Arthur Curley and Dorothy Broderick, Robert Broadus, and William Katz shows that they all develop some general principles, concentrating, as textbooks must, on broad issues rather than on the intricacies of the decision-making process. When specific selection criteria are discussed, they are treated independently; that is, the authors do not relate the various criteria to each other. The reader is left wondering which criteria are the most important and when to apply them. Finally, all three texts focus on public libraries.

In *Building Library Collections* Curley and Broderick discuss some of the principles of selection using a series of nine debate topics.[4] Under each one they present a range of contrasting viewpoints. The discussions are rarely prescriptive; indeed, they are not intended to be. Rather, they point to the diversity of opinion on such issues as high culture versus popular materials, catholicity in collecting, and demand as the governing factor in selection. Moreover, because the author's primary intention is to stimulate thought, their principles do not serve as a guide to selection.

In his textbook, *Selecting Materials for Libraries*, Broadus offers a wide-ranging exposition of the issues and practical wisdom about selecting books and most other types of library materials.[5] Although not grouped conveniently, the principles he points are (1) user needs as primary; (2) relation to existing collection; (3) relation to other libraries; (4) the sources or publishers; and (5) book-intrinsic criteria such as content, recency, veracity, reputation of the author or publisher, and format. While Broadus is a useful discussion of selection, the specific application of selection criteria is not developed.

In *Collection Development: The Selection of Materials for Libraries*, Katz advances a set of ten selection criteria.[6] These are (1) purpose, scope, and audience; (2) difficulty; (3) authority, honesty, and credibility of author and publisher; (4) subject matter; (5) comparison of a title to others in the collection; (6) timelines; (7) format; (8) price; (9) curriculum support; and (10) demand. We believe that these criteria touch upon most of the issues. However, as with the other survey texts, the relationship of the criteria to each other remains undeveloped.

Jean Boyer Hamlin, in a contributed chapter in Robert Stueart and George Miller's handbook on collection development, develops a list of nine selection criteria.[7] Her factors, paraphrased, include (1) pertinence to areas covered, (2) interest to users, (3) relationship to existing collection, (4) cost, (5) patron objections and threat of theft, (6) probable quality, (7) necessity of continuing financial commitment, (8) duplication of existing materials, and what might be called (9) "bibliothecal convenience" or ease of handling. A more tightly organized grouping would simplify the classification, since some criteria are much more narrowly focused than others. In addition, the criteria are neither well developed nor prioritized. To illustrate practical decision-making, Hamlin recasts the criteria into questions that should be asked when selecting books from a dealer's catalog. While these questions can help to refine one's thinking about a particular title, they provide no way of evaluating the results of the examination.

Recent journal literature has provided further attempts to delineate selection criteria, sometimes more focused on the decision-making process itself. Hendrik Edelman develops a model of decision-making based on the organization of library materials by source and type of publication.[8] He suggests that to this universe of published knowledge one may apply certain historical-, linguistic-, and geographical-elimination factors, correlated to the collection level descriptors. A further distinction is made between selection for short-term goals and selection for long-term goals. The main criteria, according to Delman, are established by the collection development policy. To this policy one must bring to bear the virtues of "balance, reliability, and comprehensiveness, in that order."[9] This article is very general and does not discuss specific criteria, nor how they affect individual selection decisions. The suggestions, while accurate in the main, do not yield a guide to microdecision-making; indeed, Edelman's main focus is macrodecision-making.

In an article on selection decision-making for preservation purposes, Dan C. Hazen develops another distinction.[10] Pursuing the close relationship between preservation decisions and collection development decisions, Hazen addresses five criteria that pertain both to preservation and to new-title selection. These are (1) academic activity or user demand, (2) historical precedent and tradition, (3) the volume and cost of materials, (4) the availability of alternatives to purchase, and (5) discipline-specific models of access to information. These criteria apply best to preservation decisions; for acquisition they are incomplete and lack specificity. Although most of these criteria are valid, no priority is assigned to them nor is a method of application suggested.

John N. DePew presents an explicit model of the acquisitions process, consisting of a detailed flow chart with weighted inputs and a formula that results in a selection decision.[11] Although the article does make one aware of the complexity of selection, the criteria are inadequate and not well developed. In addition, they include considerations that should not be relevant, e.g., whether the requestor will cause trouble or whether the title is a gift. Finally, the formula he presents is very arbitrary and too cumbersome.

Ross Atkinson's recent article on what actually happens when collection development librarians select a title represents one of the few attempts to describe the selection process itself.[12] His article is useful for understanding some of the dynamics of selection microdecisions and how criteria relate to each other. Atkinson sees the selection process as the interaction of a selector with a bibliographic citation; the selector resolves the decision by using three contexts, the archival (what is already in the collection), the communal (the research needs and interests of the clientele), and the thematic (what has been or is being published on he subject). While this article is stimulating, it is primarily a theoretical treatment and not intended to be a practical guide to selecting. It is also too concentrated on the bibliographic citation itself to serve as a comprehensive guide to selection decision-making.

Our view of the literature has not uncovered a practical and holistic model for microselection, the selection of materials on a title-by-title basis as is done in libraries every day. We see the need for the provision of a comprehensive and practical model that has a high level of applicability to any selection decision. The model presented in this article not only delineates and defines the appropriate criteria, but also displays them visually to show the relationship of the criteria to each other. In addition, we provide a numerical rating system to allow the librarian to rank each title and thereby relate selection to available funds.

Evolution of the Model

The model consists of the criteria discussed below, coupled with a priority system, which grew out of the tasks and opportunities faced by collection development librarians at the University of North Carolina at Chapel Hill (UNC-CH). Collection development for the main library system at UNC-CH was totally reorganized during the mid-1970s, when selection because a library responsibility. At the same time the university and library administrations greatly increased funding for acquisitions. These two developments created expanded collection development possibilities, making selectors acutely aware of the selection process and the rationale for selection decision-making. Since then, occasional budgetary reverses have given the selectors experience in the painful application of a triage system, in which all selections were classified as first, second, or third priority.

With the reorganization of collection development, long-standing cooperative acquisitions programs with neighbouring research libraries took a new lease on life.[13] This priority system has proven useful for cooperative collection development, particularly in facing the practical necessity of deciding which specific titles should be acquired locally and which should be acquired by the library holding the primary collection commitment. Within the context of board cooperative agreement, a common understanding and an explicit statement of selection criteria encourage collection development librarians to think in terms of priorities and thereby to formulate cooperative programs with a large measure of specificity.

Redefining the Selection Criteria

If, as Atkinson says, selection is difficult to describe,[14] it is also difficult to prescribe. The selection criteria presented below are the results of years of wrestling with the intellectual issues involved in the selection of library materials. We have tried to include all the relevant factors involved in selection decision-making. For the sake of clarity we have arranged the factors into six internally coherent and, insofar as possible, mutually exclusive categories, thus avoiding redundancy. At the same time the arrangement indicates relationships between the criteria. Each of the criteria causes the selector to ask specific questions about any given title; in answering the questions the selector brings objective information to bear on making the decision.

Subject

Subject constitutes the first and most important selection factor. Since all books and other library materials are about something, both collection development policies and staff are typically organized along subject lines. The selector initially discerns the subject of a work, e.g., France-History-Revolution, or Science Fiction, then evaluates the item in terms of the information or knowledge universe. At the same time, and perhaps more importantly, he or she attempts to relate the items under consideration to the program at his or her institution. How well the item supports institutional objectives and programs is the paramount consideration, but it is always seen in relation to the larger intellectual universe. Indeed, unless one knows the subject of a work, a rational selection decision cannot be made.

Intellectual Content

In actual practice, especially when selection decisions are made from a bibliographic citation, it is sometimes difficult to arrive at an informed estimate of the intellectual content of a work. Nevertheless, the question must be addressed. In assessing intellectual content, one asks how it relates to what has gone before. Is the work a key title in its field, whether a great work of literature or a seminal study? How valuable have the author's past contributions been? Is it "raw data" of the field such as statistical tables? How authoritative is the work and what is the nature of its contribution? Is it narrowly focused or a general essay? Or is the primary concern propagandistic? High intellectual content alone cannot determine the selection decision; nor can trivial or polemical works be rejected automatically, since they sometimes become the subject of research.

Potential Use

Having considered the work in terms of its subject relevance and its intrinsic intellectual integrity, the selector next reviews it in the light of his knowledge of the patrons' needs. Potential use is considered only after subject and intellectual content have been ascertained, in order to ensure that appropriate, quality materials are added. One must know what a work is about and something of the nature of its contents before one can predict level of use. What is the likelihood that the item in question will be used? What level of use justifies its acquisition? The selector should know of urgent research interests and be able to predict probable interest based on knowledge of the course offerings, research programs, and circulation patterns. There is also the category of broad, general information, material to which educated men and women will want to have recourse. These works are desirable but must take second place. At the lower end of the range are works that, because of considerations such as style or prerequisite knowledge, are deemed less accessible. From the bibliographic citation the selector can usually determine whether one use in fifty years would be the maximum expected.

Relation to the Collection

This factors echoes the concerns discussed under subject. Whereas subject relates an item to the information universe, here an item is scrutinized in terms of its relation to a specific library's collection. Typically the questions asked here are ones that will be posed by libraries, who, generally, are trained to look at the integrity of the library's collection, to fill in gaps in the collection, to establish balance and comprehensiveness in the collections, and to maintain cooperative programs with other libraries. Here there is an inherent tension: how to meet current user demands and yet continue to build upon historic collection strengths and specialties.

Bibliographic Considerations

To a certain extent you can judge a book by looking at its cover. Bibliographic considerations parallel those criteria found under intellectual content. The interrelated issues of publisher and format further refine the selection. The reputation of the publisher or sponsoring agency and the type of publication or format of the work both play an important role in any selection decision. Obviously these factors require some knowledge of the book trade. The highest priority within this category is assigned to the titles of distinguished publishing houses that over the years have built up a reputation for excellence. At the other extreme, there is a lush undergrowth of "quasi-publications" such as working papers and research reports. Between the two poles is a wide range of specialized publishing as well as the output of the major trade publishers, each of which has a reputation for quality and subject specialization.

Language

Language is a criterion because it speaks to the issue of potential use, yet it is distinct from it. Language also relates closely to the topic of the work.The major working language of a given field deserves special consideration. Similarly, the second working language of a topic will have to receive a relatively high priority. In some cases the major language of the topic will not be English. If the major language of a field is Italian, the selector cannot exclude an item in Italian if the topic is central. Does the language of the item augment or detract from the capacity of the work to inform? Travel guides in the vernacular, for example, may convey a fuller understanding of the country than English-language editions; on the other hand, a foreign-language book on computer science has little capacity to inform an English speaking audience. Perhaps the foreign-language item helps to educate the potential user about areas not well covered in the English-language press? Or, would the language of the item have to be considered distant from its topic, e.g., Italian-language studies of Czech literature? Finally, hoping to gore as few oxen as possible, we recognize that some languages are less central to scholarly inquiry than others, although factors such as user interests can cause the item to receive an overall higher ranking than the language factor alone would indicate.

Cost as a Nonfactor

Although many writers include cost as a factor, price is irrelevant to making a selection decision as distinct from a purchase decision. We agree with Atkinson that "the budget should be viewed not as a criterion for selection but rather as an influence upon the relative extent to which selection criteria are acted upon."[14] While high cost typically results in more care being taken in making the selection decision, the priorities - those items that the library must have, should have, or could have - do not change in response to budgetary limitations; they remain the same, whether money is available or not. Further, it should be noted that librarians generally select titles within specific budget lines, e.g., new subscriptions, audio-visuals, expensive titles, current books. As a consequence, a costly microform collection or multivolume set does not compete against a current book or a new journal subscription but against other possible expensive purchases. One can therefore use the proposed model to determine the relative priorities among a group of expensive titles. Finally, just as high cost should not influence a selection decision, low cost or bargain prices also should be irrelevant. If a title is ranked at priority three, its ranking does not change in response to the offer of a discount. Only when two items of equal ranking are being considered for acquisition in times of financial adversity might price determine which is actually purchased.

Using the Model

In choosing a chart or tabular form of presentation, we are attempting to provide selectors with a succinct, rapidly scannable tool for guidance in title-by-title or microselection (see Table 1). Although the model presented was developed in an academic library for the rationalization of book selection, it could be adapted with only slight modifications by any type of institution and can be applied to selection of all types of library material.

When deciding whether to acquire a title, a selector usually considers many factors of varying importance within the context of the inclusions and exclusions of a collection development policy. The factors that we consider most relevant are grouped into six columns. Each column contains a discrete set of criteria, made specific by descriptive phrases. The factors affecting selection are (1) subjects, (2) intellectual content, (3) potential use, (4) relation to collection, (5) bibliographic considerations, and (6) language. Moreover, because some selection factors are more significant than others, the columnar sets are presented from left to right in descending order of importance. Although each column represents a distinct and internally coherent set of criteria, the second three columns echo respectively the first three. Using this model one evaluates each title horizontally in terms of the six selection factors and vertically in terms of its rank within each column.

Within each column the criteria are listed in descending order of importance. We have divided the columns to create three basic levels of priority: (1) the library must have the item: the title is essential and is the first to be reviewed against available funding; (2) the library should have the item: the title is an important addition to the collection, and users could reasonably expect to find it in the library and (3) the library could acquire the title: although peripheral to the collection, the title is appropriate and there is a possibility that it will find a user.

There always will be a subjective element to selection and evaluation: it is an art - not an exact science. Nevertheless, there may be some circumstances in which one wishes to weigh each title quantitatively for the sake of comparison. In such instances we propose a method of assigning a relative value to each criterion considered in the evaluation (see Table 2). One can thereby derive a numeric rating for each selection. It seems simplest to set up the selection values so that the highest possible score totals 100 points. The cumulative score is the total of the values assigned by the selector in each of the six columns.

The first factor, subject, carries the highest number of points: any item being evaluated receives a score of 1 to 30 points for subject. Intellectual content ranks just under subject with a slightly smaller range of 25 points possible; similarly, other factors receive proportionately fewer points. If a title receives 67 to 100 points, it ranks as a first priority; if a title receives 34 to 66 points, it scores as a second priority; and if 1 to 33 points, it equals a third priority.

Table 1. Selection Criteria

	Subject	Intellectual Content	Potential Use	Relation to Collection	Bibliographic Considerations	Language
First Priority	Directly supports programs or institutional emphasis Major field of scholarship of inquiry	Key work in field Key author Major critical study Substantial new contribution to learning	Known research or program interest Patron request, based on need Probable need, based on known interest	Central to existing collection Closely related Provides specialized information about a central strength Necessary to intellectual integrity	Distinguished publisher Significant sponsoring body Specialized publisher of high quality Major trade publisher	Major language(s) of topic English and second working language(s) of topic Major foreign language accessible to users
Second Priority	Ancillary to programs Specialized topic Minor field of scholarship or inquiry	General essay Narrowly focused work Narrow intellectual perspective Popular treatment	General interest Title recommended by patron, without specific need Immediate need unlikely	Develops existing collection strength Historic collecting strength	Specialized publisher Published dissertation Popular publisher	Treatment in foreign language of topic not well covered in English Foreign language treatment of local/national issues
Third Priority	Tangential to programs Marginal area of scholarship or inquiry	Raw or unedited material Marginal or polemical work Trivial literature Propaganda	Presents problems of accessibility Infrequent use	Completes serial, series, or set held Very specialized material Assigned to cooperative partner	Research report Unpublished dissertation Working papers Pamphlets	Foreign language peripheral to topic or user Treatment in foreign language of material available in English Language accessible to tiny minority of likely users

Table 2. Selection Values

	Subject (30 points)	Intellectual Content (25 points)	Potential Use (20 points)	Relation to Collection (12 points)	Bibliographic Considerations (8 points)	Language (5 points)
First Priority	30	25	20	12	8	5
	29	24	19	11	7	4
	28	23	18	10	6	0
	27	22	17	9	0	0
	26	21	16	0	0	0
	25	20	15	0	0	0
	24	19	14	0	0	0
	23	18	0	0	0	0
	22	17	0	0	0	0
	21	0	0	0	0	0
Second Priority	20	16	13	8	5	3
	19	15	12	7	4	2
	18	14	11	6	3	0
	17	13	10	5	0	0
	16	12	9	0	0	0
	15	11	8	0	0	0
	14	10	7	0	0	0
	13	9	0	0	0	0
	12	0	0	0	0	0
	11	0	0	0	0	0
Third Priority	10	8	6	4	2	1
	9	7	5	3	1	0
	8	6	4	2	0	0
	7	5	3	1	0	0
	6	4	2	0	0	0
	5	3	1	0	0	0
	4	2	0	0	0	0
	3	1	0	0	0	0
	2	0	0	0	0	0
	1	0	0	0	0	0

The decision to assign a specific score of 16 points, rather than 25, for subject within that allocated range will be determined by subjective judgments that cannot be eliminated from the selection process. Herein lies the art of selection. We also believe that some libraries will wish to change our weighting of the criteria. This can be simply done and would allow the results to reflect local emphases more closely. In any case, such a point system could then be correlated with available funding to determine which selections are actually purchased.

By no means do we wish to suggest that every title needs to be treated with such mathematical precision. A library could limit its use to certain classes of materials that require particular selection care (e.g., reference titles); special formats (e.g., audio-visuals); expensive items (e.g., books costing more than $100); or critical budget lines (e.g., new subscriptions). Furthermore, since the first three criteria are more heavily weighted to reflect their greater importance, it will not always be necessary to go through the entire grid in order to arrive at a title's relative priority, particularly since the second three factors echo the first three and carry far less weight.

Implications of the Model

The proposed model will find its greatest utility in adding precision to and enhancing the consistency of the individual selection decisions. Consequently, use of this model can improve the quality of a library's collection development efforts. Moreover, because the schema presented here is comprehensive, holistic, and explicit, it can serve as a practical guide for training all selectors in a library and can aid in the rationalization of selection decision-making throughout a library system. If all selectors have a similar understanding of the criteria to be used and their interrelatedness, then unintended disparities in collecting levels can be minimized.

By extension, the model has applicability to cooperative collection development programs. In our experience we have found that cooperation with other libraries is most practicable when lower priority materials are under discussion. Because no library is likely to forego the purchases of first priority items, it is in the realm of less essential titles that cooperation is most likely to work. The model we have presented here can help to make sure that selectors at all participating libraries understand what kinds of materials can be acquired cooperatively.

This model also allows a library to relate selection decisions to a library's fiscal environment both generally and specifically. The model operates generally through the assignment of a first, second, or third priority, and specifically through the development - when necessary - of a precise numeric rating. This rating could then be correlated with a certain level of funding.

Finally, our schema can have a great public relations value both within the library and without. Since many departments within the library often do not fully understand the work done by collection development, this model can be used to explain to other librarians and staff how selection decisions are reached. Indeed, with the chart one can stress the rational quality of the decisions and demonstrate to colleagues that materials are being carefully chosen. The chart is also useful for educating faculty, some of whom may lack confidence in selection done by librarians. Moreover, by modeling selection in explicit and rational terms, a library can demonstrate to its parent institution as well as to outside agencies - who often view acquisitions as a bottomless pit - that the "misery" of making choices is governed by reasonable processes.

References

1   See, for example, the University of California, *Collection Development Policy Statement* (Berkeley, Calif.: University of California, General Library, 1980); Stanford University Libraries, *The Libraries of Stanford University Collection Development Policy Statement* (Stanford, Calif.: Stanford University Libraries, Collection Development Office, 1980); University of Texas at Austin. General Libraries, *Collection Development Policy* (2nd ed. Austin, Tex.: General Libraries, 1980); and Brigham Young University, Harold B. Lee Library, *Collection Development Policy Statement* (Provo, Utah: Brigham Young University, Harold B. Lee Library, 1985).

2   University of Texas at Austin. General Libraries, *Bibliographer's Manual: A Guide to the General Libraries Collection Development Program* (Austin, Tex.: University of Texas at Austin, General Libraries, 1982).

3   American Library Association. Collection Development Committee, *Guidelines for Collection Development,* ed. David L. Perkins (Chicago: American Library Association, 1979).

4   Arthur Curley and Dorothy Broderick, *Building Library Collections* (6th ed. Metuchen, N.J.: Scarecrow Press, 1985).

5   Robert N. Broadus, *Selecting Materials for Libraries* (2nd ed. New York: H.W. Wilson Company, 1981).

6   William A. Katz, *Collection Development: The Selection of Materials for Libraries* (New York: Holt, Rinehart and Winston, 1980).

7   Jean Boyer Hamlin, "The Selection Process." In *Collection Development in Libraries: A Treatise,* Part A, ed. Robert E. Stueart and George B. Miller, Jr. (Foundations in Library and Information Science, Vol. 10. Greenwich, Conn.: JAI Press, 1980), pp. 185-201.

8   Hendrick Edelman, "Selection Methodologies in Academic Libraries" *Library Resources and Technical Services* 23 (Winter 1979): 33-38.

9   *Ibid.,* p. 36.

10   Dan C. Hazen, "Collection Development, Collection Management, and Preservation." *Library Resources and Technical Services* 26 (1982):3-11.

11   John N. DePew, "An Acquisitions Decision Model for Academic Libraries." *Journal of the American Society for Information Science* 26 (1975): 230-246.

12   Ross Atkinson, "The Citation as Intertext: Toward a Theory of the Selection Process." *Library Resources and Technical Services* 28 (1984): 1098-1019.

13   For an overview, see Joe A. Hewitt, "Cooperative Collection Development Programs of the Triangle Research Libraries Network." *Resource Sharing and Information Networks* 2 (1985): 139-150.

14   Atkinson, *op. cit.,* p. 209.

15   *Ibid.,* p. 229.

CHAPTER 7

TYPES OF SELECTION RESOURCES

How to Evaluate Selection Resources

This chapter takes as its starting point the proposition that stock selectors are faced with a series of decisions, some relatively small and easy, others relatively difficult and costly, so that to increase the probability of being right more often than wrong, it is essential to be armed with as much up-to-date and accurate information as is conveniently available. This will not guarantee the selection of the necessary best books and none that are unnecessary or second-rate, but it should increase the likelihood of being right more often. As in all practical endeavours there will always come a time when the decision must be made regardless of the completeness or otherwise of the available information, so that to continue to search for more and more information beyond the necessary minimum, and for more and more expert advice and evaluation beyond what could be regarded as "reasonable" is a waste of time and effort, and is not good professional practice. As is argued elsewhere in this work, the very nature of library use will guarantee that some "selection mistakes" (in other words the selection of books that appear not to have had the level of usefulness the selector envisaged) will occur, and to attempt to avoid such "mistakes" at all costs is a counsel not of perfection but of foolishness. Nevertheless, one should aim to tread a path between perfection and foolishness, and one way of doing so is to understand the nature of selection tools.

In this chapter the various kinds of selection tools will be divided into classes (see Figure 7 below) and characteristics of the classes studied. Important characteristics of the class will be illustrated by a type specimen, and that specimen used as a model, measuring other examples by their variations from the type specimen. There are many problems with this approach including the initial problem of devising a classification scheme, deciding which are the characteristics that distinguish one group from another, deciding how to recognize and measure these characteristics, and coping with the variation of individuals from the type specimen, which makes it difficult sometimes to distinguish a variant from a specimen of a different class.

It is imperative to remember that any selection tool should do either or both of two things; if it does neither, it can be classed as worthless, and if it does both, it can be called a remarkably useful tool.

BIBLIOGRAPHIES

Evaluative Bibliographies
1. subject bibliographies
   a. total coverage
   b. selective
2. standard lists
   a. current
   b. retrospective
   c. out-of-print lists
3. guides to the literature
4. library catalogues

Alerting Bibliographies
1. national bibliographies
2. trade bibliographies
   a. USA weekly-monthly-annual
      Great Britain weekly-monthly-annual
      Australia weekly-monthly-annual
   b. government as publisher
   c. guides to periodicals

REVIEWS

Guides
1. digests
2. indexes

Journals
1. general
2. subject specialist journals
3. library journals
   a. official
   b. commercial
4. specialist book selection journals
5. newspapers
   a. tabloid
   b. quality

ADVERTISING

Display Advertisements
Direct Mail
Advance Notices

Figure 7. Classes of Selection Resources

1. It must identify the item, and provide the selector with enough information to allow him to decide what the item is; that is, it must act as an *alerting device*.

2. It must evaluate the item, or tell the selector whether the item is any good for its stated purpose, and if it is not, in what particulars it fails; that is, it must act as an *evaluating device*.

All selection tools will do the first of these in some degree, but very few do both, and of those tools that purport to do both, many must be regarded as suspect, so it is vital in any consideration of the relative value of stock selection tools that there be no confusion between these two separate, distinct and complementary functions, *alerting* and *evaluating*. A further point to be stressed is that the different nature of periodical or serial literature means that each and all of the tests applied to the various selection tools, the questions asked about them and the results expected of them must be interpreted in two sometimes conflicting ways, one for periodical literature and one for non-periodical literature.

The approach to the study of the various classes of tools used here is a mixture of the pragmatic approach, based on experience, and the logical or systematic approach, based on a theoretical construct. Overriding the approach described, and perhaps complementing it, should always be the three necessary stages in an item-by-item selection process, which is never a simple, single operation, but always a current state of affairs, at different stages of its life-cycle in various parts of the collection at any one time.

1. Preliminary identification, usually from strictly bibliographical tools such as standard lists and bibliographies, but including also tools of a different nature, advertising, publicity and booksellers' lists;

2. The quality check that is made on this preliminary selection, by the use of retrospective listing, evaluative reviews, and possible user requests. While this may well be a check on items that were not selected, there will be no control over items that perhaps ought not to have been selected in the first place, that is, the genuine mistakes, not those "pseudo-mistakes" mentioned earlier;

3. The final polishing of the selection process and its results by a retrospective review of the collection and of the selection processes, by the use of the various evaluative techniques and authoritative bibliographies and lists.

There are several sets of general questions to be asked of any selection tool:

Why does this exist at all? What can it do that is not already done elsewhere?

How well does it perform in its coverage of current publishing?

What types of material are intentionally included and excluded?

What types of material are likely to be excluded because of their very nature, not because of deliberate choice?

What subject areas are included and excluded?

What kind of information is offered about the works mentioned, and how much of it is offered?

For whom is the tool itself intended - librarians, general readers, subject specialists?

What is the physical format of the tool itself, in particular its availability in different formats, and the frequency of appearance? The format of the selection tool may bear no relationship at all to the formats of the works it covers.

What is the pattern of the cumulations? Does each cumulation supersede the earlier cumulations, or must some be kept for specified periods, for instance, pending the arrival of an annual cumulation?

How current is it?

What is the form of the classification scheme used? If it differs from the customary Dewey Decimal Classification or Library of Congress Classification, what are the details of the differences?

What are the rules for filing, and which subject headings are used?

What special methodology should be employed in order to make best use of it?

It is necessary then to decide on details of the specific tests to be applied to determine the usefulness of the tool to any particular library, remembering that conditions will change as will the tools themselves, and that last year's "useless" could become this year's "essential". This is done by the individual selector for a particular library, and the generalized questions above must be tailored to suit the particular case.

Classification of the Works

Examples of the various types, not necessarily the best of the type, the most recent, or even the most accessible will be listed; what is said about any particular work is not necessarily invalidated if a later edition exists, if it has changed its title, or has been superseded. Only a few examples are mentioned, and in practice it will be necessary to search out and evaluate all the tools relevant to a specific task. For instance, even though only one example of an "advance notice service" is mentioned, there are many such services offered, and it is part of the work of the selection librarian to discover the details of each of them, and assess the relative worth of each service in his own particular case.

With these general aims in mind, the examples will be divided into three main groups, as shown in Figure 7. Of these three groups, it can be said in general that the bibliographies can be both alerting and evaluating devices; that is, they can both identify and describe, and can also evaluate, sometimes if only by implication. The reviews ought all to be evaluative, and at the same time alerting devices, but their main purpose must be to evaluate; and advertising material is wholly alerting, so no matter what it appears to do, it cannot evaluate.

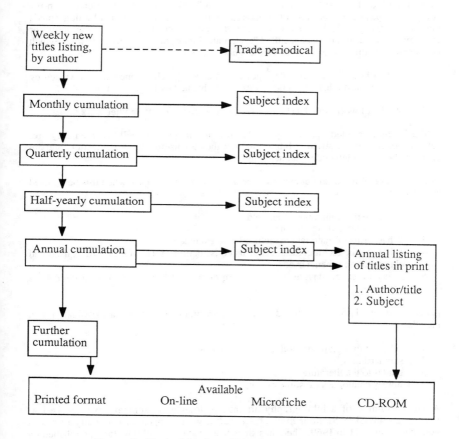

Figure 8. Typical Listing of Newly-Published Works

I. Bibliographies, or Lists of Books

There are several different meanings of the word "bibliography", which can mean the study of the physical make-up of the book, sometimes called "analytical bibliography", the study of the historical aspects of book production, called "historical bibliography", or the preparation of lists of books, called "systematic bibliography". This last group, which is of concern in this context, can be further subdivided into:

1. lists of books based on some specific criteria, e.g., about one subject; written by one author; published in one country; or published by a particular publisher;

2. the list of works cited as being used in the preparation of another work.

While it can be argued that library catalogues, no matter how well prepared they are, cannot properly be classified as bibliographies, they are useful in stock selection, and are probably best included under that heading.[1]

There are several important questions to be asked of a bibliography when it is being used as a stock selection tool:

1. What are the limitations of its field?
2. Is it selective? If so, on what basis?
3. What forms of material are included, and excluded?
4. What are the technical aspects of its construction - form of entry, rules used and classification scheme used?
5. Is it an alerting device, an evaluating device, or both, and in what degree, or neither?

(a) Evaluative. Those tools listed in the first section of this group are evaluative and include:

1. subject bibliographies, both total and selective;
2. standard lists;
3. guides to the literature;
4. library catalogues (to some extent).

A good example of a bibliography attempting total geographical coverage is J.A. Ferguson's massive *Bibliography of Australia,* which appeared originally in seven volumes from 1941 to 1969. There has since been added an eighth volume, published by the National Library of Australia in 1986, and comprising a set of addenda to the first four volumes, which cover the years 1784-1850. It aims at listing all works published outside Australia relating to Australia, as well as works published in Australia during the period. When Ferguson began this work, he intended to include all material, but after Volume 4 had been completed it was accepted that the aim of "total coverage" was no longer within the realms of possibility, and certain classes of material are specifically excluded from Volumes 5, 6 and 7. Even so, the selector must take into account the various types of material not included even in the first four volumes, as maps, charts and prints were excluded unless they were issued in book form, and articles and papers appearing in periodicals were omitted unless they were subsequently published separately.

Similar to Ferguson, but subject specific, is the *New Cambridge Bibliography of English Literature*, published in five volumes by Cambridge University Press, with various editors, from 1969 to 1977. It purports to cover all English literary works from AD 600 to AD 1950, but although it aims at completeness, various categories are excluded.

An example of the selective coverage bibliography in a specific subject is the *American Historical Association's Guide to Historical Literature*, edited by George F. Howe and others, and published in New York by Macmillan in 1961. It is imperative that the stock selector notes the criteria for the selection of items for inclusion and the extent of the limitations, some implicit rather than explicit, the classification scheme (its own), and the less than complete bibliographical detail which omits publishers' names, but does show enough to allow the selector to identify the book positively, even if it will still be necessary to go to other sources for the complete detail on which to base an order.

There are numerous examples of current standard lists, a good one being the *Fiction Catalog*, first published in New York in 1908 by the H.W. Wilson Company, and now into its eleventh edition, edited by Juliette Yaakov. The value of these lists depends entirely on the standards of the compilers, and as the *Fiction Catalog* has always been compiled from lists of books selected for public libraries in the United States of America, it naturally has a US bias. As well, the use of lists such as this will result in a form of circular selection pattern, as the list is compiled from the stocks of libraries that use it to select their stock, and also to measure the effectiveness of their stock selection programmes. There are many different standard lists, for different purposes, such as for schools, colleges, children's libraries, and it is never difficult to find a list that seems designed for a particular type of library. However, great care must be exercised to see that it does meet the criteria set down for the library's selection programme and collection development objectives, and that the standards of selection are suitable for that particular library.

There are also retrospective standard lists: each issue of *British Book News* and of *Choice*, and also some issues of *Library Journal*, will include a select list of the best books on a particular subject. The July/August 1988 issue of *Choice* has a listing of books on American education 1955-1985, for instance. These lists are evaluative, even though it is necessary to beware of the standards of the compilers. They are also alerting in that they generally provide all the detail needed for the acquisitions staff to order the books. Such lists can also be used for many other collection development purposes, such as checking the library's holdings for not only what is missing and thus must be added, but also for its strengths, assessing the collection or evaluation purposes, the establishment of a core collection, and as weeding aids. The range of subjects covered, and the standard of most reviews, make *Choice* an invaluable book selection aid in all but the smallest libraries, and it should rank high on the list of working tools of the conscientious collection development librarian.

Depending entirely on the standards of selection for inclusion, some library catalogues can be evaluative. The catalogues of deposit libraries like the British Library or the National Library of Australia are not evaluative (although invaluable for other purposes), but the carefully selected material in some special collections does reflect selection rather than simple acquisition, and to that extent their catalogues are evaluative.

(b) Alerting. The second section of this group of bibliographies comprises the national bibliographies and the trade bibliographies. They are entirely alerting devices, in that they

tell the selector what there is available, without giving any indication of the value of the material they list.

Almost every country with any kind of organized publishing trade has a national bibliography;[2] most of these major trade and national bibliographies have been available on microfiche for some years, and are also now available online through commercial databases, with the availability of the bigger bibliographies on compact disc becoming much more common, although production costs may hold back this form of access for general use in the short term. The smaller, more specific, printed bibliographies are generally not available at this time in other than the traditional printed form.

British National Bibliography, known as *BNB*, published in London by the Council of the British National Bibliography since 1950, is a good type specimen, perhaps even the archetype. The information in it is based on books lodged with the Copyright Receipt Office of the British Library. It is important to note that it is "based on" because even this work is selective, and stock selectors must note carefully the kinds of material not included. It is published weekly and monthly with annual cumulations, and a four-monthly cumulation on fiche is also available online, and lists all the information needed for ordering. The Australian equivalent, *Australian National Bibliography*, is similar in layout, purpose and coverage, and needs to be approached with precisely the same cautions in mind. It is also imperative that the stock selector remember that a national bibliography of this type may be only one facet of a very complex bibliographic network that includes such services as cooperative cataloguing, national union lists of periodicals, retrospective national union catalogues of monographs, and listings of current serials.[3]

The United States is unusual in that it does not have a national bibliography like the British *BNB* or the Australian *ANB*, both of which are of a type common in most countries with an organized book-trade and an established structure of libraries; instead the USA has a collection of catalogues providing access to the Library of Congress and to well over 1000 North American libraries which contribute details of their accessions to the scheme.

The very complex service available to stock selectors is based on the Library of Congress printed catalogues, which were first produced in 1947 (and were subsequently reprinted, with various cumulations and various titles) and totalled well over 400 volumes by the end of 1955. A subsequent cumulation, covering pre-1956 reprints, in 754 volumes, was produced from 1968 to 1981 and the user must be aware that many items not recorded in the earlier "pre-1956" printings have been gathered into the net in this vast cumulation. Production of the catalogue in book form stopped from 1982, and the *NUC* is now issued on microfiche.[4]

Next in this section come the trade bibliographies, and as the description of them becomes much more complicated they are best approached on a national basis. The general pattern is for a weekly trade journal to include, amongst its advertising and sales promotions, lists of forthcoming and recently published material derived from details provided directly by the publishers. This weekly listing is then cumulated in various ways, generally at least monthly, with other cumulations leading to annual, biennial, quinquennial and even ten-yearly cumulations, which provide an almost complete listing of material reported as published. The standards of bibliographical description, while perhaps not reaching the levels demanded by bibliographers, are sufficiently high for the purpose, and generally the descriptions provide all the necessary information for the library stock selector. This form of listing is almost always accompanied by at least one form of subject approach, based on the same material, and the information is available online as well as in the traditional printed format.

The pattern is well demonstrated by the American book-trade journal, *Publishers' Weekly*, published in New York by R.R. Bowker since 1872, which purports to list all (or most) of the works published in the United States of America, and supplies the information in a form that is designed for use by the trade in ordering. It is cumulated in a monthly, *American Book Publishing Record*, which has been issued in New York by the same publisher since 1960.

A similar publication, issued by another publisher, is the monthly *Cumulative Book Index*, published in New York by the H.W. Wilson Company since 1898. Again, this purports to list all books published in English in the USA and in Canada, and a selection of those published elsewhere. Its subtitle, *A World List of Books in the English Language*, is intended to demonstrate the extent of the coverage, and like Bowker's *Publishers' Weekly*, it is based on material supplied by the publishers of the items listed, and thus depends on those descriptions for its accuracy and coverage. Like most H.W. Wilson publications, it is in dictionary catalogue form and is extremely logical in layout and easy to use.

Another form of listing is the collation of publishers' catalogues themselves, rather than a listing of information taken from those catalogues. The annual *Publishers' Trade List Annual*, published in New York by R.R. Bowker since 1873, is the oldest. It comprises merely a collection of publishers' catalogues, to which, unfortunately, not all publishers contribute, and to be of much use needs to be combined with some form of index, such as *Books in Print*, published in New York by R.R. Bowker since 1948. Originally an author-title index to the *Publishers' Trade List Annual*, *BIP* now includes material not in that publication. Also needed so that order may be brought out of chaos is a form of subject index to these various compilations, and R.R. Bowker's *Subject Guide to Books in Print*, issued in New York since 1957, is precisely what the title says it is.

Similar publications exist in many other countries with organized book industries; for instance, in Great Britain, *Bookseller* has been issued in London by J. Whitaker since 1858, and in its earlier years carried the subtitle, *The Organ of the Book Trade*. Weekly, monthly, then with annual cumulations, it supplies the information for the listings of forthcoming and newly published books which form *Whitaker's Cumulative Book List*, and subsequently *British Books in Print*. These publications all have broad subject classes, with author and title listings, and taken together form British equivalents of the United States publications, *Publishers' Weekly, American Book Publishing Record, Cumulative Book Index,* and *Books in Print*.

There is a slight difference in *British Books in Print,* which began its life as a collection of publishers' catalogues, as did *Publishers' Trade List Annual,* but which from the 1930s has been a listing in two sequences, author and title, undergoing several changes of title in the process.

The Australian book-trade journal, *Australian Bookseller and Publisher*, published in Melbourne in various forms by D.W. Thorpe since 1921, conforms to this pattern by providing listings of forthcoming and current titles which are used to form the basis of an annual, *Australian Books in Print*; however, a slightly different approach from that used by overseas publishers underlies Thorpe's subject guide, called *Australian Books in Print by Subject*, in which the subject headings are chosen by the publishers whose books are listed, in contrast to other subject guides to books in print, which generally use more established lists of subject headings. This is not to say that the Thorpe subject headings are in any way less than satisfactory, but rather to emphasize a point which is continually being made in this chapter, that different publications have different layouts, and must be approached from different angles even when the same result is required.

A more recent publication, *International Books in Print*, published in Munich by K.G. Saur since 1979, lists works published in English outside the United Kingdom and the United States, and is an attempt to catch those publications which are not included in the two major sets of listings of books in print. Although one might expect a fair proportion of any particular nation's publishing output to be included, the very nature of the reporting process would ensure a considerable failure rate for any book selector relying on it to provide information for a detailed national coverage.

The term "trade publishers" must include the world's biggest publishers, the United States Government Printer and Her Majesty's Stationery Office in the United Kingdom. It is well known amongst reference librarians that usually the first notice that even the most interested member of the general public has of a new government publication is a mention of it in a daily paper. The reasons for this are not difficult to see when one considers the immediate nature of some government publications, their sometimes limited appeal, and the bibliographical problems of listing such an enormous output.

It is necessary to have a guide of some kind, the more detailed the better, in order to chart a path through the maze of government publications; in general, all the points that should be covered in sources of information in other areas are relevant also in the field of government publications, but additional problems may be encountered simply because of the sheer volume of the publications and the "daily or weekly" nature of some, which may not in any sense of the word be classed as "ephemera" even though they are of a slight physical nature.

To find the way around overseas government publications it is essential for the librarian to make extensive use of guides published for each specific country, a good example of which is Sears and Moody's *Using Government Publications*, published in Phoenix by Oryx Press in 1985-1986. The two volumes not only cover search strategies (an essential part of the selection operation) but also include checklists of sources, suggested methods of working through the sources, and some discussion on techniques for locating information in particular subject areas.

Periodicals, sometimes simply known as serials, magazines, or journals, have a similar pattern of useful guides. The major international directory is *Ulrich's International Periodicals Directory*, published in New York by Bowker since 1932, which lists all the necessary information for ordering, and is similar to a trade bibliography, so that the same kinds of tests need to be applied to them as to the works discussed earlier. *Ulrich's* must be used in conjunction with its partner volume, *Irregular Serials*.

The question of the bibliographical details of the periodicals under scrutiny is quite different from the problems of the suitability of those same titles for selection in the library, and the same warning as mentioned earlier must be repeated: simply identifying a periodical is not "selection", although it is a necessary part of the ordering process. There is a need for a specifically evaluative service, and a good example is that provided by William A. Katz and Linda Sternberg Katz with their *Magazines for Libraries*, first issued in 1969, which is very much an evaluative work, classified and annotated, and is useful for all libraries except perhaps the specialist. Many of the journals and selection guides mentioned earlier also include periodicals in their reviewing and evaluation processes, and they can be treated in the same manner as monographs.

II. Book Reviews

The second of the three major groups is that embracing book reviews. They ought to be evaluative, although a close study of reviews in general will leave most librarians with grave doubts about that. In fact, most are evaluative in one sense or the other, even though the standards of the evaluation may be suspect. It is obvious that a librarian cannot hope to be a "subject expert" in any more than a very limited number of fields (and even then, librarians are subject experts by virtue of their "subject interest" rather than their "professional expertise") so one must aim at being a "subject literature" expert. Because it is physically impossible to read and evaluate every book, librarians must learn to evaluate their sources of information on the "worth" of a book amongst the most important of which are the reviews. Reviews must be treated with caution, of course, but there are few real alternatives. Nevertheless (possibly because of this), one must remember that although many librarians do make considerable use of book reviews in the processes of book selection, in general they are not designed specifically for that purpose, although there are some reviews that are so designed.

Some of the points that must be taken into account in the evaluation of sources of book reviews are:

1. For what type of audience are they designed?
2. How accurate and objective are the reviews themselves?
3. Do the reviews compare the books with other titles?
4. What is the scope of the journal in which they appear?
5. How many reviews are published over given periods?
6. How relevant are the subjects covered to this library's collections?
7. What kinds of reviews are not included?
8. Are various kinds of non-print materials included?
9. How international is the coverage?
10. How timely are the reviews? The importance of timeliness of reviews varies according to the type of library. Public libraries, for instance, need earlier access to reviews because their patrons want to get to the latest "best-seller", while academic libraries may be able to wait until the reviewers have pronounced whether or not the book is worthwhile.
11. Are the reviews signed, or if they are not, is the reputation of the journal such that this is not important?
12. Can the librarian be assured that the reviewers have the competence to review the kinds of books they attempt?
13. Do the reviews conclude with specific recommendations? What is the balance between "favourable" and "unfavourable"?
14. Is the format of the book assessed?

(a) Guides. It is necessary for the book selector to have access to book reviews, and apart from the straightforward but rather haphazard method of reading the journals, one

must use the indexing and abstracting services, which fall into two groups: the digests and the indexes. *Book Review Digest*, published in New York by the H.W. Wilson Company since 1905, is one of the best-known of the first type, and displays all the faults of that type. Understandably it has a United States bias, and covers only a few journals. A recent check showed that it listed eighty-five journals, of which eight were Canadian or British, the rest being American. The entries are short, and give some idea of the flavour of the reviews, but only about 6000 books are reviewed each year.

The indexing services certainly cover more journals and more reviews, but by their very nature are not able to include a great deal of information about the review except where to find it. *Book Review Index*, published in Detroit by Gale Research Company since 1965, is a good example of this kind of location service. It is a bi-monthly with cumulations, and in 1986 listed 114,000 reviews of 63,000 different titles, the citations coming from 455 different journals. This is obviously a vastly greater coverage than that of digests such as *Book Review Digest*.

These sources can be regarded as "general", although they are useful to the specialist. There are others, such as the two US services, *Index to Book Reviews in the Humanities* and *Technical Book Review Index*, which are good examples of "specialist" indexes to book reviews. As with the other types of selection tools discussed in this chapter, it is necessary for the stock selector to be aware of the limitations of the fields covered, and the definitions current, when making use of the services. *IBRH* includes some works in foreign languages (not English), and has its own definition of the word "humanities", which may not be the same as that currently in use in the library making use of it as a selection tool. *TBRI* also has its own definition of "technical", which needs to be recognized.

(b) Journals. The tools mentioned above are alerting devices rather than evaluating devices, so the selector must also read the journals themselves, and thus subject himself to a great variety of literary efforts, ranging from full-length articles of thousands of words to what could well be the shortest review on record, comprising nine words, "the covers of this book are too far apart". These periodicals can be grouped for study in a manner similar to that used for the grouping of the other works mentioned in this chapter.

An example of the general periodical, with a limited coverage in any one area, generally with a leaning towards "literature" and employing non-subject-expert reviewers, is *Spectator*. This British political and cultural magazine is a very useful tool in its field and for the library book selector, although because of the severe space limitations it does not publish more than a very few reviews, and a considerable amount of time and effort has to be applied to gain access to a small number of evaluations.

The coverage in the subject specialist journals, like *English Historical Review*, is a little less limited, with about 50 per cent of that journal used for book reviews. In the April 1988 issue, for example, thirty-five books were reviewed and a further sixty were the subject of "short notices". While it may be an invaluable book selection tool in its discipline area, there are always the problems of assessing the reviewers themselves, and in areas of greater specialism, such as represented by this journal, the dangers associated with bias in reviewers become more and more pronounced.

Library periodicals can be subdivided into "official" and "commercial". The official journals of library associations, such as *Library Association Record* and *American*

Libraries, generally all carry reviews, written for the most part by librarians. The reviews are short, evaluative and useful, and one can expect the editorial policy to be less responsive to publisher and advertiser pressure than that of the "commercial" periodicals like *Library Journal*, the American journal published by Bowker since 1877, or the British journal, *New Library World*, now published by MCB University Press Ltd. *Library Journal's* reviews are very short, and are generally most useful, and as the journal also carries the occasional review article it is a most useful publication for the book selector, whereas *New Library World's* much chattier approach and its somewhat cavalier attitude towards the niceties of bibliographical organization make it less useful for that purpose.

Almost every newspaper carries a book section, and in general the reviews are not a great deal of use to the serious library stock selector, even though the weekend papers do allow the public librarian to be reasonably certain of what the readers are likely to be asking for on Monday morning. The editorial policy of the book page is likely to be much influenced by advertising, despite editors' protestations to the contrary, and book reviews have to be judged with that in mind. Of course, there are exceptions, and the major newspapers of the world all have good reviews; indeed, *The Times Literary Supplement*, which might well be classed as a periodical rather than as a newspaper for our purposes, has always been one of the best book selection sources, even though the scope of the books reviewed may be narrower than that of the stock of the average library.

The last subsection in this part is concerned with the specialist stock selection journals, which are designed for the library book selector, and appear generally to do the job fairly well.

Choice, published in Middletown (USA) by the Association of College and Research Libraries, is an excellent tool for all but the smallest public libraries, because of the great variety of the American colleges for which it was designed. Reviews are short and authoritative, and each issue has a long article on the best books on a particular topic; an issue in 1988, for instance, includes a review article on books about American education, while the July/August 1987 issue had an article on the bibliography of "the underground economy". There are about 6000 titles reviewed each year, and this journal must be regarded as essential for any serious library collection.

British Book News is almost a British equivalent, certainly in standard, if not in coverage or size. It is restricted to British publications, and now includes around 200 reviews per issue, still carrying its regular article on the best books on a particular topic.

III. Advertising Material

The last section to be covered is advertising, and can be divided into three parts:

1. display advertising, which comprises all the printed and graphic media intended for mass consumption, and would also include television and painted signs on the sides of racing motor cars if books were at the same level of profitability as are tobacco and alcohol;

2. publishers' blurbs which, although printed, are used for direct mailing and so cannot be classed as "mass";

3. advance notices, which are perhaps the most contentious form of advertising, in that they are designed to look as though they are some form of "official" notification; that is not to say that "advance notices" are in any way deceptive, but rather that they must always be seen for what they are, a form of advertising, regardless of the manner in which they are presented.

It must be remembered at all times that publishers and booksellers are in business to make money, and their advertising is designed to help them do just that. Marketing and distribution are among the most difficult areas of any business operation, and librarians would do well to appreciate that if very active steps are not taken by publishers and booksellers to let librarians know what is available, then there is little point in authors writing books at all, as the "best" book is of no use until someone reads it. If books are not actively and aggressively distributed, then it is unlikely that many books will find their way into libraries, and will certainly "blush unseen". Nevertheless, this need to sell does determine the purpose of the advertising, and no matter what form this advertising takes, it is still advertising. One must also beware the effect that the likely revenue from advertising might have on the editorial standards of the journals involved, reflected in the kind of conclusions reached in the books reviews, as it has been suggested that pressure can be brought to bear on review editors if the reviews are not generally favourable. It would be possible to make some kind of check on this by comparing the amount of advertising by a publisher in any particular journal with the number of reviews of that publisher's products that the journal carries, but appears not yet to have been done.

There are three basic necessities of advertising:

1. there must be a surplus of goods, for at subsistence level there is no need to advertise;

2. advertising is not needed in small communities, only where "masses" exist;

3. a medium is necessary.

The various forms of publishers' advertising can be seen to satisfy all three criteria. There is constant argument about whether advertising does or does not add to the cost of an item, but it needs only a moment's thought to establish that of course it does; but as it does increase sales (or ought to do so!), fixed costs can be spread over the greater number of units, and thus unit costs can be reduced. The obvious need is to balance the added cost of advertising against the reduction in unit costs because of increased sales, and to ensure that the scales tip in favour of an overall decrease in unit costs. The major problem is not that of selling a unique item on a single occasion, but rather of getting and keeping regular customers for articles which are almost indistinguishable from similar articles with different brand names. The tobacco companies certainly argue this way when defending cigarette advertising, but whether all books can be thought of like that is one topic that needs to be addressed by librarians involved in the subjective assessment of the value of advertising, as is the reliance that can be placed on the comments made by advertisers and their agents on the wares that they are advertising.

The most obvious form of display advertising is publishers' catalogues, which come in an amazing variety of forms and styles, and have as their purpose to make it easier for potential purchasers to buy the books. Research indicates that using publishers' advertising is a very common form of selection,[5] and depending on the librarian's acceptance of the value of "expertise", one might dismiss it all as not worthy of the attention of the selector, or alternatively accept the proposition that a considerable amount of quality selection has already taken place in the editorial offices of the publishers, in the sales offices of the distributors, and in the purchasing offices of the agents or retailers. What is certain is that all advertising, no matter what its form and no matter how much it seems to look like evaluative material, is purely alerting material, so that it will tell the librarian what there is, but it will not necessarily tell anything at all about the quality of the material or its suitability for a library.

This point needs to be stressed because some advertising material is designed to look "official" or "professional": "advance notice cards", for instance, that look just like catalogue cards, and carry annotations, are advertising just as much as are the leaflets and book jackets every accessions department gets in the mail, or the forms of display advertising mentioned above. The form of the advance notice is reasonably standard, in that the various details of each title are gathered together in a form that is convenient for librarians to use in selection and ordering, and thus is not unlike an "official" catalogue entry. Included in the information are author, title, imprint, collation, series notes, ISBN, DC or LC class numbers, pagination, date, price; most suppliers also include a series of codes representing information they have seen as useful to librarians, such as country of origin, author's approach, intended readership, language, and sometimes an annotation. A typical library supplier might offer a New Title plan with slips matched against subjects and readership levels as indicated by the library concerned, on a weekly basis. A further refinement might provide information on forthcoming mass market titles. In essence, these services provide a form of advertising that is remarkably well directed at its potential markets. The slips provide details of author, title, imprint, pagination, edition, ISBN, ISSN, Dewey and Library of Congress subject classification numbers, series information, price and details of format and binding, and may exclude publications which are judged not to have a general appeal.

References

1   G. Thomas Tanselle, "Descriptive Bibliography and Library Cataloguing." *Studies in Bibliography* 30 (1977): 1-56.

2   Barbara L. Bell, *An Annotated Guide to Current National Bibliographies* (Alexandria, Va.: Chadwyck-Healey, 1986); G.E. Gorman and J.J. Mills, *Guide to Current National Bibliographies in the Third World* (2nd rev. ed. London: K.G. Saur, 1987).

3   As an example of the way other countries follow the *BNB* pattern, one might consider the *Australian National Union Catalogue* which comprises a number of union catalogues in different formats, to which many libraries contribute, some directly by contributing information on holdings and others as a by-product of the shared cataloguing provided by the Australian Bibliographic Network (ABN). Online access is available through ABN for shared cataloguing, and also for pure reference, and libraries that do not share in ABN can get access to the various constituent parts of the *NUC* complex through services such as the *National Union Catalogue of Monographs* (*NUCOM*), a single main entry alphabetical file of monographs, covering the years to 1984, MARC NUCOM a machine-readable database developed after the closure of *NUCOM*, the *National Union Catalogue of Serials* (*NUCOS*), on card or on fiche, and *ABN Catalogue*, a fiche catalogue listing all monographs reported by libraries participating in the National Bibliographic Database.

4   Eugene P. Sheehy, ed., *Guide to Reference Books* (10th ed. Chicago, Ill.: American Library Association, 1986).

5   Peter Biskup and C.A. Jones, "Of Books, Academics and Librarians: Some Facts about the Book Selection Habits of the Teaching Staff of Two Canberra Institutions of Higher Learning." *Australian Academic and Research Libraries* 7, 3 (1976): 159-170; Kay MacLean, "A Survey of Australasian Library Selection Procedures." *Australian Academic and Research Libraries* 16 (1985): 21-31.

READINGS ON TYPES OF SELECTION RESOURCES

Three readings have been chosen to accompany this chapter, and it may not be surprising that two of them appeared as chapters in the one work, *Selection of Library Materials in the Humanities, Social Sciences and Sciences*, focusing as that work did on practical selection techniques.

Tuttle (pp. 265-277) makes the important point that not only are serials a significant part of the corpus of printed material with which the selection librarian needs to deal, but they are also quite different from monographs in that each is a continuing yet changing entity that expands, consuming space and money as it does so, and ironically almost causes more trouble when it does not arrive than when it does. Although she restricts her coverage to current American serials, she observes that the bibliographical tools needed for the selection of those serials are themselves broad in scope and coverage, and thus the lessons to be learned from the study and use of the tools can be applied successfully in other countries. The reader is advised to consider carefully Tuttle's contention that in libraries, where "...speed is a high priority...", it may be advisable to make use of an admittedly costlier online service than to use "...traditional directories". Although the information in printed directories may be out-of-date even before the library gets the directory, the question must arise here, as in every stock selection area, of the balance between the cost of an operation and its value. There is little point in paying extra money to get up-to-date information in a hurry if the rest of the selection/acquisitions/cataloguing processes cannot capitalize on the time saved. Of special importance here are her two brief sections on the evaluation of serials and on the measurement and forecasting of their use. The key to a meaningful survey, as she so rightly says, "...is a clear understanding of what constitutes use of a serial...", a point which we are at pains to stress throughout this volume.

Judy Horn (pp. 277-297) begins her paper on government publications by stressing the size and complexity of government organizations as publishers, and goes on to cover the "...basic elements in selection, evaluation and acquisition of materials...." Although she lists "...international governmental organizations, foreign governments...", she is fairly well restricted to United States government publications, which, however, in no measure detracts from the value of this paper for the collection development librarian in any country. She touches on a considerable number of the topics that are stressed in this volume, and illustrates how the questions of, for instance, the preparation of a collection development policy, the evaluation of individual items in reviewing media, or the pros and cons of title-by-title selection as against blanket selection all need to be taken into account in specific selection areas if proper collection development is to take place. Surely no conscientious collection development librarian could argue with her ultimate sentence: "Quality service is not provided by having all publications but by consciously and systematically developing a collection to meet the needs of the user."

The third reading by Macleod (pp. 297-307) presents the results of a study in which the methods by which *Library Journal* and *Choice* select books for review and reviewers for books are examined. A random selection of 2600 reviews is then chosen, and a content analysis undertaken, which shows that the key decisions were made by editors when they selected the books for review. Also significant are Macleod's conclusions that the reviews in *Choice* did not appear to be more critical or more substantive than those in *Library Journal,* that there appeared to be little difference in the quality of reviews written by college academics when compared with those written by librarians, and that anonymity did not seem necessarily to ensure more critical reviews.

Marcia Tuttle, "Serials." In *Selection of Library Materials in the Humanities, Social Sciences, and Sciences*, edited by Patricia A. McClung, 34-47. Chicago: American Library Association, 1985.

Librarians responsible for collection building work with an integrated body of information. Serial literature is a significant part of this body, used and collected together with printed monographs and nonprint formats. At the same time, serials differ from monographs. Serials continue: a subscription or standing order is invoiced and arrives until someone acts to end the commitment. Serials change: they change title, price, frequency, format, and content. Serials encroach: they consume funds needed for other materials; they spread into space reserved for acquisitions of five years hence; they get fatter and require more than their share of binding funds. Most of all, serials keep coming; when they do not, the real problems begin. These qualities of serials require that they be managed separately even while they are part of an integrated collection.

The significance of serials is increasing in library collections. As a traditionally fast means of publication, serials have always been essential to science and technology. In the last twenty years scholars writing in other disciplines have turned to serial, and particularly periodical, publication, thereby creating a demand for more titles. In April 1982, an article in the *Chronicle of Higher Education* featured some of the problems created by the "enormous proliferation of journals": increasing acadmic specialization, pressure on faculty members and researchers to publish, and few serious obstacles to starting a new journal. Libraries cannot afford to purchase all the journals they need, and scholars cannot keep up with the contents of journals in their field. Both librarians and faculty members are calling for a limit to the number of journals and for a means of evaluating serials.[1]

This discussion is limited to currently published American serials, although many of the sources mentioned are broader in scope, both geographically and chronologically. Often, more than one tool is required to ensure that the serial is identified and that the bibliographical data are current and correct. With the high incidence of change in serials, the date of the information itself (not necessarily the date of publication) is significant. The time lag between collection of data for printed directories and the appearance of the published work means that, to a certain extent, guides are obsolete by the time they reach the library.

This situation can be overcome by subscribing to online databases available from the publisher or through BRS and DIALOG, but the expense of online identification is considerably greater than the cost of printed counterparts. For example, *Ulrich's International Periodicals Directory* and *Irregular Serials and Annuals* are standard, reasonably prices sources for the identification by subject of periodicals and nonperiodical serials. Data used for these directories are available online in the Bowker Serials Database at a cost of up to $75.00 an hour, with extra charges for printed citations. Similarly, *Standard Periodical Directory (SPD)* is a good printed source for subject access to American and Canadian small-circulation, ephemeral, and processed serials, as well as to more general titles. It is available online as part of a database named Select Periodical Data, available from Oxbridge at a cost comparable to the Bowker database. Libraries where speed is a high priority may find the online services worth the extra cost; many will be best served by the traditional directories.

Printed sources exist for the identification of special types of serials. *IMS Ayer Directory of Publications* has been a standard guide to American and Canadian newspapers for more than a century, and its coverage has expanded to magazines, although *Ulrich's* and *SPD* are better sources for those. *International Directory of Little Magazines and Small Presses* is the standard work for identification of literary and political serials. For American federal document serials, *Monthly Catalog of United States Government Publications* is available in print, or online through the Government Printing Office database.

Subject access to serial titles is of more value to selectors than alphabetical arrangement. Bibliographies, periodical indexes, and abstract journals usually provide a list of serials consulted. For example, the *MLA International Bibliography* list of titles has evolved into a separate directory of serials, giving not only bibliographic information but also facts useful to scholars wishing to publish in the journals. *L'Annee Philologique* also lists titles, although these serials are not as well identified as *MLA's*.

Ulrich's International Periodicals Directory, v.1-. 1932-. New York: Bowker. Annually.

 Identification source for current journals.

 Subject arrangement.

 List of new journals.

 List of cessations.

 12-18-month lag time between collection of information and publication.

Ulrich's is a standard source for identifying current journals and is arranged by subject with a title index and liberal cross-references. It provides subscription information, ISSN, indication of where a title is indexed, a list of cessations since the last edition, and a list of new periodicals. *Ulrich's International Periodicals Directory* is updated by *Ulrich's Quarterly*.

Irregular Serials and Annuals. v.1-. 1967-. New York: Bowker. Annually.

 Identification source for current nonperiodical serials. Subject arrangement.

 List of international documents.

 ISSN finding list.

 12-18 month lag between collection of data and publication.

This is a companion volume to *Ulrich's International Periodicals Directory* and is also arranged by subject. *Irregular Serials and Annuals* gives the same bibliographic and subscription information about nonperiodical serials that *Ulrich's* gives about journals. This work includes a list of international documents and an index to ISSN for all types of serials. It is updated by *Ulrich's Quarterly*.

Standard Periodical Directory. v.1-. 1963-. New York: Oxbridge. Biennially.

 Covers current North American periodicals and annuals.

 Subject arrangement.

 Valuable for ephemeral publications.

SPD features a subject arrangement with a title index. It covers United States and Canadian serials that are published at least once every two years, and it includes some newspapers. This source is particularly valuable for small-circulation, ephemeral, and processed publications. Data are more business-oriented than *Ulrich's*.

Virtually all periodical indexes and abstract journals describe the titles included. The best give publication data, making it easy to check the serials against the library's holdings. A selection of indexes and abstract journals for examination can be made from the listing in *Ulrich's*.

Librarian selectors need to identify new serial titles more often than established titles. *Ulrich's* and *Irregular Serials and Annuals* are standard sources for older titles; *Ulrich's Quarterly*, readily available and easy to use, updates both publications. It is also part of the online Bowker Serials Bibliography database. *SPD* once had updates, but these have been discontinued.

New Serials Titles (NST) is a standard source for identifying serials, although its usefulness diminished considerably when the Classed Subject Arrangement edition was discontinued after 1980. *NST* now reproduces in alphabetical order complete bibliographic records for both current and retrospective serials entered into the OCLC database by CONSER (CON-version of SERials to machine readable form) participants.[2]

IMS Ayer Directory of Publications. v.1-. 1869-. Fort Washington, Pa.: IMS Press. Annually.
  Best source for identifying current North American newspapers.
  Geographic arrangement.
  Classified lists of newspapers.
Particularly good for information about newspapers, *IMS Ayer* also lists magazines published at least quarterly. Its scope is United States and territories, Canada, and a few other places. The work is arranged geographically, with information about each state or province and city. Among details included are circulation and editorial slant of publication. Contents include a title index and several classified lists of newspapers and magazines.

International Directory of Little Magazines and Small Presses. v.1-. 1965-. Paradise, Calif.: L.V. Fulton.
  Annually.
  Standard source for current little magazines and small presses.
  Editorial and subscription information.
  Feedback from editors.
This useful work contains in one alphabetical list detailed information about both little magazines and small presses. Subject and regional indexes increases its value. The guide includes editorial and subscription information, as well as editor and/or publisher comments.

MLA Directory of Periodicals: A Guide to Journals and Series in Languages and Literatures. 1st- ed.
  1978/79-. New York: Modern Language Assn. of America. Biennially.
  Authoritative source for international language and literature serials.
  Subscription and editorial data.
  Alphabetical arrangement.
A companion volume to *MLA International Bibliography*, this source contains subscription and editorial data on all titles in MLA's "Master List." It is arranged alphabetically by title. The selector knows that all titles included are considered worthy of being indexed by MLA.

Ulrich's Quarterly, v.1.- Spring 1977-. New York: Bowker. Quarterly.
    Subject arrangement.
    Cumulating title index.
    Lists periodicals and nonperiodical serials.
    Useful for subject selector.
This service updates both *Ulrich's International Periodicals Directory* and *Irregular Serials and Annuals* with new and additional serials. It is arranged by subject, with a title index that cumulates throughout the volume. *Ulrich's Quarterly* is a manageable printed tool for the selector working by subject.

Price Information

Most new periodical titles come to the attention of selectors through unsolicited samples and announcements from the publishers. There is nothing systematic or balanced about identification of new titles by this means, but the practice supplements the use of the sources noted above. Additionally, subscription agents and standing order vendors issue updating periodicals that list and often describe new serials. *Nijhoff Serials, EBSCO Bulletin of Serials Changes,* and *Swets Info* are examples. B.H. Blackwell sends customers an annotated list of new serials with its monthly report. Most agents will attempt to obtain free sample copies requested by the library, although some of them downplay the service.

Double-digit inflation has been the rule for American periodicals for some time. For this reason, wherever one has identified a title, it is well to check the annual catalog issued by one of the large subscription agencies to verify the price. Faxon sends its customers the *Faxon Librarians' Guide,* and EBSCO distributes its *Librarians' Handbook.* The two catalogs are published at different times during the year, so first one and then the other is likely to be more nearly current regarding price. With the changeable nature of serials and the difficulty of maintaining a file of over 150,000 titles, the accuracy of the data varies. It has been the author's experience that the Faxon guide is more likely to be correct and is easier to use, but that often the EBSCO catalog will contain exactly that piece of information that permits one to unravel a problem. The Faxon guide is easy to use because it is arranged according to cataloging entry, although it has not yet been converted to AACR2, while the EBSCO handbook seems to be arranged for nonlibrarians. These catalogs cannot replace other sources for identifying serials, because they do not give publication information and they are arranged alphabetically; however, they provide the best approximation of cost.

The Faxon and EBSCO bibliographic and publication files are available through the Linx and EBSCONET automated serials systems. Both give notice of new titles online, and Faxon has activated a component named "InfoServe" that reproduces contents pages and other data for journals of certain publishers. Libraries can subscribe to one of these systems directly from the subscription agent and can also participate in the online serials check-in feature of the system selected. Again, the cost is high and will not be attractive to all libraries.

Swets Info. Lisse, The Netherlands: Swets Subscription Service. Quarterly with annual cumulation.

    Includes new titles, with subscription information.

    Changes in serials noted.

    European emphasis.

    Subject index to new titles.

This vendor publication lists new journals, annuals, and series available through Swets. Cessations, changes, and delays are also included. Its scope is international, with a European emphasis, reflecting the vendor's specialization. Bibliographic details of new titles are given, including publisher, price, frequency, date of first issue, and ISSN. Occasionally, one-sentence descriptions appear. A useful feature for selectors is the subject index to new titles. The 1983 cumulation lists 900 new publications.

Faxon Librarians' Guide to Serials. Westwood, Mass.: Faxon, 1931-. Annually.

    Authoritative source for current price of journals.

    Arranged alphabetically by title/main entry.

    Accompanied by comprehensive microfiche, listing all titles handled by company.

Issued by a leading subscription agent, this catalog is arranged alphabetically, according to library cataloging rules. It is a good printed source for the current price of journals and for an indication of cessations, ISSN, and where a title is indexed. The catalog is not useful for selection, except as verification or identification of details about titles. Data contained in this source may be accepted as accurate at time of publication because of the authority of the company's database. The printed catalog contains only titles for which Faxon has three or more orders, but accompanying microfiche contain "low-use" titles as well.

Librarians' Handbook. v.1-. 1979/71-. Birmingham, Ala.: EBSCO Subscription Services. Annually.

    Alphabetical arrangement by serial's cover title.

    Does not follow library cataloging rules for entry.

    May contain subscription information not found elsewhere.

Arranged alphabetically by cover title of serial, this catalog contains a wealth of information drawn from the vendor's database. It lists more titles than Faxon's printed catalog, and has more information about nonperiodical serials, some of it very old. Use for selectors is in confirming or identifying details about specific serials.

Most of the sources mentioned can supply the International Standard Serial Number (ISSN). Once a selector has the ISSN, the title can be accessed in virtually any database and is uniquely identified for transactions with vendors, publishers, and patrons. The subscription agents are adding this number to their files; however, *Ulrich's* and *Irregular Serials and Annuals* have the most complete listing, because Bowker was responsible for the initial assignment of ISSN.

Evaluating Serials

The selector has any number of sources for the intelligent selection of monographs: review periodicals, scholarly journals, professional literature. Unfortunately, few scholarly or professional journals review serials. Notice of subscription information and a summary of contents is the rule. One must rely on publishers' ads, recommendations of colleagues, and sample copies. As budgets shrink, the examination of a sample journal issue by both librarian and potential user becomes mandatory so that a purchase can be defended. The factors that push subscription prices up often force publishers to charge libraries for a sample issue, in contrast to earlier times when samples were free. This is money well spent, however, for it can keep the library from committing its continuing serials funding to the wrong titles.

Librarians need reviews and other qualitative, authoritative serial review devices similar to those available for books. They need evaluations of new titles done by subject specialists and included in the standard monograph review tools. Yet, reviewing a serial involves a risk that does not exist when reviewing a monograph. The reviewer can assess only what is in hand, and one never has in hand all of an active serial. Reviews of serials can be equated with reviews of monographs only after publication has ceased, and selectors need the review during the title's early years. The reviewer cannot predict from the first issue or even the first few volumes of a serial what future content will be. This uncertainty may be a factor in the exclusion of journals from book review media.

Serials Review, the first library-oriented journal devoted to reviews of serials, contains both evaluative reviews and articles in the field of serials management, with the editor aiming for half reviews and half articles. *New Magazine Review* is another source of serial reviews, one directed primarily toward the public library. Among the evaluative sources for serials are annotated guides based on *Ulrich's* and *Irregular Serials and Annuals*, respectively: Bill Katz's *Magazines for Libraries* and Joan Marshall's *Serials for Libraries*.

Choice contains a monthly column, "Periodicals for College Libraries," compiled by Richard Centing. Titles included are all recommended and must have been published for several years; newer journals are mentioned briefly and designated "worth consideration." Each issue of *Library Journal* contains a column edited and often written by Bill Katz, reviewing new and fairly new periodicals. It is an excellent source for evaluating little magazines, but coverage of all types of new periodicals of interest to librarians is representative.

Serials Review. v.1-.1975-. Ann Arbor, Mich.: Pierian. Quarterly.

    Best source for evaluative reviews of serials, new and old.

    Subject review articles.

    In-depth reviews of a single or a few related titles.

    Signed reviews, most written by librarians.

The best source thus far for reviews of serials, this journal contains both subject review articles and in-depth reviews of one or a few related titles. A recent issue held over 150 reviews, plus evaluations of several cumulative indexes. All reviews are signed, and most are written by librarians. Serials reviewed are both established titles and new ones; little magazines and local interest periodicals are covered especially well. An index to titles reviewed appears in each issue. With vol. 10 (1984), the journal resumed publication of "Serials Review Index," listing reviews of serial publications from approximately 175 journals.

Katz, William A., and Linda Sternberg, eds. *Magazines for Libraries: For the General Reader, and School, Junior College, College, University, and Public Libraries*, 4th ed. New York: Bowker, 1982.
>   Classified arrangement.
>   Includes annotations for 6500 titles from *Ulrich's*.
>   Covers all types of journals, popular to research.

Magazines for Libraries, using a classified arrangement, annotates 6500 recommended titles from *Ulrich's*. Coverage ranges from popular to research journals, with appropriate audience noted. In addition to information found in *Ulrich's*, this source includes a journal's policy on refereeing, the extent of book review coverage, and advertising availability. It is revised every few years.

Marshall, Joan K., comp. *Serials for Libraries: An Annotated Guide to Continuations, Annuals, Yearbooks, Almanacs, Transactions, Proceedings, Directories, Services.* New York: Neal Schuman; Santa Barbara, Calif.: ABC-Clio, 1979.
>   Includes 2000 titles from *Irregular Serials and Annuals*.
>   Excludes monographic series.
>   List of special issues.

A companion volume to Katz, this work needs to be revised as often. Titles, all recommended and all annotated, are drawn from *Irregular Serials and Annuals* and presented in a subject arrangement. Monographic series are not included. A unique feature is a list of special issues published by journals. Another useful list is "When to Buy What." The guide gives appropriate audience for each entry.

Most publishers and vendors issuing regular bulletins of serials information list only title and some bibliographic details. An exception to this practice is the British subscription agent, Stevens & Brown. The company's *Quarterly Serials Bulletin* lists several pages of new serials with descriptive annotations that often include the contents of the first issue. The reviews are not usually evaluative, but they give adequate information for ordering and several paragraphs of description. Data provided by the publisher are acknowledged.

Stevens & Brown Quarterly Serial Bulletin. Godalming, Surrey: Stevens & Brown. Quarterly.
>   Complete bibliographic data and description of new journals and series.
>   Notations of serials' changes and delays.
>   Compiled from publishers' information.

This free-of-charge vendor publication contains the usual information about serials changes and delays, but in addition it has a large section devoted to new journals and several pages describing new series. These features give complete bibliographic information, usually a listing of contents or topics to be covered in the first issue, and often some description of the journal's scope and purpose, as provided by the publisher. The most useful to the selector of this type of bulletin, because of its descriptions of many new serials. A title index cumulating annually would increase its value.

Persons evaluating serial titles for library purchase can supplement any reviews located with other measures of worth. For example, coverage of a title in periodical indexes and abstract journals is an indication of both quality and ease of access. These reference works almost always contain a list of the titles consulted. It has been said, but not documented, that publishers of periodical indexes give misleading information about the titles included in an effort to enhance the appeal of the indexes. *Ulrich's* is another source of indexing information, but a recent study casts serious doubt upon the accuracy of this aspect of the guide's coverage.[3] Subscription agents' catalogs include indexing information in the listings, and the author suspects that this source may be more nearly accurate than *Ulrich's*.

Most criteria for serials selection are the same as for monograph selection, but they assume added importance because of the long-term commitment of an increasing amount of money. As with monographs, the needs of the library's users are a prime consideration. Also, the quality of the serial must be determined: is it well written, well produced, supported by a recognized editorial board? The reputation of the publisher is less significant than for a monograph, because many serials are self-published. Still, enough are produced by established companies (and this is an apparent trend in serials publishing) that one should consider the record of the publisher: are journals issued on schedule, have price increases been especially high, do issues fall apart with minimal use?

The library's environment is a strong factor in selecting serials. What resources are available elsewhere on campus, in town, or in the region? Does the library belong to the Center for Research Libraries? Is there a local consortium that could be a source of titles marginally related to the collection? Is there a similar type of library nearby, and is that library willing to lend or photocopy? The number of libraries holding a serial, as determined from union lists and the bibliographic utilities, is an indication of the popularity or perceived value of a title. The discovery that a title is held by a nearby library, perhaps a resource-sharing partner, may be reason to refrain from placing a subscription or standing order.

Some criteria are more crucial to serial than to monograph selection; for example, the cost of the journal or series. If the title is unique and meets other selection criteria, it is probably worth the cost. One must consider for serials more than for monographs whether a title fits into the collection. A monograph that is not appropriate can often be discarded and chalked up to experience; cancellation of a continuing order can create havoc within the serial acquisitions unit if the timing is bad: a letter must be written, confirmation obtained, and possibly a refund requested; encumbered funds must be liquidated and reassigned; a record of the decision must be kept so that when an unexpected issue arrives or someone else requests the title, the whole story can be explained. Conversely, an inappropriate serial order not canceled is expensive in terms of payment, processing, and space.

A serial backfile purchase is a one-time transaction, similar to the acquisition of a monograph. Because of cost, selection criteria must be applied even more stringently to the selection of backfiles than to continuing orders. Serial volumes increase in price after publication, and the cost of as little as three prior years of a scientific journal often exceeds $1000. The selector needs to assess the lasting value of the serial's content, in the context of resource sharing agreements, before placing a continuing order. If the information is ephemeral or will be generally available later, purchase of a backfile or retention of the title is not necessary. If the decision to retain or discard is not made at the time of subscription, the marginal title is likely to be routinely bound or the significant backfile never purchased.

Projecting and Measuring Patron Use

For nearly all libraries, use or potential use of the collection determines its value. Three approaches to evaluating patron use of a serials collection are use studies, citation analysis, and core lists of serials. Many articles have described serials use studies by such means as circulation counts, coloured dots, and questionnaires.[4] The key to a meaningful survey is a clear understanding of what constitutes use of a serial, but it is difficult to measure patrons' use of library serials even with a satisfactory definition of "use" and even when each item is delivered over a desk from a closed collection.

Serial citation analysis is a ranking based on the frequency with which journal articles are referred to in a specific group of titles. This technique gives the library direction in evaluating the collection, but it must be used with care, because several variables, most notably availability and access, must be accounted for. Two excellent survey essays about citation analysis appear in Stueart and Miller's *Collection Development in Libraries*.[5]

An RTSD committee, the Serials Section's ad hoc Committee to Study the Feasibility of Creating Dynamic Core Lists of Serials, has been at work since 1978. Lists already exist in several subjects, but the committee is charged with developing general criteria for the use of subject specialists in determining basic serials for undergraduate use in each major subject. Members have been wrestling with several questions concerning scope and criteria, and the committee still has not determined whether developing the lists is feasible. The concept of core lists is a good one; ideally they would be based on multiple criteria including use, citation analysis, cost, and number of subscriptions; keyed to different types of libraries according to mission and budget; compiled by librarian subject specialists; and updated often.

Acquiring Serials

Once the decision has been made to receive a serial on a continuing basis, a different set of considerations comes into play, with different problems and the need for additional sources of information. While this may be the point at which responsibility for the title passes from the selector, an understanding of the intricacies of serials acquisition facilitates communication, and therefore, receipt of the publication.

Search and Verification

The first phase of the acquisition process is searching the title against library records to ensure that a duplicate order is not being placed inadvertently. Even a subscription intended to be a duplicate is searched, because this search supplies ordering information such as source of existing order, latest price, and bibliographic information useful in cataloging.

After searching, titles new to the library are verified in databases or printed sources accepted as standard: OCLC, RLIN, *New Serial Titles, Ulrich's*, and other, more specialized tools.

Much of the verification procedure for serial orders takes place today at the computer terminal. The CONSER database, online through OCLC, gives serials catalogers increasingly useful records. These records are the best place for most libraries to check the accuracy of bibliographic and publication data on serial orders, provided they understand that CONSER participants have put more effort into building the database than updating it. The number of catalogers able to change the database is limited; most libraries are not able to improve these records except on their own tapes and catalog cards, a source of great frustration to serials catalogers. Not all OCLC serial records are CONSER records, because any library that catalogs a title unique to the database enters that record. Local records are subject to the same obsolescence as CONSER contributions, but if the CONSER and non-CONSER records are used with care, and if questionable data are checked elsewhere (as in a subscription agent's catalog), OCLC, or one of the other bibliographic networks, is the best place to verify a new serial order.

Should the title requested not be in the database, or should the details not be sufficient for verification, some searchers can go to other online sources. If the library has access to DataLink or EBSCONET, details can be checked against these databases. In some respects, these sources are better than the bibliographic utilities, because the subscription agent is more likely to list the latest price and publisher address than an OCLC record that may be several years old. However, vendors' databases do not carry the authority of files constructed by library catalogers. The Bowker Serials Bibliography database is probably midway between the bibliographic utilities and the subscription agents in authority. The printed sources derived from this file are respected, and the data more nearly current online than in printed form.

For libraries without access to the above databases, very good manual sources remain - the pre-1981 *National Union Catalog* for Library of Congress cataloging or cataloging from a cooperating library; *New Serial Titles* or the *Union List of Serials*; *Ulrich's* or *Irregular Serials and Annuals*; and other lists of serials. Periodicals and other serials that have begun publication very recently will not have had time to appear in printed sources, so the procedure for verifying new titles may be abbreviated. Before abandoning the search, one may check the vendor publications discussed earlier.

Often the use of several verification sources turns up a conflict, such as two publisher addresses or two forms of the title. In this case, it is advisable to pursue the search to see if one address or title appears significantly more often than the other and to use that one. If there are nearly equal occurrences of each, consider the authority of the sources and choose. Be sure to note the conflict and the sources, and use the alternative form later if necessary.

LINX. Westwood, Mass.: Faxon. Available online directly from the publisher.

Contains Faxon's publisher and title information files.

InfoServe module displays new journals from several international publishers.

Budgeting data available for three-year period.

This online serials system consists of several components. Those most useful for selectors are DataLinx, Faxon's publisher and title information files, and InfoServe, listings of all new titles and a forum for publishers to display their journals to *LINX* users. Since LC call number is an access point, selectors can access titles by subject. Financial data, by LC class, publisher, etc., is available for a three-year period. The system includes an electronic mail function for ordering, claiming, and communication with Faxon and other *LINX* users.

At times during the verification process, one finds information that changes the name under which the title is to be ordered. Whenever this happens, it is necessary to research library records under the new entry.

Serial Vendors

The decision to use a subscription agent or standing order vendor as an intermediary in the purchase of serials, or to deal directly with the publisher, is one each library must make based on its own needs and priorities. This decision may be a blanket policy governing all serial orders, or it may be made for specified types of orders or for each order individually. Size and scope of the serial collection are major factors in the decision. The policy that the library follows needs to be continually evaluated as computer technology and library budgets change and as vendors and their promised services change.

Until recently, many American journal publishers gave subscription agents discounts that were not available to libraries. The agents were able to pass on savings to the library customer. Rising costs and serial publishing practices have reduced or eliminated agency discounts, and the vendor now must add a service charge to the cost of publishers' prices in order to cover expenses and make a profit. The service charge is usually a percentage of the total list price of the periodicals, although some companies make other arrangements for the highest priced titles. Agents compete not only on the annual cost of subscriptions, but also on the service they give. The largest agents are extensively automated and can give almost any information or special handling the customer wants. How much of this service an agent will provide and how much will be done without additional cost depend largely on the company's willingness to please the customer.

The automated periodical fulfillment center is a relatively recent byproduct of the computer age, selling a service to publishers of mass circulation magazines. The fulfillment center contracts with a number of publishers to perform a group of related processes - receiving, entering, and filling subscriptions. By means of the economies of scale, it can do the work at lower cost than the individual publishers. Titles failing into this category can be identified from the address on the contents page to which address changes are sent. Major fulfillment centres are located n Boulder, Colorado; Des Moines, Iowa; and Marion, Ohio. A subscription address in one of these cities, especially if it is a post office box, provides the clue.

Libraries are not important to fulfillment centres, because the companies deal with mass circulation titles. *Steinbeck Quarterly* does not come from a fulfillment center, but *US News* does. Even though nearly every library in the country receives at least one copy of *US News*, those subscriptions are a small percentage of the total. Thus, library claims and complaints have very little clout.

Library problems with fulfillment center titles concern duplicate or overlapping subscriptions, gaps in receipt, and unsatisfactory claim response. In the fulfillment center everything is keyed to the coded data appearing on the mailing label. Individuals can easily renew personal subscriptions, because a copy of the label accompanies the check. Unless libraries follow the same practice, they have problems. Subscription agencies are working hard to resolve the problems, but at the present time a library has more success by placing fulfillment center orders direct. For best results, monitor the mailing labels and use the computer-produced renewal notices several weeks before the expiration date shown on the label.

Finally, the subscription or standing order request sent to the vendor should identify clearly what title the library wants to receive, when the order is to begin, the shipping and invoicing address(es), the library's order number, and (as inconspicuously as possible essential data for internal use, such as funding, routing, and searching history. This internal information can confuse the vendor, so separate it as clearly as possible from the bibliographic data and instructions to the agent or publisher. The best location for local use data is on the back of an order form or on a copy of the order that remains in the library.

This chapter is meant to guide, not to restrict. New sources of information will appear and will lead to new ways of selecting. As serials change, so do effective techniques.

References

1 Karen J. Winkler, "When It Comes to Journals, Is More Really Better?" *Chronicle of Higher Education* 24 (14 April 1982): 21-22.

2 For more about the CONSER Project, see Marcia Tuttle, *Introduction to Serials Management* (Greenwich, Conn.: JAI Press, 1983), pp. 177-183.

3 Cynthia Swenck and Wendy Robinson, "A Comparison of the Guides to Abstracting and Indexing Services Provided by Katz, Chicorel, and Ulrich." *Research Quarterly* 17 (1978): 317-319; Diana Wyndham, "An Evaluation of References to Indexes and Abstracts in Ulrich's 17th Edition." *Research Quarterly* 20 (1980): 155-159.

4 For example, see Robert Goehlert, "Periodical Use in an Academic Library: A Study of Economists and Political Scientists." *Special Libraries* 69 (1978): 51-60; W.M. Shaw, Jr., "A Practical Journal Usage Technique." *College and Research Libraries* 39 (1978): 479-484.

5 Shirley A. Fitzgibbons, "Citation Analysis in the Social Sciences." In *Collection Development in Libraries: A Treatise, Part B*, ed. Robert D. Stueart and George B. Miller, Jr. (Foundations in Library and Information Science, Vol. 10. Greenwich, Conn.: JAI Press, 1980), pp. 291-344; Kris Subramanyam, "Citation Studies in Science and Technology," in *Collection Development in Libraries*, pp. 345-72.

Selection Sources

EBSCO Bulletin of Serials Changes. Vol. 1- . Birmingham, Ala.: EBSCO Industries, 1975- ; bimonthly.

IMS Ayer Directory of Publications. Vol. 1- . Fort Washington, Pa.: IMS Press, 1869- ; annual.

International Directory of Little Magazines and Small Presses. Vol. 1- . Paradise, Calif.: L.V. Fulton, 1965- ; annual.

Irregular Serials and Annuals. Vol. 1- . New York: Bowker, 1967- ; annual.

Katz, William A., and Sternberg, Linda, eds. *Magazines for Libraries: For the General Reader, and School, Junior College, College, University, and Public Libraries.* 4th ed. New York: Bowker, 1982.

L'Annee Philologique. Vol. 1- . Paris: International Society of Classical Bibliography, 1924- ; annual.

Marshall, Joan K., comp. *Serials for Libraries: An Annotated Guide to Continuations, Annuals, Yearbooks, Almanacs, Transactions, Proceedings, Directories, Services.* New York: Neal-Schuman; Santa Barbara, Calif.: ABC-Clio, 1979.

MLA Directory of Periodicals: A Guide to Journals and Series in Languages and Literatures. 1st ed.- . New York: Modern Language Association of America, 1978/89- ; biennially.

MLA International Bibliography of Books and Articles on the Modern Languages and Literatures. 1st ed.- . New York: Modern Language Association of America, 1921- ; annual.

Monthly Catalog of United States Government Publications. Washington, D.C.: Government Printing Office, 1895- ; monthly.

New Magazine Review. Vol. 1- . North Las Vegas, Nev.: New Magazine Review, November/December 1978- ; bimonthly.

New Serial Titles: A Union List of Serials Held by Libraries in the United States and Canada. Washington, D.C.: Library of Congress, 1953- ; monthly with quarterly and longer cumulations.

Nijhoff Serials. Vol. 1- . The Hague: Martinus Nijhoff, 1979- ; quarterly.

Serials Review. Vol. 1- . Ann Arbor, Mich.: Pierian, 1975- ; quarterly.

Standard Periodical Directory. Vol. 1- . New York: Oxbridge, 1963- ; biennially.

Stevens and Brown Quarterly Serial Bulletin. Godalming, Surrey: Stevens and Brown, quarterly.

Swets Info. Lisse, Netherlands: Swets Subscription Service, quarterly.

Ulrich's International Periodicals Directory. Vol. 1- . New York: Bowker, 1932- ; annual.

Ulrich's Quarterly. Vol. 1- . New York: Bowker, spring 1977- ; quarterly.

Union List of Serials in Libraries of the United States and Canada. 3rd ed. 5 vols. New York: Wilson, 1965.

Judy Horn, "Government Publications." In *Selection of Library Materials in the Humanities, Social Sciences, and Sciences,* edited by Patricia A. McClung, 313-334. Chicago, Ill.: American Library Association, 1985.

Government organizations are the world's most prolific publishers, and the large number of governmental agencies further complicates acquisition success. This chapter covers some of the basic elements in selection, evaluation, and acquisition of materials published by the United States government, state governments, international governmental organizations, foreign governments, and local governments.

The same factors that govern selection of material for the library's collection apply to the selection of government publications. In the past, many large libraries attempted to acquire as complete a collection of government publications as possible. This provides a sense of security for the librarian and the researcher, but in an era of declining resources it is no longer possible or cost effective. We must carefully determine the levels of government and subject areas to be collected so that materials will complement the library's collection and be integrated into it. Their physical location within the library, either housed separately or merged into the collection, is irrelevant.[1]

Preparation of a written collection development policy helps to guide selection decisions that meet the needs of users. It also provides a yardstick for measuring selection activities. In addition to defining subject fields, the collection development policy should identify the levels of government to be collected. While these levels will vary depending upon the community needs, academic programs, and the resources of other libraries in the area, most larger libraries will acquire publications from local city and county jurisdictions, their state, the United States government, and selected international organizations. Publications from other states or foreign governments will usually be limited, since they tend to receive little use.

Before attempting to draft a collection policy, you should survey the literature on collection development. The book *Developing Collections of U.S. Government Publications,* by Peter Hernon and Gary Purcell, contains an overview of collection development issues and includes sample collection development policies for government publications.[2]

Government publications, for the most part, are not evaluated in standard collection development review media. However, a growing number of periodicals include review columns on government publications. These reviews, in addition to evaluating publications, also indicate where they may be obtained. Some of the periodicals currently containing evaluative reviews of government publications include *Government Publications Review* (Pergamon Press), *Documents to the People* (ALA Government Documents Round Table [GODORT]); *RQ* (ALA Reference and Adult Services Division); *Booklist* (ALA); *Serials Review* (Pierian Press); *Serials Librarian* (Haworth Press); and *Wilson Library Bulletin.*

In many instances evaluation is irrelevant since the author (issuing agency) is authoritative and the only producer of certain information. Examples include the material produced by Congress or the annual reports of various agencies. In some cases - for example, census publications - the librarian will need to evaluate compilations published by private publishers and decide whether the library should select the material as published by the government, the private publisher, or both. The sources listed above, including *Microforms Review,* evaluate and frequently offer comparisons of works issued both by the government and private publishers.

Unfortunately, relatively few publications are reviewed. If a government publication appears to fall within the collection policy parameters, select it. While you are waiting for a review to appear in the literature, the publication will probably go out-of-print. The choice in selecting large series, especially technical report series that can be quite voluminous, may not be quite so simple. Unless the library has a strong program in the subject field covered by the series, selection should be on a title-by-title basis. Before deciding to acquire the entire series, order one or two titles most pertinent to the collection policy and evaluate them. If it is a new series, wait for a number of titles to appear before making a decision. If it appears that over half the titles in the series will be heavily used by the library, you will save time and money in collecting the entire series, unless it is a very bulky collection.

The availability period for government publications will affect your selections. Few government publications are available after five years and most go out-of-print within two. The increase in government publications titles in microform, issued both by governments and private publishers, has extended the purchase period.

Resource sharing options will also impact on selection decisions, especially if there are two or more large libraries within a fifteen- to twenty-mile radius, or if several libraries are part of a larger system. An article by Bruce Morton and J. Randolph Cox describes a cooperative program for two smaller selective US depository libraries that may serve as a model for larger libraries.[3] The University of California's shared acquisitions program has made it possible for government publications departments in the system to share the costs and use of large sets, primarily microforms. Before making recommendations for purchase, the government publications librarians consult and decide the most appropriate holdings and locations; each campus receives an index. Direct loans between government publications departments facilitate the use of the materials. This has worked successfully; turnaround time among the southern campuses varies from one to three days.

General Considerations

Deciding how to acquire government publications is one of the major decisions that needs to be made. There are four basic methods of acquiring government publications: (1) exchange; (2) gift; (3) purchase; (4) depository arrangements. Using combinations of these methods increases the available options.

1. *Exchange*. Your initial request to a foreign government for free materials may result in their asking for an exchange agreement. In all except rare instances this method should be avoided. The costs involved in establishing and maintaining exchange agreements far exceed the return. Most libraries seldom have a title or collection of publications consistently available for exchange. The basic question to ask is, "Do I have a steady supply of publications that can be exchanged on a regular basis?" If the answer is not an unequivocal "yes," it is best to avoid establishing exchange agreements for government publications.

2. *Gift*. In the past, many large government publication collections were developed through this method. This, in general, is no longer possible, although you may still be able to acquire many publications by getting your library on the agency's mailing list. No publication has yet been issued that lists all free publications from all government jurisdictions; such a publication does not even exist for materials issued by the US government. This is the collection method most subject to change. What is offered free today may have a price tag on it tomorrow. The major indexes of the government jurisdictions discussed below normally indicate which items are free of charge. Write to the agency whose publications you wish to acquire and request to be put on the mailing

list for free publications. Some agencies will regularly send you their free publications; some maintain mailing lists for only certain periodical titles; and others do not maintain mailing lists. When an agency does not maintain a mailing list but has free items, each publication must be requested separately. This information about mailing lists is also not published, but is discovered by trial and error. When requesting free items, be careful to request only titles that are compatible with the collection development policy. It is easy to fall into the trap of getting on the mailing lists for publications just because they are free. Gift items frequently require more record keeping and careful monitoring.

3. *Purchase.* In the last few years the number of government jurisdictions requiring that publications be purchased has increased dramatically. No longer can we assume that a government publications collection can be built around gratis publications. Many government agencies are even requiring prepayment. To facilitate orders, some governments and vendors have deposit account options in which money is deposited in advance and drawn upon as needed. Methods of purchasing publications from each of the levels of government are described later in the chapter.

4. *Depository Arrangements.* Various government jurisdictions, including local, state, national, regional, and international governmental organizations, have established depository arrangements with libraries. Libraries designated as depositories generally receive the publications free of charge.[4] Depository types range from full (regional) to partial (selective). Designation as a full depository does not mean that the library will automatically receive everything published by that government jurisdiction, however. Many categories of publications are excluded from depository programs and, since each government jurisdiction establishes its own policies and procedures, the categories of inclusion are seldom uniform. Thus, while a library may participate in one or more depository programs, a separate arrangement will be needed for each.

Depository programs generally provide the greatest return for the least investment of time and effort required by the various acquisitions methods. However, depository arrangements may not be the best means of acquiring publications. Comparing standing order plans and individual purchases to depository receipts will help to identify potential problems. If the depository plan includes a large amount of material outside the subject areas of the collection policy and does not offer selection options, the depository arrangement will probably not be the best acquisition method. Your analysis in making this decision should also consider the costs associated with acquisitions, processing, cataloging, and space requirements of possibly extraneous materials.

Each of the methods outlined above may apply to an individual library's program. At times you may find it desirable to experiment with a combination of methods. The strategy you employ will depend upon the government jurisdiction involved.

US Government Publications

Depository Libraries. There are currently over 1300 US government depository libraries. Depository libraries are allocated primarily on the basis of Congressional and Senatorial district. The US Code, Title 44, Sections 1905-07, lists other means by which a library may become a depository. The depository library program is administered by the Library Programs Service under the superintendent of documents in the Government Printing Office (GPO).

Forty-nine regional depositories receive all items issued in the depository program. There is a limit of two regionals per state. Regionals are responsible for retaining depository materials permanently and for providing interlibrary loan and reference service for the region served.

The other libraries are selective depositories. They have the option of selecting, from approximately 6000 item numbers, the material that the library will receive. Each depository library is required to select a minimum of twenty-five percent of the available item numbers. An item number may be for one specific title, a subject group, a type of publication, or a catchall category, such as "general publications". New item selections are sent to depository libraries at least once a month. Selection of an item number establishes a "standing order" for the material included in that item number. Each depository receives an item number printout twice a year. This printout indicates each item number and notes whether the library has selected it or not, and item selections may be revised with the receipt of each printout. The "List of Items for Selection by Depository Libraries", available from the superintendent of documents, outlines the assigned item numbers, categories, and titles.

Each depository shipment contains one or more Depository Shipping Lists listing the items sent to depository libraries by superintendent of documents classification number, title, and item number. Libraries receive only those items on the list that they have selected. The *Daily Depository Shipping List* may be used by depository libraries to acquire items not selected for deposit. When publications are available for sale from the Government Printing Office (GPO) this information is usually indicated on the *Daily Depository Shipping List.* However carefully the item number selections are tailored to the collection development policy, most libraries will receive some publications that would not be selected if the material were available title by title, or by subject. This is because some item numbers are very broad. For example, the Federal Reserve Bulletin was recently assigned a separate item number after previously being included as part of the "general publications" item for the agency. Libraries desiring to select this one title had to take everything included in the general publications category. Although GPO has been refining item numbers to make them more specific, a choice must still be made between selecting an item number that provides material extraneous to the collection and not selecting the item number but acquiring only those titles relevant to the library's collection. This choice must be made on a library-by-library basis. Space availability, staffing resources, proportion of the material outside the parameters of the collection policy, ease of acquiring the publications if not received on deposit, and the availability of the publications at another area institution must be considered.

Each government agency is responsible for sending to GPO all publications except those for official use only or for strictly administrative purposes. The publications GPO receives are included in the depository program. However, not all agencies cooperate fully with this requirement, especially those with multiple regional offices, so all government publications do not get into the depository program. The publications from two large agencies, the National Technical Information Services (NTIS) and Educational Resources Information Center (ERIC), are not included in the depository program. The indexes to the publications for NTIS and ERIC are available on deposit but the publications must be purchased. There are varying degrees of overlap between what is included on deposit and what is included under the rubric of NTIS or ERIC. Technical reports from the Department of Energy are now included in the depository program.

It is difficult to outline precisely what is and what is not included in the depository program. You can safely assume that all administrative reports, such as annual reports of agencies or reports of established entitlement programs, are included. Also included on deposit are public information programs. The gray areas, in which titles will sometimes be included on deposit and sometimes will not, usually involve publications resulting from scientific and technical research, especially those done under government contract. Also included in this gray area are publications issued by regional offices.

The depository program is very active and constantly changing. Regular perusal of *Administrative Notes* from GPO and *Documents to the People,* used by GODORT, plus attendance at meetings such as the Depository Library Council and the Acquisitions and Bibliographic Control Work Group of the GODORT Federal Documents Task Force, will keep depository librarians abreast of new changes.

Philosophically, in selecting item numbers I prefer to select only those that fulfill academic program/patron needs, but during the last few years it has become increasingly difficult to acquire materials not selected on deposit. Rising costs and the substitution of microfiche for paper copy has created problems. The traditional means of acquiring nonselected items has been to scan the *Daily Depository Shipping List* and acquire a copy from the issuing agency or from the GPO Sales Program. All publications offered for sale by GPO are in the depository program. However, the sales program includes only about ten to fifteen percent of the titles issued by GPO. The remaining titles must be acquired on deposit or from the issued agency, and many issuing agencies are not retaining copies for distribution because of budget cuts. Many of these agencies are now selling their publications or charging a user or handling fee.[5]

An additional consideration is microfiche. Nearly half of the publications in the depository program are now issued in microfiche. Some item categories are available only in microfiche; others are available in dual format. Microfiche offers cost savings, especially in space. However, in the selection of microfiche, libraries should be careful to stay within the parameters of the collection policy. Microfiche cabinets take space, and a growth rate of two or more cabinets per year requires as careful consideration as creating new shelving space. The same selection criteria should be applied to microfiche as to paper with the added considerations of usage and format, when choice is available. Libraries will want to select heavily used items and reference tools in paper copy.

Individual Title Selection. Since even depository libraries must occasionally request or purchase individual titles, the following information can be used by both depository and nondepository libraries to select and acquire US government publications. As noted earlier, in addition to the depository program the GPO has a sale program. Through this program publications may be purchased from GPO in Washington, D.C., or from GPO bookstores located in major cities. The bookstores do not, however, stock all of the publications included in the program. Libraries will find it most convenient to send orders directly to the superintendent of documents in Washington, D.C. To facilitate ordering, a deposit account of at least fifty dollars may be established with GPO. The GPO bookstores will charge your orders to your deposit account.

Publications Reference File. Washington, D.C.: Government Printing Office. Bimonthly.
   Microfiche index to US government publications and subscription services offered for sale
   by the Government Printing Office (GPO).
   Bimonthly cumulation with biweekly updates of new titles (1-2 microfiche).
   Titles appear in *PRF* a minimum of 3-4 weeks after listing on the *Daily Depository Shipping List.*
   Access is by GPO stock number, Superintendent of Documents Classification Number, and title/keyword.
This source is the most up-to-date compilation of publications available from GPO, but is more of an acquisitions tool than a selection tool because each edition cumulates. Out-of-stock titles may remain on the list for up to two years. *Subject Bibliographies* are the paper equivalent of *PRF* but are not as up-to-date. For selection purposes, *New Books* and *U.S. Government Books* are easier to access.

With the exception of promotional material, GPO does not provide publications gratis. The titles of the publications that GPO has for sale appear in the *Publications Reference File (PRF).* This is a microfiche index arranged in three parts: GPO stock number, superintendent of documents classification number, and title/keyword. This contains the most current information available to libraries. However, there is a minimum delay of at least three weeks between a title's appearance on a *Daily Depository Shipping List* and the receipt of a microfiche *PRF* with that title. The *PRF* is now being sent to depository libraries bimonthly with biweekly updates of new titles added. The *PRF* may be purchased from GPO and is valuable as a reference tool as well as a selection tool.

When ordering from the *PRF,* be sure to check the status line carefully. Some titles are still included in the list but are out-of-stock. This is indicated on the left-hand side of the beginning of each entry in the *PRF.* Each entry receives an individual stock number. This is the number that should be used in ordering publications. Do not try to save time by using the stock number of a previous edition of a title in order to receive the most recent edition. Except in a few instances, this will not work. The *PRF* is also available online through DIALOG/DIALORDER. Material can be ordered directly from GPO on DIALORDER.

The *Daily Depository Shipping List* may also be utilized as a selection tool by both depository and nondepository libraries. While depository libraries may quickly scan the list for nonselected item numbers, nondepository libraries may find the *Daily Depository Shipping List,* which can be purchased on subscription, to be awkward and cumbersome to use.

Selection tools issued by the GPO include *Subject Bibliographies.* Issued free by GPO, the bibliographies provide subject access to GPO sales publications. *Subject Bibliographies* are issued on an irregular basis and, because the coverage is limited to GPO sales publications, they may be updated using the *PRF.* The GPO has discontinued *Selected New Publications* and is now issuing two titles, *New Books* and *U.S. Government Books.* These are both free titles. *New Books* is issued bimonthly and contains titles added to GPO sales since the previous issue, while *U.S. Government Books* appears quarterly and includes the 1000 most popular government publications. The information in both of these titles duplicates the *PRF* but they are easier to access for selection and contain brief annotations. The *Consumer Information Catalog* is a source for quickly locating available consumer information. Issued quarterly, this catalog contains titles of publications available from a number of federal agencies through the Consumer Information Center in Pueblo, Colorado. Less than half of the publications are free and there is a user fee for processing an order of two or more free titles. The publications with sales prices indicated are part of the GPO sales program. Those that are offered free of charge are publications for which the publishing agency has paid the printing and distributing costs. A mailing list for individual copies of the *Consumer Information Catalog* is not maintained. However, libraries may get on the bulk mailing list (twenty-five copies or more) by writing to the Consumer Information Center, Dept. 83, Pueblo, CO 81009.

The old standby, the *Monthly Catalog,* is also a useful selection tool because it contains both depository and nondepository publications. The value of this catalog has diminished as the lag between the publication date and the receipt of the *Monthly Catalog* has widened. Recently, however, an improvement in currency has been noted. Publications identified in the *Monthly Catalog* should be searched in the *PRF* to verify availability. If the title does not appear in the *PRF* and if the *Monthly Catalog* citation does not indicate that it is sold by GPO, try obtaining the publication from the issuing agency. Individual copies of congressional hearings may be obtainable from your Congressman or woman.

Another source of government publications is the National Technical Information Services (NTIS). Many government publications done under contract are included in the *Monthly Catalog* and are available from the NTIS. NTIS often makes out-of-print GPO publications available. The selection tool for titles available from NTIS is the *Government Reports Announcements and Index.*

Serials may be purchased on subscription and annuals on standing order from GPO. The *Monthly Catalog* has a separate volume containing bibliographic information for serial

---

Monthly Catalog of U.S. Government Publications. v.1- . 1895 - . Washington, D.C.,
Government Printing Office. Monthly.
Index to U.S. government publications.
Entries in MARC format according to AACR2 rules arranged by Superintendent of Document Classification Number. Entry includes issuing agency, title, GPO stock number, and price (if for sale).
6-12 month time lag between the publication date and entry in index. Hearings appear in index an average of 6 months after receipt by depository libraries.
Separate indexes by author, title, subject, series/report, contract number, stock number, and title keyword.
Monthly indexes cumulated in semiannual and annual indexes.
Separate serials volume issued annually containing titles issued three times or more per year and selected annual and monographic series titles.
This is the basic selection tool for US government publications. Time lag for indexing is the major disadvantage. It also contains some publications available only from National Technical Information Service (NTIS).

---

titles. The best selection tools is *Price List 36,* "Government Periodicals and Subscription Services." This is available free from the superintendent of documents. Not all periodicals in the depository program are available on subscription. Titles not sold by GPO or available on the depository program will not be included in the *Price List.* Some titles may be obtained through mailing lists while some, such as the *Federal Reserve Bulletin,* must be ordered from the issuing agency rather than GPO. These titles and ordering information are included in the *Monthly Catalog Serials Supplement,* issued at the beginning of each year. Commercial publishers are selling a small but growing number of titles. A recent example is the *Naval Research Logistics Quarterly,* which is being sold by John Wiley and Sons. This title is no longer available on deposit.

Nondepository libraries and depository libraries that require multiple copies of annual compilations should acquire from GPO a copy of the "Standing Order Item List". This list does not include all annual publications but does contain many of the basic reference publications, such as the *Congressional Directory, U.S. Code, Statistical Abstract,* and *Occupational Outlook Handbook.* Information on GPO standing orders may be requested from Department 40, Superintendent of Documents, Washington, D.C. Standing orders and out-of-print publications may also be acquired through government publications dealers or jobbers.[6]

Nondepository and regional publications continue to be elusive, but access tools issued by commercial publishers are of assistance in selecting, evaluating, and acquiring both

---

American Statistics Index (ASI). v.1- . 1974- . Bethesda, Md.: Congressional Information Service, Inc. Monthly with annual and quarterly cumulations.
  Abstract and index of US government statistical publications issued in two sections:
  Abstracts give full description of the content and format of each publication. Arranged by ASI accession number. Issuing agency, availability and price given.
  Index section includes subject and name category, title, and report number indexes. Keyed to *ASI* accession numbers.
  Microfiche collection of all publications included in *ASI* available.
  Also retrospective *ASI* issued in 1974 covering publications issued 1960-73.
The *ASI* is an excellent selection source for both depository and nondepository titles. Out-of-print materials may be acquired through *ASI* Documents on Demand Service. Companion titles by the same publisher are *CIS Index* and *Statistical Reference Index (SRI).*

---

depository and nondepository publications. Two primary indexes for United States government publications are *CIS Index* and *American Statistics Index (ASI). ASI* is especially useful in identifying nondepository serials and in providing the source from which the title may be obtained. The abstracts serve as an evaluation tool and assist in selection. A large number of serial titles in *ASI* are available on subscription in microfiche from the publisher (Congressional Information Service). This is an excellent means of assuring that nondepository titles are received on a regular basis, especially from those agencies that are rather casual about maintaining mailing lists. *Public Affairs Information Service Bulletin (PAIS)* is another useful selection tool for current titles. *Government Reference Books,* a biennial guide, is valuable for identifying reference materials on specific topics.

State Publications

Collections of out-of-state publications in most libraries are underutilized, yet much effort is needed to acquire and house these materials. All large libraries should collect publications from their own state. These will have a high frequency of use and, if possible, the library should participate in a depository program. However, not all states have a depository program. A 1978 article in *Documents to the People,* "Recent Developments in Depository Systems for State Government Documents," lists those states that have depository program.[7] This information has been updated in various issued of *Documents to the People.* The updates are on a state-by-state basis and appear whenever changes have occurred. Material collected from other states should be based closely on the subject parameters defined in the collection policy. The availability of such material in another nearby library should be considered. Also, federal publications sometimes summarize state information. There is an astonishing wealth of information about states in the US publications, covering a wide range of topics.

Whenever possible, larger libraries should attempt to acquire a blue book for each state. These government manuals commonly contain an overview of state activities, agencies, and addresses. A problem is that they are frequently not issued on a regular basis. however, they provide a good beginning point. A list of state blue books is included in David Parish's *State Government Reference Publications.* [8]

There is no one overall comprehensive index to all state publications, and bibliographic control varies considerably from state to state. Most states issue checklists of their publications. A list of general reference sources including state checklists can be found in *State Government Reference Publications* and also in "State Reference Sources."[9] *State Government Reference Publications* is a standard reference source that will assist libraries both with and without state collections in identifying publications issued by state governments. This volume also includes agency addresses and a subject core of state publications. If the state does not issue a checklist, contact the agencies within the state that publish material in your field of interest. If both these methods fail, the old, reliable, *Monthly Checklist of State Publications* is the next best source. This is currently the most comprehensive list of state publications available since Information Handlings Services' *Checklist of State Publications* is no longer being published. The incomplete coverage of the *Monthly Checklist* lessens its value as a selection tool, however. Although it only includes state publications issued within the last five years, the time lag is such that many publications are out-of-date before their existence is known through the *Monthly Checklist.*

In addition to using the state checklist and lists of agency publications, newspapers, especially those issued in the capital city, will contain useful articles about new reports and government activities. To assist in obtaining these reports, a telephone directory of state offices is invaluable. The best and quickest way to obtain new and popular state publications is to telephone the appropriate state agency.

State acquisition and distribution programs are well covered in the literature. A recent issue of *Government Publications Review,* devoted to state publications, contains a "state-of-the-art" article on "Distribution of State Government Publications and Information" by Margaret Lane, and David Parish's "Into the 1980's: The Ideal State Document Reference Collection."[10] A valuable article focusing upon collection development is Terry Weech's "Collection Development and State Publications."[11]

Government Publications Review. v.1- . 1973- . New York: Pergamon. Bimonthly.
  Research articles covering the field of government publications.
  Book review column in most issues.
  5-20 book reviews an issue.
  Signed reviews by librarians and scholars of commercially published books on topics of
  interest to government publications librarians.
  Government publications are reviewed in annual Notable Documents Section that appears in
  November-December issue. Includes publications issued during previous year from local,
  state, and national governments and international organizations. Includes availability and
  price.
This review provides information on both government publications and commercially published
information of interest to government publications librarians. Volumes 7-8 (1980-81) were divided
into two parts: Part A-Research and Part B-Acquisitions Guide.

An excellent nongovernmental source of acquiring statistical information published by the
states is *Statistical Reference Index (SRI),* published by the Congressional Information
Service. This is not a comprehensive index but is a good selection and acquisition tool.
The material indexed in *SRI* is available on microfiche from CIS.

International Governmental Organizations

Selection, evaluation, and acquisitions of the publications of some 300 international
governmental organizations (IGOs) that issue publications is a challenge. The *Yearbook
of International Organizations* includes a general description of an organization, its
address, publications, governmental status, and assists in determining appropriate
IGOs.[12] However, bibliographic control of international governmental publications is
generally unsatisfactory, as there is no single bibliographic source for all IGOs. Sales
brochures are available for most organizations but only the larger publishers, such as the
United Nations, UNESCO, and the Food and Agriculture Organization are
bibliographically controlled.[13]

International publications are included in selection journals and notices in professional and
technical journals that review government publications. A selection tool for publications
of international organizations is *International Bibliography: Publications of
Intergovernmental Organizations* (UNIPUB). Issued quarterly, the coverage includes all
publications sold by UNIPUB as well as other sales or unpriced publications sent by
IGOs to the editorial office of *International Bibliography* for inclusion. Arranged by
broad subjects, each issue contains information on how to acquire publications, including
addresses and a separate periodicals record. Several books and articles are useful in the
selection and acquisition of international publications, especially the writings of Luciana
Marulli-Koenig, whose column, "International Documents Roundup" in *Documents to the
People* is mandatory for keeping informed about IGO activities and publications,
especially the United Nations.[14]

International publications are acquired primarily by purchase or deposit. Except for
ephemeral or promotional material, little is available free of charge. To facilitate the sale of
their publications, the major IGOs have established sales offices or designated sales

agents in the United States. International publications are not cheap; prices are comparable to trade publications. The sales program for most of these agencies provides for the establishment of blanket or standing orders. This is definitely the best method if the categories available for purchase meet your collection needs. In ordering United Nations sales publications, you have a choice of three vendors, the United Nations Sales Office, UNIFO, and UNIPUB. The United Nations provides a quarterly billing and list of publications shipped; UNIFO sends a monthly checklist of materials that have been shipped from the UN; and UNIPUB provides packing lists of the materials they have shipped on a monthly billing. UNIPUB is the largest of the IGO vendors, handling deposit accounts and standing orders for approximately fourteen IGOs.

International Bibliography. v.1- , 1973- . New York: UNIPUB. Quarterly.
    (Title of v.1-10, 1973-82, was *International Bibliography, Information Documentation.*)
    Index to publications of international organizations.
    6-12-month time lag between publication date and entry in *International Bibliography.*
    Each issue in two parts:
    1. Bibliographic record. Arranged by title of publications under broad subject headings.
    Entry includes full bibliographic citation (publishing organization identified by acronym),
    availability, and price. Brief annotations.
    2. Periodicals record. Lists by title periodicals received at the editorial office of *International
    Bibliography.* Provides publisher and subscription information.
    Subject and title indexes.
International Bibliography is a good source for libraries interested in collecting a broad range of international publications. Annotations, while brief, are helpful. Includes not only the larger international organizations but also some of the smaller and lesser-known ones.

To further complicate the selection process, external publishing and copublishing are increasing. According to the annual report of the director general of UNESCO for 1979/80, over thirty percent of the titles issued by UNESCO were published by, or copublished with, a commercial publisher.[15] A similar picture is appearing for the United Nations. The proceedings of conferences and several periodicals are available only from private publishers. Each IGO handles this type of publishing differently. UNESCO includes most copublished titles in its standing order plan; the World Bank provides information on titles published by Johns Hopkins University and others in its *World Bank Catalog.* The United Nations primarily relies upon the commercial publisher for publicity. Some of the major publishers for the UN includes Kraus (for reprints), Pergamon, UNIFO, and Walker.[16]

Another interesting aspect of the selection process for international organizations is the difference between "publications" and "documents". At all other levels of government, these two terms are used interchangeably; at this level, however, documents refer to meeting records or internal memoranda. As examples, UNESCO has a separate subscription for documents; the European Communities Commission documents (COM) are not sent to depositories but are available on subscription from the European Communities; the World Bank documents are not included in the *World Book Catalog* and are difficult to access; documents from organizations such at NATO are confidential.[17]

Index to International Statistics (IIS). Bethesda, Md.: Congressional Information Service, Inc., 1983- . Monthly with quarterly and annual cumulations.
> Guide and index to statistical publications of 80-90 of the world's major international governmental organizations.
> English-language publications.
> Issued in two parts:
> Abstracts provide full bibliographic and availability information.
> Complete description of format and contents of publications.
> Index section includes subject, names, geographic areas; categories; issuing sources; title; and publication number indexes.
> Full text of most publications available on microfiche from the publisher.

Abstracts enhance the value of this publication as a selection tool. All major IGOs, including the United Nations system, Organization for Economic Cooperation and Development, European Community, Organization of American States, commodity organizations, development banks, and other important intergovernmental regional and special purpose organizations are included.

Official records of the United Nations are available on standing order. Not included are records designated "limited" and provisional records of the plenary minutes of the general Assembly. The provisional minutes of the committees of the General Assembly are included on standing order, as are the final verbatim records of the plenary meetings of the General Assembly. The provisional meeting records of the General Assembly are available on a separate subscription. This is worthwhile if the library needs current information, beyond that given in the *UN Chronicle,* since the UN is several years behind in issuing these minutes in the final form.

Documents of international organizations are also available in microform. Readex Corporation, which for many years issued on microprint the most complete collection of UN materials available, has now switched to microfiche. Libraries that serve Model United Nations groups will want to consider this option. The United Nations Sales Office is offering many of its series in microfiche and UNIFO also has microfiche available for United Nations publications. Congressional Information Service is now publishing *Index to International Statistics (IIS)* and provides microfiche copies of the publications indexed. *IIS,* although not comprehensive, is valuable as a selection and acquisitions tool.

Foreign Publications

Of all the levels of government, foreign government publications are most appropriate for resource sharing. Collecting foreign government publications is an area in which "one's aim will all too often exceed one's grasp."[18] Fluctuating exchange rates and shrinking library budgets can play havoc with the development of a foreign collection. Before beginning to develop a foreign collection, you should familiarize yourself with the literature on foreign government publications. With the exception of J.J. Cherns's *Official Publications: An Overview,* most articles or books cover only one specific country. Cherns's book covers the history and current government publishing practices of twenty countries as well as providing a general overview. The countries included are primarily developed countries in various parts of the world.[19] The available literature on some countries, such as Australia, Canada, Great Britain, and France, is abundant.[20] For less developed countries, it is practically nonexistent. In these instances, discussing selection and acquisition methods with colleagues who have had actual experience with these countries is invaluable. The meetings of the Foreign Documents Work Group of the GODORT International Documents Task Force are also helpful.

There is considerable overlap of information contained in foreign government publications with that found in United States and international publications. Before making a decision about what to acquire from foreign countries, become familiar with the information in international publications. You should also consider the information found in US publications, not only the well-known sources, such as the *Department of State Background Notes, Country Surveys,* and *Foreign Economic Trends and Their Implications for the United States,* but also the publications of the Foreign Information Broadcast Service, and the Joint Publications Research Service.[21] The detail of information in these nonforeign publications will not be as great as that in sources published by the foreign government, but you should carefully consider whether your patrons and programs require the greater detail. If you are uncertain whether the US and international material is sufficient, visit a library that has a strong collection in foreign government publications. Also, once a decision has been made about which countries or areas you will cover, contact librarians in institutions similar to yours to discuss acquisition methods.[22]

Bibliographic control of foreign government publications is on a country-by-country basis and ranges from nonexistent to excellent. The developed countries have national bibliographies and government printers who also issue lists of publications. Publications lists, when available, should be acquired. Also, foreign government organization manuals or blue books are useful in providing information about the organization of the government and how and where to obtain material.

Depository arrangements, with a few exceptions, are not available for foreign government publications. Deposit accounts will meet with varying success. Some countries will take the deposit and continue to send material long after the money has obviously been exhausted; others will take the money but the publications never arrive. The problems are primarily with the undeveloped countries, especially in Africa or in countries with unstable political conditions. One acquisitions method that can work well is to add foreign government publications to existing standing order or approval plans with vendors supplying material from various parts of the world. This method is probably the most cost effective, especially for undeveloped countries.

The best source of evaluation of foreign government publications is *Government Publications Review.* This is an excellent acquisitions tool and can be used to acquire a limited collection of basic foreign publications. Ordering information is normally included.

Many commercial publishers are offering foreign government materials, especially legislative and statistical material, in microform. These publications are good candidates for resource sharing. Evaluative reviews appear in *Microforms Review* as well as other government publications reviewing media.

Local Publications

All libraries should collect publications from their local area. Local publications are probably the most heavily used, on a per capita basis, of the various levels of government. If the area served is a large metropolitan city, it is easiest to acquire just the publications of that city and the county. A library surrounded by many small cities has a more difficult problem. Acquiring the publications of more than fifteen to twenty cities is nearly impossible. This number may be too high in many instances depending upon distances, publishing patterns, and subjects emphasized.

Of all the levels of government, the selection and acquisition of local publications is the most challenging and rewarding. Ideally the collection should be as comprehensive as possible; at a minimum it should include budgets, evaluative reports, proceedings, and minutes of the City Council or Board of Supervisors, annual reports, and statistical reports.

Bibliographic control is almost nonexistent. The problems in building a local collection will not be in deciding what to select, but in finding out what has been issued and acquiring it. Get an organizational directory from each of the constituencies from which you plan to acquire materials. Do not forget major special districts, such as school and water districts. Become familiar with the organization of each political entity through these directories. Request copies of the agendas for the Board of Supervisors and the City Council(s). Review the agendas for items that contain reports. Since these reports are frequently in short supply, contact the appropriate agency immediately. In order to receive these agendas regularly, it is advisable to provide the person responsible for their distribution with self-addressed, stamped envelopes.

Depending upon local conditions, it may be useful to visit the county or city offices the day following each meeting of the City Council or Board of Supervisors. Copies of reports distributed to council and board members may be returned to the file following the meeting and will be available from the city or country clerk. It is also important to read the newspaper for local events, especially small local weeklies that frequently contain more news of local government activities.

Personal contacts are extremely important in acquiring local publications. An educational process is frequently involved. Some administrators and staff must be constantly reminded of your existence and continuing needs. At first you may have problems locating the appropriate individuals and you may also be appalled by their low regard for the importance of the local information. However, persistence will pay off, and you frequently must be very persistent given the high turnover rate in some local governments. Eventually your contacts will begin to call you or send you new publications as they are issued.

Index to Urban Documents, published by Greenwood, is the only major index devoted entirely to local publications, but is limited to cities of over 100,000 population. This compilation is useful in developing a collection of local publications on specific subjects. Publications indexed are available on microfiche from the publisher. Microfiche subscriptions are also available by geographic or subject areas.

The literature contains a surprising number of books and articles on the topic of selecting and acquiring local government publications. A particularly useful article is Michael

Shannon's "Collection Development and Local Documents: History and Present Use in the United States".[23]

Conclusion

The goal in selecting government publications in any library should be to develop a "relationship between the documents collection and other library collections...[which is] that of a single resource in meeting user needs."[24] This integration is achieved by a well-written collection development policy for government publications and the adherence to such a policy in the selection process.

Libraries can no longer support comprehensive collections in all levels of government. The development of functional collections and interinstitutional cooperation demand a dynamic decision making role in the selection and acquisition of government publications. Reductions in the budgets of both libraries and governments, the growing tendency of governments to publish in microformats, publishing by commercial publishers, and interinstitutional cooperation are all important factors that influence selection decisions. Resource sharing is an area that has an untapped potential, especially among depository libraries.[25] Quality service is not provided by having all publications but by consciously and systematically developing a collection to meet the needs of the user.

References

1   Charles R. McClure, "An Integrated Approach to Government Publications Collection Development." *Government Publications Review* 8A (1981): 5-15.

2   Peter Hernon and Gary R. Purcell, *Developing Collections of U.S. Government Publications* (Greenwich, Conn.: JAI Press, 1982).

3   Bruce Morton and J. Randolph Cox, "Cooperative Collection Development between Selective U.S. Depository Libraries." *Government Publications Review* 9 (1982): 221-229.

4   United Nations depositories, since 1975, with the exception of one in each country, pay a fee. See Luciana Marulli-Koenig, "Collection Development for United Nations and Documents." In *Collection Development and Public Access of Government Documents, Proceedings of the First Annual Library Government Documents and Information Conference, Boston, 1981*, ed. Peter Hernon (Westport, Conn.: Meckler, 1982), p. 93.

5   The Department of Housing and Urban Development is an example of an agency charging a handling fee based on the number of titles requested. The Department of Defense Directorate for Information Operations and Reports has a set fee for each of its reports and requires prepayment. These defense publications recently became part of the depository program *(Daily Depository Shipping List,* Survey 82-55, 28 December 1982).

6   Ed Herman, "Directory of Government Document Dealers and Jobbers, 1981." *Documents to the People* 9 (1981): 229-234.

7   Robert F. Gaines, "Recent Developments in Depository Systems for State Government Documents." *Documents to the People* 6 (1978): 229-230.

8 David Parish, *State Government Reference Publications: An Annotated Bibliography* (Littleton, Colo.: Libraries Unlimited, 1981).

9 Peter Hernon, "State Reference Sources," *Government Publications Review* 7A (1980): 47-83.

10 Margaret Lane, "Distribution of State Government Publications and Information." *Government Publications Review* 10 (1983): 159-172; David Parish, "Into the 1980's: The Ideal State Documents Reference Collection." *Government Publications Review* 10 (1983): 213-219.

11 Terry L. Weech, "Collection Development and State Publications." *Government Publications Review* 8A (1981): 47-58. See also Margaret Lane's column in *Documents to the People*, "Scattered Notes for State Documents Librarians".

12 *Yearbook of International Organizations* (19th ed. Brussels and Paris: Union of International Associations and International Chamber of Commerce, 1981).

13 Indexes issued by these IGOs include: *UNDOC: Current Index, UNESCO List of Documents and Publications*, and *FAO Documentation: Current Bibliography*.

14 Luciana Marulli-Koenig, "Collection Development for United Nations Documents." *Government Publications Review* 8A (1981): 85-102; Luciana Marulli, *Documentation of the United Nations System* (Metuchen, N.J.: Scarecrow Press, 1979); Peter Hajnal, *Guide to the United Nations Organization, Documentation and Publishing* (Dobbs Ferry, N.Y.: Oceana, 1978); Peter Hajnal, "Collection Development: United Nations Material." *Government Publications Review* 8A (1981): 89-109; Peter Hajnal, "UNESCO Documents and Publications as Research Material: A Preliminary Report." In *Collection Development and Public Access of Government Documents*, pp. 102-133. Also see *International Documents for the 80's: Their Role and Use. Proceedings of the Second World Symposium on International Documentation, Brussels, 1980* (Pleasantville, N.Y.: UNIFO, 1982).

15 UNESCO. Director General, *UNESCO 1979-1980* (Paris: UNESCO, 1983), p. 205.

16 Some UN titles issued cooperatively by commercial publishers include: *World Trade Annual* (Walker), *Economic Bulletin for Europe* (Pergamon), *Proceedings of the World Conference of the International Women's Year, 1975* (UNIFO), *Statistical Journal of the U.N. Economic Commission for Europe* (North-Holland).

17 Peter Hajnal, "IGO Documents and Publications: Volume, Distribution, Recent Developments, and Sources of Information." *Government Publications Review* 9 (1982): 121-130.

18 Theodore Samore, ed., *Acquisitions of Foreign Materials for U.S. Librarians* (2nd ed. Metuchen, N.J.: Scarecrow Press, 1982), p. 113.

19 J.J. Cherns, *Official Publishing: An Overview* (Oxford: Pergamon Press, 1979).

20 Numerous articles have appeared in *Government Publications Review*. Some examples include: Barbara Smith, "British Official Publications: Publications and Distribution." 5 (1978): 1-12; Genevieve Boisard, "Public Access to Government Information: The Position of France." 9 (1982): 203-219; Gloria Westfall, "Access to French Publications." 8A (1981): 161-173; Frances Rose, "Publishing and Information Policies of the Government of Canada: Some Recent Developments." 5 (1978): 391-397. Pergamon Press is issuing a series of "Guides to Official Publications." Some

of the titles published in this series include: Olga B. Bishop, *Canadian Official Publications* (1981); Howard F. Coxon, *Australian Official Publications* (1980); Arthur Malthby and Brian McKenna, *Irish Official Publications* (1980); and Gloria Westfall, *French Official Publications* (1980). Also, *Documents to the People* contains columns on foreign government publications, especially Australian and Canadian publications.

21   Indexes to the Foreign Broadcast Information Service are published by Newsbank. Bell and Howell indexes the Joint Publications Research Service publications in *Transdex*.

22   To locate appropriate institutions, consult the *Directory of Government Documents Collections and Librarians* (3rd ed. Washington, D.C.: Congressional Information Service for the Government Documents Round Table, American Library Association, 1981).

23   Michael Shannon, "Collection Development and Local Documents: History and Present Use in the United States." *Government Publications Review* 8A (1981): 59-87. See also Peter Hernon, ed., *Municipal Government Reference Sources, Publications and Collections* (New York: Bowker, 1978); Yuri Nakata, Susan Smith, and William Ernst, Jr. *Organizing a Local Document Collection* (Chicago, Ill.: American Library Assn. 1979), pp. 3-12.

24   Bernard M. Fry, "Government Publications and the Library." *Government Publications Review* 4 (1977): 115.

25   Hernon and Purcell, *op. cit.,* p.57.

Selection Sources

Administrative Notes. Vol. 1- .Washington, D.C.: Supt. of Documents, 1980- ; irregular.

American Statistics Index. Vol. 1- . Bethesda, Md: Congressional Information Service, 1973- ; monthly.

Bishop, Olga B. *Canadian Official Publications.* Guides to Official Publications. Oxford: Pergamon Press, 1981.

Cherns, J.J. *Official Publishing: An Overview.* Oxford: Pergamon Press, 1979.

Coxon, Howard F. *Australian Official Publications.* Guides to Official Publications. Oxford: Pergamon Press, 1980.

Directory of Government Documents Collections and Librarians. 3rd ed. Washington, D.C.: Congressional Information Service for the Government Documents Round Table, American Library Association, 1981.

Documents to the People. Vol. 1- . Chicago, Ill.: American Library Association, 1972- ; bimonthly.

FAO Documentation: Current Bibliography. Vol. 1- . Rome: Food and Agricultural Organization of the United Nations, 1967- ; bimonthly.

Fry, Bernard M., and Hernon, Peter, eds. *Government Publications: Key Papers.* Guides to Official Publications. Oxford: Pergamon Press, 1981.

Government Publications Review. Vol. 1- . Elmsford, N.Y.: Pergamon Press, 1974- ; bimonthly.

Government Reports and Announcements. Vol. 74- . Springfield, Va.: US National Technical Information Service, 1974- ; biweekly.

Hajnal, Peter. "Collection Development: United Nations Material." *Government Publications Review* 8A (1981): 89-109.

Hajnal, Peter. *Guide to United Nations Organization, Documentation, and Publishing.* Dobbs Ferry, N.Y.: Oceana, 1978.

Hajnal, Peter. "IGO Documents and Publications: Volume, Distribution, Recent Developments and Sources of Information," *Government Publications Review* 9 (1982): 121-130.

Hajnal, Peter. "UNESCO Documents and Publications as Research Material: A Preliminary Report." In *Collection Development and Public Access of Government Documents. Proceedings of the First Annual Library Government Documents and Information Conference, Boston, 1987,* edited by Peter Hernon, 103-113. Westport, Conn.: Meckler, 1982.

Herman, Ed. "Directory of Government Document Dealers and Jobbers, 1981." *Documents to the People* 9 (1981): 229-234.

Hernon, Peter, ed. *Municipal Government Reference Sources, Publications and Collections.* New York: R.R. Bowker, 1978.

Hernon, Peter. "State Reference Sources." *Government Publications Review* 7A (1980): 47-83.

Hernon, Peter, and Purcell, Gary R. *Developing Collections of U.S. Government Publications.* Greenwich, Conn.: JAI Press, 1982.

Index to Current Urban Documents. Vol. 1- . Westport, Conn.: Greenwood Press, 1972- ; quarterly.

International Bibliography: Publications of Intergovernmental Organizations. Vol. 1- . New York: UNIPUB, 1973- ; quarterly.

Lane, Margaret. "Distribution of State Government Publications and Information." *Government Publications Review* 10 (1983): 159-172.

Lane, Margaret. "Scattered Notes for State Documents Librarians." Column in *Documents to the People,* 1981-.

Malthby, Arthur, and McKenna, Brian *Irish Official Publications.* Guides to Official Publications. Oxford: Pergamon Press, 1980.

Marulli, Luciana. *Documentation of the United Nations System.* Metuchen, N.J.: Scarecrow Press, 1979.

Marulli-Koenig, Luciana. "Collection Development for United Nations Documents and Publications." In *Collection Development and Public Access of Government Documents. Proceedings of the First Annual Library Government Documents and Information Conference, Boston, 1981,* edited by Peter Hernon, 85-102. Westport, Conn.: Meckler, 1982.

Marulli-Koenig, Luciana. "International Documents Roundup." Column in *Documents to the People,* 1980-.

Monthly Checklist of State Publications. Vol. 1- .Washington, D.C: Library of Congress, 1910- ; monthly.

Samore, Theodore, ed. *Acquisitions of Foreign Materials for U.S. Libraries.* 2nd ed. Metuchen, N.J.: Scarecrow Press, 1982.

Smith, Barbara, "British Official Publications: Publications and Distribution." *Government Publications Review* 5 (1978): 1-12.

UNDOC: Current Index. Vol. 1- . 1950- . New York: United Nations Publications, 1950- ; ten per year.

UNESCO. Director General. *UNESCO 1979-1980.* Paris: UNESCO, 1983.

UNESCO List of Documents and Publications. Vol. 1- . Paris: UNESCO, 1973- ; quarterly.

Weech, Terry L. "Collection Development and State Publications." *Government Publications Review* 8A (1981): 47-58.

Westfall, Gloria. "Access to French Publications." *Government Publications Review* 8A (1981): 161-173.

Westfall, Gloria. *French Official Publications.* Guides to Official Publications. Oxford: Pergamon Press, 1980.

Yearbook of International Organizations. 19th ed. Brussels: Union of International Associations; Paris: International Chamber of Commerce, 1981.

Further Readings

Boisard, Genevieve. "Public Access to Government Information: The Position of France." *Government Publications Review* 9 (1982): 203-219.

Dimitrov, T.D., ed. *International Documents for the 80's: Their Role and Use. Proceedings of the Second World Symposium on International Documentation, Brussels, 1980.* Pleasantville, N.Y.: UNIFO, 1982.

Fry, Bernard M. "Government Publications and the Library." *Government Publications Review* 4 (1977): 111-117.

Gaines, Robert F. "Recent Developments in Depository Systems for State Government Documents." *Documents to the People* 6 (1978): 229-230.

Marulli-Koenig, Luciana. "Collection Development for United Nations Documents." *Government Publications Review* 8A (1981): 85-102.

McClure, Charles R. "An Integrated Approach to Government Publications Collection Development." *Government Publications Review* 8A (1981): 5-15.

Morton, Bruce, and Cox, J. Randolph. "Cooperative Collection Development between Selective U.S. Depository Libraries." *Government Publications Review* 9 (1982): 221-229.

Nakata, Yuri; Smith, Susan; and Ernst, William, Jr. *Organizing a Local Documents Collection.* Chicago, Ill.: American Library Association, 1979.

Parish, David. "Into the 1980's: The Ideal State Documents Reference Collection." *Government Publications Review* 10 (1983): 213-219.

Parish, David. *State Government Reference Publications: An Annotated Bibliography.* Littleton, Colo.: Libraries Unlimited, 1981.

Rose, Frances. "Publishing and Information Policies of the Government of Canada: Some Recent Developments." *Government Publications Review* 5 (1978): 391-397.

Shannon, Michael. "Collection Development and Local Documents: History and Present Use in the United States." *Government Publications Review* 8A (1981): 59-87.

Beth Macleod, "*Library Journal* and *Choice*: A Review of Reviews." *Journal of Academic Librarianship* 7, 1 (1981): 23-28.

Library Journal and *Choice* enjoy considerable power and influence in the world of book reviewing. The two journals each review more adult books than any other single publication,[1] and they evaluate many scholarly and technical books earlier than the more specialized review sources. Librarians rely heavily upon *Library Journal* and *Choice* when choosing books for purchase, and scholarly publishers have noted a direct relationship between a good *Library Journal* or *Choice* review and sale by library suppliers.[2] Librarians are not the only ones who depend on these reviews; publishers commonly use them in advertising and, in the case of some technical publications, even rely on them to help determine the size of a particular printing.[3] For these reasons the two journals have a decided impact on both the sales of the books reviewed and the availability of these books to library users and the public.

How do the journals exercise this power, and what bases do they offer librarians and publishers for informed decision making? What sorts of criteria do their reviewers consider when evaluating books, and are there significant differences between the reviews in the two journals? In an effort to answer these questions, this article describes and compares the reviewing polices and practices of *Library Journal* and *Choice*. It deals first with the methods by which books are chosen for review, and then with the manner in which each journal chooses its reviewers. Finally, it compares the content of the reviews themselves.

Library Journal

Library Journal reviews books which might be of interest to a wide variety of institutions, from the smallest public library to the largest academic library. According to Janet Fletcher, editor of the book review section, *Library Journal* receives approximately 25,000 to 30,000 books a year, from which about 6000 are chosen for review. This figure is somewhat inflated because it includes, for some titles, both galley proofs[4] and published versions of the same books; nevertheless, it gives a general notion of the volume of books received. This may be compared with an estimated 31,520 books published in the United States in 1978, a figure which includes new editions but excludes children's books, which are received by neither *Library Journal* nor *Choice*.[5] Publishers, both domestic and foreign, send their books to *Library Journal* in hope of a review and thus publicity for their publications.

In the process of determining which 6000 of the 25,000 books will be reviewed, certain types of publications are automatically eliminated, such as textbooks, reprints, and books in languages other than English. Those that remain are then examined by one of *Library Journal's* four full-time subject editors, who may at this time send them to reviewers. Books rejected by the subject editors are examined by Janet Fletcher who either agrees or discusses with the subject editor her reasons for reconsidering the book in question. Each book is thus examined by at least two people before a decision not to review is made. Clearly this process requires summary decision making by the editors, as each must pass judgment upon several thousand books a year.

Reviewers for *Library Journal* are librarians, teaching faculty members, and, occasionally, professionals in other fields such as law or medicine. Most originally volunteer their services, some in response to occasional requests appearing in the journal's book review section. They complete a questionnaire listing their academic qualifications, professional experience, and the subjects in which they feel competent to make judgments. The payment for reviewing is a copy of the book reviewed. Turnover of reviewers is difficult to measure; some do not remain for long, but more often a reviewer stays with the job for several years. *Library Journal* reviews are signed, which means that the reviewer is identified at the end of each review by name and institutional affiliation.

Choice

Choice defines its reviewing goals more narrowly, confining its reviews to books of potential value for undergraduate libraries. The intention is to review books which would support an undergraduate curriculum. The journal receives about 18,000 to 20,000 books annually, also sent by publishers who hope for the exposure a review brings. Sometimes a publisher does not send the book itself, but instead a list of recent publications, from which an editor at *Choice* picks the books he or she would like to consider. *Choice* reviews only from the published copy, never from galley proofs. Louise Lockwood, associate editor of *Choice,* says the journal recently polled reviewers regarding their willingness to review from galleys but the reviewers preferred not to, since the proof copy generally lacks the index, plates, and sometimes other features worth examining. The price *Choice* pays for this decision is time - a journal that reviews from galleys can often publish a review just before a book's publication date or at the time of distribution. Thus, of books reviewed by both publications, reviews in *Choice* generally appear several months later than those in *Library Journal*.

The process of elimination at *Choice* is similar to that at *Library Journal*. Prime candidates for automatic exclusion are textbooks, revised editions which have not been substantially changed, collections of readings, and books judged too technical for even the most advanced undergraduate. In the past, the editor of *Choice* did a preliminary examination of the books received and then distributed then, with his decisions, to one of four subject editors who later discussed with him any differences of opinion. This policy has recently been changed so that the subject editors, rather than the main editor, are more often the first to pass judgment. No matter who sees it first, every book is examined by both the general editor and a subject editor. If there is a difference of opinion, a third view may be sought from a reviewer in the subject area. According to Lockwood, the general editor and the subject editor seldom disagree, so that only a few out of every hundred books require discussion. Disagreements, when they do arise, most often involve the question of whether a book is too advanced for an undergraduate audience. Again, as at *Library Journal*, the volume of books involved demands fairly summary decision making on the part of the editors.

Choice reviewers are "faculty members currently or formerly engaged in undergraduate teaching at academic institutions throughout the United States and Canada."[6] Most have PhDs in the subject field in which they review; the only section reviewed primarily by librarians is reference. Lockwood says that the teaching requirement for reviewers is being further refined to exclude faculty members teaching primarily graduate students, since *Choice* editors feel it is extremely important that their reviewers be college teachers at the undergraduate level.

Reviewers were originally chosen by university librarians who identified faculty members with an expressed interest in library acquisitions. As the journal grew, strong reviewers were asked to recommend colleagues. The smallest group are those who wrote *Choice* asking to be reviewers. Although the reviews are unsigned, a list of "consultants" appears at the end of each issue. This list provides the name, institutional affiliation and subject area of each contributor, but it is not possible to match reviewer and review.

Lockwood says the staff at *Choice* periodically discuss the pros and cons of unsigned reviews, but offers two primary reasons for leaving them unsigned. First, stylistic changes can be made without the reviewer's approval, thereby speeding the publication of reviews. Second, greater freedom of expression is allowed academics, especially young ones, who might feel reluctant to criticize a book by an author prominent in the field. She says that *Choice* feels reviewers are more objective when reviews are unsigned. Turnover of reviewers is similar to that at *Library Journal* and, also as at *Library Journal*, the payment for reviewing is a copy of the book reviewed.

Content of Reviews

In order to evaluate the content of the reviews themselves, it was necessary to devise a method by which they could be systematically compared. A set of criteria was formulated which might constitute an "ideal" review, and 2600 reviews - 1300 from each publication - were evaluated in the light of these criteria.[7] The 2600 reviews were randomly selected from *Library Journal* and *Choice* issues published in 1978. Each review was coded for subject of book, type of publisher, and sex of author; for *Library Journal*, the reviewer's sex and institutional affiliation were recorded. The content of each review was examined to determine, when appropriate, whether the reviewers commented on each of the following: the author, thesis, quality of writing, research, editing, nature of sources, depth of treatment, unique features of the book, and the book's value compared to others in its field. For fiction, comments on qualify of plot and characterization were noted. Finally, the reviewer's recommendation for or against purchase was recorded, as well as the type of library for which a book was recommended.

First, how did the two journals compare with regard to publishers and subject areas of the books chosen for review? Predictably, *Choice's* selections were somewhat more scholarly, although the differences when measured in broad categories were modest. Thus, 32 percent of *Choice's* books came from university presses, compared to only 19 percent of *Library Journal's* books (see Table 1). But a majority of the books reviewed by both journals were published by commercial presses - 65 percent of those in *Choice* and 81 percent of those in *Library Journal*. Neither journal reviewed many books published by organizations or by governmental agencies, although *Choice* covered a few more than *Library Journal*. Only 2 percent of the *Choice* books and 1 percent of the *Library Journal* books were published by organizations, such as the American Management Association; only 3 percent of the *Choice* books and .2 percent of the *Library Journal* books were published by governmental agencies.

Table 1. Percentage of Books Reviewed - By Publishers

Type of Publisher	*Library Journal*	*Choice*
University press	18	32
Commercial press	81	65
Private organization	1	2
Government agency	0	0
Totals	100	99*

*Total affected by rounding error.

Table 2. Percentage of Books Reviewed - By Subject

Subject	*Library Journal*	*Choice*
Social Science	43	42
Science	10	18
Humanities (excluding fiction)	28	37
Fiction	14	1.5
General reference	3	1.5
Other	2	0
Totals	100	100

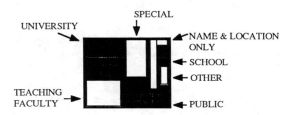

Table 3. Percentage of Library Journal Reviewers - By Occupation

Public librarian	24
University librarian	25
Special librarian	15
School librarian	2
Teaching faculty	25
Name and geographical location only	7
Other occupation	3
Total	101*

*Total affected by rounding error.

The broad difference between the two journals with regard to the subjects of books reviewed was modest and attributable in part to *Library Journal's* more extensive reviewing of fiction. A higher proportion of *Choice* books was in science (18 percent compared to 10 percent in *Library Journal*) and the humanities (37 percent compared with 28 percent in *Library Journal*) (see Table 2). There was little difference in the social sciences, as 42 percent of the *Choice* books fell into this category compared to 43 percent of *Library Journal* books. Only 1.5 percent of *Choice* books were in general reference,[8] compared to 3 percent in *Library Journal*. The big difference came in fiction, which accounted for 14 percent of *Library Journal's* reviews but only 1.5 percent of those in *Choice*. The literature bibliographer in an undergraduate library must look somewhere other than *Choice* for reviews of current fiction.

As was noted earlier, reviewers for *Choice* are primarily teaching faculty; *Library Journal* reviewers have more diverse backgrounds. In this study, most of the *Library Journal* reviewers (66 percent) were librarians, and the next largest group (25 percent), were teaching faculty at various colleges and universities (see Table 3). Seven percent were identified by name and geographical location only,[9] and the remaining 3 percent were in other occupations ranging from lawyer to clock-shop owner. Of the librarians, most worked in public or academic libraries, 37 percent and 38 percent respectively. The next largest group (22 percent) were special librarians and the remaining 3 percent school librarians. Because of *Choice's* policy of reviewer anonymity, comparable statistics for *Choice* were unavailable, but the consultant lists at the end of each issue show the reviewers to be academic specialists.

The fact that *Library Journal* relies heavily on reviewers who are librarians, whereas *Choice* uses college teachers, raises the question of whether these two groups produce different kinds of reviews. Is the college teacher reviewing for *Choice* more likely to consider certain criteria than the librarian who reviews for *Library Journal*? Is the public librarian who reviews for *Library Journal* likely to be less rigorous than his or her academic counterpart at *Choice*? In short, do academics and librarians review in different ways?

A comparison of the content of *Library Journal* and *Choice* reviews shows that in some areas there was relatively little difference between the two journals. For example, reviewers from both journals differed by less than 5 percent in the frequency with which they commented on the quality of writing, the nature of sources used, and the depth of treatment given a particular subject (see Table 4). On the other hand, a higher percentage of *Choice* reviewers did identify the author or mention other words by that person. More *Choice* reviewers also commented on the quality of editing and the quality of research.

This did not mean, however, that *Choice* reviewers were more likely to be critical in a negative sense. Indeed, their comments were more often positive than negative. For example, although *Choice* reviewers mentioned the quality of research in 52 percent of the reviews where this was appropriate, more than two-thirds of these comments involved praise and less than one-third expressed criticism.

No clear pattern emerged in the two journals regarding the content of reviews. *Library Journal* reviewers were somewhat more likely to criticize their books for bad writing or shallowness, while *Choice* reviewers complained more frequently of poor editing.[10] Surprisingly, perhaps, disagreement with an author's thesis was slightly more common in *Library Journal* reviews than in *Choice*. The *Choice* reviewer expressed disagreement or mixed judgement in only 5 percent of the reviews, compared with 7 percent in *Library Journal*. Neither percentage is high, of course, nor is the difference very significant. But since the freedom to be critical and disagree with an author's work is one of *Choice's* rationales for unsigned reviews, it is noteworthy that so few *Choice* reviewers actually took the opportunity to express negative views. Overall, indeed, there was relatively little difference between *Library Journal's* reviewers and those for *Choice* in terms of their generosity with praise or blame.

Another important element of a review for purposes of book selection is the identification of unique features which distinguish a new book from those already available on the subject. Reviewers for *Choice* were considerably more likely to provide this than reviewers for *Library Journal*. Forty-two percent of the *Choice* reviews cited one or more unique features, while only 22 percent did so in *Library Journal*.[11] Only a small percentage of the reviewers (8 percent in *Choice* and 5 percent in *Library Journal*) stated outright that the book under review added nothing to the already existing literature. This could mean either that *Library Journal* and *Choice* do succeed in reviewing the significant books, or that reviewers are lax, reluctant, or unable to identify books which offer nothing new.

Table 4. Content of Reviews - By Type of Comment*
(all figures are percentages)

	Library Journal	Choice		Library Journal	Choice
COMMENTS ON AUTHOR &/OR AUTHOR'S WORKS			**COMMENTS ON UNIQUENESS OF BOOK**		
No mention	62	49	No mention	73	51
Mention	38	51	Mentions unique		
			features	22	42
Totals	100	100	Says no unique		
			features	5	7
COMMENTS ON QUALITY OF EDITING			Totals	100	100
No mention	91	73			
Criticized	3	10	**COMMENTS ON QUALITY OF RESEARCH**		
Praised	6	17	No mention	64	48
			Criticized	13	15
Totals	100	100	Praised	23	37
COMMENTS ON QUALITY OF WRITING			Totals	100	100
No mention	53	52			
Criticized	19	13	**COMMENTS ON THESIS**		
Praised	28	35	Does not state thesis	62	65
			States thesis and		
Totals	100	100	agrees	1	1
			States thesis and		
COMMENTS ON DEPTH OF TREATMENT			disagrees or ex-		
No mention	68	73	presses mixed		
Criticized as			judgment	7	5
shallow	22	16	States thesis and is		
Praised for depth	10	11	noncommittal	30	28
Totals	100	100	Totals	100	100
COMMENTS ON NATURE OF SOURCES			*Percentages in each section include only reviews		
No mention	56	61	for which the criterion in question is appropriate.		
Mention	44	39			
Totals	100	100			

Choice states that one of its greatest services lies in "briefly comparing a new title to earlier titles in the field."[12] *Choice* reviewers were indeed more likely to do this than those in *Library Journal*, though neither publication did so in even half its reviews. In only 25 percent of *Choice* reviews and 11 percent of those in *Library Journal* was the book compared to one or more specific titles (see Table 5). Another 14 percent of the *Choice* reviews and 15 percent of those in *Library Journal* discussed the book in the context of the literature of the subject as a whole. But 55 percent of the *Choice* reviews and fully 70 percent of *Library Journal* ones compared the book neither to another book not to the literature in general. One should also note that only 4 percent of the reviews in either *Choice* or *Library Journal* recommended another book instead of the one being reviewed. This suggests a somewhat uncritical attitude if it implies that reviewers judge more than 96 percent of the books reviewed in the two journals to be as good as or better than anything previously published.

Table 5. Percentage of Books Recommended for Purchase - By Type of Library

	Library Journal	*Choice*
Not recommended	9	6
Noncommittal	17	12
Recommended (directly or by implication) without further qualification	51	32
Recommended for public libraries	4	1
Recommended for academic libraries	4	26
Recommended for public and academic libraries	4	4
Recommended for large libraries	4	1
Recommended for special libraries or special collections	8	6
Recommended for graduate libraries	0	12
Totals	101*	100

*Total due to rounding error.

When it came to recommending books for purchase, reviewers for both journals were equally generous. Only 6 percent of the books reviewed in *Choice* and 9 percent of those in *Library Journal* were given negative recommendations. Reviewers equivocated on 12 percent of the *Choice* books and 17 percent of those in *Library Journal*. The remaining titles (82 percent in *Choice* and 74 percent in *Library Journal*) were either recommended without qualification or were recommended for a specific type of library.

This high percentage of recommended books suggests an important conclusion about the function of reviews. For most books, simply getting reviewed is the main hurdle. This point has been recognized by publishers, who generally feel that exposure in the form of a review can be more important than what that review actually says.[13] In *Library Journal* and *Choice*, moreover, such exposure is most often laudatory. Thus the main task of negative selection - of determining what books librarians should not buy - is done not by the reviewers but rather by the editors in the process of choosing which books should be reviewed. Selection for review amounts in effect to a qualified endorsement by the editors. The fact that 90 percent of the books receiving negative reviews in each journal were not even reviewed by the other suggests that this system works. The purpose of a review, then, is less to determine whether any libraries should buy a given book than which libraries should buy it. In this context it is significant that 50 percent of the *Choice* reviews and 24 percent of the *Library Journal* reviews contained a recommendation for a specific type of library.

The high percentage of books recommended for purchase by *Choice* reviewers also calls into question one of that journal's principal reasons for leaving reviews unsigned - the freedom it allows reviewers to voice criticism of colleagues' books. It is possible that a more significant result of the omission of reviewers' names and institutional affiliations is the air of impersonal authority it lends to the opinions expressed. No matter how competent the review, it would possibly carry less weight if followed by the name of an unknown academic from an obscure institution. This could contribute to the tendency of many librarians to regard reviews in *Choice* more reverentially than those in *Library Journal*, an impression perhaps not wholly justified.

Other Comparisons

Because the sex and institutional affiliation of *Library Journal* reviewers were known, it was possible to investigate whether these factors appeared to affect the content of reviews. Since the author's sex was known for books reviewed in both journals, it was also possible to see whether reviewers judged works by women more harshly than those by men or vice versa.

In general, reviews by men differed little from those by women. One sex was no more likely than the other, for example, to discuss the quality of characterization, to compare a book to others, or to comment on the quality of writing or research. Men and women did not differ in their tendency to recommend that a book be purchased. In only one area was there a difference between the sexes and this was with regard to the subjects of the book reviewed. More men reviewed books in the social sciences (63 percent of the reviewers were male), and in the humanities (66 percent of the reviewers were men). More women reviewed in the sciences and fiction, as 64 percent of the reviewers in both categories were women.

Similarly, the reviewers' backgrounds seemed to have little effect on the content of reviews. Librarians of all types, college teachers, and reviewers in other occupations commented with similar frequency on aspects of the books such as depth, quality of writing, and quality of research. Public, university, special and school librarians were just as likely (or unlikely) as college teachers to compare a book to others or to recommend that it be purchased. College teachers were slightly more likely to mention quality of research, where this was an issue, than were university librarians, but they were also more likely to praise the research. Just as *Choice* reviewers, who were all academic specialists, did not review very differently from *Library Journal* reviewers, who came from diverse backgrounds, so, within the context of *Library Journal*, academics did not review very differently from librarians.

Likewise, the sex of the authors of the books had little impact on the content of the reviews, with one intriguing exception: reviewers in both journals were slightly more likely to criticize a book by a women for its shallowness, and to praise a book by a man for its depth.[14] Readers may suspect that this difference arose because more of the books by women authors were novels and many popular novels invite a charge of shallowness. But this difference held true when works of nonfiction were considered separately. Furthermore, books by women were slightly more likely to be labelled shallow by female than by male reviewers.

Sex did have one odd effect on reviewing in *Library Journal*. The editors tended very strongly to assign books to reviewers of the same sex as the author. Of the *Library Journal* books written by men, 65 percent were reviewed by men, whereas 74 percent of the books written by women were reviewed by women. Unsigned reviews made it impossible to determine if this pattern also existed in *Choice*.

Conclusion

What conclusions may be drawn from this study? First, the high percentage of positive reviews in both journals suggests that it is not the reviewers who make the hard decisions, but instead the editors in the process of choosing which books will be reviewed. Thus a small group of people hastily pass judgement on literally thousands of books. Under this system there is some chance that worthy books will go unreviewed.

Next, there seems to be little evidence that *Choice* reviews are more substantive or critical than those in *Library Journal*, nor is there much evidence revealing a qualitative difference between reviews by college teachers and those by librarians. This holds true both for comparisons of *Library Journal* and *Choice* reviews, and comparisons of *Library Journal* reviews by college teachers with *Library Journal* reviews by librarians.

In addition, contrary to *Choice's* premise, reviewer anonymity does not appear to make for more critical reviews. There was little difference in the frequency of critical comment between the signed reviews in *Library Journal* and the unsigned reviews in the positive tone of most of the reviews, and the broad similarity of reviewing styles in the two journals.

Acknowledgements

I would like to thank David Macleod of the Central Michigan University Department of History for his encouragement, support, and help in conceptualizing this project in statistical terms.

References

1   *The Bowker Annual of Library and Book Trade Information* (New York: R.R. Bowker, 1979), p. 331.

2   Abbot Friedland, "Reviews: Who Needs Them?" American Library Association Conference, Chicago, July 1976.

3   *Ibid.*

4   Galley-proof: a prepublication printing on which the author and publisher may make corrections.

5   *Bowker Annual*, p. 322.

6   *Choice* (July/August 1978): 634.

7   More specifically, I devised a codebook with 21 variables, each consisting either of one element of the bibliographical data for the books under review, or of one aspect of the books on which reviewers might comment. Price could be recorded directly and other bibliographic variables were easily coded numerically (e.g., sex of author, male = 1; female = 2; unclear or missing = 3). For variables dealing with reviewers' comments, I assigned a numerical value to each possible kind of comment. For example, variable 15 was the reviewer's comparison (or lack of comparison) of the book under review to other books. If the reviewer made no comparison, variable 15 was to be coded 0; if the reviewer compared the book to other writing on the subject but not to specific titles, variable 15 was to be coded 1; if the reviewer compared the book to specific titles, variable 15 was to be coded 2. After I had actually coded all 2600 reviews on all applicable variables, I used the university's computer services to tabulate comparisons of reviews in the two journals and to cross-tabulate variables using SPSS (Statistical Package for the Social Sciences).

8   The category "reference" was used only when a book could not be placed in a specific subject area, such as an almanac or general one-volume encyclopedia.

9   Reviewers identified by name and geographical location are generally librarians working in some other capacity, people with MLS degrees who are (temporarily) unemployed, or freelance writers. Carol Rasmussen, a subject editor at *Library Journal,* says that the identification of these reviewers is gradually being changed to more clearly reflect the person's background, such as "Jane Jones, MLS, New York, N.Y.".

10   At this point, the reader may protest that *Library Journal* probably reviews more books which are in fact shallow and badly written, since more of its books come from commercial presses, and that this accounts for the less critical tone of *Choice* reviews. In order to test the validity of these objections, the author separately compared *Library Journal's* reviews of university press books with *Choice's* reviews of university press books, and *Library Journal's* reviews of commercial press books with *Choice's* reviews of commercial press books. The differences and similarities between the two journals remained much the same.

11   As described in the previous footnote, these differences remained much the same for both commercial press and university press books from each journal.

12   *Choice* (July/August 1978): 634.

13   Allan Lang, "Reviews: Who Needs Them?" American Library Association Conference, Chicago, July, 1976.

14   Seventeen percent of books by men were criticized as shallow compared to 25 percent of those by women. Eleven percent of books by men were praised for depth compared to 10 percent of those by women.

CHAPTER 8

THE MAJOR SELECTION RESOURCES

This chapter lists in alphabetical order all those works mentioned in Chapter 7 and is intended to be used solely as a bibliographical guide to those works; a few other related items, not mentioned in Chapter 7, are also included. The details shown are those judged to be of interest to librarians as stock selectors and are not intended to be exhaustive.

American Book Publishing Record (New York: R.R. Bowker, 1960-)

This cumulates information given in *Publishers' Weekly* and since 1974 in the *Weekly Record*, which is used as a basis for *American Book Publishing Record*. Since 1965 there have been annual cumulations. A form of Dewey Decimal Classification is used, but there are separate lists of material which it is hard to fit into that scheme. There is also an author/title index, five-year and various other forms of cumulations. There were around 38,000 titles listed in the 1983 annual cumulation.

American Historical Association's Guide to Historical Literature. Edited by George F. Howe *et al.* (2nd ed. New York: Macmillan, 1961)

This supersedes the first edition of 1931, and is a " ...selective annotated bibliography of treatises and source material", that is, of both primary and secondary material. It is arranged in broad subject groups, with a sub-arrangement of material by form within the subject groups. It uses its own classification scheme, which is quite detailed. While the material is quite dated, it is an essential tool for the establishment of the value of individual titles.

Australian Books: A Select List of Recent Publications and Standard Works in Print (Canberra: National Library of Australia, 1987-)

This work began life in 1933 under a different title, and is a current reference and reading list of works dealing with Australia and of Australian authorship. The introduction does not disclose who does the selection, or what the criteria for selection are. It is classed broadly by subject.

Australian Books in Print (Melbourne: D.W. Thorpe, 1956-)

The annual volume, derived from entries in *Australian Bookseller and Publisher*, is available in one cased volume, or monthly listings are available in microfiche. The information is also included in the online service, Booknet. The listings are not exhaustive, as the editors rely on the information supplied to them by individual publishers. There is a subject guide available, *Australian Books in Print by Subject*.

Australian Books in Print by Subject (2nd. ed. Melbourne: D.W. Thorpe, 1987)

This publication is to be an annual, with the first edition having appeared in 1986. It was derived from entries in *Australian Books in Print*, and is arranged according to subject headings supplied for the individual titles by the publishers. The headings were arrived at from a survey in which publishers advised "...their preferred subject classifications". There are eighty such subject headings, very general in nature.

Australian Bookseller and Publisher (Melbourne: D.W. Thorpe, 1921-)

This is a monthly commercial journal, and carries a significant amount of advertising from publishers. The September 1987 issue was eighty-two pages in length and carried news and some "newsy" articles as well as the advertisements. There are lists of current and proposed titles, from which the annual, *Australian Books in Print*, is derived. The entries could be considered reliable indicators of subject matter, but not necessarily of quality. Entered under both author and title, they are heavily abbreviated but carry enough information for the book selector. The information is supplied by the individual publishers, which means that the editors are completely reliant on them for the accuracy, and indeed for the existence, of the information. The coverage is restricted to (1) books published in Australia, (2) books by Australian authors published overseas, and (3) books about Australia published overseas.

Australian Government Publications (Canberra: National Library of Australia, 1956-)

This publication went through a change of name in 1971, and lists printed material issued by the agencies of the Commonwealth, State and Territorial governments. It excludes non-print material, the publications of educational institutions, but otherwise is quite inclusive. It is issued monthly, with cumulations and an annual cumulation.

Australian National Bibliography (Canberra: National Library of Australia, 1961-)

Cited as *ANB*, this appears monthly with annual cumulations and four-monthly cumulations on fiche. It lists books and pamphlets published within the current year and the preceding two years, with details taken from deposit copies lodged with the National Library of Australia. It includes music, overseas publications with Australian content and government publications, but omits acts, bills and ordinances; It also omits standards and small pamphlets (fewer than five pages) unless they form part of a series. It is in three parts, a section classified by Dewey Decimal Classification, an author/title/series index, and a subject index, which uses Library of Congress subject headings. This is the official and thoroughly reliable record of Australian publications, and includes all information necessary for ordering.

Australian National Bibliography, 1901-1950 (Canberra: National Library of Australia, 1988).

This four-volume work is aimed at filling what is known to bibliographers as the "Ferguson gap", the period between the ending of the coverage of Ferguson's *Bibliography of Australia*, in 1900, and the beginning of the precursors to *Australian National Bibliography*, in 1950. Approximately 50,000 works have been listed in detail, with information taken from the National Bibliographic Database. As with all compilations of this nature, some classes of material have been omitted, but the result is nevertheless a major work which possibly provides Australia with a printed bibliography that equals the catalogues of the Library of Congress and the British Library in the coverage of its chosen field. Some care will need to be taken with it, as the fact that about 20 per cent of the entries were supplied by libraries other than the National Library of Australia could mean some inconsistency in detailed descriptions.

Book Review Digest (New York: H.W. Wilson Company, 1905-)

One of the best-known of the first type of guides to book reviews, it displays all the faults of the type. It has a United States of America bias (which while not a "fault" lessens its usefulness in other countries); it covers only a small number of journals; the 1987 annual issue listed eighty-five journals, of which three were Canadian and five were British, the rest being from the United States. There are ten issues per year, with various forms of cumulations over the years of its existence. Currently there are four cumulations each year, the fourth being the bound annual. In the order of 6000 titles are included each year, mainly with a public library orientation. As with all such publications, care must be taken with the list of exclusions: government publications, textbooks, technical, science and law are omitted, but general science is included. The various permutations of number of reviews needed before a work can be included need consideration. Children's books need three reviews; non-fiction need two; adult fiction needs four; and some reference books need only one. The reviews must have appeared in the eighteen months after publication of the book, and at least one must be from a United States or Canadian journal. Full bibliographical details of the books are shown, with brief descriptive notes and some limited excerpts from the reviews. The arrangement is the normal dictionary order, with Dewey Decimal Classification numbers and Sears *List of Subject Headings* used. A four-volume author/title index was issued in 1976.

Book Review Index (Detroit, Mich.: Gale Research Company, 1965-)

This differs from the "digest" form, as represented by *Book Review Digest*; it is a bi-monthly with cumulations of various sorts ending in a bound annual volume. The 1986 annual volume contained about 114,000 review citations of about 63,000 books and periodicals (slightly fewer than in 1984, when 128,000 reviews of 68,000 different titles were listed), the citations coming from 460 different journals, including some newspapers. This is obviously a vastly greater coverage than is possible from works in the form of digests. Included are all publications over fifty pages in length reviewed in the selected sources, with children's books and poetry excepted from this length limitation. The publishers make regular changes in their definitions to accommodate changing demands, so it is necessary for the selector to be aware of what is current at any time. There was a master cumulation 1965-1984 issued in ten volumes in 1985.

Books in Print (New York: R.R. Bowker, 1948-)

This was originally an author-title index to *The Publishers' Trade List Annual*, but now includes material not in that work, and has a subject guide, called *Subject Guide to Books in Print*. It is also available (in various forms) in microfiche and on computer files. The 1986-1987 issue comprised (1) three volumes of authors, (2) three volumes of titles, (3) one volume of publishers, (4) four volumes of subject index, and (5) a two-volume supplement.

Bookseller (London: J. Whitaker, 1858-)

This is a weekly, with monthly then annual cumulations, and in its earlier days carried the subtitle "The Organ of the Book Trade". It now consists mainly of advertising, but does include author and title listings in a list called "Publications of the Week", which is itself cumulated as *Whitaker's Books of the Month and Books to Come*. These entries form the basis of *Whitaker's Cumulative Book List*, and all subsequently appear in *British Books in Print*, which is available on fiche and also bound in four volumes. The entries are grouped into broad subject classes, and provide all the detail necessary for ordering.

British Book News (London: The British Council, 1940-)

This is restricted to British publications, and recent issues carry in the order of 190-200 reviews; the November 1986 issue contained reviews of 190 titles, plus its usual listing of recent best books, this one being on "British Pop and Rock". The reviews are signed, although there is no identification beyond the signature, and the reviews all carry the necessary detail for ordering. There is also a small section on periodicals, and a small news section. Dewey Decimal Classification is used, with the numbers taken from the British Library's CIP data. The work is also available on microfiche and microfilm.

British Books in Print (London: J. Whitaker, 1874-)

This began as a collection of publishers' catalogues, and from the 1930s has been a listing in two sequences, author and title. It has undergone several changes of title, and has been produced by computer since the early 1970s. Details include author, title, editor, reviser, publication date or the date of the latest edition, size, pages, various details of the format, price and ISBN - in fact, all that is needed for ordering. The 1988 edition includes 450,000 titles and a directory of 13,000 publishers in its 8500 pages, which are spread over four volumes.

British National Bibliography (London: Council of the British National Bibliography, 1950-)

Cited as *BNB*, this is the official and thoroughly reliable listing of all publications received by the Copyright Receipt Office of the British Library. It is a subject catalogue, arranged according to the Dewey Decimal Classification, and catalogued according to the Anglo-American Rules, and lists and describes every new work published in the United Kingdom, with the usual list of classes not included. The entries show series details as well as the full imprint for each work, and include the International Standard Book Number, as well as its own *BNB* number. There is an author/title index and a subject index, which are excellent examples of their genre. It is published weekly, with various cumulations, including an annual cumulation.

Canadian Books in Print: Author and Title Index, 1967- (Toronto: University of Toronto Press, 1967-)

This annual publication comprises a listing of English language books, and of French language books issued by publishers who normally publish only English language books. Since 1980 it has been supplemented by three complete and up-to-date microfiche editions each year. The subject approach is through *Canadian Books in Print: Subject Index.*

Canadian Books in Print: Subject Index, 1976- (Toronto: University of Toronto Press, 1976-)

This is an annual which offers access by subject to works included in *Canadian Books in Print: Author and Title Index.*

Canadian Catalogue of Books, Published in Canada, as well as Those Written by Canadians, with Imprint 1921-1949 (2 vols. Toronto: Toronto Public Library, 1959)

This is a reprint of the English language sections of annual lists issued by Toronto public libraries, re-issued in 1959 in two volumes, Volume 1 covering 1921-1939, Volume 2 covering 1940-1949. It was succeeded by *Canadiana* from 1951.

Canadian Publishers' Directory (Toronto: Key Publishing, 1935-)

Issued twice per year, this is a supplement to *Quill and Quire,* the Canadian book-trade journal, and lists the usual commercial details of publishers in Canada.

Canadiana (Ottawa: National Library of Canada, 1951-)

This monthly publication took over the listing of Canadian works previously covered by *Canadian Catalogue of Books.* It is cumulated annually, with annual indexes to each of its constituent parts until 1968, after which each annual index covers all six parts.

Choice (Middletown, Conn.: Association of College and Research Libraries, 1964-)

This is an excellent tool for all but the smallest public libraries because of the great variety of American colleges for which it was designed. The reviews are short, authoritative and signed, and each issue has a long article devoted to the bibliography of a particular subject area, the July/August 1988 issue carrying a bibliographic essay on writings on American education, 1955-1985. There are separate sections for periodicals and non-print material, and the whole work is arranged in classified form, with cumulative indexes. There are about 600 titles reviewed each month, and while it is said to be restricted to "scholarly and academic" books, it is difficult to imagine a library with any pretensions to adequacy that would not benefit from using this tool. The bibliographic essays are designed to help librarians and faculty "...assemble the published work in an established, new or emerging discipline to develop library collections...."

Cumulative Book Index (New York: H.W. Wilson, 1898-)

This work was first published in 1898, and was kept up-to-date by a series of supplements to the fourth edition, published in 1928, which appeared every four or five years. It has been issued in various numbers of volumes and cumulations, but since 1969 has been an annual and now appears in eleven monthly issues, with the bound annual cumulation. It purports to list all books published in English in the United States of America and Canada, and a selection of those published elsewhere, and one should note its subtitle, *A World List of Books in the English Language*. It is arranged in what is recognized as a "standard H.W. Wilson" arrangement, the dictionary form, with entries for authors, titles and subjects interfiled in one alphabetical order. The omissions, which include government documents, periodicals, editions limited to fewer than 500 copies, privately published genealogy, local directories, prospectuses, tracts, tests, propaganda, maps, sheet music, cheap paperbacks and ephemera, must be noted. Generally (but not always) all necessary detail is provided, but because some entries are based on information provided by the publishers, it cannot be regarded as bibliographically precise.

English Historical Review (London: Longman, 1886-)

This is an academic journal, which includes book reviews as part of its service to its subject area. Its apportioning of space for reviews is quite generous, with about 50 per cent being used for book reviews in one form or another, but nevertheless it also seems to be devoting less space than it did in previous years. In the January 1977 issue, for example, eighty-nine books were reviewed, but by the April 1988 issue that number had dropped to reviews of thirty-five books and sixty short notices (which, however, are themselves often longer and more substantial than are the regular reviews in some other publications). There were also nine pages of "other publications", listing around 150-160 titles. This must be regarded as an invaluable and indispensable selection tool in its subject area.

Ferguson, J.A. *Bibliography of Australia* (8 vols. Canberra: National Library of Australia, 1975-1986)

This work was published originally by Angus and Robertson in seven volumes from 1941 to 1969, and was reprinted in facsimile by the National Library of Australia from 1975 to 1986; the eighth volume was added in 1986 and comprises a set of addenda to the first four volumes, which cover the years 1784-1850. It aims at listing all works published outside Australia relating to Australia, as well as works published in Australia during the period. When Ferguson began this work, he intended to include all material, but after Volume 4 it was accepted that the aim of "total coverage" was no longer within the realms of possibility, and certain classes of material are specifically excluded from Volumes 5, 6 and 7. Even so, the selector must take into account the various types of material not included even in the first four volumes, as maps, charts and prints were excluded unless they were issued in book form, and articles or papers appearing in periodicals were omitted unless they were subsequently published separately.

Fiction Catalog. Edited by Juliette Yaakov. (11th ed. New York: H.W. Wilson Company, 1986)

The first edition of this work was produced in 1908, and its basic design has not changed markedly since then, with the main volume being kept up-to-date by annual supplements of around 500-600 volumes until the next edition is made available. The book lists those works of fiction recommended for selection by public libraries, and features annotations and analytical entries, sometimes including excerpts from relevant reviews, the works for listing being chosen by consultant librarians. This work is unusual for H.W. Wilson publications in that it is not arranged in their normal dictionary form, but comprises two sections, the first arranged alphabetically by author with the full bibliographical details and the second a title/subject index. An interesting point about the 1986 edition is that around 2000 of the 5000 titles are out of print.

Index to Book Reviews in the Humanities (Williamstown, Mich.: Thomson, 1960-)

This annual has made several changes in its definition of "humanities" over the years of its existence, and currently has a fairly restricted definition. It does include some foreign language material.

International Books in Print, 1987: English Language Titles Published outside the United States and the United Kingdom (6th ed. 2 vols. Munich: K.G. Saur, 1986)

First published in 1979, this work lists over 160,000 books published in English outside the United Kingdom and the United States. A separate listing shows details of the more than 6000 publishers who supply the information. As in all earlier editions, they have relied on responses from specific requests, but it would appear that publishers are now responding without a great deal of prompting, and the completeness of coverage should improve. Included are monograph fiction and non-fiction, microforms and other non-book material, and non-trade publications. The "...tendency is to exclude publications of less than 50 pages...", so some pamphlets and ephemera may well be missed. Specifically excluded are magazines and journals, schoolbooks, teaching aids, maps, posters, puzzle books, calendars, popular guide books and music scores. Various new features added to the later editions make it essential that the selector keeps up-to-date on the techniques needed to get maximum value from this volume.

International Information: Documents, Publications, and Information Systems of International Governmental Organizations. Edited by Peter I. Hajnal (Englewood, Colo.: Libraries Unlimited, 1988)

This is a collection of ten chapters, each one concentrating on a separate aspect of the information dissemination systems that are needed to make available to the public the confusing mass of publications issued in various formats by international bodies other than the various government publishing offices. Its wealth of detail and its focus will certainly make it an essential desk-book for stock selectors.

Irregular Serials and Annuals: An International Directory (13th ed. New York: R.R. Bowker, 1987)

Designed to provide information on serials and continuations such as proceedings and transactions of various societies, yearbooks, handbooks and annual reviews, this compilation contains information on over 34,000 serials. Again the librarian must note the exclusions, items mainly administrative in content, and the criteria for selection, which cover material issued annually or less frequently, irregular publications or publications which have been issued at least once under the same title. One interesting inclusion is the first publication of an item of which it is planned to continue publication, so that it is wise to search here for all new serials.

Katz, William A., and Katz, Linda Sternberg. *Magazines for Libraries* (5th ed. New York: R.R. Bowker, 1986)

This evaluative work first appeared in 1969, and covers the areas specified in its title. It is classified and annotated, and is useful for all libraries except perhaps the specialist, with about 6500 periodicals being evaluated in this latest edition.

Library Association Record (London: The Library Association, 1899-)

This is the official journal of The Library Association, and includes news, advertisements and some articles. The June 1987 issue included twelve reviews, signed by identified reviewers, and thirteen short notices in a section called "Book Briefs". The reviews sometimes include minimal bibliographical detail, and there is little consistency in this area, so there is a need occasionally to supplement the information. Nevertheless, as the reviews are written by librarians for librarians, one can assume that the evaluations are trustworthy for selection purposes.

Library Journal (New York: R.R. Bowker, 1877-)

This is a commercial journal, but of such venerable stature that it may be easy to overlook the essential profit-making objective of its existence. The reviews are very short, and are generally most useful, not least because many of them appear before the works themselves are published, and thus give the stock selector a form of "advance notice" of a perhaps more evaluative nature than those services operated by publishers and library supply agencies. The journal also carries the occasional article listing the best books on a particular subject. The reviews, of which around 6500 appear annually, are arranged in a broad subject classification, and since 1968 have been cumulated and published as *Library Journal Book Reviews* in New York by R.R. Bowker.

Library Journal Book Reviews (New York: R.R. Bowker, 1968-)

This is an annual cumulation of the book reviews originally appearing in *Library Journal*; the reprinted reviews are classified, and indexes of authors and titles are included.

Muir, Marcie. *Bibliography of Australian Children's Books* (2 vols. London: Andre Deutsch, 1970; Sydney: Hutchinson, 1976)

A major work of scholarly bibliography, this attempts to include all children's books relating to Australia irrespective of place of publication, and all children's books written by an Australian, regardless of subject matter, but excludes school textbooks and books of religious instruction.

National Union Catalog [US] (known as *NUC*) is based on listings of accessions in over 1000 North American libraries, including the Library of Congress, and is certainly even more bibliographically complex than is the Australian *NUC*. It began with the publication from 1942 to 1946 of *A Catalog of Books Represented by Library of Congress Printed Cards Issued to July 31, 1942*, in 167 volumes; a supplement was issued in forty-two volumes in 1948, bringing the listing to the end of 1947. Further supplementary listings, bearing different titles but all being essentially alphabetical listings of the books in the Library of Congress and subsequently other North American libraries, were issued by different publishers from 1953 to 1961. A cumulative author listing, covering all pre-1956 imprints included in these volumes, was issued from 1968 to 1980 by Mansell in London, in 685 volumes, with a supplementary sixty-eight volumes in 1980-1981.

A similar cumulation, covering the period 1956-1967, was published from 1970 to 1972 by Rowman and Littlefield in Totowa, New Jersey in 125 volumes. From 1968 to 1982 the listings were in the form of monthly, quarterly and annual cumulations, with some quinquennial cumulations, 1968-1972 and 1973-1977. No cumulation for the period after 1977 seems yet to have been produced, and the publication of the catalogue in traditional printed form stopped with the 1982 issues.

The period from 1983 to date is covered by *National Union Catalog. Books*, published in microfiche since 1983 by the Library of Congress in Washington. A complete listing of the various compilations of this massive catalogue is covered in the tenth edition of *Guide to Reference Books*, edited by Eugene P. Sheehy (Chicago, Ill.: American Library

Association, 1986, items AA123-AA131) to which the reader in search of more detailed information is referred.[1]

National Union Catalogue [Australia] is a complex arrangement of several parts, comprising a number of different union catalogues in different formats, to which many libraries contribute, some directly by contributing information on holdings and others as a by-product of the shared cataloguing provided by the Australian Bibliographic Network (ABN). Online access is available through ABN for shared cataloguing, and also for pure reference, and libraries that do not share in ABN can get access to the various constituent parts of the *NUC* complex through services such as the *National Union Catalogue of Monographs (NUCOM)*, a machine-readable database (MARC NUCOM), and the *National Union Catalogue of Serials (NUCOS)*, on card or on fiche. The various parts are:

1. *NUCOM (National Union Catalogue of Monographs)*, a single main entry alphabetical card file of monographs, in three original files covering the years to 1984, which are regarded as the "retrospective *NUCOM*". This is also available on microfilm.

2. MARC NUCOM is a separate machine-readable file of monographs that was developed after the closure of *NUCOM*, and is available on fiche.

3. *ABN Catalogue*, a fiche catalogue listing all monographs reported by libraries participating in the National Bibliographic Database (NBD).

4. *NUCOS (National Union Catalogue of Serials)* is also derived from the NBD and is the current listing of serials held in participating libraries, which since 1985 have not been listed in ABN.

New Cambridge Bibliography of English Literature (5 vols. London: Cambridge University Press, 1969-1977)

This five-volume work has appeared with various editors, and it aims to cover all English literary works, both primary and secondary, from AD 600 to AD 1950, claiming to "...aim at completeness in its own terms", so it is important to understand what those terms are. The material that is excluded comprises unpublished dissertations and their published abstracts, ephemeral journalism, encyclopedia articles, reviews of secondary works, brief notes of less than crucial interest to scholarship, and sections of general works, and is notable because its exclusion is generally based on some perceived standards leading to the exercise of scholarly judgment, and not merely on the basis of size or format, as is common in other publications that exclude certain classes of works.

New Library World (Bradford: MCB University Press Ltd, 1898-)

This is a much chattier journal, which started life as *Library World* and changed its title in 1971 and its publisher in 1987. It is a commercial journal, which does not share the stature of other commercial library journals, but which nevertheless, as its almost one century of existence attests, does fill a need in the profession. The July 1987 issue included nine book reviews, signed, although the reviewers were not always identified, and had ten titles listed in a column called "Research", and a further seven in one called "Commercial and Technical", some serials being included in these ranks. Another nineteen were included in a column called "Back Burner", a type of "book notes", which oddly enough uses the almost totally incomprehensible classification scheme devised by the Classification Research Group, one title carrying the following as its class number "ThM(7)MdpML&LvxEkjOtmZp"; in contrast, the August 1988 issue, using the same headings, included one review in "Reviews", eleven short notices in "Back Burner", and mainly news items in "Research". The CRG classification scheme appears to have been dropped. The changes that have taken place in this periodical are a good example of the need for regular re-assessment of the value of a working tool.

Publishers' Trade List Annual (New York: R.R. Bowker, 1873-)

This work is basically a collection of publishers' catalogues, to which unfortunately not all publishers contribute. As it omits material "outside the trade", it is essential to keep track of its definition of "outside". The number of volumes issued each year varies, and some volumes are available on microfiche. Because of the number and arrangement of the catalogues, it is necessary to have access to *Books in Print* in its various forms, which acts as an index to this work.

Publishers' Weekly (New York: R.R. Bowker, 1872-)

This is the American book-trade journal, and purports to list all (or most) of the works published, in a form that can be used for ordering. The information contained in it is used to form *American Book Publishing Record*, and since 1974 the weekly listings of new books have appeared as a separate publication called *Weekly Record*. It includes announcements of new and forthcoming titles, and has special issues.

Quill and Quire: The Magazine of the Canadian Book Industry (Toronto: Key Publishing, 1935-)

As its subtitle indicates, this is the Canadian book-trade journal, and includes book reviews as well as the normal publishers' advertising. It is available also in microfiche, and is supplemented by *Canadian Publishers' Directory*.

Sears, Jean L., and Moody, Marilyn K. *Using Government Publications* (2 vols. Phoenix, Ariz.: Oryx Press, 1985-1986)

This is designed to be used as a practical tool especially for librarians without experience in the problems of locating and using government publications. The first volume covers search strategies, using the ideas of "subject search" and "agency search", and the second volume covers the problems of finding and using statistics and other material for which special techniques are necessary, such as historical searching and the location of patents and trade marks. This is a necessary tool for those wishing to use government documents in any manner.

Serials Directory (2nd ed. 3 vols. Birmingham, Ala.: EBSCO Publishing, 1987)

A recent addition to the range of tools available to the selection librarian, this conforms to the current pattern in that it is taken from information held in the parent company's computer databases. Its three volumes include a listing of periodicals alphabetically by title inside various subject groupings, an alphabetical title index, a listing of titles that have ceased publication, and an index of International Standard Serial Numbers (ISSNs). It is kept up-to-date by a quarterly cumulative paperback, called *Update*, which is divided into seven sections, mirroring the arrangement of the *Serials Directory*. The *Update* is numbered so that the user should find it necessary to go to only two sources, the *Directory* and the current *Update*. Including as it does around 120,000 entries, it will certainly challenge the more established directories, such as *Ulrich's*.

Spectator (London: The Spectator, 1828-)

This is one of the venerable British political and cultural journals, which over the years has carried a succession of reliable and authoritative reviews.

Subject Guide to Books in Print (New York: R.R. Bowker, 1957-)

There can be no question of the content of this work: it is precisely what the title says it is, using Library of Congress subject headings and references, but omitting items that are not given subject headings by the Library of Congress, such as poetry, drama and fiction.

Technical Book Review Index (Pittsburgh, Pa.: JAAD Publishing, 1917-1929, 1935-)

This is an index to book reviews in technical subjects, and should be noted for its expansion of the definition of works suitable for inclusion. It is an annual author index only.

Times Literary Supplement (London: Times Newspapers, 1902-)

This has always been regarded as one of the best book selection sources for libraries with any major collections of general works, although it can be said to favour the literary rather than the technical, and its prestige is determined by the quality of the reviews rather than their number, with the issue of 14 August 1987 carrying reviews of seventy-four books, as well as a listing of newly received works. The reviews are now signed (this was not always the case), but there is no further identification of the reviewers, and one is left with a distinct impression that if one does not know who the reviewers are, one has no right to be reading *TLS*, as it is universally known. This is an essential selection tool for all but the very smallest libraries.

Ulrich's International Periodicals Directory (26th ed. New York: R.R. Bowker, 1987)

This is the twenty-sixth edition of a work that first appeared in 1932. Its title and frequency have varied over the years, but its aims have not, and it still attempts to list all the necessary information for ordering periodicals. The current edition is a two-volume work, comprising a classified listing of periodicals by title, with a title index, and including many useful lists, such as a subject guide to abstracting services, a list of the subject headings used, with a cross-index, and a list of periodicals available online. It is generated from Bowker's International Serials Database, which comprises about 140,000 entries, with details of over 59,000 publishers in almost 200 countries; most of the information in this database is recycled in different formats, and is available in printed form, online, on microfiche and on CD-ROM. It can be considered in the same light as a trade bibliography, and it is kept up-to-date between editions by *Ulrich's Quarterly*, published by the same organization since 1977.

Weekly Book Newsletter (Melbourne: D.W. Thorpe, 1976-)

This is a newsletter aimed at bookshops, and supplies items of trade news and information as well as details of the latest books. The entries are included free of charge to the publishers, and form the basis of the more detailed entries that appear in Thorpe's *Australian Bookseller and Publisher*.

Whitaker's Cumulative Book List (London: J. Whitaker, 1924-)

This is based on the trade journal, *The Bookseller*, and is a quarterly, cumulative, with a two-volume annual, and is kept up-to-date by weekly lists in *The Bookseller*. It is a classified list, with a title index, and includes such listings as a subject guide to abstracting services, a list of subject headings, and a list of periodicals available online. As is common with modern directories, it is generated from the parent company's database, which is also used to produce similar directories, and makes information available in traditional printed form, online, on microfiche and on CD-ROM.

Reference

1   Eugene P. Sheehy, ed. *Guide to Reference Books* (10th ed. Chicago, Ill.: American Library Association, 1986).

CHAPTER 9

WEEDING OF LIBRARY MATERIALS

What Is Weeding?

Any discussion of the problems and techniques of weeding library collections must begin with the consideration of the proposition that the size of a library's collection has no necessary connection with the value of that collection, a proposition that comes closer and closer to a statement of fact when one considers the different characteristics of the items that are being counted. It is certainly necessary to go through the collection in any library on a regular basis, and to weed material simply to make room for other material, but that should not be regarded as the only reason for weeding collections, or indeed even as the most important reason.

Weeding is the process of removing material from the open shelves of a library and re-assessing its value in terms of current needs. Once the material has been removed it can be relegated, discarded, transferred to group storage, or disposed of by sale. There are many reasons for weeding other than lack of space, and to ignore these is to contribute to the confusion over the difference between the size of a collection and its value. If size is to be regarded as the measure of value, then lack of storage space becomes the only reason for weeding and it is thus logical that a general resistance to weeding and also a general resistance to the "self-renewing library" concept will develop. On the other hand, if the intrinsic merit of the books themselves, rather than their number, is taken to be the measure of the value of a collection, then there are many reasons for weeding apart from lack of space, a possible acceptance of the "self-renewing library" concept, and an acceptance of weeding as a good and desirable part of collection building, not simply as an unavoidable necessary evil. The closer the librarian is in attitude to one or other of these contradictory approaches, the more radically different will be the aims and purposes of the weeding programme, and thus of course the steps taken in operation of the programme itself. Because of this one can argue that the most important aspect of any weeding programme is contained initially in the determination of the value of the individual books to the collection. Studies have demonstrated that work done on the collections of some German research libraries badly damaged in the Second World War showed that in many cases as much as 40 per cent of the collection was considered not worth replacing, and other studies seem to indicate that 99 per cent of the circulation requirements of a particular library could be met by between 25 and 40 per cent of its collection.[1] Needless to say, one must remember that these later calculations were made on the basis of "circulation requirements", and as is argued constantly throughout this book, circulation must never be taken as a measure of value.

The measures used in these calculations require some basic assumptions, such as:

1. the use of a book is a measure of its value;

2. past use of books is a valid indicator of likely future use;

3. circulation figures are an indication of the actual "use" of an item;

4. measurements of "use" in the library are indicators of use outside the library, which in some cases can be as high as ten or eleven times the use of similar material as measured by counting loans;

5. the effect of browsing should at least be taken into account, even if it cannot be measured.

It seems to be a basic assumption underlying methods of analysis of use or user statistics that the value of an item is directly proportionate to use that is made of it, but both common sense and studies in the field suggest that availability of material, rather than perceived ideas of value, is probably the most significant factor affecting material use, certainly in enough cases to make measurement of use a doubtful method of measuring value, even though such measurement may well be a good indicator of levels of availability. To calculate value of a library collection in terms of its use is almost to guarantee the maintenance of the status quo, and to stress the importance of what was done in the past, but to ignore the more important consideration of what perhaps ought to have been done. It can be argued, for instance, that instead of working to reduce the size of academic libraries, academic librarians should work towards enlarging the outlook of the users, academics and students alike.

In all, it is probably true that most librarians can always find a valid reason for keeping material they want to keep, and that to them the idea of weeding is distasteful. One should also remember that many users may feel this way, so it pays the librarian working on a weeding programme not to overlook the political ramifications of any kind of operation designed to remove stock from the shelves, for to suggest to a user that his favourite material is in some way second-class or unimportant and can be relegated or stored elsewhere can easily be taken as denigrating or insulting.

Throughout this chapter reference will be made to the various operations of weeding in the following terms; it does not matter which terms are used for these operations, so long as there is general agreement on the operations themselves:

1. *relegation,* in which the material is removed from the open shelves, or from easy access, and stored in stacks, or at some remote location;

2. *discarding,* in which references to the material are removed from the records, and the material itself is destroyed;

3. *transference of the material to group storage,* in which case there could be common ownership of the material and access to it, or alternatively the library

could retain ownership, even though there might be some form of common storage;

4.   *transference of the ownership*, in which case access could be possible if the material is transferred to another library, but difficult or impossible if it is transferred to private ownership, by sale to the public.

Criteria for weeding should be essentially those that are used in the first place for selection, ensuring that in general the emphasis is on qualitative judgment rather than on quantitative, so it is essential to begin by looking at the library's objectives. For instance, if a library is working towards a comprehensive collection in any area, then there is no justification for discarding any material at all. Material may be relegated or shifted to a compact storage area, but it should never be discarded. On the other hand, if the library is designed as a working collection, in that books are bought for use, then after that period of usefulness is over, and specific titles are superseded, it is pointless and counter-productive to retain material that no longer justifies its shelf space. Alas, in practice the choice is never as simple as that, and compromises will always have to be made between the need to keep currently unused items in case of possible future use and the need to maximize current availability by the removal of unused material.

It follows then that there are many reasons why collections should be weeded, and although there is a great deal written about it, and at least a few practical guides to the processes, weeding, one of the most practical of all the topics the library collection manager has to deal with, is also one of the most neglected in practice.

The problem of storage space generally heads the usual lists of criteria for subjective weeding, a close study of which will in fact show that they should be regarded as reasons for weeding rather than criteria for choice of item to be weeded. Some of these reasons for weeding are:

1.   the material and the information may be out-of-date;

2.   the material may be worn out physically;

3.   better editions of a specific title may be available, even though the content may be the same;

4.   community needs may have changed;

5.   institutional objectives may have changed so that library objectives must change also;

6.   unwanted material can get in the way and has a "hindrance effect";

7.   costs of storage.

Indeed, as has been stressed earlier in this work, because of the multiplicity of reasons for the lack of use of a book it is more important to work out why a book is not being used, not merely to record the fact that it is not, because lack of use in many cases is a result of the processes of change in user needs or user requirements, rather than of initial poor selection by the librarian. The ultimate aims of weeding must be to increase accessibility, to improve efficiency and to reduce costs. The first step therefore is to ensure that the primary collection will consist of core material which is likely to retain a certain percentage of likely future use, while the non-core material can be sent to some form of secondary storage. The associated questions, which are how to determine what is this core collection, and precisely what percentage of use is to be the target, are those that turn the process of weeding from a purely mechanical operation that could be left to staff less qualified, and thus presumably lower paid, into a set of subjective processes that require the use of professional judgment, technical expertise and a considerable amount of tact and common sense.

It is necessary to study in some detail the operations used in weeding, as methods and purposes are much more intertwined in this area than in some other library operations. In doing so one should not assume that quantitative methods of weeding are necessarily incompatible with the various qualitative methods. The subjective approach, one of the most common, needs rules, guidelines, principles and the exercise of the minimal amount of professional expertise, and relies on a series of decisions being made about titles on the basis of their age and the length of time they have been on the shelf since the last loan, known as the "shelf-time period". It presents a series of problems.

1. There must be an assumption that the measure of the use of a book is a measure of its value to society, an assumption which we argue is of doubtful validity.

2. While it may not be difficult to produce figures that indicate classes of books that have not been used in the past, and thus are likely not to be used in the future, it may not be possible to do the same for individual items, as it cannot be assumed that simply because a book has not been used in the past, it will not be used in the future.

3. The definition of "use" needs to be settled. Circulation figures will provide details of loans, but this is not necessarily an indication of the actual use of each item, as has been stressed in Chapter 5.

4. The problems of measuring use of material inside the library are different from those of measuring use outside the library.

5. Any measures of past use show what was done, and do not necessarily take into account the more important questions of what ought to have been done in the past, and what ought to be done in the future.

It is because the use of various mathematical formulae is as yet of questionable validity, and the formulae themselves are too complex, and also that combinations of these various methods have not yet been shown to be better than the straight "shelf-time period" method favoured by some writers in the area that it can be suggested that weeding based solely on this method could be quite effective, because future use patterns can be reliably predicted. In particular, the use of shelf-time period could be combined with methods based largely on the age of the individual items to produce a cheap and effective method of weeding.

Whatever methods are used, the cost of operating the weeding programme is going to be one of the most important factors to be considered - cost of identifying material, removing it, altering location records, disposing of the material or storing it elsewhere, retrieving it when necessary, and rectifying the inevitable mistakes.

It is interesting to note that the system set up at Yale University in the early 1960s seemed to work reasonably well, while nothing that has been published since would indicate that any system has yet been proposed that is likely to be much better.[2] The operators at Yale established criteria for selection of material that required the exercise of a certain amount of expert judgment on the part of the weeder, and the initial selection was made on the basis of the following characteristics of monographs:

1. out-of-date scientific and technical matter;

2. books on highly specialized topics essentially covered in other works;

3. biographies of obscure people;

4. textbooks from the undergraduate browsing collection that had not been borrowed for three years.

At the end of their project they had found that it was easier to choose specific titles rather than specific small groups within a subject field, that it was not possible to specify large groups, either by subject or by form, and that it was best for librarians to make the initial choice which was later checked by academics. Projects completed in other institutions, while agreeing essentially with these results, have shown that there are considerable differences in the agreement rate between librarians and academics in different subject discipline areas, with the highest rate of agreement in the sciences, falling away to the lowest rate of agreement in the humanities, which only emphasizes the point made continually in these studies, that different methods are needed for different situations. In all there are two important guidelines that any weeding programme could do well to follow:

1. that the likelihood of future use be the sole criterion for weeding, and

2. that the best method of establishing likely future use is "shelf-time period", defined as the time the material has remained on the shelf since last issue or, in the case of very recently bought material, since its accession.

The problem with using these measures is that before the librarian can move to the calculation of various time periods, there is the need to tidy shelves before doing any kind of shelf count, the need to simplify the various procedures, the requirement that the data be accurate, the need for books to be brought up from various storage areas before counting so they can be taken into account, the fact that weeding must take place immediately after the individual titles have been identified, and the need to adjust the entries in the catalogues.

Periodicals and Serials

It has been one of the truisms of librarianship in recent years, especially but not only in the world of the academic library, that the cost of periodicals is rising so swiftly and inexorably that the subscription bill is set fair to take up the entire allocation of funds for stock, to the extent that if periodicals subscriptions are not reduced, there is danger that the allocation for monographs will disappear. It is more noticeable in discussions on periodicals than those on monographs that the cost of purchase and storage is regarded as the most important factor, and the relative value of the material seems to be of less importance than it is when monographs are discussed. The other major factor in weeding of periodicals is the use of citation analysis in the determination of suitable titles.

The processes of deciding on the titles for cancellation are usually long and tortuous, the most important factors to be taken into account being:

1. who should make the decisions, the alternatives ranging from leaving the responsibility solely to librarians, through involvement of the teaching staff, to sole responsibility being left to academics;

2. the relative importance of the results of citation analysis and use studies;

3. factors specific to the individual titles, such as price, language of publication, coverage by indexing services, availability for borrowing elsewhere and relationship to the teaching curriculum.

Other factors that have been mentioned are the reputation of the publisher, predicted future use, and a calculation of cost per shelf-unit or per item-use. Possibly the only area of agreement in the whole discussion is that no one factor can be relied on solely, or even to the same extent as perhaps "past use" can be relied on for monograph weeding. Much talk has been expended on the possible assignment of weightings to the various widely differing criteria in order to allow for a final points score to be awarded. Again, as has been mentioned before in this book, it is important for the librarian not to overlook the political value of involving all parties in the selection-weeding procedure. Even though the use of detailed decision models may not necessarily result in a more accurate final decision in terms of cost or space savings, the fact that, for instance, teaching staff have been asked for their opinions, and those opinions have been taken into account, may weigh more heavily in the final acceptance by academic staff of a reduced list of titles than any more "objective" method that the library may have used.

The question of the usefulness of citation analysis in general for the determination of the value of quoted sources, quite apart from the question of whether it in fact measures accurately even the use of those sources, has been covered elsewhere in this volume, but it is important to note the specific application of such studies to the question of journal use and non-use, and thus the eligibility of a particular title for weeding. Even though it may be accepted that there exists a fairly high correlation between the use of individual monograph volumes used in the library and the use of volumes taken out on loan, and thus that circulation figures could be regarded as a reliable indicator of "in-library" use, it is quite likely that a different situation exists with periodicals. They are used "in-library" to a much greater extent than are monographs, each volume is part of a set rather than an individual work and photocopying probably distorts what might otherwise have been a "normal" use pattern. It is also necessary to take into account the "impact factor", the ratio between the number of articles published in a journal and the number cited, as a large monthly with many papers must be cited more than a small quarterly even though the quality of the papers might be lower. There is also little doubt that problems of differential access to articles through indexing and abstracting journals will affect citation rankings to such an extent that analysis of citations can be of very little use in comparing journals which have been covered by the indexing services with those that have not. A further point is that such studies may be of very little use in collection management if they measure only raw use, and ignore various factors such as subscription costs, the staff costs of claiming for lost issues, and the normal costs of receiving, processing, binding and storage. In fact what really counts is "use per monetary unit", or expressed another way "use per shelf-space unit".

For practical purposes it is essential also to take into account factors such as the gaps in the holdings of any specific title, the relationship of the title to the entire collection, whether or not it is covered by an available indexing service and the absolute necessity of browsing facilities for those titles not so covered. Further points generally mentioned in this context include the likely availability on inter-library loan of a title under consideration for weeding, and the general problems of the now well documented phenomena of scattering and of obsolescence, which can be interpreted by the journal weeder so that it is possible to nominate some titles for relegation almost entirely on the basis of their reputation for a low count of useful articles, and other titles because of their absolute age. Whatever criteria are used, the factors that should be used to judge the relevance of those criteria must be those also used in relation to the weeding of monographs.

The Concept of the "Self-renewing Library"

This approach to the management of academic libraries arose as a result of the report of the Working Party of the University Grants Committee (UGC) set up in Britain in 1975 with the specific task of looking into "...the minimum essential capital requirements of university libraries (excluding copyright libraries) in regard to reader places and storage, in the light of current limitations on UGC capital resources, with particular reference to possible ways of providing for the remote storage of books and periodicals in repositories to avoid the necessity for a continual expansion of central library facilities."[3] The intention was to make certain that any future building expansion went into low-cost storage rather than into the usual high-cost library building, and to exempt the copyright libraries, at the universities in both Oxford and Cambridge, from these restrictions. The Committee, referred to now by the name of its Chairman as the Atkinson Committee, recommended the "self-renewing library", one that would not grow beyond a certain size because it balanced its new accessions by the withdrawal of "...obsolete or unconsulted material..." each year, allowing, however, for a slight overrun because of the increase in the amount being published each year and also for the need for permanent retention of at least some of each year's publications. The main concept was that of a library of a certain limited size that would maintain itself at very close to that size by discarding each year as much material as it took in, and that concept attracted a considerable amount of criticism. Most of this criticism was directed at the proposition that the optimum size established for each library would be tied to student numbers, a suggestion that appeared at the time (and still does) to ignore the very real need for more than adequate library services in order that university-based research in all fields can continue.

The report of that Working Party has probably been the most contentious issue in the academic library world in the last decade, and still attracts both criticism and support. It is of interest in this volume because it challenges the position of the university library as solely a depository and moves towards the idea of the library as an active service facility, a position that supports the idea that what is important in library service is the ability of the collection to satisfy users, not the number of books in it. Despite its theoretical attractions, however, the "self-renewing library" is a concept that makes practical sense only if the library under discussion begins with a stock which was satisfactory, both in terms of value and in terms of number of volumes, in the first place, precisely the problem that this chapter has attempted to address.

Some Practical Approaches

It might be thought that a simple but effective method could be for individual experts to rank books in order of current and expected future value, but this would be prohibitively expensive, and there are many reasons for regarding the opinions of experts as suspect if they are not substantiated by other more objective measurements. Alternatives suggested are for the books to be judged by a small panel of experts, or for the history of their past use to be examined, and decisions made on the basis of expected future use. It is likely that a combination of two or more different methods would be the most effective. One seminal study set out to determine whether the two different methods might produce different results, and set the stage for two decades of discussion by establishing that a system based on the objective study of the past use of the book more accurately ranked books by probable future use than did a form of assessment by any single expert, and that such a system was a satisfactory basis for weeding in certain areas of the sciences, and could be used also in some areas of the humanities, with the same kinds of doubts about its use when one is dealing with periodicals.[4]

One of the basic problems in the practical application of the various methods of weeding is that of balancing two different and opposing concepts, the strictly utilitarian approach that libraries should collect material for use, and the archival approach to the preservation of the written word;[5] in the large deposit libraries this may be no problem, as most are expressly forbidden by law to dispose of material (indeed one such large library may not even allow material to leave its premises, so that the production of the national bibliography of that country must take place on the site of its national library), but many smaller libraries, even those that have legal and accounting restrictions on the disposal of material, still face the problem of disposing of books that an earlier exercise of professional judgment determined were valuable, but which have proven in practice to be of minimal interest to users. It is obvious that much care must be taken in the application of any kinds of prescriptive formulae to the weeding of collections, as many arguments can be found to support the proposition that obsolescence is more important than inappropriate selection as an explanation for unused material, and that the factors that contribute to that obsolescence are largely independent of the age of the material or of its present use patterns, a position that suggests it can be dangerous to rely too much on those factors for weeding decisions.

Any practical weeding programme should be based on models that satisfy at least these criteria:

1. the assumptions are logically sound as well as statistically valid;

2. the methods recommended are simple both to understand and also to operate in practice;

3. the results are likely to be more useful than those which might have been obtained from the use of even simpler techniques.

Certain basic assumptions can then be made in the design of the programme.

It is possible to predict possible future use with a reasonable degree of accuracy, if not for individual items, then at least for small discrete classes of books.

Past use of any one item is a reliable indicator of likely future use of that item.

The most reliable indicator of past use is the length of time the item has remained on the shelf since its last use, with certain safeguards to protect newly acquired books, and certain reservations about the various definitions of "use".

Provided the groupings are logical, circulation counts of small groups of books can be reliable indicators of use of these books inside the library.

It is necessary to determine a level of use that establishes a core collection to satisfy a predetermined percentage of present demand on the collection.

Each library must design its own models, and establish its own criteria, although these could well be based on those in use in other weeding programmes.

The gains made in the savings of storage space, and the increased accessibility of books left on the open shelves are enough to justify the losses in availability, the costs of the weeding processes, and the cost to users as well as to the library of making available material stored on remote locations.

Two practical applications of the various criteria and methods used in the weeding of certain libraries provide an example of how one might go about a similar exercise. In the first study, described by Ford and involving academic libraries in the United Kingdom, the prime factors influencing the weeding policies were seen to be the objectives of the library, which in most cases are at least based on, if not determined by, those of the parent body, and the need to involve academic staff in the operation.[6] Other factors were the availability of nearby large collections that could be used for material that the individual libraries did not have, the need to allow for browsing, which, inefficient though it may be as a research method, is still a favourite tool, and the political necessity of maintaining collections that covered at least a large range of subjects.

The weeding criteria set up were:

1. likelihood of use was the most important factor; it was assumed this had been taken into account at the time of purchase, as it was the practice to allocate titles to particular locations on acquisition;

2. expediency was next most important; "special collections" were selected for relocation in the first instance, with "age of the item" ranking high in the list. The physical format of the material was a factor, with pamphlets, audio-visual material and periodicals all presenting themselves as prime targets;

3. evidence of use was most important in the selection of periodicals, but the problems this presented with books meant it was necessary for this method to be reserved solely for the identification of candidates for relegation, with the

selection being made on the basis of subjective judgment by librarians or academics.

Although the use of other academic criteria was mentioned, it is difficult to find evidence of their actual use in these applications, and it can be seen that the three basic criteria, form of publication, age, and use, were applied in various combinations.

The second study is that described by McKee, in which the objective was both to maintain an active collection in a suburban branch public library in Canada and also to increase its circulation. In this case the strictly utilitarian approach was adopted from the outset, with the plan being to remove from the collection those books that did not circulate during a predetermined time.[7] The usual assumptions, that past use is a good predictor of future use, and that a core collection of material which is being used could be maintained, were made. An arbitrary decision was made to relegate material that had not circulated during the past two years, with some specified exceptions - Canadian books, which were given a shelf-life of three years, local history, which was not weeded at all, and books which had been in the collection for less than three years. The process of putting coloured dots on the spines, which was seen as being both cheap and visually efficient, meant that in all only about 8 per cent of the total collection had to be considered for weeding, the whole operation took an estimated 10 per cent of the time that might have been necessary if a more traditional system were used, and a non-subjective method, which could be implemented by non-professional staff, was made operational. The experiment was seen to establish that a reduction in the stock of the library had resulted in an increase in the circulation figures, and the conclusion was drawn that the method was effective in increasing circulation. It is this approach taken by McKee rather than that followed by Ford that informs the largely pragmatic series of steps described in the following Appendix. Here the intention is to outline the specific set of practices needed to weed the collection in an "average" public library. As in earlier examples provided in this text, variations will arise as a result of unique local situations; this outline should be treated only as a set of likely guidelines.

Appendix. Outline of Steps in Implementing a Weeding Programme in a Small Library (see summary in Figure 9)

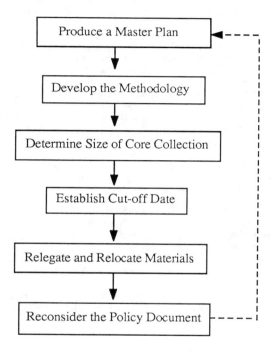

Figure 9. Stages in Implementing a Weeding Programme

Produce a Master Plan

It is necessary first of all to set out the guidelines that will control the complete weeding process, and due consideration must be given to the factors that determine those guidelines. The guidelines will take into account the average physical life expectancy of a book in the library; children's books may last six months, adult fiction two years, adult non-fiction four to five years depending on the subject matter. Important also are the concepts of changing needs of the users, as continued relevance of the stock to user needs will be a major factor. While basic works in subjects such as history, politics and literature may well remain despite possible low use, more transitory books on contemporary politics, fashions, and travel will be candidates for discard, as will be the best-sellers in the fiction section. There should be no question of any attempt by a small public library to maintain any reference works other than the latest, and any material that may be of research value rather than of current interest should be offered to larger libraries. Local history will need different treatment, and the weeding policy will need to take account of local or regional collections; in general, it may be accepted that local history is a *local* concern, and that even the smallest public library has a duty to preserve local material.

Limitations of space, the need to keep an attractive and modern collection easily available, and the local political ramifications of the methods of disposal of unwanted material, are all telling factors; the decision could thus be made to maintain a core collection that will satisfy between 95 and 99 per cent of present circulation, while keeping on the shelves at least a "token" collection of the classics in each field, in a clean modern edition; to maintain a working local history collection; and to offer discards first of all to a regional library and then by sale to the public. It is accepted that only a minimal reference service can be offered, and no attempt is to be made to provide other than a first level of reference material.

While it seems that a lack of suitable storage space is generally the telling factor in a decision to consider weeding a collection, it is possible that other factors may be present, and the policy planning should consider at least whether a change of emphasis of the collection could be indicated; perhaps local needs and demands have changed to the extent that the emphasis on certain specific subject areas could be altered, so that a more balanced collection might result without the need to make drastic changes to storage arrangements. Re-arrangement of existing shelving, major changes to the building layout, even a new or altered building may well be indicated - it should never be accepted without due consideration of alternatives that the only (or even the most acceptable) answer to over crowded shelves always is to remove some books. Assuming this consideration of alternatives has been done, and the costing of the alternatives does indicate the most acceptable course of action is the reduction of stock on the shelves, the next step will be a consideration of the cheapest and most effective method by which this reduction can be achieved.

Develop the Methodology

The next level of discussion of options then is the consideration of the kinds of methods available for the selection of the items to be removed. A perusal of the literature will surely lead the librarian to the conclusion that no more effective method has yet been devised for weeding the collections in a small public library than some kind of variation of the basic method described by Slote,[8] that of measuring the length of time a book has remained on the shelf without use and then using this measurement to identify each item as a candidate for removal; the resulting collection will be the "core collection" which will attract the predetermined level of borrowing. The original collection now will have been divided into two distinct groups: the core collection, which will comprise books that will not be considered for weeding, and the non-core collection, items in which can be considered as candidates for weeding.

The method has the appeal of being easy to design because the various discrete steps are not complex, cheap to administer because the bulk of the work can be done by clerical staff, and effective because it does identify those items which have attracted past use and thus are likely to continue to be used. It does, of course, have the major disadvantage that it fails to identify books that are not being used until after they have been selected and have sat on the shelf for some time; there remains no known method of original book selection that will ensure the selection only of books that will be used and the passing over of those that will not be used. In addition the method does not in any way establish that a book will be used once it is borrowed, or that any form of "use" results in an acceptable level of user satisfaction. Nevertheless, given the comparatively low cost of the method, and the ease with which a check in the form of a subjective evaluation of each selected item can be built in, it is difficult to see an alternative to the method or the circumstances outlined in this example.

The details of the methods to be used in carrying out the various steps of the weeding programme will be affected by the relative cost of different methods, the availability of existing suitable records or the cost of preparing alternative records, the availability of staff at the appropriate level (there is an assumption that junior staff cost less than do senior staff, and that clerical staff cost less than do professional staff, a set of assumptions that may not always be valid), and the length of time available for the entire programme. It is unlikely that a computer-based circulation system is in operation, so that any variation of a "computer circulation control method" is out of the question, and the spine-marking method would take too long to complete, so it is likely that one of the simplest methods outlined by Slote, that of marking bookcards, will be most appropriate, at least for the establishment of the initial selection of candidates.

There are various other criteria which could be used to determine the prime candidates, but most would not be appropriate in this context; age of a book, in itself, has not been shown to be a good indicator of a lack of relevance; obsolescence could be a useful indicator but would require a sophisticated checking system and the untiring vigilance of a team of subject experts for its proper application; use and user studies also require a sophisticated system for their application, and as well have been shown in recent years to be based on a set of doubtful assumptions about "use";[9] citation analysis studies would be quite inappropriate as well as being costly to apply; and most of the arithmetical formulae that have been suggested over the years have not been demonstrably more accurate in their identification of items suitable for relegation than the much simpler and much less costly method being examined here.

Determine Size of the Core Collection

The next step is the determination of the level of future loans, expressed generally as a percentage of current circulation that will be regarded as providing an acceptable level of service after the weeding has been completed; this percentage figure will be determined only by educated guesswork, very much affected by attitudes on library policy, objectives and type of service. Once the level of future circulation is decided, it is then necessary to translate this figure into an expression of the number of titles that will be needed to maintain that circulation, referred to as the "core collection".

In this present example, where the policy decisions discussed earlier have resulted in a high lending, low reference approach to service, and a subsequent satisfaction rate of between 95 and 99 per cent of current loan figures from the core collection, it is estimated that between 70 and 90 per cent of current stock may need to be retained. It is necessary then to plan subsequent operations so that a chart can be prepared showing the date of the previous issue of each book as it is currently issued, so that the shelf-time (the period of time each book has spent on the shelf prior to its current issue) can be measured.

Establish Cut-off Date

Simple charts, as shown below, can be designed, and the *previous* issue date noted, either at the time of the current issue or perhaps in order to lessen confusion at the issue desk, at the time of return. When a sufficiently large number of dates is recorded, the decision can be made as to which cut-off date should be selected in order to preserve the percentage issue figures previously determined. In this case we would assume that approximately 1000 loans were made in the January and February 1989, and each day a Daily Checksheet is kept with the *previous* issue date recorded for each item that is returned (see Figure 10). At the end of the data-gathering period the totals are transferred to a Cumulative Checksheet, and totals and percentages are calculated (Figure 11). It can be seen that in order to maintain a core collection that would satisfy 97 per cent of current circulation, those books that had not been issued in the period between December 1986 and the date of the exercise could be marked as candidates for weeding.

Now that the cut-off date has been determined, staff can be employed to mark the spines of books on the shelves that have not circulated since that date - that is to say, those prime candidates for weeding. At this stage, it could be desirable to leave the marked books on the shelves for a further period so that any that are subsequently presented for borrowing can be examined to see if any pattern emerges to explain why a book appears to be "breaking the rules"; otherwise they could be removed immediately from the shelves and set up for that subjective final examination mentioned earlier.

Relegate and Relocate Materials

Once the decision has been made to weed a title, arrangements need to be made for the location records to be altered, various ownership marks to be cancelled, and the unwanted items disposed of according to the policy decisions made earlier. In the case of this small public library under discussion, it is assumed that the books will be divided into two groups: (a) those obviously suitable for any form of local or state subject specialization or group storage scheme, in which nominated libraries or groups of libraries agree to keep at least one copy of any work on a cooperative basis; and (b) those thought suitable only for discard. Local storage and staffing conditions will determine whether the library will keep these items while advising other libraries of their existence, so that donations could be arranged, or whether the discards will go immediately to the pulping mill or for sale.

Once the method of selection of these candidates is established, the details of the evaluative judgment to be exercised by professional staff need to be spelled out, as it cannot be stressed too strongly that the initial selection of candidates for weeding must be complemented by a professional evaluation of each candidate. Some items will need to remain despite lack of use, for a variety of reasons, which could include the relative rarity of the edition, a need to maintain some kind of subject balance, or the fact that an item may have been donated by an influential citizen or may have some kind of association value. In cases such as these a subjective value judgment will be needed which may over-rule the original shelf-time selection. Ideally, it would be expected that the criteria taken into account in the selection of new titles would be precisely those taken into account in this subjective evaluation; in many ways, this would be less difficult than initial selection, as the evaluators would have the benefit of hindsight in their attempt at assessing the value of the book and would also have the book in hand, a factor regarded as of some importance by many selectors.

Reconsider the Policy Document

After a suitable period, depending on local circumstances but in general not less than twelve months, it would be desirable to repeat the exercise of identifying and marking the books, carrying out once again the same steps as detailed here to see if there were any significant change in the circulation figures or in the cut-off date. In any specific subject area a marked and sustained drop in overall circulation could indicate that the wrong books had been weeded, whereas a strong initial increase in circulation followed by a decline would almost certainly show that too few desirable books had been left in the subject area and they had been "read out" too quickly. An increase in the use of books in a specific subject area followed by an increase in a related subject area could indicate too few titles had been left in the first area, thereby forcing readers to seek out alternative titles, while an overall drop in ᴄirculation figures, spread evenly over the entire book stock, would almost certainly show that the initial weeding had been too severe. Whatever the results of this evaluation of the weeding programme, it is likely that at least some changes may be needed to the policy document as a result of the weeding experiences, as well as those made necessary by the normal effluxim of time. If the original policy document accurately reflected the aims and objectives of the library and the desires of its community of users, no more than minor changes necessitated by normal external pressures and by changes in usage patterns reflecting the newly refurbished collection, should be needed.

DAILY CHECKSHEET

Date: 3 Jan. 1989   Class: 920

Previous issue date		Enter one mark for each book with previous issue date	Daily total
1988	Dec	ⅡⅡⅡ ⅡⅡⅡ ⅡⅡⅡ / ⅡⅡⅡ ⅡⅡⅡ ⅠⅠⅠ	28
1988	Nov	ⅡⅡⅡ ⅠⅠⅠ	8
1988	Oct	ⅠⅡⅡⅡ ⅡⅡⅡ Ⅰ	11
1988	Sep	ⅡⅡⅡ ⅡⅡⅡ ⅡⅡⅡ	15
1988	Aug	ⅠⅠⅠ	3
1988	July June May Apr Mar Feb Jan	ⅠⅡⅡⅡ ⅠⅠ ⅠⅠ ⅠⅡⅡⅡ	7 2 5
1987	Dec Nov Oct Sep Aug July	Ⅰ Ⅰ Ⅰ	1 1 1
1987	Jan to June		
1986	July to Dec	Ⅰ	1
1986	Jan to June		
		Total	83

Figure 10. Sample Daily Checksheet

CUMULATIVE CHECKSHEET AND CUT-OFF DATE CALCULATOR

Date loans recorded: Jan. / Feb. 1989   Class: 920

Previous issue date	Total number of books	Cumulative total	Percentage of current circulation loss if this cut-off date is chosen
Before June 1986	5	5	0.5
1986 July-Dec	22	27	2.8 CUT-OFF DATE ?
1987 Jan-June	41	68	7.0
1987 July	11	79	8.1
August	15	94	9.7
September	19	113	12
October	20	133	14
November	27	160	17
December	33	193	20
1988 January	20	213	22
February	41	254	26
March	31	285	29
April	20	305	31
May	40	345	36
June	40	385	39
July	45	430	44
August	55	485	50
September	105	590	61
October	85	675	69
November	97	772	79
December	200	972	100

Figure 11. Sample Cumulative Checksheet

References

1   J. Periam Danton, *Book Selection and Collections: A Comparison of German and American University Libraries* (New York: Columbia University Press, 1963); Richard A. Trueswell, "A Quantitative Measure of User Circulation Requirements and Its Possible Effect on Stack Thinning and Multiple-copy Determination." *American Documentation* 16 (January 1965): 20-25.

2   Lee Ash, *Yale's Selective Book Retirement Program* (Hamden, Conn.: Archon Books, 1963).

3   Great Britain. University Grants Committee, *Capital Provision for University Libraries: Report of a Working Party* (London: HMSO, 1976).

4   Herman H. Fussler and Julian L. Simon, *Patterns in the Use of Books in Large Research Libraries* (Chicago, Ill.: University of Chicago Press, 1969).

5   It should be noted here that this distinction has no connection with that more common one of the difference between demand and value, that is to say, the argument mentioned before in this book over the conflict between supplying material because readers ask for it, and supplying material that professional librarians feel ought to be on the shelves because it has intrinsic value.

6   Geoffrey Ford, "Stock Relegation in Some British University Libraries." *Journal of Librarianship* 12, 1 (January 1980): 42-55.

7   Penelope McKee, "Weeding the Forest Hill Branch of Toronto Public Library by the Slote Method: A Test Case." *Library Research* 3 (1981): 283-301.

8   Stanley J. Slote, *Weeding Library Collections - II* (2nd ed. Littleton, Colo.: Libraries Unlimited, 1982).

9   Abraham Bookstein, "Sources of Error in Library Questionnaires." *Library Research* 4, 1 (1982): 85-94.

READINGS ON WEEDING OF LIBRARY MATERIALS

Stueart (pp. 342-350) takes an overall look at the processes of weeding, and attempts a review of the nature and purpose of the operation. Asking the question why weeding is avoided so assiduously in practice, he answers that the primary reason is that staff may not understand the importance of weeding in helping achieve the objectives of the institution. He argues that a collection retirement policy must be developed alongside the collection development policy, and stresses that the maximization of space should not be the only reason for weeding. He includes eight points he believes should be covered in any list of criteria for weeding, lists those that seem to be foremost in the minds of librarians sending material for storage, and makes mention of the importance of costing the operation of weeding.

Reed-Scott (pp. 350-356) begins with the statement that there is no simple answer to the question of how best to carry out an effective weeding programme, and no programme that will suit all libraries, because any programme must be based on local factors. The important point is made that any such programme will be a compromise between the ideal in-depth review and the achievable local review, restrained as it must be because of a need for immediate results. The three essential steps in such a programme, the analysis of needs, the analysis of options, and the setting of achievable goals, are outlined in such a way that it is less difficult than it might be for the practising librarian to take this paper and use it as an outline for a workable programme. The author lists weeding criteria, options for relegation, questions to be asked about staffing, and some practical weeding methodologies, stressing the need for cooperation with users at all times.

The paper by Neame (pp. 356-364) has been included because it is an excellent example not only of the intensely pragmatic nature of a weeding programme, but also of the importance of most of the factors that have been discussed in this chapter in getting the total programme accepted by the faculty at a small college. Faced with the problem of reducing the total cost of periodicals subscriptions, the college library staff began by choosing those titles with the highest subscription costs and circulated the details among the faculty, and found themselves surprised by the helpful attitude of some academics and the proprietorial resentment expressed by some others. The necessity of considering not only the cost in money of keeping certain titles regardless of "use factors", but also of the possible lack of faculty support should those expensive titles be dropped, are well expressed in this short paper.

Robert D. Stueart, "Weeding of Library Materials - Politics and Policies." *Collection Management* **7,** 2 (1985): 47-58.

It is somewhat of a cliche to say that weeding is one of the most important components of a collection management program. At the same time, weeding is one of the most sensitive issues facing librarians today. Why then is this process so highly recommended in theory and so rigorously ignored or avoided in practice? The reasons are many, and include politics, priorities, and other perceived problems associated with the process. Many of us fear criticism for making discarding mistakes, little realizing that such mistakes are more likely to occur when weeding has been delayed to the point that pressures prevent a thorough reflection on the process. Clearly patrons and staff both find weeding distasteful as either an undesirable necessity or an unreasonable imposition. This is partly because they lack an understanding of the primary importance of weeding in achieving the goals, objectives, and programs of the institution. Further complicating the issue is the fact that these are likely to be unstated or, if stated, not clearly and generally understood. In such a setting, the necessary connection is often not made between maintaining "current collections" and "throwing away old books" in meeting the primary objective of providing an effective collection. Certainly, without some guidelines based on institutional objectives, no comprehensive selection and deselection program can be successful. Therefore, once the commitment has been made to pursue a deselection program, the needs of patrons and their patterns of use of the collection must be ascertained so that a collection suited to the community's needs is maintained. A number of ways of identifying those user needs and use patterns will be discussed later in this paper.

The scientific approach should be employed in developing a weeding program so that decisions are based on facts and not simply on fancies or hunches. The unique role each type of library performs is an important variable that has a bearing on approaches to the problem and on the criteria to be established. For example public libraries, unless they purport to be research institutions, will probably find it easier to justify removal of materials from their active collections than will major academic libraries.

Before getting too far into a discussion of what this amorphous concept means, one must have a working definition for the removal process, whether it is called retirement, pruning, reverse selection, negative selection, deselection, weeding, or one of several other terms used in the literature. Anyone who follows the topic in *Library Literature* knows that the heading still used is "Discarding of books, journals, etc." I personally preferred the British term "relegation" until I checked the dictionary to find that it means to exile or banish, so my search goes on for an acceptable term. Two of the most common terms, "weeding" and "discarding", are sometimes used interchangeably, but in fact are not synonymous. "Discard" means complete removal from the collection and is thus only one aspect of weeding. Materials are usually discarded because they are available in multiple copies, are out of date, discredited, no longer suitable for a particular library, are scattered portions of serial runs, are now available in microtext, uncatalogued, unfit for further use because of physical condition, or, finally, are considered "trash". In this last case the thin dividing line between discarding and censorship must be recognized.

Whether one admits it or not, all libraries participate routinely in the discard of materials. It has become imperative as the rate of obsolescence of information has accelerated and as budgets for maintaining collections have decreased. Much out of date information, whether in a book on building construction published before new stress codes came into law or in a medical book discussing diseases before newer miracle drugs appeared, has accumulated on our libraries' shelves. Too often such volumes have remained on the shelves because of the feeling that some information is better than none at all or, much more disturbingly, because of a library's drive for quantity at the expense of quality. Libraries that compare themselves with others have begun to abandon the "bigger is better" syndrome promulgated more notably by ARL libraries. There has been a shift in perception of prestige as reasonable individuals realize that libraries must develop weeding policies to maintain quality. The author is reminded of the time when he was first starting in the profession as an acquisitions librarian at the University of Colorado. The library was approaching its millionth volume acquisition, and the call went out for an appropriate title to celebrate the occasion. One anonymous - for obvious reasons - staff member suggested a new title that had only recently appeared: *How to Lie with Statistics*.

Just as a collection development policy must be prepared so that a collection of quality is developed, so a collection retirement policy must be prepared to assure continued quality in the collection. Bonk and Magrill remind us that "In all libraries which do not pretend to be permanent depositories of all that has been published, weeding the collection becomes as important a part of the maintenance of the library as the initial selection."[1] Therefore the whole process is linear. On the one hand, one must evaluate materials before purchasing them, and, on the other hand, one must re-evaluate their usefulness to the collection and then remove them, if they have lost their value. This removal requires judgement just as selection does, and involves added pressures that the initial purchase did not.

This leads us to the definition of the second te-m. "Weeding", a more generic term, means, along with discarding, reclassification to a more specific number, shifting to storage, transferring to another institution if there is a cooperative collection development program, or perhaps, transfer to another section or unit of the library such as special collections or rare books.

If written objectives have been formulated, then it is possible to develop weeding guidelines that can be applied initially by support personnel. If no decision is required for removal of material because of intellectual content as opposed to status, certain types of materials - superseded editions, multiple copies, materials in disrepair - can easily be spotted by pages or other support staff members in either the routine maintenance process or through a systematic approach. All such decisions on removal should receive follow-up scrutiny by professionals, either specially-designated ones or subject area specialists or reference or branch librarians.

Should weeding be done as a discrete project or as a systematic part of a collection management project? The two different approaches bring to mind the story of the New Yorker who was lost in the backwoods of Maine, until he came upon a crossroads where a farmer was working in the field. Upon asking which road led to Bangor, and being told "The one up theah and the one down theah," he asked naively, "Does it make any difference which one I take?" and was told, "Not to me it doesn't". One could probably take that same stance in relation to weeding - it doesn't matter, as long as all factors have been considered. A crash project will probably require additional staff, while it is possible that a systematic ongoing project will not. The size of the collection and the purpose of the assessment are also considerations. The discrete project with the primary objective of creating more space within the active collection is most frequently seen today. Despite the fact that such projects are relatively easy to accomplish, they often create confusion by putting pressure on all units - cataloguing, circulation, stack maintenance, binding, etc.

Each library is so different from all others that it is impossible to offer one general statement of guidelines on weeding for all to follow, but it is possible to talk about factors and criteria that relate to all types of libraries. When looked at in its broadest sense, the whole weeding problem is an organisation problem: it is the physical availability of materials in relation to those who need to use them. With that thought in mind, it is interesting to note that in the past, the most often cited reason for developing a weeding policy has been that of space limitations. The concept of "one book in/one out" has become popular for those collections that have serious space problems and that have abandoned the usual overwhelming concern for statistics. But several alternatives to the one in/one out concept have been employed, including:

1. Building a new library or a new addition, which we all know, few funding authorities are prone to consider these days.
2. Finding storage space outside the library, which requires thorough maintenance and presents inherent delivery and preservation problems.
3. Rearranging space within the existing library, which is most likely to take away from user or staff space.
4. Using microforms or other replication and miniaturization techniques for some original materials.

Each of these in its own way involves weeding decisions, based on hard information combined with a bit of speculation and guesswork, but also the alienation of patrons, particularly faculty in academic institutions. Despite the existence of these alternatives, material may still have to be discarded as a last resort.

Maximum space utilization is not the only reason for developing weeding programs. Redundancy in a collection, shifts in goals and emphasis of the institution, the physical deterioration or obsolescence of materials, and even the need to generate income may provide other rationales. In its own way, each of these is multifaceted. For instance, the term obsolescence is not specific enough because it most often defines a decline in use only and not necessarily in value. For this reason, many librarians would cast aside the emphasis on use in favour of assessing the true value of an item and determined by its users in its own context. This argument would further demand that individual titles be examined with a knowledge of the whole collection. Are other books on the subject available? Is money available for more satisfactory and up-to-date materials in the area? Is something better than nothing? Wilmarth Lewis said, "It doesn't bother me in the least that in the future many of my books will stand unopened for many years on end. Counting the number of times a book is used as a criterion of value is to reduce a research library and its purpose to absurdity: on that basis the most valuable books in it are its telephone books. Every great library has tens of thousands of books that may not be called for once in a decade. Paradoxically, it is these books that make it great."[2] This quotation provides an important cautionary note in pointing out the different problems that research libraries face and the pitfalls of evaluating all subject areas with the same criteria. The value of a book cannot be determined by use studies or other quantitative means alone.

Cost can be a major factor in determining the appropriate weeding strategy. Is it cheaper to continue to house certain types of lesser-used materials in high-use areas, to store them, or to discard them and rely on cooperative arrangements? Several cost models have been developed by individual libraries to predict such costs, including the hidden cost to users of time delay. For instance, the University of California, Berkeley, has decided that certain categories of materials published more than twenty years ago that have circulated one or more times in the last twenty-one years should be stored. Those that have not circulated in the last twenty-one years should be discarded with reliance on interlibrary loan since, even with ILL charges, it is less expensive than maintaining them on the shelves. A good discussion of cost models appears in Lancaster's *The Measurement and Evaluation of Library Services*.[3] The retrospective conversion of files, a time consuming and expensive experience, is made more efficient by a previous weeding of the collection to avoid needless duplication of materials. This is but one example of a variety of peripheral cost considerations that are likely to come to light as one plans a total collection management program.

Questions of what, when, and how to weed, along with the factors of cost and policies, can be dealt with only on an individual library basis. For instance, the decision to discard earlier almanacs, yearbooks, or even encyclopedias would be approached quite differently by a small public library than by a large research library. Likewise, the cost involved would be different for each of those libraries. Even the question of systematic, continuous removal versus the discrete project approach would be viewed differently by each library.

Any thorough list of weeding criteria should include the following:

1. The condition of the item. Is it worth repairing or replacing?
2. The elapse of time since the item last circulated. Can a cutoff date be identified for subject groups within the collection?
3. The availability of multiple copies of the same edition or the duplication of the item's content in some other form.
4. The age of material and its accession date in the library.
5. The language of materials.
   The author is reminded of a newspaper collection developed at Penn State in order to attract an economist with a specialization in East European economics. He never came, but in the meantime the library had placed orders for five years of about twelve newspapers in Russian.
6. The availability of materials elsewhere, either through a local consortium, a national one (such as theses through the Center for Research Libraries), or other sources.
7. The coverage of material in indexes and abstracts as well as its citation frequency.
8. The gross characteristics of a group of materials.

Regarding subject group weeding, it is more difficult to weed whole subject areas than individual titles, even if the interest of users has shifted completely away from the subject. This is substantiated by research. Yale found it easier to choose specific titles for retirement rather than specific small groups of materials within a subject field. This was partly because of the historical importance of certain titles, the interdisciplinary nature of some subjects, and the possible relevance of an individual book to several subjects. Yale also found that it was impossible to isolate an entire group, either by subject or form, for storage, and that it was better for a librarian to make the initial choice of books to be weeded and then forward the list to faculty members for comment.[4]

This last point is much debated. What should be the role of the faculty in the deselection of materials? In most cases faculty should be involved when evaluating journal titles if not individual monographic titles. But it is crucial to point out diplomatically to faculty members that one is less likely to find that a desired volume has been sent to storage or discarded than to find that the volume is out on loan to another borrower or in use in the library. Faculty objections that browsing is limited can be countered by emphasizing that much important research takes place in universities outside North America where stacks are closed and browsing is not permitted. In addition, by maximizing the chance of finding relevant materials, browsing can be made more efficient. Removing low use materials should increase the user success rate, decrease use frustration in search time and effort, and facilitate stack maintenance.

Perhaps the criterion for weeding that has been most discussed and studied is that of "use". Almost twenty-five years ago, the Yale "Selective Book Retirement Program" resulted in the removal of between 20,000 and 60,000 items per year. It was later determined that only three per cent of the stored materials were ever requested.[5] More recently the infamous Pittsburgh study indicated that forty per cent of materials purchased never circulate.[6] Numerous other reports have bombarded us with statistics on use and non-use. We are told that, according to the Bradford distribution, twenty per cent of the collection provides for eighty per cent of its use,[7] and by Trueswell that ninety-nine per cent of the needs are supplied by one half of the collection.[8] If we could identify the core collection before it was acquired, rather than through use over time, we would be in better shape when selection becomes the issue. However, we have not been able to predict accurately the use of materials before purchase, and therein lies the dilemma. We know that the core should not be weeded, regardless of what other factors come into play. It is sacred, but certainly all non-core items are candidates for weeding. This statement is made even though the word "normally" ought to be inserted in it, since there are valid permanent shelf-sitters in every library, whether they be works by local authors or gifts by influential patrons.

We know that in-house use plays an important role in this consideration, but one that is difficult to establish, and that serials, reserves, and reference collections receive greater use in-house than other materials do. Citation studies have attempted to identify core journals, particularly in the sciences, but now also in the social sciences. Any discussion of use and citation studies must take into consideration the "half-life" of serials, that half-life being their use beyond the cut-off point that identified their period of most active use. Studies such as that at Lancaster University, with its fifteen/five method, have developed formulae for retiring journals. At Lancaster, it was decided that all serials whose last fifteen years of publication had not circulated during the last five years should be retired.[9]

As budgets have stabilized or shrunk, as subscription costs have spiraled, and as unused periodical volumes continue to take up valuable space in active collections, the one thing that we know with certainty is that periodical weeding has become essential. How to decide which titles should be retired is the issue. Many libraries have successfully used the Delphi technique of consulting faculty experts to resolve some of their problems. This technique, for instance, was used for the science/technology core journal collection evaluation at Stanford University.[10] Other studies, such as the one at Arizona State, which found that in microbiology seventy-six per cent of the journals indexed in *Current Contents - Life Sciences* were used while only twenty-six per cent of the journals being used are not indexed, supplement our knowledge about criteria for weeding periodicals.[11]

Many libraries have then concentrated on storing their least-used materials. A recent study on storage facilities in ARL libraries reports that the following criteria, in descending order of frequency, are the most prevalent:

1. Use
2. Publication date
3. Availability of new edition of updated information
4. Availability of microform editions
5. a. Availability of other copies in the collection
   b. Condition
   c. Language
6. a. Size
   b. Value as recognized by knowledgeable staff
   c. Intrinsic value
   d. Relationship to collection scope.[12]

If a wholesale storage program is to be instituted, one must establish some agreement on how much or what percentage of the collection to store and whether the cut-off date for storage should be the same for all subjects. For instance, if a classified book in the PT humanities collection has not circulated in the last ten years, should it be retired along with an RC-classed science volume that likewise has not circulated during that period? A nagging question is the shelf-time criteria for any subject. If a book has not circulated for example, within the last twenty-five years, is it likely to circulate in the next twenty-five? What if it has not circulated in ten or even five, or perhaps one year? What if it has circulated once in that twenty-five years? Does the time on the shelf between uses tell us anything, and how do we establish in-house library use of each library? Evaluation of shelf time criteria is certainly a slow, methodical process whose usefulness can be questioned. Some, such as Slote, believe that the most recent shelf-time period should be the sole criterion for weeding and for identifying useful core collections.[13] Others feel that there are multiple factors - subject area, patron considerations, language, citation analysis, subject specialists' opinions, etc.

McGrath, in his studies, has found a correlation between subjects of books used within the library and subjects of books borrowed.[14] Similar findings came from earlier studies by Morse at MIT and by others.[15] To develop a policy one must combine such knowledge with such findings as those of the landmark study by Fussler and Simon in *Patterns of the Use of Books in Large Research Libraries,*[16] in which it is maintained that all subject areas cannot be considered the same in weeding. This conclusion is based on the varying agreements and disagreements among experts within the University of Chicago and outside, who said that past use of materials in areas such as chemistry and economics could be used as predictors of future use of those materials, but that it was not possible to make similar predictions in other subjects, such as English and American literature. In other words, one must agree that an arbitrary retirement age of materials in all subject areas is probably not desirable and that in-house use of materials, such as the use of journals in the sciences, is likely to be heavier in certain subject areas than in others. These considerations must be weighted with other factors that relate to individual libraries, however, so that each library, although it can draw on some inferences and use them as guidelines, must develop its own statistics using proven methodologies.

Another consideration is the more costly one of calculating use, unless extensive circulation statistics are computerized, or one can rely on staff to pull volumes when the circulation record is in the volume. Many studies have supported the thesis that circulation history is a better weeding criterion than date of publication, although it is more expensive to exercise. A study fifteen years ago estimated that it cost about forty cents to weed by publication date.[17] Ash, in his study five years earlier estimated two and a half times that amount to weed by circulation.[18] Those estimates would be much higher today, and have been cited as examples of the kinds of costs one will encounter.

In the discussion so far, only slight mention has been made of certain types of materials such as newspapers, special collections, and government reports, all of which are very different in their use and staying power from materials in the general collection. For example, state and federal documents may be part of a depository agreement which prohibits their being discarded, even if they are out of date.

Finally, the actual cost of weeding depends upon the nature of the materials to be weeded and the methods to be used. It costs more to weed monographs than periodicals because individual rather than block decisions are required. Any calculation of such costs should include:

1. The education of staff. There is almost no section of the library that should not be consulted before discarding materials - reference serials records, circulation, subject/area specialists, binding, cataloguing, etc.
2. The education of faculty, a most delicate political process and one already referred to.
3. Record changing, which can be more expensive than one would assume. At this point, one must decide whether every card in the catalog should indicate the disposition of materials or whether a simple notation, in the circulation record, is enough.
4. Developing a suitable storage facility and moving materials to it - determining appropriate storage facilities, environmental controls, shelf size needed, moving companies or staff time needed, etc.
5. Retrieving materials once they have been removed to storage - time delays, communications costs, vehicles, staff time, etc.

At the same time, the cost of not weeding materials must also be considered. This calculation should include:

1. Maintenance - dusting, preserving, shelf-reading, repairing, taking inventory, and catalog maintenance.
2. Prime shelf space.
3. Insurance on superfluous volumes.
4. Promulgation of out-of-date information.
5. Frustration factor for users.
6. Space limitations.

All of the above are important. Any large scale weeding program should probably be carried out in conjunction with network members and national organizations such as USBE, and can probably be constructed so that part of the costs are recouped through sales to those organizations, or perhaps through individual library book sales. This suggestion is made recognizing the complicated regulations that some state-supported institutions face in attempting such activities.

Finally, here are a couple of mottos to ponder. The first, "When in doubt, throw it out" is certainly countered by "If you do, God help you." Somewhere between these extremes a balance must be achieved in this most important aspect of collection development and management.

References

1   Wallace J. Bonk and Rose Mary Magrill, *Building Library Collections* (5th ed. Metuchen, N.J.: Scarecrow Press, 1979), p. 314.

2   Wilmarth Lewis, *Collectors Progress* (New York: Alfred A. Knopf, 1951), p. 252.

3   Frederic W. Lancaster, *The Measurement and Evaluation of Library Services* (Washington, D.C.: Information Resources Press, 1977).

4   Lee Ash, *Yale's Selective Book Retirement Program* (Hamden, Conn.: Linnett Books, 1963).

5   *Ibid.*, p. 28.

6   Allen Kent et al., *Use of Library Materials: The University of Pittsburgh Study* (New York: Marcel Dekker, 1979), p. 9.

7   Ferdinand F. Leimkuhler, "The Bradford Distribution." *Journal of Documentation* 23 (1967): 199.

8   Richard W. Trueswell, "A Quantitative Measure of User Circulation Requirements and Its Possible Effect on Stack Thinning and Multiple Copy Determination." *American Documentation* 16 (January 1965).

9   Michael K. Buckland et al., *Systems Analysis of a University Library, Lancaster, England* (University of Lancaster Library Occasional Papers, No. 14. Lancaster: University of Lancaster, 1970), p. 52.

10 Stanford University, *The Libraries of Stanford University, Collection Development Policy Statement, 1980*, ed. Paul H. Mosher (Stanford, Calif.: Stanford University Libraries, 1980), p. 6.

11 Arizona State University Library, *Collection Analysis Report* (Tempe, Ariz.: Arizona State University, 1978), p. 24.

12 Association of Research Libraries, Office of Management Systems, Systems and Procedures Exchange Center, *Remote Storage* (SPEC Kit 39. Washington, D.C.: Association of Research Libraries, 1977), pp. 5-6.

13 Stanley J. Slote, *Weeding Library Collections* (Littleton Colo.: Libraries Unlimited, 1975), p. 120.

14 William E. McGrath, "Correlating the Subjects of Books Taken out of and Books Used within an Open-stack Library." *College and Research Libraries* 32 (1971): 280.

15 Jeffrey A. Raffel and Robert Shisko, *Systematic Analysis of University Libraries: An Application of Cost-benefit Analysis to the MIT Libraries* (Cambridge, Mass.: MIT Press, 1969).

16   Herman H. Fussler and Julian L. Simon, *Patterns in the Use of Books in Large Research Libraries* (Rev. ed. Chicago, Ill.: University of Chicago Press, 1969.

17   Raffel and Shisko, *op. cit.*

18   Ash, *op. cit.*, p. 52.

Jutta Reed-Scott, "Implementation and Evaluation of a Weeding Program." *Collection Management* **7, 2 (1985): 59-67.**

Careful management of a library's collections requires an effective, ongoing weeding program. How can such a program be carried out? There is no simple answer, and there is no best way to weed a collection, because a library's weeding program must be closely related to its mission, goals and programs, the users served by the library, its space limitations, and the characteristics of its collections. While it is useful to consider another library's weeding program - Brigham Young University Library or Stanford University Libraries provide excellent examples - such a model can serve only as a point of departure in designing a local program.

A weeding program must be based on careful assessment of a multiplicity of local factors such as the depth, scope and age of the collections, academic programs, and staff constraints. In most libraries, weeding will be a compromise between the in-depth review of the collections that would be done under ideal circumstances, and the more limited assessments of priority areas that promise the most immediate results, such as increased space or enhanced browsability.

With local requirements and constraints playing a critical role, a planned and structured approach is of vital importance to the success of a weeding program. To reduce the hazards implicit in weeding, three essential steps should be included in the initial planning process: (1) analysis of needs (2) analysis of options and (3) determination of what is feasible.

A careful analysis of why the collection needs to be weeded is the first step in developing a weeding program. The extensive library literature on the subject lists several general reasons for weeding.[1] These include relieving crowded stacks and making room for new acquisitions; discarding outdated, superseded and useless materials; enhancing browsing capability; and ensuring the continued usefulness of the collection. These are general goals that each institution needs to translate into specific goals.

Most libraries are not in a position to go through the stacks from A to Z. Rather, libraries are usually faced by a tight space crunch in a specific stack section. Two reasons underscore the importance of identifying priority areas for weeding. First, a library can more easily measure progress in these specific areas, and second, much of the design of the weeding program will flow from the initial goals.

A case in point is the weeding program in the Dartmouth College Library, where the collection development librarians had explored the development of a large scale weeding program. For a long time, nothing much happened. Then in 1982, the Library contracted with an outside vendor to undertake the retrospective conversion of 100,000 titles. The collection development staff decided not only to take an inventory, but also to weed the collection prior to the conversion. This decision resulted in very specific goals and a very specific timetable. Moreover, it dictated the weeding methods that the Library could use.

The second step in implementing a weeding program is the evaluation of available options, including discarding materials, removing some of the materials to storage, and replacing materials with alternate formats, in most cases, microforms.

For many libraries, a combination of these three options will be used. Although for some libraries removal of older materials to storage may not be an option, and in others, replacement of hardcopy materials with microform may not be feasible for economic reasons, all libraries will find it useful to explore the general options and to develop detailed guidelines that direct the actual weeding. To cite one example, if a library decided to weed primarily duplicated titles, such a weeding program requires a very different staffing pattern from that required if a library decided to evaluate the continued usefulness of titles in the collection.

Weeding Criteria

Central to the evaluation of available options is the determination of criteria for weeding. These include use of hard data such as circulation counts and soft data such as user consultations. An excellent summary of weeding criteria is found in the ALA "Guidelines for the Review of Library Collections".[2] These guidelines analyze various options that are available in weeding and list the advantages and disadvantages of different approaches.

The most difficult criterion for weeding material is the determination of the continued value or quality of the item. In considering the value of a given title, a bibliographer should weigh its relevance to the subject; its historical importance; the availability of the information in other editions of the work or in other, perhaps more current works on the subject; the age of the work; its citation in standard bibliographies; and its frequency of use. It is evident that this process is highly dependent on the sound judgement and knowledge of the individual bibliographer. Not only must the librarian be familiar with the literature of a given subject before making weeding decisions, but he or she must also be aware of any cross or inter-disciplinary use of the material considered for weeding.[3]

Because the value/quality approach to weeding is often seen as lacking objectivity, many libraries focus on use as a more objective criterion, based on the assumption that past use is indicative of future use patterns. Numerous studies have attempted to establish quantitative measures of obsolescence and declining use, but the available evidence suggests that use cannot be the sole criterion in weeding. Lack of use is only one element that should be considered with more qualitative factors. There are many reasons why use alone gives incomplete justification for weeding a title. Library experience suggests that changes in user populations or in university educational programs may affect use. A striking example of this is the changing pattern of use of the mining collection at MIT. During the 1960s, after the academic program on mining was discontinued, interest in mining research at MIT was minimal, and for ten years a fairly sizable collection in mining sat unused on the shelves. But with the advent of the energy crisis in the 1970s, these little-used materials became library best-sellers. Suddenly, a collection that had not seen any use for a long time was in constant circulation.

A second caveat is that so many of the use studies have been carried out in the sciences and in technology. Collections in the social sciences and in the humanities show different use patterns.

Moreover, although use is viewed as an objective criterion, there are value judgements inherent in the reliance on this factor. As Phyllis Dain asked: "Is it better to have collections that are frequently used? Worse to have collections infrequently used ...? What of the quality of use? Is one person's need for relatively esoteric materials less important than many persons' need for more commonly known or easily available materials?"[4] There are no universal answers to these questions. Each library must evaluate its needs and determine the appropriate role for use data in making weeding decisions.

Relegation to Storage

In many libraries an important component of the weeding program is the removal of lesser-used materials to storage. While it is not easy to decide what to move to storage, a bibliographer - in case of a mistake - at least has a chance to re-evaluate that decision. To cite another example from the Dartmouth College Library, the library staff there identified 150,000 volumes for relegation to storage on the basis of carefully established criteria. But on the day of the move, a student urgently needed a journal volume that appeared not to have been used for ten years. Although the timing of the student's request was awkward, it was possible simply to recall the item from storage.

The following options for moving material to storage are listed in terms of the ease with which they can be implemented.

One option, that can be implemented easily and economically, is a block move. For instance the Cornell University Libraries decided to move their "Cornelliana" to storage. The major advantage here is that one decision can allow the library to move a very large portion of materials with little staff review. The obvious disadvantage is that a block of materials may include valuable titles that should really not be sent to storage.

Another option is the use of a cut off date for serials. For example, the Dartmouth College Library relegated to storage many serial titles published prior to 1950, the rationale being that with one decision, a bibliographer could transfer 50, 60 or even 100 volumes. Clearly this approach is much easier than selecting title-by-title. Moreover, the changing of records is simplified. Another advantage to moving serials by cutoff date is that it gives library users some sense of what is in storage.

Still other options include moving foreign language books that are no longer of current interest, moving sets of an author's complete works where the library has later editions, or moving older editions.

Staffing for Weeding

The third step in the development of a weeding program should be a determination of what is feasible. This means looking at available staff, determining the structure of the program, and establishing a timetable.

Inevitably, this raises a set of questions, the most important of which is: who is actually going to do the work? It is suggested that weeding is part of a collection development librarian's responsibility and that it is an important aspect of the selection function.

Because of the heavy workload of collection development librarians, the availability of support staff or student staff is vital. Many preliminary tasks can be carried out by non-professional staff, and the primary responsibility of the collection development librarian should be deciding whether or not to weed pre-selected titles.

The structure of a weeding program must be clearly defined. Major questions that need to be addressed are: Will this be an ongoing program? will it be an ad hoc program in response to an urgent need? or will it be a stop-and-go program? Other important issues center around the comprehensiveness of the program and the integration of the weeding effort with current library activities.

While an ongoing, integrated weeding program is undoubtedly preferred, a realistic understanding of what is feasible, given staff workloads, is essential to the success of a weeding program.

Probably few libraries have the resources to carry out a comprehensive program such as the Stanford University Libraries have implemented.[5] The Stanford staff plan is to review the total collection over a period of ten years. The program allows the libraries not only to weed the collection, but also to identify weak areas in the collection, to identify preservation candidates, and to identify materials that should go to storage. While the Stanford weeding program can serve as a model, libraries must fashion weeding strategies based on their own financial and staff resources.

Finally, it must be recognized that the collection development librarian's decision to weed a volume will have an impact on technical services. Determining whether the catalog department can cope with the record changing is another important step in the planning process.

While the specific considerations in planning a weeding program differ from library to library, all libraries will find it useful to analyze their needs, evaluate available options, and determine staffing workloads before beginning the weeding program.

Weeding Methodologies

Libraries, over a number of years, have developed many different techniques for weeding, all of which are limited in some way. In the final analysis there is no scientifically based method for weeding, just as there are no precise standards for measuring the quality of library collections. Experience suggests that any one approach used in weeding would probably not work in all fields, and that a weeding program should use a combination of different techniques. What are some of these techniques? Probably the most frequently used tool in weeding is data obtained from the library's circulation system - either from an automated system or a manual system. Using circulation data can achieve two things: identification of little-used portions of the collection and documentation of the use pattern over time (if records for all circulations have been kept). There are dangers in relying on circulation data, not only in the inherent problem of weighing the significance of use data, but also in the fact that circulation data give only a partial picture of use. A recent use study once more documented the significance of in-house use and concluded that "the use of collections of research libraries is greater than would be indicated by circulation statistics alone, perhaps as much as six times greater".[6]

Recognizing that circulation systems give incomplete information on use, libraries have devised other methods. In one of these, called "the dot method", a dot is put on the spine as volumes are reshelved to identify material that has been used. While this method has been applied primarily in small special libraries, some large universities have also experimented with it.

Probably the most frequently used method for weeding is shelf scanning. Bibliographers go to the shelves, and through a direct visual examination of the volumes, determine which volumes should be weeded, which should be moved to storage, and which are in need of repair.

This title-by-title review has several advantages. Direct examination of the collection provides much information on the size, scope, depth, and currency of the material. This approach also builds on the bibliographer's knowledge. Still other advantages are that it gives immediate relevant results and that it can be carried out over an indefinite period of time.

It is evident from reviewing library literature that this approach depends upon the experience and the knowledge of the bibliographer. But in making a value judgement on the continued use of the material, a danger exists that this judgement will be based on an assessment that reflects the bibliographer's personal values rather than the ongoing needs of the users. We all know that determining the potential use of materials in a research library, or, for that matter, in any library, is very difficult. Henry James' motto of "the prudent virtue of keeping", must be balanced against the fact that library users benefit from a carefully orchestrated weeding program. There are no short cuts for knowing the collections, understanding the subject, and using prudent judgement.

Recognizing that bibliographers' weeding decisions may have a long-term impact on the collection, a number of libraries have returned to an approach where the bibliographers work in consultation with the faculty. In this process the librarian can bring the knowledge of the book trade and of the collections, and the faculty can provide the added expertise in the subject. Libraries that use this approach find several advantages: the library maintains a better understanding of faculty research interests, the process expands faculty knowledge of the contents of the collection, and perhaps most importantly, faculty awareness of weeding will help to overcome the political problems that weeding a collection may entail. By gaining the support of the faculty for removing materials, either to storage or for discard, potential misunderstandings are avoided.

The libraries that have used faculty in weeding also point out that there are some pitfalls in the approach. The most serious obstacle is finding faculty members who are willing to go to the shelves and commit the time and effort required for weeding. An equally important concern is that faculty interests and knowledge of the collection may be focused too narrowly and that the faculty may not view weeding within the broader context of meeting all user needs.

To overcome these potential problems, some libraries use a two-step process: The librarian identifies the candidates for weeding, and the faculty review these preliminary weeding decisions. Stanford University Libraries staff, for example, uses this two-step process. As part of their ongoing weeding program, each book designated either for weeding or for storage is flagged, and the flags remain in the book for a year. During that time a user, either a faculty member or a student, who believes that the particular book should remain in the collection may remove the flag and indicate to the bibliographer why he or she feels that the book should remain in the collection. The benefits of this process are not only the review of the weeding decisions, but also the support of the library users for the weeding program.

Cooperative arrangements may also provide opportunities for weeding. A case in point is the Boston Library Consortium serials review project. This project allowed institutions to identify and weed serials titles that are little-used in their home institution, with the assurance that the titles would still be available in the area.

Preservation and Weeding

Preservation and collection management are closely linked. A number of available studies suggest that about a third of the collections in large research libraries are so brittle and fragile that they can no longer be used. Other studies estimate that at the end of the century half of these research collections will be so brittle that they cannot be used.

The obvious point is that preservation is not a local problem: preservation is a national problem. Some solutions are emerging from national programs such as the efforts of the Research Library Group, the Association of Research Libraries, and a number of other cooperative groups. But the national efforts build on local initiatives, and a weeding program can be a first step toward establishing a preservation plan. Frequently, weeding provides a good opportunity to look at the collection and to identify deteriorating materials.

At the same time, the preservation problem is so overwhelming, and the available techniques are so time-consuming and expensive, that bibliographers must identify priorities and evaluate treatment options. An important benefit of weeding is the examination of the collection and the strengthening of preservation activities.

Conclusion

Weeding is a vital part of collection management, but we can probably all agree that it needs more attention than it has received. Effective implementation of a weeding program builds on the planning process and requires clarification of goals, and design of a workable plan of action. By necessity, implementation of a weeding program will take time and will be a dynamic process, but it will assure the ongoing effectiveness of the collection.

References

1   A useful summary of the literature is: Barbara A. Rice, "Weeding in Academic and Research Libraries: An Annotated Bibliography." *Collection Management* 2 (1978): 65-71.

2   "Guidelines for the Review of Library Collections." In American Library Association, Collection Development Committee, *Guidelines for Collection Development*, ed. David L. Perkins (Chicago, Ill.: American Library Association, 1979).

3   The dangers of weeding are highlighted in: J. Wesley Miller, "Throwing out Belles Letters with the Bathwater." *American Libraries* 15 (1984): 384-385.

4   Phyllis Dain, "The Profession and the Professors." *Library Journal* 105 (1980): 1703.

5   See Paul H. Mosher, "Collection Evaluation in Research Libraries: The Search for Quality, Consistency and System in Collection Development." *Library Resources and Technical Services* 23 (1979): 16-32.

6   Gary S. Lawrence and Anne R. Oja, *The Use of General Collections at the University of California* (Berkeley, Calif.: University of California Systemwide Administration, 1980), p. viii.

Laura Neame, "Periodicals Cancellation: Making a Virtue out of Necessity." *Serials Librarian* **10, 3 (1986): 33-42.**

Most college and university librarians have, at some point, examined the more expensive, impressive, and largely unread journals in their undergraduate collections with the strong urge to purge them from the shelves. Unfortunately the resulting cries of anguish and outrage from faculty members who consider the exercise a mutilation of their subject areas and an infringement of their rights give all but the boldest of us pause.

Cancellation for lack of sufficient funds, however, may, as many have discovered, provide an excellent opportunity for ridding the library of the more inexcusably arcane of academic annals. It allows the application of a consistent and systematic cancellation process; and such a project can provide the bedrock for a rational and controlled approach to future collection development in the periodicals area. Also, in institutions without a strong tradition of library directed collections development for periodicals, such a project can assist the library in affirming its right to the determination of collection growth.

In the last few years, the combined impact of decreasing library budgets and increasing costs have made cancellations an absolute necessity, and the truth of the matter is, that journal cancellations are rarely initiated willingly. As Herbert White has said, the process usually begins with a suggestion concerning the size of savings to be achieved.[1] Although this may not be the best possible reason, it is to some extent comforting to know exactly how many dollars can be released from those committed to periodicals; it gives a concrete goal towards which to work; and it provides an introduction to the realities of periodicals cancellations in the first memo sent to faculty on the subject.

Cutting Back While Keeping the Periodicals Use Study in Its Place

Librarians who deal principally with the user of the library collection tend to take a rather different view of cancellation than does the faculty member. To the instructor, the journal's important in its field, the uniqueness of its subject coverage, the number of times it is cited in scholarly articles, and even its appearance in postgraduate thesis work can be more important than the fact that there is no record of his or her students ever having used the periodical in question.

Librarians cannot of course rely on their own memories concerning levels of periodicals use. For this reason use studies are an essential and objective way of gathering user information. Such studies have been the backbone of journal cancellation projects since the early seventies. Use studies involve a record of the number of times a periodical title has circulated and the number of times it has been removed from the shelf or microform cabinet. Trueswell's 80/20 rule (20% of library titles will receive 80% of the use)[2] is as true for journals as for books, a fact repeatedly affirmed in the literature, [3, 4, 5, 6] and low use is, of course, a very strong reason to cancel. It cannot, however, be relied on exclusively in making periodicals collection decisions.[7, 8]

There are, moreover, problems inherent in over-reliance on use studies, as is so with any method of measurement, and these are sure to be pointed out to the librarian by faculty members. Some of them are as follows:

1. The period of measurement may not cover the time period in which a course using a particular journal is taught.
2. Multiple subscriptions to a title can show a higher use rate because of greater availability. Similarly, the length of a periodical's backrun can affect level of use.
3. In-library use, measured by reshelving statistics are not accurate, as many readers often reshelve in spite of signs advising them against this.
4. Items are removed from shelves for reasons other than the desire to peruse a particular article. The fact that it was taken from the shelf, while an indication of probable use, is not a guarantee.

The most important factor, however, is that cancellation decisions based solely on use statistics are unlikely to gain the support of the faculty. Not only do faculty people make all of the above arguments against the validity of use statistics, but some argue that use is a minor or even totally irrelevant consideration in deciding which of their journals to cancel. A librarian, therefore, who wishes to cancel solely on the basis of lack of use of a journal can expect stiff opposition to the proposal. It is very difficult to see $300.00 per annum spent on a quarterly publication, knowing full well that it is untouched from one year to the next; however, good reasons can exist for not basing its cancellation on this fact alone.

The Reaction of Faculty

The failure of use study reports as a tool in convincing faculty of the need to cancel is well demonstrated by a report by Barbara Rice from the University of New York in 1979. Unused science titles were placed in broad subject groupings and the lists circulated to the departments. However, as Rice states, "not all departments were willing to discontinue any subscriptions or discard any back issues."[9] This is not an uncommon experience.

Astounding as it may seem to librarians, faculty do not seem to attach as much importance to actual use as to their own possible needs and to the integrity of what they see as their department's subscriptions.

While to the librarian it seems wrong to continue to pay for a title that receives no use, the typical faculty member rarely shares this point of view. He or she may have initiated subscriptions to a number of journal titles, most of them to the type never destined for a high level of use. One of the reasons for this is that few faculty members seem to consider level of difficulty an important consideration in journal selection. As a result, undergraduate libraries sometimes carry journals suitable only for doctoral level studies. Few, moreover, consider accessibility through indexing, which also has a heavy impact on journal use. One can hardly wonder, therefore, that these become upset when a list of low use journals circulates through their department. Title after title on the list has been ordered by members of the department, and each has an annual use of 0 or 1. It is only natural that they object, first by questioning the validity of the use study methodology and second by denying that journal use should be a factor in cancellation decisions.

It can be seen that discontent and conflict are real possibilities when the librarian attempts to cancel titles based on a criterion accepted more or less as valid by librarians, but not considered legitimate by the faculty. A good example of this occurred at California State University, Los Angeles,[10] as reported by Barbara Case in an article in *The Serials Librarian* in 1979. An extremely thorough four part use study was undertaken, but when the library circulated the resulting list of low use titles for comment, the reaction was explosive. Faculty challenged the right of the library to make any cancellation decisions whatsoever. In the end, recognition of the right of the library to cancel titles after faculty consultation was sustained, but only after considerable conflict and the appearance of the library director before the Academic Senate.

Control over Collection Development: The Real Issue

As the California State experience illustrates, the issue of cancellation is ultimately the issue of the library's authority to make the final decision on collection holdings. While faculty input is solicited, and feedback from it integrated into the final cancellation list, the ultimate responsibility here belongs to the library. The fact that the library is charged with responsibility for spending the periodicals budget is enough to confirm this arrangement.

Cost and Value as Additional Cancellation Criteria

Cost of the subscription and value of the journal as defined by the librarian and through faculty feedback are important additional criteria to consider in making cancellation decisions. As proposed by Roger R. Flynn in his report on a study at the University of Pittsburgh in 1979,[11] these additional criteria are more effective than use alone in determining cancellations.

Cost in particular is extremely valuable. In 1975, Line and Sandison recommended that librarians ask how many uses per monetary unit each journal provides.[12] However logical an approach this may be, it is not one that has been generally adopted. To quote Herbert S. White, "while it is true that the cancellation of one expensive journal would eliminate the necessity of cancelling several cheaper ones, libraries seem not to choose this option."[13] If, however, an attempt is made to cancel chiefly high cost, low use items in order to eliminate fewer titles in total, the result is generally cost effective, as the most costly journals tend, with some notable exceptions, not to be as well used. Journals costing in excess of the average cost per title can be considered "high cost," and should become cancellation candidates unless use or value factors intervene.

Value factors as a third consideration are also important. This is the area in which feedback from faculty and a recognition of faculty concerns are important. Faculty arguments for journal retention should be considered carefully. Legitimate professional development needs do not necessarily translate into a consistent high use level of the periodicals involved. There are also periodicals so central to a particular discipline that they should be retained in spite of low use levels. A journal may be the only one covering a vital subject area, for instance, or it may have a potential for higher use as a result of changes in course offerings. The faculty member is often in a better position than the librarian to recognize these concerns, and opportunity and time should be given for their expression.

The Method

Okanagan College, in British Columbia, Canada, serving students in the first two years of academic and career programs, needed to cut $8000 from a $27,000 periodicals budget. There were 578 subscriptions at an average cost of $46.15. After the process was completed, 105 subscriptions had been cancelled with an average cost of $79.04. The average cost of the subscriptions remaining was $38.84. There is not doubt that the project succeeded in cancelling high cost items (see Table 1).

Table 1. Cancellations: A Comparison of Costs and Savings

Before Cancellations		
Subscription total	578	
Cost total	$26,674.64	
Average cost per item	$ 46.21	
After Cancellations		
Subscription total	473	
Cost total	$18,373.77	
Average cost per item	$ 39.90	
Cancelled Items		
Cancelled Total	105	(39 duplicate subscriptions)
Savings total	$8,300.87	
Average cost of cancelled item	$79.04	

Titles costing over $50.00 were considered cancellation candidates and were then subjected to use and value criteria. Naturally some high cost titles could not be cut. One hundred subscriptions of 578, or 17% of the total were presented to a meeting of faculty department heads along with an explanation of cancellation criteria and budget information. A memo was then circulated to all departments listing potential cancellations in their area and asking for comment within a certain time period (see Table 2).

The majority of the faculty provided useful feedback, making reasonable cases for journal retention, suggesting changes in the paper/microform copy configuration, and naming other titles they felt could also be cancelled. Many were surprised by the cost of some of their favourite journals, and realized reluctantly that we could no longer afford to subscribe.

There were negative reactions, however, over the method by which periodical cuts were determined. Departmental representatives, particularly in those areas commanding a large share of the periodicals budget, wished to see the percentage of cutbacks applied equally to each department. This is a possible cutback method, and one described by Jacqueline Maxin as having been instituted at Clarkson,[14] but it presupposes a well balanced and representative collection. At Okanagan College it would not have been possible, for while some departments were extremely well represented in the periodicals area, others had very little.

Table 2. Sample of Cancellation Recommendations Circulated to Faculty

Subject:	*Psychology*		
Title	Cost*	Reason for Cancellation	Use per Annum
Cognitive Therapy and Research	$132.60	Price, low use, specialized	0
Journal of Applied Psychology	104.00	Price, low use	2
Journal of Behavioural Medicine	97.50	Price, low use, specialized	1
Journal of Youth and Adolescence	204.10	2 subscriptions, cancel 1	12

NOTE: Examples of high use in this area:

Child Development	($115.50)	35
Developmental Psychology	($141.10)	26
Psychology Today	($ 25.50)	102

*Cost reflects American exchange rates where applicable.

As a result of a strong feeling that the periodicals appearing in their subject area literally were theirs, some faculty felt that they were bearing the brunt of the program. It was necessary for the library to reemphasize the importance of the criteria used in cancellation and to make clear that each journal was being judged on its own merits, with no reference to the department that happened to have originated the subscription request. It was necessary also to point out that while input was welcome, the final decision belonged to the librarians. In the end, the principle of ultimate library responsibility for periodicals collection decisions was well demonstrated, and the overall success of the project was evident in the results produced by it (see Table 3).

Table 3. Cancellation Criteria for Periodicals

Results

At Okanagan College, the periodicals cancellation project was one of the first concerted efforts made in forming a logical and consistent periodicals collection policy after a long period when subscriptions were rarely dropped, and periodicals added chiefly on the strength of the case made for it by the individual faculty member.

As a result of the newness of the procedure, questions were raised as to the legitimacy of the librarian's role in cancellation and periodical selection decisions. However, as opportunity was provided for faculty input, and reasonable cases for journal retention were made, the program's outcome was positive.

The result in financial terms was likewise positive. A significant number of periodicals were saved through identifying and cancelling one high-priced journal in place of several lower-price ones. In addition, care was taken through application of use statistics to cancel only low-use journals, thus avoiding the cancellation of high-cost, high-use items. Finally, the application of value factors resulted in a finetuning of the final list.

Although some compromises were made in arriving at cancellation decision, major pitfalls were avoided. The library did not abdicate its responsibility to the students and the college by delegating the hard choices that needed to be made to the academic departments, nor did it provoke confrontation and revolt by being inflexible and uncompromising in the face of faculty concerns. The expectation now exits that collection development work will continue to be initiated and directed by the library.

The Next Step

At Okanagan College, the next logical step to the building of a strong periodicals collection was undertaken in the following year, when subscriptions were initiated to over 130 periodicals identified as having high use and value potential by the library. This was done by comparing Okanagan College holdings with those of two other colleges of similar size. Factors checked were cost, indexing access, level of ILL requests, and course applicability. The resulting list of new periodical titles had an average cost of only $30.00 per annum. Their appearance in the library has occasioned only positive comment from faculty members who have noticed the additions to their subject area. While there have been some queries as to the criteria for selection, no question has been raised as to the wisdom of the choices, nor as to the right of the library to make such selection decisions - a state of affairs that the previous cancellations project and the care taken in presenting the library's position helped to foster. Two years after the initial cancellations project, Okanagan College has 615 periodical subscriptions and a periodicals budget of $27,000. More new subscriptions were added than items dropped, and this was done at half the previous outlay.

In conclusion, it can be asserted with some confidence that the expectation exists in academic institutions that collection development is an ongoing process and that it will be directed by the library. The explicit recognition of control over the collection as an important and central role for the library is a vital goal to keep in mind while in the midst of what can be a confusing and painful process. If successful, a periodicals cancellation project can result not only in a pared-down, healthy list of holdings, but also can ease the way for future selection and deselection decisions and even increase the strength and importance of the library in its academic community.

References

1 Herbert S. White, "Factors in the Decision by Individuals and Libraries to Place or Cancel Subscriptions to Scholarly and Research Journals." *Library Quarterly* 50, 3 (1980): 287-309.

2 Richard W. Trueswell, "Some Behavioural Patterns of Library Users: The 80/20 Rule." *Wilson Library Bulletin* 14, 1 (1968): 458.

3 Charles N. Wenger and Judith Childress, "Journal Evaluation in a Large Research Library." *Journal of the American Association for Information Science* 28, 5 (1977): 293-299.

4 Michael J. Pope, "Use of Periodical Backfiles in a Community College Library." *Community/Junior College Research Quarterly* 2, 2 (1978): 163-177.

5 Carol A. Johnson and Richard W. Trueswell, "The Weighted Criteria Statistics Score: An Approach to Journal Selection." *College and Research Libraries* 3, 4 (1978): 287-292.

6 Jacqueline A. Maxin, "Periodical Use and Collection Development." *College and Research Libraries* 40, 3 (1979): 248-253.

7 Barbara A. Rice, "Science Periodicals Use Study." *Serials Librarian* 4, 1 (1979): 35-47.

8 Patricia Stenstrom and Ruth McBride, "Serial Use by Social Science Faculty: Survey." *College and Research Libraries* 40, 5 (1979): 426-431.

9 Rice, *op. cit.*, p.43.

10 John B. Wood and Lynn M. Coppel, "Drowning Our Kittens: Deselection of Periodicals in Academic Libraries." *Serials Librarian* 3, 3 (1979): 317-331.

11 Roger R. Flynn, "The University of Pittsburgh Study of Journal Usage: A Summary Report." *Serials Librarian* 4, 1 (1979): 25-33.

12 Maurice B. Line and Alexander Sandison, "Practical Interpretation of Citation and Library Use Studies." *College and Research Libraries* 26, 5 (1975): 287-292.

13 White, *op. cit.*, p. 305.

14 Maxin, *op. cit.*, pp. 248-253.

PART 4

SELECT BIBLIOGRAPHY ON COLLECTION DEVELOPMENT AND SELECTION

SELECT BIBLIOGRAPHY

This bibliography lists a wide range of publications in the areas of collection development, policy formulation, collection evaluation, use and user studies, selection of library materials, weeding and related topics. It does *not* include the specific selection aids described and listed in Chapters 7 and 8, nor does it seek to be comprehensive. Additional references may be located through several of the bibliographies included in this list and in the standard indexing and abstracting services for library science literature. The materials in this bibliography have been classified according to their use within the context of this volume, and each item appears under only one heading.

1. Bibliographies and Literature Reviews

Albright, John B. "A Bibliography of Community Analysis for Libraries." *Library Trends* 24 (1976): 619-643.

Almony, Robert A., Jr. "The Concept of a Systematic Duplication: A Survey of the Literature." *Collection Management* 2, 2 (1978): 153-165.

Broadus, Robert N. "Evaluation of Academic Library Collections: A Survey of Recent Literature." *Library Acquisitions: Practice and Theory* 1, 3 (1977): 149-155.

Davis, Richard A., and Bailey, Catherine A. *Bibliography of User Studies.* Philadelphia, Pa.: Drexel Institute of Technology, Graduate School of Library Science, 1964.

DeLoach, Marva L., and DeLong, Dianne S. "Collection Development in School Library/Media Centers: A Selected and Partially Annotated Bibliography." In *Collection Management for School Library Media Centers,* edited by Brenda H. White, 5-36. New York: Haworth Press, 1986.

Ford, Geoffrey, ed. *User Studies: An Introductory Guide and Select Bibliography.* Occasional Papers, No. 1. University of Sheffield, Centre for Research on User Studies, 1977.

Godden, Irene P.; Fachan, Karen W.; and Smith, Patricia A., comps. *Collection Development and Acquisitions, 1979-1980: An Annotated, Critical Bibliography.* Metuchen, N.J.: Scarecrow Press, 1982.

Nisonger, Thomas E. "Annotated Bibliography of Items Relating to Collection Evaluation in Academic Libraries." *College and Research Libraries* 43, 4 (1982): 300-311.

Powell, Ronald R. *The Relationship of Library User Studies to Performance Measures: A Review of the Literature*. Occasional Papers, No. 181. Champaign, Ill.: University of Illinois, Graduate School of Library and Information Science, 1988.

Rice, Barbara A. "Weeding in Academic and Research Libraries: An Annotated Bibliography." *Collection Management* 2, 2 (1978): 65-71.

Rodwell, John. *A Review of the Recent Literature on the Assessment of Library Effectiveness*. Kensington, N.S.W.: University of New South Wales, School of Librarianship, 1975.

Rossi, Gary J. "Library Approval Plans: A Selected, Annotated Bibliography." *Library Acquisitions: Practice and Theory* 11, 1 (1987): 3-34.

Roy, Loriene. "Does Weeding Increase Circulation? A Review of the Related Literature." *Collection Management* 10, 1/2 (1988): 141-156.

Schorr, Alan E. *Federal Documents Librarianship, 1879-1987*. Juneau, Alaska: Denali Press, 1988.

Seymour, Carol A. "Weeding the Collection: A Review of Research on Identifying Obsolete Stock Part I: Monographs." *Libri* 22, 2 (1972): 137-148.

Seymour, Carol A. "Weeding the Collection: A Review of Research on Identifying Obsolete Stock Part II: Serials." *Libri* 22, 3 (1972): 183-189.

Stecher, G. "Library Evaluation: A Brief Survey of Studies in Quantification." *Australian Academic and Research Libraries* 6, 1 (1975): 1-19.

Welsch, Erwin K. "A Social Scientific View of Collection Development: A Review Article." *Collection Management* 4, 3 (1982): 71-84.

Wiemers, Eugene, Jr., *et al.* "Collection Evaluation: A Practical Guide to the Literature." *Library Acquisitions: Practice and Theory* 8, 1 (1984): 65-76.

Wood, D.N. "User Studies: A Review of the Literature from 1960-1970." *Aslib Proceedings* 23 (1971): 11-23.

2. General Studies on Collection Development and Management
(See also Sections 3, 7, 11-13)

Adams, John. "More than 'Librarie Keepers'." In *Books, Libraries and Readers in Colonial Australia: Papers from the Forum on Australian Colonial Library History Held at Monash University, 1-2 June 1984,* edited by Elizabeth Morrison and Michael Talbot, 93-101. Clayton: Graduate School of Librarianship, Monash University, 1984.

Altan, Susan. "Collection Development in Practice in an Independent School." *Catholic Library World* 54 (1982): 110-112.

Auchmuty, J.J. "The University Library from a Vice-Chancellor's Point of View." *Australian Academic and Research Libraries* 9, 1 (1978): 1-6.

Australia. Committee of Inquiry into Public Libraries. *Public Libraries in Australia: Report of the Committee of Inquiry into Public Libraries.* Canberra: Australian Government Publishing Service, 1976.

Baatz, Wilmer H. "Collection Development in 19 Libraries of the Association of Research Libraries." *Library Acquisitions: Practice and Theory* 2, 2 (1978): 85-121.

Baughman, James, *et al.* "A Survey of Attitudes toward Collection Development in College Libraries." In *Collection Development in Libraries: A Treatise, Part A,* edited by Robert D. Stueart and George B. Miller, Jr., 89-138. Foundations in Library and Information Science, Vol. 10. Greenwich, Conn.: JAI Press, 1980.

Biggs, M., and Biggs, V. "Reference Collection Development in Academic Libraries: Report of a Survey." *RQ* 27 (1987): 67-79.

Bob, Murray L. "Aspects of Collection Development in Public Library Systems: A Critical View." *Bookmark* 38 (1980): 374-377.

Brewer, J. Gordon. "Selection, Management and Exploitation of Stock." *College Librarianship: The Objectives and the Practice,* edited by A. Rennie McElroy, 221-240. Handbooks on Library Practice. London: Library Association Publishing, 1984.

Bryant, Bonita. "The Organizational Structure of Collection Development." *Library Resources and Technical Services* 31, 1 (1987): 111-122.

Buzzard, Marion L., and Whaley, John J. "Serials and Collection Development." *Drexel Library Quarterly* 21, 1 (1985): 37-49.

Cline, Hugh F., and Sinnott, Loraine T. *Building Library Collections: Policies and Practices in Academic Libraries.* Lexington, Mass.: Lexington Books, 1982.

Clinton, Alan. *Printed Ephemera: Collection, Organization and Access.* London: Clive Bingley, 1981.

Cogswell, James A. "The Organization of Collection Management Functions in Academic Research Libraries." *Journal of Academic Librarianship* 13, 5 (1987): 268-276.

Corrall, Sheila, ed. *Collection Development: Options for Effective Management. Proceedings of a Conference of the Library and Information Research Group, University of Sheffield, 1987.* London: Taylor Graham, 1988.

Crowe, Cathryn; Kent, Philip; and Paton, Barbara, eds. *Collection Management in Academic Libraries: Papers Delivered at a National Seminar, Surfers Paradise, Queensland, 16th-17th February 1984.* Sydney: Library Association of Australia, University and College Libraries Section, 1984.

Curley, Arthur, and Broderick, Dorothy M. *Building Library Collections*. 6th ed. Metuchen, N.J.: Scarecrow Press, 1985.

Current Issues in Fine Arts Collection Development. Occasional Papers, No. 3. n.p.: Art Libraries Society of North America, 1984.

Downs, Robert B. "Collection Development for Academic Libraries: An Overview." *North Carolina Libraries* 34 (1976): 31-38.

Dudley, Norman H. "Collection Development: A Summary of Workshop Discussions." *Library Resources and Technical Services* 23, 1 (1979): 52-54.

Dudley, Norman H. "Organizational Models for Collection Development." In *Collection Development in Libraries: A Treatise, Part A*, edited by Robert D. Stueart and George B. Miller, Jr., 19-33. Foundations in Library and Information Science, Vol. 10. Greenwich, Conn.: JAI Press, 1980.

Edelman, Hendrik. "Redefining the Academic Library." *Library Journal* 101, 1 (1976): 53-56.

Evans, G. Edward. *Developing Library and Information Center Collections*. 2nd ed. Library Science Text Series. Littleton, Colo.: Libraries Unlimited, 1987.

Ezennia, Steve E. "Problems and Achievements in Collection Building and Management in Anambra State, Nigeria." *Collection Management* 10, 1/2 (1988): 157-168.

Feller, Siegfried. "Developing the Serials Collection." In *Collection Development in Libraries: A Treatise, Part B*, edited by Robert D. Stueart and George B. Miller, Jr., 497-523. Foundations in Library and Information Science, Vol. 10. Greenwich, Conn.: JAI Press, 1980.

Gardner, Richard K. *Library Collections: Their Origins, Selection and Development*. New York: McGraw-Hill Book Company, 1981.

Great Britain. University Grants Committee. *Capital Provision for University Libraries: Report of a Working Party*. London: HMSO, 1976. [Atkinson Report]

Great Britain. University Grants Committee. *Report of the Committee of Libraries*. London: HMSO, 1976. [Parry Report]

Grebey, Betty. "Core Collections in Small Media Centers." In *Collection Management for School Library Media Centers*, edited by Brenda H. White, 83-90. New York: Haworth Press, 1986.

Griffin, Mary Ann. "Collection Development to Information Access: The Role of Public Services Librarians." *RQ* 24, 3 (1985): 285-289.

Hajnal, Peter. "Collection Development: United Nations Material." *Government Publications Review* 8A (1981): 89-109.

Hannaford, William E. "Toward a Theory of Collection Development." In *Collection Development in Libraries: A Treatise, Part B*, edited by Robert D. Stueart and George B. Miller, Jr., 573-583. Foundations in Library Information and Science, Vol. 10. Greenwich, Conn.: JAI Press, 1980.

Hazen, Dan C. "Collection Development, Collection Management and Preservation." *Library Resources and Technical Services* 26, 1 (1982): 3-11.

Hensley, Charlotta C. "The Role of the Serials Librarian in Collection Development and Management in Academic Libraries in the United States: A Commentary." In *Advances in Serials Management*, Vol. 2, edited by Marcia Tuttle and Jean G. Cook, 117-158. Greenwich, Conn.: JAI Press, 1988.

Hernon, Peter. "Developing the Government Publications Collection." In *Collection Development in Libraries: A Treatise, Part B*, edited by Robert D. Stueart and George B. Miller, Jr., 291-344. Foundations in Library and Information Science, Vol. 10. Greenwich, Conn.: JAI Press, 1980.

Hernon, Peter, and Purcell, Gary R., eds. "Collection Development for Government Publications." *Government Publications Review* 8A, 1/2 (1981): entire issue.

Hernon, Peter, and Purcell, Gary R. *Developing Collections of U.S. Government Publications*. Greenwich, Conn.: JAI Press, 1982.

Hodge, Stanley P., and Ivins, Marilyn. "Current International Newspapers: Some Collection Management Implications." *College and Research Libraries* 48, 1 (1987): 50-61.

Hoffman, Andrea. "Collection Development Programs in Academic Libraries: An Administrative Approach." *Bookmark* 35 (1979): 121-125.

Hoffman, Frank W. *The Development of Library Collections of Sound Recordings*. New York: Marcel Dekker, 1979.

Horton, Allan. "National Collection Building." *Australian Academic and Research Libraries* 11, 3 (1980): 161-166.

Jaramillo, George R. "Computer Technology and Its Impact on Collection Development." *Collection Management* 10, 1/2 (1988): 1-14.

Johnson, Richard G. "The College Library Collection." In *Advances in Librarianship*, Vol. 14, edited by Wesley Simonton, 143-174. Orlando, Fla.: Academic Press, 1986.

Kaegbein, Paul. "National Collection Building in the Federal Republic of Germany." *Journal of Academic Librarianship* 13, 2 (1987): 81-85.

Kaser, David. "Standards for College Libraries." *Library Trends* 31 (Summer 1982): 7-18.

Kennedy, Gail A. "The Relationship between Acquisitions and Collection Development." *Library Acquisitions: Practice and Theory* 7, 3 (1983): 225-232.

Kohl, David F. *Acquisitions, Collection Development and Collection Use: A Handbook for Library Management.* Handbooks for Library Management. Santa Barbara, Calif.: ABC-Clio, 1985.

Koops, Willem R.H., and Stellingwerff, Johannes, eds. *Developments in Collection Building in University Libraries in Western Europe: Papers Presented at a Symposium of Belgian, British, Dutch and German University Librarians, Amsterdam, 31st March-2nd April 1976.* Munich: Verlag Dokumentation, 1977.

Kroll, Rebecca. "The Place of Reference Collection Development in the Organizational Structure of the Library." *RQ* 25, 1 (1985): 96-100.

Kronick, David A. "Preventing Library Wastelands: A Personal Statement." *Library Journal* 107, 4 (1980): 483-487.

Laughlin, Mildred K. "Collection Development in Elementary School Library Media Centers." In *Collection Management for School Library Media Centers,* edited by Brenda H. White, 55-60. New York: Haworth Press, 1986.

Lee, Sul H., ed. *Serials Collection Development: Choices and Strategies.* Library Management Series, No. 5. Ann Arbor, Mich.: Pierian Press, 1981.

Lynden, Frederick C. "Financial Planning for Collection Management." *Journal of Library Administration* 3, 3/4 (1982): 109-120.

McCleary, H. "Practical Guide to Establishing a Business Intelligence Clearing House." *Database* 9, 3 (1986): 40-46.

McClure, Charles R."An Integrated Approach to Government Publications Collection Development." *Government Publications Review* 8A (1981): 5-15.

Magrill, Rose Mary, and East, Mona. "Collection Development in Large University Libraries." In *Advances in Librarianship,* Vol. 8, edited by Michael H. Harris, 1-54. New York: Academic Press, 1978.

Magrill, Rose Mary, and Hickey, Doralyn J. *Acquisitions Management and Collection Development in Libraries.* Chicago, Ill.: American Library Association, 1984.

Malhan, Inder Vir. "The Management of Library Collections and Services in Scientific and Technical Libraries in India." *Collection Management* 10, 1/2 (1988): 169-180.

Marulli-Koenig, Luciana. "Collection Development for United Nations Documents." *Government Publications Review* 8A (1981): 85-102.

Marulli-Koenig, Luciana. "Collection Development for United Nations Documents and Publications." In *Collection Development and Public Access of Government Documents. Proceedings of the First Annual Library Government Documents and Information Conference, Boston, 1981,* edited by Peter Hernon, 85-102. Westport, Conn.: Meckler, 1982.

Miller, Marilyn L. "Collection Development in School Library Media Centers: National Recommendation and Reality." *Collection Building* 1 (1978): 25-48.

Miller, William, and Rockwood, D. Stephen. "Collection Development from a College Perspective." *College and Research Libraries* 40, 4 (1979): 318-324.

Miranda, Michael. "Developing College Business and Economics Collections." *Collection Management* 10, 1/2 (1988): 53-62.

Mount, Ellis, ed. *Collection Development in Sci-Tech Libraries.* New York: Haworth Press, 1984.

New Zealand Library Association. *Standards for Public Library Service in New Zealand.* Rev. ed. Wellington: New Zealand Library Association, 1980.

Osburn, Charles B. *Academic Research and Library Resources: Changing Patterns in America.* Westport, Conn.: Greenwood Press, 1979.

Pankake, Marcia. "From Book Selection to Collection Management: Continuity and Advance in an Unending Work." In *Advances in Librarianship*, Vol. 13, edited by Wesley Simonton, 185-238. Orlando, Fla.: Academic Press, 1984.

Pojman, Paul E. "Collection Develoϸment in Elementary School Libraries: Current Practice." *Catholic Library World* 58, 6 (1987): 262-265, 282.

Prostano, Emanuel T., and Prostano, Joyce S. *The School Library Media Center.* 2nd ed. Library Science Text Series. Littleton, Colo.: Libraries Unlimited, 1977.

Root, Nina J. "Decision Making for Collection Management." *Collection Management* 7, 1 (1985): 93-101.

Sankowski, Andrew. "The Challenge in Developing Academic Library Collections." *Catholic Library World* 58, 6 (1986): 269-272.

Schad, Jasper G., and Tanis, Norman E. *Problems in Developing Academic Library Collections.* New York: R.R. Bowker Company, 1974.

Serebnick, Judith, ed. *Collection Management in Public Libraries.* Chicago, Ill.: American Library Association, 1986.

Sohn, Jeanne. "Collection Development Organizational Patterns in ARL Libraries." *Library Resources and Technical Services* 31, 2 (1987): 123-134.

Spyers-Duran, Peter, and Mann, Thomas, eds. *Shaping Library Collections for the 1980s.* Phoenix, Ariz.: Oryx Press, 1980.

Steele, Colin, ed. *Steady-state, Zero Growth and the Academic Library: A Collection of Essays.* London: Clive Bingley, 1978.

Stoica, Ion. "The Place and Role of the Library within the University System." *Libri* 27, 4 (1977): 352-340.

Stueart, Robert D., and Miller, George B., Jr., eds. *Collection Development in Libraries: A Treatise.* 2 vols. Foundations in Library and Information Science, Vol. 10, Parts A and B. Greenwich, Conn.: JAI Press, 1980.

Thomas, Lucille C. "Building School Library Media Collections." *Bookmark* 41 (1982): 16-19.

Thomas, Sarah E. "Collection Development at the Center for Research Libraries: Policy and Practice." *College and Research Libraries* 46, 3 (1985): 230-235.

Totterdell, Barry, ed. *Public Library Purpose: A Reader.* London: Clive Bingley, 1978.

Van Orden, Phyllis J. *The Collection Program in Schools: Concepts, Practices and Information Sources.* Library Science Text Series. Englewood, Colo.: Libraries Unlimited, 1988.

Van Orden, Phyllis J., and Phillips, Edith B., eds. *Background Readings in Building Library Collections.* 2nd ed. Metuchen, N.J.: Scarecrow Press, 1979.

Weech, Terry L., ed. "Standards for Library and Information Services." *Library Trends* 31, 1 (1982): entire issue.

White, Brenda H., ed. *Collection Management for School Library Media Centers.* New York: Haworth Press, 1986.

White, Peter. "Only the Best Will Do." *Australian Library Journal* 25, 4 (1976): 145-149.

Yu, Priscilla C. "Chinese Theories on Collection Development." In *Advances in Library Administration and Organization,* Vol. 7, edited by Gerard B. McCabe and Bernard Kreissman, 59-72. Greenwich, Conn.: JAI Press, 1988.

3. Policy Development
(See also Sections 2, 10, 12)

Adams, Helen R. "Media Policy Formulation and Adoption in a Small School District." *Wisconsin Library Bulletin* 7 (1981): 11-13.

Adams, Helen R. *School Media Policy Development: A Practical Process for Small Districts.* Littleton, Colo.: Libraries Unlimited, 1986.

American Library Association. Collection Development Committee. *Guidelines for Collection Development,* edited by David L. Perkins. Chicago, Ill.: American Library Association, 1979.

Bartle, F.R., and Brown, W.L. "Book Selection Policies for Public Libraries." *Australian Library Journal* 32, 3 (1983): 5-13.

Boyer, Calvin J., and Eaton, Nancy L., eds. *Book Selection Policies in American Libraries: An Anthology of Policies from College, Public and School Libraries.* Austin, Tex.: Armadillo Press, 1971.

Brigham Young University, Harold B. Lee Library. *Collection Development Policy Statement.* Provo, Utah: Brigham Young University, Harold B. Lee Library, 1985.

Bryant, Bonita. "Collection Development Policies in Medium-sized Academic Libraries." *Collection Building* 2, 3 (1980): 6-26.

Buzzard, Marion L. "Writing a Collection Development Policy for an Academic Library." *Collection Management* 2, 4 (1978): 317-328.

Capital Planning Information. *Trends in Public Library Selection Policies.* British National Bibliography Research Fund Reports, No. 29. London: British Library, 1987.

Cargill, Jennifer S. "Collection Development Policies: An Alternative Viewpoint." *Library Acquisitions: Practice and Theory* 8, 1 (1984): 47-49.

Carpenter, Eric J. "Collection Development Policies: The Case for." *Library Acquisitions: Practice and Theory* 8, 1 (1984): 43-45.

Coleman, Kathleen, and Dickinson, Pauline. "Drafting a Reference Collection Policy." *College and Research Libraries* 38, 3 (1977): 227-233.

Donahue, Mary K., *et al.* "Collection Development Policy Making." *Collection Building* 6, 3 (1984): 18-21.

Dowd, Sheila T. "The Formulation of a Collection Development Policy Statement." In *Collection Development in Libraries: A Treatise, Part A,* edited by Robert D. Stueart and George B. Miller, Jr., 67-87. Foundations in Library and Information Science, Vol. 10. Greenwich, Conn.: JAI Press, 1980.

Evans, Robert W. "Collection Development Policy Statements: The Documentation Process." *Collection Management* 7, 1 (1985): 63-73.

Feng, Y.T. "The Necessity for a Collection Development Policy Statement." *Library Resources and Technical Services* 23, 1 (1979): 39-44.

Ferguson, Anthony W., *et al.* "The RLG Conspectus: Its Uses and Benefits." *College and Research Libraries* 49, 3 (1988): 197-206.

Ferguson, Anthony W.; Grant, Joan; and Rutstein, Joel. "Internal Uses of the RLG Conspectus." *Journal of Library Administration* 8, 2 (1987): 35-40.

Fergusson, David G. "You Can't Tell the Players without a Program (Policy)." *North Carolina Libraries* 41 (1983): 80-83.

Flesch, Juliet. "Collection Development at Melbourne University Library." *Australian Academic and Research Libraries* 14, 11 (1983): 21-27.

Futas, Elizabeth W. "Issues in Collection Building: Why Collection Development Policies?" *Collection Building* 3, 1 (1981): 58-60.

Futas, Elizabeth W., ed. *Library Acquisitions Policies and Procedures.* 2nd ed. Phoenix, Ariz.: Oryx Press, 1984.

Genoni, Paul. "Information Management in the Legal Environment: The Case for Collection Development." In *Proceedings of the Second Asian-Pacific Special and Law Librarians' Conference, September 28-October 2, 1987, Sheraton Brisbane Hotel and Towers, Brisbane, Australia,* 94-104. [Sydney]: National Special Libraries Section, Library Association of Australia, and the Law Librarians' Group, 1987.

Giblon, Della L. "Materials Selection Policies and Changing Adult Needs." *Catholic Library World* 53 (1982): 288-289.

Gorman, G.E. "Principles and Procedures for Collection Development with Special Reference to Theological Libraries." *Australasian College Libraries* 5, 2/3 (1987): 63-73.

Guyatt, Joy. *Towards a Collection Development Policy: A First Essay.* St Lucia: University of Queensland, Tertiary Education Institute, 1987.

Hanger, Stephen. "Collection Development in the British Library: The Role of the RLG Conspectus." *Journal of Librarianship* 19, 2 (1987): 89-107.

Hazen, Dan C. "Modelling Collection Development Behavior: A Preliminary Statement." *Collection Management* 4, 1/2 (1982): 1-14.

Hellenga, Robert R. "Departmental Acquisitions Policies for Small College Libraries." *Library Acquisitions: Practice and Theory* 3 (1979): 81-84.

Horacek, John. "Collection Development Policies." In *Collection Management in Academic Libraries: Papers Delivered at a National Seminar, Surfers Paradise, Queensland, 16th-17th February 1984,* edited by Cathryn Crowe, Philip Kent and Barbara Paton, 11-18. Sydney: Library Association of Australia, University and College Libraries Section, 1984.

Johnston, Dick. "Book Selection Policies." *Michigan Librarian* 28 (1962): 12-13.

Koenig, Dorothy A. "Rushmore at Berkeley: The Dynamics of Developing a Written Collection Development Policy Statement." *Journal of Academic Librarianship* 7, 6 (1982): 344-350.

Lake, Albert C. "Pursuing a Policy." *Library Journal* 90 (1965): 2481-2494.

Lea, A.R. "Selection Policies - South Australian CAE's." *Australian Academic and Research Libraries* 14, 11 (1983): 28-36.

Library Board of Western Australia. *Book Provision and Book Selection Policy and Practice.* Perth: Library Board of Western Australia, 1982.

MacAllister, J. "Selection Policies of State Libraries." *Australian Academic and Research Libraries* 14, 1 (1983): 8 - 14.

McLachlan, Jo. "The Future of Collection Development Policies in Australia." In *Collection Management in Academic Libraries: Papers Delivered at a National Seminar, Surfers Paradise, Queensland, 16th-17th February 1984*, edited by Cathryn Crowe, Philip Kent and Barbara Paton, 19-30. Sydney: Library Association of Australia, University and College Libraries Section, 1984.

Matheson, Ann. "The Planning and Implementation of Conspectus in Scotland." *Journal of Librarianship* 19, 3 (1987): 141-151.

Meyer, Betty J., and Demos, John T. "Acquisition Policy for University Libraries: Selection or Collection." *Library Resources and Technical Services* 14, 3 (1970): 395-399.

Monroe, Margaret. "The Library's Collection in a Time of Crisis." *Wilson Library Bulletin* 36, 5 (1962): 372-374.

National Library of Australia. *National Library of Australia Selection Policy*. Development of Resource Sharing Networks: Networks Study No. 17. Canberra: National Library of Australia, 1981.

Oberg, Larry R. "Evaluating the Conspectus Approach for Smaller Library Collections." *College and Research Libraries* 49, 3 (1988): 187-196.

Osburn, Charles B. "Planning for a University Library Policy on Collection Development." *International Library Review* 9, 2 (1977): 209-224.

Osburn, Charles B. "Some Practical Observations on the Writing, Implementation and Revision of Collection Policy." *Library Resources and Technical Services* 23, 1 (1979): 7-15.

Palais, Elliot S. "Use of Course Analysis in Compiling a Collection Development Policy Statement for a University Library." *Journal of Academic Librarianship* 13, 1 (1987): 8-13.

Reed-Scott, Jutta. *Manual for the North American Inventory of Research Library Collections*. 1985 ed. Washington, D.C.: Association of Research Libraries, Office of Management Studies, 1985.

Research Libraries Group. *RLG Collection Development Manual*. 2nd ed. Chicago, Ill.: Research Libraries Group, 1981.

Riverina College of Advanced Education. Information Resources Centre. *Policy Statements and Guidelines*. Wagga Wagga: Riverina College of Advanced Education, 1982.

St. Joseph Public Library. *Materials Selection and Collection Review Policy*. St. Joseph, Mo.: St. Joseph Public Library, n.d.

Sexton, M. "The Selection Policy of the National Library of Australia." *Australian Academic and Research Libraries* 14, 1 (1983): 1- 7.

Stanford University. *The Libraries of Stanford University Collection Development Policy Statement, 1980,* edited by Paul H. Mosher. Stanford, Calif.: Stanford University Libraries, 1980.

State Library of New South Wales. *Draft Collection Development Policy.* Sydney: State Library of New South Wales, 1988.

State Library of Tasmania. *Public Library Objectives.* Hobart: State Library of Tasmania, 1981.

State Library of Victoria. *State Library of Victoria Selection Policy.* Melbourne: Library Council of Victoria, 1986.

Taylor, Mary M., ed. *School Library and Media Center Acquisitions Policies and Procedures.* Phoenix, Ariz.: Oryx Press, 1981.

"Trends in Public Library Selection Policies." *Library Association Record* 90 (1988): 31.

University of California, Berkeley. *Collection Development Policy Statement.* Preliminary ed. Berkeley, Calif.: University of California Library, 1980.

University of Melbourne. *The University of Melbourne Library Collection Development Policy.* Parkville: University of Melbourne Library, 1983.

University of Texas at Austin, General Libraries.*Collection Development Policy* . 2nd ed. Austin, Tex.: University of Texas at Austin, General Libraries, 1980.

William Paterson State College of New Jersey. Sarah Byrd Askew Library. *Collection Development Policy.* Wayne, N.J.: William Paterson State College of New Jersey, 1982.

Wood, D.N. "Local Acquisition and Discarding Policies in the Light of National Library Resources and Services." *Aslib Proceedings* 29, 1 (1977): 24-34.

4. Collection Evaluation
(See also Sections 5-6, 12)

Armbrister, Ann. "Library MARC Tapes as a Resource for Collection Analysis: The AMIGOS Service." In *Advances in Library Automation and Networking*, Vol. 2, edited by Joe A. Hewitt, 119-135. Greenwich, Conn.: JAI Press, 1988.

Arthur, Anthony J. *Collection Development: A Report to the Swinburne Librarian.* 2 vols. Hawthorn, Vic.: Swinburne Ltd, 1985.

Arthur, Anthony J. "Collection Management - an Australian Project." *Australian Academic and Research Libraries* 17, 1 (1986): 29-38.

Ash, Lee. "Old Dog; No Tricks: Perceptions of the Qualitative Analysis of Book Collections." *Library Trends* 33, 3 (1985): 385-395.

Association of Research Libraries. *Collection Analysis Project: Reports.* 6 vols. Washington, D.C.: Association of Research Libraries, 1978-1980.

Association of Research Libraries. Office of Management Studies. Systems and Procedures Exchange Center. *Collection Description and Assessment in ARL Libraries.* SPEC Kit 87. Washington, D.C.: Association of Research Libraries, 1982.

Association of Research Libraries. University Library Management Studies Office. *Collection Analysis in Research Libraries: An Interim Report on a Self-study Process.* Washington, D.C.: Association of Research Libraries, 1978.

Baughman, James C. "Toward a Structural Approach to Collection Development." *College and Research Libraries* 38, 3 (1977): 241-248.

Behar, Sol, *et al. Collection Analysis Project Interim Report* (Berkeley, Calif.: University of California, The General Library, 1978).

Bland, R.N. "The College Textbook as a Tool for Collection Evaluation, Analysis and Retrospective Collection Development." *Library Acquisitions: Practice and Theory* 4 (1980): 193-197.

Bolgiano, Christina E., and King, Mary K. "Profiling a Periodicals Collection." *College and Research Libraries* 39, 2 (1978): 99-104.

Bonn, George S. "Evaluation of the Collection." *Library Trends* 22, 3 (1974): 265-304.

Burr, Robert L. "Evaluating Library Collections: A Case Study." *Journal of Academic Librarianship* 5, 5 (1979): 256-260.

Burton, R.E., and Kebler, R.W. "The 'Half-life' of Some Scientific and Technical Literatures." *American Documentation* 11 (1960): 18-22.

Buzzard, Marion L., and New, D.E. "An Investigation of Collection Support for Doctoral Research." *College and Research Libraries* 44 (1983): 469-475.

Cassata, Mary B., and Dewey, Gene L. "Evaluation of a University Library Collection: Some Guidelines." *Library Resources and Technical Services* 13, 4 (1969): 450-457.

Clapp, Verner W., and Jordan, Robert T. "Quantitative Criteria for Adequacy of Academic Library Collections." *College and Research Libraries* 26, 5 (1965): 371-380.

Coale, R.P. "Evaluation of a Research Library Collection: Latin American Colonial History at the Newberry." *Library Quarterly* 35 (1965): 173-184.

Comer, Cynthia. "List Checking as a Method for Evaluating Library Collections." *Collection Building* 3, 3 (1981): 26-34.

Danton, J. Periam. *Book Selection and Collections: A Comparison of German and American University Libraries.* New York: Columbia University Press, 1963.

Detweiler, Mary Jo. "Availability of Materials in Public Libraries." In *Library Effectiveness: A State of the Art*, 75-83. Chicago, Ill.: American Library Association, 1980.

Downs, Robert B. "Technique of the Library Resources Survey." *Special Libraries* 32, 7 (1941): 113-115.

Eckman, Charles. "Journal Review in an Environmental Design Library." *Collection Management* 10, 1/2 (1988): 69-84.

Evaluating the School Library Media Program. Chicago, Ill.: American Association of School Librarians, 1980.

Faigel, Martin. "Methods and Issues in Collection Evaluation Today." *Library Acquisitions: Practice and Theory* 9, 1 (1985): 21-35.

Fast, Betty. "Looking at the 'Balanced' Collection." *Wilson Library Bulletin* 50 (1976): 370-371.

Freiband, Susan J. "Evaluation of Reference Collections in Public, Community College and High School Libraries." *Collection Management* 3, 4 (1979): 353-361.

Futas, Elizabeth W. "The Role of Public Services in Collection Evaluation." *Library Trends* 33, 3 (1985): 397-416.

Futas, Elizabeth W., and Intner, Sheila S., eds. "Collection Evaluation." *Library Trends* 33, 3 (1985): [entire issue].

Gabriel, M.R. "Online Collection Evaluation, Course by Course." *Collection Building* 8, 2 (1987): 20-24.

Gardner, Jeffrey J., and Webster, Duane E. *The Collection Analysis Project: Operating Manual for the Review and Analysis of the Collection Development Function in Academic and Research Libraries. CAP Manual.* Washington, D.C.: Association of Research Libraries, University Library Management Studies Office, 1978.

Gardner, Jeffrey J., and Webster, Duane E. *The Collection Analysis Project: An Assisted Self-study Manual.* Washington, D.C.: Association of Research Libraries, 1980.

Gaver, Mary V. *Services of Secondary School Media Centers: Evaluation and Development.* ALA Studies in Librarianship, No. 2. Chicago, Ill.: American Library Association, 1971.

Golden, B. "A Method for Quantitatively Evaluating a University Library Collection." *Library Resources and Technical Services* 18 (1974): 268-274.

Goldhor, Herbert. "Analysis of an Inductive Method of Evaluating the Book Collection of a Public Library." *Libri* 23, 1 (1973): 6-17.

Goldhor, Herbert. "A Report on an Application of the Inductive Method of Evaluation of Public Library Books." *Libri* 31, 2 (1981): 121-129.

Gore, Daniel. "Curbing the Growth of Academic Libraries." *Library Journal* 106, 20 (1981): 2183-2187.

Hall, Blaine H. *Collection Assessment Manual for College and University Libraries.* Phoenix, Ariz.: Oryx Press, 1985.

Hall, Blaine H. "Writing the Collection Assessment Manual." *Collection Management* 6, 3/4 (1984): 49-61.

Heinzkill, Richard. "Retrospective Collection Development in English Literature: An Overview." *Collection Management* 9, 1 (1987): 55-65.

Henige, David. "Epistemological Dead and Ergonomic Disaster? The North American Collections Inventory Project." *Journal of Academic Librarianship* 13, 4 (1987): 209-213.

Holt, Mae L. "Collection Evaluation: A Managerial Tool." *Collection Management* 3, 4 (1979): 279-284.

Intner, Sheila S. "Responsibilities of Technical Service Librarians to the Process of Collection Evaluation." *Library Trends* 33, 3 (1985): 417-436.

Katz, William A. "A Way of Looking at Things." *Library Trends* 33, 3 (1985): 367-385.

Lancaster, F. Wilfrid. *If You Want to Evaluate Your Library....* Champaign, Ill.: University of Illinois, Graduate School of Library and Information Science, 1988.

Lancaster, F. Wilfrid, and Mehrotra, R. "The Five Laws of Librarianship as a Guide to the Evaluation of Library Services." In *Perspectives in Library and Information Science,* Vol. 1, 26-39. Lucknow: Print House, 1982.

Levitan, Karen M. "Resource Development and Evaluation: A Focus on Research." *School Media Quarterly* 3 (1975): 316-318, 323-326.

Loertscher, David V. "Collection Mapping: An Evaluation Strategy for Collection Development." *Drexel Library Quarterly* 21 (1985): 9-21.

Loertscher, David V. "The Elephant Technique of Collection Development." In *Collection Management for School Library Media Centers,* edited by Brenda H. White, 45-54. New York: Haworth Press, 1986.

Loertscher, David V., ed. "Measures of Excellence for School Library Media Centers." *Drexel Library Quarterly* 21 (1985): entire issue.

Loertscher, David V., and Land, Phyllis. "An Empirical Study of Media Services in Indiana Elementary Schools." *School Media Quarterly* 4 (1975): 8-18.

McGrath, William E. "Collection Evaluation - Theory and the Search for Structure." *Library Trends* 33, 3 (1985): 241-266.

McInnis, R. Marvin. "The Formula Approach to Library Size: An Empirical Study of Its Efficacy in Evaluating Research Libraries." *College and Research Libraries* 33, 3 (1972): 190-198.

McLachlan, Jo, and Trahn, Isabella. "A Method of Collection Evaluation for Australian Research Libraries." *University of New South Wales Library Annual Report* (1982): 51-61.

Magrill, Rose Mary. "Evaluation by Type of Library." *Library Trends* 33, 3 (1985): 267-295.

Metz, Paul. "Duplication in Library Collections: What We Know and What We Need to Know." *Collection Building* 2, 3 (1980): 27-33.

Moran, Michael. "The Concept of Adequacy in University Libraries." *College and Research Libraries* 39, 2 (1978): 85-93.

Mosher, Paul H. "Collection Evaluation in Research Libraries: The Search for Quality, Consistency, and System in Collection Development." *Library Resources and Technical Services* 23, 1 (1979): 16-32.

Mosher, Paul H. "Collection Evaluation or Analysis: Matching Library Acquisitions to Library Needs." In *Collection Development in Libraries: A Treatise, Part B*, edited by Robert D. Stueart and George B. Miller, Jr., 527-545. Foundations in Library Information and Science, Vol. 10. Greenwich, Conn.: JAI Press, 1980.

Mosher, Paul H. "The Nature and Uses of the RLG Verification Studies." *College and Research Libraries News* 46, 7 (1985): 336-338.

Mosher, Paul H. "Quality and Library Collections: New Directions in Research and Practice in Collection Evaluation." *Advances in Librarianship*, Vol. 13, edited by Wesley Simonton, 211-238. Orlando, Fla.: Academic Press, 1984.

Mostyn, G.R. "The Use of Supply-demand Equality in Evaluating Collection Adequacy." *California Librarian* 35 (1974): 16-23.

Murray, William, *et al.* "Collection Mapping and Collection Development." *Drexel Library Quarterly* 21 (1985): 40-51.

Nisonger, Thomas E. "Editing the RLG Conspectus to Analyze the OCLC Archival Tapes of Seventeen Texas Libraries." *Library Resources and Technical Services* 29, 4 (1985): 309-327.

Nisonger, Thomas E. "An In-depth Collection Evaluation at the University of Manitoba Library: A Test of the Lopez Method." *Library Resources and Technical Services* 24 (1980): 329-338.

O'Connell, John B. "Collection Evaluation in a Developing Country: A Mexican Case Study." *Libri* 34, 1 (1984): 44-64.

Pacific Northwest Collection Assessment Manual. Salem, Ore.: Oregan State Library Foundation, 1986.

Piccininni, James C. "Using the Higher Education General Information System (HEGIS) to Enhance Collection Development Decisions in Academic Libraries." *Collection Management* 10, 1/2 (1988): 15-24.

Rice, Barbara A. "Evaluation of Online Databases and Their Uses in Collections." *Library Trends* 33, 3 (1985): 297-325.

Rippingale, Ray. "Managing the Book Selection Process: Derbyshire's Stock Assessment Programme." *Public Library Journal* 2, 3 (1987): 40-46.

Robinson, William C. "Evaluation of the Government Documents Collection: A Step-by-step Process." *Government Publications Review* 9, 2 (1982): 131-141.

Robinson, William C. "Evaluation of the Government Documents Collection: An Introduction and Overview." *Government Publications Review* 8A, 1/2 (1981): 111-125.

Rosenberg, K.D. "Evaluation of an Industrial Library: A Simple-minded Technique." *Special Libraries* 60 (1969): 635-638.

Rossi, Peter H., and Freeman, Howard E. *Evaluation: A Systematic Approach.* 3rd ed. Beverly Hills, Calif.: Sage Publications, 1985.

Russel, John H. "The Library Self-survey." *College and Research Libraries* 17, 2 (1956): 127-131.

Segal, Joseph P. *Evaluating and Weeding Collections in Small and Medium-sized Public Libraries: The CREW Method.* Chicago, Ill.: American Library Association, 1980.

Shiels, Richard D., and Alt, Martha S. "Library Materials on the History of Christianity at Ohio State University: An Assessment." *Collection Management* 6, 3/4 (1984): 107-117.

Stielow, F.J., and Tibbo, H.R. "Collection Analysis and the Humanities: A Practicum with the RLG Conspectus." *Journal of Education for Library and Information Science* 27 (1987): 148-157.

Stiffler, Stuart A. "Core Analysis in Collection Management." *Collection Management* 5, 3/4 (1983): 135-149.

Strain, Paula M. "Evaluation [of a Special Library] by the Numbers." *Special Libraries* 73, 3 (1982): 165-172.

Vandergrift, Kay E. "Selection: Reexamination and Reassessment." *School Media Quarterly* 6, 2 (1978): 103-111.

Wainwright, Eric J. "Collection Adequacy: Meaningless Concept or Measurable Goal?" In *Collection Management in Academic Libraries: Papers Delivered at a National Seminar, Surfers Paradise, Queensland, 16th-17th February 1984,* edited by Cathryn Crowe, Philip Kent and Barbara Paton, 1-10. Sydney: Library Association of Australia, University and College Libraries Section, 1984.

Wainwright, Eric J., and Dean, John E. *Measures of Adequacy for Library Collections in Australian Colleges of Advanced Education: Report of a Research Project Conducted on Behalf of the Commission on Advanced Education.* 2 vols. Perth: Western Australian Institute of Technology, 1976.

Watson, Phillip, ed. *Profiling a Periodicals Collection.* Melbourne: Footscray Institute of Technology, 1979.

Wenger, Charles B., and Childress, Judith. "Journal Evaluation in a Large Research Library." *Journal of the American Society for Information Science* 28, 5 (1977): 293-299.

Wenger, Charles B., *et al.* "Monograph Evaluation for Acquisitions in a Large Research Library." *Journal of the American Society for Information Science* 30 (1979): 88-92.

West, C. Eugene, and Lincoln, Tamara. "A Critical Analysis and Evaluation of Russian Language Monographic Collections at the University of Alaska-Fairbanks." *Collection Management* 10, 1/2 (1988): 39-52.

5. Citation Analysis
(See also Sections 4, 7, 12)

Adewole, S. "Selecting Livestock Periodicals through Citation Analysis Techniques." *Information Processing and Management* 23, 6 (1987): 629-638.

Atkinson, Ross. "The Citation as Intertext: Toward a Theory of the Selection Process." *Library Resources and Technical Services* 28, 2 (1984): 109-119.

Atkinson, Ross. "The Language of the Levels: Reflections on the Communication of Collection Development Policy." *College and Research Libraries* 4, 2 (1986): 140-149.

Baughman, James C. "Some of the Best in Sociology: A Bibliographic Checklist Created by the Unusual Technique of Citation Counting." *Library Journal* 98, 18 (1973): 2977-2979.

Bennion, Bruce C., and Karschamroon, S. "Multivariate Regression Models for Estimating Journal Usefulness in Physics." *Journal of Documentation* 40 (1984): 217-227.

Brittain, J. Michael, and Line, Maurice B. "Sources of Citations and References for Analysis Purposes: A Comparative Assessment." *Journal of Documentation* 29, 1 (1973): 72-83.

Broadus, Robert N. "The Application of Citation Analyses to Library Collection Building." In *Advances in Librarianship*, Vol. 7, edited by Melvin J. Voigt and Michael H. Harris, 299-335. New York: Academic Press, 1977.

Brookes, B.C. "Obsolescence of Special Library Periodicals: Sampling Errors and Utility Contours." *Journal of the American Society for Information Science* 21 (1970): 320-329.

Cline, Gloria S. "Application of Bradford's Law to Citation Data." *College and Research Libraries* 42, 1 (1981): 53-61.

Fitzgibbons, Shirley A. "Citation Analysis in the Social Sciences." In *Collection Development in Libraries: A Treatise, Part B*, edited by Robert D. Stueart and George B. Miller, Jr., 291-344. Foundations in Library and Information Science, Vol. 10. Greenwich, Conn.: JAI Press, 1980.

Gleason, Maureen L., and Deffenbaugh, James T. "Searching the Scriptures: A Citation Study in the Literature of Biblical Studies: Report and Commentary." *Collection Management* 6, 3/4 (1984): 107-117.

Griscom, R. "Periodical Use in a University Music Library: A Citation Study of Theses and Dissertations Submitted to the Indiana University School of Music from 1975-1980." *Serials Librarian* 7, 3 (1983): 35-52.

Hafner, A.W. "Primary Journal Selection Using Citations from an Indexing Service Journal: A Method and Example from Nursing Literature." *Bulletin of the Medical Library Association* 64 (1976): 392-401.

Hawkins, D.T. "The Percentage Distribution: A Method of Ranking Journals." *Proceedings of the American Society for Information Science* 16 (1979): 230-235.

Koenig, Michael E.D. "Citation Analysis for the Arts and Humanities as a Collection Management Tool." *Collection Management* 2, 3 (1978): 247-261.

Line, Maurice B. "Rank Lists Based on Citations and Library Uses as Indicators of Journal Usage in Individual Libraries." *Collection Management* 2, 4 (1978): 313-316.

Line, Maurice B., and Sandison, Alexander. "Practical Interpretation of Citation and Library Use Studies." *College and Research Libraries* 36, 5 (1975): 393-396.

Lopez, Manuel D. "The Lopez or Citation Technique of In-depth Collection Evaluation Explicated." *College and Research Libraries* 44, 3 (1983): 251-255.

McCain, K.W., and Bobick, J.E. "Patterns of Journal Use in a Departmental Library: A Citation Analysis." *Journal of the American Society for Information Science* 32 (1981): 257-267.

Mankin, C.J., and Bastille, J.D. "An Analysis of the Differences between Density-of-use Ranking and Raw-use Ranking of Library Journal Use." *Journal of the American Society for Information Science* 32 (1981): 224-228.

Martyn, John. "Citation Analysis." *Journal of Documentation* 31, 4 (1975): 290-297.

Nisonger, Thomas E. "A Test of Two Citation Checking Techniques for Evaluating Political Science Collections in University Libraries." *Library Resources and Technical Services* 27, 2 (1983): 163-176.

Palais, Elliot S. "The Significance of Subject Dispersion for the Indexing of Political Science Journals." *Journal of Academic Librarianship* 2, 2 (1976): 72-76.

Pan, Elizabeth, "Journal Citations as a Predictor of Journal Usage in Libraries." *Collection Management* 2, 1 (1978): 29-38.

Pravdic, Nevenka, and Oluic-Vukovic, Vesna. "Application of Overlapping Technique in Selection of Scientific Journals for a Particular Discipline - Methodological Approach." *Information Processing and Management* 23, 1 (1987): 25-32.

Sandison, A. "Densities of Use, and Absence of Obsolescence, in Physics Journals at MIT." *Journal of the American Society for Information Science* 25 (1974): 172-182.

Sandison, A. "Obsolescence in Biomedical Journals." *Library Research* 2 (1981): 347-348.

Satariano, W.A. "Journal Use in Sociology: Citation Analysis versus Readership Patterns." *Library Quarterly* 48 (1978): 293-300.

Scales, Pauline A. "Citation Analyses as Indicators of the Use of Serials: A Comparison of Ranked Title Lists Produced by Citation Counting and from Use Data." *Journal of Documentation* 32, 1 (1976): 17-25.

Smith, Linda C. "Citation Analysis." *Library Trends* 30 (1981): 83-106.

Stankus, Tony, and Rice, Barbara A. "Handle with Care: Use and Citation Data for Science Journal Management." *Collection Management* 4 (1982): 95-110.

Stinson, E.R., and Lancaster, F. Wilfrid. "Synchronous versus Diachronous Methods in the Measurement of Obsolescence by Citation Studies." *Journal of Information Science* 13 (1987): 65-74.

Subramanyam, Kris. "Citation Studies in Science and Technology." In *Collection Development in Libraries: A Treatise, Part B*, edited by Robert D. Stueart and George B. Miller, Jr., 345-372. Foundations in Library and Information Science, Vol. 10. Greenwich, Conn.: JAI Press, 1980.

Sullivan, M.V., *et al.* "Obsolescence in Biomedical Journals: Not an Artifact of Literature Growth." *Library Research* 2 (1980/1981): 29-45.

6. Use and User Studies
(See also Sections 4, 7, 12)

Adam, Ralph. "Meeting the Information Needs of Social Scientists." *Information Scientist* 9, 4 (1975): 141-148.

Aguilar, William. "The Application of Relative Use and Interlibrary Demand in Collection Development." *Collection Management* 8, 1 (1986): 15-24.

American Library Association. Public Library Development Project. *Output Measures for Public Libraries: A Manual of Standardized Procedures.* 2nd ed. Chicago, Ill.: American Library Association, 1987.

Association of Research Libraries. Office of Management Studies. Systems and Procedures Exchange Center. *User Surveys and Evaluation of Library Surveys.* SPEC Kit 24. Washington, D.C.: Association of Research Libraries, 1976.

Association of Research Libraries. Office of Management Studies. Systems and Procedures Exchange Center. *Surveys.* SPEC Kit 71. Washington, D.C.: Association of Research Libraries, 1981.

Attman, Ellen, *et al. A Data Gathering and Instruction Manual for Performance Measures in Public Libraries.* Chicago, Ill.: Celadon Press, 1976.

Baker, David, ed. *Student Reading Needs and Higher Education.* London: Library Association, 1986.

Beeler, M.G. Fancher. *Measuring the Quality of Library Service.* Metuchen, N.J.: Scarecrow Press, 1974.

Blaxter, K. L., and Blaxter, M.L. "The Individual and the Information Problem." *Nature* 246 (1973): 335-339.

Bookstein, Abraham. "On the Complexity of Asking Questions: Difficulties in Interpretation of Library Surveys." In *Library Effectiveness: A State of the Art; Papers from a 1980 ALA Preconference,* 35-48. Chicago, Ill.: Library Administration and Management Association/American Library Association, 1980.

Bookstein, Abraham. "Sources of Error in Library Questionnaires." *Library Research* 4, 1 (1982): 85-94.

Borkowski, Casimir, and MacLeod, Murdo J. "The Implications of Some Recent Studies of Library Use." *Scholarly Publishing* 11 (1979): 3-24.

Bradburn, N.M., and Sudman, S. *Improving Interview Method and Questionnaire Design.* San Francisco, Calif.: Jossey-Bass, 1979.

Broadbent, Marianne. "Who Wins? Who Loses? User Success and Failure in the State Library of Victoria." *Australian Academic and Research Libraries* 15, 2 (1984): 65-80.

Broadus, Robert N. "Use Studies of Library Collections." *Library Resources and Technical Services* 24, 4 (1980): 317-324.

Buckland, Michael K. *Book Availability and the Library User.* New York: Pergamon Press, 1975.

Buckland, Michael K. "On Types of Search and the Allocation of Library Resources." *Journal of the American Society for Information Science* 30, 3 (1979): 143-147.

Buckland, Michael K., *et al. Systems Analysis of a University Library.* University of Lancaster Library Occasional Papers, No. 14. Lancaster: University of Lancaster, 1970.

Budd, John. "Libraries and Statistical Studies: An Equivocal Relationship." *Journal of Academic Librarianship* 8, 5 (1982): 278-281.

Burns, Robert W., Jr. "Library Use as a Performance Measure: Its Background and Rationale." *Journal of Academic Librarianship* 4, 1 (1978): 4-11.

Busha, Charles H., and Harter, Stephen P. *Research Methods in Librarianship: Techniques and Interpretation.* Library and Information Science Series. New York: Academic Press, 1980.

Byrd, Gary D.; Thomas, D.A.; and Hughes, Katherine E. "Collection Development Using Interlibrary Loan Borrowing and Acquisitions Statistics." *Bulletin of the Medical Library Association* 70, 1 (1982): 1-9.

Campbell, D.T., and Fiske, D.W. "Convergent and Discriminant Validation by the Multitrait-multimethod Matrix." *Psychological Bulletin* 56 (1959): 81-105.

Carpenter, Ray. "A Study of Adult Public Library Patrons in North Carolina." *North Carolina Libraries* 35 (1977): 24-36.

Chen, C.C. "The Use Patterns of Physics Journals in a Large Academic Research Library." *Journal of the American Society for Information Science* 23 (1972): 254-270.

Christiansen, Dorothy E.; Davis, C. Roger; and Reed-Scott, Jutta. "Guide to Collection Evaluation through Use and User Studies." *Library Resources and Technical Services* 27, 4 (1983): 434-440.

Chweh, Steven S. "User Criteria for Evaluation of Library Service." *Journal of Library Administration* 2, 1 (1981): 35-46.

Ciliberti, A.C., *et al.* "Material Availability: A Study of Academic Library Performance." *College and Research Libraries* 48 (1987): 513-527.

Clark, Philip M. *New Approaches to the Measurement of Public Library Use by Individual Patrons.* Occasional Papers, No. 162. Champaign, Ill.: University of Illinois, Graduate School of Library and Information Science, 1983.

Daniel, Evelyn H. "Performance Measures for School Librarians." In *Advances in Librarianship*, Vol. 6, edited by Melvin J. Voigt and Michael H. Harris, 1-51. New York: Academic Press, 1976.

D'Elia, George. "The Development and Testing of a Conceptual Model of Public Library User Behavior." *Library Quarterly* 50 (1980): 410-430.

DeProspo, Ernest R., *et al. Performance Measures for Public Libraries.* Chicago, Ill.: American Library Association, 1973.

DeProspo, Ernest R., *et al. Performance Measures for Public Libraries: A Procedures Manual for the Collection and Tabulation of Data.* New Brunswick, N.J.: Rutgers University, Bureau of Library and Information Science Research, 1974.

Detweiler, Mary Jo. "Planning - More than Process." *Library Journal* 108, 1 (1983): 23-26.

DuMont, Rosemary R., and DuMont, Paul F. *Assessing the Effectiveness of Library Service.* Occasional Papers, No. 152. Champaign, Ill.: University of Illinois, Graduate School of Library and Information Science, 1981.

Estabrook, Leigh S. "Valuing a Document Delivery System." *RQ* 26, 1 (1986): 58-62.

Evans, G. Edward. "Book Selection and Book Collection Usage in Academic Libraries." *Library Quarterly* 40, 4 (1970): 297-308.

Evans, G. Edward; Borko, Harold; and Ferguson, Patricia. "Review of Criteria Used to Measure Library Effectiveness." In *Reader in Library Management*, edited by Ross Shimmer, 166-180. London: Clive Bingley, 1976.

Flynn, Roger R. "The University of Pittsburgh Study of Journal Usage: A Summary Report." *Serials Librarian* 4, 1 (1979): 25-33.

Ford, Geoffrey. "Research in User Behaviour in University Libraries." *Journal of Documentation* 29, 1 (1973): 85-106.

Fry, Bernard M., and White, Herbert S. *Publishers and Libraries: A Study of Scholarly and Research Journals.* Lexington, Mass.: D.C. Heath, 1976.

Fry, Edward B. "A Readability Graph for School Libraries. Part I." *School Libraries* 19, 1 (1969): 13-16.

Fussler, Herman H., and Simon, Julian L. *Patterns in the Use of Books in Large Research Libraries.* Rev. ed. Chicago, Ill.: University of Chicago Press, 1969.

Garfield, E. "Which Medical Journals Have the Greatest Impact?" *Annals of Internal Medicine* 105 (1986): 313-320.

Goehlert, R. "Book Availability and Delivery Service." *Journal of Academic Librarianship* 4 (1978): 368-371.

Gordon, Martin. "Periodicals Use at a Small College." *Serials Librarian* 6 (1982): 63-73.

Govan, James F."Community Analysis in an Academic Environment." *Library Trends* 24, 3 (1976): 541-556.

Greene, Robert J. "The Effectiveness of Browsing." *College and Research Libraries* 38, 4 (1977): 313-316.

Grosser, Kerry. "Library Usage Habits amongst Melbourne's Tertiary Students." *Australian Academic and Research Libraries* 19, 1 (1988): 1-14.

Handfield, Carey, and Hamilton-Smith, Elery. *Libraries and People in Melbourne: A Study for the Library Council of Victoria.* Melbourne: Library Council of Victoria, 1975.

Hardesty, Larry. "Use of Library Materials at a Small Liberal Arts College." *Library Research* 3 (1981): 261-282.

Harris, Michael H., and Sodt, James. "Libraries, Users and Librarians: Continuing Efforts to Define the Nature of Public Library Use." In *Advances in Librarianship*, Vol. 11, edited by Michael H. Harris, 109-133. New York: Academic Press, 1981.

Hayes, R.M. "The Distribution of Use of Library Materials: Analysis of Data from the University of Pittsburgh." *Library Research* 3 (1981): 215-260.

Herner, Saul, and Herner, Mary. "Information Needs and Uses in Science and Technology." *Annual Review of Information Science and Technology* 2 (1967): 1-34.

Hindle, A., and Buckland, Michael K. "In-library Book Usage in Relation to Circulation." *Collection Management* 2 (1978): 265-277.

Hodowanec, George V. "Library User Behavior." *Collection Management* 3, 2/3 (1979): 215-232.

Jain, A.K. "Sampling and Data Collection Methods for a Book-use Study." *Library Quarterly* 39 (1969): 245-252.

Jenks, George M. "Circulation and Its Relationship to the Book Collection and Academic Departments." *College and Research Libraries* 27 (1966): 211-218.

Kahn, R.L., and Cannell, C.F. *The Dynamics of Interviewing.* New York: John Wiley and Sons, 1957.

Kantor, Paul B. "Availability Analysis." *Journal of the American Society for Information Science* 27, 5 (1976): 316-318.

Kantor, Paul B. "Demand-adjusted Shelf Availability Parameters." *Journal of Academic Librarianship* 7, 2 (1981): 78-82.

Kantor, Paul B. *Objective Performance Measures for Academic and Research Libraries.* Washington, D.C.: Association of Research Libraries, 1984.

Kantor, Paul B. "Vitality: An Indirect Measure of Relevance." *Collection Management* 2, 1 (1978): 83-95.

Kaske, Neal K. "An Evaluation of Current Collection Utilization Methodologies and Findings." *Collection Management* 3, 2/3 (1979): 187.199.

Kent, Allen, *et al. Use of Library Materials: The University of Pittsburgh Study.* New York: Marcel Dekker, 1979.

Kim, Choong Ham, and Little, Robert D. *Public Library Users and Uses: A Market Research Handbook.* Metuchen, N.J.: Scarecrow Press, 1987.

Knightly, John J. "Overcoming the Criterion Problem in the Evaluation of Library Performance." *Special Libraries* 70, 4 (1979): 173-178.

Krikelas, James. "Information-seeking Behaviour: Patterns and Concepts." *Drexel Library Quarterly* 19, 2 (1983): 5-20.

Kronus, Carol L. "Patterns of Adult Library Use: A Regression and Path Analysis." *Adult Education* 23 (1973): 115-131.

Lack, Clara R. "Can Bibliotherapy Go Public?" *Collection Building* 7 (1985): 27-32.

Lancaster, F. Wilfrid. "Evaluating Collections by Their Use." *Collection Management* 4, 1/2 (1982): 15-43.

Lancaster, F. Wilfrid. *The Measurement and Evaluation of Library Services.* Washington, D.C.: Information Resources Press, 1977.

Langlois, Dianne C., and Von Schulz, Jeanne V. "Journal Usage Survey: Method and Application." *Special Libraries* 63 (1973): 239-243.

Leedy, Paul D. *Practical Research: Planning and Design.* 3rd ed. New York: Macmillan, 1985.

Leimkuhler, Ferdinand F. "The Bradford Distribution." *Journal of Documentation* 23 (1967): 197-207.

Line, Maurice B. "The Ability of a University Library to Provide Books Wanted by Researchers." *Journal of Librarianship* 5, 1 (1973): 37-51.

Line, Maurice B., and Sandison, A. "'Obsolescence' and Changes in the Use of Literature with Time." *Journal of Documentation* 30 (1974): 283-350.

Line, Maurice B., and Vickers, S. *Universal Availability of Publications.* Munich: K.G. Saur, 1983.

Lubans, John. "Library User Studies." In *Encyclopedia of Library and Information Science,* Vol. 16, 147-160. New York: Marcel Dekker, 1975.

Lynch, Mary Jo. "Measurement of Public Library Activity: The Search for Practical Methods." *Wilson Library Bulletin* 57 (1983): 388-393.

McClure, Charles R. "A View from the Trenches: Costing and Performance Measures for Academic Library Public Services." *College and Research Libraries* 47, 4 (1986): 324.

McGrath, William E. "Circulation Studies and Collection Development: Problems of Methodology, Theory and Typology for Research." In *Collection Development in Libraries: A Treatise, Part B,* edited by Robert D. Stueart and George B. Miller, Jr., 373-403. Foundations in Library and Information Science, Vol. 10. Greenwich, Conn.: JAI Press, 1980.

McGrath, William E. "Correlating the Subjects of Books Taken out of and Books Used within an Open-stack Library." *College and Research Libraries* 32, 4 (1971): 280-285.

McGrath, William E. "Measuring Classified Circulation According to Curriculum." *College and Research Libraries* 29 (1968): 347-350.

McGrath, William E. "The Significance of Books Used According to a Classified Profile of Academic Departments." *College and Research Libraries* 33 (1972): 212-219.

McIntyre, L.B. *Stock Failure in RMIT Central Library 1978-1981.* Melbourne: Royal Melbourne Institute of Technology, Department of Librarianship, 1981.

McMurdo, George. "User Satisfaction." *New Library World* 81, 958 (1980): 83-85.

Mancall, Jacqueline C., and Drott, M. Carl. *Measuring Student Information Use: A Guide for School Library Media Specialists.* Littleton, Colo.: Libraries Unlimited, 1983.

Mann, Peter, ed. *Books and Undergraduates: Proceedings of a Conference Held at Royal Holloway College, University of London, 4-6 July 1975.* London: National Book League, 1976.

Mann, Peter H. "Identifying User Needs." In *Alternative Futures: Proceedings of the 20th Biennial Conference of the Library Association of Australia, 26-30 August 1979,* 34-45. Sydney: Library Association of Australia, 1979.

Mansbridge, J. "Availability Studies in Libraries." *Library and Information Science Research* 8 (1986): 299-314.

Martyn, John. "Unintentional Duplication of Research." *New Scientist* 377 (1964): 338.

Maxin, Jacqueline A. "Periodical Use and Collection Development." *College and Research Libraries* 40, 3 (1979): 248-253.

Metz, Paul. *The Landscape of Literatures: Use of Subject Collections in a Library.* Chicago, Ill.: American Library Association, 1983.

Mick, Colin K.; Lindsey, George N.; and Callahan, Daniel. "Toward Usable User Studies." *Journal of the American Society for Information Science* 31, 5 (1980): 347-356.

Moll, Joy K., ed. *Collection Management: Special Issue on Bibliometrics* 2, 3 (1978): entire issue.

Morse, P.M. "Demand for Library Materials: An Exercise in Probability Analysis." *Collection Management* 1 (1976/1977): 47-78.

Moser, C.A., and Kalton, G. *Survey Methods in Social Investigation.* 2nd ed. London: Heinemann, 1971.

Mueller, Elizabeth. "Are New Books Read More Than Old Ones?" *Library Quarterly* 35 (1965): 166-172.

Nimmer, R.J. "Circulation and Collection Patterns at the Ohio State University Libraries 1973-1977." *Library Acquisitions: Practice and Theory* 4 (1980): 61-70.

Norton, Robert, and Gautschi, David. "User Survey of an International Library: Expectations and Evaluations." *Aslib Proceedings* 37 (1985): 195-206.

Oakeshott, P., and White, B. *Impact of New Technology on the Availability of Publications.* London: British Library, 1984.

Oldman, Christine, and Wills, Gordon. *The Beneficial Library.* Bradford: MCB Books, 1977.

Orr, Richard H. "Measuring the Goodness of Library Services: A General Framework for Considering Quantitative Measures." *Journal of Documentation* 29, 3 (1973): 315-332.

Orr, Richard H., *et al.* "Development of Methodologic Tools for Planning and Managing Library Services, II: Measuring a Library's Capability for Providing Documents." *Bulletin of the Medical Library Association* 56, 3 (1968): 241-267.

Osburn, Charles B. "Non-Use and Loser Studies in Collection Development." *Collection Management* 4, 1/2 (1982): 45-53.

Passman, S. *Scientific and Technological Communication.* Oxford: Pergamon Press, 1969.

Payne, S.L. *The Art of Asking Questions.* Princeton, N.J.: Princeton University Press, 1951.

Pope, Michael J. "Use of Periodical Backfiles in a Community College Library." *Community/Junior College Research Quarterly* 2, 2 (1978): 163-177.

Powell, Ronald R. *Basic Research Methods for Librarians.* Library and Information Science Series. Norwood, N.J.: Ablex Publishing Company, 1985.

Powell, Ronald R. "Library Use and Personality: The Relationship between Locus of Control and Frequency of Use." *Library and Information Science Research* 6, 2 (1984): 179-190.

Power, C.J., and Bell, G.H. "Automated Circulation, Patron Satisfaction and Collection Evaluation in Academic Libraries - A Circulation Analysis Formula." *Journal of Library Automation* 11 (1978): 366-369.

Public Libraries Research Group. *Output Measurement.* PLRG Publications, No. 1. London: Public Libraries Research Group, 1974.

Raffel, Jeffrey A., and Shisko, Robert. *Systematic Analysis of University Libraries: An Application of Cost-benefit Analysis to the MIT Libraries.* Cambridge, Mass.: MIT Press, 1969.

Ramsden, Michael J. *Performance Measurement of Some Melbourne Public Libraries.* Melbourne, Vic.: Library Council of Victoria, 1978.

Rice, Barbara A. "Science Periodicals Use Study." *Serials Librarian* 4, 1 (1979): 35-47.

Roberts, Michael. "A Barometer of 'Unmet Demand': Interlibrary Loans Analysis and Monographic Acquisitions." *Library Acquisitions: Practice and Theory* 8, 1 (1984): 31-42.

Saracevic, Tefko; Shaw, W.M.; and Kantor, Paul B. "Causes and Dynamics of User Frustration in an Academic Library." *College and Research Libraries* 38, 1 (1977): 7-18.

Sargent, Seymour H. "The Uses and Limitations of Trueswell." *College and Research Libraries* 40, 5 (1979): 416-423.

Schwarz, Philip J. "Demand-adjusted Shelf Availability Parameters: A Second Look." *College and Research Libraries* 44, 4 (1983): 210-219.

Selltiz, C.; Wrightsman, L.S.; and Cook, S.W. *Research Methods in Social Relations.* 3rd ed. New York: Holt, Rinehart and Winston, 1976.

Shaw, W.M., Jr. "A Practical Journal Usage Technique." *College and Research Libraries* 39 (1978): 479-484.

Skelton, Barbara. "Scientists and Social Scientists as Information Users: A Comparison of Results of Science User Studies with the Investigation into Information Requirements of the Social Sciences." *Journal of Librarianship* 5, 2 (1973): 138-156.

Snow, Christine. "Architects' Wants and Needs for Information Demonstrated through a University-based Information Service." *Aslib Proceedings* 27, 3 (1975): 112-123.

Soper, Mary E. "Characteristics and Use of Personal Collections." *Library Quarterly* 46, 4 (1976): 397-415.

Stenstrom, Patricia, and McBride, Ruth B. "Serial Use by Social Science Faculty: A Survey." *College and Research Libraries* 40, 5 (1979): 426-431.

Strain, Paula M. "A Study of the Usage and Retention of Technical Periodicals." *Library Resources and Technical Services* 10 (1966): 295-304.

Stroud, Janet G., and Loertscher, David V. "User Needs and School Library Service." *Catholic Library World* 49 (1977): 162-165.

Tobin, J.C. "A Study of Library 'Use Studies'." *Information Storage and Retrieval* 10 (1974): 101-113.

Trochim, M.K., *et al. Measuring the Circulation Use of a Smaller Academic Library Collection: A Manual.* Chicago, Ill.: Associated Colleges of the Midwest, 1980.

Trueswell, Richard W. "User Circulation Satisfaction vs. Size of Holdings at Three Academic Libraries." *College and Research Libraries* 30 (1969): 204-213.

Urquhart, John A., and Schofield, J.L. "Measuring Readers' Failure at the Shelf." *Journal of Documentation* 27, 4 (1971): 272-286.

Urquhart, John A., and Schofield, J.L. "Measuring Readers' Failure at the Shelf in Three University Libraries." *Journal of Documentation* 28 (1972): 233-241.

Wender, Ruth W. "Counting Journal Title Usage in Health Sciences." *Special Libraries* 70, 5 (1979): 219-226.

Wilson, Pauline C. *A Community Elite and the Public Library: The Uses of Information in Leadership.* Westport, Conn.: Greenwood Press, 1977.

Wilson, Pauline C. "Information-seeking Activity of Selected Members of Community Groups Seeking Social Change." Ph.D. dissertation, University of Michigan, 1972.

Yerbury, Hilary. "Is Library Use Using a Library?" *Australian Library Journal* 33, 2 (1984): 19-23.

Zweizig, Douglas. "Community Analysis." In *Local Public Library Administration,* 2nd ed., edited by Ellen Altman, 38-46. Chicago, Ill.: American Library Association, 1980.

Zweizig, Douglas. "Measuring Library Use." *Drexel Library Quarterly* 13 (1977): 3-15.

Zweizig, Douglas, and Dervin, Brenda. "Public Library Use, Users, Uses: Advances in Knowledge of the Characteristics and Needs of the Adult Clientele of American Public Libraries." In *Advances in Librarianship,* Volume 7, edited by Melvin J. Voigt and Michael H. Harris, 231-255. New York: Academic Press, 1977.

Zweizig, Douglas, and Rodger, Eleanor Jo. *Output Measures for Public Libraries.* Chicago, Ill.: American Library Association, 1982.

7. Selection and Evaluation of Library Materials
(See also Sections 2, 5-6, 8-12)

Axford, H. William. "The Economics of a Domestic Approval Plan." *College and Research Libraries* 32, 5 (1971): 368-375.

Baker, Sharon L. "Does the Use of a Demand-oriented Selection Policy Reduce Overall Collection Quality? A Review of the Evidence." *Public Library Quarterly* 5 (1984): 29-49.

Barber, Raymond W., and Mancall, Jacqueline C. "The Application of Bibliometric Techniques to the Analysis of Materials for Young Adults." *Collection Management* 2 (1978): 229-241.

Barrette, Pierre P. "Selecting Digital Electronic Knowledge: A Process Model." *School Library Media Quarterly* 10, 4 (1982): 320-336.

Bell, Jo-Ann, *et al.* "Faculty Input in Book Selection: A Comparison of Alternative Methods." *Bulletin of the Medical Library Association* 75, 3 (1987): 228-233.

Belland, John C. "Factors Influencing Selection of Materials." *School Media Quarterly* 6, 2 (1978): 112-119.

Biskup, Peter, and Jones, Catherine A. "Of Books, Academics and Librarians: Some Facts about the Book Selection Habits of the Teaching Staff of Two Canberra Institutions of Higher Learning." *Australian Academic and Research Libraries* 7, 3 (1976): 159-170.

Bob, Murray L. "The Case for Quality Book Selection." *Library Journal* 107, 16 (1982): 1707-1710.

Broadus, Robert N. *Selecting Materials for Libraries.* 2nd ed. New York: H.W. Wilson, 1981.

Brownson, Charles W. "Mechanical Selection." *Library Resources and Technical Services* 32, 1 (1988): 17-29.

Burr, Robert L., *et al.* "Six Responses to 'A Rationalist's Critique'." *Journal of Academic Librarianship* 7, 3 (1981): 144-151.

Byrd, Gary D., and Koenig, Michael E.D. "Systematic Serials Selection Analysis in a Small Academic Health Sciences Library." *Bulletin of the Medical Library Association* 66 (1978): 397-406.

Cabeceiras, James. *The Multimedia Library: Materials Selection and Use.* Library and Information Science Series. New York: Academic Press, 1978.

Calhoun, John, and Bracken, James K. "An Index of Publisher Quality for the Academic Library." *College and Research Libraries* 4, 3 (1983): 257-259.

Calmes, Alan. "New Confidence in Microfilm." *Library Journal* 111, 15 (1986): 38-42.

Cargill, Jennifer S., and Alley, Brian. *Practical Approval Plan Management*. Phoenix, Ariz.: Oryx Press, 1979.

Cenzer, Pam. "Library/Faculty Relations in the Acquisitions and Collection Development Process." *Library Acquisitions: Practice and Theory* 7, 3 (1983): 215-219.

Chisholm, Margaret E. "Selection of Media." In *Collection Development in Libraries: A Treatise, Part B*, edited by Robert D. Stueart and George B. Miller, Jr., 469-496. Foundations in Library and Information Science, Vol. 10. Greenwich, Conn.: JAI Press, 1980.

Craig, James. "Evaluating Materials: A System for Selection of Non-Print Materials." *Media Spectrum* 9 (1982): 5-6.

D'Aniello, Charles. "Bibliography and the Beginning Bibliographer." *Collection Building* 6, 2 (1984): 11-19.

Danton, J. Periam. "The Subject Specialist in National and University Libraries with Special Reference to Book Selection." *Libri* 17, 1 (1967): 42-58.

DePew, John N. "An Acquisitions Decision Model for Academic Libraries." *Journal of the American Society for Information Science* 26 (1975): 230-246.

De Vilbiss, Mary Lee. "The Approval-built Collection in the Medium-sized Academic Library." *College and Research Libraries* 36, 6 (1975): 487-492.

Dhawan, S.M.; Phull, S.K.; and Jain, S.P. "Selection of Scientific Journals: A Model." *Journal of Documentation* 36, 1 (1980): 24-30.

Dickinson, Dennis W. "A Rationalist's Critique of Book Selection for Academic Libraries." *Journal of Academic Librarianship* 7, 3 (1981): 138-143.

Dickinson, Dennis W. "Subject Specialists in Academic Libraries: The Once and Future Dinosaurs." In *New Horizons for Academic Libraires*, 438-444. New York: K.G. Saur, 1979.

Dobbyn, Margaret. "Approval Plan Purchasing in Perspective." *College and Research Libraries* 3, 6 (1972): 480-484.

Dudley, Norman. "The Blanket Order." *Library Trends* 18, 3 (1970): 318-327.

Dukes, Robert J., Jr. "Faculty/Library Relations in Acquisitions and Collection Development: The Faculty Perspective." *Library Acquisitions: Practice and Theory* 7, 3 (1983): 221-224.

Edelman, Hendrik. "Selection Methodology in Academic Libraries." *Library Resources and Technical Services* 23, 1 (1979): 33-38.

Ellison, John W. "Non-Print Selection: A Combination of Methods." *Catholic Library World* 54 (1982): 119-121.

England, Claire, and Fasick, Adele M. *ChildView: Evaluating and Reviewing Materials for Children.* Littleton, Colo.: Libraries Unlimited, 1987.

Evans, G. Edward, and Argyres, Claudia White. "Approval Plans and Collection Development in Academic Libraries." *Library Resources and Technical Services* 18, 2 (1974): 35-50.

Fisher, William H. "Use of Selection Committees by California Academic Libraries." *Journal of Academic Librarianship* 10, 2 (1984): 94-99.

Garland, Kathleen. "The Brillouin Information Measure Applied to Materials Selection." *Collection Management* 3, 4 (1979): 371-380.

Gill, Philip. "Book Selection: By What Criteria and with What Objective?" *Library Review* 28 (1979): 3-7.

Grochmal, Helen M. "Selection Criteria for Periodicals in Microform." *Serials Librarian* 5 (1981): 15-17.

Hamlin, Jean B. "The Selection Process." In *Collection Development in Libraries: A Treatise, Part A*, edited by Robert D. Stueart and George B. Miller, Jr., 185-201. Foundations in Library and Information Science, Vol. 10. Greenwich, Conn.: JAI Press, 1980.

Hannabuss, Stuart. "Resources for Love: Intimate Thoughts on Stock Selection." *Assistant Librarian* 80, 1 (1987): 6-9.

Hannigan, Jane A. "The Evaluation of Microcomputer Software." *Library Trends* 33, 3 (1985): 327-348.

Hardesty, Vicki H. "Selection Protection." *Indiana Media Journal* 7 (1985): 5-9.

Hartz, Frederic R. "Selection of School/Media Materials." *Catholic Library World* 47 (1976): 425-429.

Hearne, Betsy G. *Choosing Books for Children: A Commonsense Guide.* New York: Delacorte Press, 1981.

Helmer, D.J., and Mika, J.J., comps. *Selecting Materials for School Library Media Centers.* Chicago, Ill.: American Association of School Librarians, 1985.

Hill, Bonnie Naifeh. "Collection Development: The Right and Responsibility of Librarians." *Journal of Academic Librarianship* 3, 5 (1977): 285-286.

Horn, Judy. "Government Publications." In *Selection of Library Materials in the Humanities, Social Sciences and Sciences*, edited by Patricia A McClung, 313-334. Chicago, Ill.: American Library Association, 1985.

Hulbert, Linda Ann, and Curry, David Stewart. "Evaluation of an Approval Plan." *College and Research Libraries* 39, 6 (1978): 485-491.

Jenks, George M. "Book Selection: An Approach for Small and Medium-sized Libraries." *College and Research Libraries* 33, 1 (1972): 28-30.

Johnson, Carol A., and Trueswell, Richard W. "The Weighted Criteria Statistic Score: An Approach to Journal Selection." *College and Research Libraries* 39, 4 (1978): 287-292.

Katz, William A. *Collection Development: The Selection of Materials for Libraries.* New York: Holt, Rinehart and Winston, 1980.

Katz, William A. *Magazine Selection: How to Build a Community-oriented Collection.* New York: R.R. Bowker, 1971.

Kevil, L. Hunter. "The Approval Plan of Smaller Scope." *Library Acquisitions: Practice and Theory* 9 (1985): 13-20.

Kim, Ung Chon. "Participation of Teaching Faculty in Library Book Selection." *Collection Management* 3, 4 (1979): 333-352.

Leonardt, Thomas W., ed. *Approval Plans in ARL Libraries.* Washington, D.C.: Association of Research Libraries, Office of Management Studies, 1982.

Losee, Robert M. "A Decision Theoretic Model of Materials Selection for Acquisition." *Library Quarterly* 57, 3 (1987): 269-283.

McClung, Patricia A., ed. *Selection of Library Materials in the Humanities, Social Sciences, and Sciences.* Chicago, Ill.: American Library Association, 1985.

McCullough, Kathleen. "Approval Plans: Vendor Responsibility and Library Research: A Literature Survey and Discussion." *College and Research Libraries* 33, 5 (1972): 368-381.

McCullough, Kathleen; Posey, Edwin D.; and Pickett, Doyle C. *Approval Plans and Academic Libraries: An Interpretive Survey.* Phoenix, Ariz.: Oryx Press, 1977.

MacLean, Kay. "A Survey of Australasian Library Selection Procedures." *Australian Academic and Research Libraries* 16, 1 (1985): 21-31.

McNiff, Philip. "Book Selection and Provision in the Urban Library." *Library Quarterly* 38, 1 (1968): 58-69.

Messick, Frederic M. "Subject Specialists in Smaller Academic Libraries." *Library Resources and Technical Services* 21, 4 (1977): 368-374.

Moody, Marilyn K. "Selecting Documents: Using Core Lists of Item Selections." *RQ* 26 (1987): 305-309.

Norman, Ronald V. "A Method of Book Selection for a Small Public Library." *RQ* 17 (1977): 143-145.

Ottness, Harold M. "Wanderlust and Fireside: Building a Travel Collection." *Library Journal* 113, 8 (1988): 33-36.

Pasterczyk, Catherine E. "A Quantitative Methodology for Evaluating Approval Plan Performance." *Collection Management* 10, 1/2 (1988): 25-38.

Peasgood, Adrian N. "Towards Demand-led Book Acquisitions? Experiences in the University of Sussex Library." *Journal of Librarianship* 18, 4 (1986): 242-256.

Purcell, Gary R. "United States Government Publication Collection Development for Non-depository Libraries." *Government Publications Review* 8A, 1/2 (1981): 31-45.

Quinn, Kenneth. "Using DIALOG as a Book Selection Tool." *Library Acquisitions: Practice and Theory* 9, 1 (1985): 79-82.

Rada, Roy, *et al.* "Computerized Guides to Journal Selection." *Information Technology and Libraries* 6 (1987): 173-184.

Ranganathan, S.R. *Library Book Selection.* New Delhi: Indian Library Association, 1952.

Reidelbach, John H., and Shirk, Gary M. "Selecting an Approval Plan Vendor: A Step-by-Step Process." *Library Acquisitions: Practice and Theory* 7, 2 (1983): 115-122.

Reidelbach, John H., and Shirk, Gary M. "Selecting an Approval Plan Vendor II: Comparative Vendor Data." *Library Acquisitions: Practice and Theory* 8, 3 (1984): 157-202.

Reidelbach, John H., and Shirk, Gary M. "Selecting an Approval Plan Vendor III: Academic Librarians' Evaluations of Eight United States Approval Plan Vendors." *Library Acquisitions: Practice and Theory* 9, 3 (1985): 177-260.

Roper, Fred W. "Selecting Federal Publications." *Special Libraries* 65 (1974): 326-331.

Rouse, Roscoe. "Automation Stops Here: A Case for Manmade Book Collections." *College and Research Libraries* 31, 3 (1970): 147-154.

Rowell, John, and Heidbreder, Ann M. *Educational Media Selection Centers: Identification and Analysis of Current Practices.* ALA Studies in Librarianship, No. 1. Chicago, Ill.: American Library Association, 1971.

Rutledge, John, and Swindler, Luke. "The Selection Decision: Defining Criteria and Establishing Priorities." *College and Research Libraries* 48, 2 (1987): 123-131.

Ryland, John. "Collection Development and Selection: Who Should Do It?" *Library Acquisitions: Practice and Theory* 6, 1 (1982): 13-17.

Sandler, Mark. "Organizing Effective Faculty Participation in Collection Development." *Collection Management* 6, 3/4 (1984): 63-72.

Scheppke, James B. "Public Library Book Selection." *Unabashed Librarian* 52 (1984): 5-6.

Sive, Mary R. *Media Selection Handbook.* Littleton, Colo.: Libraries Unlimited, 1983.

Smith, Eldred R. "Out-of-print Booksearching." *College and Research Libraries* 29, 4 (1968): 303-309.

Smith, Lotsee P. "The Curriculum and Materials Selection: Requisite for Collection Development." In *Collection Management for School Library Media Centers,* edited by Brenda H. White, 37-44. New York: Haworth Press, 1986.

Spaulding, F.H., and Stanton, R.O. "Computer-aided Selection in a Library Network." *Journal of the American Society for Information Science* 27 (1976): 269-280.

Spiller, David. *Book Selection: An Introduction to Principles and Practice.* 4th ed. London: Clive Bingley, 1986.

Spofford, Ainsworth R. "A Guide to Book Selection." In *Ainsworth Rand Spofford: Bookman and Librarian,* edited by John T. Cole, 110-127. The Heritage of Librarianship Series, No. 2. Littleton, Colo.: Libraries Unlimited, 1975.

Spreitzer, Francis F. ed. *Microforms in Libraries: A Manual for Evaluation and Management.* Chicago, Ill.: American Library Association, 1985.

Spyers-Duran, Peter, ed. *Approval and Gathering Plans in Academic Libraries.* Littleton, Colo.: Libraries Unlimited for Western Michigan University, 1969.

Spyers-Duran, Peter, and Gore, Daniel, eds. *Economics of Approval Plans.* Westport, Conn.: Greenwood Press, 1972.

Stankus, Tony. "Looking for Tutors and Brokers: Comparing the Expectations of Book and Journal Evaluators." *Library Trends* 33, 3 (Winter 1985): 349-365.

Stankus, Tony, ed. *Scientific Journals: Issues in Library Selection and Management.* New York: Haworth Press, 1987.

Subramanyan, K. "Criteria for Journal Selection."*Special Libraries* 66, 8 (1975): 367-371.

Swisher, Robert, *et al.* "Involving Young Adults in Fiction Selection." *Top of the News* 40 (1984): 163-170.

Tanselle, G. Thomas. "Descriptive Bibliography and Library Cataloguing." *Studies in Bibliography* 30 (1977): 1-56.

Tauber, Maurice F. "The Faculty and the Development of Library Collections." *Journal of Higher Education* 32 (1961): 454-458.

Thomas, Lawrence. "Tradition and Expertise in Academic Library Collection Development." *College and Research Libraries* 48 (1987): 487-493.

Tuttle, Marcia. "Serials." In *Selection of Library Materials in the Humanities, Social Sciences and Sciences,* edited by Patricia A McClung, 34-47. Chicago, Ill.: American Library Association, 1985.

Veaner, Allen B. *The Evaluation of Micropublications: A Handbook for Librarians.* Chicago, Ill.: American Library Association, 1971.

Vidor, David L., and Futas, Elizabeth W. "Effective Collection Developers: Librarians or Faculty?" *Library Resources and Technical Services* 32, 2 (1988): 127-136.

Warwick, J.P. "Duplication of Texts in Academic Libraries: A Behavioural Model for Library Management." *Journal of Librarianship* 19, 1 (1987): 41-52.

Weller, Ann C. "The 'Instructions to Authors' Section as an Aid in Serials Collection Development." *Serials Librarian* 11, 3/4 (1986/1987): 143-154.

Whitehead, Robert J. *A Guide to Selecting Books for Children.* Metuchen, N.J.: Scarecrow Press, 1984.

Whittaker, Kenneth. *Systematic Evaluation: Methods and Sources for Assessing Books.* London: Clive Bingley, 1982.

Wilden-Hart, Marion. "The Long-term Effects of Approval Plans." *Library Resources and Technical Services* 14, 3 (1970): 400-406.

Woodbury, Marda. *Selecting Materials for Instruction.* 3 vols. Littleton, Colo.: Libraries Unlimited, 1979-1980.

Woolls, E. Blanche. "Selecting Software." In *The Microcomputer Facility and the School Library Media Specialist,* edited by E. Blanche Woolls and David V. Loertscher, 14-24. Chicago, Ill.: American Library Association, 1986.

Woolls, E. Blanche; Loertscher, David V.; and Shirey, Donald. *Evaluation Techniques for School Library/Media Programs: A Workshop Outline.* Pittsburgh, Pa.: University of Pittsburgh Press, 1977.

Yates, Jessica. "Book Selection for Young People in the Public Library: A Survey." *Assistant Librarian* 80, 4 (1987): 55-62.

8. Reviews and Reviewing
(See also Section 7)

Arbetman, L. "Reviewing the Books School Children Read: Censorship or Selection?" *Georgia Social Science Journal* 14 (1983): 1-4.

Batt, Fred. "The Folly of Book Reviews." In *Options for the 80s: Proceedings of the Second National Conference of the Association of College and Research Libraries,* edited by Michael D. Kathman and Virgil F. Massman, 269-277. Foundations in Library and Information Science, Vol. 17A and B. Greenwich, Conn.: JAI Press, 1981.

Crow, Sherry R. "The Reviewing of Controversial Juvenile Books: A Study." *School Library Media Quarterly* 14, 2 (1986): 83-86.

Fisher, Susan. "Book Reviews in Five Library Journals: A Comparative Analysis." *Australian Library Journal* 30, 3 (1981): 87-96.

Furnham, A. "Book Reviews as a Selection Tool for Librarians: Comments from a Psychologist." *Collection Management* 8, 1 (1986): 33-43.

Katz, Bill, and Kinder, Robin, eds. *The Publishing and Review of Reference Sources.* New York: Haworth Press, 1987.

Lekachman, Robert. "No, but I Read the Reviews."*Wilson Library Bulletin* 39, 4 (1964): 325-330.

Macleod, Beth. "*Library Journal* and *Choice*: A Review of Reviews." *Journal of Academic Librarianship* 7, 1 (1981): 23-28.

Merritt, LeRoy C.; Boaz, Martha; and Tisdel, Kenneth S. *Reviews in Library Book Selection.* Detroit, Mich.: Wayne State University Press, 1958.

Muirden, Geoff. "The Art of Book Reviewing." *Australian Author* 12, 2 (1980): 10-12.

Murphy, Marcy, and Rehman, Sajjad ur. "The Reviewing of Management Literature." *Library Quarterly* 57, 1 (1987): 32-60.

Orwell, George. "Confessions of a Book Reviewer." In his*Collected Essays, Journalism and Letters,* Vol. 4, 181-184. London: Secker and Warburg, 1950.

Palmer, Judith L. "A Comparison of Content, Promptness and Coverage of New Fiction Titles Reviewed in *Library Journal* and *Booklist*." In *Advances in Library Administration and Organization,* Vol. 7, edited by Gerald B. McCabe and Bernard Kreissman, 89-133. Greenwich, Conn.: JAI Press, 1988.

Prawer, Michelle. "The Treatment of Novels in the Reviewing Literature." *Australian School Librarian* 22, 3 (1985): 78-83.

Ream, Daniel. "An Evaluation of Four Book Review Journals." *RQ* 19, 2 (1979): 149-153.

Schmitt, John P., and Saunders, Stewart. "Assessment of *Choice* as a Tool for Selection." *College and Research Libraries* 44, 5 (1983): 375-380.

Serebnick, Judith. "Book Reviews and the Selection of Potentially Controversial Books in Public Libraries." *Library Quarterly* 51, 4 (1981): 390-409.

Silver, Linda R. "Criticism, Reviewing and the Library Review Media." *Top of the News* 35, 2 (1979): 123-130.

Simon, Rita J., and Mahan, Linda. "A Note on the Role of Book Review Editors as Decision Makers." *Library Quarterly* 39, 4 (1969): 353-356.

Walford, A.J., ed. *Reviews and Reviewing: A Guide.* London: Mansell Publishing, 1986.

"What Makes a Good Review? Ten Experts Speak." *Top of the News* 35, 2 (1979): 146-152.

9. Selection Tools
(See also Section 7 and note at beginning of bibliography)

American Library Association. *Books for College Libraries: A Core Collection of 40,000 Titles.* 2nd ed. Chicago, Ill.: American Library Association, 1975.

Bell, Barbara L. *An Annotated Guide to Current National Bibliographies.* Alexandria, Va.: Chadwyck-Healey, 1986.

Bennion, Bruce C. "The Use of Standard Selection Sources in Undergraduate Library Collection Development." *Collection Management* 2, 2 (1978): 141-152.

Binder, Michael B. *Videotext and Teletext: New Online Resources for Libraries.* Greenwich, Conn.: JAI Press, 1985.

Borchardt, Dietrich H., ed. *Australian Official Publications.* Melbourne: Longman Cheshire, 1979.

Brandon, Alfred N., and Hill, Dorothy R. "Selected List of Books and Journals for a Small Medical Library." *Bulletin of the Medical Library Association* 69, 2 (1981): 185-193.

Burns, Elizabeth. "Religious Periodicals: A Recommended Collection." *Serials Review* 7, 1 (1981): 9-32.

Cherns, J.J. *Official Publications: An Overview.* Oxford: Pergamon Press, 1979.

Churukian, Araxie P. "Current National Bibliographies from the Near East as Collection Development Tools." *Library Resources and Technical Services* 30, 1 (1986): 72-78.

Gorman, G.E. "African National Bibliographies as Selection Sources." *International Library Review* (1989): in press.

Gorman, G.E., and Mills, J.J. "Evaluating Third World National Bibliographies as Selection Resources." *Library Acquisitions: Practice and Theory* 12, 1 (1988): 29-42.

Gorman, G.E., and Mills, J.J. *Guide to Current National Bibliographies in the Third World.* 2nd rev. ed. London: K.G. Saur, 1987.

Grove, Pearce S., ed. *Nonprint Media in Academic Libraries.* Chicago, Ill.: American Library Association, 1975.

Harrington, Michael. "Access to Australian Commonwealth Publications." *Library Acquisitions: Practice and Theory* 10, 4 (1986): 335-350.

Katz, William A., and Katz, Linda Sternberg. *Magazines for Libraries*. 5th ed. New York: R.R. Bowker, 1986.

Morehead, Joe. *Introduction to United States Public Documents*. 3rd ed. Littleton, Colo.: Libraries Unlimited, 1983.

National Library of Australia. *Guide to the National Union Catalogues of Australia*. 5th ed. Canberra: National Library of Australia, 1985.

Olle, James G. *Introduction to British Government Publications*. 2nd ed. London: Association of Assistant Librarians, 1973.

Schmeckebier, Laurence F., and Eastin, Roy B. *Government Publications and Their Use*. 2nd rev. ed. Washington, D.C.: Brookings Institution, 1969.

Serials Directory: An International Reference Book. 3 vols. Birmingham, Ala.: EBSCO, 1986.

Sheehy, Eugene P., ed. *Guide to Reference Books*. 10th ed. Chicago, Ill.: American Library Association, 1986.

Sive, Mary R. *Selecting Instructional Media: A Guide to Audiovisual and Other Instructional Media Lists*. 3rd ed. Littleton, Colo.: Libraries Unlimited, 1983.

Smith, Adeline Mercy. *Free Magazines for Libraries*. Jefferson, N.C.: McFarlane, 1980.

Teague, Edward H. "Fine Arts Periodicals as Book Selection Sources." *Art Documentation* 4, 3 (1985): 120-122.

10. Censorship and Intellectual Freedom
(See also Sections 3, 10)

American Library Association. Office for Intellectual Freedom. *Intellectual Freedom Manual*. 2nd ed. Chicago, Ill.: American Library Association, 1983.

Amey, L.J. "In Defense of Intellectual Freedom: What to Include in a School Library Collection Policy." *Emergency Librarian* 15 (1988): 9-13.

Asheim, Lester E. "Not Censorship but Selection." *Wilson Library Bulletin* 28, 1 (1953): 63-67.

Asheim, Lester. "The Public Library Meets the Censor." *Texas Library Journal* 55 (1979): 44-48.

Asheim, Lester E. "Selection and Censorship: A Reappraisal." *Wilson Library Bulletin* 58, 3 (1983): 180-184.

Association for Educational Communications and Technology. Intellectual Freedom Committee. *Media, the Learner and Intellectual Freedom: A Handbook.* Washington, D.C.: Association for Educational Communications and Technology, 1979.

Before and after the Censor: A Resource Manual on Intellectual Freedom. Lansing, Mich.: Michigan Association for Media Studies and Michigan Library Association, Intellectual Freedom Committees, 1987.

Bosmajian, Haig A. *Censorship, Libraries and the Law.* New York: Neal-Schuman, 1983.

Burress, Lee, and Jenkinson, Edward B. *The Students' Right to Know.* Urbana, Ill.: National Council of Teachers of English, 1982.

"Censorship in the Eighties." *Drexel Library Quarterly* 18, 1 (1982): entire issue.

Censorship Litigation and the Schools: Proceedings of a Colloquium Held January 1981. Chicago, Ill.: American Library Association, Office of Intellectual Freedom, 1983.

Clark, Elyse. "A Slow, Subtle Exercise in Censorship." *School Library Journal* 32, 7 (1986): 93-96.

Cohen, Barbara. "Censoring the Sources." *School Library Journal* 32, 7 (1986): 97-99.

Cronin, Mary J. *Performance Measurement for Public Services in Academic and Research Libraries.* Occasional Papers, No. 9. Washington, D.C.: Association of Research Libraries, 1985.

Dailey, Jay E. *The Anatomy of Censorship.* New York: Marcel Dekker, 1973.

Davis, James E. *Dealing with Censorship.* Urbana, Ill.: National Council of Teachers of English, 1979.

Donelson, Kenneth L. "Shoddy and Pernicious Books and Youthful Purity: Literary and Moral Censorship, Then and Now." *Library Quarterly* 51, 1 (1972): 4-19.

Foley, Robert. "The Community's Role in Dealing with Censorship." *Educational Leadership* 40, 4 (1983): 51-55.

Jenkinson, David. "Censorship Iceberg: Results of a Survey of Challenges in Public and School Libraries." *Canadian Library Journal* 43 (1986): 7-21.

Jones, Frances. *Defusing Censorship: The Librarian's Guide to Handling Censorship Conflicts.* Phoenix, Ariz.: Oryx Press, 1983.

Kamhi, Michele M. "Censorship vs. Selection - Choosing the Books Our Children Shall Read." *Educational Leadership* 39, 3 (1981): 211-215.

Kirchner-Dean, Otto. "Book Selection and the Democratic Dialogue." *Library Journal* 91 (1966): 2765-2767.

Merritt, LeRoy C. *Book Selection and Intellectual Freedom.* New York: H.W. Wilson Company, 1970.

Moon, Eric, ed. *Book Selection and Censorship in the Sixties.* New York: R.R. Bowker, 1969.

Oboler, Eli M. *Defending Intellectual Freedom:The Library and the Censor.* Contributions in Librarianship and Information Science, No. 32. Westport, Conn.: Greenwood Press, 1980.

Person, Pamela H. "Censorship: The Attack on School Libraries." *Louisiana Library Association Bulletin* 45 (1983): 159-204.

Pope, Michael. *Sex and the Undecided Librarian: A Study of Librarians' Opinions on Sexually Oriented Literature.* Metuchen, N.J.: Scarecrow Press, 1974.

Poppel, Norman, and Ashley, Edwin M. "Toward an Understanding of the Censor." *Library Journal* 111, 12 (1986): 39-43.

Pringle, Laurence. "Balance and Bias in Controversial Books." In *Beyond Fact*, compiled by Jo Carr, 165-168. Chicago, Ill.: American Library Association, 1982.

Procuniar, Pamela E. "The Intellectual Rights of Children." *Wilson Library Bulletin* 51 (1976): 163-167.

Robotham, John S., and Shields, Gerald. *Freedom of Access to Library Materials.* New York: Neal-Schuman, 1982.

Sorenson, Gail P. "Removal of Books from School Libraries 1972-1982: Board of Education v. Pico and Its Antecedents." *Journal of Law and Education* 12 (1983): 417-441.

Stahlschmidt, Agnes D. "A Democratic Procedure for Handling Challenged Library Materials." *School Library Media Quarterly* 11, 3 (1983): 200-203.

Tollefson, Alan M. "Censored and Censured: Racine Unified School District vs. Wisconsin Library Association." *School Library Journal* 33, 7 (1987): 108-112.

Watson, Jerry J., and Snider, Bill C. "Book Selection Pressure on School Library Media Specialists and Teachers." *School Media Quarterly* 9 (1981): 95-108.

Watson, Jerry J., and Snider, Bill C. "Educating the Potential Self-censor." *School Media Quarterly* 9 (1981): 272-276.

West, Celeste. "Secret Garden of Censorship: Ourselves." *Library Journal* 108, 15 (1983): 1651-1653.

White, Howard D. "Majorities for Censorship." *Library Journal* 111, 12 (1986): 31-38.

Woods, L.B. "Censorship Is a Subversive Activity." *Show-Me Libraries* 31 (1980): 5-9.

Woods, L.B., and Salvatore, Lucy. "Self-censorship in Collection Development by High School Library Media Specialists." *School Media Quarterly* 9, 2 (1981): 102-108.

11. Acquisitions
(See also Sections 2, 7, 11)

Bender, Ann. "Allocation of Funds in Support of Collection Development." *Library Resources and Technical Services* 23, 1 (1979): 45-51.

Blackwell, Richard M. "Bookselling in a Depression after a Devaluation." *Australian Academic and Research Libraries* 14, 3 (1983): 144-148.

Collins, Judith, and Finer, Ruth. "National Acquisition Policies and Systems." *Interlending Review* 10, 4 (1982): 111-118.

Collins, Judith, and Finer, Ruth. *National Acquisition Policies and Systems: A Comparative Study of Existing Systems and Possible Models.* Wetherby: IFLA International Office for UAP, 1982.

Dole, Wanda V. "Gifts and Block Purchases: Are They Profitable?" *Library Acquisitions: Practice and Theory* 7, 3 (1983): 247-254.

Evans, Glyn T. "The Cost of Information about Library Acquisitions Budgets." *Collection Management* 2, 1 (1978): 3-23.

Gehringer, M.; Peterson, T.; and Williamson, J.A. "Getting the Ungettable: Hard to Locate Federal Documents." *Law Library Journal* 72 (1979): 659-673.

Kilton, Thomas D. "Out-of-print Procurement in Academic Libraries: Current Methods and Sources." *Collection Management* 5, 3/4 (1983): 113-134.

Landesman, Margaret. "Selling Out-of-print Books to Librarians." *AB Bookmans Weekly* 74 (1984): 3184-3192.

Lane, Alfred H. *Gifts and Exchange Manual.* Westport, Conn.: Greenwood Press, 1980.

McGrath, William E.; Huntsinger, R.S.; and Barber, G.R. "An Allocation Formula Derived from a Factor Analysis of Academic Departments." *College and Research Libraries* 30 (1966): 51-62.

Melcher, Daniel, and Saul, Margaret. *Melcher on Acquisition.* Chicago, Ill.: American Library Association, 1971.

Mitchell, Betty J. "A Systematic Approach to Performance Evaluation of Out-of-Print Book Dealers: The San Fernando Valley State College Experience." *Library Resources and Technical Services* 15, 2 (1971): 215-222.

Piekarski, Helen. "Acquisitions of Out-of-Print Books for a University Library." *Canadian Library Journal* 26 (1969): 346-352.

Schenck, William Z. "Acquiring Library Materials as Efficiently, Inexpensively, and Quickly as Possible: Exploring Possibilities within the Impossible Dream." *Library Acquisitions: Practice and Theory* 1, 3 (1977): 193-199.

Scudder, Mary C. "Using *Choice* in an Allocation Formula in a Small Academic Library." *Choice* 24, 10 (1987): 1506-1511.

Sheehan, Joy. "Library Supply in Australia." *Library Acquisitions: Practice and Theory* 10, 3 (1986): 219-226.

Voigt, Melvin J. "Acquisition Rates in University Libraries." *College and Research Libraries* 36, 4 (1975): 263-267.

Weatherford, Richard. "Computers in the Antiquarian Book Trade." *AB Bookmans Weekly* 79 (1987): 397-402.

Werking, Richard J. "Allocating the Academic Library's Book Budget: Historical Perspectives and Current Reflections." *Journal of Academic Librarianship* 14, 3 (1988): 140-144.

12. Weeding

(See also Sections 2-7, 13)

Ash, Lee. *Yale's Selective Book Retirement Program.* Hamden, Conn.: Archon Books, 1963.

Association of Research Libraries. Office of Management Studies. Systems and Procedures Exchange Center. *Remote Storage.* SPEC Kit 39. Washington, D.C.: Association of Research Libraries, 1977.

Bayly, Cynthia. "A Withdrawals Policy." *School Library Bulletin* 14 (1982): 88-89.

Bedsole, Danny T. "Formulating a Weeding Policy for Books in a Special Library." *Special Libraries* 49, 5 (1958): 205-209.

Bostic, Mary J. "Serials Deselection." *Serials Librarian* 9, 3 (1985): 85-101.

Broadus, Robert N. "A Proposed Method for Eliminating Titles from Periodical Subscription Lists." *College and Research Libraries* 46, 1 (1985): 31-35.

Broude, Jeffrey. "Journal Deselection in an Academic Environment: A Comparison of Faculty and Librarian Choices." *Serials Librarian* 3, 2 (1978): 147-166.

Burrell, Quentin L. "A Third Note on Aging in a Library Circulation Model: Applications to Future Use and Relegation." *Journal of Documentation* 43, 1 (1987): 24-45.

Calgary Board of Education. Educational Media Team. "Weeding the School Library Media Collection." *School Library Media Quarterly* 12 (1984): 419-424.

Cooper, Marianne. "Criteria for Weeding of Collections." *Library Resources and Technical Services* 12, 3 (1968): 339-351.

Doyen, Sally E. "Guidelines for Selective Weeding of a Multi-media Collection." *Ohio Media Spectrum* 22, 2 (1980): 45-49.

Durey, Peter. "Weeding Serials Subscriptions in a University Library." *Collection Management* 1, 3/4 (1976/1977): 91-94.

Ellsworth, Ralph E. *Economics of Book Storage in College and Research Libraries.* Washington, D.C.: Association of Research Libraries, 1969.

Ellsworth, Ralph E. *The Economics of Compact Storage.* Metuchen, N.J.: Scarecrow Press, 1969.

Engeldinger, Eugene A. "Weeding of Academic Library Reference Collections: A Survey of Current Practice." *RQ* 25, 3 (1986): 366-371.

Evans, G. Edward. "Limits to Growth or the Need to Weed." *California Librarian* 38 (1977): 8-16.

Fisher, Willliam H. "Weeding the Academic Business/Economics Collection." *Behavioral and Social Sciences Librarian* 4 (1985): 29-37.

Ford, Geoffrey. "Stock Relegation in Some British University Libraries." *Journal of Librarianship* 12, 1 (1980): 42-55.

Goldstein, Cynthia H. "Study of Weeding Policies in Eleven TALON Resource Libraries." *Bulletin of the Medical Library Association* 69 (1981): 311-316.

Gordon, Anitra. "Weeding - Keeping up with the Information Explosion." *School Library Journal* 30 (1983): 45-46.

Grefshein, S.; Bader, S.; and Meredith, P. "User Involvement in Journal De-selection." *Collection Management* 5, 1/2 (1983): 43-52.

Hayden, Ron. "If It Circulates, Keep It." *Library Journal* 112, 10 (1987): 80-82.

Hickman, Roger. "The Self-renewing Library." *Library Review* 29 (1980): 176-183.

Houghton, Tony. *Bookstock Management in Public Libraries.* London: Clive Bingley, 1985.

Hulser, Richard P. "Weeding in a Corporate Library as Part of a Collection Management Program." *Science and Technology Libraries* 6 (1986): 1-9.

Johnson, Steve. "Serial Deselection in University Libraries: The Next Step." *Library Acquisitions: Practice and Theory* 7, 3 (1983): 239-246.

Lancaster, F.Wilfrid. "Obsolescence, Weeding and the Utilization of Space." *Wilson Library Bulletin* 62, 9 (1988): 47-49.

Lawrence, Gary S. "A Cost Model for Storage and Weeding Programs." *College and Research Libraries* 42, 2 (1981): 139-147.

McGaw, Howard F. "Policies and Practices in Discarding." *Library Trends* 4, 3 (1956): 269-282.

McKee, Penelope. "Weeding the Forest Hill Branch of Toronto Public Library by the Slote Method: A Test Case." *Library Research* 3, 3 (1981): 283-301.

McReynolds, Rosalee. "Limiting a Periodicals Collection in a College Library." *Serials Librarian* 9 (1984): 75 - 81.

Mahoney, Kay. "Weeding the Small Library Collection." *Connecticut Libraries* 24 (1982): 45-47.

Maxin, Jacqueline A. "Weeding Journals with Informal Use Statistics." *Deacquisitions Librarian* 1, 2 (1976): 9-11.

Miller, J. Wesley. "Throwing out Belles Lettres with the Bathwater: A Patron Protests What He Considers Boorish Weeding of Library Collections." *American Libraries* 15, 6 (1984): 384-385.

Mosher, Paul H. "Managing Library Collections: The Process of Review and Pruning." In *Collection Development in Libraries: A Treatise, Part A*, edited by Robert D. Stueart and George B. Miller, Jr., 159-181. Foundations in Library and Information Science, Vol. 10. Greenwich, Conn.: JAI Press, 1980.

Mount, Ellis, ed. *Weeding of Collections in Sci-Tech Libraries*. New York: Haworth Press, 1986.

Neame, Laura. "Periodicals Cancellation: Making a Virtue out of Necessity." *Serials Librarian* 10, 3 (1986): 33-42.

Poller, Marian. "Weeding Monographs in the Harrison Public Library." *Deacquisitions Librarian* 1, 1 (1976): 1, 6-7.

Reed, Mary Jane Pobst. "Identification of Storage Candidates among Monographs." *Collection Management* 3, 3 (1979): 203-214.

Reed-Scott, Jutta. "Implementation and Evaluation of a Weeding Program." *Collection Management* 7, 2 (1985): 59-67.

Routh, Spencer. "Storage and Discard." In *Collection Management in Academic Libraries: Papers Delivered at a National Seminar, Surfers Paradise, Queensland, 16th-17th February 1984*, edited by Cathryn Crowe, Philip Kent and Barbara Paton, 31-39. Sydney: Library Association of Australia, University and College Libraries Section, 1984.

Simon, J.L. "How Many Books Should Be Stored Where? An Economic Analysis." *College and Research Libraries* 28 (1967): 93-103.

Slote, Stanley J. *Weeding Library Collections - II.* 2nd rev. ed. Littleton, Colo.: Libraries Unlimited, 1982.

Snowball, G.J., and Sampedro, J. "Selection of Periodicals for Return to Prime Space from a Storage Facility." *Canadian Library Journal* 30 (1973): 490-492.

Stankus, Tony. "Journal Weeding in Relation to Declining Faculty Member Publishing." *Science and Technology Libraries* 6 (1986): 43-53.

Stayner, Richard A., and Richardson, Valerie E. *The Cost-effectiveness of Alternative Library Storage Programs.* Clayton: Graduate School of Librarianship, Monash University, 1983.

Stoljarov, J.N. "Optimum Size of Public Library Stocks." *Unesco Bulletin for Libraries* 27 (1973): 22-28, 42.

Stueart, Robert D. "Weeding of Library Materials - Politics and Policies." *Collection Management* 7, 2 (1985): 47-58.

Swartz, Linda Jo. "Serials Cancellations and Reinstatements at the University of Illinois Library." *Serials Librarian* 2 (1977): 171-180.

Taylor, Colin R. "A Practical Solution to Weeding University Library Periodicals Collections." *Collection Management* 1, 3/4 (1976/1977): 27-45.

Thompson, Frances. "Closing Libraries Using the District Dispersal Method." *School Library Media Quarterly* 12 (1984): 169-173.

Trueswell, Richard W. "Determining the Optimal Number of Volumes of a Library's Core Collection." *Libri* 16 (1966): 49-60.

Trueswell, Richard W. "A Quantitative Measure of User Circulation Requirements and Its Possible Effect on Stack Thinning and Multiple Copy Determination." *American Documentation* 16 (1965): 20-25.

Trueswell, Richard W. "'The Uses and Limitations of Trueswell': A Comment." *College and Research Libraries* 40, 5 (1979): 424-425.

Turner, Stephen J. "Trueswell's Weeding Technique: The Facts." *College and Research Libraries* 41, 2 (1980): 134-138.

Urquhart, John A., and Urquhart, N.C. *Relegation and Stock Control in Libraries.* Newcastle upon Tyne: Oriel Press, 1976.

Wezeman, F. "Psychological Barriers to Weeding." *ALA Bulletin* 52 (1958): 637-639.

White, Herbert S. "Factors in the Decision by Individuals and Libraries to Place or Cancel Subscriptions to Scholarly and Research Journals." *Library Quarterly* 50, 3 (1980): 287-309.

Williams, R. "Weeding an Academic Lending Library Using the Slote Method." *British Journal of Academic Librarianship* 1 (1986): 147-159.

Williamson, Marilyn L. "Seven Years of Cancellations at Georgia Tech." *Serials Librarian* 9, 3 (1985): 103-114.

Wood, John B., and Coppel, Lynn M. "Drowning Our Kittens: Deselection of Periodicals in Academic Libraries." *Serials Librarian* 3, 3 (1979): 317-331.

13. Cooperative Collection Development and Resource Sharing
   (See also Sections 2, 12)

Abbott, Peter, and Kavanagh, Rosemary. "Electronic Resource Sharing Changes Interloan Patterns." *Library Journal* 111, 16 (1986): 56-58.

Ballard, Thomas H. *Failure of Resource Sharing in Public Libraries and Alternative Strategies for Service.* Chicago, Ill.: American Library Association, 1986.

Ballard, Thomas H. "Public Library Networking: Neat, Plausible, Wrong." *Library Journal* 107, 7 (1982): 679-683.

Brewer, Karen; Pitkin, Gary; and Edgar, Neal. "A Method for Cooperative Serials Selection and Cancellation through Consortium Activities." *Journal of Academic Librarianship* 4, 4 (1978): 204-208.

Dannelly, Gay N. "Coordinating Cooperative Collection Development: A National Perspective." *Library Acquisitions: Practice and Theory* 9, 4 (1985): 307-315.

De Gennaro, Richard. "Copyright, Resource Sharing and Hard Times: A View from the Field." *American Libraries* 8, 8 (1977): 430-435;

Dougherty, Richard M. "Library Cooperation: A Case of Hanging Together or Hanging Separately." *Catholic Library World* 46 (1975): 324-327.

Duggan, Maryann. "Library Network Analysis and Planning." *Journal of Library Automation* 2 (1969): 157-175.

Fiels, Keith M. "Coordinated Collection Development in a Multitype Environment: Promise and Challenge." *Collection Building* 7, 2 (1985): 26-31.

Fjallbrant, Nancy. "Rationalization of Periodical Holdings: A Case Study of Chalmers University Library." *Journal of Academic Librarianship* 10, 2 (1984): 77-86.

Forcier, Peggy. Building Collections Together: The Pacific Northwest Conspectus." *Library Journal* 113, 7 (1988): 43-45.

Graneek, J.J. "The Pros and Cons of Rationalization." In *The Rationalization of Library Resources in Australia,* 10-16. Australian Humanities Research Council Occasional Paper, No. 10. Sydney: Sydney University Press for the Australian Humanities Research Council, 1967.

Gwinn, Nancy E. "Cooperative Collection Development: National Trends and New Tools." *Art Documentation* 4, 4 (1985): 143-147.

Gwinn, Nancy E., and Mosher, Paul H. "Coordinating Collection Development: The RLG Conspectus." *College and Research Libraries* 44, 2 (1983): 128-140.

Jaffe, Lawrence L. "Collection Development and Resource Sharing in the Combined School/Public Library." *Collection Management* 7, 3/4 (1985): 205-215.

Kaiser, John R. "Resource Sharing in Collection Development." In *Collection Development in Libraries: A Treatise, Part A*, edited by Robert D. Stueart and George B. Miller, Jr., 139-157. Foundations in Library and Information Science, Vol. 10. Greenwich, Conn.: JAI Press, 1980.

Luquire, William, ed. *Coordinating Cooperative Collection Development: A National Perspective*. New York: Haworth Press, 1986.

Mosher, Paul H., and Pankake, Marcia. "A Guide to Coordinated and Cooperative Collection Development." *Library Resources and Technical Services* 27, 4 (1983): 417-431.

Shaw, W.M., Jr. "A Journal Resource Sharing Strategy." *Library Research* 1 (1979): 19-29.

Sohn, Jeanne. "Cooperative Collection Development: A Brief Overview." *Collection Management* 8, 2 (1986): 1-9.

Stam, David H. "Collaborative Collection Development: Progress, Problems and Potential." *Collection Building* 7, 3 (1986): 3-8.

Stam, David H. "Think Globally - Act Locally: Collection Development and Resource Sharing." *Collection Building* 5 (1983): 18-21.

Stockdale, N. "The Rationalization of Library Resources." In *The Rationalization of Library Resources in Australia*, 3-9. Australian Humanities Research Council Occasional Paper, No. 10. Sydney: Sydney University Press for the Australian Humanities Research Council, 1967.

INDEX

ABN
  see Australian Bibliographic Network

ABN Catalogue, 261n3, 318

academic libraries
  adequacy of collections in, 166-73
  and cooperative collection
    development, 221-2, 231, 232,
    239, 245
  and faculty accountability, 218-
    19, 222, 229, 232
  faculty selection in, 213, 214-15,
    216-22, 225-36
  librarian selection in, 215-16, 220,
    222, 225-36
  model against faculty selection in,
    231-3
  model for faculty selection in, 219-20
  needs analysis and, 167-8
  purposes of, 166-7
  and research needs, 220-2, 231
  selection in, 190-1, 213, 214-24,
    225-36
  and self-renewing concept, 329-
    30
  weeding in, 329-30, 331-2, 341,
    356-63

academic staff
  see faculty

acquisitions policies
  see also collection development
    policies
  and collection development
    policies, 27-9, 45
  and selection policies, 27-9, 45

Adams, J., 4, 9, 10-16

Adams, J.R.G., 16

Administrative Notes (of GPO), 282

advertising material
  aims of, 260
  basic necessities of, 260-1
  as selection resource, 248, 250, 259-
    62
  types of, 259-60

ALA
  see American Library Association

American Book Publishing Record, 255,
  309, 319

*American Historical Association's Guide
  to Historical Literature*, 253, 309

American Libraries, 258-9

American Library Association (ALA), 6,
  22-3, 30, 33, 34, 35-6, 68, 87, 88,
  89, 94, 95, 96-7, 98, 99, 101, 106,
  130, 131, 134, 135, 139, 166, 168,
  177, 207-10, 237, 351

American Statistics Index (ASI), 285

ANB
  see Australian National Bibliography

Anderson, H.C.L., 15

approval plans
  and selection, 192-3, 194, 231

Arizona State University
  weeding of collections at, 346

Armstrong, E. La T., 16

Arthur, A.J., 119, 130, 131-40

ASI
  see American Statistics Index

book reviews, cont.
  as guides, 257-8
  journals containing, 258-9, 297-307
  policies and practices of journals
    containing, 297-307
  purposes of, 304
  and reviewer anonymity, 305, 306
  as selection resources, 248, 250, 257-9
  and sex of authors, 305-6, 307n14

Book Selection and Collections, 232-3

Booklist, 278

Booknet, 310

Books in Print (BIP), 255, 312, 319

Bookseller, 255, 312, 321

Bookstein, A., 124, 149, 157, 158-65

Boorstin, D., 39

Boston Library Consortium
  serials review project of, 355

Boston Public Library, 17

Bowker Serials Bibliography database,
  265, 267, 274

Bowker's International Serials Database,
  321

Bradford's law, 152, 156n9, 346

Bride, T.F., 13, 14-15

Brigham Young University (BYU), 174,
  175, 178-81, 350

Britain
  national bibliography of, 254, 261n3,
    313

British Book News, 253, 259, 312

British Books in Print, 255, 312

British Council, 312

British Library, 253, 254, 311, 312, 313
  Copyright Receipt Office of the, 254,
    313

British National Bibliography (BNB),
  254, 261n3, 313

Broadbent, M., 136

Broadus, R.N., 185-6, 237

Broderick, D.
  see Curley and Broderick

Brown, W.L.
  see Bartle and Brown

browsing, 123, 137, 324

BRS, 265

Building Library Collections, 237

Burr, R.L., 225-7

Burr, R.L., *et al.*, 213, 225-36

BYU
  see Brigham Young University

BYU *Manual*
  see Collection Assessment Manual

California State University, Los Angeles
  weeding programme at, 358

Camberwell-Waverley, 40

Cambridge University Press, 253, 318

*Canadian Books in Print: Author and
  Title Index*, 313

Canadian Books in Print: Subject Index,
  313

*Canadian Catalogue of Books, Published
  in Canada*, 313

Canadian Publishers' Directory, 313, 319

Canadiana, 313

CAP Manual
  see Collection Assessment Manual

Cargill, J., 7, 9, 24-5

Carpenter, E., 9, 21-3

Case, B., 358

Case Western Reserve University, 180

Catalog of Books Represented by Library of Congress Printed Cards Issued to July 31, 1942, 317

censorship, 95, 144, 199

Centing, R., 270

Central Gippsland Regional Library Service, 42

Checklist of State Publications, 286

Cherns, J.J. 289

Choice, 253, 259, 263-4, 270, 297-307, 314
  and choice of books for review, 298-9, 300
  and choice of reviewers, 298-9, 301, 302
  and content of book reviews, 299-305, 307n10
  institutional affiliation of reviewers for, 305
  reviewers for, 263-4, 297-307
  reviews in, 263-4, 297-307
  sex of reviewers for, 305

Chronicle of Higher Education, 265

Chweh, S.S., 122, 155

circulation studies, 135, 150-1, 180
  see also user studies
  advantages of, 151
  disadvantages of, 151

CIS
  see Congressional Information Service

CIS Index, 285

citation analysis, 152-3, 169, 170, 273, 328-9, 346
  advantages of, 152-3
  disadvantages of, 153
  of periodicals, 328-9
  of serials, 273, 328-9
  and weeding of periodicals, 328-9 and weeding of serials, 328-9

Clapp-Jordan formula, 155n1, 169

client-oriented studies, 168, 170-1, 177, 179-80
  see also user studies
  disadvantages of, 171
  and opinionnaires, 179-80

collection adequacy
  see collection evaluation

collection analysis
  see collection evaluation

Collection Analysis Project (CAP), 168, 174

collection assessment
  see collection evaluation

Collection Assessment Manual, 174, 175, 178-81

collection development
  see also collection development policies
  in nineteenth century Australian libraries, 10-16

Collection Development: The Selection of Materials for Libraries, 237

Collection Development in Libraries, 273

"Collection Development and Local Documents: History and Present Use in the United States", 292

collection development policies
  see also collection evaluation; selection; weeding
  and acquisitions policies, 27-9, 45
  arguments against, 9, 24-5
  arguments for, 3-7, 9, 17-23
  case studies of formulation of, 94, 100-1, 102-15, 133-4
  and collection levels, *see* collection levels
  communication functions of, 5-6, 9, 21-2
  components of, 30-6
  content of, 27-36, 37-84
  data forms for, 88-9
  determination of preliminary matters concerning, 86, 87-9
  dissemination of, 86, 92

"International Documents Roundup, 287

international governmental organizations (IGOs)
acquisition of publications of, 287-9
and copublishing arrangements, 288
sales agents for publications of, 288
selection of publications of, 287-9

International Information, 316

International Standard Serial Number (ISSN), 269, 320

"Into the 1980's: The Ideal State Document Reference Collection", 286

Irregular Serials and Annuals, 256, 265, 266, 267, 268, 269, 270, 271, 274, 316

ISSN
see International Standard Serial Number

J. Whitaker, 255, 312, 321

JAAD Publishing, 320

Johns Hopkins University, 232, 288

Joint Publications Research Service, 290

Jones, F., 199

K.G. Saur, 256, 315

Kantor, P.B., 170, 180

Katz, W.A., 192, 237
see also Katz and Katz; Katz and Sternberg

Katz, W.A. and Katz, L.S., 257, 316

Katz, W.A. and Sternberg, L., 270

Kenner, Professor Hugh, 232

Key Publishing, 313, 319

Koenig, D.A., 88, 94, 102-15, 153

L'Annee Philologique, 266

LAA
see Library Association of Australia

Lancaster, F.W., 168, 174, 345

Lancaster University
weeding of collections at, 346

Lane, M., 286

LC Classification: National Shelflist Count, 23

Leland Stanford Junior University, 103

librarians
as experts, 5
as clerks, 5
in nineteenth century Australia, 10-16

Librarians' Handbook, 268, 269

Librarians in New South Wales, 10

librarianship, "laws" of, 186-7

libraries
see also academic libraries; national libraries, public libraries; school libraries; special libraries
and collection development policies, *see* collection development policies
and collection evaluation, *see* collection evaluation
collection levels in, *see* collection levels
communication among, 6
and complaints, *see* complaints
differing interpretations of "use" of, 160-2, 164-5, *see also* use studies
donations to, *see* gifts
and gifts, *see* gifts
and information needs, 122-8
in nineteenth century, 4, 9, 10-16
and resource sharing, 6, 22-3, 98, 103-4, 110-11
size and value of collections in, 323-4
use of questionnaires in research on, 158-65
and use studies, 323-4
and user needs, 122-8
and user satisfaction, 140-4

non-quantifiable measures
and collection evaluation, 153-5;
advantages of, 154;
disadvantages of, 154

Northeast Ohio Major Academic Libraries
(NEOMAL), 23

NST
see New Serials Titles

NTIS
see National Technical Information
Services

NUC
see National Union Catalog

NUCOM
*see National Union Catalogue of
Monographs*

NUCOS
*see National Union Catalogue of
Serials*

NZLA
see New Zealand Library Association

Occupational Outlook Handbook, 285

OCLC, 274

O'Donovan, D., 13-14

Office of Management Studies, 170

Official Publications, 289

Okanagan College [British Columbia]
cancellation of periodicals at, 359-63
faculty and weeding decisions at,
360-3
periodicals collection policy at, 359-
63

*Operational Standards for Public
Libraries in Western Australia,* 45

Organ of the Book Trade, The, 255, 312

Orr, R.H., 169, 180

Oryx Press, 256

Osburn, C.B., 233-4

Parish, D., 286

*Patterns of the Use of Books in Large
Research Libraries,* 347

Peabody Library, 232

periodicals
see also serials
cancellation of, 356-63
cancellation criteria for, 361
cost of, 358-9
and use studies, 357
value of, 358-9
weeding of, 327-9, 341, 346, 356-63

Poulos, A., 229-31

PRF
see Publications Reference File

Price List, 284-5

pruning
see weeding

*Public Affairs Information Service
Bulletin (PAIS),* 285

Public Library Manifesto, 39

Public Library Objectives, 39, 40

Public Service Board (Victoria), 48

public libraries
selection in, 38-48, 187-8
weeding in, 332, 333-9

Publications Reference File (PRF), 283,
284

Publishers' Trade List Annual, 255, 312,
319

Publishers' Weekly, 255, 309, 319

Purcell, G.
see Hernon and Purcell

"quality versus demand" debate
see selection

Simon, J.L.
    see Fussler and Simon

Slote, S.J., 148, 347

SPD
    see Standard Periodical Directory

special libraries
    selection in, 191-2

Spectator, 258, 320

Spiller, D., 194, 196

SRI
    see Statistical Reference Index

St. Joseph Gazette, 64-5

St. Joseph Public Library, 34, 37, 58-67
    clientele of, 59-60
    complaints handling at, 66
    criteria for materials selection and
        collection review at, 60-1
    gifts to, 66-7
    selection policy of, 58-67

Stam, D.H., 231-3

Standard Periodical Directory (SPD),
    265, 266, 267

Standards for Public Library Service in
    New Zealand, 40

"Standing Order Item List", 285

standing orders
    and selection, 193-4

Stanford University Libraries
    weeding programme of, 346, 350,
        353, 355

State Government Reference
    Publications, 286

State Library of Tasmania, 38, 39, 40, 43

State Library of Victoria, 31, 34, 37, 48-
    58
    collection levels in selection policy of,
        56-7
    determinants of selection policy of,
        50-1

State Library of Victoria, cont.
    materials acquired for, 54-6
    purposes of selection policy of, 51-2
    role of, 50
    selection policy of, 31, 34, 37, 48-58
    users of, 52-4

State Library of Victoria Selection Policy,
    31, 34, 37, 48-58

"State Reference Sources", 286

State University of New York (SUNY),
    94
    College at Purchase, 100-1
    formulation of collection development
        policy statement at, 100-1

state publications
    selection of, 285-7

Statement on Freedom to Read, 207-10

Statistical Abstract, 285

Statistical Reference Index (SRI), 285,
    287

Steinbeck Quarterly, 275

Sternberg, L.
    see Katz and Sternberg

Stevens & Brown Quarterly Serials
    Bulletin, 271

Stevens & Brown, 271

Stueart, R.D., 341, 342-50
    see also Stueart and Miller

Stueart, R.E. and Miller, G.B., Jr., 237-
    8, 273

Subject Bibliographies, 283

Subject Guide to Books in Print, 255,
    312, 320

SUNY
    see State University of New York

surveys
    and data analysis, 127
    and data for collection, 125-6
    design of, 124-8

surveys, cont.
    methodology in, 125-6
    objectives of, 124-5
    and population sample, 126-7
    purpose of, 124-5
    replication of, 127
    and review of previous research, 125

Swets Info, 268, 269

Swinburne Library, 130, 131-40
    browsing use of, 137
    collection management project at, 131-40
    collection evaluation at, 135-6
    collection levels at, 134
    collection development groups at, 135, 138, 139
    Collection Management Librarian at, 134
    collection management plan at, 135
    discard of materials at, 136, 138
    funding at, 138
    periodicals use at, 137
    selection at, 139
    use studies at, 135-6, 137
    user studies at, 135-6

Swindler, L.
    see Rutledge and Swindler

Tasmanian Library Board, 39

TBRI
    see Technical Book Review Index

Technical Book Review Index (TBRI), 258, 320

Thomson, 315

Times Literary Supplement, The, 259, 320

Times Newspapers, 320

Toowoomba Municipal Library, 43

Toronto Public Library, 313

trade bibliographies, 254-6

Trueswell, R.A., 150, 346, 357

Tulk, A.H., 14

Tuttle, M., 263, 265-77

U.S. Code, 285

U.S. Government Books, 283

UGC
    see University Grants Committee

Ulrich's International Periodicals Directory, 4, 256, 265, 266, 267, 268, 269, 270, 271, 272, 274, 320-1

Ulrich's Quarterly, 266, 267, 268, 321

UN Chronicle, 289

UNESCO, 39, 287, 288

UNIFO, 288, 289

Union List of Serials, 274

UNIPUB, 287, 288

United Nations, 287-8, 289
    Sales Office of, 288, 289

United States of America
    depository libraries for government publications in, 280
    government publications in, 263, 277-85
    and lack of national bibliography, 254

United States Government Printer
    see Government Printing Office

University of California at Berkeley, 34, 88, 91, 94, 102-15, 344-5
    academic environment at, 102-3
    collecting levels at, 106-7, 112-14
    and cooperative collection development, 279
    development of collection development policy statement at, 102-15
    and resource sharing between libraries, 103-4, 110-11
    size of collection at, 103
    weeding of collection at, 344-5

University of Chicago
    use studies at, 347

University Grants Committee, 329-30

University of London
specialized research libraries at, 191

University of New South Wales, 170-1

University of New York, 357

University of North Carolina at Chapel
Hill (UNC-CH), 239

University of Pittsburgh
journal use at, 358

University of Texas at Austin Library,
236

University of Toronto Press, 313

Update, 320

US News, 275

use studies, 90, 91, 122-8, 131-40, 147-
56, 157, 179-80, 353-4, 357-9
see also client-oriented studies; user
studies
and design of surveys, 124-8, 148
and non-quantifiable measures, 153-5
problems in, 148-9
and weeding,323-4, 326, 328, 344,
346-8, 351-2, 353-4, 357-9

user satisfaction
see also user studies
and delay in delivery of a document,
142-3, 144
and ethical issues, 144
and restricted access to the librarian,
143, 144

user studies, 90, 91, 122-8, 130, 131-
46, 147-56, 157, 158-65, 166-73,
179-80
see also circulation studies; client-
oriented studies; collection-oriented
studies; document delivery tests; in-
house use studies; shelf availability
tests; use studies
and academic libraries, 166-73
and design of surveys, 124-8, 148
differing interpretations of questions
asked in, 158-65
disadvantages of, 140-6

user studies, cont.
methodology in, 124-8, 140-6, 148,
157, 158-65
and non-quantifiable measures, 153-5
people's understanding of questions
asked in, 158-65
problems in, 148-9
and quality of library service, 140-2
and user satisfaction, 140-6

Using Government Publications, 256,
319

Van Orden, P.J., 32

verification studies, 151-2
advantages of, 152
disadvantages of, 152

Wade Shire Library, 39-40

Wainwright, E.J., 155, 157, 166-73

Walker, R.C., 14

Webster, D.E.
see Gardner and Webster

Weech, T., 286

weeding, 136, 138, 197, 199, 204,
223n13, 323-40, 341-63
in academic libraries, 329-30, 331-2,
341, 356-63
aims of, 325-6
and analysis of options, 341, 350,
351
and archival approach, 330, 355
basic assumptions in programmes for,
331
and citation analysis, 328-9, 346
and collection evaluation, 223n13
cost of, 326, 341, 344-5, 347-8
criteria for, 325-7, 331-2, 341, 344-
7, 348, 351-2
definition of, 323, 342-3
and discarding, 324, 336, 343
faculty and, 341, 345-6, 354-5, 357-
63
feasibility of, 341, 350, 351, 353
guidelines for, 327
and local factors, 341, 350
and needs analysis, 341, 350